Notes On The Rubrics Of The Roman Ritual

NOTES ON THE RUBRICS

OF

THE ROMAN RITUAL

REGARDING

THE SACRAMENTS IN GENERAL,

BAPTISM, THE EUCHARIST, AND EXTREME UNCTION.

BY THE

REV. JAMES O'KANE,

SENIOR DEAN, ST. PATRICK'S COLLEGE, MAYNOOTH.

With the Approbation of
His Eminence JOHN CARDINAL McCLOSKEY, Archbishop of New York.

———•———

NEW YORK:

P. O'SHEA, AGT.,

45 WARREN STREET.

1883.

Nihil obstat.

EDMUNDUS J. O'REILLY, S. J.,
Censor Theolog. Deputatus.

Imprimatur.

✠ PAULUS CARD. CULLEN,
Archiepiscopus Dubliniensis.

PREFACE.

It has been part of my duty, for several years, to give Lectures on the Rubrics of the Ritual to the Senior Class of Divinity Students. In preparing for these Lectures, I had occasion to consult the principal authorities on the various subjects treated; and in order to save the trouble of frequent references, I usually made a note of what seemed to me valuable for the purpose, either of explaining the text of the Rubric, or of drawing out the instructions contained in it.

The Rubrics which regard the Sacraments in general, Baptism, the Eucharist, and Extreme Unction, claimed special attention, because they treat of those duties of the ministry that present, perhaps, most difficulties to a priest on the mission. It was suggested to me that a work explaining these Rubrics, and at the same time taking into account the difficulties that stand in the way of observing them to the letter in a country like Ireland, would supply a want felt by many priests. With a view, therefore, to compiling a work of the kind, I some time ago revised and considerably extended my notes on these Rubrics, intending ultimately to condense and recast them, using probably the Latin language as best suited to many of the subjects of which they treat. But, having consulted one on whose judgment I place great reliance, I was induced to prepare them for the press in their present form—that in which they were first written—as, on the whole, the best for the purpose intended. The want of the more exact and methodical arrangement which I had contemplated, I have made an effort to supply in some degree by means of a copious Index.

The text of the Rubrics, which is that of the "Propaganda" edition of the Ritual (ROMÆ, MDCCCXLVII), is divided, in each chapter, into sections printed in distinctive type. The Notes on the several Rubrics or sections contain the substance of what I could glean, in the way already intimated, from the authorities consulted. For the satisfactory explanation of many Rubrics, I found it necessary not to confine myself to the mere ceremonial, but to touch on theological questions of great practical importance, and occasionally to notice questions of interest as to the origin, history, or meaning of particular ceremonies. A reference is given in every case to the works cited, so that the reader is put at once in the way of getting fuller information, should he desire it. Far, then, from wishing to present anything new or original, I have endeavored to give a voucher, if possible, for every statement, and to use, where I could do so conveniently, the very words of the authority cited.

What might here be said on the importance of the subject-matter of the volume, as well as on the sources from which the Notes are taken, will be found in the Introductory Chapter and in the Appendix.

It only remains for me to acknowledge my obligations to the Very Rev. Edmund O'Reilly, the learned Father Provincial of the Society of Jesus, for much valuable assistance in the treatment of several questions, as well as for the great care and trouble taken by him in revising the sheets as they passed through the press. His name is a sufficient guarantee that the book contains nothing opposed to sound theology. But if any expression has escaped me, at variance, even remotely, with the teaching and spirit of the Church, I hereby unreservedly condemn and retract it.

MAYNOOTH COLLEGE,
  Feast of the Epiphany, 1867.

PREFACE

TO THE SECOND EDITION.

THIS volume has been received by the clergy with a degree of favor which I did not dare to expect, the first edition having been exhausted in a few months.

Since its publication I have had communications in reference to many of the subjects treated, from several priests of experience on the mission. I also had valuable opportunities of observation and inquiry during some weeks spent in Rome. But neither of these sources of information has suggested any change of importance to be made in bringing out a new edition.

The Sacred Congregation of Rites, however, having examined the work, directed changes to be made in a few sentences, as may be seen by the subjoined Decree. These changes, I need not say, have been carefully made. A change has been made also, n. 609, on account of a decision of the S. R. C., there referred to. A foot-note is added, p. 303; and an important instruction from the Propaganda, regarding the Blessed Eucharist, is inserted in the Appendix. In almost all else this edition is an exact reprint of the first, to which the Decree of the Sacred Congregation refers.

MAYNOOTH COLLEGE,
Feast of St. Thomas Aquinas 1866.

PREFACE

TO THE THIRD EDITION.

In this Third Edition I have made a few changes, rendered necessary by recent decisions of the Roman Congregations. One of these decisions regards the confession of converts on being received into the Church. Another regards Communion at a Requiem Mass. These, by settling points on which there had been previously a diversity of practice, called for certain changes in Nos. 464-6, 766-9. The rest required little or no change, and are noticed chiefly in foot-notes, while all the decisions referred to are given in the Appendix.

Considering the Decree of the Sacred Congregation prefixed to the volume, I feel that I should hardly be justified in making any change not strictly necessary. It is owing to that Decree that the work has been so favorably received, both in this country and in America, and has been even translated into French.

The numbers containing what is of most practical importance are, in this edition, each marked with an asterisk. This arrangement will be a convenience to those who may wish to pass over the rest, and will perhaps serve, in great measure, the purposes of a compendium.

MAYNOOTH COLLEGE,
Feast of the Purification of the Blessed Virgin, 1872.

DECRETUM.

SACRA RITUUM CONGREGATIO, exquisito prius voto Censoris Theologi specialiter deputati declarandum censuit, ex parte Liturgica nihil obstare quominus vere commendabile et accuratissimum hoc opus cui titulus, *Notae super Rubricis Ritualis Romani*, a R. D. Jacobo O'Kane, Anglica Lingua exaratum iterum typis mandetur, servatis sequentibus conditionibus, nimirum.

PAG. 253.[1]—Corrigatur locus in quo asseritur modo ubique et etiam Romae praevalere usum iterum baptizandi sub conditione qui ex Protestantismo ad unitatem Catholicam redeunt. Siquidem Romae juxta Decretum Sacrae Universalis Inquisitionis *in singulis casibus examinari debet* an iterum sit conferendus Baptismus.

PAG. 434.[2]—Defendit usum praebendi communionem Fidelibus in Missis Defunctorum cum particulis praeconsecratis—Debet addi:-- *attamen haec quaestio nondum decisa manet : et donec aliter a Sacra Congregatione Rituum statutum fuerit standum est praxi in unaquaque Dioecesi receptae.*

PAG. 504.[3]—Asserit posse poni Sanctissimam Eucharistiam in sacculo ubi privatim deferre permittitur. *In hoc casu adamussim servetur quod praescribit Rubrica.* . . . . .

PAG. 525.[4]—Asserit in Hibernia Sacerdotes posse deferre plures particulas consecratas privatim de domo in domum quin vocati fuerint ad visitandos infirmos. Quum haec praxis paucis abhinc annis prohibita fuerit a Sacra Congregatione de Propaganda Fide, *immutanda est haec assertio, ac reformanda juxta hoc Decretum.*

Datum ex Secretaria Sacrorum Rituum Congregationis, die XIV Februarii, anni MDCCCLXVIII.

D. BARTOLINI, S.R.C. Secretarius.

(Loco Sigilli.)

---

[1] No. 457, III. [2] No. 707-709. [3] No. 806 No. 838.

CONTENTS.

CHAPTER I.

INTRODUCTION.

CHAPTER II.

SACRAMENTS IN GENERAL.

CHAPTER III.

SACRAMENT OF BAPTISM.

CONTENTS.

CHAPTER IV.

ORDER OF INFANT BAPTISM.

CHAPTER V.

BAPTISM OF ADULTS.

CHAPTER VI.

ORDER OF ADULT BAPTISM.

CHAPTER VII.

ORDER FOR SUPPLYING THE CEREMONIES OMITTED IN BAPTISM.

CHAPTER VIII.

RITE WHEN A BISHOP BAPTIZES.

CHAPTER IX.

BLESSING OF THE FONT.

CHAPTER X.

BLESSING OF WOMEN AFTER CHILDBIRTH.

CHAPTER XI.

SACRAMENT OF THE EUCHARIST.

CHAPTER XII.

ORDER OF HOLY COMMUNION.

CHAPTER XIII.

PASCHAL COMMUNION.

CHAPTER XIV.

COMMUNION OF THE SICK.

NOTES

RUBRICS OF THE ROMAN RITUAL.

CHAPTER I.

INTRODUCTION.

§ I. ORIGIN AND MEANING OF "RUBRICS."

*1. In the law books of the ancient Romans the titles
and inscriptions were marked in red with a kind of mineral
called "Rubrica," and hence the word "Rubricæ," applied
at first to the titles or inscriptions, came in the end to signify
the laws themselves.[1] The liturgical books which regulated
the solemn offices of the Church were marked in the same
way; and as in course of time they came to be almost the
only books so marked, the word "Rubrics" came to signify
almost exclusively the laws contained in these books.[2]

2. The word "Liturgy," from its etymology—λέῖτος and
ἔργον—signifies "public service," or "public ministry."
Applied to the offices of religion, it signifies, primarily, that
greatest and most excellent of all—the oblation of the holy
sacrifice, or the mass. But it is used also in a more extended
signification, as comprising not only the mass, and the
ceremonies immediately pertaining to the mass, but the
canonical hours, the administration of the sacraments, and
other public functions of the clergy.[3]

[1] Vid. Facciolati, *Lexicon*, v. *Rubrica*.
[2] Vid. Fornici, *Instit Liturg. Notiones Præviæ*, pag. 3.
[3] Fornici, ibid. pag. 1. Vid. Bouix, *De Jure Liturgico*, pars. i. cap. '.
et cap. ii. 6°.

3. The liturgical books contain these offices with the rubrics to be observed in them. Those now in use in the Western or Latin Church are—1° The Missal, containing the mass, with the method of ordering it, and the rites and ceremonies to be observed in celebrating it. 2° The Breviary, containing the canonical hours with the method of ordering the office for each day, and the manner of reciting it. 3° The "Ceremoniale Episcoporum," containing instructions on the manner of performing certain solemn functions in cathedral or collegiate churches, when the bishop or some dignitary officiates. 4° The Pontifical, containing the functions and the ceremonies to be observed in the functions that (if we except a few for which special faculties are sometimes given) are performed only by a bishop. 5° The Ritual, containing the rites and ceremonies to be observed in administering the sacraments (except confirmation and orders, which are administered only by a bishop,)[1] the office for the dead, and certain benedictions and processions. Nominally there are other liturgical books in use, but in reality they are these, or portions of these, as e. g., the "Antiphonarium," the "Graduale," etc., etc.

4. There are various liturgical books in use in the Greek and other Oriental churches, but the only one of these we may have occasion to refer to, is the Greek Euchologium, which contains the rites and ceremonies observed in the administration of the sacraments. It is, in fact, at once Ritual, Missal, and Pontifical.[2]

5. The distinction between "Rite" and "Ceremony" is not very accurately fixed. By "ceremony" some understand the sacred action with all its circumstances, and by "rite" the manner of performing the action, or the rules to be observed in performing it, so that the "ceremony" is the actual application of the "rite," or the actual observance of the rules laid down for the sacred action.[3] Others understand by "rite" all the words and actions that are substantial in the sacred function, and by "ceremony" those that are accidental.[4]

6. The two words, however, according to Catalani[5] and Fornici,[6] are generally used in the same sense—viz., to

[1] Vid. infra, chap. ii. § xvii.
[2] Cfr. Bouix, *De Jure Liturgico*, pars iv. cap. i.
[3] Baruff., Tit. i. n. 3; Catal., Tit. i. § ii. n. xiv.
[4] Vid. Fornici, l. c. pag. 2.
[5] Loc. cit.   [6] Loc. cit.

signify, Fornici says, the laws to be observed in public religious worship. It would be, perhaps, more exact to say that
by "Rite" or "Ceremony" is now commonly understood any
religious function performed according to certain laws fixed
by the Church. These laws, as has been stated, are contained in the Rubrics.

*7. For the present we are concerned only with the
rubrics of the Roman Ritual. The book is so called because it gives the sacred functions which it contains according
to the *Rites* used at Rome, and was published under this
title by the authority of Pope Paul V, as appears from the
bull *Apostolicæ Sedi*, given at the commencement of the
Ritual.[1]

8. It is shown by Bouix[2] that all the liturgies used
throughout the Western Church, except the Ambrosian,
retained at Milan, and the Mozarabic, used in Toledo, were
commonly called "Roman," before the correction made by
St. Pius V. They were so called, because they all agreed
substantially with the liturgy used in Rome, though differing
in many things from it, as well as from each other. Those
that had been in use in any church for two hundred years, at
the time of the correction, were allowed to be retained as
they were, and may therefore still, in a certain sense, be called "Roman," as they were called before. Since the correction, however, the Roman Liturgy is usually understood to be
the corrected Liturgy, unless where the contrary is expressed
or implied by the context. Hence it is that many of the
liturgical books, which differ considerably from the Roman,
and are now spoken of as opposed to the Roman, were nevertheless, before the correction, included under the general
name of "Roman."

*9. The rubrics, which regard the sacraments, embody
the teaching and instructions of the Church on the qualifications and duties of the minister, the dispositions of the recipient, and the ceremonies to be performed in the actual administration. It is plain, therefore, that a knowledge of these
rubrics is indispensable to a priest.

10. He acquires a good deal of this knowledge in his
theological studies, for a considerable part of the theology
that relates to the sacraments is occupied with the discus-

---

[1] Baruff., l. c. n. 5, et seq. Vid. Gardellini, *Annot. in Dec. S. R. C.,*
27 Aug. 1836, sub Dub. i. in *Rhedonen.,* n. 4780.
[2] *De Jvre Liturgico,* pars iv. cap. ii. § 2, prop. 1ª 2ª et 7ª.

sion of questions which are necessarily involved in the rubrics. A slight examination of the matter will show that the most approved decisions on these questions are sometimes embodied in the rubric, sometimes the best commentary on the text of the rubric. This is true, especially of the rubrics, which regard the duties of the minister and the dispositions of the recipient. There is this advantage in connecting the decisions of theology with the explanation of the rubric, that by doing so both are likely to be better remembered. The priest has the ritual constantly in his hand, and a glance at the rubric may suffice to recall to his mind the decisions connected with it; and again, this very circumstance will induce him to recur frequently to the text of the rubric. Commentators on the rubrics, therefore, usually discuss both the moral questions which the rubrics involve and the ceremonies which they prescribe.

11. But, besides, there is a great deal in the rubrics regarding the sacraments, which is not touched on at all, or touched on very slightly, in theological treatises. This is the case with nearly all the ceremonies that do not affect the validity or integrity of the sacrament. Yet many of these ceremonies are of great importance, and must be strictly observed by the priest, who is consequently bound to know the rubrics which prescribe them. The study of, at least, these rubrics is distinct from the study of theology, but still is necessary to the priest, who is charged with the duty of administering sacraments.

12. Accordingly, we find that "the rubrics" not only form a special branch of study in ecclesiastical colleges, but are made the subject of frequent ecclesiastical conferences by the clergy on the mission.

§ II. OBLIGATION OF THE RUBRICS.

*13. Rubrics in general are divided into "preceptive" and "directive." Preceptive rubrics are those which bind under sin. Directive rubrics do not bind under sin, but simply direct what is to be done by way of counsel and instruction. This is the distinction as commonly understood, and as the words themselves seem to imply.

14. But some authors understand by "preceptive" rubrics those that bind under grievous sin; and by "directive," those that bind under venial sin, at least in the sense, that to violate them without any reasonable cause would be a venial

sin. Cavalieri [1] seems to understand them in this sense. St. Liguori [2] rejects this explanation as incongruous. In referring to any author on the obligation of the rubrics, it is necessary to ascertain in what sense he uses the words; otherwise, his opinion might easily be misunderstood.

*15. It is certain that the rubrics which regard the administration of the sacraments are, with few exceptions, preceptive. Some prescribe what is required for the substance and integrity of the sacraments. Some prescribe what is known from other sources, as *e. g.*, from the decrees of councils, or the teaching of theologians, to be of strict precept. Some are expressed in a form which leaves no doubt as to the intention of the Church to make them preceptive.

*16. With regard to the rest, there are strong reasons for holding that, with the exceptions to be noticed presently, they, too, are preceptive. This is justly inferred from the canon of the Council of Trent, cited in the very first paragraph of the rubrics themselves:—" *Si quis dixerit, receptos* " *et approbatos Ecclesiæ Catholicæ Ritus in solemni Sacra-* " *mentorum administratione adhiberi consuetos, aut contemni,* " *aut sine peccato a Ministris pro libito omitti, aut in novos* " *alios per quemcumque Ecclesiarum pastorem mutari posse,* " *anathema sit.*"[3] St. Liguori [4] infers from these words that the rubrics to be observed in the actual celebration of Mass are preceptive; and it is evident that the words apply with equal force, and even more directly and explicitly, to the rubrics that regard the administration of the sacraments. The Roman Ritual introduces the canon in a way which leaves no doubt as to its application:

" UT EA QUÆ ex antiquis Catholicæ Ecclesiæ institutis, et sacrorum " canonum summorumque Pontificum decretis, DE SACRAMEN- " TORUM RITIBUS AC CÆREMONIIS HOC LIBRO PRÆSCRI- " BUNTUR, qua par est diligentia ac religione custodiantur et ubique " fideliter serventur illud ante omnia scire et observare convenit QUOD " SACROSANCTA TRIDENTINA SYNODUS DE IIS RITIBUS " DECREVIT IN HÆC VERBA: *Si quis,*" *etc.*

These words show that the Tridentine canon applies, at least, to what is prescribed by the rubrics in the actual solemn administration of the Sacraments, and, consequently, these rubrics at least are preceptive. But, in order to observe these,

[1] *Opera Liturgica*, tom. v. cap. ii. *De Rubricis*, n. 2 in fine
[2] Lib. vi. n. 399. *Tertia Sententia*, in fine.   [3] Sess. vii. can. 13.
[4] Lib. vi. n. 399, *Quarta Sententia*.

there are others that must be observed, and that consequently must be, at least so far, acknowledged to be preceptive.

*17. We here suppose the rubrics of which there is question to be the rubrics sanctioned by the Church. That these are, for the Latin Church, the rubrics of the Roman Ritual is justly inferred from the words cited, for these words clearly convey that the rites required by the Canon of Trent to be observed are the rites prescribed *in this book*, i. e., *in the Roman Ritual*. If the Canon of Trent could still apply to rites different from those of the Roman Ritual, it surely could not be put forward as a powerful motive why those prescribed in the Roman Ritual should be everywhere faithfully observed. The words by which the canon is introduced must, therefore, be understood to restrict the "approbatos ritus," from that time forth, to the rites prescribed in the rubrics which follow.[1] But we shall discuss the question more fully by and by.

18. A decree of Benedict XIII seems to convey clearly enough that the rubrics of the ritual regarding the administration of the sacraments are preceptive even in the most minute details. The decree, it is true, is not addressed to the whole Church, but is given amongst the acts of the council which this Pope held at Rome in the year 1725. At the same time it must be acknowledged to have great weight in the present matter. Its words are: "Cum invisi-
"bilia Dei per visibilia Religionis ac pietatis signa quæ
"cæremoniarum nomine censentur, intellecta conspiciuntur,
"Pastoralis nostri muneris curam ad hoc intendimus, et ab
"omnibus fieri volumus, et mandamus, ut in sacramentorum
"videlicet administratione, in missis et divinis officiis cele-
"brandis, aliisque ecclesiasticis functionibus obeundis non
"pro libito inventi et irrationabiliter inducti, sed recepti et
"approbati Ecclesiæ Catholicæ ritus *qui, in minimis etiam,*
"*sine peccato negligi, omitti vel mutari haud possint,* peculiari
"studio ac diligentia serventur; quamobrem Episcopis dis-
"tricte præcipimus ut contraria omnia quæ in ecclesiis seu
"secularibus seu regularibus (iis exceptis quæ Rituali, vel
"Missali, vel Breviario utuntur a S. Sede probato) contra
"præscriptum Pontificalis Romani et Cæremonialis Episco-
"porum vel rubricas Missalis, Breviarii, et *Ritualis* irrepsisse
"compererint, detestabiles tanquam abusus et corruptelas
'prohibeant et omnino studeant removere, quavis non obstante

[1] Vid. Bouix, *De Jure Liturg.*, pars iv. cap. iii. § v. punct. iv. 3*.

"interposita appellatione vel immemorabili allegata con-
"suetudine; cum non quod fit sed quod fieri debet sit
"attendendum."[1]

*19. What Benedict XIV says, speaking of the Rubrics
of the Missal, is evidently applicable to the Rubrics of the
Ritual as well, especially seeing that, in the decree of Benedict XIII just cited, both are regarded as equally binding.
In his work, *De Sacrificio Missæ*,[2] Benedict XIV says: "Ips.
"communis omnium sententia docet rubricas esse leges præ-
"ceptivas quæ obligant sub mortali *ex genere suo* ut loquun-
"tur theologi, ita tamen ut immunis sit a mortali qui eas
"non servat per invincibilem omnimodam imprudentiam et
"aliquando etiam propter parvitatem materiæ." These
words express precisely the conclusion which, we think,
should be adopted in practice on the obligation of the rubrics
that regard the sacraments.

*20. We have said there are exceptions. We must, of
course, except those rubrics which are expressed in a form
indicating that they are merely directive. We must except
those also which there is good authority for regarding as
directive. In a matter of this kind we need not expect
always to have certainty. We must very often be content
with a greater or less degree of probability. Treating of the
distinction between "preceptive" and "directive" as it affects
the rubrics of the Missal, Janssens uses the following words,
which clearly apply with equal force to the rubrics of the
Ritual: ". . . Rubricarum mens tum ex subjecta materia
"tum ex Pontificum aut S. R. C. decretis tum ex communi
"Ritualistarum consensu; tum etiam aliunde colligi potest,
"idque sæpissime certo, aliquando tamen probabiliter tan-
"tum, aut solum sub dubio, prout et saepe fit in re
Theologicâ."[3]

21. Some would except all those rubrics, of which the
matter is so minute and trifling as not to be fit matter for
a precept. The opinion of certain authors, cited by Merati,[4]
would favor this exception. Such rubrics, no doubt, ought
to be excepted, if they can be pointed out. But it would be
difficult, not to say impossible, to point out any such rubrics.
The words of the decree above cited[5]—*etiam in minimis*—
go to prove that there are no such rubrics. However minute

---

[1] Conc. Rom. 1725, tit. xv. cap. i. Labbe, curante Coleti, tom. xxi.
pag. 1874, Venetiis, 1733.   [2] Lib. iii. cap. xiii. n. 3.
[3] *Explan. Rub. Miss. Rom., Introductio practica*, § 2. n. 13.
[4] Pars iii. tit. xi. n. 1. *Tertia sententia*.   [5] Supra, n. 18.

the thing may be, there may be still good reason to make it matter of precept.[1]

*22. It is to be remembered, however, that in the non-observance of a preceptive rubric, according to the words of Benedict XIV just cited, not only want of advertence, but also the lightness of the matter, excuses from grievous sin; in other words, the rubric binds only *sub veniali* when the matter is of light importance. Now, when there is no scandal or contempt, any reasonable cause suffices to exempt from an obligation *sub veniali*, imposed by the ecclesiastical law; and, therefore, the non-observance of a rubric, when the matter is of light importance, is free from sin as often as there would be any notable inconvenience in observing it.[2]

*23. On the other hand, grievous sin might be committed by a number of transgressions or omissions against the rubrics in matters which, separately, would be of light importance, but, taken together, are enough to constitute the matter of grievous sin.[3]

24. When the meaning of a rubric is doubtful or obscure, and also in cases for which no provision is made in the rubric, there are three authorities to which recourse may be had for our guidance. These are—1° The decrees of the Sacred Congregation of Rites; 2° Custom; 3° The opinions of Rubricists or Commentators on the Rubrics.

§ III. DECREES OF THE SACRED CONGREGATION OF RITES.

25. The authority and the functions of this congregation are clearly set forth in the bull of Sixtus V, *Immensa æterni Dei*,[4] by which it was instituted along with many other congregations. The words of the bull, which regard the Congregation of Rites, are: "Quinque itidem Cardinales delegi-"mus, quibus hæc præcipua cura incumbere debeat, ut veteres "ritus sacri ubivis locorum, in omnibus Urbis, Orbisque "Ecclesiis, etiam in capella nostra Pontificia, in Missis, "divinis officiis, sacramentorum administratione, cæterisque "ad cultum pertinentibus, a quibusvis personis diligenter "observentur, cæremoniæ si exoleverint restitutantur, si de "pravatæ fuerint reformentur."[5]

---

[1] Cfr. Falise, *Cours Abrégé de Liturgie Pratique, Introduction pag.* 5.
[2] Cfr. St. Lig., lib. v. n. 170 et n. 173; lib. vi. n. 285 in fine, et 1. 347 in fine.
[3] De Herdt, pars. 6. n. 1, in fine. Cfr. St. Lig., lib. vi. n. 400.
[4] 11 Kalen. Feb., 1857. Bullarium Romanum. Edit. Car. Coque-lanes, Roma, 1747.   [5] § *Congregatio Vta.* n. 1.

26. It might be justly inferred from these words that the decrees of the Sacred Congregation are to be regarded as having the authority of the Sovereign Pontiff. But all doubt on the point is removed by the following answer, formally approved by the present Pope:—"An decreta a Sacra Con- "gregatione emanata, et responsiones quæcunque ab ipsa "propositis dubiis scripto formiter editæ, eandem habent "auctoritatem, ac si immediate ab ipso summo Pontifice pro- "manarent, quamvis nulla facta fuerit de iisdem relatio "Sanctitati Suæ? Resp. *Affirmative.*"[1] Another answer of the Sacred Congregation[2] explains the meaning of the words, "scripto formiter editæ." It declares that all decrees and responses are to be regarded as "scripto formiter editæ," that are signed by the Prefect and Secretary of the Sac. Cong., and also that all those in the collection of Gardellini are to be regarded as such.

*27. The Sacred Congregation, then, in the words of Cavalieri,[3] "pollet facultate per Sedem Apostolicam Sibi "factâ interpretandi et declarandi concessiones Pontificias, "Rubricas et quæcunque Decreta ac dubia, quæ circa eccle- "siasticos ritus, cæremonias, ac divina officia insurgant, et "circa eadem disponendi prout circumstantiæ et temporum "et congruentiarum varietas exposcunt."

28. It is to be observed that, under the general name of "Decreta Sac. Cong.," we are to understand as included not only decrees strictly so called, but also the resolutions, declarations, or responses of any kind that emanate from the Sacred Congregation. This is evident from the collection of Gardellini, which is entitled, "Decreta Authentica Congregationis Sacrorum Rituum," though it contains many that are not decrees in the strict sense.

29. The Decrees of the Sacred Congregation, considered as to their form, are of two kinds. Some are general, addressed to the whole Church, as *e. g.*, those in the beginning of the Missal and Breviary. Others, and by far the greater number, are in the form of answers to individuals or to particular churches, and even take their names, or the titles by which they are cited, from these churches, as *e. g.*, *in Mechli- nensi, in Baltimorensi,*[4] etc. But, though they are thus, in

---

[1] Die 23 Maii, 1846. *Ord. Prædicat.*, ad. 7; and this answer was confirmed and approved by His Holiness on the 17th July following, n. 5051.   [2] 8 April, 1854. *Romana.* n. 5202.
[3] Tom. i. cap. vi. Decr. 3. n. 12.   [4] Gardellini, *passim.*

form, particular, they are nearly all, in substance and intent, general and applicable everywhere throughout the Church. *Nearly all,* we say, for we must except those that imply a dispensation or privilege, or are given on account of special local circumstances.

*30. We cannot do better than give here the words of Cavalieri, which express the common opinion on this subject: "Habent Sac. Rit. Cong. Decreta ut, licet ad particularium "personarum instantias aut quæsita emanata ea sint, ad nor-"mam et exemplum pro iisdem et aliis similibus casibus in "Ecclesiâ universali deserviant, nisi peculiaris adsit ratio vel "inspecta sit aut circumstantia, quæ Decreta penitus particu-"larizet, et ultra personas vel ecclesias pro quibus emanarunt, "protendi ea non sinat. Talis est se in sacris ritibus diri-"gendi praxis omnium ecclesiarum. Talis est sensus omnium "Doctorum qui de sacris ritibus vel cæremoniis scripsere; et "si talis non foret procedendi ratio, vel nulla vel nimis incon-"stans ac varia eorundem sacrorum rituum, ac cæremoniarum "extaret norma ac regula, cum fere omnia eorundem directiva "Decreta ad instantiam particularium personarum sint emanata, "et admodum perpauca sint Decreta generalia."[1]

31. Some decrees are simply declaratory of the sense of the rubric. These bind as the rubrics themselves bind—being preceptive when the rubric is preceptive, and directive when the rubric is directive.[2]

32. Others are not purely declaratory of the sense, but prescribe what is only obscurely implied in the rubric or remotely deduced from it; or, perhaps, something for which the rubric makes no provision at all. Decrees of this kind are admitted by all to be preceptive when they are rigorously *decrees,* or whenever they have appended to them the clause "*servetur,*" "*servari mandavit,*" or the like. But when they are merely answers to doubts proposed, and are issued without any such clause, Merati[3] teaches, that though they are to be received with great respect, and to be preferred to any contrary opinion of authors, they are still to be regarded as only directive. St. Liguori[4] seems to adopt this opinion of Merati, and it is the opinion followed by De Herdt.[5] Some, however, maintain that all, even those that have no such clause, are preceptive.[6]

---

[1] Tom. i. cap. vi. *Decr.* 3, n. 4. Cfr. Fornici, *Notiones prœviœ,* pag. 4. De Herdt, pars i n. 3. ii. Gardellini *in Instruct. Clement.,* § 12. n. 4.
[2] De Herdt, l. c. iii.   [3] Pars iii. tit. xi. n. iii.   [4] Lib. vi. u. 401.
[5] L. c. cit.   [6] Cfr. Falise, *Introduction,* § ii

33. It is evident that the determination of the point depends altogether on the *intention* of the Sacred Congregation; for, according to what has been already stated,[1] there can be no doubt about its *power*. There are good reasons in favor of the opinion that the Sacred Congregation *has* the intention of making its decrees preceptive, even when it does not use the clause "*servari mandavit,*" or the like, but the authority above cited is enough to make the other opinion probable.

34. The decrees of the Sacred Congregation, like other laws, to be binding, must be sufficiently promulgated. Those that are merely declaratory are sufficiently promulgated in the rubric itself, and require only to be known as authentic.[2]

Those that prescribe anything new must be promulgated in the usual way.[3] The general decrees are published at Rome; the others are published in the particular churches to which they are addressed.

35. It is a disputed question whether decrees of this kind, addressed to particular churches, but of general application in the sense before explained,[4] are to be regarded as binding elsewhere, even though they be not solemnly promulgated to the entire Church. St. Liguori seems inclined to the opinion that they are not;[5] but he afterwards modifies this opinion by adding, that when such decrees are universally known, and are thus, in fact, promulgated by long usage and the constant reference of authors to them, they are binding on all.[6] Now, most of the decrees of the Congregation of Rites, and especially those of general application, may be truly said to be promulgated in this way, since the publication of the "Decreta Authentica Cong. Sac. Rit." by Gardellini.[7]

36. It is highly probable, therefore, that such decrees, though addressed to particular churches, are, at the present day, sufficiently promulgated to be binding. But even if they do not, in strictness, bind through defect of sufficient promulgation, it is at least highly laudable to observe them when there is no doubt about their authenticity.[8]

37. We may here observe that the decrees cited in the course of this work, and in the Appendix, are, unless when the contrary is expressed, taken from the third edition of

---

[1] Sup. n. 26, 27. [2] Cfr. St. Lig., lib. i. n. 200, *His positis.*
[3] St. Lig., l. c. [4] Sup. n. 29, 30.
[5] Lib. i. n. 106. Quaer. 2, *Secunda Sententia.*
[6] *Elenchus Quæstionum recentius reformatarum, Quæst.* ii. et in nota.
l. c. Edit. Mechlin, 1845. [7] Vid. sup., n. 26.
[8] Cfr. Bouix, *De Jure Liturg.,* pars ii. sect. ii. cap. vi.—*Scholium.*

Gardellini.[1] Certain decrees which, in the preceding editions, were published as supplementary to some of the volumes, are, in this edition, given and numbered in their proper places according to their dates. The numbers, consequently, in this edition are not the same as in the preceding editions; but this can cause no great inconvenience, as the titles and dates of the decrees are still the same. Even the numbers will be found generally to correspond, if from any proposed number in this third edition there be taken 146 or 149, the number of decrees previously published as supplementary. There can be no doubt about the authenticity of a decree given in this "Collection," for it has the requisite approval of the Sacred Congregation and the Sovereign Pontiff.

38. Gardellini has appended notes to several of the decrees. These notes have no public authority, but they derive great weight from the character and position of the writer, who was Assessor of the Congregation of Sacred Rites. His continuators also have appended valuable notes to some of the decrees issued since his time; that is, since May, 1826, the date of the latest decree given by Gardellini himself.

39. The most important of these decrees have been arranged in alphabetical order by Falise, the learned author of *Cours Abrégé de Liturgie Pratique*," and published in a small volume, which has already gone through several editions. The missionary priest will find it a very useful book.

*40. It has been decided that decrees of the Sacred Congregation have the effect of derogating from any, even immemorial, usage to the contrary ; but in any particular case recourse may be had to the Sacred Congregation for a toleration of the usage.[2]

*41. With respect to certain decrees which appear to be opposed to each other, Gardellini observes, in his preface, that the contradiction will be found, on a careful consideration of all the circumstances, to be in most of them only apparent; what is granted in one set of circumstances, *e. g.*, being refused in another, etc. But there are a few instances in which the Sacred Congregation has really changed or modified previous decrees, and in such cases we are to be guided by the latest issued on the subject.[3]

[1] Romæ, Typis S. Congregationis de Propaganda Fide, MDCCCLVI.
[2] 11 Sept. 1847. *In Angelop.*, ad. 16., n. 5102.   [3] Cfr. Decr. 28 Apr. 1741, n. 4110, *et Annot.* u 4542, ad. 4, 27 Sept 1817.

§ IV. CUSTOM.

*42. The Rubrics, if we except a few which regard the matter and form of the sacraments, are ecclesiastical laws, and, like other ecclesiastical laws, are affected by "custom."

43. We must here suppose the general principles regarding custom laid down by theologians and canonists in the treatise "*De Legibus.*" Custom may be in strict accordance with the law, *secundum legem;* or it may be beside, or go beyond, the law, *præter legem;* or it may be at variance with the law, *contra legem.*[1]

44. Custom which is in accordance with the law, that is, in the present matter, with the rubric, is the best interpreter of the rubric, according to the well-known axiom, "*optima est legum interpres consuetudo.*"[2] The actual practice of those who know the law, and who *bona fide* intend, in what they do, to fulfil the law, is a very good evidence of the sense in which the legislator wished his law to be understood.

45. When, therefore, the meaning of a rubric is doubtful, the actual practice of Rome is an excellent means of determining that meaning. The clergy there know the law, and intend to carry it out in their practice; and moreover, their practice is under the very eye of the supreme authority. The usage of Rome is, therefore, justly regarded as decisive in the matter of sacred rites. So it was regarded by Benedict XIV, who, when Archbishop of Bologna, condemned a certain practice in that city on the ground that it was opposed to the usage of Rome, which he says "Sacrorum Rituum magistra merito appellatur."[3]

46. Custom which goes beyond the rubric, "*præter legem,*" i. e., which requires something not contained or implied in the rubric, but yet not at variance with it, may have all the conditions necessary to make its observance licit, or even obligatory.

47. It is a matter of little moment whether we are to regard custom with these conditions as sufficient of itself to induce an obligation, or as merely the evidence of an unwritten law from which it has its origin. The former is the

---

Suarez, *De Legibus*, lib. vii. cap. iv.
[2] *l. Si de interpretatione ff. de Legib.*, apud Reiffenstuel, tom. '. lib L Decret., tit. iv. n. 8.　　　　[3] *Instit.* xxx. n. 23.

opiniou of Suarez,[1] and is the one commonly received. The latter is the opinion of Cardenas,[2] which is developed and maintained at great length by the "Mélanges Théologiques."[3]

48. Whatever be the source of the obligation, it is certain, at all events, that "custom" has sometimes the force of law; and that this is the case in ceremonies as well as in other matters, appears from certain decrees of the Sacred Congregation,[4] and might be inferred from the words of the rubric regarding local usages in the marriage ceremony.

49. These two kinds of custom present little difficulty in the matter of ceremonies. The chief difficulty is in determining how far custom of the third kind, "*contra legem,*" can justify a departure from the rubrics, or how far any existing custom at variance with the rubrics can be licitly retained.

*50. There can be little doubt that custom, with certain conditions, can abrogate any human law. "Nihil magis "tritum," says Benedict XIV,[5] "quam legem quamlibet "humanam, etiam canonicam, posse contrariâ consuetudine "quæ sit rationabilis et legitimo præscripta, abrogari, juxta "textum in cap. final. *de Consuetudine.*"

51. The conditions required are expressed in the words "*rationabilis et legitime præscripta,*" which are the words of the text referred to, taken from the decretal of Gregory IX. But all are not agreed as to what precisely must be understood as included under these words. Benedict XIV., in another place in the same work,[6] explains them thus. Having stated that custom may abolish a law, he adds, that for this it must have certain conditions:—"Et primo quidem ut sit "rationabilis, hoc est, neque juri divino, neque naturali con- "traria nec expresse a jure reprobata, aut in legislatoris con- "temptum invecta: deinde ut a majori communitatis parte "libere et sponte sit inducta, pluribusque ac continuis actibus "frequentata animo legem tollendi: ac demum ut adsit "consensus legislatoris non quidem expressus et *personalis,* "qualem cum aliis necessarium voluit Pontius, lib. 6 de "Matrim., cap. 6, n. 7, sed consensus legalis et juridicus, qui

---

[1] *De Legibus,* lib. vii., cap. 14, et seq.

[2] *Crisis Theol.,* tract. iii. *de Legibus et præceptis,* disp. xxiii. cap. v. art. v. vi. et viii.

[3] IIme Serie. Art. "*De la coutume en Rubriques,*" pag. 208 et seq.

[4] 15 Sept. 1668, *in Conversan.,* n. 2448,—13 Jul., 1675, *in Aquil.,* n. 276.

[5] *De Synod. Diœc.,* lib. xii. cap viii. n. 8.   [6] Lib. xiii. cap. v. n. 5.

"nimirum jam habetur per leges et canones omnem consuetu-
"dinem populi moribus inductam approbantes, eique vires
"tribuentes abrogandi legem: quod communissime sentiunt
"doctores congesti a Suarez cit. lib. 7, cap. 18, num. 14."
These words, taken in connection with the preceding extract,
show that, to be "legitime præscripta," according to Benedict
XIV, the custom must prevail amongst the greater part of
the community with the intention of abrogating the law, and
must also have (at least constructively) the consent of the
legislator.

*52. The chief point, after all, in this matter is, to ascer-
tain whether the custom opposed to any law has the sanction
of the legislator; because, as the same great authority states,
"Quod consuetudo prævaleat contra legem superioris, id
"oritur ex ipsomet superioris consensu qui eam etiam suæ
"legi obviantem, cum rationabilis et diuturna est, statuit tole-
"randam."[1] It is then justly observed by Falise,[2] that all
the other conditions laid down and discussed by theologians
and canonists are no more than the preamble, as it were, to
that consent of the legislator, whether express or by legal
construction, from which, and from which alone, custom
derives its efficacy.

*53. From all this, then, it is evident that no custom,
however widespread or long-continued, can be allowed to
prevail against the rubric, unless so far as the legislator,
that is, the Sovereign Pontiff, by himself, or by the Congregation of Rites as his organ,[3] consents to, or tolerates that
custom.

*54. The whole inquiry is thus practically reduced to
the simple question of fact, viz: In what, and how far, does
the Holy See consent to any existing custom at variance with
the rubrics?

To answer this question satisfactorily, it is necessary to say
a word on each of the liturgical books separately.

55. And, first, with regard to the Missal.‐ The bull of
St. Pius V, *Quo primum*,[4] given at the commencement of the
Missal, prohibits the use of any other than the Missal then
published, and all customs at variance with its rubrics, in all
churches, "in quibus missa conventualis alta voce cum choro,
"aut demissa, celebrari juxta Romanæ Ecclesiæ ritum con-
suevit vel debet"—that is to say, throughout the whole Latin

---

[1] Lib. xii. cap. viii. n. 8.
[2] *Introduction au Cours Abrégé de Liturgie*, § iv.
[3] Vid. supra. n. 24.   [4] Pridie idus Julii, 1570.

Church.[1] It excepts only those churches in which a different usage had been followed for two hundred years previously. After declaring that churches in which other Missals had been in use for this period, are permitted to follow the ancient usage, the bull proceeds—. . . "ex aliis vero omnibus "ecclesiis præfatis eorumdem missalium usum tollendo, "illaque penitus et omnino rejiciendo, ac huic missali nostro "nuper edito, nihil unquam addendum, detrahendum aut "immutandum esse decernendo, sub indignationis nostræ "pœna, hac nostra perpetua valitura constitutione statuimus ' et ordinamus. Mandantes, ac districte omnibus et singulis ". . . . illis in virtute sanctæ obedientiæ præcipientes "ut, cæteris omnibus rationibus et ritibus ex aliis missalibus "quantumvis vetustis hactenus observari consuetis in posterum "penitus omissis, ac plane rejectis, missam juxta ritum, mo- "dum, ac normam quæ per missale hoc a Nobis nunc traditur, "decantent ac legant," etc., etc.

56. It appears, therefore, that a custom at variance with the rubrics of the Missal has the sanction of the Holy See, and can be licitly retained, provided it had existed for two hundred years before the date of this bull. It is true, this is not exactly the case of custom abolishing a law, but rather of custom in certain places preventing a general law from being extended to these places. But the effect is the same. Such a custom, where it exists, may be regarded as one at variance with the rubric, and yet having the consent of the Holy See.

57. But it is evident from the words cited, that this con- sent cannot be claimed for any other custom, either then ex- isting or afterwards introduced, against the rubric of the Missal. If there could be any doubt on the point, it is re- moved by several decrees of the Congregation of Rites, in which all such customs are declared to be abuses. Thus, in the decrees, printed by order of Urban VIII, at the com- mencement of the Missal we have these words: "Demum "renovando decreta alias facta, mandat Sacra Congregatio in "omnibus et per omnia servari Rubricas Missalis Romani, non "obstante quocunque prætextu, et contraria consuetudine quam abusum esse declarat." Other decrees of the same import may be seen in Gardellini.[2] There is one rubric,

---

[1] Vid supra, n. 8.
[2] In *Oscen.*, 15 March, 1591, ad. 10, n. 15,—14 June, 1845, *Ord. Discal.*, n. 5018.

however, which may perhaps be excepted; that, namely, which regards the purification to be administered to the laity after communion. We shall have occasion to refer to it in treating of the similar rubric given in the Ritual.[1]

58. All that has been said regarding the Missal, is equally applicable to the Breviary. The bull, *Quod a nobis*, printed at the commencement of the Roman Breviary, contains similar provisions, and almost in the very same words, regarding the obligation of using it, except where another had been in use for two hundred years. The decrees of the Sacred Congregation also insist, in similar terms, on the strict observance of its rubrics.[2]

59. The bull of Clement VIII, *Ex quo in Ecclesia Dei*, given at the commencement of the " Pontificale Romanum," orders, in like manner (but without any exception in favor of custom, however ancient), the strict observance by all who exercise Pontificalia, of what is there prescribed for the various functions contained in it, and prohibits any change or modification whatever.

60. With regard to the "Cæremoniale Episcoporum," the bulls printed at the commencement of it are no less clear and decisive as to the strict obligation of following what it prescribes. To show that no custom can be allowed to prevail against it, it is enough to cite the following words of a decree of the Sacred Congregation, dated so recently as 12 Dec., 1832.[3] " Cæremonialis Episcoporum legem a summis " Pontificibus Clemente VIII, Innocentio X, et Benedicto " XIV, latam et confirmatam, hujusmodi indolis esse, ut a " nulla contraria consuetudine abrogari valeat, accedentibus " præsertim non paucis S. R. C. decretis."

61. It had been declared in previous decrees,[4] that the " Cæremoniale" does not do away with laudable immemorial customs. If by " laudable customs" we can understand any that are opposed to the Cæremoniale, and not simply those that are in accordance with it, or at least reconcilable with it, they must be, in the strictest sense, *immemorial ;* otherwise, their observance is not lawful.[5]

*62. And now we come to consider the question of cus-

[1] Vid. infra. chap. xii. § I.
[2] 16 March, 1658 *in Jacen.*, n. 1868,—17 Nov. 1674, *in Veronen.*, n. 2719,—28 Sept. 1675, *in Compostell.* ad 5, n. 2749.
[3] *In Pisana*, n. 4696.
[4] 11 Jun. 1605, *in Hispan.*, n. 266—17 Jun. 1606, *in Elbor.*, n. 318.
[5] Vid. Bouix. *De Jure Liturg.*, para iv. cap. 3, § iv.

tom as it affects what is prescribed by the Roman Ritual. It is not easy, it must be confessed, to determine how far the consent or toleration of the Holy See is extended to customs at variance with the rubrics of the Ritual.

*63. The bull of Paul V, *Apostolicæ sedi*, printed at the commencement of the Ritual, is as follows : " Apostolicæ Sedi " per abundantiam divinæ gratiæ, nullis suffragantibus meritis, " præpositi, Nostræ sollicitudinis esse intelligimus, super " universam Domum Dei ita invigilando intendere, ut op- " portunis in dies magis rationibus provideatur, quo, sicut " admonet Apostolus, omnia in ea honeste, et secundum " ordinem fiant, præcipue vero quæ pertinent ad Ecclesiæ Dei " Sacramentorum administrationem, in qua religiose observari " Apostolicis traditionibus, et SS. Patrum Decretis constitutos " Ritus et Cæremonias pro Nostri officii debito curare omnino " tenemur. Quamobrem fel. rec. Pius Papa V, Prædecessor " noster, hujus Nostri tunc Sui officii memor, ad restituendam " sacrorum Rituum observationem in sacrosancto Missæ " Sacrificio, divinoque Officio, et simul ut Catholica Ecclesia " in Fidei unitate, ac sub uno visibili capite B. Petri suc- " cessore Romano Pontifice congregata, unum psallendi et " orandi ordinem, quantum cum Domino poterit, teneret, " Breviarium primum, et deinde Missale Romanum, multo " studio et diligentia elaborata pastorali providentia edenda " censuit. Cujus vestigia eodem sapientiæ spiritu secutus simi- " lis memoriæ Clemens Papa VIII, etiam Prædecessor Noster, " non solum Episcopis, et inferioribus Ecclesiæ Prælatis " accurate restitutum Pontificale dedit, sed etiam complures " alias in Cathedralibus et inferioribus Ecclesiis cæremonias " promulgato Cæremoniali ordinavit. · His ita constitutis, " restabat, ut uno etiam volumine comprehensi, sacri et sinceri " Catholicæ Ecclesiæ Ritus, qui in Sacramentorum adminis- " tratione, aliisque Ecclesiasticis functionibus servari debent, " ab iis, qui curam animarum gerunt, Apostolicæ Sedis " auctoritate prodirent, ad cujus voluminis præscriptum, in " tanta Ritualium multitudine, sua illi ministeria tamquam ad " publicam et obsignatam normam peragerent, unoque ac fideli " ductu inoffenso pede ambularent cum consensu. Quod " quidem jampridem agitatum negotium, postquam Generalium " Conciliorum græce latineque divina gratia editorum opus " morari desivit, sollicite urgere Nostri muneris esse exis- " timavimus. Ut autem recte, et ordine, ut par erat, res " ageretur, nonnullis ex Venerabilibus Fratribus nostris S. " R. E. Cardinalibus, pietate, doctrina et prudentia præstan

"tibus, eam demandavimus, qui cum consilio eruditorum
"virorum, variisque præsertim antiquis et quæ circumferuntur,
"Ritualibus consultis, eoque in primis, quod vir singulari
"pietatis zelo, et doctrina bonæ memoriæ Julius Antonius
"S. R. E. Cardinalis S. Severinæ nuncupatus, longo studio,
"multaque industria et labore plenissimum composuerat, rebus-
"que omnibus mature consideratis, demum divina aspirante
"clementia, quanta oportuit brevitate, Rituale confecerunt.
"In quo cum receptos et approbatos Catholicæ Ecclesiæ
"Ritus suo ordine digestos conspexerimus, illud sub nomine
"Ritualis Romani merito edendum publico Ecclesiæ Dei bono
"judicavimus. Quapropter hortamur in Domino Venerabiles
"Fratres Patriarchas, Archiepiscopos, et Episcopos, et dilectos
"Filios eorum Vicarios, necnon Abbates, Parochos universos,
"ubique locorum existentes, et alios, ad quos spectat, ut in
"posterum tamquam Ecclesiæ Romanæ filii, ejusdem Ecclesiæ
"omnium matris et magistræ auctoritate constituto Rituali
"in sacris functionibus utantur, et in re tanti momenti, quæ
"Catholica Ecclesia, et ab ea probatus usus antiquitatis
"statuit, inviolate observent.
"Datum Romæ apud S. Mariam Majorem, sub Annulo
"Piscatoris, die xvii. Junii MDCXIV. Pontificatus Nostri
anno X.

"*S. Cobellutius.*"

*64. Now, it must be evident that the use of the Roman
Ritual, to the exclusion of every other, is not here insisted on
in terms like those of the bull *Quo primum* above cited[1] regarding the use of the Missal, or the similar terms employed
regarding the use of the Breviary, Pontifical, and Cæremoniale.
Instead of *mandantes* . . . *in virtute sanctæ obedientiæ
præcipientes, etc., etc.,* we have here merely . . . *hortamur in Domino* . . . . ut in posterum . . . .
utantur, etc. . . . . Accordingly, some theologians have
maintained that the use of the Roman Ritual, though
earnestly recommended, is not of precept, that whatever it
contains of precept is of precept *aliunde,* and that the rest is
prescribed only *de decentiâ.* This opinion is cited by St.
Liguori without disapproval.[2] Catalani, while he extols the
authority of the Roman Ritual, holds, nevertheless, that particular churches may use their own ritual . . . "modo
"ritus laudabiles sint ac probati, nihilque contineant quod
"Christianæ doctrinæ, bonisque moribus adversetur."[3]

[1] Supra, n. 55. [2] Lib. vi. n. 285, *Dub.* 4. [3] *Præf. ad Lectorem,* n. xi.

According to De Herdt,[1] the Church has approved of the Roman Ritual, and wishes to have it used everywhere, but does not impose it as of precept. He infers this, (a) from the words of the bull, which merely exhort, but do not command; (b) from a decree of the Sacred Congregation, in which, in reply to the Archbishop of Manilla, it expresses only a desire "*placere sibi*" that the observance of the Roman Ritual be introduced if it had not been so already;[2] and (c) from the notorious fact that other rituals, or, as they are sometimes called, pastorals, are used in some places with the knowledge, and with at least the toleration, of the Holy See. He cites a decree of the third synod of Mechlin, approved by the Holy See, in which it is ordered that " In administrandis sacramen- " tis pastorale suæ Ecclesiæ cathedralis omnes sequantur, et " eo deficiente, Ecclesiæ metropolitani, nihil temere addendo, " demendo, vel immutando." This decree, however, is of little weight, because the synod was held in 1608, six years before the publication of the Roman Ritual.[3]

*65. On the other hand, there are good reasons for hold- ing that the use of the Roman Ritual is obligatory every- where throughout the Latin Church. The words of the bull, it is true, do not formally convey a precept, but, on careful examination, it will be seen that they suppose or employ one. The Pontiff commences by declaring that he is strictly bound by his office to take care that, in the administration of the sacraments, the rites and ceremonies established by apostolic tradition and the decrees of the fathers be religiously ob- served; . . that, as his predecessors had published the Breviary, Missal, Pontifical, and Ceremonial, it remained only to have published, by the authority of the Holy See, a Ritual, according to which, as a public and authorized standard, amidst such a multitude of rituals, those who have care of souls should perform their sacred functions. Having stated what means were taken to prepare it, he proceeds to say that, see- ing it to contain the received and approved rites of the Catho- lic Church, he publishes it under the title of the Roman Ritual for the public good of the Church of God. *In quo cum receptos et approbatos Catholicæ Ecclesiæ ritus suo ordine digestos conspexerimus, illud sub nomine Ritualis Romani merito edendum publico Ecclesiæ Dei bono judicavimus.* Wherefore he exhorts all . . . . for the future, as

---

[1] Pars vi. n. 1.   [2] 2 Maii, 1626, *in Manilien.*, n. 629.
[3] Cfr. Mélanges Théologiques, VIme série, pag. 340.

children of the Roman Church, to use in their sacred functions the ritual established by the authority of the same Church, the mother and mistress of all, etc. *Quapropter hortamur in Domino, etc.*, as above.[1]

Now the canon of the Council of Trent, previously cited, declares that, in the solemn administration of the sacraments, there is a strict obligation of observing the received and approved rites of the Catholic Church, and the bull here expressly affirms that those rites are contained in the Roman Ritual. Whence it plainly follows that in the administration of the sacraments, there is a strict obligation of observing what is prescribed in that Ritual. It is true that, in this matter, a certain latitude ought, perhaps, to be admitted. It may be contended that rites differing from each other in some details could, nevertheless, all be "recepti et approbati" in the sense of the canon. But there is no sufficient security that those contained in any ritual published without the sanction of the Roman Pontiff are "recepti et approbati."[3]

To make the use of the Roman Ritual preceptive, then, at least as far as the administration of the sacraments is concerned, the Pontiff may have judged it sufficient to declare that it contains the "receptos et approbatos Ecclesiæ Catholicæ ritus," the canon of Trent having already defined that there is an obligation of observing these.

66. This interpretation is confirmed by the consideration, that one declared object of the Pontiff is to secure uniformity in the administration of the sacraments and other ecclesiastical functions, by fixing one amongst the various rituals then in use as a standard to which all should conform. Such an object could hardly be attained, or could be attained only very imperfectly, unless the standard ritual were made obligatory everywhere. From the word *ubique*, in the first paragraph of the rubrics above cited,[4] Baruffaldi[5] infers the intention of the Church to secure uniformity by making the Roman Ritual obligatory everywhere. In another part of his commentary also[6] he urges the same reason, and insists on the obligation of pastors to use the Roman Ritual and no other.

67. According to this view, the "*hortamur in Domino*" is to be understood, not as a mere counsel, but as an earnest exhortation to do what had just been sufficiently declared to be of strict obligation.[7]

[1] Supra, n. 63.   [2] Supra, n. 16.   [3] Vid. supra, n. 17.
[4] Supra, n. 16.   [5] Tit. ii. n. 9.   [6] Tit. ii. n. 84 et seq.
[7] Cfr. Clericati *de Extrema Unctione*, Decis. 66, n. 19 et seq.

68. We have before cited[1] the decree of Benedict XIII, in which bishops are strictly ordered to prohibit, and to labor zealously to remove as a detestable abuse, whatever they may find opposed to the Rubrics of the Ritual. This decree, whose authority, as has been said,[2] is of the greatest weight, appears to leave no doubt that there is a strict obligation of using the Roman Ritual everywhere except in those churches which are excepted in the decree itself, viz., those in which the Holy See has sanctioned the use of a different ritual.

69. Since the time of Benedict XIII, the Congregation of Rites has issued several decrees which clearly enough convey the same thing. Thus it has frequently answered: "Servetur Rituale Romanum;" "Juxta Rituale Romanum;" "Juxta Ritualis Romani Rubricam;"[3] "Illi soli libri adhi- "bendi, et in illis tantum benedictionibus, quæ Rituali Romano sunt conformes."[4]

Again, amongst the decrees regarding prohibited books at the beginning of the Index, we have "§ IV. 1, Benedictiones "omnes ecclesiasticæ, nisi approbatæ fuerint a Sac. Rit. Con. "7 Rituali Romano additiones omnes factæ aut faciendæ post "reformationem Pauli V, sine approbatione S. R. C."[5]

70. It would be impossible, we think, to reconcile these declarations and decrees with the supposition that custom, or episcopal authority in any diocese, is enough to justify a departure from the Rubrics of the Roman Ritual, or to justify the use of any other ritual at variance with it.

71. But all doubt on this point would appear to be removed by certain recent answers of the Sacred Congregation—one to the Bishop of Troyes, cited by the "Mélanges Théologiques,"[6] which declares that the laws of the Roman Ritual affect the whole Church: "Rituale "Romanum," it says in referring to it, "cujus leges uni- "versam afficiunt Ecclesiam;" another to the Curé of Bar- sur-Aube, declaring that he may use the Roman Ritual notwithstanding the prohibition of his bishop;[7] and another

---

[1] Sup., n. 18. [2] Loc. cit.
[3] 1 Dec. 1742, *Nullius Fasani*, n. 4133;—23 Maii, 1835, *Ord. Min.*, n. 474º, ad. 1;—12 Mart. 1836, *in Trident.*, n. 4777, ad. 13.
[4] 7 April, 1832, *in Arminen.*, n. 4681, ad 5.
[5] Vid. "*Index Librorum Prohibitorum,*" in "*Dictionnaire des Hérésies,*" Migne, Paris, 1853, pag. 935.   [6] VIᵐᵉ *Série*, 3ᵐᵉ Cahier, p. 339.
[7] 22 Maii, 1841, *in Trecen.*, given by Falise in the *Alphabetical Com- pendium* (vid. supra n. 39), V. *Rituale Romanum*, and referred there to No. 4779 in Gardellini, though we could not find it in our copy of Gar- dellini (Editio tertia, Roma, MDCCCLVI).

to a canon of Mans,[1] in which it is declared that the canons or other priests of the diocese could not, with a safe conscie ce, infringe or neglect the preceptive rules of the Roman Ritual, nor would the authority of the bishop be sufficient to justify them in doing so.

*72. We conclude, therefore, that, although on account of the reasons and authorities above stated,[2] it cannot be said to be perfectly certain, it is at least far the more probable opinion, that the Roman Ritual is obligatory everywhere throughout the Latin Church, and that the Holy See alone can authorize any change or modification in what it prescribes. Whatever doubt there may be as to the obligation imposed by the bull of Paul V, there can hardly be a reasonable doubt as to the obligation expressed or implied in the subsequent decrees and declarations above cited.

73. To the argument from the sanction or toleration of a different ritual in some places, it may be answered: 1° The approval by the Holy See of a different ritual in a particular place, serves only to confirm the general obligation (which is all we contend for) of using the Roman, according to the principle "exceptio firmat regulam." The decree of Benedict XIII, above cited,[3] expressly refers to such exceptions. 2° Some of these rituals differ from the Roman only by the addition of certain customary ceremonies, in themselves laudable, such, e. g., as the rubric of the Roman Ritual itself expressly wishes to have observed in the celebration of marriage. The Ritual published for the use of the English clergy,[4] may perhaps be taken as an example. Others differ from it only by the omission or abbreviation of certain ceremonies authorized by special indult or dispensation from the Holy See, as, e. g., the ritual published for the use of the clergy in the United States.[5] 3° The toleration extended to certain rituals published by episcopal authority, and differing considerably from the Roman, proves nothing but the forbearance of the Holy See. While it declares, on every con venient opportunity, the obligation of the Roman Ritual, it does not enforce the obligation by severe penalties. That is all. And there may be good reasons for this forbearance. It may be that in some places the observance of the Roman

---

[1] 10 Jan. 1852, in Cenomanen., n. 5165, ad 4.
[2] Supra, n. 64.   [3] Sup., n. 18.
[4] Ordo administrandi Sacramenta, etc., . . . ex Rituali Romano . . . nonnullis adjectis ex Antiquo Rituali Anglicano. Derbiæ, Richardson, 1856.   [5] Excerpta ex Rituali Romano, etc.—Baltimori, 1860.

Ritual would interfere with long-established customs, which the people are attached to, and would not willingly give up, and that it is a less evil to tolerate such customs, than to run the risk of suddenly interfering with them. But the obligation of the Roman Ritual, though suspended, so to speak, by the circumstances, still exists, and requires that at least an effort be made to prepare the way for its introduction. And here we may, not improbably, find a reason why the bull of Paul V concludes, as it does, by earnestly exhorting, instead of commanding, etc. There was a great variety of rituals then in use, as the bull itself states; and there was, consequently, a great variety of usages in different parts of the Church. Perhaps, then, the Pontiff—knowing the great difficulties there might be in some places in conforming at once to the Roman Ritual, and abolishing customs of long standing—judged it expedient to adopt the form he did adopt; that is, to state reasons from which not only the importance, but the strict obligation, of following the Roman Ritual might be apparent, and yet to urge its actual observance only in such terms as would leave the bishops and pastors considerable latitude in respect to the time and circumstances in which they would introduce it. The decree of the Sacred Congregation, referred to by De Herdt,[1] is in perfect accordance with this supposition. The Sacred Congregation contents itself at that time—hardly twelve years after the publication of the Ritual—with expressing a desire, but does not yet think it expedient to insist, as it might, that, in the case proposed, the Roman Ritual should be observed. The tone of subsequent decrees, as we have seen, is very different.

74. In all this discussion we have considered the obligation of the Roman Ritual only as it regards the administration of the sacraments. The bull declares that it contains the received and approved rites of the Church, and as the Council of Trent has defined that, in the solemn administration of the sacraments, these rites cannot be omitted "pro libito" without sin, it evidently follows that the priest, in such administration, is bound to comply with the rubrics of the Roman Ritual. But if another ritual be approved of by the Holy See for a particular place, it may, of course, be followed in that place, because any change or omission, being duly authorized, would not then be "pro libito."

75. It is to be observed, however, that the arguments

---

[1] 2 Maii, 1626—Vid. supra. n. 64.

adduced, except the one from the Canon of Trent, apply not only to the rubrics that regard the administration of the sacraments, but to those that regard the other ecclesiastical functions as well. Thus, the bull itself having stated what had been done for the other liturgical books, says : . . . "resta-"bat ut, uno etiam volumine comprehensi, sacri et sinceri "Catholicæ Ecclesiæ ritus, qui in sacramentorum administra-"tione, *aliisque ecclesiasticis functionibus* servari debent ab "iis qui curam animarum gerunt, Apostolicæ sedis auctoritate "prodirent," etc. ; and concludes by urging the use of the ritual then published, not merely in the administration of the sacraments, but *in sacris functionibus*, which must be under-stood as comprehending all the ecclesiastical functions con-tained in the Ritual.

The decree of Benedict XIII also applies to the other functions as well as to the administration of the sacraments, as is evident from the words ;[1] and the same may be said of the decrees of the Sacred Congregation[2] some of which regard, not the administration of the sacraments, but other functions.

*76. Supposing, then, this general obligation of the Ro-man Ritual, we come at length to the question, How far the consent of the Holy See has been given to any custom at variance with what the Roman Ritual prescribes.[3] The answer may be collected from what has been said. 1° That consent is expressly given to the laudable customs observed in particular places in the celebration of marriage. The ceremony of marriage, as given in the Roman Ritual, is very short and simple, and such customs being additions to it, may, perhaps, be regarded as at variance with the rubric ;[4] though in strictness they are rather to be looked on as in accordance with it, since the rubric itself expresses a wish that they be observed. 2° The rituals approved of by the Holy See for use in particular places, such, *e.g.*, as the rituals referred to parenthetically in the decree of Benedict XIII,[5] differ from the Roman, chiefly by embodying in their rubrics certain customs peculiar to those places. The approval, there-fore, of such rituals may be regarded as giving consent to the customs which they contain.

*77. But we doubt if the consent of the Holy See can be claimed for any other customs that could be looked on as

[1] Supra, n. 18.　　[2] Supra, n. 69.　　[3] Vid. supra, n. 54.
[4] Vid. supra, n. 69, in fine.　　[5] Supra. n. 18.

in any way at variance with the rubric of the Roman Ritual. *Consent*, we say, because there may be, and there have been often, granted indults or dispensations in virtue of which such customs are allowed to be continued for a time; but of course, as soon as the indult ceases, the rubric or law of the ritual revives with all its force.

*78. We have still, however, to consider whether custom, though it may want that consent which is necessary to make it prevail against the rubric, does not, mediately and indirectly, justify the neglect of what the rubric prescribes, by making it very difficult, or morally impossible, to observe it. This is a question of the greatest importance as regards Ireland, and countries similarly circumstanced.

*79. In Ireland the Roman Ritual of Paul V was introduced immediately after its publication. Amongst the statutes of Clonmacnoise, avowedly taken from previous synodical decrees of the province of Armagh,[1] we have the following " 7. Statuimus et ordinamus omnibus sacerdotibus hujusce " dioecesis in administratione sacramentorum, solo Rituali " Romano, et non alio uti." These statutes are dated Oct. 7 1624, only ten years after the date of the bull *Apostolicæ Sedi*.[2] In the statutes of Tuam, A. D. 1631, it is ordered that, " 18. Omnes et singuli hujus Provinciæ Tuamensis " eodem Rituali Romano Pauli Papæ V utantur."[3] In another synod of Tuam, A. D. 1660, we find the following : " 4. " Decernitur sacramenta administranda esse juxta sacros Can- " receptasque rubricas Ritualis Romani Pauli V, et laudabilem " praxim orthodoxæ ecclesiæ in Hybernia, ac proinde hac in " parte omnes abusus, præsumptiones anticanonicas, et cor- " ruptelas abolendas esse."[4] The " laudabilis praxis," here mentioned, is probably the use of a few ceremonies taken from the old Ritual of Sarum, which were generally observed throughout the country . In the synod of Drogheda, held in February, 1614, it was ordered that, in the administration of the sacraments and other sacred functions, priests should observe strictly . . . " as far as possible, all the ceremonies of " the holy Roman Catholic Church, and at least admitting no " change from them, except those of the Ritual of Sarum, ' which has been tolerated for a long time in this province

---

[1] Vid. *Collections on Irish Church History from the MSS. of the V. Rev. Lawrence Renehan*, by Rev. Daniel M'Carthy, p. 146, et seq.
[2] Supra, n. 63.   [3] *Collections, etc.*, Appendix D, p. 499.
[4] *Ibid.* p. 501.

"and throughout the kingdom."[1] The Sarum rites are still observed in the celebration of marriage, and one or two other sacred functions, and hence the edition of the Roman Ritual used by the Irish clergy contains a few extracts from the Ritual of Sarum.

*80. But the operation of the penal laws against the Catholic religion made it impossible to carry out many things prescribed by the rubrics. With regard to some rubrics, there was an absolute impossibility of observing them, inasmuch as there were no churches and very few clergy. With regard to others, the difficulty of observing them was so great, that the bishops were obliged to seek and to use extensive faculties of dispensing in them. Mass was celebrated, and baptism with the solemn ceremonies, as well as the other sacraments, was administered in private houses; and this often under an apprehension of danger so great that, on these occasions, some of the faithful were usually posted as sentinels at convenient places to guard against a sudden surprise, and the consequent arrest, or perhaps the massacre, of all concerned.[2]

*81. Again, all the clergy were educated in continental countries, and some had been employed in pastoral duties in those countries before entering on their mission in Ireland. These, in many instances, learned the use of diocesan or provincial rituals, differing from the Roman in many details, and embodying usages peculiar to the diocese or province in which they had been officiating. On coming to Ireland, they brought with them these usages, and taught them to others, and transmitted them to their successors, many of whom had no other knowledge of ceremonies than what they acquired in this way. It is easy to see that such a state of things, continued through several generations, should naturally give rise, as it did, to many omissions, and to many practices at variance with the rubrics.

*82. It could not be expected that customs thus established would disappear at once with the persecution from which they sprung. The toleration granted to the Catholics could affect such customs only by very slow degrees. When churches began to be erected, they were at first so few and so remote from the houses of many of the parishioners, so poor also, and so badly provided with vestments and other requisites, that little or no change could yet be made. Besides,

[1] *Collections*, etc., Appendix A, p. 429.
[2] Vid. *Ibid.*, Lives of the Primates Maguire, M'Mahon. and O'Reilly, pp. 84–103.

the number of clergy was very small compared with the population. Each priest was consequently charged with the care of so many souls, often scattered over an extensive district, that in administering the sacraments he was obliged, in most cases, to shorten the ceremonies—in fact, to adopt as his general rule what the rubric permits only in cases of necessity, or what the Holy See permits by special faculties granted to bishops and vicars-apostolic in missionary countries. This is the reason why, in the epitome of the Roman Ritual published for the use of the Irish clergy, many important rubrics were omitted. They could not, in the circumstances of the country, be observed, and their insertion, therefore, would needlessly increase the size and expense of the volume.

83. Thank God, this state of things exists no longer. The improvement, slow at first, has been very notable and very rapid of late years. Churches have been multiplied, and the clergy very much increased in number, while a great zeal for sacred ceremonies has been manifested everywhere throughout the country, especially since the Synod of Thurles. The improvement is still going on, and we may hope that many years will not elapse until every trace of the mutilation caused by the penal laws will have disappeared from our ritual observances.

*84. As yet, however, neither the churches nor the clergy are sufficiently numerous to make it possible to comply with all the rubrics of the Ritual as they are carried out in some Catholic countries. There are parishes where many of the old customs are still justified by necessity. There are others in which the same customs, though not justified by a strict necessity, are, nevertheless, so interwoven with the habits of the people and of the older clergy, that they could not be suddenly abolished without causing great inconvenience and great dissatisfaction. Now, in circumstances like these, it may be fairly contended, that custom, though it does not abolish the law of the rubric, suspends its obligation until the difficulties in the way of its observance are removed.

*85. It is for the bishop to judge of the nature and extent of these difficulties, and to take such measures as prudence may suggest for their removal. The Sacred Congregation, consulted on a case of the kind, left the bishop to deal with it as he might judge prudent in the circumstances. This was the purport of the answer given to the Bishop of

Monte Pulciani, when there was question of a custom at variance with express decrees of the Sacred Congregation: "Pro gratia speciali, non obstantibus decretis, Episcopus "pro suo arbitrio et prudentia juxta particulares casus et "circumstantias indulgeat."[1] And Gardellini observes, with reference to a somewhat similar answer concerning communion at a Requiem Mass, that it is not unusual for the Sacred Congregation to act in this way, in order to avoid offence or scandal: "Novum non est ut S. C. prudenti "aliqua discretione utatur in iis quæ in sacris ritibus quam- "dam possunt aut moderationem aut indulgentiam admit- "tere, ad effectum evitandi admirationem offensionemve et "scandala."[2]

*86. It is certain, at all events, that no priest should undertake to change an existing custom, where such change would involve the danger of offence, without having previously consulted the bishop. But where there is no such danger— where there is question simply of the observance of rubrics that were previously slurred over or neglected—there is no reason why he may not, and should not, endeavor to comply with them as exactly as circumstances permit.

*87. We cannot do better than give here the words of the Synod of Thurles, in reference to this important matter: "Optaret hæc Synodus ut ea omnia quæ, ob temporum "calamitates, Ecclesiæ legibus minus conformia, præsertim "in sacramentorum administratione, inducta sunt, ad normam "generalis disciplinæ quam citissime reducerentur; verum "cum, ut ait S. Augustinus, 'quæ utilitate juvant, novitate "'quandoque perturbant,' sequentia tantum ad renovationem "disciplinæ hac in re spectantia monenda aut statuenda "censet.

"1º Ritus omnes præscripti in Rituali Romano, Rubricis "Missalis, et Pontificali Romano pro Sacramentorum admin- "istratione, quantum circumstantiæ hujus regionis permittunt, "accurate observentur," etc.[3]

88. In explaining some of the rubrics, we shall have occasion to notice a few of the difficulties that are still in the way of a full compliance with what is prescribed, and to suggest means by which, in many instances, at least, these difficulties might be diminished or altogether removed.

---

[1] 22 Jul. 1848, *in una Montis Politiani*, n. 5130.
[2] *In fine annotationis* ad Dub. ix. *Panormit.*, 12 April, 1823, n. 4594.
[3] *De Sacramentis*, pag. 16.

§ V. RUBRICISTS.

89. It is evident that, in explaining the meaning of any rubric, we must attach great weight to the opinions of writers who have made the rubrics a special study, or who have specially treated the questions which the particular rubric may chance to involve. The Sacred Congregation has sometimes answered a question by directing those who proposed it, to consult approved writers on the rubrics. Thus, to a question regarding the genuflections to be made in presence of the Blessed Sacrament exposed, it concludes the answer by the words, "pro reliquis consulantur Rubricistæ."[1]

90. When these writers are unanimous, or nearly so, in giving a certain meaning to a rubric, or in inculcating a certain obligation, as implied in a rubric, or connected with it, it may be taken as a sure sign that the rubric has that meaning, or involves that obligation. Such unanimity is, in truth, but the expression in words of the sentiments of the Church, or of that approved custom which, as has been previously stated,[2] is the best interpreter of laws. Just as the unanimous consent of theologians is an evidence of what the Church teaches regarding any point of faith or morals,[3] so here the unanimity of interpreters may be taken as an evidence of the meaning which the Church intends to convey in the words of her law.[4]

91. But since there is question here, for the most part, of positive laws, which the Church may enforce, modify, or revoke, according to circumstances, it is clear that the authority of rubricists, even if unanimous, must yield to a declaration of the Church herself, and therefore is of no weight against a decree of the Sacred Congregation, which, as we have seen,[5] is in this matter the organ of the Church. When we speak, therefore, of the weight to be attached to their authority, we suppose that it is not contravened by any clear declaration of the Church.[6]

92. When rubricists are divided in opinion, we must consider the authority on each side, the character of the writers, and the reasons they give. We should also take into account

---

[1] 12 Nov. 1831, in una Marsorum. ad 53, n. 4669.
[2] Sup. n. 44.
[3] Vid. Melchiorem Canum De Locis Theol., lib. viii. cap. iv. n. 3.
[4] Falise, Cours Abrégé de Liturgie Pratique, Introduction, § iii. n. 9, 10.
[5] Sup. n. 26.   [6] Falise, l. c. 3º.

the time and the place in which they wrote. As there is question of interpreting the rubrics of the Roman Ritual, it may be fairly assumed that those who knew best the Roman practice, ought to be the best interpreters of the Ritual. Modern writers also, *cæteris paribus*, should have greater authority, as they alone can be acquainted with those recent decrees which have set at rest so many questions, formerly the subject of warm discussion.[1] There are many points on which as yet no clear decision has been given, and regarding which there are different opinions. In treating of these points, though we often indicate a preference for some one opinion, we endeavor to state the others fairly, that the reader may decide for himself.

93. In the Appendix will be found a notice of the principal works which we have consulted, and from which we have, in a great measure, compiled the "Notes." Here we shall merely say that we cite no authority at second-hand, except in a few instances; and in these we are careful to give a reference to the work in which we have found the authority cited.

[1] Falise, l. c. 4º.

CHAPTER II.

ON WHAT MUST BE OBSERVED GENERALLY IN THE ADMINISTRATION OF THE SACRAMENTS: "DE IIS, QUÆ IN SACRAMENTORUM ADMINISTRATIONE GENERALITER SERVANDA SUNT."

§ I.—Ut ea quæ ex antiquis Catholicæ Ecclesiæ institutis, et sanctorum Canonum Summorumque Pontificum Decretis, de Sacramentorum Ritibus ac Cæremoniis hoc libro præscribuntur, qua par est diligentia ac religione custodiantur, et ubique fideliter observentur; illud ante omnia scire, et observare convenit, quod Sacrosancta Tridentina Synodus, sess. vii. can. 13, de iis Ritibus decrevit in hæc verba : *Si quis dixerit, receptos et approbatos Ecclesiæ Catholicæ ritus in solemni Sacramentorum administratione adhiberi consuetos, aut contemni, aut sine peccato a Ministris pro libito omitti, aut in novos alios per quemcumque Ecclesiarum Pastorem mutari posse, anathema sit.*

94. The meaning of this first paragraph of the rubrics, and the obligation imposed by the canon of the Council of Trent here cited, have been noticed in the preceding chapter.[1] The rubric itself, it will be seen, here asserts that what the Ritual prescribes regarding the sacraments is taken from the ancient established usage of the Catholic Church, the decrees of the Sovereign Pontiffs, and the sacred canons. This is substantially the same as what is asserted in the bull *Apostolicæ Sedi ;* viz., that the Ritual contains the received and approved rites of the Catholic Church.[2]

95. The Canon of Trent is thus immediately and directly applied to *the rites prescribed in this Ritual to be observed* in the solemn administration of the Sacraments.[3]

These rites, therefore, may not "be contemned, or without "sin be omitted at pleasure by the ministers, or be changed "by every pastor of the churches into other new ones."[4]

96. It is evident that to maintain the proposition condemned by the Canon of Trent would be implicitly to maintain that

---

[1] Sup., n. 16.   [2] Vid. supra. chap. i. n. 65.
[3] Vid. Falise, *Cours Abrégé*, etc., 3me partie, Introduction. n. 6.
[4] Vid. *Canons and Decrees of the Council of Trent*, translated by the Rev. J. Waterworth.

the Church has not power to institute ceremonies or require their observance under pain of sin, which is an error in faith.[1]

97. "Nor is it without reason," says the Catechism of the Council of Trent, "that the administration of the Sacra-"ments has been, at all times, from the earliest ages of the "Church, accompanied with certain solemn ceremonies. "There is, in the first place, the greatest propriety in mani-"festing towards the sacred mysteries such a religious "reverence as to appear to handle holy things holily. The "ceremonies themselves also display more fully, and place as "it were before the eyes, the effects of the Sacraments, and "impress more deeply on the minds of the faithful the holi-"ness of these things. They also elevate to the contempla-"tion of sublime things the minds of the spectators who "observe them with attention, and excite within them senti-"ments of faith and charity."[2]

§ II.—Cum igitur in Ecclesia Dei nihil sanctius aut utilius, nihilque excellentius aut magis divinum habeatur, quam Sacramenta ad humani generis salutem a Christo Domino instituta, Parochus, vel quivis alius Sacerdos, ad quem eorum administratio pertinet, meminisse in primis debet, se sancta tractare, atque omni fere temporis momento ad tam sanctæ administrationis officium paratum esse oportere.

. 98. "Of the many definitions, each of them seemingly "apt and appropriate, which may serve to explain the nature "of a Sacrament, there is none," says the Catechism of the Council of Trent,[3] "more simple and perspicuous than that "of St. Augustine, a definition which has since been adopted "by all scholastic Doctors: ' A Sacrament,' says he, ' is a "' sign of a sacred thing;' or, as has been said in other words, "but to the same purport, A Sacrament is a visible sign of "an invisible grace, instituted for our justification." Some, while adopting this definition in substance, make it more clearly and accurately applicable to the Sacraments of the Old as well as of the New Law, by putting it in some such form as the following, which is that of Coninck,[4] and is perhaps the most exact definition of a Sacrament in general : " Res vel cæremonia sacra sensibilis ad aliquam sanctitatem "pro statu ecclesiæ tunc existentis convenientem hominibus suo ·· usu conferendam et ad veram sanctitatem significandam legi-"time stabiliterque instituta."

---

[1] Vid. Perrone, De Sacramentis in genere, cap. iv.
[2] Pars ii. cap. i. n. 18, Donovan's Translation, Rome, 1839.
[3] Pars ii. cap. i. n. 4.   [4] De Sacram. in genere, Art. iv. Dub. i. n. 17 Edit. Rhotomagi, MDCXXX.

9). The Sacraments of the Old Law conferred only legal sanctity. Those of the New Law confer true internal sanctity. The Sacraments of the New Law, as the Rubric here states, were instituted by Christ for the sanctification and salvation of men. "Through them," says the Council of Trent,[1] "all "true justice either begins, or, being begun, is increased, or, "being lost, is repaired." Nothing in the Church, therefore, is more holy, nothing demands to be treated with greater reverence. The parish priest, or any other priest who is charged with the administration of the Sacraments, must always bear this in mind, as he is here admonished, and be prepared at all times to fulfil this sacred duty.

*100. During the first three centuries of the Church, the pastoral duties were performed by the bishop, who resided in the chief city of his diocese, and was assisted by a number of priests who lived with him. It was not until the fourth century that priests were charged with the care of particular districts. This was the origin of the present parochial system, which was formed by degrees as the faithful increased in number, and were scattered through the villages and country districts at a distance from the chief cities.[2]

*101. It is the right and the duty of the parish priest, according to the canons, to administer the sacraments to his flock, and as a general rule no other can lawfully administer them in his parish without his permission.

*102. But the bishop has still all the rights of an ordinary pastor throughout every part of his diocese, and the Pope is the supreme pastor of the universal Church; so that a priest may be authorized by either of them to administer sacraments independently of the parish priest.

*103. Hence it is that regulars, in virtue of privileges conferred on them by the Holy See, commonly hear confessions and administer the Eucharist in their churches independently of the parish priest; but their privileges do not extend to the other sacraments (except as regards persons who belong to the order, and cases of necessity), nor even to the Eucharist, when there is question of paschal communion or the viaticum.[3]

§ III. Quamobrem illud perpetuo curabit, ut integre, caste, pieque vitam agat; nam etsi Sacramenta ab impuris coinquinari non possint, neque a pravis Ministris eorum effectus impediri: impure tamen et indigne ea ministrantes, in æternæ mortis reatum incurrunt.

[1] Sess. vii. De Sacrament. Proœmium, Waterworth's Translation.
[2] Vid. Devoti. Inst. Can., lib. i. tit. iii. sec. x. Bouix, De Parocho, Pars i. sect. i. cap. iv.   [3] St. Lig., lib. vi. n. 239, 240.

104. It was an error of the Donatists, refuted by St. Augustine, and condemned by the Church in the fourth century, that a sacrament could not be validly conferred by a person in mortal sin. This error was revived by Wickliff, and condemned in the Council of Constance. Amongst the articles of Wickliff, condemned by that Council, the fourth asserts: "Si episcopus vel sacerdos est in peccato mortali, "non ordinat, non conficit, non consecrat, non baptizat."[1] The same error having been adopted by the Anabaptists, was again condemned in the Council of Trent.[2]

105. But, though the sacrament be valid, the minister who confers it in the state of mortal sin is guilty of a grievous crime. This is quite certain in the case of a priest who administers a sacrament solemnly, and "ex officio."[3] Some theologians maintain that he would not be guilty of mortal sin by merely giving Holy Communion, because, as they say in this case, "non conficit sacramentum."[4] Benedict XIV cites this opinion, but says the contrary is to be held.[5] St. Liguori[6] also holds that the priest in such a case would be guilty of mortal sin; though he admits, as more probable, that the sin is not multiplied numerically, but only aggravated by the number of communicants.

106. When baptism is administered in case of necessity by a laic, or even by a priest, not in the state of grace, it is the opinion of many theologians, with St. Thomas, that he is not guilty of mortal sin. St. Liguori[7] admits this opinion as probable, but thinks it intrinsically more probable, with Lacroix and others, that the administration of the sacrament even in this case is *per se* a mortal sin, on account of the great irreverence, though *per accidens* the minister may be excused, as he may be called on so suddenly as to be unable previously to elicit an act of contrition.[8] But this excuse can hardly be admitted in case of the pastor, who is bound "ex officio," and may be called on at any moment to administer the sacraments. He should be at all times in a condition to administer them, as he is warned in the preceding rubric, in words taken from the instructions of St. Charles Borromeo, and quoted by St. Liguori.[9] With regard to marriage, St.

---

[1] Concil. Constant. sess. viii. *Articuli Joannis Wickliff.* Labbe, vol. xvi. page 119.
[2] Sess. vii., can. xii.   [3] St. Lig., lib. vi. n. 31.
[4] Lugo, *De Sacramentis*, Disp. viii. n. 155.
[5] *De Sacrif. Missæ*, lib. iii. cap. xix. n. 2.   [6] Loc. cit. n. 35.
[7] Lib. vi. n. 32.   [8] Loc. cit. n. 33.   [9] Ibid. *A fortiori.*

Liguori maintains, as more probable also, that the parties contracting would sin grievously, not only by receiving the sacrament, but by administering it, in a state of mortal sin.[1]

§ IV.—Sacerdos ergo, si fuerit peccati mortalis sibi conscius (quod absit,) ad Sacramentorum administrationem non audeat accedere, nisi prius corde pœniteat: sed si habeat copiam Confessarii, et temporis locique ratio ferat, convenit confiteri.

107. If a priest, then, should unhappily be conscious of mortal sin, he must not dare to administer any sacrament without having previously made an act of contrition, or gone to confession. The words of the rubric, "convenit confiteri," do not imply an obligation of going to confession, even when he has the opportunity.

108. If he has to say Mass, he is bound to confess, however contrite he may believe himself to be;[2] but this is by a special precept, affecting those who are about to receive the Eucharist, and commonly understood by theologians to be even a divine precept, implied in the words of the Apostle:[3] "Probet autem seipsum homo," etc.[4]

109. But, when there is question of administering a sacrament, even the Eucharist, it is sufficient that he make an act of contrition, or of sorrow which he "bona fide" believes to be contrition,[5] though confession is recommended if he has an opportunity. This is the more probable opinion, and the one more commonly held by theologians. St. Liguori even proves it from the words of this very rubric, "convenit confiteri," which merely recommend confession, but do not impose it as an obligation.[6]

110. Some, however, insist on the obligation of confessing, because, 1°, the reasons why confession is required in the case of one about to receive the Eucharist, may be applied whenever the state of grace must be recovered, before administering or receiving any sacrament. 2°, Because a person in the state of sin cannot have true contrition, if, having an opportunity of confessing, he declines to avail himself of it, since true contrition includes a desire of going to confession.

111. These reasons, however, are not conclusive; for we have just seen that there is a special positive precept affecting

[1] Loc. cit. n. 32. *Infertur* 2.
[2] Conc. Trid. Sess. xiii., *De Euch.*, can. xi.   [3] 1 Cor. xi. 28.
[4] St. Lig. lib. vi. 255, 256.   [5] Baruff., Tit. ii. n. 39.   St. Lig., lib. vi. n. 6, and n. 269. Vid. Suarez, Disp. xvi. sect. iii. 5 et 6.
[6] Lib. vi. n. 34. Cfr. Bouvier, *De Sacram.*, cap. v. § ii. Quær 2, 2°.

those who are about to receive the Eucharist, which does not exist with regard to those who administer it, nor with regard to those who either administer or receive any other sacrament.[1] The motive of the precept may be the more effectually to secure purity of conscience in the communicant, and this motive may be more or less applicable in the other cases, it is true; but this does not suffice to extend the precept to them. The second reason, though specious, is not solid. Contrition, it is true, includes the "*votum sacramenti*," as the Council of Trent teaches,[2] and therefore the desire of confessing and receiving absolution—but at what time? Catalani[3] says, as soon as possible—"quam primum." Few, however, would maintain this opinion. It is enough to have the purpose of confessing *when the precept of confession urges*, and it cannot be shown that a purpose of confessing any sooner is required. A person, therefore, may have true contrition, and thereby recover the state of grace, though he has no intention of going to confession immediately, or on the first opportunity, provided the precept of confession does not urge just then.

112. And here we may see the effect of the special precept regarding the Eucharist: it renders it impossible that any one, conscious of mortal sin, and being about to receive communion, can have true contrition, if, having the opportunity, he neglects to fulfil the precept of confession *which just then urges*. But, in the other cases, there is no such reason to prevent his having true contrition.

113. In all this we have been considering what the priest is strictly bound to, in order to avoid sacrilege. But in reference to his obligations generally, it may be said with perfect truth, that he cannot preserve the necessary purity of conscience unless he makes it his constant study to live "integre, "caste, pieque," as is stated in the preceding rubric; and the priest who does so, should he have the misfortune of falling into any grievous sin, will hardly fail to have recourse at once to the tribunal of penance, as the surest and most efficient means of recovering the state of grace; for few, as the Catechism of the Council of Trent teaches,[4] have that perfect contrition which suffices to blot out sin.

§ V.—Quacumque diei ac noctis hora, ad Sacramenta ministranda vocabitur, nullam officio suo præstando, præsertim si necessitas urgeat,

---

[1] Catalani, Tit. i. cap. i. § iv. n. viii., *Secundo quia*. etc. Delahogue, *De Sac. in genere*, cap. vi. art. ii. *Præterea ipsa contritio*. etc.
[2] Sess. xiv. cap. 4.   [3] Loc. cit.   [4] Pars ii. cap. v. n. 30.

moram interponat, ac propterea populum sæpe, prout sese offert occasio,
præmonebit, ut cum sacro ministerio opus fuerit, se quamprimum
advocet, nulla temporis, aut cujuscumque incommodi habita ratione.

114. A pastor or priest charged with the care of souls is
bound to reside within the limits of his parish, and in the
parochial house, if there be one. This is the general rule, to
which few exceptions are allowed.[1] If there be no fixed
parochial residence, his house should be so situated that the
parishioners can have easy access to him when they require
him to administer the sacraments.[2] The statutes of each
province or diocese usually determine everything that pertains
to the obligation of residence. The priest is, of course,
bound to comply with the statutes of the diocese in which he
serves.

*115. But it is of the greatest importance that he should
also attend to the admonition of the present rubric. No
doubt it may sometimes happen that the priest is sent for
without any real necessity; that the person he is called on
to visit is unwilling or unfit to receive the sacraments, etc.,
etc.; but yet the only safe rule is to obey the summons without
hesitation or delay. Better surely to make ten visits that are
not strictly necessary, than fail in one that is so. Hence, he
is here admonished to give notice to the people, from time to
time, that they should have no difficulty in calling on him at
once when his ministrations are required. This notice might
seem superfluous in some places, but there is no place in
which it is not useful; for it always emboldens those who
might otherwise be afraid or unwilling to call on him until
the last moment.

116. Theologians discuss whether or not the pastor is bound
to administer the sacraments even at the risk of his life, as in
time of pestilence, etc. They are agreed that he is, when
there is question of the sacraments necessary to salvation,
as Baptism or Penance; but it is probable that he is not,
when there is question of any of the other sacraments. Even
Baptism and Penance he may administer " per alios," and in
some circumstances he should do so, in order that he himself
may hear the confessions of those who would otherwise be
afraid to come near him, lest they might catch the infection.[3]

[1] Bouix. De Parocho, pars v. cap. ii. § vii.
[2] St. Lig., lib. v. n. 121 et 124, Parochi autem.
[3] St. Lig., lib. vi. n. 233. Vid. Benedict XIV. De Synod. Diœc., lib.
xiii. cap. x. t. n. 6.

§ VI.—Ipse vero antequam ad hujusmodi administrationem accedat, paululum, si opportunitas dabitur, orationi, et sacræ rei quam acturus est, meditationi vacabit, atque ordinem ministrandi, et cæremonias pro temporis spatio prævidebit.

*117. Before administering any sacrament he is here recommended to pray and to reflect for a few moments on the sacred act he is going to perform. No particular prayer is prescribed, but the "*Veni Sancte Spiritus*," etc., is very appropriate. It is the prayer recommended by St. Charles.[1] The words, "si opportunitas dabitur," like the words in the Rubric of the Missal, "pro temporis opportunitate,"[2] show, according to Baruffaldi,[3] that there is no strict obligation; but it is plain that a compliance with what is here recommended is the best means of securing the gravity and reverence with which these holy functions should be performed.

*118. It is very important, too, and especially for any one of little experience on the mission, to read attentively beforehand the rubrics regarding the sacrament he is going to administer, that he may have clearly before his mind what he is to do, and how he is to do it. This precaution would often prevent embarrassment to the priest himself, and consequent scandal to those who witness the ceremony; for few cases occur in which he shall not be instructed by the rubric how he is to act.

§ VII.—In omni Sacramentorum administratione superpelliceo sit indutus, et desuper stola ejus coloris quem Sacramenti ritus exposcit; nisi in Sacramento Pœnitentiæ ministrando occasio vel consuetudo, vel locus interdum aliter suadeat.

119. In administering the sacraments the priest must be vested in surplice and stole. This is the general rule to which the rubric admits only one exception, apart from cases of necessity. No mention is here made of the soutane, or "vestis talaris," because this is supposed to be the ordinary dress of the priest; but where it is not, of course it should be put on, as the surplice is worn only over a soutane, or at least a garment which can fairly be called a "vestis talaris."

*120. There is some variety in the size and form of the surplice in different places. That which is called the French surplice has no sleeves, but, instead of them, wings or pendants from the shoulders reaching almost to the ground.

---

[1] *Act. Eccl. Mediol.*, Pars iv. § *Instructiones generales de Sacramentorum administratione*, p. 408.
[2] *De Prep. Sacerd.*, n. 1.
[3] *Rit. Rom. Com.*, tit. ii. n. 42.

What is called the Roman surplice is usually shorter and has wide sleeves. The form described by Gavantus[1] and Bauldry,[2] after the instructions of St. Charles, is the one most commonly adopted. There is no general law, however, fixing the precise shape, and each one should follow the approved custom of his diocese. The first Provincial Council of Baltimore prescribed for the American clergy a particular form of surplice, which it described in its decree as the form used in Rome. But the Sacred Congregation observed that the form described could not be affirmed to be the only form used in Rome, and directed the decree to be altered, so as to order simply : " Superpelliceum esse debere modestum, deco-"rum et sacris functionibus conveniens."[3]

*121. The rochet differs from the surplice in being generally shorter, and always having tight sleeves.[4] It is a vestment which properly belongs to bishops, and can be worn by inferior dignitaries only when they have special permission from the Holy See.[5] But in the administration of the sacraments, even by canons who may have the use of the rochet, the surplice must be worn, according to several decisions of the Sacred Congregation.[6] Bishops alone who are not members of a religious order, can wear the stole over the rochet.[7]

*122. The surplice, according to Gavantus,[8] from the etymology of the word, "superpelliceum," and its color, being a white robe thrown over the garments (tunicas pelliceas, Gen. iii. 21), that became necessary in consequence of the sin of Adam, signifies the innocence and purity with which we are clothed in putting on the second Adam. Hence the bishop, in conferring tonsure, puts the surplice on each one, saying, " Induat te Dominus novum hominem qui secundum Deum " creatus est in justitia et sanctitate veritatis."[9] And it is a laudable custom, recommended by Baruffaldi,[10] to recite the same prayer while putting on the surplice, changing a single word, and saying, " Induat me Dominus," etc.

---

[1] De mensuris propriis Sacræ Supellectilis, pars v.
[2] De forma et mensuris Eccl. Supell.
[3] Sacræ Congregationis de Propagandâ Fide Instructio circa decreta a Synodo Provinciali Baltimoriensi edita. In decreto 32°. Vid. Append.
[4] Gavantus, Par. 2, Tit. 1, n. 2, lit. z.
[5] Macri, Hierolex., v. Rochettum.
[6] 12 Jul. 1628, in Dub. Urbis ad 1, n. 753.—31 Mai, 1817, ad 1, Dub. addit., n. 4536.—10 Januar. 1852, in Cenoman., ad 5, n. 5165.
[7] Vid. infra, chap. viii. § iii.   [8] Loc. cit. lit. a.
[9] Pontif. Rom., De clerico faciendo.
[10] Tit. ii. u. 48.

*123. The stole is put on over the surplice, so as to fit rather close to the neck, and hang straight over the shoulders in front. It is always worn in this manner over the surplice.[1] But when worn over an alb, with or without a cope, at the altar or elsewhere, it should be always crossed on the breast as it is in vesting for Mass, unless when the celebrant is a bishop, or has the privilege of wearing the pectoral cross.[2] It must be of a color suited to the sacrament that is to be administered. What this color is, we shall see in treating of each sacrament. There are five ecclesiastical colors—viz., white, red, green, violet, and black—and of these we may here observe that violet is used for Penance, Extreme Unction, and the first part of the ceremony of Baptism; white for the Viaticum, the Marriage ceremony, and the second part of Baptism; and the color of the office of the day for the Eucharist, when not administered as the Viaticum.

*124. The stole, which was originally a complete garment covering the whole body, assumed its present form after the introduction of the alb.[3] It signifies, mystically, the cords by which our Lord was bound, or the cross which was laid on his shoulders. Morally, it signifies the yoke of Christ and the virtue of obedience.[4] Putting on the stole, the priest should kiss it in the centre, and recite the prayer of the Missal as in vesting for Mass, "*Redde mihi Domine stolam,*" etc.[5] This prayer is very appropriate, since it is only by submitting to the yoke of Christ that we can recover what we lost by the disobedience of our first parents.[6]

*125. In requiring the use of the surplice and stole, the rubric makes one exception. It does not insist on their use in administering the sacrament of Penance, when the circumstances of time, place, etc., might make it inconvenient, or when there is a custom against it. Baruffaldi[7] observes that many religious hear confessions in the habit of their order In these countries the surplice is seldom worn in the confessional, but the stole commonly is. Another exception, of course, is the administration of Baptism in case of necessity.[8] With regard to the other sacraments, we shall see hereafter[9]

---

[1] Baruff., l. c. n. 49.   [2] Merati, pars ii. tit. i. n. xxxi.
[3] Merati, pars ii. tit. i. n. xxviii.
[4] Gavantus, pars ii. tit. i. Rub. 6, *Expositio Vestium.* Benedict XIV. *De Sacrif. Miss.*, cap. x. n. 7. De Herdt, l. c. n. 51.
[5] Baruff., n. 48.   [6] Benedict XIV. l. c.   [7] Loc. cit. n. 56.
[8] Baruff. l. c. Vid. infra, cap. iii. § xiii.
[9] Infra. chap. xvi. § v.

how far necessity can justify their administration without
surplice and stole.

§ VIII.—Adhibebit quoque unum saltem, si habeat, vel plures Clericos,
prout loci et Sacramenti ratio postulabit, decenti habitu, et superpelliceo
pariter indutos.

*126. The rubric, no doubt, contemplates clerks or clerics
in the strict canonical sense, i. e., persons who have received
at least the tonsure, for these alone have the privilege of
wearing the surplice, according to Baruffaldi,[1] Catalani,[2]
Baldeschi,[3] and others. The Council of Trent expresses a
wish that a number of clerics should be attached to every
parochial church;[4] and if such were the case, the view of
these authors might be strictly adhered to. But it is the case
in very few instances at present, and the functions of clerk
are now nearly everywhere performed by laics in soutane and
surplice. Seeing that the practice has the sanction, or at
least the toleration, of the bishops, and that it contributes so
much to the decorous celebration of public worship, Cavalieri[5]
would not venture to condemn it; neither would De Herdt.[6]
Even St. Charles Borromeo, so exact in all that regards ritual
observances, allowed it in churches not having a sufficient
number of clerics.[7]

127. Those selected for the purpose should be carefully
instructed in the ceremonies and duties they are required to
perform when serving Mass, or assisting in the administration
of the sacraments. There is no parish in Ireland, and there
are few places in any country, in which the priest may not
easily find some intelligent boys whom he could instruct in
this way; and their assistance, while it would comply with
the rubric, would make the ceremony easier for himself, and
give it an imposing effect, which it otherwise could not have.
If a number of such boys be once well instructed in any
parish, the succession can be easily kept up, as the older and
more experienced would train the others. There should be
one clerk at least to assist when a sacrament is conferred,
but it would be desirable to have two or more on occasions
of greater solemnity. Their duties will be mentioned in
treating of each sacrament.

[1] Loc. cit. n. 60.   [2] Tit. i. § viii. n. iii.
[3] Esposizione delle Sacre Ceremonie, tom. i. cap. xii. n. 1.
[4] Sess. xxiii. cap. 17. De Ref.
[5] Tom. iv. cap. iv. in Decr. xiii. n. 19.   De Communione Fidelium.
[6] Tom. i. par. i. n. 50, vi.
[7] Act. Eccl. Mediol., pars iv.   Instr. de Sacr. Commun. p. 607.

128. In no circumstances can a female be allowed simply to perform the duties of a clerk in the administration of the sacraments.[1] But in a convent the chaplain may be accompanied by one of the nuns,[2] not to minister in the strict sense, but to render such assistance as may be necessary.[3]

§ IX.—Curabit etiam, ut sacra supellex, vestes, ornamenta, linteamina, et vasa ministerii integra, nitidaque sint et munda.

129. He must take care that the vestments, vessels, and other requisites be kept perfectly clean, and in good order. Every parochial church should be in charge of some intelligent person, who would act as sacristan, and whose duty it would be to keep the furniture of both church and sacristy in proper order; but it still is necessary, as Baruffaldi observes,[4] for the priest himself to see that this important duty is not neglected. If the vestments, linens, sacred vessels, etc., be not rich or costly, they should be at least "integra, nitida, et munda," as the rubric prescribes. This is the answer of Cardinal Bellarmine to the excuse that might here be pleaded on the score of poverty.[5]

§ X.—In Sacramentorum administratione, eorum virtutem, usum ac utilitatem, et cæremoniarum significationes, ut Concilium Tridentinum præcepit, ex Ss. Patrum et Catechismi Romani doctrina, ubi commode fieri potest, diligenter explicabit.

130. The Council of Trent expressly commands bishops and parish priests to explain to the people, in a manner suited to their capacity, the efficacy and use of the sacraments.[6] The words of the Council seem to imply that this should be done when any sacrament is about being administered; and most rituals contain a brief instruction on the subject, to be then addressed to the people. This time is undoubtedly very appropriate, and is recommended as such by the Catechism of the Council of Trent,[7] whenever there is a considerable number of the faithful present, because, seeing the rite performed before them, they are in a condition to profit better by the instructions they receive. It is not required that he should each time touch on every point, but, as the Catechism suggests,[8] he may select one point now, another again, and so on.

131. But the pastor should take other opportunities also

[1] Baruff., n. 58.　Catal., tit. i. § viii. n. iii.
[2] Baruff., n. 60., Catal., loc. cit. Falise, 3ᵐᵉ partie, *Parag. prelim.*, n. 6.
[3] De Herdt, pars vi. n. 2. iv.　　　　　[4] Loc. cit. n. 62.
[5] *De Gemitu Columbæ*, lib. ii. cap. v. apud Catal., loc. cit. § ix. n. ii.
[6] Sess. xxiv. cap. 7, De Ref.　　[7] Pars ii. cap. ii. n. 2.　　[8] Loc. cit.

of giving instructions on this important subject. He could do so in short familiar lectures before or after mass or vespers on Sundays. In these he could fully explain the necessity of the sacraments, the dispositions with which they must be received, and the ceremonies to be observed in their administration, particularly those ceremonies in which the recipient or the assistants are to take part. While he would thus comply with an important duty of his office, he would save himself a good deal of trouble and annoyance in the actual administration of the sacraments.

132. Everything pertaining to this matter is explained in the Roman Catechism, or Catechism of the Council of Trent, which is here recommended, and in which the pastor will find abundant materials for all his instructions. This book, compiled by the ablest theologians of the day,[1] was published by St. Pius V, pursuant to a decree of the Council of Trent, expressly for the use of pastors; and, besides its great authority on this account, it will be found the most convenient book that can be referred to; for, though of moderate size, it contains a perfectly clear and methodical statement of all the points of Catholic doctrine and practice in which the pastor should instruct his flock.

§ XI.—Dum Sacramentum aliquod ministrat, singula verba, quæ ad illius formam et ministerium pertinent, attente, distincte, et pie, atque clara voce pronuntiabit. Similiter et alias orationes et preces devote ac religiose dicet; nec memoriæ, quæ plerumque labitur, facile confidet, sed omnia recitabit ex libro. Reliquas præterea Cæremonias ac Ritus, ita decenter, gravique actione peraget, ut adstantes ad cœlestium rerum cogitationem erigat, et attentos reddat.

133. The importance of attending to what is prescribed in this rubric is apparent from reading it. A mistake in a single word of the form might render the sacrament invalid. It is the duty of the minister, therefore, to pronounce the words, as he is here directed, clearly and distinctly. It is unnecessary to discuss how far the change, suppression, or addition of a word or syllable affects the validity of the form. The rule is, that any change which alters the meaning is to be regarded as a substantial one, rendering the sacrament null; but any which leaves the meaning intact is to be regarded as accidental, which, though it may be illicit, does not destroy the validity.[2] Hence, as the meaning of words that are

---

[1] Vid. *The Catechism, etc., translated into English.* by Rev. J. Donovan. Rome, 1839. Preface.   [2] Gury, ii. n. 198, 199.

spoken is more easily affected, so is the form more easily vitiated, by a change at the commencement of any word than by one at the end;[1] but all danger is avoided by pronouncing the words as here directed. The other prayers prescribed are of less importance, and accordingly we see that in them the rubric is not so exact about the "singula verba," but it requires them to be said with religious attention, and will not allow the minister to trust to his memory, but will have him recite them from the book. He should always use the ritual in Baptism, Extreme Unction, and Matrimony, in which the prayers and ceremonies are of considerable length; but he can easily dispense with it in Penance, and in giving Holy Communion, as in these the forms are so short and so frequently used by him, that, at least after a little practice, there is no danger of mistake in trusting to his memory.[2]

*134. The words of the form should be pronounced while the matter is being applied. In the Eucharist the words of the form require that the matter be *physically* present when they are pronounced. In the other sacraments it suffices that the form be pronounced and the matter applied at *morally* the same time. It is not required, *e. g.*, in Baptism, that the water be actually falling on the head when the word "*baptizo*" is being pronounced. The rubric even directs that the water be poured on in naming the persons of the Blessed Trinity.[3]

*135. The admonition regarding the manner of performing the ceremonies is well worthy of notice. The demeanor of the priest cannot but be closely observed by those who are present, and if it gives evidence of piety and a lively faith, it is sure to produce a salutary impression on them; but if, on the contrary, it gives evidence of carelessness or want of gravity, it cannot fail to give great disedification, and thus defeat the very end for which these sacred ceremonies have been instituted.[4]

§ XII.—Ad ministrandum procedens, rei quam tractaturus est, intentus sit, nec de iis, quæ ad ipsum non pertinent, quidquam cum alio colloquatur: in ipsaque administratione actualem attentionem habere studeat, vel saltem virtualem, cum intentione faciendi quod in eo facit Ecclesia.

136. We must carefully distinguish *attention* from *inten-*

[1] Lacroix, lib. vi. pars i. n. 36. Gury, l. c.   [2] Catal., § xi. n. 31.
[3] Infra, chap. iv. § xvii. Vid. St. Lig., lib. vi. n. 9.
[4] Vid. supra, n. 97.

tion—the former being defined "an act of the intellect,
"considering what a person is doing;" the latter, "an act of
"the will tending to some desired end."[1] The distinction,
however, is understood from the words themselves, as easily,
perhaps, as from any definition of them. In administering a
sacrament, the priest, according to the rubric, should endeavor
to have actual, or at least virtual, attention. It is hard to
understand how there can be attention at all, unless it be
actual. St. Liguori maintains that it is impossible.[2] By
virtual attention, the rubric most probably means the absence
of *voluntary* distraction. The explanation of Baruffaldi[3]
almost comes to this; and it is in this sense virtual attention
seems to be used by La Croix.[4] Attention in the act of conferring a sacrament is not necessary to its validity; but to be
voluntarily distracted is at least a venial sin, and, in the consecration of the Eucharist, is very probably a mortal sin.[5]
Attention is required chiefly in pronouncing the form and in
reciting the prayers. It may be directed: 1° to the words,
so as to pronounce them well; 2° to the sense of the words,
which is better; 3° to God and to the object of the sacred
rite, which is best of all.[6]

137. It has been defined by the Council of Trent, that in
conferring a sacrament the minister must have the intention
of doing what the Church does.[7] There are various ways in
which a person may be conceived to have an intention in
doing a thing. 1° He may have an *actual* intention at the
moment he does it. 2° He may have a *virtual* intention, *i. e.*,
he may do it in *virtue* of an actual intention which he had,
and which still continues in some effect, though he does not
think of it: as, *e. g.*, if a priest leaves his house with the intention of baptizing a child, and *in virtue* of this intention
goes to the church and performs the ceremony, though in the
act he is quite distracted, and does not reflect on what he is
doing. 3° He may have an *habitual* intention, *i. e.*, he may
have had the intention, and may not have retracted it; but
yet it does not continue in any effect, nor can it be said that
the act is performed in virtue of it. 4° He may have what
is called an *interpretative* intention; *i. e.*, he may be so
disposed in doing the act, that *if* he had adverted to it, he
would have had such an intention in doing it. These seem

[1] Gury ii. n. 202, 203.   [2] Lib. vi. n. 14.   [3] Tit. ii. n. 73.
[4] Lib. vi. p. i. n. 84.   [5] St. Lig., l. c.
[6] St. Lig., lib. v. n. 176. *Attentio autem.*
[7] Sess. vii. can. xi. *De Sac. in genere.*

to be the distinctions as laid down by St. Liguori,[1] according
to whom it is certain that neither the habitual nor the interpretative intention is sufficient; that the actual intention is
not required; but that the virtual is required, and is quite
sufficient.[2]

138. So much for the intention as it is an act of the mind.
With respect to the object of this intention, it must be "to
"do what the Church does," and the intention may be directed
to this object in two ways, explicitly and implicitly. A well-
instructed pious Catholic, in baptizing an infant, would have
the *explicit* intention of "doing what the Church does;"
while a heretic, or an infidel, not believing in the true
Church or in the efficacy of the sacrament, but yet intending,
in the act of baptizing, to do what is done amongst Christians,
would have the *implicit* intention of "doing what the
"Church does," and such implicit intention suffices for the
validity.[3]

139. It is quite certain, then, that a virtual implicit intention is sufficient; but it is a question amongst divines whether
this intention must be *internal*, or whether it be not enough
for the validity to perform the external rite seriously and in
proper circumstances, even though the minister should mentally exclude the intention of doing what the Church does.
This is the famous question of the *external* and *internal* intention, which was for a time warmly debated in the schools.
It is generally admitted now, that the weight of authority and
reason is completely in favor of the necessity of the internal; and
the other opinion barely escapes condemnation by Alexander
VIII, who condemned the proposition: "Valet Baptismus
"collatus a ministro qui omnem ritum externum formamque
"baptizandi observat, intus vero in corde suo apud se resol-
"vit: Non intendo facere quod facit Ecclesia."[4] At least it
cannot be denied, according to Benedict XIV, that this is a
very severe blow to it;[5] and should there be, in any case,
sufficient reason to think that the internal intention was wanting in the administration of Baptism, or any other sacrament
that cannot be iterated, the sacrament should be again conferred conditionally, or if time permit, the Holy See should
be consulted.[6] The question, however, is very speculative,
for in practice the internal intention is hardly ever wanting.

[1] Lib. vi. n. 15.   [2] Loc. cit. n. 16, 17, 18.   [3] Ibid. n. 29.
[4] 7 Dec. 1690. Denzinger, *Enchiridion Symbolorum et Definitionum*,
c xxviii. n. 1185.   [5] *De Syn. Diœc.,* lib. vii. cap. iv. n. 8.
[6] Ibid. n. 9.

§ XIII.—Illud porro diligenter caveat, ne in Sacramentorum admin
istratione aliquid quavis de causa vel occasione, directe vel indirecte exigat, aut petat; sed ea gratis ministret, et ab omni simoniæ, atque avaritiæ
suspicioue, nedum crimine, longissime absit. Si quid vero nomine elee-
mosynæ, aut devotionis studio, peracto jam Sacramento, sponte a Fidelibus offeratur, id licite pro consuetudine locorum accipere poterit, nisi
aliter Episcopo videatur.

140. The priest must not only be free from the crime of
simony, the essential malice of which consists in estimating a
spiritual thing at a temporal price,[1] but he must also be careful to keep himself free from the least suspicion of it; and on
the occasion of administering a sacrament, therefore, he must
take care to avoid exacting the customary oblations in any
way that might leave him open to such a suspicion. It is
enough to cite here the admonition of the Synod of Thurles,
which may serve as a practical commentary on this rubric:
"In oblationibus quæ ex veteri et recepto usu fieri solent oc-
"casione administrationis quorundam Sacramentorum, caveant
"Parochi ne aliquid fiat quod simoniam aut avaritiam
sapiat. Sacramenta vero nunquam denegentur eo sub præ-
"textu quod oblationes istæ dandæ non sint; alioquin
"noverint delinquentes se ad arbitrium Ordinarii esse puni-
"endos."[2]

§ XIV.—Fidelibus alienæ Parochiæ Sacramenta non ministrabit, nisi
necessitatis causa, vel de licentia Parochi, seu Ordinarii.

*141. A parish priest can *validly* administer the sacraments
to all who present themselves within the limits of his parish.
There could be no difficulty about any except the sacrament
of penance, but it is certain that he has jurisdiction to hear
in his own parish the confessions, not only of his own parishioners, but of any who present themselves. Indeed any
priest, at the present day, who is authorized to hear confessions in a parish, is understood, by the universal custom of
the Church, to have authority to hear there all who present
themselves to him, no matter from what place they may come.[3]
A parish priest can hear the confessions of his own parishioners everywhere, even outside his own diocese;[4] but he
cannot hear the confessions of others beyond the limits of his
own parish, unless where he is understood by custom, as is

[1] Busemb. apud St. Lig., lib. iv. n. 49. *Unde Patet.* Suarez. *De
Simonia,* cap. l. n. 1.
[2] *De Sacramentis,* n. 5.
[3] St. Lig., lib. vi. n. 564, et 569. Benedict XIV. *Instit.,* xviii. n. 9.
[4] Gury, vol. ii. n. 541. Bouix, *De Parocho,* pars iv. cap. iv. n, 8.

the case in many places, to have jurisdiction in every part of the diocese.[1]

*142. He can *licitly* confer sacraments on those of another parish: 1° In case of necessity, but this can ordinarily apply only to Baptism and Penance; 2° When there is an express or implied understanding with the parish priest, for then in reality he acts "de licentia." 3° By custom he can not only validly but licitly hear their confessions, even in paschal time, when they come to him in his own parish;[2] and he can also give them Communion, unless it be the Paschal Communion, which they are bound to receive from their own pastor.[3] He cannot lawfully administer sacraments to them in other cases without the permission of their parish priest or Ordinary.[4]

§ XV.—Omnes autem qui Sacramenta suscipiunt, loco et tempore opportuno monebit, ut remoto inani colloquio, et habitu, actuque indecenti. pie ac devote Sacramentis intersint, et ea qua par est reverentia suscipiant.

143. The admonition here recommended should be given in general terms, so as not to mark out any individual.[5] It is to be given "loco et tempore opportuno." and perhaps it could be most conveniently given in the instructions already mentioned.[6] By this means the risk of giving offence to individuals would be avoided.

§ XVI.—Librum hunc Ritualem, ubi opus fuerit, semper cum ministrabit, secum habebit, Ritusque et Cæremonias in eo præscriptas, diligenter servabit.

144. We have treated in the preceding chapter[7] of the obligation of using the Roman Ritual, and observing all that is prescribed by its rubrics. The priest is here admonished that he should always have a copy of it with him when he is about to administer a sacrament.[8]

§ XVII.—Cæterum illorum tantum Sacramentorum, quorum administratio ad parochos pertinet, Ritus hoc opere præscribuntur, cujusmodi sunt Baptismus, Pœnitentia, Eucharistia, Extrema Unctio, et Matrimonium. Reliqua vero duo Sacramenta Confirmationis et Ordinis, cum propria sint Episcoporum, Ritus suos habent in Pontificali præscriptos. Et ea quæ de iis atque aliis Sacramentis scire, servare, et docere Parochi debent, cum ex aliis Libris, tum præcipue ex Catechismo Romano sumi possunt. Siquidem hic de iis fere tantum agere instituti operis ratio postulat, quæ ad ipsorum quinque Sacramentorum ritus pertinent.

---

[1] St. Lig., lib. vi. n. 544. *Dub.* 2. Lacroix, lib. vi. pars ii. n. 153e. Bouix, l. c. n. 4. [2] St. Lig. n. 564.
[3] St Lig.. n. 300. Vid. infra, chap. xiii. § i.
[4] Vid. infra. chap. xvi. § i. [5] Baruff., tit. ii. n. 80.
[6] Supra, n. 131. [7] Vid. n. 65, et seq. [8] Vid. supra, n. 133.

145. The Ritual treats only of those sacraments that are administered by priests. What regards Confirmation and Orders, which are conferred only by bishops, may be found in the "Pontificale Romanum." But though the priest is not the minister of these sacraments, it may be his duty to explain to the people the doctrine which relates to them,[1] and especially it is the duty of the pastor to prepare the children of his parish for the worthy reception of the sacrament of Confirmation, and hence he is here referred to such books as may enable him to fulfil his duty in this respect; but, above all, to the Roman Catechism, or Catechism of the Council of Trent, the advantages of which we have had occasion to point out before.[2]

§ XVIII.—Postremo, quisquis Sacramenta administrare tenetur, habeat libros necessarios ad officium suum pertinentes, eosque præsertim, in quibus Parochialium functionum notæ ad futuram rei memoriam, ut ad finem hujus Ritualis habetur.

*146. The books here specially referred to are the Parochial registers, of which there are five, according to the Roman Ritual, to be kept in the manner prescribed at the end of the Ritual itself, viz: 1° of Baptisms; 2° of Confirmations; 3° of Marriages; 4° of every family with its members, noting the sacraments received by each, called the "Liber Status Animarum;" 5° of the faithful departed. At least the registers of Baptisms and Marriages must be kept with great care, and the Synod of Thurles directs parish priests to keep them in the manner prescribed by the Roman Ritual, "ad normam Ritualis Romani."[3]

147. With regard to other books which treat of matters pertaining to the duties of his office, it is enough to observe that it is impossible for any priest to fulfil the duty of administering the sacraments and instructing the people, unless he be devoted to sacred study,[4] and, therefore, unless he have a supply of good books. Speaking of Pastors, the Synod of Thurles says: "Lectioni præterea attendant et supellecti-"lem librorum ecclesiasticorum sibi comparent; saltem sacra "Biblia, et unum integrum Theologiæ cursum, canones "Concilii Tridentini, Catechismum Romanum, et vitas "Sanctorum habeant et assidue versant."[5]

[1] Baruff. n. 91.   [2] Supra, n. 132.
[3] De Parochis, n. 27.
[4] Vid. St. Lig., Praxis Confessarii, n. 18, prope finem.
[5] De Vita et Honestate Clericorum, n. 23.

"Sacerdotes, jam ad munera ecclesiastica admissi," says the Synod of Westminster, "non ideo studiis præcipue "sacris, valedicant: sed cum ex ore sacerdotis scientiam "populi requirere debeant (*Mal.* ii. 7), sint assidui in lectione "S. Scripturæ et theologiæ tam dogmaticæ quam moralis et "asceticæ. Ita fiet, ut, gregem instruentes, non inanibus "verbis hominum tantum pulsabunt aures, non contra "inimicos dimicabunt velut aerem verberantes, sed et illos "fructuose vero vitæ pane nutrient, et hos solida argu-"mentatione profligabunt."[1]

[1] Decr. xxiv. *De Vita et Honestate Clericorum*, 19°.

CHAPTER III.

ON THE ADMINISTRATION OF THE SACRAMENT OF BAPTISM: "DE SACRAMENTO BAPTISMI RITE ADMINISTRANDO."

§ I.— Sacrum Baptisma, Christianæ Religionis et æternæ vitæ janua quod inter alia novæ Legis Sacramenta a Christo instituta, primum tenet locum, cunctis ad salutem necessarium esse, ipsa Veritas testatur illis verbis : *Nisi quis renatus fuerit ex aqua et Spiritu Sancto, non potest introire in regnum Dei (* Joan. 3). Itaque summa ad illud opportune, riteque administrandum ac suscipiendum diligentia adhibenda est.

148. Baptism is defined by the Catechism of the Council of Trent, " Sacramentum regenerationis per aquam in verbo:" " The Sacrament of regeneration by water in the word ; " *i. e.*, the sacrament by which we are spiritually regenerated or born again, by an ablution of water with the prescribed form, " Ego te baptizo in Nomine Patris," etc. It had various other names besides Baptism amongst the early Fathers and ecclesiastical writers. It is called the Sacrament of Faith, of Illumination, etc.[1]

149. By Baptism we are cleansed from original sin, made members of the Church, children of God, and heirs to the kingdom of heaven. " By nature," says the Catechism of the Council of Trent,[2] " we are born from Adam children of " wrath, but by Baptism we are regenerated in Christ children " of mercy ; for he gave power to men, to be made the sons of " God, to them that believe in his name, who are born, not of " blood, nor of the will of the flesh, nor of the will of man, " but of God" (*John*, i. 12, 13). This spiritual regeneration, then, by Baptism, is absolutely necessary to salvation, as has been defined by the Council of Trent,[3] and as is clearly inferred from the words of our Lord here cited, " *Nisi quis renatus*," etc.: " Unless a man be born again of water and the Holy Ghost, he cannot enter into the kingdom of God."[4]

150. The word *water* in this text has always been understood by the Fathers in the literal sense, and the Council of

[1] Vid. Bellarmine, *De Bapt.*, cap. i.
[2] Pars. ii. cap. ii. n. 5.
[3] Sess. vii. cap. 5 *De Bapt.*
[4] John, iii. 5.

Trent[1] has anathematized those who, with Calvin,[2] distort its
meaning by taking it metaphorically. We see that our
Lord himself baptized, as is related in the same chapter[3]
(though by the ministry of his disciples, as appears from
what the Evangelist afterwards states);[4] that he commissioned
his apostles to baptize,[5] and that they did baptize all who re
ceived the gospel,[6] while the nature of the baptism administer
ed is evident from the history of the baptism of the eunuch,
and of the Gentile converts,[8] in which there is distinct men
tion of water. There can be no doubt, therefore, that the
meaning of our Saviour's words, " to be born again of water,"
is simply " to be regenerated by Baptism," and this is declared
necessary to salvation.

151. Moreover, the expression implies that it is necessary,
not merely as the fulfilment of a precept is necessary, because
its voluntary omission would be a sin, *necessitate præcepti ;*
but that it is absolutely necessary as a means positively con-
ducing to salvation, so that without it salvation could not be
attained, even though its omission were involuntary, *necessitate medii.* This is shown by the universality of the form,
" *Nisi* QUIS," etc., by which it extends to all, even those to
whom a precept could not be addressed, as infants, but still
more perhaps by the implied assertion, that this regeneration
is as necessary to spiritual life and admission into the kingdom of God, as birth according to the flesh is to natural life ;
an assertion which is confirmed by what our Saviour immediately adds : " That which is born of the flesh is flesh,
" and that which is born of the Spirit is spirit,"[9] for what St.
Paul so clearly expresses[10] is here understood, viz., " that flesh
" and blood cannot possess the kingdom of God."[11]

152. But though Baptism is thus necessary to salvation,
its defect in those who, through no fault of their own, are unable to receive it, may be supplied in two ways, according to
the common doctrine of the Fathers : 1° by an act of perfect
charity, which includes the desire of Baptism, and which is
called *Baptismus Flaminis ;* 2° by martyrdom, which is called *Baptismus Sanguinis,* and by which even infants, who are
put to death for Christ, as were the Holy Innocents, may be

[1] Sess. vii. can. 2. *De Baptismo.*
[2] *Instit.,* lib. iv. cap. 15, cit. apud Tournel., *De Baptismo,* Quæstio
I. art. ii.　[3] Vv. 23, 26.　[4] Chap. iv. 2.　[5] Matth. xxviii. 19.
[6] Acts. ii. 41.　　[7] Acts, viii. 36.　　[8] Acts. x. 47.
[9] John, iii. 6.　　　　　　　　[10] 1 Cor. xv. 50.
[11] Vid. Corn. A Lapide, *Comment.* in Joan. iii. 6.

saved.[1] There is no other means of supplying for the Baptism of water, or *Baptismus Fluminis*, which is always meant by the word Baptism, when used simply and without any adjunct, and which alone is a sacrament.

153. It is here said to be "Christianæ Religionis et æternæ "vitæ janua," for although without it salvation may be attained in the two cases we have mentioned, no one properly belongs to the body of the Church, or is capable of receiving any other sacrament, without the spiritual character which it alone impresses on the soul.[2]

§ II.—Cum autem ad hoc Sacramentum conferendum alia sint de Jure divino absolute necessaria, ut materia, forma, minister; alia ad illius solemnitatem pertineant, ut Ritus ac Cæremoniæ, quas ex Apostolica et antiquissima traditione acceptas et approbatas, nisi necessitatis causa, omittere non licet; de iis aliqua præmonenda sunt, ut sacrum hoc ministerium rite ac sancte peragatur.

154. In every sacrament three things are essential, the matter, the form, and the minister: "Hæc omnia Sacramenta "tribus perficiuntur, videlicet rebus tanquam materia, verbis "tanquam forma, et persona ministri conferentis Sacramentum "cum intentione faciendi quod facit Ecclesia: quorum si ali- "quod desit non perficitur sacramentum."[3] The words, matter, and form, as applied to the sacraments, were introduced by the Scholastics, being found in no writer earlier than the thirteenth century;[4] but the things signified by them were always distinguished. In every sacrament there is a something to be determined, which we now call the "matter," and which in ancient writers is called "res," "elementum," etc.; and there is that which determines it, which we now call the form, and which in ancient writers is called the "verbum," since it, at least ordinarily, consists in words. This distinction is clearly expressed in the well known citation from St. Augustine: "Detrahe verb- "um et quid est aqua nisi aqua? Accedit verbum ad elementum "et fit Sacramentum."[5] The minister, too, is essential, for he must apply the matter and form with the intention of doing what the Church does.[6] In the administration of Baptism, besides what is essential to the Sacrament, certain rites and ceremonies, which have been in use from the earliest

[1] St. Lig., lib., vi. n. 95 et seq. Vid. Bellarmine, *De Bapt.*, cap. vi.
[2] St. Lig., lib. vi. n. 79. Cfr. Murray, *De Ecclesia*, Disp. iii. sec. vii.
[3] Decret. Eugenii IV., *Ad Armenos*. Labbe, vol. xviii. p. 547.
[4] Baruf., tit. iv n. 1. Drouin. *De Re Sacramentaria*, cap. i. § 4.
[5] *Tract 30 in Joan.*, cit. ap. Drouin. l. c.   [6] Vid. supra, n. 137.

times, are to be observed. The rubrics proceed to give instructions on all these in order.

THE MATTER OF BAPTISM.

DE MATERIA BAPTISMI.

§ III. -Ac primum intelligat Parochus, cum hujus Sacramenti materi sit aqua vera ac naturalis, nullum alium liquorem ad id adhiberi posse.

155. The matter of a sacrament is distinguished into "remote" and "proximate;" the remote being that which is applied or used, the proximate being the application or use of the remote, in the act of administering.[1] Thus, in Baptism, water is the remote matter, and ablution with water is the proximate matter.

*156. That water alone is the matter of Baptism, is proved by the reasons already mentioned in treating of its necessity.[2] Any liquid which can be, simply and properly speaking, called " water," whether it be hot or cold, salt or fresh, is sufficient for the validity of the sacrament. The admixture of any other ingredient does not interfere with the validity, provided the liquid still retains, in common estimation, the nature and properties of water. This is the rule by which theologians determine whether any proposed liquid be sufficient or not for the matter of the sacrament.[3] But in case of necessity even doubtful matter may, and should be, used, when no other can be had.[4]

157. Many very congruous reasons are assigned by the Fathers and theologians, why water was selected by Christ in preference to any other element. " In the first place, water, " which is always at hand, and is easily procured by all, " was a most fit matter of a sacrament necessary to all, without " exception, to attain life;[5] next, water admirably expresses " the effect of Baptism, for, as water washes away uncleanness, " so also does it strikingly illustrate the virtue and efficacy of " Baptism, which washes away the stains of sin. Moreover, " as water is extremely well adapted to cool bodies, so does " Baptism in a great measure extinguish the ardor of the " passions."[6]

---

[1] Vid. Gury, vol. ii. n. 196.
[2] Supra, n. 150.
[3] Vid. St. Lig., lib. vi. n. 103.
[4] Ibid. *Et hic sedulo*, etc.
[5] The translation from which we copy has "maintain," but this is probably a misprint for "attain;" the original being "ad consequendam vitam."
[6] Cat. Conc. Trid., pars ii. cap. ii. n. 10.

§ IV.—Aqua vero solemnis Baptismi sit eo anno benedicta in Sabbato
Sancto Paschatis, vel Sabbato Pentecostes, quæ in fonte mundo nitida
et pura diligenter conservetur; et hæc, quando nova benedicenda est,
in Ecclesiæ, vel potius Baptisterii sacrarium effundatur.

*158. Though common water, as has been said, is sufficient
for the validity of the sacrament, the water used in the
administration of solemn Baptism should have been blessed
on the Holy Saturday, or on the Saturday of Pentecost, im
mediately preceding. Merati shows that the custom of bless
ing the water used in Baptism has existed in the Church
form the earliest times;[1] and according to the common opinion
of theologians, there is an obligation *sub mortali* of using
blessed water in solemn baptism.[2]

*159. On the days above mentioned, the water is blessed
according to the form prescribed in the Roman Missal; at
other times it is blessed according to the form prescribed in
the Ritual,[3] and should always be preserved with great care in
the baptismal font. What remains when new water is to be
blessed, should be poured into the sacrarium of the church,
or that of the baptistery, if it have one annexed;[4] and even
what is used, as we shall see, should be poured, or allowed to
fall, into the same place.[5]

§ V.—Si aqua benedicta tam imminuta sit, ut minus sufficere videatur,
alia non benedicta admisceri potest, in minori tamen quantitate.

*160. It is doubtful whether one or two drops of water would
suffice.[6] According to the common opinion there must be an
ablution, which supposes the water to flow on the part to
which it is applied.[7] When the supply in the font is insuf-
cient, it is here stated that common water may be added, but
it must be in less quantity.

*161. Since there is no restriction as to the number of
times, it would seem that this addition of common water in
small quantities may be made as often as is necessary, though
the quantity of unblessed water thus added may, in the end,
exceed that of the blessed water which remained in the font
when the first addition was made. This is the opinion of
Cavalieri.[8] In was expressly decided with respect to the holy

[1] Pars ii. tit. x. n. xxxvii. Vid. infra, chap. ix. § vi.
[2] Vid. St. Lig., lib. v. n. 102, *in fine in parenth.*
[3] Infra, chap. ix.   [4] Vid. infra, § xxxii.   [5] Infra, § xii,
[6] St. Lig., n. 107. *Quær.* vi.   [7] Billuart, *De Bapt.*, dis. i. art.
iii. § iii. Collet, *De Bapt.*, art. ii. concl. i.   [8] Tom. iv. cap. xii.
Dec. x. n. v.

oils, that unblessed oil may be added in this way.[1] And if this be true of what is essential to the sacrament of Extreme Unction,[2] we may infer that the same will hold for the baptismal water, in which the benediction is by no means required for the validity.

§ VI.—Si vero corrupta fuerit, aut effluxerit, aut quovis modo defecerit, Parochus in fontem bene mundatum ac nitidum recentem aquam infundat, eamque benedicat ex formula quæ infra præscribitur.

*162. Provision is here made for the case in which the water becomes unfit for use, or the supply, from whatever cause, altogether fails. Water that has been for a considerable time stagnant often becomes corrupt,[3] and might be injurious to infants if used in their baptism.[4] The font, too, may be leaky or porous, so as to retain the water but a short time, and the present rubric directs what is to be done in such cases. The font is to be thoroughly cleansed, the putrid water, if any remains, being thrown into the sacrarium; and a new supply having been poured in, is to be blessed according to the formula given hereafter.[5]

*163. A mucous film is soon formed on the surface of the font from the oils used in the benediction. This does not render the water unfit for use, but it may be removed, according to Baruffaldi,[6] without any injury or irreverence, just as the oil used in the consecration of a chalice. It may be removed with a little cotton, and burned or thrown into the sacrarium.

§ VII.—Sed si aqua conglaciata sit, curetur ut liquefiat: sin autem ex parte congelata sit, aut nimium frigida, poterit parum aquæ naturalis non benedictæ calefacere, et admiscere aquæ baptismali in vasculo ad id parato, et ea tepefacta ad baptizandum uti, ne noceat infantulo.

*164. Water in the solid state, as ice, cannot be used for Baptism, for there cannot be an *ablution* with it in this state; at least it is very doubtful matter, and can be used, therefore, only in case of necessity, and then *sub conditione*.[7] But if it be dissolved in the act of application it is certainly valid.[8]

*165. The rubric here directs that if the water in the font be congealed, it must be liquefied before use. This may be

---

[1] Sac. Cong. Conc. Sept. 23, 1862. Vid. infra, § xxxv.
[2] Vid. chap. xv. § iii.　　　[3] Baruff., tit. iv. n. 13.
[4] Baruff., ibid. n. 16.　　*[5] Chap. ix.　　[6] Tit. iv. n. 10.
[7] St. Lig., n. 104, *Dub.* 4°.　　·[8] Lacroix, lib. vi. p i. n. 262.

done in various ways. A little may be taken from the font, and reduced, by the application of heat, to the liquid state;[1] or, as the rubric here directs, a little common water may be heated, and mixed with some taken from the font, in a vessel provided for the purpose. The same should be done, even when the water is not frozen, if it be too cold to be poured, with safety, on the child; but the common water used should always be less in quantity than that taken from the font, as is directed by St. Charles, in his instructions,[2] and as might be inferred from a preceding rubric.[3] In the Greek Church warm water is used, according to Goar,[4] not only to guard against danger to the infant, but also because the warmth is regarded as a symbol of the fervor of grace produced by Baptism.

ON THE FORM OF BAPTISM: "DE FORMA BAPTISMI."

§ VIII.—Quoniam Baptismi forma his verbis expressa: *Ego te baptizo in nomine Patris, et Filii, et Spiritus Sancti*, omnino necessaria est, ideo eam nullo modo licet mutare, sed eadem verba uno et eodem tempore quo fit ablutio pronuntianda sunt.

166. We have already[5] mentioned the rules by which one may determine what change in the form of a sacrament is to be regarded as substantial, and what as merely accidental. We shall add merely, that when the change is such as to leave it doubtful whether or not the sense is substantially altered, the validity very often depends on the intention of the minister.[6]

*167. It is never lawful to change the words of the form as here given in the rubric. It is admitted, however, that the omission of the pronoun "Ego" would not invalidate the sacrament.[7] Neither would the omission of the *et* before *Filii*, nor, according to the more probable opinion, of the preposition *in;* but this last omission, as it would leave the validity doubtful, could not be excused from mortal sin.[8] All the other words are essential.

[1] Rit. Leod. et. past. Brug. apud De Herdt, p. vi. n. 3, § vi.
[2] *Act. Eccl. Mediol.*, pars vi. *Instructiones de Bapt. administrationis*, p. 410.
[3] Supra, n. 160.
[4] *ΕΓΧΟΛΟΓΙΟΝ*, sive *Rituale Graecorum Illustratum, In Baptismatis Officium Notae*, n. 24, pag. 366.
[5] Supra, n. 133.   [6] Cfr. Lacroix, lib. vi. pars i. n. 38.
[7] St Lig., lib. vi. n. 112.   [8] Ibid. *Dub.* 2, *in fine.*

*168. St. Liguori seems to suppose that the word ' Amen"
is as much a part of the form as the pronoun " Ego," for he
says the omission of neither one nor other would invalidate
the sacrament, nor exceed a venial sin.[1]   The same is supposed by several theologians whom he cites.   It is evidently
supposed by Lacroix[2] and by Gury.[3]

Now the truth is, that the word " Amen " does not belong
to the form at all, nor is it given in any correct edition of the
Ritual.   The authority of the theologians, however, and especially of St. Liguori, suggested a doubt on the matter, which
was proposed to the Sacred Congregation, and answered as
follows: " Plures Theologi inter quos Sanctus Alphonsus
" Maria de Ligorio sentiunt veniale esse omittere vocem,
" ' Amen' in fine formæ Baptismi, quæ tamen vox non repe-
" ritur in Rituali Romano: quæritur ergo utrum adhibenda sit
" vel omittenda?"   Resp: " Strictim in casu servetur Rituale
Romanum."[4]   It is not permitted, therefore, to add the word
" Amen " to the form.

169. The Apostles are stated to have baptized " in nomi-
" ne Jesu Christi,"[5] and these words were understood by some
to be the form which they used.   If this interpretation be
admitted, it must be said, with St. Thomas,[6] that the Apostles
did so in virtue of a special revelation, in order that the name
of Christ might be thus more highly honored.[7]   But it is
much more probable that the words mean simply that the
Apostles administered the Baptism instituted by Christ, and
therefore with the form instituted by him.   That they baptized with the explicit mention of the three divine persons,
may be inferred from Acts, xix, where the question of St.
Paul clearly implies that those who received the Baptism of
Christ must have heard the name of the Holy Ghost.[8]

170. The form must be pronounced while the matter is being applied, that is, at morally the same time.[9]

§ IX.—Latinus Presbyter latina forma semper utatur.

171. The form above given is that which a priest of the
Latin Church is bound to use.   In some of the ancient
Liturgical books used in France, certain words are added

[1] Loc. cit.   [2] Loc. cit. n. 43.   [3] Vol. ii. n. 241.
[4] 9 Jun. 1853, in Cochin., ad 2, n. 5188.
[5] Acts, ii. 38, viii. 12, etc.   [6] 3 p. qu. 66, art. 6, ad 1.
[7] Vid. Cat. Conc. Trid., p. ii. cap. ii. n. 15.
[8] St. Lig.; n. 112, Dub 3.   Vid. Bellarmine, De Bapt., lib. i cap. 3.
[9] Vid. supra, n. 134.

after "Spiritus Sancti," as, "ut habeas vitam æternam—
"Amen;" "in remissionem peccatorum, ut habeas vitam
"æternam;" "ut habeas vitam æternam, in sæcula sæculo-
"rum."[1] Such additions do not affect the validity, but they
are no longer in use anywhere, nor are they at present allowable, as is plain from the answer of the Sacred Congregation
before cited.[2]

172. In the Greek Church the form used is "Baptizatur
servus Christi in nomine Patris," etc.; or, as it is in the
Euchologium, or Ritual of the Greeks: "Baptizatur servus
"Dei in nomine Patris," etc. This form is declared valid in
the decree of Eugene IV, "Pro instructione Armenorum."[3]
Though the form "Baptizetur," etc., in the imperative mood,
is likewise declared valid in the same decree, at least according to a common reading, and is often mentioned as the form
used by the Greeks, it is maintained by Arcudius,[4] that this
form is not, and never was, in use amongst them. Cardinal de Lugo maintains the same;[5] so also does Collet.[6]

"Baptizatur," etc., is the only form found in the "Eucholo-
"gium," published and commented on by Goar;[7] and the
same is to be said of that which is cited by Martene.[8] In the
ΕΥΧΟΛΟΓΙΟΝ ΜΕΓΑ[9] the words of the form are: "Βαπτίζεται
ὁ δωῦλος τοῦ θεοῦ (ὁ δεῖνα) εἰς τὸ ὄνομα," etc. The indicative
is also the only form given in a Compendium of Theology
published for the use of ecclesiastical students in the schis-
matic Russo-Greek Church.[10] It says: "Forma Baptismi
(ex antiqua praxi Ecclesiæ Græcæ et nostræ Russicæ) hæc
"est: Baptizatur servus Dei in nomine Patris et Filii et
"Spiritus Sancti."[11]

It is worthy of note that the word "Baptizetur," in the
text of the decree of Eugene IV, as given by Labbe,[12] is
marked by an asterisk, referring to the word "Baptizatur"
printed in the margin, which intimates that "Baptizatur" is
another, and perhaps the correct reading. The words are:
"Forma autem est: *'Ego te Baptizo in nomine Patris et Filii*

---

[1] Martene, *De Ant. Eccl. Rit.*, lib. i. cap. i. art. xiv. n. 15.
[2] Sup. n. 168.   [3] Labbe, vol. xviii. pag. 547.
[4] Apud Catal., tit. ii. cap i. § ix. n. ii.
[5] *De Sacramentis*, disp. ii. sec. vi. n. 109.
[6] *De Baptismo*, cap. iv. art iii. Conclusio i.
[7] *ΕΥΧΟΛΟΓΙΟΝ*, sive *Rituale Græcorum Illustratum.* Officium
Sancti Baptismatis, pag. 350 et seq.
[8] *De Ant. Eccl. Rit.*, lib. i. cap. i. art. xviii. ord. xxii. et seq.
[9] Edit. EN BENETIA, 1834.   [10] Petropoli, 1799.
[11] Cap. lvii. *De Baptismo*, § 10.   [12] Loc. cit.

"'*et Spiritus Sancti.*' Non tamen negamus quin et per illa
 "verba: *Baptizetur talis servus Ch·isti
*Baptizatur. "in nomine Patris et Filii et Spiritus
 "Sancti; vel, baptizatur manibus meis talis,
"in nomine Patris et Filii et Spiritus Sancti, verum perficia-
"tur baptisma."

Goar says that the similarity of "Baptizetur" to the Greek
verb gave rise to the error. "Propter dictionis Βαπτίζεται
"affinitatem ad aliam vocem Latinam 'Baptizetur,' commenti
"sunt quidam Graecos in Baptismate deprecatoriâ vel impera-
rativâ forma uti."[1]

§ X.—Cum Baptismum iterare nullo modo liceat, si quis sub conditione, de quo infra, sit baptizandus, ea conditio explicanda est hoc
modo: *Si non es baptizatus, ego te baptizo in nomine Patris, etc.* Hac
tamen conditionali forma non passim aut leviter uti licet, sed prudenter;
et ubi, re diligenter pervestigata, probabilis subest dubitatio infantem
non fuisse baptizatum.

*173. When Baptism is to be administered conditionally,
the condition should be expressed as is here directed. According to Natalis Alexander,[2] Baptism was not administered
conditionally before the eighth century; but Benedict XIV
refutes this opinion, and shows that the use of conditional
Baptism was frequent from the very beginning, though the
condition was only implied in the intention, and not expressed
in words, previous to the eighth century.[3] The conditional
form, however, is not to be used unless when, after diligent
inquiry, there is a prudent reason for doubting whether the
sacrament was validly administered before.

174. The Catechism of the Council of Trent warns pastors
against the error of supposing that they are free to baptize
conditionally any child that is presented to them. They are
strictly bound to inquire whether it has been previously
baptized, and if so, to ascertain, as well as they can, whether
the Baptism was validly conferred; and it is only when,
after this diligent inquiry, a doubt still remains as to the
validity, that they should proceed to baptize conditionally.
If they act otherwise, the use of the conditional form will
not save them from being guilty of sin and incurring an
irregularity.[4]

[1] *In Baptismatis Officium Notæ*, n. 20, page 365.
[2] *Hist. Eccl.*, sec. iv. cap. iv. art. 12.
[3] *Syn. Diœc.*, lib. vii. cap. vi. n. 1.
[4] Pars ii. cap. ii. n. 57. Bened. XIV, l. c. n. 3. Vid. St. Lig., lib.
vi. n. 122.

§ XI.—Baptismus licet fieri possit aut per infusionem aquæ, aut per immersionem, aut per aspersionem ; primus tamen, vel secundus modus, qui magis sunt in usu, pro Ecclesiarum consuetudine retineantur ; ita ut trina ablutione caput baptizandi perfundatur, vel immergatur in modum Crucis uno et eodem tempore quo verba proferuntur, et idem sit aquam adhibens et verba pronuntians.

175. In the Latin Church, Baptism is now generally conferred by effusion (called also infusion and affusion), *i. e.*, by pouring water on the head in the manner hereafter directed.[1] For many centuries it was much more commonly conferred by immersion, and it would be difficult to fix the time when Baptism by immersion fell into disuse: it was common enough so late as the fourteenth century, as appears from the statutes of several synods mentioned by Martene,[2] and it is still retained as part of the Ambrosian rite at Milan.[3]

176. Immersion has been always in use amongst the Greeks. It is the only mode of Baptism given in the Euchologium,[4] though Goar testifies that very frequently they baptize by effusion.[5] In the Russo-Greek Church, according to the Compendium of Theology above referred to,[6] both modes are in use: "Modus quo baptismus in nostra Ecclesia "peragitur duplex est . . . alter immersionis, alter ablutionis."[7]

177. It is quite certain that, from the very beginning, Baptism was frequently conferred by effusion, as *e. g.*, in the case of those who were baptized in sickness, and who were called "Clinici;" and, at all events, since the thirteenth century, this is the ordinary mode of conferring it in the Latin Church.[8]

178. Baptism by aspersion or sprinkling is not in use, but there can be no doubt of its validity. It is the common opinion of theologians that this was the mode used by the Apostles in baptizing the multitude of converts mentioned, *Acts*, cap. ii. v. 41. This whole matter is briefly but clearly stated in the Catechism of the Council of Trent, which directs the pastor to explain that, "by the common custom and "practice of the Church, there are three ways of administer-"ing Baptism—immersion, effusion, and aspersion; and that, "administered in any of these three ways, it is valid; for in

[1] Infra, chap. iv. § xvii.
[2] *De Ant. Eccl. Rit.*, lib. i. cap. i. art. xiv. n. 6.
[3] Ibid. n. 5.   Vid. infra, chap. iv. § xviii.
[4] Vid Martene. lib. i. cap. i. art. xviii. Ord. xxii. et seq.
  In Baptismatis Officium Notæ, n. 24, page 365.   [6] Supra, n. 173.
  Cap. lvii. § 6.   [8] Vid. Perrone, *De Bapt.*, cap. i. prop. ii.

"Baptism water is used to signify the spiritual ablution which
"it accomplishes, whence Baptism is called by the Apostle a
"'laver' (*Ephes.* v. 26); but ablution is not more really ac-
"complished by immersion, which was long in use from the
"earliest period of the Church, than by effusion, which we
"now see to be the general practice, or aspersion, the manner
"in which there is reason to believe Peter administered
"Baptism, when on one day he converted and baptized three
"thousand persons (*Acts,* ii. 41)."[1]

*179. The water is to be poured on the head, or the head
is to be immersed three times, each time in the form of a
cross.[2]　The triple ablution here prescribed is not essential
to the sacrament, but it should not be omitted except in case
of necessity.[3]

*180. The form should be pronounced while the matter is
being applied, so that they be physically, or at least morally,
united.　It has been already stated[4] that strict physical
simultaneousness is not essential to the validity, but at least
there must be a moral union, otherwise the words of the form
would not be verified, nor would the sacrament, consequently,
be valid; and for the same reason it is essential that the same
person apply the water and pronounce the form.[5]

§ XII.—Ubi vero Baptismus fit per infusionem aquæ, cavendum est
ne aqua ex infantis capite in fontem, sed in sacrarium Baptisterii prope
ipsum fontem extructum defluat, aut in aliquo vase ad hunc usum parato
recepta, in ipsius Baptisterii, vel in Ecclesiæ sacrarium effundatur.

*181. The water which is poured on the head in Baptism
should never be permitted to fall back into the font from
which it is taken.　It should either fall immediately into the
sacrarium of the baptistery, or be received in a basin or vessel
provided for the purpose, and be afterwards poured into the
sacrarium of the baptistery or of the Church.　The object of
the rubric is to preserve the water from impurities, and to
prevent the danger of infection.[6]

*182. Immediately adjoining the baptismal font, and on
the same or a somewhat lower level, so that the head of the
infant may be conveniently held over it while the water is
being poured on, there should be constructed a "sacrarium,"
or basin communicating with the earth by means of a pipe.

[1] Pars ii. cap. ii. n 17.　　　[2] Vid. infra, cap. iv. § xvii. et § xviii.
[3] Vid. infra, cap. iv. § xxvi.
[4] Supra, n. 134.　　　　　　[5] St. Lig., lib. vi. n. 119.
[6] Baruff., tit. v. n. 22.　De Herdt, pars vi. n. 4. § iv.

The font itself is sometimes divided into two compartments, one of which communicates with the earth and
serves as the sacrarium.   This arrangement is very convenient, and has been adopted in most of the fonts recently
constructed.[1]

*183. Should Baptism be administered in a church which
has no baptismal font,[2] or the font of which has no sacrarium
immediately annexed, the water flowing from the head of the
child ought to be received in a vessel, as here directed, and
afterwards poured into the sacrarium.   Should it be administered in a private house, the water ought to be received in
like manner, and conveyed to the sacrarium of the baptistery
or church; or, if this be found too inconvenient, it may be
thrown into the fire, as is directed by the Constitutions of
St. Edmund of Canterbury.[3]   Whether the water used has
been blessed or not, it should be disposed of in this way, since
it has been used as the matter of the sacrament; and the
reason assigned in the Constitutions is simply "*propter reve-*
"*rentiam Baptismi.*"

ON THE MINISTER OF BAPTISM: "DE MINISTRO BAPTISMI."

‡ XIII.—Legitimus quidem Baptismi minister est Parochus, vel
alius Sacerdos a Parocho, vel ab Ordinario loci delegatus; sed quoties
infans, aut adultus versatur in vitæ periculo, potest sine solemnitate a
quocumque baptizari in qualibet lingua, sive Clerico, sive Laico, etiam
excommunicato, sive fideli, sive infideli, sive Catholico, sive hæretico,
sive viro, sive fœmina, servata tamen forma et intentione Ecclesiæ.

‡184. According to the ancient discipline of the Church,
the solemn administration of Baptism was generally confined
to the bishop, who, nevertheless, occasionally committed it to
priests and deacons.[4]   Since the institution of parishes,[5] however, the priests appointed to the care of them are, by the
very fact, commissioned to administer the sacraments, though
a reservation was made as to the solemn administration of
Baptism on Easter Saturday and the eve of Pentecost; and
this reservation is, with respect to the baptism of adults, still
continued in many churches.[6]   But, if we except this reservation, it is, according to the present discipline, the undoubted
right of the parish priest to baptize all who belong to his

[1] Vid. infra, § xxxii.   [2] Vid. infra. § xxx.   [3] Apud. Martene,
De Antiquis Ecclesiæ Ritibus, lib. i. cap. i art. xiv. n. 4.   [4] Catal.,
tit. ii. cap. i. § xiii. n. iii. et iv.   Martene, cap. i. art. iii. n. 2, et seq.
[5] Vid. supra, n. 101.   [6] Catal., l. c. n. v.   Vid. infra. § xxix.
et chap. v. § viii.

parish. Any other priest who baptizes one of them without his leave, or the leave of the Ordinary of the diocese, is guilty of mortal sin, the case of necessity of course excepted.[1] The leave, however, need not always be expressed; it is enough that it can be reasonably presumed.[2]

In case of necessity, Baptism may be conferred by any human being who has the use of reason, and knows how to apply the matter and form.[3] "And here truly may we ad-"mire the supreme wisdom and goodness of our Lord, who, "this sacrament being necessary for all, as he instituted water "as its matter, than which nothing can be more common, "wished also, in like manner, that no one should be excluded "from its administration."[4] We have already seen[5] what words are essential to the form, but they may be pronounced in any language or dialect. It seems difficult to understand how an infidel or heretic can have the necessary intention of doing what the Church does, but it has been above explained how they can have the intention implicitly.[6]

§ XIV.—Sed si adsit Sacerdos, Diacono præferatur. Diaconus Subdiacono, Clericus laico, et vir fœminæ, nisi pudoris gratia deceat fœminam potius, quam virum baptizare infantem non omnino editum, vel nisi melius fœmina sciret formam et modum baptizandi.

*185. The order here prescribed in the rubric binds *sub gravi*, so far as it prohibits a laic to baptize, if a priest be present and willing to do so; but it is probable that a departure from it in any other way, when a priest is not present, does not exceed a venial sin.[7]

A deacon can baptize solemnly when he is specially commissioned by the bishop or parish priest; but theologians commonly teach that this commission should not be given unless for very grave reasons, as, *e. g.*, on account of the great number to be baptized while the priest is disabled by sickness, or too much occupied in hearing confessions, preaching, and other pastoral duties, as might easily happen in missions amongst infidels.[8] Without such a commission, a deacon is not permitted to baptize solemnly, even when called on in case of necessity, and would incur an irregularity by doing so.[9] Hence St. Liguori inclines to the opinion, that a laic baptizing in presence of a deacon would not be guilty of more than a venial sin.[10] It is manifest that, in some cases,

[1] St. Lig., lib. vi. n. 115. *Not.* iv.   [2] Ibid. *Not.* ii.   [3] St. Lig., n. 113.
[4] Cat. Conc. Trid., pars. ii. n. 24.   [5] Supra, n. 167.
[6] Supra, n. 136.   [7] St. Lig., n. 117.   [8] St. Lig., lib. vi. n. 116.
[9] St. Lig., l. c. *Dub.* 2.   [10] Lib. vi. n. 117, *Dub.* 3.

such as the rubric mentions below,[1] modesty requires that, if possible, no other than a female be the minister, even though a priest were at hand.[2]

§ XV.—Quapropter curare debet Parochus, ut Fideles, præsertim obstetrices, rectum baptizandi ritum probe teneant et servent.

*186. Pastors are strictly bound to take care that the faithful, and especially midwives, be well instructed in the manner of administering the sacrament. The obligation here mentioned in the rubric has been inculcated by innumerable provincial and diocesan synods.[3] It is enough to cite the words of the Synod of Thurles: "Cum Baptisma ad salutem "necessarium sit, Dei benignitate factum est ut a quolibet "homine valide conferri possit. Curandum itaque est a Paro- "chis ut singuli fideles, præsertim vero obstetrices, modum et "formam illius ministrandi norint, ut in casu necessitatis illud "rite conferant."[4]

187. It is important also that no one should be permitted to perform the office of midwife, who does not hold the Catholic doctrine on the necessity of Baptism. Nothing short of this will insure sufficient care for the safety of the child in cases of difficult parturition. It is appalling to think of the disregard for infant life avowed and acted on by some practitioners,[5] and it is the undoubted duty of the pastor to prevent, as far as he can, the employment of such persons.[6]

§ XVI.—Pater aut Mater propriam prolem baptizare non debent, præterquam in mortis articulo, quando alius non reperitur qui baptizet; neque tunc ullam contrahunt cognationem, quæ matrimonii usum impediat.

*188. The minister of Baptism, even when conferred privately or in case of necessity, contracts a spiritual relationship with the child and its parents, which is a diriment impediment to marriage with any of them.[7] This is of no practical importance when the minister is in holy orders, unless in the case wherein the relationship should be mentioned in confession;[8] but it is of great importance as regards Baptism conferred by a laic, whose subsequent marriage with

[1] § xviii.   [2] Baruff., Tit vi. n. 16.
[3] Vid. Catal., tit. ii. cap. i. § xiv. n. ii. et iii.   [4] De Baptismo, 6°.
[5] Vid. "The Dublin Review," No. lxxxvii March, 1858, and No. lxxxix. Sept. 1858, Art. Obstetric Morality.
[6] Cfr. Synod. Thur., De Baptismo in fine.   [7] St. Lig., lib. vi. n. 149.
[8] Vid. St. Lig., lib. iv. n. 450.

the child or its parent would be null, unless a dispensation from the impediment were previously obtained.

*189. The present rubric directs that a child should not be baptized by its parent, unless in the case of extreme necessity here mentioned. In any other case, the parent who baptizes is certainly guilty of grievous sin, unless excused by ignorance;[1] but theologians are divided as to whether or not there results any impediment to the use of marriage. The greater number, with St. Thomas, hold that there does, and the rubric here, by excepting the case of necessity, seems to imply the same; but St. Liguori[2] cites many authors in favor of the opposite opinion, to which he himself seems inclined.

190. The same decision is to be given if the husband baptizes the child of his wife by another man, or the wife the child of her husband by another woman; for the impediment, if contracted at all, is contracted in this case as well as when the child belongs to both.[3]

191. All this, however, proceeds on the supposition that the parties are already married, for, if they be not, there is no doubt that, even in case of necessity, there would result a diriment impediment to their subsequent marriage.[4]

It may be doubted whether in this case the parent is prohibited more than any other laic from conferring Baptism. De Lugo discusses the question, whether a father could licitly stand sponsor for his illegitimate child, and he decides it in the affirmative, laying down as a general principle that the prohibition of the canons extends to the children of one's present lawful consort, whether they be the issue of the present marriage or not, but that it does not extend to others, because in the case of no other does any inconvenience result from the spiritual relationship contracted.[5] The same reasoning appears to be perfectly applicable to the case in which the parent baptizes his or her illegitimate child. The Catechism of the Council of Trent, however, assigns one reason why the parent of a child should not act as sponsor, which seems to hold good even when the child is illegitimate, viz.: "To mark more "strongly the great difference that exists between this spirit-'ual and the carnal bringing up of youth."[6] At all events, the decision of De Lugo could not be acted on, if the father

---

[1] St. Lig., lib. VI. n. 150.
[2] Loc. cit. *Secunda Sententia.*
[3] Vid. Carrière, *De Matrimonio,* n. 695.
[4] Baruff., n. 21. Carrière, n. 697, *Dicitur* 2°.
[5] *Resp. Mor.,* lib. i. *Dub.* v. n. 4. [6] Pars ii. cap. ii. n. 29.

of an illegitimate child were already bound to marry the mother, in virtue of a promise, or in order to repair an injury, as may easily happen.[1] In such a case, to contract the relationship would be to put an obstacle to the fulfilment of his obligation.

ON THE BAPTISM OF INFANTS: "DE BAPTIZANDIS PARVULIS."

§ XVII.—Opportune Parochus hortetur eos ad quos ea cura pertinet, ut natos infantes, sive baptizandos sive baptizatos, quamprimum fieri poterit, ea qua decet Christiana modestia, sine pompæ vanitate deferant ad Ecclesiam, ne illis Sacramentum tantopere necessarium nimium differatur cum periculo salutis, et ut iis, qui ex necessitate privatim baptizati sunt, consuetæ cæremoniæ ritusque suppleantur, omissa forma et ablutione.

192. The exhortation here recommended as to the time and manner of presenting infants for Baptism, might be conveniently introduced into the instructions before mentioned.[2] Since Baptism is absolutely necessary to salvation,[3] it follows that infants should be baptized; and seeing the many accidents to which they are exposed, and the great number that die in infancy, it is manifestly expedient that their baptism be not long deferred. The rate of infant mortality varies in different countries, and even in the same country is considerably affected by the circumstances of the parents. But it is ascertained, from reliable statistics, that fully one-third of the infants born alive die before completing their fifth year.[4] In a paper read by Dr. Fraser before the Association for the Promotion of Social Science,[5] it was stated that, in Glasgow, during the month of July, 1860, the mortality of infants under five years was as high as 55 per cent. And in another paper, read by Dr. Gairdner on the same occasion, it was shown, as the result of a great number of returns carefully selected, that the mortality *within the first year after birth*, ranges from 15, as the lowest, up to nearly 30[6] per cent.[7]

There are good reasons, therefore, why the rubric should prescribe, as it does here, that infants be presented for Baptism as soon as possible. Several provincial synods have or-

---

[1] Vid. St. Lig., lib. iv. n. 641, et seq. Carrière, *De Justitia*, n. 1356, et seq.   [2] Sup. n. 131.   [3] Vid. supra, n. 149 et seq.
[4] Vid. Encyclopædia Britannica, 8th edition, art. *Mortality*.
[5] Transactions of the National Association for the Promotion of Social Science for 1860, p. 648.
[6] Accurately 29.641.   [7] Ibid. p. 632.

dered it within a limited time. St. Charles ordered it before
the ninth day, and that, too, under pain of excommunication.[1]
Benedict XIV ordered the same, and under the same
penalty, for Bologna, when he was archbishop of that
city.[2]

*193. It is certain that parents, or those who have the
charge of infants, are guilty of grievous sin, if they put off
their baptism for a long time, unless there be some weighty
reason to excuse them. It is difficult to determine what
delay would amount to a mortal sin, but the more common
and the more probable opinion, according to St. Liguori,
requires it to exceed ten or eleven days.[3]

*194. Though the infant may have received a private
baptism, the rubric directs that it be brought to the church as
soon as possible, to have the usual ceremonies supplied. To
neglect this would be a grievous sin, according to St. Liguori.[4]

When a priest baptizes an infant in a private house, Collet
teaches[5] that he should apply all the usual ceremonies if
there be no danger of the infant's death before the sacrament
is conferred. But it is certain that even in such circumstances he is not, at least as a general rule, permitted to perform
any of the ceremonies which precede baptism: these must be
performed in the church. This is the general law expressed
or supposed in the Ritual, and confirmed by several decrees of
the Sacred Congregation.[6]

*195. In missionary countries, however, where the houses
of the faithful are often at a great distance from the church,
and where there is reason to fear that the children might not
afterwards be brought to the church, to have the ceremonies
supplied, it is permitted to the missionaries to administer the
sacrament with all the ceremonies in private houses, according
to an instruction of Pius VI.[7] In Ireland, until recently, this
custom very generally prevailed; but the Synod of Thurles
has abolished it, and decreed that, in future, Baptism be conferred only in the church. The Synod adds, however, by way
of exception: " Quod si infantes in periculo mortis sint aut si
" longe degunt ab Ecclesiis, ita ut ad eas tuto ferri non possunt,
" tunc morem jam inductum necessitas mutari non sinit."[8]

---

[1] *Act. Eccl. Mediol.*, pars i. Concil. Prov. i. *Quæ pertinent ad Bapt. administ.*, p. 7.   [2] *Instit.*, xcviii. n. 8.   [3] Lib. vi. n. 118, *Not.* ii.
[4] Lib. vi. n. 144, *in parenth.*   [5] *De Bapt.*, cap. v. Quæres 3°.
[6] Vid. infra, cap. iv. § xxvi.
[7] Cit. apud " Analecta Juris Pontificii," Nov. 1855, p. 1304.
[8] *De Baptismo*, 7°.

This would certainly seem to allow a priest, baptizing in case of necessity in a private house, to follow the old custom of performing all the ceremonies.[1]

§ XVIII.—Nemo in utero matris clausus baptizari debet. Sed si infans caput emiserit, et periculum mortis immineat, baptizetur in capite; nec postea, si vivus evaserit, erit iterum baptizandus.

*196. An infant is not to be baptized until fully born, unless when there is reason to fear that it may not be born alive. In cases of difficult parturition, therefore, such as are here contemplated, it is important to know when Baptism may be conferred.

It is certain, in the first place, that the infant cannot be baptized if it is still enclosed so that water cannot reach it; but if it can be reached through the enclosure even by means of an instrument, so that water can be poured or sprinkled on it, the baptism would probably be valid, and, therefore, in case of necessity, might be conferred conditionally.[2]

Those who maintain that the baptism in this case would be invalid, rely chiefly on the argument used by St. Augustine against the heretics who maintained that the ablution of the mother's body would suffice for the baptism of the infant in her womb, viz., "that it must be first *born*, before it can be *born again*." But it is replied that it may be said, in a theological sense, to be "natus" when it is alive in the womb, as in the expression of the Scripture, "*Quod in ea natum est de Spiritu Sancto est;*"[3] and it may be added that, in the case supposed, there is incipient parturition. Benedict XIV discusses the question at great length, and concludes that pastors should instruct midwives, in such a case of extreme necessity, to administer Baptism conditionally.[4]

*197. There is no doubt about the validity of the baptism when water is poured on the head. And therefore it should be conferred absolutely in the case here mentioned in the rubric, and should not be repeated, unless when there is reason to fear, as there often is, according to Cardinal Gousset,[5] that the midwife or other person conferring it in such trying circumstances may have omitted something essential, in which case it should, of course, be repeated conditionally. The words of the rubric, "si caput emiserit," ought to be rigorously

[1] Vid. infra, cap. iv. § xxvii.   [2] St. Lig., lib. vi. n. 107.
[3] Matth. i. 20.   Vid. St. Lig., n. 107. *Secunda Sententia.*
[4] *Synod. Diœc.* lib. vii. cap. v. . . . . .
[5] *Théologie Morale,* vol. ii. No. 82.

verified, because it was decided by the Sacred Congregation of the Council, that if a fœtus in the womb be baptized on the crown or top of the head, baptism should be repeated conditionally after the birth: " Fœtus in utero supra verticem bap-"tizatus post ortum denuo sub conditione baptizetur."[1]

§ XIX.—At si aliud membrum emiserit, quod vitalem indicet motum, in illo, si periculum impendeat, baptizetur; et tunc si natus vixerit, erit sub conditione baptizandus eo modo quo supra dictum est: *Si non es baptizatus, ego te baptizo in nomine Patris, etc.* Si vero ita baptizatus, deinde mortuus prodierit ex utero, debet in loco sacro sepeliri.

*198. Baptism on any other part than the head is doubtful, and, therefore, it is directed that, if conferred in necessity, it be repeated conditionally, though it is commonly held that baptism on any principal part, as the shoulder or breast, would be valid.[2] The rubric does not say that it is to be conferred conditionally in the first instance, but we believe it should, at least when the water reaches only a hand or foot, or some small part.[3]

*199. The conditional baptism conferred in any of these cases gives a right to ecclesiastical sepulture, which, as a general rule, is conceded, unless when there is a clear and certain ground of exclusion.[4]

§ XX.—Si mater prægnans mortua fuerit, fœtus quamprimum caute extrahatur. ac, si vivus fuerit, baptizetur: si fuerit mortuus, et baptizari non potuerit, in loco sacro sepeliri non debet.

*200. It is needless to observe that the greatest caution is necessary in doing what is here prescribed. There must be a certainty of the mother's death before any incision is attempted, otherwise it is evident there would be a risk of taking away or shortening her life; and this is never lawful, not even to procure the baptism of the infant.[5] But when it is quite certain that she is dead, the fœtus should be extracted without delay, if there be the least hope that it is still alive.

201. It may be useful to dwell a little on this important matter, since priests on the mission are so often obliged to give advice and direction as to what should be done in the distressing case here supposed.

It is evident from the Catholic doctrine regarding the

---

[1] 12 Julii, 1794, cit. apud Falise, *Decreta Authentica Sac. Rit. Cong.* v. *Baptisma*, in notn.   [2] St. Lig. lib. vi. n. 107, Quær. iv.
[3] St. Lig., l. c. Quær. iii. in fine.   [4] Cfr. Ferraris, *V. Sepultura.* n. 172, et seq.   [5] St. Lig., lib. vi. n. 106. *Omnino tenendum.* Gousset, vol. ii. n. 83. Bouvier, *Abrégé d'Embryologie,* Q. v. 2.

necessity of baptism, that there is a strict obligation of doing
all that can be done in the circumstances to give the infant a
chance of receiving it.[1] Some writers condemn the Cæsarean
operation as useless, maintaining that the infant in the womb
must die at the same time with the mother; but this opinion
is exploded, and all theologians are agreed in inculcating
what is here prescribed in the rubric.[2] Numberless instances
prove that the infant may be alive in the womb a considerable
time after the mother's death. Bouvier mentions that infants
have been taken out alive twenty-four and even forty-eight
hours after the death of the mothers.[3]

202. It was formerly believed that, to preserve the infant's
life, the mouth of the deceased should be kept open till the
operation has been performed, and a recommendation to this
effect is found in most authors.[4] But it has been ascertained,
according to Bouvier,[5] that this is quite useless, and that the
only thing necessary is, to prevent, if possible, the cold which
follows death from reaching the infant. This is best effected
by applying warm clothes to the part where the infant is;
and care should be taken to do so, if it be necessary to wait
some time for a person to perform the operation.

203. The operation should be performed by a surgeon, if
one can be had. In defect of a surgeon, it should be performed by the nurse in attendance or some other female. If
there be no one else, it may be performed by a man, but in
no case, according to Bouvier, should it be attempted by a
priest, above all, by a young priest.[6] At least, according to
Cardinal Gousset,[7] the priest is not bound to perform it, even
if there be no one else.

The exception as regards the priest is not made by any
other writer that we have seen. Dens[8] expressly says that,
in defect of any other to perform it, "incumbit parocho
"eandem operationem facere." Debreyne[9] is of the same
opinion, and says this is the opinion of the older theologians.
He observes that Bouvier himself, in the earlier editions of
his book, excepted the case in which it would be impossible

[1] Vid. supra, n. 149 et seq.
[2] Benedict XIV, *De Synod. Diœc.*, lib. xi. cap. vii. n. 12.
[3] *Op. cit.*, Quest. vii. 2°. Vid. "Dublin Review," No. lxxxvii, March
1858. Art. *Obstetric Morality*, pag. 127.
[4] St. Lig., l. c. Dacroix, lib. vi. pars i. n. 293, etc.
[5] *Op. cit.*, Q. vi. 2°.   [6] *Op. cit.*, Q. viii.
[7] Vol. ii. n. 48.   [8] *De Baptismo*, n. 24.
[9] *Traité Pratique d'Embryologie Sacrée*, chap. ii. § iii.

to get another to do it.   No doubt, such an operation is extremely unsuited to the priestly character; but if we suppose a case in which there is good reason to believe that the infant is alive in the body of the deceased mother, while there is no one but the priest to perform the operation, it is hard to see why he might not, and should not, perform it if he can, since the eternal salvation of the infant is here at stake.

204. At all events it is certain that the pastor is bound to instruct, with regard to this obligation, those of his flock whom it may concern, as mothers, nurses, surgeons, and such as are employed in any way about women at the time of their confinement.   His own prudence must direct him as to the time and circumstances in which the instructions may be given.[1]

205.   He should take care also that those who might be required to perform the operation, in defect of a surgeon, be instructed as to the manner of performing it.   For the instruction of such persons, Bouvier gives the following directions:—1° The incision should be made on the side that appears most prominent, lengthwise, and not across.   It may be made with a razor when there is no surgical instrument. 2° It should be about six or seven inches long.   The flesh having been cut through, and the entrails that may be met with set aside, the matrix must be opened very gently, so as not to hurt the infant.   When the matrix is sufficiently opened, conditional baptism should be administered with tepid water, lest the infant might die on exposure to the air.   It should then be taken out, and when the membrane which envelops it is removed, it should be again baptized conditionally.[2]

*206. If baptism has not been administered before extraction, and if the fœtus when extracted be alive, it should be baptized absolutely.   In case of doubt, if it shows the least sign of life, however equivocal, it should be baptized conditionally, "Si vivis," etc.[3]   But if it be certainly dead, baptism should not be attempted, nor should it be buried in consecrated ground, as is plain from the present rubric.   If it be found dead in the womb, however, it should not be removed, but be buried with the mother.[4]

207. We may here observe that the Cæsarean operation has been often successfully performed on the living subject

---

[1] Vid. Bouvier, Op. cit., Qu. vii. n. 1, 2.   St. Lig. n. 106.   His opera pretium.
[2] Bouvier, Op. cit. Qu. ix.
[3] St. Lig., n. 124.
[4] Bouvier, Qu. ix. 4°.

in France and other countries of the Continent. Several instances are related by Clericati,[1] and the statistics of modern practice show that the operation was successful in more than two-thirds of the cases in which it was performed, though these included many in which it was not tried until the life of the patient was almost despaired of.[2] In this way the lives of both mother and child are often saved, when otherwise both must have been lost, or one sacrificed to preserve the other.

208. If we suppose a case, then, in which there is an experienced surgeon prepared to undertake the operation, while it is certain, 1° that the danger to the mother's life is not increased by it, and 2° that it is the best, if not the only chance of extracting the infant alive; the mother would be plainly bound, in charity to her infant, to submit to it. Bouvier says she should be earnestly exhorted to do so, but not compelled under pain of being refused the sacraments. Better leave her *in bona fide*. At all events, in practice it can hardly occur that all the conditions are so certainly placed as to leave no doubt about her obligation.[4]

209. The operation is comparatively rare either in these countries or in America. The reason is one which shows what little account is generally made of Christian faith and morality in certain surgical schools. It is, that practitioners are commonly taught to have recourse to another operation, by which the infant is ruthlessly destroyed in order to save the mother, or even, perhaps, to spare her extraordinary pain.[5] With us, therefore, a surgeon can hardly be found willing to attempt the Cæsarean section while the mother is living, and consequently with us a priest can hardly be called on to deal with the case above mentioned.

210. But he is called on, and is bound to do all he can, to prevent any operation which directly tends to destroy the infant's life. Such an operation is never lawful, unless it be ascertained beyond doubt that the infant is already dead in the womb. If surgical skill can supply no other remedy, the case must be left to the efforts of nature and to Providence. If in these circumstances the mother dies, the Cæsarean opera-

[1] *De Baptismo*, Decis. xli. n. 5, et seq.
[2] Vid. "Dublin Review," March, 1858, No. lxxxvii. pag. 117.
[3] *Op. cit.*, Qu. v. n. 3.
[4] Bouvier, l. c. Gousset, vol. ii. n. 84. Vid. St. Lig., n. 106, *circa medium*. Gury, vol. ii. n. 259.
[5] Vid. "Dublin Review," No. lxxxvii. Art. *Obstetric Morality*.

tion should be performed after death, and Baptism administered to the fœtus, according to what has been said above.

211. The same rule, as regards baptism, is to be followed in case of abortion, no matter how early the stage of pregnancy. It is now the common opinion that the fœtus is animated from the moment of conception, or a few days after; and the rule generally received is, in every case of abortion to baptize the fœtus, absolutely, if it shows evident signs of life; conditionally, if there is reasonable ground for doubting whether it be alive or not.[1] The Congregation of the Holy Office, in reference to cases proposed in this matter, gave the following decision: "In casibus propositis (nempe de baptismo "fœtûs abortivi) si suppetat rationabile fundamentum dubi-"tandi, an fœtus ille sit animatus animâ rationali, tunc potest "et debet baptizari sub conditione; si vero non suppetat "rationabile fundamentum, nullatenus potest baptizari.

"Ad videndum autem an sit rationabile fundamentum talis "dubii, consulendi sunt Medici et Theologi in facti contin-"gentiâ, sive in casibus particularibus."[2] It is not to be baptized, for instance, if it does not present even the first lineaments of a human body, for all are agreed: "Non "debere baptizari carneam massam quæ nullam habeat or-"ganorum dispositionem."[3]

Jerome Florentinius, who was the first to write a formal dissertation on the subject,[4] maintained that, on account of the doubt about the time of animation, conditional baptism should be administered to the fœtus in case of abortion, no matter how soon after conception it may take place. This dissertation was received with great applause in all the schools of Theology.[5] But the author was directed by the Sacred Congregation of the Index, to limit his propositions to fœtus, ... "in quibus apparent prima vitæ humanæ delinea-"menta;"[6] and he accordingly declares in the commencement of his dissertation that such is his meaning. He further adds (by direction, as it would seem, of the same authority), that he has no intention of binding others under pain of sin to

---

[1] St. Lig., n. 124. Bouvier, *Abrégé d'Embryologie*, Quæst. i. n. 3ᶜ.

[2] Die 5 Aprilis, an. 1715. The decision, in the words cited, was sent, not long ago, in answer to a priest who had made application to Rome on the subject. [3] St. Lig., l. c.

[4] *Disputatio de ministrando Baptismo Humanis fœtibus abortivis*, given in extenso, by the "Analecta Juris Pontificii," VIᵐᵉ Série, pag. 1280, et seq., Rome, 1863.

[5] Vid. "Analecta," Vᵐᵉ Série, *Sacrement de Baptême*, chap. v. pag 1112 et seq. [6] "Analecta," l. c. pag. 1138.

adopt his opinion in practice, nor of introducing any new
rite: "Deinde adverto me neminem, quoad praxim attinet,
"sub mortali obligare, sed tantum rationes speculative id
"suadentes exponere, ac in suspenso relinquere, sicuti nec in-
"ducere novum aliquem ritum in Ecclesiam; cum id ad Sac.
Rit. Congregationem, Summumque Pontificem spectet."[1]

Cangianila, in his *Embryologia Sacra,* adopting the view
of Florentinius, gives minute instructions as to the manner of
administering baptism in the various cases that may occur.
This work, which is commended by Benedict XIV,[2] has
supplied nearly all that is found in subsequent writers on the
subject.[3]

212. If the foetus be enveloped in the secundines, it should
be baptized in this state conditionally: "Si tu es capax," etc.;
for, on the one hand, such a baptism is probably valid,[4] and
on the other, there is danger of instant death from exposure
to the air on the membrane being opened.[5] The baptism
thus conferred being doubtful, the foetus should be again
baptized conditionally when the membrane is opened.[6]
Bouvier[7] observes that the foetus, though alive, may be so
feeble as to be unable to bear the application of cold water,
and in this case tepid water, if at hand, should be used.
Again, it may be so small that it cannot be baptized in the
usual way, and in this case he recommends that it be baptized by immersion; but care must be taken, as far as possible, that nothing be done which would tend to deprive it of
life. It cannot live long, it is true, but it would be unlawful
to do anything that would directly hasten its death.[8]

213. Since 1831 the practice has been introduced in France,
of causing the child to be born prematurely when it is foreseen that it cannot be born alive at the end of the natural
term. This method has been found very successful in saving
the lives of both mother and child, when the birth is not
caused till after the seventh month. And it is not only lawful, but highly laudable, to have recourse to it, when it is
already known from experience that the child, if full-sized,
cannot be brought forth alive.[9]

---

[1] *Disput. cit.* apud "Analecta," pag. 1290.
[2] *De Synodo Diœc.,* lib. xi. cap. vii. n. 13.
[3] Vid. *Dissert. Theolog. De Baptizandis Abortivis* apud Dens, § Appendice ad *Tractatum De Baptismo.* Edit. Mechliniæ. 1830.
[4] Benedict XIV., *De Syn. Diœc.,* lib. vii. cap. v. n. iii.
[5] Bouvier, *Op. cit.,* Qu. ii. n. 2º.   [6] Bouvier, l. c. Gousset,
vol. ii. n. 85.   [7] Loc. cit., n. 3 and 4.   [8] Bouvier, l. c.
[9] Bouvier, Qu. v. n. 3º.   "Dublin Review," loc. cit. p. 118.

§ XXI.—Infantes expositi et inventi, si re diligenter investigata de eorum Baptismo non constet, sub conditione baptizentur.

*214. The priest is strictly bound to make diligent inquiry about the baptism of such children as are here mentioned;[1] and they are to be baptized conditionally, unless there be satisfactory proof that they have been already validly baptized. The same rule is to be observed with regard to infants baptized in case of necessity by midwives or other laics; the doubt, if after proper inquiry any still remains, being always resolved in practice by conferring conditional baptism.[2]

*215. If the children of non-Catholic parents be presented to a priest for baptism, with the consent of one of the parents, they should, by all means, be baptized when there is hope that they shall be educated as Catholics, care being taken to have a Catholic sponsor. But if such children be in probable danger of death, they should be baptized without any hesitation.[3] Of course the baptism should be conferred *sub conditione* when there is a doubt whether the child was validly baptized before.

§ XXII.—In monstris vero baptizandis, si casus eveniat. magna cautio adhibenda est, de quo, si opus fuerit, Ordinarius loci, vel alii periti consulantur, nisi mortis periculum immineat.

Monstrum, quod humanam speciem non præ se ferat, baptizari non debet; de quo si dubium fuerit, baptizetur sub hac conditione: *Si tu es homo, ego baptizo, etc.*

216. With respect to this rubric we cannot do better than cite what St. Liguori says:[4] "Quando dubitatur an monstrum "sit homo, baptizandum absolute, si caput sit humanum, licet "membra sint ferina; sub conditione vero, si caput sit ferinum, "et membra humana; hoc vero si prodierit ex congressu viri "cum fœmina; nam si prodierit ex viro cum bestia (quod in- "credibile puto) tunc baptizari semper deberet sub conditione; "secus si ex fœmina et bruto, tunc enim nullo modo bapti- "zandum, quia non descenderet ex Adam, utpote non concep- "tum ex semine virili." Debreyne[5] denies the possibility of procreation such as is supposed here, and lays down as the rule to be observed in practice, that the issue of a woman, no matter what shape or appearance it presents, may be baptized conditionally.

[1] Vid. supra, n. 174.　　[2] St. Lig., n. 135, 136. Syn. Thurl., De Bapt. n. 11.　　[3] Syn. Thur., l. c. n. 9°.　　[4] Lib. vi. n. 125.
[5] *Traité Pratique d'Embryologie Sacrée*, chap. ii. § vii.

§ XXIII.—Illud vero, de quo dubium est, una ne aut plures sint personæ, non baptizetur, donec id discernatur: discerni autem potest, si habeat unum vel plura capita, unum vel plura pectora; tunc enim totidem erunt corda et animæ, hominesque distincti, et eo casu singuli seorsum sunt baptizandi, unicuique dicendo: *Ego te baptizo, etc.* Si vero periculum mortis immineat, tempusque non suppetat ut singuli separatim baptizentur, poterit Minister, singulorum capitibus aquam infundens, omnes simul baptizare, dicendo: *Ego vos baptizo in nomine Patris, et Filii, et Spiritus Sancti.* Quam tamen formam in iis solum, et in aliis similibus mortis periculis ad plures simul baptizandos, et ubi tempus non patitur ut singuli separatim baptizentur, alias nunquam licet adhibere.

Quando vero non est certum in monstro esse duas personas, quia duo capita et duo pectora non habet distincta; tunc debet primum unus absolute baptizari, et postea alter sub conditione, hoc modo: *Si non es baptizatus, ego te baptizo in nomine Patris, et Filii, et Spiritus Sancti.*

217. The rubric here requires no explanation. The rules it lays down for forming the judgment, and the instructions it gives as to what should be done in the several cases, are very clear and precise, insomuch that St. Liguori[1] is satisfied with quoting the words.

ON THE SPONSORS: "DE PATRINIS."

§ XXIV.—Parochus, antequam ad baptizandum accedat, ab iis, ad quos spectat, exquirat diligenter, quem, vel quos Susceptores seu Patrinos elegerint, qui infantem de sacro fonte suscipiant, ne plures quam liceat, aut indignos, aut ineptos admittat.

218. It has been the practice in the Church, from the very earliest times, to have certain persons assisting at the solemn administration of baptism, to answer for the infant, making profession of the Christian faith in its name, and to receive it from the hands of the minister when baptized at the sacred font. They assisted in like manner at the baptism of adults, except that the adults themselves were required to answer the interrogations. Hence they were called "Sponsores," "Fidejussores," "Susceptores," and sometimes also "Offe-"rentes."[2] They are mentioned by Tertullian, *Lib. de Bapt.*, cap. xviii., St. Basil, *Epist.* 128, and in several places by St. Augustine.[3]

In later times they have been usually called "Patrini," since they undertake the office of spiritual parents towards those for whom they are sponsors at the sacred font. In English they are called "God-fathers" and "God-mothers" as well as Sponsors; and very commonly, amongst the hum-

---

[1] Loc. cit. in fine.   [2] Martene, *De Antiquis Ecclesiæ Ritibus,* lib. l. cap. i. art. xvi. n. 11, 12.   [3] Citat. apud Martene, l. c.

bler classes, "Gossips," which is the old Saxon name by which they were designated.[1]

219. "Let all sponsors, then," says the Catechism of the Council of Trent, "at all times recollect that they are bound "principally to exercise a constant vigilance over their "spiritual children, and to take particular care that in those "things that belong to the formation of a Christian life, they "approve themselves throughout life such as their sponsor "promised they should be by the solemn ceremony."[2]

It is not surprising, therefore, that the pastor is here directed to make diligent inquiry regarding the person or persons selected as sponsors, and to admit no one who is not duly qualified. He ought to make this inquiry before he commences the ceremony, as he would then have less difficulty in setting aside one whom he might ascertain to be unfit. The inquiry should be made of the parents, who have the right of selecting the sponsors. The priest cannot refuse to admit those who are designated, if they are duly qualified; but should he refuse, and appoint others, his act, though sinful, would be valid.[3] If he be careful to instruct the faithful, as he is required to do by the Catechism of the Council of Trent,[4] on the duties and qualifications of sponsors, it will rarely happen that any one is presented as sponsor whom he will find it necessary to reject.

§ XXV.—Patrinus unus tantum, sive vir, sive mulier, vel ad summum unus et una adhibeantur, ex Decreto Concilii Tridentini; sed simul non admittantur, duo viri, aut duæ mulieres, neque baptizandi pater, aut mater.

*220. According to the decree of the Council of Trent, only one, or at most two, a male and a female, should be admitted to act as sponsors,[5] and St. Liguori[6] teaches that the pastor would be guilty of grievous sin if he admits a greater number. The object of the decree is to prevent a too great extension of the impediment arising from the spiritual relationship contracted by the sponsors with the infant and its parents.[7] If a greater number, however, be selected, the priest may permit them to be present and even to touch the child, provided he designates two who are to be the real sponsors, and gives notice that they alone contract the spiritual relationship.[8]

[1] Worcester's Dictionary, v. Gossip.   [2] Pars ii. cap. ii. n. 28.
[3] St. Lig., lib. vi. n. 146.   [4] Loc. cit.   [5] Sess. xxiv. De Reform.
Matrim., cap. ii.   [6] Lib. vi. n. 154, in fine.   [7] St. Lig., loc. cit.
Carrière, De Matrimonio, n. 602.   [8] St. Lig., loc. cit.

221. But if, notwithstanding the decree, a greater number be simply admitted to act as sponsors, it is a question amongst theologians whether all contract the relationship. St. Liguori[1] resolves it thus: If all be designated, and if they touch the child *successively*, only the first two contract the relationship; but if they touch it *simultaneously*, all contract it. If none be designated, all who touch contract it; because, according to him, the decree of Trent implies: 1° that no more than two should be designated; and 2° that in case two thus designated shall act, no others who after them may touch the child shall, in any circumstances, contract the relationship, but it does not abrogate the provisions of the ancient canons with regard to other cases.

*222. When there are two sponsors, they should be of different sexes, according to the rubric—not two males, nor two females. There is a certain congruity in this, from the analogy between the spiritual and natural parentage, as is explained by St. Thomas.[2] A violation of the rubric would be a grievous sin, according to St. Liguori, if the sponsors admitted be of a different sex from that of the child; but it would not exceed a venial sin if they be of the same sex.[3] By a constitution of Urban II, a husband and wife were prohibited from acting together as sponsors, but this constitution is no longer in force, and they are now freely admitted.[4]

When there is only one sponsor, it is usual to select one of the same sex with the child; but there is no obligation, since the words of the rubric, taken from the decree of Trent, leave the choice free.[5]

*223. The father or mother is prohibited from acting as sponsor; and this, according to the Catechism of the Council of Trent, "to mark more strongly the great difference that "exists between the spiritual and the carnal bringing up of "youth."[6] But if either *does* act as sponsor, would there arise an impediment to the use of marriage? Most theologians affirm that there would, and assign this as a reason for the prohibition here mentioned in the rubric. St. Liguori,[7] however, seems inclined to the opposite opinion, for he includes this case, and that in which the parent baptizes, under the same question; and although, in the discussion, he seems to speak only of the case in which the parent baptizes, he mani-

[1] Lib. vi. n. 154.   [2] 3 part. ques. lxvii. art. vii.
[3] Lib. vi. n. 155, Dub. 2.   [4] Ibid. n. 157.   [5] Ibid. n 155, Dub. 1.
[6] Pars ii. cap. ii. n. 29.   [7] Lib. vi. n. 150.

festly supposes the decision to apply equally to both cases, especially since the canon, *Si vir* 2. *de cognat. spirit.*, which is quoted by him, and, indeed, by all theologians and canonists, in treating the question, regards precisely the case of a parent being sponsor.[1]

§ XXVI.—Hos autem Patrinos saltem in ætate pubertatis, ac Sacramento Confirmationis consignatos esse, maxime convenit.

*224. From the duties attached to the office of sponsor, it is fitting that those who undertake it be not mere children, but have attained the age of puberty, which is, according to the canons, fourteen years complete for males, and twelve for females;[2] and also that they have received the sacrament of confirmation. In the fifth provincial council of Milan, under St. Charles, parish priests are ordered to require these conditions.[3] The words of the rubric, "maxime convenit," do not, however, imply a strict obligation, and theologians generally are satisfied with requiring that the person acting as sponsor should have been baptized, and have attained the use of reason, being at least seven years old.[4] At all events, there need be no great difficulty in admitting one sponsor under the age of puberty, with another who has attained it.[5]

225. We must, of course, except places where the provisions of the rubric are enforced by a special law, as would seem to be the case in England, for the Synod of Westminster has the following decree: "Non admittantur patrini "vel matrinæ qui non sint Catholici vel qui a jure excludun- "tur; nimirum, impuberes, excommunicati majori excom- "municatione, nondum confirmati, qui paschalis communionis "præceptum non adimplent; demum ecclesiastici. Curet "sacerdos ut, propter periculum fidei infantium facile ob- "venturum post mortem parentum, ambo, quoties fieri possit, "adhibeantur."[6]

226. To act as sponsor validly, and thereby contract the spiritual relationship, it is necessary, 1° that the person be designated, or at least in some way admitted to act as such;[7] 2° that he have the intention of so acting; 3° that by himself or his procurator (for he can depute another to act in his

---

[1] Vid. supra, n. 189.   [2] Cfr. Carrière, *De Mat.*, n. 901.
[3] *Act. Eccl. Mediol.*, pars i. concil. prov. v. *Quæ ad Baptism.cm pertinent*, pag. 178.   [4] St. Lig., n. 146. Gousset, vol. ii. n 111.
[5] Cfr. Bouvier, *De Bapt.*, cap. vii. art. i.
[6] *Acta et Decreta Primi Concil. Provinc. Westmon.*, De Baptismo, n. 5
[7] Vid supra, n. 231.

name),[1] he hold up or physically touch the child while it is
being baptized, or immediately receive it from the hands of
the priest;[2] 4° that the baptism be conferred solemnly.[3]

227. According to St. Liguori, sponsors may be admitted
in private baptism, and he would even prefer to have them
"præstantius adhibetur."[4] Falise says they should not be
admitted, because the ritual makes no mention of them in
what it has regarding baptism in necessity.[5] The Sacred
Congregation of the Council has declared, according to
Ferraris, that "pro baptismo privato susceptores Ecclesia non
"instituit;" but Ferraris himself infers nothing more from
the declaration than that it is no sin to confer private baptism
without a sponsor.[6] Bouvier says merely: "In baptismo pri-
"vato non adhibetur patrinus nec matrina."[7] There is no
decision, then, nor any sufficient authority, as far as we know,
to make it clear that sponsors *should not* be admitted in private
baptism; but at least it is certain that they are not required,
and that, if admitted, they contract no relationship.

228. They are required, however, when the ceremonies are
supplied in the church; for the "Ordo supplendi," etc.,
plainly supposes them to be present;[8] and although they
contract no impediment,[9] it is more probable, according to
Bouvier,[10] that they are bound to look after the Christian
education of the child. The Ritual of Toulon has a formal
admonition to this effect, in the "Ordo supplendi," etc.[11]

§ XXVII.—Sciant præterea Parochi, ad hoc munus non esse admit-
tendos infideles, aut hæreticos, non publice excommunicatos, aut inter-
dictos, non publice criminosos, aut infames, nec præterea qui sana mente
non sunt, neque qui ignorant rudimenta Fidei. Hæc enim Patrini
spirituales filios suos, quos de Baptismi fonte susceperint, ubi opus
fuerit, opportune docere tenentur.

229. From what has been already said regarding the duties
and obligations that belong to the office of sponsor,[12] it is
easy to see that those here mentioned in the rubric are unfit to
be intrusted with it, and therefore cannot be lawfully admitted
to it. The priest should ascertain whether those presented
have a sufficient knowledge of the Christian doctrine; and
with this view, it is often expedient to ask them a few ques-

---

[1] St. Lig., n. 153.   [2] St. Lig., n. 148.   [3] St. Lig., n. 149.
[4] St. Lig., n. 147.   [5] *Cours Abrégé*, etc., 3ᵐᵉ part. sec. i. chap. i.
[6] v. n. 5.   [6] Verb. *Baptismus*, art. vii. n. 7, edition Migne.
[7] *De Bapt.*, cap. vii. art. 1, 2°.   [8] Infra, chap. vii. § ii.
[9] Vid. infra, chap. iv. § xxix.   [10] Loc. cit. 5°.
[11] Tit. ii. § iv. in fine.   [12] Supra, n. 219.

tions from the Catechism. There is no doubt that sponsors are bound to give a Christian education to their spiritual children, as is here stated in the Ritual, and as is more fully explained in the Catechism of the Council of Trent,[1] which cites the words of St. Augustine on the subject: "'They "'ought' (says he), 'to admonish them to observe chastity, "'love justice, cherish charity; and, above all, they should. "'teach them the Creed, the Lord's prayer, the Ten Command- "'ments, and the first rudiments of the Christian religion.'— "Serm. 163, De Temp.—"Hence," the Catechism adds,[2] "it is "not difficult to decide who are inadmissible to this holy guar- "dianship: to those who are unwilling to discharge its duties "with fidelity, or who cannot do so with care and accuracy, "this sacred trust should not be confided."

230. Theologians, however, commonly teach, with St. Thomas,[3] that sponsors are bound to fulfil these duties only when there is reason to think that they are neglected by the parents or others on whom they naturally devolve in the first instance; and hence, generally speaking, sponsors need have no anxiety about the discharge of these duties towards the children of Christian parents.[4]

*231. We may observe that an infidel, in the strict sense —that is, one who is unbaptized—cannot act validly as sponsor; at least he does not contract the spiritual relationship which is a matrimonial impediment;[5] and the same is to be said of one whose mind is unsound, or who is incapable of a human act;[6] but the others here mentioned could act validly, though it is unlawful to admit them.

*232. In mixed communities, where Catholics and Protestants live together, and often even intermarry, a Protestant is sometimes selected to act as sponsor, and this is a cause of great embarrassment to the priest. He cannot, however, in any circumstances, admit one who is not a Catholic. Laymann, and one or two others, speaking of Germany, hold that he might, in cases where the refusal would give very great offence; but in this they are opposed to the common opinion of theologians.[7]

In such circumstances, the priest might appoint a Catholic sponsor who would really act as such, and permit the Protestant to be present merely as a witness, taking care to note

· Pars ii. cap. ii. n. 28. ² Loc. cit. n. 29.
³ 3 part, quæs. lxvii. art. viii. ⁴ St. Lig., n. 147.
⁵ Carrière, De Mat., n. 680. ⁶ Ibid., n. 688.
⁷ Vid. St. Lig., n. 156. Lacroix, lib. vi. p. i. n. 373.

this in the registry; or he may omit in the ceremony whatever regards the sponsor, and have none at all.[1] Better, according to Dens,[2] to baptize solemnly without a sponsor, than admit a heretic to act as such ; and Bouvier would apply the same rule to all who are clearly excluded by the rubric.[3] If the priest has been careful to inquire beforehand, and ascertain who are to be presented as sponsors, he will probably find some pretext for setting aside those who are unfit, without giving any offence.

§ XXVIII.—Præterea ad hoc etiam admitti non debent Monachi, vel Sanctimoniales, neque alii cujusvis Ordinis Regulares a sæculo segregati.

233. The secular clergy are not excluded from the office of sponsor by this rubric, but they have been sometimes excluded by diocesan or provincial statutes, as, *e. g.*, that of Milan, cited by Catalani,[4] and that of the Synod of Westminster, above cited.[5] Some have doubted whether the priest who baptizes could at the same time act as sponsor, since he should thus respond to the interrogations put by himself, etc. It is very probable, however, that he can do so by substituting another to give the responses and act in his place.[6] Even this subtitution is unnecessary when there is a godmother, for she can answer the interrogations.[7]

234. It is certain that a sponsor can act by means of a proxy, and, in this case, the principal, and not the proxy, contracts the relationship, according to a decision of the Sacred Congregation.[8]

THE TIME AND PLACE OF ADMINISTERING BAPTISM: "DE TEMPORE ET LOCO ADMINISTRANDI BAPTISMUM."

§ XXIX.—Quamvis Baptismus quovis tempore, etiam interdicti, et cessationis a Divinis, præsertim si urgeat necessitas, conferri possit ; tamen duo potissimum ex antiquissimo Ecclesiæ ritu sacri sunt dies, in quibus solemni cæremonia hoc Sacramentum administrari maxime convenit ; nempe Sabbatum Sanctum Paschæ, et Sabbatum Pentecostes, quibus diebus Baptismalis Fontis aqua rite consecratur. Quem ritum, quatenus fieri commode potest, in adultis baptizandis, nisi vitæ periculum imminent, retineri decet, aut certe non omnino prætermitti, præcipue in Metropolitanis, aut Cathedralibus Ecclesiis.

[1] Lacroix. l. c.   [2] *De Baptismo*, n. 42 in fine.
[3] *De Bapt*, cap. vii. art. i. n. 2°.   [4] Tit. ii. cap i. § xxvii. n. ii.
[5] Supra, n. 225.   [6] Lacroix, l. c. n. 353.
[7] Vid. Revue Théologique, IVᵐᵉ Série, 5ᵐᵉ Cahier, Julliet, 1860, p. 404.   [8] Vid. St. Lig., n. 153. Carrière, *De Matrimonio*, n. 604.

235. According to the discipline of the Church in the first ages, the solemn administration of baptism took place only twice a year, being confined to the vigils of Easter and Pentecost. Martene proves this by the testimony of the most ancient writers, and decrees of early popes.[1] In the Greek Church the feast of the Epiphany was added, at least as early as the fourth century.[2] In Ireland, also, the decree of the synod of St. Patrick regarding the time of baptism mentions the Epiphany as well as Easter and Pentecost: "Octavo die "catechumeni sunt, postea solemnitatibus Domini baptizan-"tur. id est, Pascha et Pentecoste et Epiphania."[3] In Gaul, at the close of the sixth century, there were already five days fixed on for the purpose, the feasts of the Nativity of our Lord and of St. John the Baptist having been added to the three already mentioned;[4] and in some parts of Spain, at a still earlier period, baptism was conferred not only on these feasts, but on all feasts of apostles and martyrs.[5]

236. In case of necessity, however, or when there was reason, from any cause, to apprehend that a catechumen could not be baptized on one of the appointed days, it was conferred, without hesitation, on any day. As the number of adults to be baptized diminished, and that of infants increased, with the gradual establishment of Christianity in each country, the discipline restricting baptism to particular solemnities was gradually relaxed on account of the danger in case of infants, until it altogether ceased. Certain it is, at all events, that it had ceased almost everywhere about the close of the tenth, or beginning of the eleventh, century. In one of the canons enacted in the reign of King Edgar, priests were directed to administer baptism whenever they were called on, and to admonish the faithful that the baptism of infants should not be deferred beyond thirty-seven days at most.[6] What is required by the present discipline and practice throughout the Church has been above stated.[7]

237. Some vestiges of the ancient usage still remain in the benediction of the font and other ceremonies prescribed for the vigils of Easter and Pentecost. "On these vigils alone," says the Catechism of the Council of Trent,[8] "except in cases of "necessity, it was also the practice of the ancient Church to

---

[1] De Antiquis Ecclesiæ Ritibus, lib. i. cap. i. art. i.   [2] Ibid., n. iv.
[3] Synod. Sti. Patricii, cap. xix. Qua ætate baptizandi sunt, apud Wilkins. Concilia Magnæ Brittaniæ et Hiberniæ, vol. i. pag. 5: Londini, MDCCXXXVII.   [4] Martene, loc. cit. n. vii.   [5] Martene, n. x.
[6] Martene, l. c. n. xv.   [7] Supra, n. 193.   [8] Pars. ii. cap. ii. n. 61.

"administer baptism. But although, on account of the dan-
"ger to which common life is exposed, the Church has deemed
"it expedient not to continue this custom, she has still most
"religiously observed the solemn days of Easter and Pente-
"cost, as those on which the baptismal water is to be conse-
"crated." She wishes also to give a fuller significance to
the ceremonies and prayers, by the administration of solemn
baptism on these days. In the Canon of the Mass on these
festivals, there are words which refer to those who are supposed to be recently baptized; and the "Cæremoniale Epis-
"coporum" even prescribes[1] that no infant be baptized in the
church for eight days before, except in case of necessity.
This provision of the "Cæremoniale," however, according to
a recent annotator,[2] is not attended to even in Rome, on
account of the danger in case of infants. But it certainly is
the wish of the Church, as the present rubric shows, that, at
least in cathedrals, if at all convenient, adults should be presented for baptism on these vigils. Hence in Rome there are
always some adult converts in readiness for these occasions,[3]
and the same is the case in many other cities, the bishops
reserving for this purpose the baptism of those adults that
may be preparing at the time.[4]

§ XXX.—Ac licet, urgente necessitate, ubique baptizare nihil impediat; tamen proprius baptismi administrandi locus est Ecclesia, in qua
sit Fons Baptismalis, vel certe Baptisterium prope Ecclesiam.

238. In the first ages, when the Christians had no churches,
baptism was administered wherever a supply of water could
be found. After the time of Constantine, its administration
came gradually to be restricted to the churches and baptisteries; and this usage was adopted and everywhere enforced
by the canons, so that baptism could not be lawfully administered elsewhere, except in case of necessity.[5] The rubrics
of the ritual are in exact conformity with the ancient canons;[6]
and many provincial synods, recently celebrated, have taken
measures to carry out what is thus prescribed, as far as circumstances permit. It is sufficient to refer to the Synod of
Thurles,[7] the Synod of Westminster,[8] and the Synod of Bal-

---

[1] Lib. ii. cap. xxvii. n. 18.   [2] Cérémonial des Evêques Expliqué, in
loc. cit. note (2).   [3] Cfr. Catal., tit. ii. cap. i.§ xxix. n. i.
[4] Vid. Cavalieri. tom. iv. cap. xxii. De Fonte Baptismali, in Decr
iv. n. iv.   [5] Martene, lib. i. cap. i. art. ii. Catal., § xxx. n. vii.
[6] Catal., loc. cit.   [7] De Baptismo, n. 7 et 8.
[8] Decr. xvi. De Baptismo, n. 1° et 4°.

timore.[1] "Meminerint parochi," says the Synod of Thurles,
"Rituale Romanum et Ecclesiæ consuetudinem exigere ut
"aqua in Baptismo adhibenda, infuso Oleo et Chrismate
"benedicatur, vel Sabbato Sancto, vel Sabbato Pentecostis,
"vel, si necessitas exigat, alio tempore ante Baptismi adminu-
"istrationem.   Caveant itaque ut quam primum fontes baptis-
"males in Ecclesiis Parochialibus erigantur et custodiantur,
"apud quos Baptismus conferatur, et omnia quæ ad hujus
"sacramenti administrationem in Rituali Romano præscribun-
"tur, accurate serventur."[2] We shall have occasion to treat
of the baptismal water, and the manner of blessing it, with
the infusion of oil and chrism, hereafter.[3] The synod orders
a baptismal font to be constructed in every parochial church,
and the Synod of Westminster orders the same for every
church, "cui annexa est cura animarum."[4]

239. Baptismal fonts were first constructed in turret-shaped
buildings, called baptisteries, apart from, but contiguous to,
the churches.   These baptisteries were, in some instances,
very spacious, and contained several fonts, some for men, and
others for women, being provided also with altars, at which
the divine mysteries were celebrated, and the newly-baptized
received the holy communion.[5] Many of these buildings are
still to be seen in Italy. From about the sixth century,
however, fonts were commonly constructed within the principal
churches, being placed near the entrance on the left, in
chapels which are usually called baptisteries, as well as the
buildings just mentioned.[6] They were mostly confined to the
cathedrals, in which the bishops themselves baptized, and
immediately afterwards confirmed the neophytes; and in some
cities, to the present day, they are restricted to two or three
churches, to which all must be brought for baptism.[7] Benedict XIV, when Archbishop of Bologna, insisted on the immemorial right of his metropolitan church, which required all
the children of the city to be brought to it for baptism, and
prohibited the parish priests of other churches from conferring
baptism unless in case of necessity.[8]

*240. Hence the rubric assigns, as the proper place for
baptism, not every church, but the church *in which there is a*

[1] Provin. I^m Decr. xvi.   [2] Loc. cit. n. 8º.
[3] Infra, cap. ix.   .   [4] Loc. cit. n. l.
[5] Martene, lib. i. cap. i. art. ii. n. vi. et seq.
[6] Vid. Revue Théologique, Ire Serié, 4mo Cahier, Nov. 1856, p. 550.
[7] Martene, loc. cit. n. xv. Cavalieri, *De Fonte Baptismali,* in Decr.
l. n. vii. and vi'i.   [8] *Instit.,* xcviii. n. 12.

font, or the baptistery. Generally speaking, however, there should be a font in every parish church, and every parish priest has the right to baptize the children of his parish.[1] In Ireland, since the destruction or usurpation of her ancient churches, there were very few baptismal fonts until recently; but they have been constructed, or are in course of construction, in almost every parish church at present; and the same may be said of England and America, pursuant to the decrees of the synods above-mentioned.

§ XXXI.—Itaque, necessitate excepta, in privatis locis nemo baptizari debet, nisi forte sint Regum aut magnorum Principum filii, id ipsis ita deposcentibus, dummodo id fiat in eorum Capellis seu Oratoriis, et in aqua Baptismali de more benedicta.

*241. The parish church or baptistery, then, is the only place in which baptism can be administered, except in the two cases here mentioned: 1st, In necessity, in which case baptism may be administered anywhere, but without the ceremonies. These are afterwards to be supplied in the church.[2] 2d, When there is question of the children of kings and princes: in this case, at the special request of the parents, baptism may be conferred with all the ceremonies in their oratories or private chapels. The water, however, cannot be blessed in a private chapel, but must be brought from the font of the parish church.[3] If any of the baptismal water remains, it should be brought back to the church and poured into the font; and what has been used should be thrown into the sacrarium.[4] The rubric, we may observe, is merely permissive; leave must be asked and obtained in every case from the Ordinary of the place.[5]

242. It may be doubted whether, in this matter, all magnates, nobles, and men of great property can be regarded as " magni principes," to whom the favor may be extended. Catalani thinks they cannot;[6] and it is not easy to see how, in strictness, they can. But where there is a custom of extending the favor to them, St. Liguori would tolerate it.[7] At all events, it is probable that the bishop can dispense in particular cases.[8] When a distinguished person is expected

[1] Vid. supra, n. 184.　　　　　[2] Vid. supra, n. 194, 195.
[3] Baruff., tit. ix. n. 20.　Catal., tit. ii. cap. i. § xxxi. n. ii.
[4] Baruff., and Catal., ll. cc.　Vid. supra, n. 183.
[5] Baruff., n. 19.　Catal., l. c.　　　[6] Loc. cit. n. ii.
[7] Lib. vi. n. 118. *Not.* iii.
[8] Vid. Revue Théologique, Ire Série, pp. 276, et seq.

to act as sponsor, if it be necessary to wait some time for him, the bishop could give leave to have baptism privately administered in the house, and the solemn ceremonies afterwards supplied in the church.[1]

In all other cases the law of the Church must be strictly observed. It is evidently *in materia gravi*, and the deliberate transgression of it, therefore, cannot be excused from grievous sin.[2]

§ XXXII.—Baptisterium sit decenti loco et forma, materiaque solida. et quæ aquam bene contineat, decenter ornatum, et cancellis circumseptum, sera et clave munitum, atque ita obseratum, ut pulvis vel aliæ sordes intro non penetrent, in eoque, ubi commode fieri potest, depingatur imago Sancti Joannis Christum baptizantis.

243. We have already seen[3] that "Baptisterium" is the name given to the place containing the baptismal font, whether it be a chapel within the church, or a building apart. But here it must be understood, at least in the first part of the sentence, to designate the font itself, or basin which contains the water. The rubric prescribes what is to be observed regarding it; and, first, that it be constructed in a suitable place. St. Charles orders that it be placed near the entrance of the church, on the left, in conformity with ancient usage, unless from the plan of the building the bishop may think it expedient to have it placed at the other side.[4] The place set apart for it should be railed off, and, if possible, form a distinct chapel, adorned with a representation of St. John baptizing Christ.

Its position near the entrance is convenient for the ceremonies to be observed,[5] as we shall see; and, moreover, serves to remind us that by baptism we enter into the Church. Benedict XIII, in the Synod of Rome, ordered the strict observance of what the ritual prescribes regarding the place of the baptismal ceremony. "Quia Baptismus est janua "Sacramentorum et porta per quam in Christi Ecclesiam "intramus, sciant Parochi non vane a Rituali Romano præ- "scribi, ut baptizandorum catechismus ad Ecclesiæ januam, "his, cum patrinis, extra existentibus, peragatur. Ipsis "itaque districte præcipimus ut ritum omnino servent eundem, "nec unquam committant, contrarius ultra procedat abusus:

[1] Cfr. Benedict XIV, *Instit.*, xcviii. n. 13.
[2] St. Lig., n. 142. [3] Supra, n. 239.
[4] *Act. Eccl. Mediol.*, pars i. Concil. Prov. iv. *Quæ pertinent ad Sacramentum Baptismi*, p. 108. [5] Vid. infra, § liv.

"quemadmodum et alter ille, domi scilicet infantes baptizandi
"extra necessitatem, quæ si unquam eveniat, erit ab Episcopo
"probanda."[1]

*244. With respect to the material of which the font should
be made, the rubric merely prescribes that it be solid, and
such as will keep in the water; and, therefore, it may be of
any kind that is not porous, unless some special material be
required by diocesan or provincial statute. All the ancient
fonts were of stone;[2] and St. Charles[3] prescribes that the
material be marble or hard stone: "Fons baptismalis e
"marmore aut solido lapide constet."

The Synod of Westminster recommends this instruction
of St. Charles, and gives it in the appendix to its decrees, so
that the material seems to be defined in England. The
Synod of Thurles gives no special instruction on the subject;
and in Ireland some fonts have been made of metal, though
stone or marble is generally preferred, and is, on the whole,
more suitable, as being more in accordance with ancient
usage, and also free from the inconvenience of rust, which
sooner or later attacks the metal.

245. In shape, the ancient fonts were circular,[4] and being
designed for baptism by immersion, were also large and deep.
The fonts now in use for baptism by effusion are also circular or
elliptical. The division into two parts, as recommended by
the Ritual of Toulon,[5] is very convenient, and has been of
late generally adopted. This form, amongst others, is minutely described in the instructions of St. Charles. In shape,
according to the instruction, the font should be oval: "Forma
"ovata sit ac longe cubitos duos et uncias octo pateat; late
"cubitum unum et uncias duodecim;" that is, about three
feet six inches by two feet four inches, of our measure. The
interior should be divided into two circular basins, of the same
dimensions, and separated about two inches at the edges; the
one which is nearer to the high altar, to contain the baptismal
water; the other, to receive the water poured on the head,
and communicating with the earth, to serve as the sacrarium.
The whole should be supported on a perforated pillar, through
which the water from the second basin may pass to a small
cistern under ground.[6]

[1] Concil. Roman., tit. xxvi. cap. iii. apud Labbe, vol. xxi. p. 1895.
[2] Catal., tit. ii. cap. i. § iv. n. xxi. [3] Loc. cit. [4] Catal., tit. ii.
cap. i. § iv. n. xxii. [5] Tit. i. § xi. apud Dictionaire des Cérémonies,
tom. i. Art. Baptême. [6] Act. Eccl. Mediol., pars iv. Instruct. Fabric.
Eccl. cap xix. § De Baptisterii forma tertia, pag. 483, 484.

246. The Ritual of Toulon[1] would have the basin which holds the water larger than the other, and it is usually made so; but it would also have it lined with lead or tin, or have a vessel of this material, or of tinned copper, inserted in the stone. De Herdt recommends the same.[2] Many of the ancient fonts used in England were lined with lead. Indeed, according to a recent writer on the subject,[3] all that were not of granite or very hard stone were so lined.

Such lining with metal is quite unnecessary, if the font be of hard stone or marble, as is described by St. Charles. He would permit the use of metal in this way, when the font is observed to be leaky or porous, but only until another is constructed of proper material.[4]

*247. The font should have a lid, which may be of wood or metal, fitting closely, so as to exclude dust, flies, etc. If it be constructed with two basins as described, the lid need not cover that which serves as the sacrarium. In the instructions of St. Charles[5] it is directed that the lid be flat, only one half opening, the other being fastened, and the whole surmounted by a dome or canopy, within which the holy oils should be kept. The Rubric says nothing of this, and, therefore, leaves considerable latitude as to the shape and construction of the covering. It requires, however, that the baptistery be under lock and key, by which, therefore, either the lid of the font or the entrance to the baptistery ought to be secured.

ON THE HOLY OILS AND OTHER REQUISITES: "DE SACRIS OLEIS ET ALIIS REQUISITIS."

§ XXXIII.—Sacrum Chrisma, et Sanctum Oleum, quod et Catechumenorum dicitur, quorum usus est in Baptismo, eodem anno sint ab Episcopo de more benedicta Feria V, in Cœna Domini.

248. The chrism, which is a mixture of oil and balsam,[6] and the oil of catechumens used in baptism, must have been blessed by the bishop on the preceding Holy Thursday.

The use of the holy oils in baptism may be traced to the earliest times, as is shown by Catalani.[7] The anointing of the catechumens before baptism is mentioned by St Justin

---

[1] Loc. cit.　　　　　　　　　　[2] Pars vi. n. 3, § i.
[3] F. A. Paley, M.A. *Illustrations of Baptismal Fonts*, introduction, pag. 24.
[4] Concil. Provin. iv., § *Quæ pertinent ad Sacram. Baptismi*, pag. 108.
[5] Loc. cit.　[6] Vid. St. Lig., lib. vi. n. 162.　[7] Tit. ii. cap. i. § xxxiii.

Martyr, St. Chrysostom, etc.[1] With respect to the unction
with chrism after baptism, we may observe that, in the beginning, the bishop, as we have seen,[2] was usually the minister,
and he signed the neophytes on the forehead with chrism immediately after baptizing them, so that the chrism used by
the bishop was in reality for the sacrament of confirmation.
The vertical unction by priests was introduced, according to
Bellarmine,[3] to supply in some way for this, when the bishop
was absent, and when, consequently, confirmation could not
be immediately conferred as usual. It is said to have been
instituted by Pope Sylvester I.[4] Innocent I, in a letter regarding this matter, says that priests may anoint those whom
they baptize with chrism blessed by the bishop; but they
must not apply it to the forehead, as this is reserved to
bishops.[5] From the Sacramentary of St. Gregory, it appears
that the vertical unction was applied by a priest, even when
the bishop was present, and confirmed the neophytes immediately after.[6] The same may be also inferred from the Sacramentary of Pope Gelasius.[7] There can be no doubt, therefore, about the great antiquity of this vertical unction with
chrism, distinct from the sacrament of confirmation. It is to
be applied even by the bishop when he baptizes, though he
may confer the sacrament of confirmation immediately after.[8]

249. The chrism must be blessed by the bishop. A simple
priest may be delegated by the pope to confer confirmation,
but it is doubtful whether he could be empowered to bless the
chrism, which is necessary for the sacrament.[9] In the Greek
Church the priest blesses the oil of catechumens just before
using it; but, although he administers the sacrament of confirmation immediately after baptism, the chrism which he
uses must have been blessed by the bishop.[10] In the vertical
unction, there is no sacrament, it is true, but the chrism to be
used is the same as that which is required for confirmation.

250. The consecration of the oils takes place on Holy
Thursday, and, according to the present usage, is not permit-

---

[1] Cit. apud Martene, lib. i. cap. i. art. vi. n. xv. et art. xiii. n. xxi.
[2] Supra, n. 184.   [3] De Baptismo, cap. xxvii.
[4] Martene, lib. i. cap. i. art. xv. n. ii.
[5] Cit. apud St. Lig., vi. n. 163, Dub. 2.
[6] Chardon, Histoire des Sacrements, liv. Ire sec. Ire part. 2^d chap. x.
[7] Apud Martene, cap. i. art. xviii. ord. iv.
[8] Pontificale Romanum, Ritus Pontif. pro Baptismo Adultorum Rubricæ in fine.   [9] St. Lig., lib. vi. n. 163, Dub. 2.
Vid. Benedict XIV, Synod. Diœc., lib. vii. cap. viii.
[10] Guar, in Baptismatis officium Nota, nota 11, pag. 363

ted on any other day.[1] The bishop is assisted in the ceremony by twelve priests, seven deacons, and seven sub-
deacons.[2] In cases of necessity, however, dispensations are
granted both as to the day and the number of assistants.[3] In
Ireland bishops have the faculty: "Consecrandi olea cum
"quinque saltem sacerdotibus, non tamen extra diem Cœnæ
"Domini nisi necessitas aliud urgeat."[4]

§ XXXIV.—Curet Parochus ut ea suo tempore quam primum habeat,
et tunc vetera in ecclesia comburat.

*251. The parish priest is strictly bound by the canons to
procure the holy oils every year from his own bishop, and not
from any other, unless with his own bishop's consent.[5] He
must take care to procure them as soon as possible after they
are consecrated, since he requires them for the benediction of
the font on Holy Saturday. The functions of this day should
never be omitted in parochial churches, according to a decree
of the Sacred Congregation. Where the number of clergy
is insufficient to carry out the ceremonies of the Missal, they
should be performed according to the small ceremonial of
Benedict XIII.[6]

The Sacred Congregation has expressly condemned the
custom prevailing in some places, of deferring the distribution
of the oils until after Low Sunday.[7] In a note to the decree
condemning this custom, the annotator observes that the holy
oils should be distributed so that they may be available for
the benediction of the font on Holy Saturday. He cites the
"quamprimum" of the rubric, and says that it must be interpreted by the obligation of using the new oils on Holy
Saturday. Nothing, according to him, but the necessity
arising from great distance, difficult roads, or the like, could
justify a delay beyond that time on the part either of those
who receive, or of those who distribute them.

252. Benedict XIV, while archbishop of Bologna, earnestly exhorted the parish priests of his diocese who had
baptismal fonts to be blessed, to procure the holy oils in time
for the ceremonies of Holy Saturday. But he did no more

---

[1] Catal., tit. ii. cap. i. § xxxiii. n. v.
[2] Pontif. Romanum, *De officio in Feria V. Cœnæ Domini.*
[3] S. C. R., 23 Jan. 1644, *in Emonien.*, n. 1486; 9 Mart. 1765, *in
Ramaten.*, n. 4325.　　　　　　　　　[4] Formula vitæ n. 28.
[5] Catal., tit. ii. cap. i. § xxxiv. n. 1. Cavalieri, vol. iv. cap. xxvi.
De sacris oleis, in Decr. i. n. iii.
[6] 22 Jul. 1848, *in una Ord. Carm.*, n. 5132.
[7] 16 Dec. 1826, *in una Gandav.*, ad. iv. n. 4623.

than exhort and recommend; and, as the time of distribution
for all in the city and diocese, he fixed from Holy Thursday
till " Sabbatum in Albis :"—" A feria quinta in Cœna Domini,
" statim ac oleum sacratum fuerit, usque ad Sabbatum in
" Albis pro ipso accipiendo tempus statuitur omnibus qui vel
" in civitate aut in diocesi versantur.   Parochos tamen Dioce-
" sanos, qui baptismalem fontem suis in Ecclesiis habent,
" magnopere hortamur satagere omni studio, ut Oleum a
" nobis eadem feria quinta consecratum statim obtineant, quo
" utantur Sabbato majoris hebdomadæ, cum benedictio Fontis
" Baptismalis instituitur, quæ sacrum Chrisma necessario re-
" quirit; et valde commendandi sunt, si tunc recens Chrisma
" a nobis sacratum adhibeant."[1]

253. These words seem to convey that the old oils should
be used for the benediction of the font on Holy Saturday, if
the new oils, no matter from what cause, have not been procured in time.   They are understood in this sense by Cavalieri ;[2] but, according to a recent decree of the Sacred Congregation, it is necessary to take the circumstances into
account, and make a distinction.   Either there is a prospect
of getting the holy oils within a short time, a week or ten
days suppose, or there is no prospect of getting them within
a reasonable time.   In the former case, the infusion of the
oils should be omitted in the ceremony of blessing the font,
and be supplied privately as soon as the oils are procured.
In the latter, the oil and chrism of the preceding year are to
be used, and the water thus blessed is to be preserved in the
font, and used until the vigil of Pentecost, even though the
new oils may have been obtained in the meantime.

Such is the latest decision of the Congregation of Rites on
the question.[3] This decision is given by the "Analecta
" Juris Pontificii,"[4] by the " Revue Théologique,"[5] and also
in the last edition of the Sac. Rit. Cong. Decreta, etc.,
alphabetico ordine disposita, etc., by Falise.[6] It may be seen
on reading it,[7] that it serves to reconcile two previous decisions
apparently at variance, but of whose authenticity there can
be no doubt; one directing that the holy oils, if not procured
in time for the blessing of the font on Holy Saturday, should

---

[1] Instit., lxxxi. n. 5.
[2] Loc. cit. n. vi.
[3] 12 Aug. 1854, in Lucionen., ad. 79 et 80.
[4] IIme Série, p. 2188 et seq.   [5] VIme Série, Février, 1859, pag. 27.
[6] Editio 4ta, MDCCCLXII.   V. Baptisma, n. 7.
[7] Vid. Decret. in Appendice.

be afterwards poured in, "privatim et separatim;"[1] the other deciding that, when they cannot be procured, the oils of the preceding year are to be used.[2] Of these two decrees it declares that the former proceeds on the supposition that the holy oils are only accidentally detained, and that there is a prospect of getting them within a short time; while the latter proceeds on the supposition that they could not be procured in the diocese, or in any of the neighboring dioceses. This supposition was plainly involved in the case proposed to the Sacred Congregation, for it regarded a diocese in Spain during the civil wars, when most of the sees in the country were deprived of their pastors. Now the fact of its thus reconciling two apparently conflicting decisions, together with its being cited by the authorities mentioned, makes us look on the authenticity of the decree as all but certain, although a slight doubt may still be suggested by its being omitted in the last edition of the "Decreta Authentica," etc., by the Propaganda press, since that edition gives the decrees down to 29th November, 1856.[3]

*254. When the new oils have been procured, what remains of the old oils should be burned. If there be any contained in bottles or other vessels destined to hold the usual supply for the year, it should be burned in the lamp before the blessed sacrament; but what is contained absorbed in cotton in the oilstocks for ordinary use, should be burned with the cotton containing it, as is directed by the rubric of the Pontificale Romanum.[4] The cotton, before it is burned, may be squeezed over the lamps, and the ashes should be thrown into the sacrarium.[5]

§ XXXV.—Veteribus Oleis, nisi necessitas cogat, ultra annum non utatur: ac si deficere videantur, et Chrisma, aut Oleum benedictum haberi non possit, aliud Oleum de olivis non benedictum adjiciatur, sed in minori quantitate.

*255. As soon as the oils are blessed on Holy Thursday, the use of the oils of the preceding year should cease, unless a case of necessity arises before the new oils are procured. If there be no prospect of getting them within a reasonable time, it has been decided, as we have seen,[6] that the old oils

---

[1] 12 April, 1755, in *Lucana*, ad 3ᵐ n. 4252. Vid. Gardellini, *Annotationem in Decr. Sac. Cong. Rit.*, 16 Dec. 1826, in *Gandaven.*, *Ques.* v. ad iii. n. 4623.   [2] 23 Sept. 1837, in *Oriolen.*, ad 1ᵐ et 3ᵐ, n. 4820.
[3] Vid. supra, n. 37.   [4] Para iii. *De Officio in Feria* V. in fine.
[5] Caval.. l. c. n. viii.   [6] Supra, n. 253.

are to be used in blessing the font. It is further decided,
n the same decree, that they are to be used also for the
unctions in baptism.[1] There is, therefore, no difficulty in this
case.

*256. But if the oils can be procured within a few days,
and if in the meantime an infant be presented for baptism,
what should be done ? There are two difficulties in the case :
one, with regard to the water to be used ; and the other,
with regard to the oil and chrism. 1° With regard to the
water : If the baptism takes place before the font is blessed
on Holy Saturday, the old baptismal water still remains, and
of course should be used. If it takes place after, the choice
is between common water and the water of the font, which, as
we suppose, is blessed, but as yet without the infusion of the
holy oils.[2] We should prefer to use the water of the font,
though we do not think there is any *obligation* of using it,
since it is not, in strictness, baptismal water.[3] But it would
be best of all, in the circumstances we here suppose, to reserve a little of the old baptismal water for such contingencies,
until the new oils are procured. This is recommended by
Romsée,[4] and the " Revue Théologique."[5] 2° With regard
to the unctions : these are to be deferred until the new oil
and chrism are obtained. This appears to follow from the
decision that has been cited ;[6] for if, in the case supposed, the
old oils are not to be used in blessing the baptismal water,
it may be reasonably inferred that they should not be used
in the baptismal unctions. This is also clearly supposed by
St. Liguori.[7] On account of the necessity of deferring the
unctions, it would be desirable that the baptism also should
be deferred, as it should not be separated from the unctions without a grave reason. St. Liguori[8] decides that,
if the delay is only for a few days, baptism ought to be deferred ; but if it be necessary to wait for the oils ten or eleven
days, baptism may be administered, and the unctions afterwards supplied. He speaks only of the unctions, and seems
to suppose that the other ceremonies are applied when baptism
is conferred, as is recommended in an opinion cited, apparently with approval, by Lacroix.[9] But it is probable that the
other ceremonies may be deferred with the unctions ; so that ulti-

---

[1] 23 Sept. 1837, *in Oriolen.*, ad 4ᵐ n. 4820.   [2] Vid. supra, n. 253.
[3] Vid. infra, chap. iv. § xxvii.   [4] *Praxis Divini Officii*, tom. iii.
De Sabbato Sancto, § iii. in fine.   [5] IVᵐᵉ Série, Février, 1859, pag ℀.
[6] Supra, n. 253.   [7] Lib. vi. n. 141.   [8] Loc. cit.
[9] Lib. vi. pars i. n. 342.

mately the case we are discussing may be resolved in practice, by either putting off the baptism for a few days until the new oils are procured, or conferring it, as the rubric directs, for the case of necessity,[1] leaving the usual ceremonies to be supplied when the new oil and chrism are obtained.

*257. Should the supply of chrism or oil become short during the year, more should be got from the cathedral or other place where a quantity is usually kept in reserve.[2] If, however, there be any difficulty in procuring it in this way, or if there be not time to wait, unblessed oil may be added, but in less quantity. In Ireland, during the operation of the penal laws, the priests were obliged to have recourse frequently to this means of keeping up a supply of the holy oils. Amongst the ordinances drawn up for their direction about the middle of the seventeenth century, we find one prescribing that the quantity of unblessed oil added each time shall not exceed a third part.[3] Great care should be taken that the oil be pure, " Oleum ex olivis," as is mentioned in the rubric.

*258. It is plain, from the words, that it may be added to the chrism as well as to the other oils, and it may be added too, not once merely, or twice, but as often as may be found necessary, even although the quantity of unblessed oil thus added may in the end exceed the quantity first blessed. This was expressly decided by the Sacred Congregation of the Council.[4] But there must be *bona fide* necessity, such as is supposed in the rubric; for it was decided by the Congregation of Rites that it would not be lawful, *e. g.*, on Holy Thursday to add a quantity of unblessed oil to what had just been consecrated.[5]

§ XXXVI.—Chrisma et Oleum sacrum sint in suis vasculis argenteis, aut saltem stanneis, bene obturatis; quæ vascula sint inter se distincta, et propriam unumquodque inscriptionem habeat majusculis litteris incisam, ne quis error committatur.

*259. The necessity of attending to what is here prescribed is obvious. In baptism there is no question of the validity of the sacrament, but it is not so in confirmation and extreme unction. A mistake with regard to the vessel in either of these would render the validity of the sacrament at least

---

[1] Vid. infra, chap. iv. § xxvi.
[2] Cfr. Catal., tit. ii. cap. i. § xxxv. n. ii.
[3] *Collections on Irish Church History*, page 122.
[4] 23 Sept. 1632, cit. apud Falise, *Decreta Authentica*, etc. V. Oleum in nota, n. 6.　　　[5] 7 Dec. 1844, in una *Patav.*, ad 4ᵐ; u. 5000.

doubtful.[1] Even in baptism the mistake is a serious one. Should it occur, Baruffaldi[2] would have the unction afterwards supplied. This ought to be done, if the error be detected at the moment, and can be at once repaired; but, otherwise, we are inclined to the opinion of Falise, who thinks it too severe to insist on the repetition, seeing that, 1° one oil is probably a *valid* substitute for another, even where there is question of a sacrament;[3] 2° that there is here question of a rite, the omission of which does little or no injury; and 3° that the repetition would often be an occasion of murmur or scandal.[4] To guard against mistake, the rubric here directs that the vessels containing the holy oils be marked with letters, so as to be easily distinguished.

*260. They should be of silver, or, at least, of tin or pewter; they must not be of glass or any other brittle material, lest they be broken and the contents spilled; nor of iron, brass, or other very oxidable metal, from which the oil would easily contract impurities.[5]

§ XXXVII.—Ad usum vero quotidianum minora habeantur vascula ex argento, si fieri potest, aut stanno, sive separata, sive etiam conjuncta; apte tamen distincta, et bene cooperta, et cum suis inscriptionibus, ut supra, ne Parochus aberret, et unum pro altero sumat, quod cavere debet diligenter.

*261. Besides the vessels for containing the yearly supply, there should be smaller ones to contain what may be required for daily use. The material prescribed by the rubric for these is the same as for the others, but being much smaller, they can be had of silver at much less expense; and few are made of any other material. They may be, according to the rubric, either separate or joined together. In missionary countries they are usually made to be joined by a screw; and, with a third compartment containing the "oleum infirmorum," likewise screwed on, they form a cylinder about one inch in diameter, and three or three and a-half inches long, commonly called "oilstocks." The compartments are perfectly distinct, and marked, each with its appropriate letter.

*262. It was usual to put only a single letter on each—I, on that containing the "oleum Infirmorum;" B, on that containing the "oleum Catechumenorum," or oleum Baptizandorum; and C, on that containing the Chrism. This, we

[1] St. Lig., lib. vi. n. 162 et 709. Vid. chap. xv. § iii.
[2] Tit. x. n. 19.   [3] Vid. chap. xv. § iii.
[4] *Cours Abrégé,* 3ᵐᵉ partie, chap. i. § i. n. 8, note.
[5] Vid. Baruff., tit. x. n. 16 et seq.

may observe, is hardly sufficient, for it might easily happen that the compartment marked C would be mistaken for that containing the " oleum Catechumenorum;" and to our certain knowledge the mistake was actually made in some instances. It is much better, therefore, to have the first two or three letters engraved on each—as, INF., CAT., CHR. St. Charles ordered the inscriptions to be respectively: CHR., CATH., and EXT. UNC.[1]

We may observe, also, that, although formerly it was convenient for priests in Ireland to have the three joined together, there is now no reason why the two required for baptism should not be kept apart from the third, which is required for the sick.[2]

§ XXXVIII.—In ea igitur ex majoribus vasculis Chrismatis et Olei, quod sufficiat, infundatur, atque ut effusionis periculum caveatur, commodum erit in his vasculis bombacium, seu quid simile habere, Oleo sacro et Chrismate separatim perfusum, in quo pollex, cum opus est, ad inungendum immittatur.

*263. The oilstocks should always be provided, as here directed, with a little cotton, or some like material, which may absorb the oil, and thus prevent the danger of effusion; and, at the same time, when pressed with the thumb, yield enough for the unctions. A little flax, or a small piece of sponge, would do equally well.[3]

*264. The rubric supposes that a little is poured into the oilstocks out of the larger vessels as occasion may require; but it may happen that the priest has no vessels except the oilstocks, and that there is no other supply for the year except what is put into them when the oils are distributed after Holy Thursday. If the supply be insufficient, he must, in this case, either go to the cathedral to have the oilstocks replenished, or add a little unblessed oil in the manner already mentioned.[4]

*265. There is no reason, however, why every parish church should not have its supply of holy oils as well as its baptismal font. The larger vessels should be filled at the place of distribution, and brought back in time for Holy Saturday.[5] In fact, the quantity which oilstocks of the usual size could contain, would hardly suffice for the benediction of the font on that day, to say nothing of what is

[1] Act. Eccl. Mediol., Instruct. Supell. Eccles., lib. ii. pag. 530.
[2] Vid. inf. § xxxix.
[3] Baruff., tit. x. n. 22, 23. Catal., tit. ii. cap. i. § xxxviii. n. l.
[4] Supra, n. 257.   [5] Vid. supra, n. 251.

required for the vigil of Pentecost, or may be necessary at other times for blessing the baptismal water.[1] It is hardly possible, therefore, to carry out what is prescribed by a preceding rubric regarding the water to be used in baptism,[2] without attending to what is here prescribed regarding the oils.

§ XXXIX.—Hæc vascula ita parata, in loco proprio, honesto, ac mundo, sub clave ac tuta custodia decenter asserventur, ne ab aliquo, nisi a Sacerdote, temere tangantur, aut eis sacrilege quispiam abuti possit.

266. At the end of the Mass at which the holy oils are blessed, the bishop admonishes the priests to keep them carefully, as the canons prescribe.[3] The oil and chrism used in baptism should be kept under lock and key, and if possible in the baptistery, which is undoubtedly the best place for them.[4] St. Charles gives very minute instructions on this subject. He would have the vessels inclosed in a box with the lid fitting closely, and kept in what he calls a "ciborium,"[5] which means a kind of press or safe, erected over the font.[5]

If they cannot be conveniently kept in the baptistery, they should be kept at least somewhere within the church. The rubric, it is true, does not mention the church, but this must be understood from the words it uses, and from the universal custom, as is observed by the continuator of Gardellini, in a note to a decree of the Sacred Congregation in this matter.[6] Perhaps the reason why the rubric does not say that the place must be within the church is, because the baptistery (in which they certainly may be kept) is in some instances a building apart from the church.[7] They cannot be put into the tabernacle with the Blessed Sacrament, as was decided by the Sacred Congregation of Bishops.[8] But it is recommended by many to place them in a safe near the altar, where the Blessed Sacrament is kept, as there would thus be a lamp burning before or near them.[9]

*267. Priests are permitted to keep the "oleum infi- "morum" in their houses, when they live at a considerable

---

[1] Vid. chap. ix. § vi.   [2] Supra, n. 158.
[3] Pontificale Romanum, p. iii., *De Officio in Feria* V. *Cœnæ Domini*, in fine.   [4] Baruff., tit. x. n. 24.
[5] *Instr. Supell. Eccl.*, lib. ii. pars. ii. p. 530. Concil. Prov. iv. p. 108.   [6] 16 December, 1826, *in una Gandav.*, *Dub. Quæs.* iii. n. 4623.
[7] Vid. supra, n. 239.
[8] 3 Maii, 1693, cit. apud Caval., tom. iv. cap. vi., Decr. xiii. n. 1.
[9] Cfr. *Annotat. cit.* in Decr. Sac. Cong., 16 Dec. 1826.

distance from the church,[1] and in the country parishes of
Ireland they generally do so; but the same reason does not
exist for keeping along with it the oil and chrism used in
baptism. These, except in rare cases, can be used only in
the church;[2] and we are convinced that the exceptional
cases are not sufficient to justify a priest in keeping them in
his house. Hence, we think that a little vessel of silver, containing the "oleum infirmorum" alone, might, in most cases,
be conveniently substituted for the oilstocks that have been
hitherto in use; two other little vessels of the same kind, for
the chrism and oil of catechumens, being kept in the baptistery, or in a safe near the altar of the Blessed Sacrament.
In England the Synod of Westminster has ordered that in
all new churches a proper place be prepared for them in the
baptistery.[3]

268. Laics are not permitted to touch these vessels unless
in case of necessity. Baruffaldi says that a laic is guilty of
grievous sin if he does so.[4] This decision seems to us very
severe. The offence, we think, does not exceed a venial sin,
unless where there is contempt. At all events, the decision
must be understood of the case in which they actually contain
the holy oils; for as they are not consecrated, nor even blessed, there seems no reason why they may not when empty be
handled by any one.[5]

The sacrilegious abuse here referred to is probably that of
applying the holy oils to medicinal purposes, or as charms,
etc. It appears from several canons that such superstitious
practices prevailed at certain periods;[6] and hence in the
admonition of the bishop already mentioned, the priests are
specially warned to guard against this profanation.[7]

§ XL.—Parochus, quantum fieri potest, curet, ne per laicos, sed per
se, vel per alium Sacerdotem, vel saltem per alium Ecclesiæ ministrum
hæc Olea deferantur: caveat item, ne de iis quicquam ulli unquam tribuat
cujusvis rei prætextu.

269. The preceding rubric is to guard against any sacrilegious abuse of the holy oils. This is to secure due reverence for them. Catalani cites a series of canons and decrees,
from the fourth council of Carthage, in 398, downwards for

---

[1] Sac. Cong., 16 Dec. 1826, in una Gandav., ad Dub. Quæs. iii. a.
1623.   [2] Vid. chap. iv. § xxviii.
[3] Dec. xvi. De Baptismo, 2°.
[4] Tit. x. n. 25.   [5] Vid. chap. xi. § v.
[6] Cfr. Catal., tit ii. cap. i. § xxxix. n. ii. et seq.
[7] Pontificale Romanum, loc. cit.

several centuries, ordering that none but priests, or others in
holy orders, should carry the holy oils from the place where
they are distributed to the several churches.[1] In the fourteenth century the practice had been introduced of allowing
them to be carried by inferior clerics; but this was forbidden
by several provincial councils, amongst the rest, by that of
Milan, under St. Charles.[2] The present rubric requires the
ancient discipline to be observed as far as possible.

By "ministrum" Catalani[3] thinks we should understand a
deacon or subdeacon. Baruffaldi[4] allows it to include inferior
clerics. At all events, it is plain from the words, "quantum
fieri potest," that the rubric permits the oils to be carried by
an inferior cleric, or even by a laic, when no other can be had.[5]
None is to be given away under any pretence, and this for the
reason already stated.[6]

§ XLI.—Sal, quod in os baptizandi immittendum est, sit benedictum
sua peculiari benedictione, quæ infra præscribitur; neque utatur sale
exorcizato ad benedicendam aquam; sitque prius bene confractum et
attritum, siccum ac mundum. Sal ita benedictum nemini tradatur,
neque etiam iis qui benedicendum attulerint reddatur, sed ad alios baptizandos servetur, aut in sacrarium abjiciatur.

270. According to Martene,[7] no mention is made of the
salt given to the catechumens, by any of the early Greek
Fathers, except Origen, who seems to make an allusion to it
once, nor is it mentioned in the Euchologium of the Greeks.
But amongst the Latins its use dates from the earliest times.
It is distinctly mentioned by St. Augustine in his Confessions,
by Venerable Bede, and subsequent writers.[8] It should be
"sal naturale,"[9] that is, such as is used for seasoning food,
and as is commonly understood by the word itself without an
adjunct.

*271. There are two benedictions of salt given in the
Ritual—one for baptism, the other for holy water; and care
must be taken that the salt used in baptism has been blessed
according to the special form given hereafter.[10] It should be
reduced to a fine powder, as is here directed by the rubric, so
that a very small quantity may be easily administered.

---

[1] Loc. cit. § xl. n. i. et ii.   Cfr. Caval., tom. iv. cap. xxvi. De Sacris
Oleis, in Decr. i. n. iii. et iv.
[2] Act. Eccl. Mediol., pars i. Concil. Provin. ii. Dec. ix. p. 52, et pars
ii. Synod. Diœc. ii. Dec. xiv. p. 270.   [3] Loc. cit. n. iv.
[4] Tit. x. n. 29.   [5] Vid. chap. xv. § xiii.   [6] Supra, n. 268.
[7] De Ant. Eccl. Rit., lib. i. cap. i. art. vi. n. xiv.
[8] Cit. apud Martene, ibid.   [9] Baruff., tit. x. n. 33.   Catal., tit. ii.
cap i. § xli. n. iii.   [10] Cap. iv. § v.

What is blessed at one time may serve for several baptisms, if it be kept clean and dry ; but the rubric directs that it be kept exclusively for this purpose, or else thrown into the sacrarium, and not given away under any pretext, most probably lest it might be employed for some superstitious purpose.[1] It must not be given even to those who may have brought it to be blessed. If they wish to have some blessed salt, the priest may bless some for them, using the benediction given in the Ritual, or at the end of the Missal, "Ad "quodcumque comestibile."[2]

§ XLII.—Cum igitur Baptismi Sacramentum jam administrandum est, hæc in promptu esse debent.

272. The rubric now gives a summary of the things that should be at hand in the baptistery, or in a convenient place near the font, when baptism is about being conferred. The priest who is to perform the ceremony should carefully read over this summary, and see that everything required is in readiness, so that there may be no interruption or delay when he has once commenced.[3]

§ XLIII.—Vascula sacri Olei Catechumenorum, et Chrismatis.

*273. It would be convenient to have a table near the font, on which several of the things required might be placed before the commencement of the ceremony. Amongst these should be the small vessels containing the oil and chrism, which have been before described.[4]

§ XLIV.—Vasculum cum sale benedicendo, vel jam, ut dictum est, benedicto.

*274. The salt is required soon after the commencement, and before the child is admitted within the church. This vessel, then, which may be a small plate or salver, should be placed on a table within the porch. or near the door, according to circumstances,[5] or it may be held by a clerk.

§ XLV.—Vasculum, seu cochlear ex argento, vel alio metallo nitidum, ad aquam Baptismi fundendam super caput baptizandi, quod nulli præterea alii usui deserviat.

*275. The water should be poured on the head, not with the hand, but out of a ladle or small vessel provided for this purpose, and used for no other. This vessel, according to our rubric, should be of silver, or some other metal not easily

---

[1] Baruff., n. 34. Catal., l. c. n. iv.   [2] De Herdt. pars vi. n. 4, ii.
[3] Baruff., n. 36, 37.   [4] Supra, n. 261.   [5] Vid. infra, § liv.

tarnished. It may be made also of shell, according to Baruffaldi.[1] Pewter or tin (*stannum*) is mentioned by many[2] as a suitable material; and that it is so may be inferred from the rubric regarding the vessels for containing the holy oils.[3]

St. Charles gives minute instructions as to its form. According to these, it should be furnished with a pretty long handle, somewhat bent, and a lip or spout, through which the water might be easily poured in a gentle, steady stream.[4] It should be also large enough to hold what may suffice for a single baptism, as it would be inconvenient to be obliged to dip it into the font while pronouncing the form.[5]

§ XLVI.—Pelvis, seu bacile ad excipiendam aquam ex capite defluentem, nisi statim in sacrarium defluat.

*276. Nothing is prescribed as to the material of this basin. It may be of earthenware, but should be reserved for the use of the baptistery exclusively. We have already seen, however, that the sacrarium may be situated so as to render any such vessel unnecessary.[6]

§ XLVII.—Gossipium, alio nomine bombacium, seu quid simile, ad abstergenda loca sacris Oleis inuncta.

*277. The cotton, flax, or other material to be used for wiping the parts anointed, should be placed on a small dish or salver beside the holy oils on the table. When used, it should be put back again on the dish, and after the ceremony is concluded it should be burned, and the ashes thrown into the sacrarium.[7]

XLVIII.—Stolae duae, ubi commode haberi possunt, una violacea, et altera alba, ut infra notatur, mutanda; sin minus, una saltem adhibeatur.

*278. Baruffaldi justly observes that there are few churches so poor as not to be able easily to provide the two stoles required for the ceremony, and is very severe on the negligence or parsimony of those pastors who fail to do so.[8] The white stole may be left on the table beside the font; the violet stole is put on with the surplice at the commencement, and exchanged for the white one at the proper time.[9]

*279. The present rubric tolerates the use of the same stole during the whole ceremony. In this case it may be

---

[1] Tit. x. n. 39.   [2] Baruff., l. c. De Herdt, pars vi. n. 4. iii.
[3] Supra, n. 260.   [4] *Act. Eccl. Mediol.*, pars iv. Inst. Fab. Eccl. cap. xix. *De Baptisterio*, pag. 480.   [5] Baruff., l. c. De Herdt. l. a.
[6] Supra, n. 182.   [7] Vid. infra, chap. iv. § xxiv.
[8] Tit. ii. n. 54. et tit. x. n. 41.   [9] Chap. iv. § xv.

either white or violet, but we should prefer, with **Falise**[1]
and De Herdt, who cites the pastoral of Bruges,[2] to have it
double—white on one side, and violet on the other—so that
it might be reversed at the time marked for the exchange,
and thus be equivalent to two stoles. Baruffaldi[3] seems to rep-
robate the use of this double stole; but, on examining his
words, it will be seen that he does so only when it is adopted
as a matter of choice, or from a motive of parsimony, in preference to two distinct stoles; but he does not imply that it
is not preferable to a single stole of one color.

XLIX.—Medulla panis, qua inuncti Sacerdotis digiti, cum manus
lavat, abstergantur; et vas pro manum lotione post Baptismum, quod
huic tantum usui deservire debet.

*280. A crumb of bread, or a little dry meal, is the best
means of removing the oil from the fingers. This, as well
as the basin for washing the priest's hands, may be placed on
a corner of the table already mentioned, or in any other convenient place in the baptistery. The rubric seems to require
that the basin be reserved for this use exclusively. At least
it should not be used for any merely profane purpose; but
we would not condemn its being used for receiving the water
flowing from the head, and conveying it to the sacrarium.[4]

*281. It is strange, as Catalani observes,[5] that the rubric,
notwithstanding its minuteness, makes no mention of the
towel, which, manifestly, should be in readiness for drying the
hands. There should be another towel also for the purpose
of drying the child's head after the water has been poured on
it.[6]

§ L.—Alba vestis in modum pallioli, seu linteolum candidum, infantis
capiti imponendum.

*282. It is the custom in most places for the parents or
sponsors to bring with them this white linen garment. It is
usually a piece of plain linen, about the size of a small hand-
kerchief, though it was formerly a complete garment, which
was worn by the neophytes for some time after their baptism.[7]
It should be placed on the table beside the holy oils, so as
to be at hand when required. It would be well to have one
or two at all times in the baptistery, lest in some instance
those who bring the child should come without one.[8]

---

[1] *Du Sacrement de Baptême*, § i. n. 10.   [2] Pars vi. n. 4, vi.
[3] Loc. cit.   [4] Supra, n. 183.   [5] Tit. ii. cap. i. § xlvii. n. L.
[6] Baruff., tit. x. n. 48.   Vid. infra, chap. iv. § xvii.
[7] Vid. chap. iv. § xxii.   [8] Baruff., tit. x. n. 45.

§ LI.—Cereus, seu candela cerea, baptizato ardens tradenda.

*283. The wax-candle, as well as the linen garment, is presented by the parents or sponsors, according to the custom existing in many places.[1] Such a custom might be made a convenient means of supplying wax-candles for the use of the altar in parishes where no provision exists for the purpose. The candle should be placed on the table with the rest. The rubric does not require that it be lighted from the commencement of the ceremony, though this is prescribed in some rituals, as in that of Ghent.[2] St. Charles, in his instructions,[3] required that during the ceremony there should be two lighted candles on the table, or, if convenient, on the altar of the baptistery. In this matter each one may follow the approved custom of his diocese, but the rubric requires no more than that the candle be burning when it is presented by the priest.

§ LII.—Hic denique Ritualis liber sit paratus; et item liber Baptismalis, in quo baptizati describuntur.

*284. The ritual to be used is no other than the Roman. We have already discussed the obligation of observing what it prescribes, as far as circumstances permit.[4] Generally speaking, there can be nothing to prevent an exact compliance with all that it prescribes regarding baptism when solemnly administered in the church. The ritual itself warns the minister not to trust too easily to his memory, but to recite everything out of the book,[5] which he should, therefore, have at hand, as he is here directed. He should have in readiness also the baptismal register, in which he is to inscribe the names of the baptized and of the sponsors, in the manner prescribed at the end of the ritual.

§ LIII.—Omnibus igitur opportune præparatis, Sacerdos ad tanti Sacramenti administrationem, lotis manibus, superpelliceo et stola violacea indutus, accedat; Clericum unum seu plures, si potest, secum adhibeat, superpelliceo pariter indutos, qui sibi ministrent.

*285. All things being prepared, both in the baptistery and at the church porch, the priest, already vested in soutane,[6] washes his hands, and then puts on a surplice and violet stole. Baruffaldi[7] would prefer that he should vest and unvest at the font, but we believe the sacristy will, generally

---

[1] Baruff., n. 49.   Catal., tit. ii. cap. i. § li.
[2] De Herdt, pars vi. n. 5. xx.
[3] *Act. Eccles. Mediol.*, pars iv. § *De iis quæ Parochus servet et paret antequam Baptismum ministret*, pag. 415.   [4] Vid. chap. i. n. 65, et seq.
[5] Supra, n. 133.   [6] Vid. supra, n. 119.   [7] Tit. x. n. 54.

speaking, be found the most convenient place, the vestments being usually kept there. The clerk or clerks who are to attend him, should be already vested in soutane and surplice,[1] and be prepared to present him with the water and towel, and assist him in vesting.

*286. Should baptism be administered, as is often the case, immediately after Mass, it may be asked, whether the priest may not, in such circumstances, retain the alb and stole, having laid aside the chasuble and maniple. We think that in strictness he may, especially since, according to Catalani,[2] the surplice is but a substitute for the alb, which was formerly in use. He cannot do so, however, unless the stole be violet, as is plain from the rubric; and again, the trouble of changing it for a white stole at the time marked[3] will be much greater in consequence of its being fastened by the cincture.[4] We think, therefore, that, in the case supposed, it is not only more in accordance with the letter of the rubric, but on the whole more convenient for the priest himself, to lay aside the alb and put on a surplice.

287. No mention is made in our text of the cap or berretta, but De Herdt says that the priest goes towards the porch "tecto capite et junctis manibus."[5] The Ritual of Toulon[6] also prescribes that the priest wear his cap at the commencement, and directs him at what parts he is to uncover afterwards during the ceremony. We shall give these directions as they occur under each rubric. They are the same, with one or two exceptions, as those given in the Roman Ritual regarding the use of the mitre when the bishop baptizes.[7] The priest may, if he chooses, wear his cap according to the directions thus given; but we think the silence of our rubric on the point is sufficient to show that there is no obligation of wearing the cap at any part of the ceremony.

§ LIV.—Ita paratus accedat ad limen Ecclesiæ, ubi foris expectant qui infantem detulerunt.

288. The priest thus vested, and preceded by the clerk or clerks, advances to the door or porch of the church, being careful to make the usual reverences in passing the high altar, or any other on his way. Those who present the child for baptism should be in waiting at the door, for the rubric clearly supposes that it is kept outside the church until it is

---

[1] Vid. supra, n. 126, 127.   [2] Tit. ii. cap. i. § liii. n. ii.
[3] Infra, chap. iv. § xv.   [4] Vid. supra. n. 123.
[5] Pars vi. n. 5,   [6] *Baptême*, tit. ii. § ii.   [7] Vid. chap. viii. § iv.

introduced with the ceremony mentioned hereafter.[1] It may
be brought, however, within the porch, if there be one, as it
is still outside the church.[2] The candidates for baptism were
kept outside the church, or place of assembly of the Christians, even from the earliest times, as is proved from Tertullian, *De Cor. Mil.*, *cap.* 3, and St. Cyril of Jerusalem, *Catech.*
1, referred to by the Catechism of the Council of Trent,
which assigns the reason of the exclusion in these words:
" The person to be baptized is carried, or, as also happens,
" conducted, to the door of the church, and is strictly forbid-
" den to enter, as unworthy to be admitted into the house of
" God, until he shall have cast off the yoke of the most de-
" grading servitude, and devoted himself unreservedly to
" Christ the Lord, and to his most just sovereignty."[3]

*289. But what is to be done if there be no porch, and if
the state of the weather, or other circumstances, should make a
strict compliance with the rubric seriously inconvenient? In
this case, we think the child may be brought inside. Indeed,
this is expressly permitted by the Ritual of Toulon,[4] and by
the rituals published for the use of several dioceses in Belgium; as those of Mechlin, Bruges, Ghent, etc., cited by De
Herdt.[5] The child, however, should be kept near the door,
for the only safe rule in this and other such cases is to adhere to the rubric, if not strictly, at least as far as circumstances will allow; and we shall see that, after having entered the church, the priest and sponsors are required by the
rubric to recite the " Credo " and " Pater Noster " *while they
are going to the font.*[6]

§ LV.—Interroget, nisi de his bene sibi constet, an sit suæ Parochiæ,
masculus, an fœmina, an sit domi baptizatus, et a quo, et quam rite, et
qui sint compatres qui infantem teneant, pro eoque respondeant, quos pie
ac decenter assistere, ac prout opus fuerit, pro baptizando ad interrogationes respondere admoneat.

290. From what has been already stated, it is plainly the
duty of the priest to ascertain all the particulars regarding
the child presented for baptism, which he is here directed to
ask, viz., whether it belongs to his parish, because, if not,
he has, generally speaking, no right to baptize it;[7] its sex,
because of the name to be given, and the gender to be used
in the prayers, and because it is congruous, though not strictly

[1] Chap. iv. § viii.   [2] Baruff., tit. x. n. 55.
[3] Pars. ii. cap. ii. n. 62.   Vid. *Decret.* Benedicti XIII, supra, n. 243.
[4] Tit. ii. § i.   [5] Pars vi. n. 5, i.
[6] Infra, chap. iv. § x.   [7] Vid. supra, n. 194.

required, that the sponsor, if there be only one, should be of the same sex;[1] whether it has received a private baptism, and from whom, that he may know whether he is now to baptize it absolutely, or conditionally, or at all;[2] who are the sponsors, that he may know whether they are admissible,[3] and that he may instruct them how to assist with becoming reverence, and to respond to the interrogations.

§ LVI.—Et quoniam iis qui baptizantur, tanquam Dei filiis in Christo regenerandis, et in ejus militiam adscribendis, nomen imponitur, curet ne obscœna, fabulosa, aut ridicula, vel inanium deorum, vel impiorum ethnicorum hominum nomina imponantur, sed potius, quatenus fieri potest, Sanctorum, quorum exemplis Fideles ad pie vivendum excitentur, et patrociniis proteguntur.

291. As in the ancient law, names were imposed in circumcision, so, under the Christian dispensation, names are given in baptism.[4] In the early ages, catechumens were required to give in their names, and have them inscribed on the register of the church for some time before receiving baptism.[5] From this it is inferred, with some probability, that the names given in baptism were frequently imposed or adopted long before.[6] It is certain, at all events, as Martene proves at length,[7] that the custom of giving a name in baptism prevailed from the beginning. The converts from paganism usually laid aside their old names and received others, while the children of Christian parents either had no names previously, or changed those they had for new ones, or at least had them again imposed and ratified in baptism.

*292. The priest is directed by the rubric to take care that the name given be such as may become one who is regenerated in Christ and enlisted as his soldier. "To the person "baptized," says the Catechism of the Council of Trent, "is "given a name, which should be taken from some one whose "eminent piety and religion have given him a place in the "catalogue of the saints; for this similarity of name will "easily serve to stimulate to the imitation of his virtues and "the attainment of his holiness, and to hope and pray that he, "who should be the model of his imitation, may also, by his "advocacy, become the guardian of his safety of soul and "body. Wherefore, those are to be reprehended who so in-"dustriously search for, and distinguish their children by, the

[1] Supra. n. 222.   [2] Supra, n. 174.
[3] Supra, n. 229.   [4] Baruff., tit. x. n. 64.
[5] Martene, *De Ant. Eccl. Rit.*, lib. i. cap. i. art. x.
[6] Martene, ibid.   [7] Loc. cit.

" names of heathens, of those particularly who were the most
" conspicuous for their crimes; for they thus show what little
" regard they have for the pursuit of Christian piety, who
" seem to be so enamored with the memory of impious men,
" as to wish to have such profane names everywhere echo in
" the ears of the faithful."[1]

293. The names of the Old Testament were generally
adopted by the heretics of modern times, especially by the
Puritans, in preference to the names of Christian saints.[2]
When one of these is converted, or when any adult, having
a name not found in the calendar or martyrology, is about to
receive baptism, there may be some difficulty about changing
the name. The words of the rubric, as Baruffaldi observes,[3]
do not imply a rigorous precept, but an admonition to the
priest to do what he can to have every one baptized by the
name of a saint; and should it happen that there are special
reasons for giving or retaining another name—as in the case
where an inheritance or a legacy might be made to depend
on it—the priest need have no hesitation in allowing it.
Indeed it is justly observed by the same author,[4] that hardly
a name can be thought of which has not been borne by some
one of the faithful, now amongst the saints, though not mentioned in the calendar. At all events, a name that is insisted on may be easily admitted, by adding or prefixing to it
the name of a saint. The name received in baptism may
be changed in confirmation; and, accordingly, many change
the names they had, or take others in addition, when they are
confirmed.[5]

§ LVII.—His igitur expeditis, et accepto nomine baptizandi, positi,
si infans fuerit, super brachium dexterum illius qui eum defert, Parochus
ad Baptismum procedat, in hunc modum nominatim interrogans.

294. The infant to be baptized is placed so as to rest, or
be borne up, on the right arm of the person holding it; and
this, as Baruffaldi states,[6] for the greater convenience of the
minister, and because the right arm is reputed more honorable than the left. The Ritual of Toulon directs the child to
be held by the godfather, the godmother being on his left,
and holding it at the same time by the feet.[7] Catalani also
supposes that it is held up by the godfather.[8] In Ireland it

[1] Pars ii. cap. ii. n. 76.   [2] Cfr. Catal., tit. ii. cap. i. § lvi. n. viii.
[3] Tit. x. n. 65.   [4] Loc. cit. n. 66.
[5] Baruff., tit. x. n. 68. Catal., tit. ii. cap. i. § lvi. n. ix.
[6] Tit x. u. 70.   [7] Tit. ii. § i. n. i.   [8] Cap. ii. § ix. u. ii. in fine.

is usually held up by the godmother, the godfather standing
at her right.   The priest takes his place at the door opposite
them, standing with his back turned to the high altar,[1] and
with his cap on,[2] holding the ritual in his hand, or having it
held before him by the clerk, proceeds with the ceremony as
directed in the order.

[1] Rit. Leod. apud De Herdt, p. vi. n. 5, iii.   [2] Rit. Toul., l. c.

CHAPTER IV.

ORDER FOR THE BAPTISM OF INFANTS: "ORDO BAPTISMI PARVULORUM."

§ I.—N. *Quid petis ab Ecclesia Dei?* Patrinus respondet: *Fidem.* Sacerdos: *Fides quid tibi præstat?* Patrinus respondet: *Vitam æternam.* Sacerdos: *Si igitur vis,* etc.

295. The ceremonies prescribed by the ritual to be observed in baptism, have been in use from the earliest times, and most of them may be traced to the apostolic age, as is shown by abundant extracts from the Fathers and ancient liturgies, given by Catalani and Martene, but they were not always applied in the same order. It appears from the "Ordines" given by Martene,[1] that the unctions, insufflations, etc., in some ancient rituals, precede, and in others follow, the interrogations or catechetical instructions on the doctrines of the Christian faith, of which a profession is to be made in baptism.

"This practice of instruction," says the Catechism of the Council of Trent, "originated, beyond all doubt, in the com-
"mand of our Lord addressed to his Apostles: 'Go ye into
"'the whole world, and teach all nations; baptizing them in
"'the name of the Father, and of the Son, and of the Holy
"'Ghost: teaching them to observe all things whatsoever I
"'have commanded you' (*Matth.* xxviii. 19, 20; *Mark,* xvi.
"15); words from which we may learn that baptism is not to
"be administered until at least the principal heads of our
"religion are explained. But, as the catechetical form con-
"sists of many interrogations, if the person to be instructed
"be an adult, he himself answers; but if he be an infant, the
"sponsor answers according to the prescribed form, and makes
"the solemn engagement for the child."[2]

In the present case, then, addressing the infant by its name, the priest says:—N. (*i. e.,* Joannes, Maria, etc.): *Quid*

---

[1] *De Antiquis Ecclesiæ Ritibus,* lib. i. cap. i. art. xviii.
[2] Pars ii. cap. ii. n. 63, 64.

petis ab Ecclesia Dei ? The sponsor answers: *Fidem.* Priest: *Fides quid tibi præstat ?* Sponsor: *Vitam æternam.* Priest: *Si igitur vis ad vitam ingredi,* etc., etc.

*296. When a great many names are given to an infant, as it would be inconvenient to repeat them all every time the letter N is marked in the ritual, the priest may follow the rule laid down by the Council of Baltimore.[1] In the first interrogation he may mention all the names if he thinks it expedient; but in the rest of the ceremony let him mention only what may be commonly known as the Christian name, taking care that all be inscribed in the baptismal register.[2]

*297. According to Baruffaldi,[3] these questions are to be proposed in Latin, exactly as they are given in the ritual But a custom has pretty generally prevailed, of proposing them in the vernacular, or at least of repeating them in the vernacular, since sponsors, for the most part, are unable to answer in Latin. The editions of the ritual used in Ireland, England, and America, give a translation of the questions and answers annexed to the Latin form. That which has been published for the use of the English Church, pursuant to a decree of the Synod of Westminster,[4] does not differ in this respect from those that preceded. The compendium published for the use of the clergy of the United States, likewise gives a translation of the questions in English, French and German. This compendium[5] was published according to a decree of the third Provincial Council of Baltimore, with the approval of Gregory XVI.

It is worthy of note, that, in the fourth Provincial Council of Baltimore, it was directed that, in the edition of the ritual to be published, there should be inserted at the foot of the page a translation, approved by the archbishop, of certain interrogations and prayers, so that it might be used when expedient—*the Latin form, however, never being omitted;* and, in the decree of the fifth Council, which approved of the ritual published, the priests were strictly ordered. . . . "Lati-"nam formam precum nunquam omittere."[6]

*298. The Congregation of Rites has been several times consulted on this subject, and has invariably insisted on a

[1] Provinciale, i. Decr. xiii.   [2] Vid. Decret. in Appendice.
[3] Tit. x. n. 69, and Tit. xi. n. 2.   [4] Derby, 1856.
[5] "*Excerpta ex Rituali Romano pro administratione sacramentorum* "*ad commodiorem usum Missionariorum in Septentrionalis America* "*Fœderatæ Provinciis.*" Editio tertia, Baltimori, 1860.
[6] Decr. viii. q. v. in Appendice.

strict adherence to the form given in the Roman Ritual.
The last answer we have seen on the subject is given to a
question proposed on the 12th September, 1857, and seems
quite decisive against the lawfulness of translating the interrogations at all : " Utrum in collatione baptismi interroga-
" tiones possint fieri vernacule, vel saltem vernacule iterari
" postquam Latine factæ fuerint ?   Resp. : Quoad interroga-
" tiones quæ baptismi ordinem præcedunt vel sequuntur, ac
" pro quibus Rituale nullam exhibit formulam : *Affirmative.*
" Quoad interrogationes quæ in ipsomet baptismi ordine
" occurrunt, ac pro quibus formulæ in Rituali extant : *Negative*
" *ad utramque partem.*"[1]

*299. To proceed in strict conformity with this decision,
no one should be admitted to act as sponsor who is not instructed to answer the interrogations in Latin ; and this would,
undoubtedly, cause great inconvenience and great dissatisfaction in places where the contrary practice has long prevailed.
It is not impossible, however, that the decision may be intended to guard against the danger of introducing incorrect
and unauthorized translations ; and that when a sponsor,
otherwise qualified, is unable to answer the interrogations in
Latin, it may still be lawful for the priest to repeat them in
the vernacular, *according to an approved translation,* such as
is given in the rituals above referred to.[2]

300. But at least it is certain that the priest is never justified in simply *omitting* the Latin, and *substituting* a translation, in any of the interrogations or prayers of the ritual.
The translation, when used, must be merely added " explica-
" tionis causâ."   The whole of this is very well put in the
following decree of the first provincial Synod of Baltimore :
" Statuimus juxta Ritualis Romani præscriptum, in sacramen-
" tis administrandis et in defunctorum sepulturâ, sacerdotes
" omnino teneri ad adhibendam linguam Latinam : et si cen-
" suerint expedire, explicationis causâ, eorum quæ recitant
" adjungere versionem linguâ vernaculâ, eam tantum versio-
" nem adhibendam esse, quæ fuerit ab Ordinario sancita.
" Ubicumque autem consuetudo aliqua invaluerit huic Decreto
" adversa, eam quamprimum abrogandam statuimus."[3]

301. It may be well to observe that the National Synod
(*Concilium Plenarium*) of the whole United States of North
America, held at Baltimore in 1852, formally adopted the

---

[1] 12 Sept. 1857, *in Molinen.*, ad 17, apud Falise, *Decreta Authentica
etc., v. Baptisma.*   [2] Supra, n. 297.   [3] Decr. xx.

decrees of the seven provincial Synods of Baltimore, and declared them to be binding everywhere throughout the states and territories subject to the general government.[1]

§ II.—Deinde ter exsufflet leniter in faciem infantis, et dicat semel: *Exi ab eo* (vel *ab ea*) *immunde, etc.*

302. From the insufflations and exorcisms used before the baptism of infants, as well as before that of adults, St. Augustine proves original sin against the Pelagians;[2] and that they were used everywhere throughout the Church from the time of the Apostles, is placed beyond all doubt by this and the other testimonies cited by Martene.[3]

303. In reference to the ceremony mentioned in the present rubric, as well as to the exorcisms used in baptism generally, the Catechism of the Council of Trent says:—"The exor-"cism follows, which is composed of words of sacred and "religious import, and of prayers to expel the devil, and to "weaken and crush his power; wherefore the priest breathes "three times into the face of him who is to be initiated, that "he may expel the power of the old serpent, and may catch "the breath of lost life."[4] This ceremony was not always performed by the bishop or priest who administered the sacrament, but often by a deacon, exorcist, or even a simple cleric.[5]

*304. According to the rubric, the priest blows gently on the face of the child three times, and then says, once, *Exi ab eo,* etc. Baruffaldi[6] directs this to be done with the mouth fully open, "ore lato," and not with the mouth nearly closed, "ore 'stricto:" in other words, he requires the priest to breathe, rather than blow, gently; and this, that the air exhaled may not be too cold. We think, however, that the word in the rubric means to blow, as a person, *e. g.*, would blow dust off a book or paper. This is its ordinary meaning; and in the ceremony for baptizing adults, the rubric itself directs the priest first to blow, "exsufflet," and afterwards to breathe, "halet," on the face of the person to be baptized, thus plainly distinguishing between the two.[7]

§ III.—Postea pollice faciat signum Crucis in fronte et in pectore infantis. dicens: *Accipe signum Crucis tam in fronte ✠ quam in corde ✠; sume Fidem cœlestium præceptorum; et talis esto moribus, ut templum Dei jam esse possis. Oremus. Preces nostras, etc.*

---

[1] Decr. ii.   [2] *Epistola* 194, ad Sixtum. *De Symbolo ad Catechumenos,* lib. i. cap. 5, cit. apud Catal., tit. ii. cap. ii. § ii. n. i.   [3] *De Antiquis Ecclesiæ Ritibus,* lib. i. cap. i. art. vi. n. viii.   [4] Pars ii. cap. ii. n. 65.   [5] Martene, l. c. n. ix.   [6] Tit. xi. n. 3.   [7] Vid. infra, chap. vi. § v.

305. The frequent use of the sign of the cross, from the very commencement of Christanity, is proved by the testimony of the most ancient writers, and is admitted by Protestants themselves. It is enough to refer to the well-known passage of Tertullian,[1] in which he says :—" Ad omnem pro-" gressum atque promotum ; ad omnem aditum et exitum ; " ad vestitum, calciatum, ad lavacra, ad mensas, ad lumina, " ad cubilia, ad sedilia ; quæcumque nos conversatio exercet, " frontem crucis signaculo terimus."   St Augustine expressly mentions that the catechumens were signed with the sign of the cross before baptism,[2] and the same is inferred from St. Basil.[3]

306. The signing of several parts of the body shows, according to the Catechism of the Council of Trent, " that, by " the ministry of baptism, the senses of the person baptized " are opened and strengthened to enable him to receive God, " and to understand and observe his precepts."[4]   As to the parts signed, there was a considerable diversity of usage in different churches from the earliest times ;[5] and even still the pastorals or rituals of particular places direct signs to be made which are not mentioned in our rubrics.[6]

307. The priest should make the sign of the cross directed by the present rubric, with his right thumb (the other fingers being joined and extended) on the forehead at the word "*fonte*," and on the breast at the word "*corde*." He should make it in such a way that the first line be drawn downwards and the other from right to left (of the child). This will naturally be the case if he stands as he ought, in front of the person holding the child.

308. The rubric does not say whether the breast of the child should be uncovered at this ceremony.   De Herdt[7] here lays it down as a general rule, that when the parts to be signed are covered, it is sufficient to make the sign outside the dress ; and he cites for this the rituals of Bruges, Liege, etc.

309 In reciting the prayer which follows, *Preces nostras*, etc., the priest should be uncovered,[8] and remain so till after the blessing of the salt.

---

[1] *Lib. de Corona Militis*, c. 3, cit. apud Perrone, *De Cultu Sanctorum*, cap. vi.
[2] *De Symb. ad Catech.*, ii. cap. i., apud Catal., tit. ii. cap. ii. iii. n. i.
[3] *De Spiritu Sancto*, cap. 27, apud Catal., ibid.
[4] Pars ii. cap. ii. n. 67.   [5] Catal., cap. i. § iii. n. ii.
[6] Vid. De Herdt, pars vi. n. 5, v.   [7] Loc. cit.
[8] Rit Toul., tit. ii. § i. n. 3.

§ IV.—Deinde imponat manum super caput infantis, ac dicat: *Oremus. Omnipotens,* etc.

*310. The imposition of hands on catechumens is a ceremony of great antiquity, mentioned by Sulpicius Severus, *De Vita Sti Martini,* c. 10, and other ancient writers cited by Martene.[1] It is also mentioned, with the prayer which here accompanies it, in many ancient rituals given by the same author.[2]

The priest puts his right hand over the head of the child, having the fingers joined together and extended,[3] and says the prayer, *Omnipotens,* etc. He may touch the head gently, as is directed by the ritual of Toulon;[4] but this is not necessary, it is enough that the hand be extended over it.[5] He may keep it so extended during the prayer, but the rubric does not require this.[6]

§ V.—Deinde Sacerdos benedicit sal. quod semel benedictum alias ad eumdem usum deservire potest. Benedictio Salis: *Exorcizo te, creatura salis,* etc.

*311. We need not repeat what has been already said regarding the salt used in baptism.[7] It must be blessed according to the form given here. A very small quantity, if carefully preserved from dust and moisture, would suffice for a great many baptisms; and, of course, the benediction here mentioned is omitted while the supply lasts. In performing the ceremony, the priest turns to the table where the salt to be blessed is already placed,[8] and standing, with head uncovered and hands joined,[9] recites the prayer, making the sign of the cross over the salt at the words marked in the ritual; for which purpose he separates his hands, placing the left on the table or on his breast, and making the sign with the right.

312. In the rubrics of the Missal we have minute instructions as to the manner of making the sign of the cross in blessing any person or object. The right hand is to be stretched out, all the fingers being joined together and extended, and the little finger directed to the person or object to be blessed. In signing himself, the priest should always put his left hand

[1] *De Ant. Eccl. Rit.,* lib. i. cap. i. art. iv. n. vii.
[2] Art. vii. ord. iv. v.   [3] De Herdt, pars vi. n. 5, § vi.
[4] Tit. ii. § i. n. 4.   [5] Baruff., tit. xi. n. 9. De Herdt, l. c.
[6] Vid. infra, chap. vi. § xi. et § xxiii.
[7] Supra, n. 270, 271.   [8] Vid. supra, n. 274.
[9] Rub. Missal., *Die* iv. *Cinerum.* Vid. De Herdt, pars v. n. 37, vii.

below his breast; but in other benedictions, if he be at the
altar, he should put his left hand on the altar. The words
of the rubric as they are found in the Missal,[1] are :

"Cum seipsum signat semper sinistram ponit infra pectus; in aliis
"benedictionibus cum est ad Altare, et benedicit oblata, vel aliquid aliud,
"ponit eam super Altare, nisi aliter notetur. Seipsum benedicens,
"vertit ad se palmam manus dextræ, et omnibus illius digitis junctis et
"extensis, a fronte ad pectus, et ab humero sinistro ad dextrum, signum
"crucis format. Si vero alios, vel rem aliquam benedicit, parvum
"digitum vertit ei, cui benedicit, ac benedicendo totam manum dextram
"extendit, omnibus illius digitis pariter junctis, et extensis: quod in
"omni benedictione observatur."

313. The rubric does not say where he should keep his left
hand in blessing any object when he is not at the altar. If
he be at a table, we are inclined to think, from analogy, that
he should put it on the table; in other circumstances, we
think he should put it under his breast, for it would be very
unbecoming to have it suspended in the air, as is observed by
Merati on the above rubric. Besides, the rubric itself[2] directs
the priest to put the left hand under the breast in giving the
benediction before the last Gospel, from which it may be, not
unreasonably, inferred, that he should do the same whenever
he has nothing before him on which to rest it.

§ VI.—Deinde immittat modicum salis benedicti in os infantis, dicens:
N. *Accipe sal sapientiæ : propitiatio sit tibi in vitam æternam.* R. *Amen.*
Sacerdos: *Pax tibi.* R. *Et cum spiritu tuo. Oremus. Deus Patrum
nostrorum,* etc.

*314. After the blessing of the salt the priest puts on his
cap,[3] and then, taking with the thumb and index finger of
his right hand a very small quantity—a few grains—of the
blessed salt, he puts it into the mouth of the child, saying:
"Jacobe, Catharina, etc., *Accipe sal,*" etc. Baruffaldi observes
that he must be careful to put in only very little, lest the
child might be injured by it.[4]
The meaning of the ceremony is explained by the Catechism
of the Council of Trent. "When salt," it says, "is put into
"the mouth of the person to be baptized, it evidently imports
"that, by the doctrine of faith and the gift of grace, he
"should be delivered from the corruption of sin, experience a
"relish for good works, and be delighted with the food of
"divine wisdom."[5]

[1] *Rit. Celeb. Miss.,* iii. n. 5.   [2] Ibid. xii. n. 1.
[3] Rit. Toul., tit. ii. § i. n. 6.   [4] Tit. xi. n. 20.   [5] Pars ii. cap. ii. n. 66.

315. In reciting the prayer which follows, "*Deus patrum* "*nostrum*," etc., he should be uncovered[1] and keep his hands joined,[2] the clerk holding the ritual open before him.

At the end of the prayer he again puts on his cap,[3] and proceeds with the exorcism which immediately follows, keeping his hands joined, except when he makes the sign of the cross over the child (which he is to do with his right hand, placing the left hand on his breast),[4] while he pronounces the name of each of the persons of the Blessed Trinity, as marked in the ritual.

§ VII.—Hic pollice in fronte signat infantem, dicens: *Et hoc signum*, etc.

*316. A rubric is here inserted in the form of the exorcism, directing the priest to make the sign of the cross on the child's forehead, saying: "*Et hoc signum sanctæ Crucis*," ✠ etc. It would not suffice to mark the cross in the text where it is to be made, because the sign is here to be made, not with the hand over the child, as in those immediately preceding, but with the thumb on the child's forehead in the manner before directed.[5]

317. De Herdt, speaking of the crosses marked in the Missal as directions to make the sign at certain words, observes that the word or syllable which precedes the cross should be pronounced in the act of drawing the first line, and that which follows, in drawing the transverse line.[6] This rule seems to express very well the direction implied in the mark, and it would be well to follow it in practice. At least, care should be taken that the words are pronounced, and the sign made at morally the same moment.

§ VIII.—Mox imponit manum super caput infantis, et dicit: *Oremus. Æternam ac justissimam*, etc.

318. On this rubric we have only to repeat what has been said above.[7] He takes off his cap before extending his hand, and remains uncovered while reciting the prayer.[8]

§ IX.—Postea Sacerdos imponit extremam partem stolæ super infantem, et introducit eum in Ecclesiam, dicens: N. *Ingredere*, etc.

319. It is supposed that, up to this time, the child has been outside the church.[9] The priest is here directed to put the

[1] Rit. Toul., tit. ii. § i. n. 6.   [2] Falise, *Cours Abrégé*, etc., 3me part. chap. i. § iv. n. 3.   [3] Rit. Toul., l. c.   [4] Vid. supra, n. 313.
[5] Supra, n. 307.   [6] Pars i. n. 45, i. 4.   [7] Supra, n. 310.
[8] Rit. Toul., tit. ii. § i. n. 8.   [9] Vid. supra. n. 288.

extremity of his stole over it, and thus in a manner lead it into the church, while he says the words: *Petre, Maria,* etc., *Ingredere in Templum,* etc.

320. This imposition of the stole, according to Baruffaldi,[1] signifies protection against the assaults of the demons. It is not prescribed in any of the ancient rituals. According to the Ambrosian ritual and the Instructions of St. Charles,[2] the priest should not touch the child with the stole, but merely give a sign to have it enter, while he goes before saying: "*Ingredere fili in domum Dei, audi Patrem tuum docentem te* "*viam scientiæ.*"[3]

*321. Our rubric does not say which extremity of the stole is to be used. De Herdt recommends the left (which is to be simply laid on the child's breast), in order, as he says, that the priest may be at the right in entering the church.[4] Indeed, the left extremity is expressly mentioned by the rubric of the Pontifical, in the ceremony of baptizing adults. This arrangement is very convenient if the child be carried by the godfather, for the priest could easily walk at the godfather's right, having the left extremity of the stole placed on the child; but it is not quite so convenient when the child is carried, as it usually is, by the godmother. In this case, the left side of the stole must be extended, so that, passing in front of the godfather, it may reach the child.

322. He puts on his cap at the end of the preceding prayer, and wears it entering the church, but takes it off as soon as he has entered.[5]

§ X.—Cum fuerint Ecclesiam ingressi, Sacerdos procedens ad fontem, cum Susceptoribus conjunctim, clara voce dicit: *Credo in Deum,* etc.

323. Many ceremonies not here mentioned were prescribed by several ancient rituals.[6] One, which was very common, is still retained according to the usage of certain churches—that of reading the Gospel, *Matthew,* chap. xi., from the 25th verse to the end; or, more commonly, *Matthew,* chap. xix., verses 13, 14, and 15; making, at the beginning, the sign of the cross on the child's forehead, lips, and breast, and putting the book to its lips at the end. This is still prescribed in many diocesan rituals in Belgium and other places on the Continent.[7]

---

[1] Tit. xi. n. 22. [2] *Act. Eccl. Mediol.,* pars iv. § *Ordo Baptismi Parvulorum,* pag. 417. [3] Cfr. Catal., tit. ii. cap. ii. § ix. n. ij. [4] Pars vi. n. 5, viii. [5] Rit. Toul., l. c. n. 9. [6] Vid. Catal., § x. n. i. et seq. [7] De Herdt, pars vi. n. 5, ix.

The ritual of St. Ambrose, used in Milan, directs that the infant, after being brought into the church, be placed on the ground near to, and with its feet turned towards, the font, while the "Credo" and "Pater Noster" are recited by the ministers and sponsors, looking towards the altar.[1]

324. According to our rubric, the priest, having entered the church, must, while proceeding to the font, recite conjointly with the sponsors, and in a clear, distinct voice, the "Apostles' Creed" and the "Pater Noster." A profession of faith was always required from those who were about to receive baptism, as is proved from the most ancient rituals and the testimony of several Fathers, and especially of St. Augustine.[2]

This is evidently in accordance with the institution of Christ, referred to by the Catechism of the Council of Trent, already cited,[3] and is strikingly illustrated in the baptism of the eunuch by Philip.[4] Adults are required to make this profession themselves, but infants make it through their sponsors, as St. Augustine states in his work against the Donatists.[5]

325. The "Credo" and "Pater Noster" should be recited in Latin by the sponsors as well as by the priest. If they cannot recite them in Latin, they are usually permitted to recite them in the vernacular. How far this usage is to be tolerated may be inferred from what has been said regarding the interrogations.[6] The same decision may evidently be applied here.

§ XI.—Ac deinde, antequam accedat ad Baptisterium, dicat: Exorcismus. *Exorcizo te,* etc.

*326. When they come near the baptismal font, if they have not yet finished the Pater Noster, they should turn towards the high altar, and remain standing until they conclude it.[7] Then the priest, having put on his cap,[8] turns towards the child, and reads the exorcism, making the sign of the cross in the manner already explained.[9]

§ XII.—Postea Sacerdos digito accipiat de saliva oris sui, et tangat aures et nares infantis: tangendo vero aurem dextram et sinistram dicat *Ephpheta, quod est adaperire:* deinde tangit nares, dicens: *In odorem suavitatis: Tu autem,* etc.

[1] *Act. Eccl. Mediol.,* § *Ordo Baptismi Parvulorum,* pag. 417.
[2] *Confess.,* lib. viii. cap. ii. apud Catal., § x. n. iii.
[3] Supra, n. 295.   [4] Act. Apost., cap. viii.
[5] Lib. iv. cap. 24, apud Catal., 1. c. n. iv.   [6] Supra, n. 297, et seq.
[7] Rit. Toul., tit. ii. § i. n. 9. Falise, *Sacr. de Baptême,* § iv. n. 3.
[8] Rit. Toul., 1. c. n. 10.   [9] Supra, n. 317.

327. The ceremony of touching the catechumens with spittle is clearly referred to by St. Augustine, *Tract*, 44, *in Joannem*, speaking of the blind man whom our Lord restored to sight, after having rubbed on his eyes clay mixed with spittle;[1] and by other Fathers, cited by Martene.[2] It is prescribed in many very ancient rituals given by the same author.[3]

328. The mystic signification is explained by the Catechism of the Council of Trent: "His nostrils and ears are next "touched with spittle, and he is immediately sent to the "baptismal font, that, as sight was restored to the blind man "mentioned in the Gospel, whom the Lord, after having "spread clay over his eyes, commanded to wash them in the "waters of Siloe; so also we may understand that the "efficacy of the sacred ablution is such, as to bring light to "the mind to discern heavenly truth."[4]

*329. In performing this ceremony, the priest, still covered,[5] puts his right thumb[6] to his lips, touching it with the point of his tongue, and having thus moistened it with saliva, touches the lobe of the right ear, saying: "*Ephpheta;*" that of the left, saying: "*Quod est adaperire;*" then the nostrils, one after the other, saying: "*In odorem*" (at the right), "*suavitatis*" (at the left), and continuing, "*Tu autem,*" etc. We believe this to be the most approved manner of performing the ceremony, for there is some diversity of opinion and practice regarding it. The rubric seems to be clear enough as to the manner of taking the saliva, but De Herdt observes[7] that several Belgian rituals direct it to be put first into the hollow of the left hand, and then taken with the thumb and index of the right. The same direction is found in the ancient ritual of Limoges, given by Martene.[8] In applying the saliva it is not necessary to make the sign of the cross with the thumb, this not being prescribed as it is in anointing.[9] As to the parts of the ear to be touched, we may follow the rule given for extreme unction, in which all agree that the lobes are to be anointed.[10]

330. The above distribution of the words is the one given by De Herdt,[11] Falise,[12] and the Ritual of Toulon.[13] Baruffaldi

[1] John, ix. 7.   [2] *De Ant. Eccl. Rit.*, lib. i. cap. i. art. vi. n. xvi.
[3] Art. vii. ordo vi.   Art. xviii. ord. vi. et xviii.
[4] Pars ii. cap. ii. n. 68.   [5] Rit. Toul., §. c. n. 11.
[6] Vid. infra, chap. vi. § xxviii.   [7] Pars vi. n. 5, x.
[8] Lib. i. cap. i. art. xviii. ordo xviii.
[9] De Herdt, 1. c   [10] Vid. chap. xvi. § xiii.   [11] Loc. cit.
[12] *Du Sacrement de Baptême*, n. iv. n. 3.   [13] Tit. ii. § i. n. 11.

says[1] that the words, "*quod est adaperire*," may be omitted, as they are merly explanatory of the word, "*Ephpheta;*" but in this he is followed by no other writer. He observes that they are printed in a different type. But, whatever was the case in his time, the "*Propaganda*" edition and all correct editions of the ritual at present give the words in the same type with the others.

The chief diversity is with respect to touching the nostrils. De Herdt[2] says both should be touched together; but Falise[3] and the Ritual of Toulon[4] prescribe that they be touched one after the other; and this, we think, is the more exact method, and the one usually followed in practice.[5]

§ XIII.—Postea interrogat baptizandum nominatim, dicens: N. *Abrenuntias Satanæ?* Respondet Patrinus: *Abrenuntio.* Sacerdos: *Et omnibus operibus ejus?* Patrinus: *Abrenuntio.* Sacerdos: *Et omnibus pompis ejus?* Patrinus: *Abrenuntio.*

*331. After the preceding ceremony, the priest wipes his thumb with a towel,[6] and having entered the baptistery, which is supposed to be railed off,[7] gets the holy oils in readiness and arranges the other requisites, if all be not already prepared, in the manner before explained.[8] In the meantime the nurse or godmother uncovers the head, shoulders, and breast of the child.[9] The priest then, standing with his face looking towards the high altar,[10] and having the sponsors opposite him, puts the interrogations in Latin,[11] saying, "Joannes, Catharina, *Abrenuntias Satanæ?*" etc.

332. This public and solemn renunciation of the devil immediately before baptism is expressly mentioned by Tertullian, *De Cor. Militis*, cap. iii.; St. Basil, who says it is handed down by tradition, *De Spiritu Sancto*, cap. xxvii.; and other ancient authors cited by Catalani.[12] It was made by the catechumen standing and looking towards the west, and immediately after he turned round with his face to the east.[13]

" In three distinct interrogatories," says the Catechism of the Council of Trent, "the person to be baptized is formally "asked by the priest: 'Dost thou renounce Satan? and all "'his works? and all his pomps?' to each of which he, or the "sponsor in his name, replies: 'I renounce.' He, therefore,

---

[1] Tit. xi. n. 34.   [2] Loc. cit.   [3] Loc. cit.   [4] Loc. cit.
[5] Vid. inf. chap. xvi. § xiv.   [6] Rit. Toul., tit. ii. § i. n. 11.
[7] Supra, n. 243.   [8] Supra, n. 273, et seq.
[9] Rit. Toul., l. c.   [10] De Herdt, pars vi. n. 5, xii.
[11] Vid. supra, n. 297, et seq.   [12] Tit. ii. cap. ii. § xiii. n. 1.
[13] Martene, lib. i. cap. i. art. xiii. n. viii.

"who is to be enrolled under the banner of Christ, must
"first enter into a holy and religious engagement that he
"abandons the devil and the world, and will ever detest
"them as his worst enemies."[1]

§ XIV.—Deinde Sacerdos intingit pollicem in oleo Catechumenorum,
et infantem ungit in pectore, et inter scapulas in modum Crucis, dicens:
Ego te linio, ✠ etc.

*333. The priest now uncovers,[2] and having laid aside his
cap, or given it to the clerk, dips his right thumb into the
oil of catechumens, and anoints the child on the breast and
between the shoulders, making the sign of the cross on each
part with his thumb in applying the holy oil; and at the
same time saying the words, *" Ego te linio,"* etc.

*334. Only a single cross is marked in the ritual, at least
in any copy we have seen; but the words of the rubric are
understood to imply that the sign is to be made on each of
the parts in the act of anointing it.   The mark is usually
put between the words *linio* and *oleo,* thus: *" Linio ✠ oleo,"*
from which it might, perhaps, be inferred, that both the unctions should take place while pronouncing these words; but
as the child must usually be turned for the unction between
the shoulders, we think the pause between the words would
be rather long.   We should, therefore, prefer the distribution
of the words which is given by the Ritual of Toulon,[3] viz.;
anointing the breast, he says: *" Ego te linio ✠ oleo salutis ;"*
then anointing between the shoulders, he continues: *"in
"Christo Jesu ✠ Domino nostro ut habeas vitam æternam.
"Amen."*

335. The unctions in baptism have been in use from the
earliest times,[4] but they were not always confined to the parts
here mentioned.   According to an ancient sacramentary cited by
Catalani,[5] they were extended to the ears and nostrils; and
in the Oriental Church the whole body was anointed, as
expressly stated by St. Cyril of Jerusalem, *Cat. Myst.*, ii. n
3, and St. John Chrysostom, *Hom.* 6 *ad Coloss.*, cited by
Martene.[6]

336. The Euchologium still used in the Greek Church,
prescribes the unction of the forehead, breast, back (τὰ μετά-
φρενα, between the shoulders), ears, feet, hands, and lastly
of the whole body, as may be seen in the *"ΕΥΧΟΛΟΓΙΟΝ*

1 Pars ii. cap. ii. n. 69.   3 Rit. Toul., 1. c. n. 13.
2 Loc. cit.   4 Vid. supra, n. 248.
5 Tit. ii. cap. ii. § xiv. n. iii.   6 Lib., i. cap. i. art. xiii. n. xi.

ΜΕΓΑ."[1] The unction of the entire body is likewise prescribed in the several "Ordines" of the Greeks given by
Martene, except the one that relates to baptism in necessity.[2]

337. The mystic meaning of the ceremony as now performed,
is thus explained by the Catechism of the Council of Trent :[3]
" The person to be baptized is next anointed with the oil
" of catechumens on the breast and between the shoulders :
" on the breast, that, by the gift of the Holy Ghost, he may
" cast off error and ignorance, and may receive the true faith,
" ' for the just man liveth by faith ' (*Galat.* iii. 11); on the·
" shoulders, that, by the grace of the Holy Spirit, he may
" shake off negligence and torpor, and engage in the perform-
" ance of good works; for ' faith without works is dead '
" (*James,* ii. 26)."

Hic deponit Stolam violaceam, et sumit aliam albi coloris.	§ XV.—Subinde pollicem et inuncta loca abstergit bombacio, vel re simili; et interrogat expresso nomine baptizandum, Patrino respondente. N. *Credis in Deum,* etc.

*338. Immediately after the unctions the priest wipes his
thumb and the parts anointed, with a little cotton or flax, or
some similar material, which he should have at hand for the
purpose.[4] According to the letter of the rubric, he first wipes
his thumb; and this is certainly convenient, because, having
the thumb free, he can more easily wipe the parts anointed.
But we think it might be sometimes, and perhaps generally,
more convenient to wipe the oil off the breast immediately
after applying it; because otherwise there is danger of its
coming in contact with the dress or the hand of the person
holding the infant, in turning it for the unction between the
shoulders; just as in extreme unction it is recommended to
wipe the oil from the right ear, before anointing the left.[5]

*339. After this he takes off the violet stole and puts on a
white one. Violet is the color used by the Church as expressive of sorrow and affliction; white, as expressive of joy
and innocence.[6] Violet is therefore suited to the condition of
the catechumen, and white to the state of the neophyte regenerated by baptism.[7]

The rubric directing the change is usually printed in small
type in the margin as we give it; but in some editions it has

---

[1] 'Ακολουθία του 'Αγίου Βαπτίσματος.
[2] Lib. i. cap. i. art. xviii. ordo xxii. et seq.   [3] Pars ii. cap. ii. n. 70.
[4] Vid. supra, n. 277.   [5] Vid. infra, chap. xvi. § xii.
[6] Gavant., pars i. tit. xviii. *Rub.* 2 et *Rub.* 5.   [7] Baruff., tit. xi. n. 37.

been printed as a distinct paragraph in the same type as the rest, and immediately before "Subinde pollicem," etc. It is printed in this way in the edition published by order of Benedict XIV,[1] which is that followed by Catalani. But in whatever way it be printed, it is right, as Catalani himself observes,[2] that the priest should wipe off the oil before he changes the stole, as he could not conveniently do so without the use of his right thumb. If the stole which he has be a double one—violet on one side, and white on the other—he should reverse it.[3]

*340. Having on the white stole, he puts the interrogations: "Joannes, Maria, etc.: *Credis in Deum Patrem,*" etc. The interrogations on the chief articles of the Creed were put to catechumens when they were just beside the font about to receive baptism, as appears from the ancient ceremonials cited by Martene.[4] They were often put so as to require a full and explicit profession of Catholic doctrine, in opposition to some spreading heresy of the time, as Arianism, Nestorianism, etc.[5]

341. The practice in these countries has been to put those questions in the vernacular, or at least to repeat them in the vernacular. Catalani says[6] that the vernacular should be used here, and also in the renunciations above mentioned, citing as his authority the statutes of St. Boniface, Archbishop of Mentz. But there can be no doubt that, according to the decision of the Sacred Congregation already cited, they are to be put in Latin, for that decision comprehends all the interrogations for which formulæ are given in the ritual.[7]

§ XVI.—Subinde expresso nomine baptizandi, Sacerdos dicit: N. *Vis baptizari?* Respondet Patrinus: *Volo.*

342. On this rubric it is enough to cite the words of the Catechism of the Council of Trent: "When the sacrament is "now to be administered, the priest asks the person to be "initiated if he will be baptized; and on receiving an answer "in the affirmative from him, or, if an infant, from the spon- "sor, he immediately performs the salutary ablution, in the "name of the Father, and of the Son, and of the Holy "Ghost: for as, by voluntary obedience to the serpent, man "justly incurred sentence of condemnation, so the Lord will "have none but the voluntary soldier enrolled under his

---

1 Romæ, 1752.   2 Tit. ii. cap. ii. § xv. xvi. n. i.
3 Rit. Toul., tit. ii. § i. n. 14.   Vid. supra, n. 279
4 Lib. i. cap. i. art. xviii.   5 Catal., tit. ii. cap. ii. § xvi. n. vii.
6 Loc. cit. n. x.   7 Vid. supra, n. 298, et seq.

" banner, that, by a spontaneous obedience to the divine
" commands, he may attain eternal salvation." [1]

§ XVII.—Tunc Patrino, vel Matrina, vel utroque (si ambo admittantur) infantem tenente, Sacerdos vasculo, seu urceolo accipit aquam
baptismalem et de ea ter fundit super caput infantis in modum Crucis,
et simul verba proferens, semel tantum distincte, et attente dicit.   N.
Ego te baptizo in nomine Patris, ✠ fundat primo, *et Filii,* ✠ fundat
secundo, *et Spiritus* ✠ *Sancti,* fundat tertio.

*343. To act as sponsor validly, and contract the spiritual
relationship, it is necessary to touch the child physically; [2]
and hence both sponsors, when two are admitted, are here
required to hold it while the priest pours on the water.   It is
held with the face downwards, and so that the water poured
on the head may fall into the sacrarium, or the vessel destined
to receive it, but by no means into the font. [3]

The Ritual of Toulon directs that the godfather hold the
child by the body, the godmother holding it by the feet. [4]   But
in places where it is usually held up by the godmother, the
godfather is required merely to put his right hand on or
under the child's right shoulder, and this is as much as is required by the word " *tangit,*" which is used in the canons, as
well as " *tenet,*" " *levat,*" [5] etc.

*344. The child being held in this manner, the priest
takes the water out of the font with a ladle or ewer, [6] and
pours it on the child's head, making with the little stream, as
it falls on the head, the sign of the cross at the word *Patris,*
another at the word *Filii,* and a third at the words *Spiritus
Sancti ;* being careful, as here directed, to pronounce the
form distinctly and with attention. [7]

The priest then dries the child's head, rubbing it gently
with a towel, which should be at hand for this purpose, and
used for no other. [8]

345. If the hair be thick, which, generally speaking, can
happen only in the case of adults, it is a useful precaution to
furrow the hair with the fingers of the left hand, while the
water is poured on with the right, [9] for, should it touch the
hair alone, and not the skin, the baptism would be at least
doubtful." [10]

---

[1] Pars ii. cap. ii. n. 72.
[3] Vid. supra, n. 181.
[6] Vid. St. Lig., lib. vi. n. 148.
[7] Vid. n. 167, et seq.
De Herdt, pars vi. n. 5, xvi.
[10] St. Lig., lib. vi. n. 107, *Quær.* iii.

[2] Vid. supra, n. 226.
[4] Tit. ii. § ii. n. 11, et n. 15.
[6] Supra, n. 275.
[8] Baruff., tit. xi. n. 44.
[9] De Herdt, n. 5, xvii.

§ XVIII.—Ubi autem est consuetudo baptizandi per immersionem, Sacerdos accipit infantem, et advertens ne lædatur, caute immergit, et trina mersione baptizat, et semel tantum dicit: N. *Ego te baptizo*, etc.

346. We have already seen that immersion is the mode of baptizing still used throughout the Eastern Church. It is prescribed by the Ambrosian rite, and as such is still used at Milan.[1] It is in use also in the cathedral and parochial churches of Benevento, as we learn from the Pontificale Romanum;[2] but, we believe, in no other part of the Latin Church.

The following minute instructions as to the manner of baptizing by immersion, are given by St. Charles:[3] "The "priest takes the child from the sponsor with both hands, "having the right next the head, and keeping it on its back "with the face up (*supinum*); then he dips the back part of "the head (*occiput*) three times into the water in the form of a "cross, pronouncing the words, 'N. *Ego te baptizo*,'" etc.

The "Ordo" including this rubric is given at length by Martene,[4] as well as in the "Instructions" of St. Charles just cited. In another paragraph of the same "Instructions," it is permitted to confer baptism by effusion on an infant in imminent danger of death.[5]

Great care, of course, must be taken, as our rubric directs, lest the child be in any way injured, as it easily might be, in baptizing by immersion.

§ XIX.—Mox Patrinus, vel Matrina, vel uterque simul infantem de sacro Fonte levant, suscipientes illum de manu Sacerdotis.

347. In the case of baptism by immersion, the sponsors do not hold the child while it is being immersed, but they receive it from the hands of the priest after it has been immersed, as the rubric here directs; and it is from this circumstance they are said "*suscipere*," "*levare de sacro fonte*," etc., while they are said "*tenere*," "*tangere*," etc., from what they are required to do in baptism by effusion.

§ XX.—Si vero dubitatur an infans fuerit baptizatus, utatur hac forma: N. *Si non es baptizatus*, etc.

348. Under a preceding rubric we have treated of the

---

[1] Vid. supra, n. 175, et seq.
[2] *Pontificalis Ritus pro Baptismo Adultorum.*
[3] *Acta Mediol. Eccles.*, pars iv. § *Ordo Baptismi Parvulorum*, pag. 417.   [4] Lib. i. cap. i. art. xviii. ord. xxi.
[5] § *De modo administrandi Baptismum*, pag. 411.

conditional form, and the circumstances in which it is to be used,[1] and we need not repeat what has there been said on the necessity of careful inquiry in every case of doubt.

§ XXI.—Deinde intingit pollicem in sacro Chrismate, et ungit infantem in summitate capitis in modum Crucis, dicens: *Deus Omnipotens, Pater Domini nostri Jesu Christi, qui te regeneravit ex aqua et Spiritu Sancto, quique dedit tibi remissionem omnium peccatorum* (hic inungit), *ipse te liniat Chrismate salutis* ✠ *in eodem Christo Jesu Domino nostro in vitam æternam.* R. *Amen.* Sacerdos dicit: *Pax tibi.* R. *Et cum spiritu tuo.*

*349. The child's head having been dried, the priest dips his right thumb into the little vessel of chrism, and saying the prayer, *Deus Omnipotens*, etc., anoints the crown of the head in the form of a cross, at the words, " *Ipse te liniat Chrismate salutis* ✠ *in eodem,*" etc.

We have already treated of this vertical unction with chrism, its antiquity, and the probable cause of its introduction.[2] Here we shall merely add the explanation of the ceremony given by the Catechism of the Council of Trent: "The person being now baptized, the priest anoints with "chrism the crown of his head, to give him to understand "that from that day he is united as a member to Christ, his "head, and ingrafted on his body; and that therefore is he "called a Christian from Christ, but Christ from chrism. St. "Ambrose observes that what indeed the chrism signifies, the "prayers then offered by the priest sufficiently explain."[3]

§ XXII.—Tum bombacio, aut re simili abstergit pollicem suum, et locum inunctum, et imponit capiti ejus linteolum candidum loco vestis albæ, dicens: *Accipe vestem,* etc.

350. Here, as well as after the unction with the oil of catechumens,[4] he uses only a little cotton or other such material for removing the oil; but at the end of the ceremony he uses crumbs of bread, to rub off any that might still adhere to his fingers.[5]

351. According to Martene, a small veil or fillet was formerly tied on the head of the baptized immediately after the unction with chrism.[6] Baruffaldi[7] says this was in use till the end of the eleventh century, when the practice was introduced of rubbing off the chrism immediately after its application, as here directed in the rubric. Catalani, however, on the present

---

[1] Supra, 173–174.   [2] Vid. supra, n. 248.   [3] Pars ii. cap. ii. n. 73.
[4] Supra, n. 338.   [5] Vid. infra, xxiv.
[6] *De Ant. Eccl. Rit.*, lib. i. cap. i. art. xv. n. vi.   [7] Tit. xi. n. 52

rubric,[1] maintains that there was no veil or fillet in use distinct from the white garment which is here mentioned; otherwise, he says, there should be a special form to be used in putting it on, whereas there is no form prescribed but the one, *Accipe vestem*, etc.   This reason does not appear to be of great weight.   The distinct veil is prescribed in the order for the baptism of adults, as Catalani himself observes in his commentary on the rubric that refers to it,[2] and yet no form is there given, except the *Accipe vestem*, etc.[3]

This veil was probably of the same kind as that which is ordered by the rubric of the Pontifical, to be tied on the head after confirmation, and which, according to ancient usage, was worn for seven days,[4] though the time was afterwards shortened; and in the end it became usual to dispense with the bands altogether, and to wipe off the chrism immediately after the bishop conferred the sacrament.[5]

*352. The newly-baptized were clothed in white garments, which they continued to wear for some time after baptism, as is expressly mentioned by St. Ambrose, *De Mysteriis*, cap. 7; St. Augustine, *serm.* 223, *qui est 5 in Vig. Pasch.*; and other ancient writers cited by Martene.[6]   The vigils of Easter and Pentecost were, as we have seen,[7] the great days fixed for the solemn administration of baptism.   The neophytes wore the white garments in which they were clothed on Easter eve, until the Saturday following, which, from this circumstance, was called "Sabbatum in Albis," the next day being called "Dominica in Albis," probably because they did not lay aside the white garments until after the Sunday.[8] It is highly probable that the name "Whitsunday," or Whitsuntide," by which Pentecost Sunday is known in England, owes its origin in like manner to the white garments worn by those who were baptized on the vigil.[9]

*353. We have a vestige of this ancient observance in the ceremony prescribed by the present rubric, as indeed the rubric itself clearly indicates, when it says that the "linteolum candidum" is "loco vestis albæ."   A small piece of clean linen serves for the purpose, and it is usually presented by

---

[1] Tit. ii. cap. ii. § xxiii. n. vi.   [2] Tit. ii. cap. iv. § liii. n. i. et ii.
[3] Vid. infra, cap. vi. § xxxviii.   [4] Catalani, *Pontificale Romanum Commentariis Illustratum*, pars prima, tit. i. § viii. n. i.
[5] Catal., ibid, n. ii.   [6] Art. xv. n. v.   [7] Supra, n. 235.
[8] Fornici, *Inst. Liturg.*, pars ii, cap. 40.   *De temp. Paschali.* Vid Catal., *Rituale Romanum*, etc., tit. ii. cap. iv. § liv. n. iv.
[9] Wheatly, *Book of Common Prayer*, etc. cap. v. sect. xxiii. § 2.

the parents or sponsors; but, to guard against disappointment, there should always be one in the baptistery.[1]

"The Holy Fathers teach," says the Catechism of the Council of Trent, "that this symbol signifies the glory of "the resurrection, to which we are born again by baptism; "the brightness and beauty with which the soul, purified "from the stains of sin, is invested in baptism; and the "innocence and integrity which the person baptized should "preserve through life."[2]

§ XXIII.—Postea dat ei, vel Patrino, candelam accensam, dicens: *Accipe lampadem*, etc.

*354. The priest then puts into the hand of the infant, or, if he cannot do so conveniently, gives to be held by the sponsor,[3] a lighted candle, saying, "*Accipe lampadem*," etc. Reference is made by several ancient writers to the lights which the neophytes carried in their hands immediately after baptism;[4] and the present ceremony is what still remains of that ancient usage in the baptism of infants.

355. Some rituals, as that of Ghent,[5] require the candle to be lighted from the commencement of the ceremony. This, however, is not prescribed by our rubric, which merely requires that it be lighted when it is presented.[6] The words of the priest, in presenting it, contain an evident allusion to the parable of the virgins, who, "taking their lamps, went "out to meet the bridegroom and the bride;"[7] and the mystic meaning is thus explained by the Catechism of the Council of Trent: "A lighted candle is next put into the "hand, showing that faith inflamed by charity, and received "by him in baptism, is to be fed and augmented by the "pursuit of good works."[8]

§ XXIV.—Postremo Sacerdos dicet: N. *Vade in pace*, etc.

356. This parting salutation is supposed by some to be derived from the ancient custom mentioned by St. Cyprian,[9] according to which the minister gave a kiss to the newly-baptized, immediately after conferring the sacrament. Martene, however, found no mention of it in any other ancient

---

[1] Baruff. tit. x. n. 45.   [2] Pars ii. c. ii. n. 74.
[3] De Herdt, pars vi. n. 5, xx. Rit. Toul., tit. ii. § i. n. 20.
[4] Cfr. Martene, lib. i. cap. i. art. xv. n. ix.
[5] Cit. apud de Herdt, 1. c.   [6] Vid. supra, n. 283.
[7] Matthew, xxv. i.   [8] Pars ii. cap. ii. n. 75.
[9] *Ep.* 59 *ad Fidum*, apud Martene, art. xv. n. i.

writer, and supposes it to have been peculiar to the African Church.[1] Whatever may have been its origin, it is, at all events, a very appropriate conclusion of the ceremony.

*357. The priest should now take the piece of cotton, or other material used in wiping the parts anointed, and have it burned on a metal dish, or in some other way, so that the ashes may be thrown into the sacrarium; he should do this himself, unless there be some other in holy orders to do it for him.[2] Then he rubs his thumb, and any other finger that may have touched the holy oil, with the crumbs of bread, which a preceding rubric directs to be in readiness,[3] and washes his hands, taking care that the water used in washing them be afterwards thrown into the sacrarium.[4] After this he closes the font, and puts the holy oils into the place where they are kept.[5] In the meantime the child will have been dressed, and he should then proceed with the admonitions as directed below.[6]

358. The Ritual of Toulon[7] directs that, before the admonitions, the infant be presented at one of the altars of the church, where the priest, placing the right extremity of the stole over its head, reads the beginning of St. John's Gospel: "In principio erat Verbum," etc. This is also prescribed in the ancient ritual of Limoges, given by Martene,[8] and was a usual ceremony in many places.[9] The practice is still observed in several dioceses of France, according to Cardinal Gousset;[10] but it is evidently unauthorized by the Roman Ritual, and can be justified only by special indult, or by custom in the sense before explained.[11]

§ XXV.—Si vero fuerint plures baptizandi, sive masculi, sive foeminæ, in Catechismo masculi statuantur ad dexteram, foeminæ vero ad sinistram; et omnia pariter dicantur ut supra in proprio genere, et numero plurali. Verum prima nominis interrogatio, exsufflatio, Crucis impressio, seu signatio, tactus aurium et narium cum saliva, abrenuntiationis interrogatio, unctio Olei Catechumenorum, interrogatio de Fide seu Symbolo, et ipse Baptismus, inunctio Chrismatis, candidæ vestis impositio, atque accensæ candelæ traditio, singulariter singulis, et primum masculis, deinde foeminis fieri debent.

359. Baruffaldi seems to think that this rubric is practically of very little importance, for, according to him, nothing short

---

[1] Loc. cit.   [2] Rit. Toul., tit. ii. § i. n. 20.   [3] Supra, n. 280.
[4] Rit. Toul., l. c. De Herdt, n. 5, xxi.   [5] Rit. Toul., l. c.
[6] Infra, § xxix. et seq.   [7] Loc. cit.   [8] De Ant. Eccl. Rit., lib. i. cap. i. art. xviii. ord. xviii.
[9] Vid. Catal., tit. ii. cap. ii. § xxv. Append. n. xii.
[10] Vol. ii. n. 101, in fine.   [11] Vid. supra, chap. i. n. 76, et seq.

of urgent necessity, as in the case of the conversion of a multitude of infidels, would justify a priest in baptizing a number together in the manner here contemplated: "Nonnisi urgen-"tissima causa hæc Rubrica et ejus Regulæ sunt adhibendæ," etc.[1] This opinion is not maintained by any other writer of note, and it has evidently no foundation in the rubric. The rubric makes no such restriction, but simply directs what is to be done when a number are presented for baptism at the same time.

Baruffaldi cites Clericati in favor of his opinion, but, on referring to Clericati in the part cited,[2] it will be seen that he speaks of the case in which the sacrament is conferred on a number together,—"*unica vice et sub unica forma;*" and this, he says, though valid, is illicit, being prohibited by the Church, unless in case of urgent necessity,[3] though she permits the exorcisms and other prayers to be recited for a number together in the plural. And he gives in proof of the permission this very rubric of the ritual, "Si vero," etc.

360. A priest need have no hesitation, therefore, in availing himself of this rubric in order to shorten the ceremony, whenever a number of children are to be baptized together. There is no good reason why he should not, any more than there is why he should not avail himself of the similar rubrics, when a number of adults are to be baptized together;[4] or than there is why a bishop should not avail himself of the like rubrics in the Pontifical, which are very clear and explicit on this matter.[5]

361. There is some difficulty, however, in determining the exact meaning of the rubric when we come to apply it to the several parts of the "Ordo." The most satisfactory way of explaining it, perhaps, is to go through the entire "Ordo," and point out in detail, as well as we can, the changes that are to be made. We shall take as our guide in this the rubrics of the "Ordo Baptismi Adultorum," which, as we shall see, are very explicit on most points,[6] and those of the "Pontificale Romanum," which professedly give in detail the directions that are indicated here only in general terms.[7]

*362. First of all, when children of both sexes are to be

---

[1] Tit. xi. n. 56. edit. Ancona, 1757.
[2] *De Baptismo*, Decis. xxxiv. num. 1-3,
[3] Vid. supra, chap. iii. § xxiii.
[4] Vid. infra, chap. vi.
[5] Vid. *Pontif. Rit. pro Baptismo Parvulorum,* et *Pontif. Rit. pro Baptismo Adultorum,* in Pontificali Romano.
[6] Infra, chap. vi. § ii. et seq.
[7] Vid. *Pontif. Rit. pro Baptismo Parvulorum.* Rubricas in fine.

baptized, the males are placed on the right, and the females on the left; that is, as the rubric is usually understood, the males are placed on the right of the females, though there are reasons for understanding it differently.[1] The priest, then, vested and attended, as before explained, comes to the door or porch of the church, where the sponsors with the infants ought to be in waiting.[2]

*363. Commencing with the first of the male children, he puts the interrogation, "N. *Quid petis ?*" etc., in the singular number, and proceeds exactly as in the baptism of one as far as the words, "*ut templum Dei jam esse possis*," inclusively. He does the same with the next in order, and so on to the last on his extreme right. This is the order to be followed in baptizing a number of adults, according to the rubric of the Ritual.[3] It is also the order to be observed according to the rubrics of the Pontifical.[4]

An order of baptism for a number of infants together is given at full length in the "Epitome Ritualis Romani," published for the use of the clergy in Scotland.[5] It has the question, "*Fides quid* VOBIS *praestat ?*" and the exhortation, "*Si igitur* VULTIS," etc., addressed to all in common. We do not know what authority this "Epitome" may have, but, in this point, it does not accord with the Ritual or Pontifical.

*364. Then he says the prayer, "*Preces nostras*," etc., for all in common, and in the plural number. This prayer is expressly directed to be said in the plural for a number of adults;[6] and the rubric of the Pontifical, "Pro Baptismo Parvulorum," has in brackets the words, "In plurali pro omnibus," immediately before it.

*365. For "*hunc electum tuum*," "*hos electos tuos*" should be substituted in every case except that in which all are females, when the words "*has electas tuas*" are used; and the same rule is to be observed for the similar changes in the other prayers. The rubric of the Pontifical is very explicit on this: "Quod si fuerint masculi et foeminae simul baptizandi, omnia dicantur in numero plurali, sed in genere masculino, etiam si sint plures foeminae quam masculi."[7]

*366. It may be asked whether the names of all should be distinctly mentioned where the letter N occurs in the

[1] Vid. chap. vi. § viii.   [2] Vid. supra. n. 288, et seq.
[3] Vid. chap. vi. § viii.   [4] *Pro Baptismo Parvulorum.*
[5] Glasgow, Margey, 1859.   [6] Infra. chap. vi. § xi.
[7] *Pro Bapt. Parv.*, in fine.

prayers. We have seen no authority on the question, but we think they ought; at least, we take this to be most in accordance with the rubric. If the number, however, be very great, so that the names could not easily be remembered, we are inclined to think they may be omitted. Of course the name is always mentioned in the interrogations, for these are put "singulariter singulis."[1]

*367. We have already seen that the imposition of the hand, prescribed by the rubric, does not require physical contact;[2] and hence it might be inferred that, in the present case, it is enough to extend the hand over all in common. Besides, "manus impositio" is not mentioned among the ceremonies to be applied "singulariter singulis," from which De Herdt infers that it may here be applied to all in common.[3] We had no doubt about the correctness of this conclusion till we referred to the rubric of the Pontifical, which distinctly prescribes that the hand be imposed here, "singulariter singulis." This must be looked on as decisive, however specious the above reasons may be; for the Pontifical[4] professes to give in the proper places the directions which are put together here in the ritual, and there is no reason to suppose that the ceremony as performed by a bishop differs in this point from the ceremony when performed by a priest.

*368. Having, then, imposed his hand on the head of each, he says the prayer, "*Omnipotens sempiterne*," etc., for all in common. This prayer is preceded in the Pontifical by the notice, "In plurali pro omnibus;" and in the "Order for "Adults" it is directed to be said in the plural for a number.[5]

*369. No change is made in the blessing of the salt. It is administered to each separately, with the words, "N. *Accipe*," etc. . . . . "*Pax tecum*," etc.

*370. Then the prayer, "*Deus Patrum*," etc., is said for all in the plural, and so is the exorcism, as far as the words, "*vocare dignatus est;*" the remaining words, "*Et hoc signum*," etc., being said in the singular, while the sign of the cross is being made on the forehead of each. All this is distinctly prescribed in the Pontifical.[6]

*371. The prayer, "*Æternam ac justissimam*," etc., is said for all in common; but before it the priest is to impose his hand on the head of each separately, as is prescribed here-

---

[1] Vid. supra, n. 296.　　[2] Supra, n. 301.　　[3] Pars vi. n. 7.
[4] *Pro Bapt. Parvul.*, in fine.　　[5] Vid. infra, chap. vi. § xi.
[6] Rub. in loc.

after in the Order for Adults,[1] and as is marked in the Pontifical.[2]

*372. Then placing the left extremity of his stole on the first of the children, or, if there be only two or three, placing it so that it may touch each of them,[3] he introduces all into the church, saying in the plural : N. et N., etc. *"Ingredimini,"* etc.

373. Having recited the "Credo" and "Pater Noster," with all the sponsors advancing towards the font, before entering the baptistery, he says the exorcism for all in common, *"Exorciso te . . . ab his plasmatibus,"* etc.

374. He touches with saliva the ears and nostrils of each, saying, *"Ephpheta,"* etc. In the present case it would be convenient to adopt the method before mentioned,[4] of putting some saliva in the hollow of the left hand. He would thus avoid the necessity of putting the thumb to his lips after having used it in applying the saliva to the first child.

*375. Having dried his fingers with a towel, he then interrogates each, "N. *Abrenuntias,"* etc.; and this done, he anoints each with the oil of catechumens, on the breast and between the shoulders, saying, *"Ego te linio,"* etc.

*376. Having then wiped his thumb and the parts anointed, he changes his stole, and proceeds to interrogate on the Creed and baptize them one by one.

*377. When all are baptized, he applies the vertical unction to each, and after he has applied it to all, he removes the oil from his thumb.

He then presents the white garment and the lighted candle, and gives the parting salutation, *"Vade,"* etc., to each in succession, and concludes with the admonitions to the sponsors and parents, etc., in common.

*378. For those who are often required to baptize a number together, it would be very convenient to have the "Ordo" with all the changes given at full length. In defect of this, we would recommend them to note the changes in the margin of the common "Ordo" in the ritual which they use.

§ XXVI.—Si infans, vel adultus ægrotus adeo graviter laboret, ut periculum immineat ne pereat antequam Baptismus perficiatur, Sacerdos, omissis quæ Baptismum præcedunt, eum baptizet, ter, vel etiam semel infundens aquam super caput ejus in modum Crucis, dicens : *Ego te baptizo, in nomine Patris,* ✠ etc.

*379. In case of necessity, or when there is danger that

---

[1] Infra, chap. vi. § xxiii.   [2] Rub. in loc.   [3] Vid. chap. vi. § xxiv.
[4] Supra, n. 329.

the person to be baptized may die before the preceding ceremonies could be completed, all that precedes the baptism
itself, that is, all that precedes the application of the matter
and form of the sacrament, should be omitted; and the priest
should at once pour on the water and pronounce the form in
the manner before explained.[1]

*380. If the danger be very imminent, it is enough to pour
on the water once, as the triple ablution is not essential;[2] and
it is hardly necessary to observe with Baruffaldi[3] that the two
ablutions omitted are not to be afterwards supplied.

*381. The case here provided for might occur even in the
church itself, as, e. g., when an infant that has been brought
to the church is observed to be in danger of death.   In such
circumstances, the priest should at once put on the white stole
and commence by pouring on the water, proceeding (unless
the infant be dead) with the other ceremonies to the end, as
directed in the following rubric.[4]   Then, if the infant be yet
living, and if it be not necessary to remove it from the church
to apply remedies or the like, he puts on the violet stole, and
supplies what has been omitted in the manner prescribed hereafter.[5]   This we take to be the order he should follow, for the
rubrics here are quite general, comprising every case in which
it may be necessary to commence by applying the matter and
form.

*382. When a priest, however, is called on to baptize, in
a case of necessity, in a private house, or in any other place
than the church, it is certain that he is not allowed to perform
any of the ceremonies which precede the application of the
matter and form, even though there be no danger of the infant's death until all the ceremonies could be completed.   He
should vest in a white stole, and, after pouring on the water,
apply the ceremonies which follow, leaving those that precede,
and for which the violet stole is worn, to be afterwards supplied in the church.   This has been expressly decided by the
Sacred Congregation.[6]   What exceptions may be admitted
we shall consider under the next rubric.

§ XXVII.—Si non habeatur aqua baptismalis, et periculum impendeat, Sacerdos utatur aqua simplici.

*383. If the baptismal water be at hand, or can be easily
procured, it ought to be used, as, e. g., when the case of ne-

---

[1] Supra, n. 344.   [2] St. Lig., lib. vi. n. 107, *Quær.* v.
[3] Tit. xi. n. 60.   [4] Intra, § xxviii.   [5] Chap. vii
[6] 23 Sept. 1820.   *In Calagur et Calceat.*, n. 4572.

cessity arises in the church itself, or in a house near it. Many
hold that, even in private baptism, there is an obligation *sub
gravi* of using consecrated water when it can be had. Gury,[1]
citing the Salmanticenses and others, thinks this the more probable opinion. But St. Liguori,[2] Lacroix,[3] and others whom
they cite, hold the contrary. St. Liguori says:[4] "In baptis-
"mo privato probabile est licere uti aqua non consecratâ."
It is practically certain, then, that the obligation of using
consecrated water in private baptism, is at most *sub veniali*,
but all are agreed that it is at least laudable to use it when
it can be had.

De Herdt maintains[5] that no one who has not deacon's
orders is permitted to baptize with consecrated water. But
the authors we have just cited make no distinction as regards
the minister, and seem to apply the same rule whether a priest
or laic administers the private baptism. St. Liguori, citing
the opinion of Collet, says that "baptismus adhuc necessitate
"domi conferendus, debet curari, ut fiat aqua benedicta sive
"lustrali ob majorem decentiam."[6] It rarely happens that
any other than a priest can get consecrated water, since the
font is kept locked;[7] but in case it can be had, we think it
should be used even by a laic.

When baptismal water cannot be had, the rubric here says
that he may use common water. Collet[8] recommends the
use of holy water in such circumstances as more becoming,
and approximating more to the practice of the Church. St.
Lignori, in the words just cited, seems to approve of this. It
would appear, from a statement in the "Revue Théologique,"[9]
that the use of holy water in private baptism by laics is com
mon in France and Belgium. But, whatever may be said of
local usages, it is evident from our rubric that, at least, there
is no general obligation to use holy water, or any other than
common water, when baptismal water is not at hand.

*384. It is not permitted, unless in virtue of special facul-
ties, to bless baptismal water anywhere except in the church.[10]
We have already seen[11] that the baptismal font should be
blessed according to the form prescribed in the Missal, on
Holy Saturday and the eve of Pentecost. At any other time,

---

[1] Vol. ii. n. 253.
[2] Lib. vi. pars i. n. 263.
[3] Pars vi. n. 3, ii.
[*] Vid. sup. n. 247.
in necessitate," etc.
[10] Or Baptistery, vid. supra, n. 239.

[*] Lib. vi. n. 102, *in parenth.*
[4] *Hom. Apost.* Tract. xiv. n. 8.
[6] Loc. cit. n. 102, in fine.
[8] *De Baptismo,* cap. iii. Art. i. " *Qui domi*
[9] IVme Série, pag. 24.
[11] Supra, n. 159.

should the font be exhausted, it ought to be blessed according
to the form given in the ritual,[1] and the rubrics of this form
clearly imply that the ceremony takes place in the church.
Even when, by special permission, baptism is solemnly
administered in a private oratory, the water is not to be
blessed there, but to be carried from the font of the parochial
church.[2] The present rubric provides for the case in which a
priest baptizes in necessity, and has not baptismal water, and
it tells him that in this case he is to use common water.
There is no rubric, then, or general law, as far as we know,
which requires, or even allows, a priest to bless water for
baptism outside the church.

*385. In missionary countries, however, and in places where
there are no baptismal fonts, special faculties are granted, in
virtue of which baptism is usually administered with all the
ceremonies in private houses, and the water blessed for the
occasion, if there be not a supply of what had been previously
blessed.

*386. During the operation of the penal laws, and until
very recently, such a custom prevailed pretty generally in
Ireland and England. But measures were adopted by the
Synod of Thurles,[3] and the first Synod of Westminster,[4] to
abolish the custom wherever the provisions of the ritual regarding the place of baptism could be conveniently carried
out.

*387. "Ob præteritorum temporum calamitates," says the
Synod of Thurles, "usus in hanc regionem inductus est
"baptisma in domibus privatis conferendi. Cum sine magno
"incommodo in pluribus locis hæc consuetudo aboleri nunc
"possit, præcipimus ut in locis prædictis hoc sacramentum in
"Ecclesiis, in posterum conferatur. Quod si infantes in
"periculo mortis sint, aut si longe degunt ab Ecclesiis, ita ut
"ad eas tuto ferri non possint, tunc morem jam inductum
"necessitas mutari non sinit."[5] This decree must be understood of baptism with the ceremonies before, as well as after,
the application of the matter and form, for this is the baptism
which was conferred in private houses according to the custom.
It is plain from the words that the old custom may still be
retained: 1° in places where it cannot be abolished "sine
"magno incommodo," and of this the bishop in each diocese
must, of course, be the judge ; 2° when a priest is called on to

---

[1] Infra, chap. ix.   [2] Supra, n. 241.   [3] *De Baptismo*, 7°, 8°.
[4] Decr. xvi. *De Baptismo*, n. 4.   [5] Loc. cit.

.baptizo an infant in danger of death, or at a great distance from the church.

*388. The Synod of Westminster also, while prescribing the observance, generally, of the law of the ritual, excepts the case in which baptism is administered at a station remote from the church or chapel, and visited by the priest either at stated times, or when he is called on.[1] In such circumstances, baptism is still administered with all the ceremonies, "*extra* "*ecclesiam.*"

*389. The custom prevailing in the United States of America was pretty nearly the same as in England and Ireland. The decree of the first provincial Synod of Baltimore, referring to the custom, directs that care be taken, as far as possible, to have the sacrament of baptism conferred in the church; but leaves it entirely to the bishops and missionary priests to determine the circumstances in which such a regulation might be enforced.[2]

It is worthy of note, that the decree, in its first form, ordered that, in towns where there is a church, baptism be administered only in the church, but was altered to its present form by direction of the Sacred Congregation. The words, which will be found with the decree in the Appendix, are important as showing clearly that the Sacred Congregation is unwilling to interfere suddenly with an established usage, even when that usage is opposed to the provisions of the rubric regarding the administration of the sacraments.

*390. When a priest, then, in any of these exceptional cases, baptizes solemnly, it may be asked what kind of water he should use. Of course, if he can get water from the baptismal font, he should use it;[3] but if not, is he to bless water for the baptism in the place where he is? We are inclined to think he should; for the water used ought to be consecrated water, if it can be conveniently obtained, even when baptism is conferred without the solemnities, as is plain from what has been said; and there is, evidently, a still stronger reason why it should be blessed, when baptism is conferred, as we here suppose it to be, with all the solemnities, though outside the church, for such baptism is really that " baptismus solemnis," in which, according to the common opinion, there is an obligation, *sub mortali*, of using blessed water.[4] "Curandum est," says Benedict XIV, "ne, extra

[1] Loc. cit. Vid. Decr. in Appendice.
[2] Decr. xvi. q. v. in Appendice.   [3] Supra, n. 383.
[4] St. Lig., lib. vi. n. 141.   Vid. supra, n. 158.

"casum necessitatis justique timoris ab infidelibus incussi,
"communis et naturalis aqua, vel etiam ea quæ pro lustra-
"tionibus benedicitur, in baptismi administratione adhibeatur,
"ac temere omittatur usus aquæ ad hunc præcise effectum
"benedictæ juxta præscriptum Ritualis Romani."[1] Now, we
are much mistaken, if the same custom which justifies the
administration of baptism with the solemnities in a private
house, or anywhere outside the church, does not justify also
the blessing of baptismal water in the same place, when a
supply cannot be had from the font.

*391. The form of blessing to be used in such circum-
stances is that which is prescribed in the ritual,[2] unless in
places where the use of a shorter form is allowed by special
indult.

392. In the United States of America, the form used is
one prescribed by the first Council of Baltimore, and approved
by Pius VIII. We give in the Appendix the form as published in the ritual for the use of the American clergy.[3] It
will be seen that, though very short, it does not dispense with
the infusion of the holy oils.

393. In an epitome of the Roman Ritual published for the
use of the clergy in Scotland,[4] there is an abbreviated form,
in which there is no mention of the infusion of the oils. A
form similar to this was in use in some parts of Ireland before
the Synod of Thurles. It consisted simply of the prayers
prescribed by the Roman Ritual for the blessing of the font,
omitting the Litany, the infusion of the oils, and, of course,
the words to be used in the infusion.

*394. We may conclude, then, that in any diocese or dis-
trict where an abbreviated form of blessing is in use with the
knowledge and approval of the bishop, it may be used in the
case we are now considering; while in other places the form
given in the Roman Ritual must be adhered to.

395. The decree of the Synod of Thurles, cited in a
previous part,[5] would seem, at first sight, to prevent in
Ireland the use of any other form than that of the Roman
Ritual; but probably it may be understood with the limitation expressed in the preceding paragraph, n. 7, which we
have given above;[6] and in this sense it would not extend to
the cases in which the synod itself permits the custom of

[1] Constit. *Inter omnigenas*, § 20.
[2] Editio Tertia. Baltimori, 1860.
[3] Supra, n. 238.
[4] Infra, chap. ix.
[5] Glasgow, Margey, 1859.
[6] Supra, n. 387.

baptizing solemnly in private houses to be continued, and in which it may be necessary to bless water for the occasion. In these cases it would still be left to the bishop to determine how far it is necessary or expedient to continue the observance of the old custom, as regards the blessing of the water as well as the other ceremonies.

396. Since the Synod of Thurles, however, other synods have been held; and in one of these, for the province of Dublin, the ceremonies are prohibited outside the church, and a strict adherence to the Roman Ritual as regards baptism, is enjoined everywhere throughout the province. " Si aliquando " contigerit Parochum aut ejus vicarium vocari ad baptizan- " dum infantem vita periclitantem in privata domo, is accepta " aqua benedicta de Fonte Baptismali (si tamen commode fieri " potest) statim accedat, et Baptismum administret absque " cæremoniis in Rituali Romano præscriptis, quæ tamen, si " baptizatus postea vixerit, et cum primum convaluerit, in " Ecclesia suppleri omnino debeant, servatâ in omnibus " Decreti 23 Septembris 1823 formâ editi a Sacra Congrega- " tione Rituum."[1]

*397. Wherever, then, in Ireland, the old custom has been thus expressly abolished, the priest, when required to baptize outside the church, must adhere to the present rubrics, omitting the ceremonies that precede baptism, and using common water when he cannot get water from the font.[2]

§ XXVIII.—Deinde, si habeat Chrisma, liniat eum in vertice, dicens : *Deus Omnipotens*, etc.

Postea dat ei linteolum candidum, dicens : *Accipe vestem*, etc.

Ac demum dat ei ceream candelam accensam, dicens : *Accipe lampadem*, etc.

Si supervixerit, suppleantur alii ritus omissi.

*398. It is plain from this rubric that all the ceremonies which follow the application of the matter and form, and which have been treated of above,[3] should, if they can conveniently, be performed by the priest, even when he baptizes in necessity outside the church. It may easily happen that he has not with him the holy chrism, nor does the rubric impose any obligation of bringing it with him when he is called on to baptize in such circumstances; but if he has it with him—" si

---

[1] *Acta et Decreta Conc. Prov. Dublinen.* Dublini habiti mense Junio, 1853. *Decr.* 10. The Decree of the S. C. R. referred to is, no doubt, the one that has been cited above, n. 382, and will be found in the Appendix, so that 1823 must be a misprint for 1820.

[2] Vid. supra, p. 383.   [3] Supra, n. 349, et seq.

"habeat Chrisma"—he should use it, and not wait till the child, if it survives, be afterwards brought to the church.

*399. If he has not the chrism, it may be asked whether he should at least perform the other ceremonies, of presenting the garment and the lighted candle. We have not seen this question discussed, but we believe that in such circumstances it is the usual and the approved course to leave all to be afterwards supplied in the church in the manner directed by the ritual.[1]

§ XXIX.—Admonendi sunt Susceptores de spirituali cognatione quam contraxerunt cum baptizato, baptizatique patre et matre; quæ cognatio impedit Matrimonium, ac dirimit.

*400. Baruffaldi observes[2] that it may be useful sometimes to give this admonition to the sponsors before the ceremony commences, for some might be unwilling to act as sponsors if they knew the relationship they were about to contract, and the matrimonial impediment resulting from it. But, however they may have been instructed on the subject previously, the priest must not omit, at the conclusion of the ceremony, to give them the admonition here prescribed, telling them that they have contracted a spiritual relationship with the child and its parents, such as to prevent a marriage between the godfather and the child, or its mother; and between the godmother and the child, or its father. This is the precise extent of the impediment which results, and which renders such marriage null, unless a dispensation has been previously obtained;[3] but no impediment arises between the sponsors themselves.[4]

401. It has been already stated[5] how the relationship affects the minister; but no relationship, and consequently no impediment, is contracted by the sponsors, unless when baptism is administered solemnly, with all the ceremonies.[6] Although sponsors, if admitted in a private baptism, contract no impediment,[7] it must not be supposed that baptism in a private house with all the ceremonies, such as we have before mentioned,[8] is to be regarded as a private baptism.

402. The impediment is not contracted by those who act as sponsors when the ceremonies are merely supplied, according to an express declaration of the Sacred Congregation of

---

[1] Vid. infra, chap. vii.   [2] Tit. xi. n. 62.
[3] Carrière, *De Matrimonio*, n. 679.   [4] Ibid.
[5] Supra, n. 188.   [6] St. Lig., lib. vi. n. 149. Carrière, n. 684.
[7] St. Lig., l. c. Vid. supra, n. 227.   [8] Supra, n. 365.

the Conncil.[1] It is probably not contracted even when the same persons have been permitted to act as sponsors in the private baptism previously conferred.[2]

403. It is, of course, doubtful whether or not it be contracted when the baptism is conferred conditionally. In this case, if the doubt be merely negative, the impediment arises, according to the common opinion; but if it be positive, e. g., if it be known that baptism has been privately administered, though there is a doubt about its validity, it is very probable the impediment is not contracted.[3] In such a case as this, and generally when there is a solid probability, according to canonists and theologians, not mere probability of fact, against the existence of an impediment established only by the ecclesiastical law, St. Liguori teaches that it may be assumed practically not to exist, or to be removed by the Church.[4]

§ XXX.—Curet Parochus parentes infantis admoneri, ne in lecto secum ipsi, vel nutrices parvulum habeant, propter oppressionis periculum; sed eum diligenter custodiant, et opportune ad Christianam disciplinam instituant.

*404. Attention to this admonition is of the greatest importance, for experience proves that many infants are suffocated by being allowed to sleep in the same bed with their parents or nurses. This abuse was noticed as destructive to infant life, and prohibited as such from an early period by the canon law.[5] It was severely censured in several provincial and diocesan synods, and not unfrequently made a reserved case.[6] It was made a reserved case in a synod of the province of Armagh, held in 1670, under Primate Oliver Plunkett.[7] St. Charles, in the fourth Council of Milan, enacted that those who keep in the same bed with themselves infants of less than a year old, without adopting certain precautions, to be specified by the pastor, shall incur excommunicaton *ipso facto*.[8]

405. We have the more reason to admire the wisdom and tenderness of the Church in her efforts to ward off this danger

[1] Cit. apud Carrière, n. 682.   [2] Collet apud Carrière, n. 685.
[3] St. Lig., n. 151.   [4] Lib. vi. n. 901.
[5] Cfr. Reiffenstuel, lib. v. *Decretal.* Tit. x. n. 11.
[6] Baruff., tit. xi. n. 65. Catal., tit. ii. cap. ii. § xxxiv. n. iii.
[7] Cap. viii. *De Casibus Ordinario reservatis,* 2°. Vid. *Collections on Irish Church History,* etc., pag. 161.
[8] *Act. Eccl. Med.,* pars i. conc. prov. 4. *Quæ pertinent ad Sacramentum Baptismi,* pag. 110.

to infants, when we consider certain facts that have been recently brought out by the registration of deaths in England. It appears that, during the seven years, 1848–1854, of 8,277 who are returned as having died from "hanging and suffocation," 2,826, or more than a third, were children under one year;[1] and, although it is not stated, it can hardly be doubted that most of these were suffocated in bed. Dr. Lankester, in an analysis of the verdicts returned by coroners' juries in London, from 1st August, 1862, till the 31st July, 1863, states that, out of 1,080 inquests in all, no less than ninety were held on children who met their death, according to the verdict returned, by "suffocation from lying in bed with the "mother." Of these, four were newly born, seven between one and five years, and seventy-nine under one year. " In a "very large proportion of these cases," he observes, "the "mother falls asleep with her babe upon her breast, and the "child is thus suffocated in the act of sucking. Sometimes "the child is found dead between the father and mother. "In such a position, even when the clothes are adjusted "before sleep comes on, the infant is likely to be easily "covered over, by the restlessness of either of its parents."[2]

406. It would be difficult, no doubt, to insist on a strict compliance with what our rubric prescribes, amongst the very poor, who are badly provided with beds, clothing, etc.; but at least their attention should be called to the matter, and they should be earnestly exhorted to take all the precautions they can, in their circumstances, to guard against danger. St. Liguori[3] cites with approval the opinion of Collet and others, that if the infant cannot otherwise be kept sufficiently warm, and if the mother or nurse is certain that she is not in the habit of changing her position during sleep, the practice of keeping the infant in bed with her may be free from any fault.

XXXI.—Commonendi sunt etiam parentes, et alii, si opus fuerit, n filios Hebræis, aliisve infidelibus, vel hæreticis mulieribus ullo modo lactandos aut nutriendos tradant.

407. The mother is evidently bound by the law of nature to suckle her infant, and there must be a just cause to exempt her from complying with this obligation. The milk of the mother, and not that of a strange woman, is provided by nature as the nutriment best suited to the child. To with-

[1] Eighteenth Annual Report of the Registrar-General in England
[2] *Social Science Review*, June, 1864, p. 516.   [3] Lib. vi. n. 160.

hold this nutriment, then, unless for very good reasons, is to act against the dictates of nature, and to do an injury to the child, which, according to all theologians, is at least a venial sin.[1] Amongst the excusing causes, St. Liguori mentions delicacy of health, and the custom which may exist amongst persons of the same rank.[2]

*408. In all cases, however, in which an infant is confided to a nurse, care must be taken that a proper person be selected. The neglect of parents in this particular may easily amount to grievous sin.[3] It is not enough that she be sound and healthy, she should also be of good moral dispositions; and to make sure of this, as well as to guard against any danger to the faith or morals of the child, should it be in any way under her charge after the period of infancy, care ought to be taken that she be a good practical Catholic.

409. The qualities of the nurse have proverbially a great influence, not only on the health, but on the temper and dispositions of the child. It is not without reason that persons are often said to have imbibed such or such a disposition with their mother's milk. If it be true that certain dispositions are often transmitted from the parent to the child, we cannot be surprised if the dispositions of the nurse, too, are sometimes conveyed with the nourishment which she supplies to it. Whatever may be said of the question physiologically, there can be no doubt about the fact;[4] and it is the duty of the pastor to instruct parents in their obligations on this head, as is here directed by the ritual. It may be useful to remind them of these obligations immediately after the baptism of the child; but, as was before observed,[5] he may do so at other times, and perhaps he might do so with greater fruit, and with less danger of offending individuals, by speaking of the matter in a general instruction.

§ XXXII.—Antequam infans ex Ecclesia asportetur, aut Susceptores discedant, eorum nomina, et alia de administrato Baptismo ad præscriptam formam in Baptismali libro Parochus accurate describat.

*410. It is not without reason that the priest is here admonished to make the usual entry in the baptismal register before the parties withdraw from the church. If he does not do so, he may easily forget the names, or even neglect the

---

[1] Vid. A. Lapide, *Commentarium* in Gen. xxi. 7.
[2] Lib. iv. n. 336, 2 in parenth.   [3] Busembaum, apud St. Lig., l. c.
[4] Cir. Catal., tit. ii. cap. ii. § xxxv. n. ii.   [5] Supra, n. 131.

matter altogether. Hence the "liber baptismalis" is reckoned amongst the things that should be in readiness when baptism is about to be administered.[1] The Synod of Thurles directs that the register be kept in the manner prescribed by the ritual.[2] It is unnecessary to dwell on the importance of accuracy in this matter, since the weightiest interests, such as the proof of marriages, the transmission of property, etc., may often depend on it.

§ XXXIII.—Additamentum.

411. Before concluding this chapter, it may not be uninteresting to note that, according to the ancient discipline of the Church, confirmation and holy communion were administered immediately after baptism, even to infants.[3] When the bishop himself baptized, he confirmed the neophyte immediately after baptism, anointing him on the forehead with chrism. It was to supply for this, in some way, when the bishop was absent, and when, therefore, the sacrament of confirmation had to be deferred, that priests were permitted to anoint the crown with chrism; and it was thus the vertical unction was introduced and prescribed amongst the ceremonies of solemn baptism.[4]

412. When baptism came to be generally administered by priests,[5] the newly-baptized, infants as well as adults, were presented to the bishop to be confirmed, when he visited the several districts of his diocese.[6] A good illustration of this is given in the life of St. Cuthbert, cited by Lingard.[7] Martene cites the decrees of several ancient synods, which order parents, under severe penalties, to present their children for confirmation when they have the opportunity. Amongst others, he cites one of a synod held at Oxford in 1287, which provided "that, if, through the negligence of a parent, a child "be not confirmed before it is three years of age, the parent "be obliged to fast on bread and water every Friday until "the child shall have received confirmation."[8]

413. This usage of administering confirmation, even to infants, as soon as convenient after baptism, was generally

---

[1] Chap. iii. § lii.   [2] *De Parochis*, n. 27.
[3] Martene, lib. i. cap. i. art. xv. n. xi. Bened. XIV, *De Synod. Diœc.*. lib. vii. cap. x. n. 3, et cap. xii. n. 1.   [4] Vid. supra, n. 248.
[5] Vid. supra, n. 184.   [6] Martene, lib. i. cap. ii. art. i. n. iv.
[7] *History and Antiquities of the Anglo-Saxon Church*, chap. vii. page 322.   [8] Loc. cit. n. vi.

observed throughout the Latin Church until the thirteenth cen
tury. After this time a different custom began to prevail,
and it was judged more expedient not to confirm children
until they had attained the use of reason.[1] "It is to be
"observed," says the Catechism of the Council of Trent,
"that, after baptism, the sacrament of confirmation may,
"indeed, be administered to all; but that, until children
"shall have reached the use of reason, its administration
"were inexpedient. If not, therefore, to be postponed to the
"age of twelve, it is most proper to defer this sacrament to
"at least that of seven."[2] This, then, is the general rule at
present.

414. But there are two cases in which the bishop may still
lawfully, and even laudably, confirm children before they
have attained the use of reason. 1° When an infant is in
danger of death. 2° When there is reason to fear that there
will not be an opportunity of having the sacrament conferred
for a very long time afterwards.[3] These exceptional cases
show, according to Benedict XIV,[4] that there is no opposition
between the Catechism of the Council of Trent, which gives
the general rule in the above extract, and the Roman Pontifical, which clearly supposes that infants may be confirmed, and
directs what is to be done when they are presented for confirmation.[5]

415. In the Greek Church there is still a rigid adherence
to the ancient discipline. The priest, immediately after conferring baptism, instead of applying the vertical unction, as
is done in the Latin Church, confers the sacrament of confirmation. He is directed by the "Euchologium"[7] to make the
sign of the cross with chrism on the forehead, and also on the
eyes, nostrils, mouth, and ears—the breast also, and the hands
and feet, according to some ordines, as in the ΕΥΧΟΛΟΓΙΟΝ
ΜΕΓΑ[6]—pronouncing the words, Σφραγὶς δωρεᾶς Πνεύματος
'Αγίου, "Signaculum doni Spiritus Sancti," which are the form
of the sacrament.[7]

416. It is true that a bishop is the ordinary minister of
confirmation, and that a simple priest has not the same power

---

[1] Benedict XIV. De Synod. Diœc. lib. vii. cap. x. n. 3.
[2] Pars ii. cap. iii. n. 18.   [3] St. Lig., lib. vi. n. 178. Benedict
XIV, l. c. n. 5, et seq.   [4] Loc. cit. n. 8.
[5] De Confirmandis, Rubricæ, § 1.
[6] 'Ακολουθία τοῦ 'Αγίου Βαπτίσματος. Cfr. Martene, lib. i. cap. i.
art. xviii. ord. xxii. et seq. et cap. ii, art. iii. n. x.
[7] Vid. Perrone, De Confirmatione, cap. iii.

of conferring it that a bishop has ;[1] but it canno be doubted that a simple priest can administer it, when he is delegated by the Roman Pontiff;[2] and Benedict XIV clearly conveys that the priests in the Greek Church are so delegated, at least tacitly, unless where there is evidence to the contrary, as is the case with respect to some districts.[3]

417. With regard to holy communion, it is quite certain that, according to the ancient discipline, it was administered to infants after baptism.[4] It was administered to them " sub " specie vini." At first it was usual to put the chalice to the infant's mouth, as may be inferred from a passage of St. Cyprian, in his book *De Lapsis*.[5] But afterwards a different practice was introduced. The priest dipped his finger into the chalice, and put it thus moistened with the sacred blood into the mouth of the infant, who would naturally suck it. In some churches the priest used, instead of his finger, a spoon, which he moistened and presented in the same way.[6]

418. It would appear from Martene that this use of the spoon was generally adopted, for it is still continued by the Greeks and other Oriental Churches that adhere to the ancient usage of administering communion to infants.[7] Goar, describing the present practice of the Greeks, says : " Cochleari, " quod Λάβιδα dicunt, sacro sanguine intincto, guttulam e " calice eductam pueri lingua exsugendam apponunt; et si " quidem extra liturgiam aliquem initiant ægrotis sacramenta " reservata depromunt ; sin liturgia celebretur, ex ipsis specie- " bus consecratis."[8]

419. In the Latin Church, the practice of giving communion to infants after baptism was common until the tenth century, and had not altogether ceased even in the twelfth, as is clearly shown by Martene,[9] and Benedict XIV,[10] who, however, observes that it had completely disappeared in the thirteenth. In reference to the ancient usage, as well as to the existing discipline, the Council of Trent has the following : " Denique eadem sancta Synodus docet parvulos usu rationis

---

[1] Concil. Trid., sess. xxiii. can. vii.
[2] Benedict XIV, lib. vii. cap. vii. n. 4.   St. Lig., lib. vi. n. 170.
[3] Cap. ix. n. 2, et seq.
[4] Martene, lib. i. cap. i. art. xv. n. xi. et seq. Benedict XIV, lib. vii. cap. xii. n. i.   [5] Cit. apud Martene, l. c. n. xv.
[6] Martene, loc. cit.
[7] Loc. cit. Vid. etiam, lib. i. cap. iv. art. x. n. xiv.
[8] *ΕΥΧΟΛΟΓΙΟΝ*, etc., *De Pueri post Baptismum ablutione*, not. 5, pag. 374.   [9] Loc. cit.   [10] Loc. cit.

"carentes, nulla obligari necessitate ad sacramentalem
"Eucharistiæ communionem; siquidem per baptismi lavacrum
"regenerati et Christo incorporati, adeptam jam filiorum Dei
"gratiam in illa ætate amittere non possunt. Neque ideo
"tamen damnanda est antiquitas, si eum morem in quibusdam
"locis aliquando servavit: ut enim sanctissimi illi patres sui
"facti probabilem causam pro illius temporis ratione habue-
"runt: ita certe, eos nulla salutis necessitate id fecisse, sine
"controversia credendum est."[1]

420. Besides confirmation and communion, it was usual, according to the ancient observance, at least in the Western Church, to administer also milk and honey to the newly-baptized, as Martene shows from the testimony of Tertullian, St. Jerome, and others.[2] Catalani[3] observes that this ceremony, as appears from a formula for blessing the milk and honey, given in an ancient Roman Ordo which he cites, was designed to signify, mystically, that the neophyte, having left the Egypt of darkness and sin, had entered the Church, a land abounding in spiritual blessings.

[1] Sess. xxi. cap. iv. *De Communione.*   [2] Lib. i. cap. i. art. xv. n. xvi.
[3] Tit. ii. cap. ii. § xxv. Appendix, n. x.

CHAPTER V.

ON THE BAPTISM OF ADULTS.—"DE BAPTISMO ADULTORUM."

§ I.—Si quis adultus sit baptizandus, debet prius, secundum Apostolicam regulam, in Christiana Fide, ac sanctis moribus diligenter instrui, et per aliquot dies in operibus pietatis exerceri, ejusque voluntas et propositum sæpius explorari, et nonnisi sciens et volens, probeque instructus baptizari.

421. We have seen that the Church requires infants to be presented for baptism with as little delay as possible;[1] but when an adult is to be baptized, she requires him to be previously well-instructed and prepared, so that there may be no doubt as to his intention and disposition in receiving the sacrament. Hence, according to the ancient discipline, all adult candidates for baptism were obliged to receive a certain course of instructions in the Christian doctrine, from which they were called "Catechumens," *i. e.*, persons under instruction. They were distinguished into several classes or grades, according to their progress; but there is some diversity of opinion as to the number of these grades, and the names by which they were known. According to Catalani[2] and Fornici[3] there were three: 1° the "Audientes," who merely heard the public instructions in the Church, and were obliged to leave with the pagans and public penitents, not being yet enrolled amongst the catechumens properly so called. 2° The catechumens themselves, also called "Genuflectentes," who knelt in the church, and over whom certain prayers were pronounced. 3° The "Electi" or "Competentes," who were judged fit to receive baptism at the Easter or Pentecost next following.

422. The duration of the catechumenate varied in different churches, and it does not appear that it was at any time fixed by a uniform discipline: it was left to the prudence and discretion of the bishop to determine it according to circumstances.[4] There was some diversity of practice also as regards the ceremonies observed in the admission of catechumens and in the subsequent stages of their probation; but

[1] Supra, n. 192. [2] Tit. i. cap. ii. § i. n. vi. [3] Pars iii cap. viii.
[4] Martene, *De Antiq. Eccl. Rit.*, lib. i. cap. i. art. viii. n. i. ii. iii.

is evident from Martene,[1] that, generally speaking, they included all those ceremonies that are still used by the Church in the solemn administration of baptism, though they were then applied at intervals during the preparation, and not, as at present, all together when the sacrament is conferred. The ceremonies were comprised under the general name of "Scrutinia," so called because they implied a careful scrutiny as to the dispositions of the catechumens.[2]

423. This ancient discipline regarding the catechumens naturally fell into disuse as the spread and establishment of Christianity diminished the number of adult baptisms, and it ceased, at least as to its form, in the ninth or, at latest, the eleventh century.[3] So far, however, as it required the instruction of the person to be baptized in the Christian doctrine and in the dispositions necessary for the worthy reception of the sacrament, it is still retained, and never was, nor ever could be, dispensed with. In the case of adults, instruction must always precede the administration of the sacrament, and this, as our rubric says, "secundum Apostolicam regulam," for so the Apostles did: they first preached and instructed, and then baptized. This rule is justly inferred from the words of Christ Himself: "Go, teach all nations; baptizing them," etc., as is observed by the Catechism of the Council of Trent, in the passage already cited.[4]

*424. By the world *adult* we are here to understand any one who has attained the perfect use of reason: "qui adulta "ætate sunt, et perfectum rationis usum habent."[5] This is presumed with regard to all who have completed their seventh year.[6]

425. The duty of instructing the catechumens was often performed by the bishop, but more frequently by priests, deacons, or persons in minor orders, and sometimes even by laics.[7] At present the missionaries in infidel countries are very glad to avail themselves of the services of any one who is himself sufficiently instructed to undertake the office of catechist;[8] and it is a matter of no great moment by whom the duty is performed, if it be efficiently performed.

426. Great care must be taken, according to the rubric, not

---

[1] Art. vi. per totum.   [2] Ibid. art. xi.
[3] Martene, art. xi. n. iv.   [4] Supra, n. 295.
[5] Catech. Conc. Trid., pars ii. cap. ii. *De Baptismo*, n. 35.
[6] Baruff., tit. xii. n. 8, et seq.
[7] Martene, lib. i. cap. i. art. v. n. ii.
[8] "Annals of the Propagation of the Faith," passim.

only to instruct the candidate in the Christian doctrine and precepts, but also to ascertain, as far as possible, his dispositions, his wishes, and intentions in presenting himself for baptism. "The faithful," says the Catechism of the Council of Trent, "are also to be instructed in the dispositions for " baptism, and are to be taught that, in the first place, they " must desire and purpose to receive it; for as in baptism we " die to sin, and engage to enter upon a new manner and dis- ' cipline of life, it is fit that it be administered to those only ' who receive it of their own free will and accord, and is " to be forced upon none. Hence we learn from holy tradi- "tion, that it has been the invariable practice of the Church " to administer baptism to no one without previously asking "him if he will receive it. This will even infants are pre- "sumed not to be without, for the will of the Church, who "answers for them, cannot be doubtful."[1]

427. An intention of receiving baptism is necessary in adults even for its validity.[2] In treating of that which is required in the minister of a sacrament, we mentioned the several kinds of intention distinguished by theologians,[3] and we may here observe, that in the recipient what is called the *habitual* intention suffices for the validity of baptism.[4] It might seem that the intention of receiving baptism, if it exists at all, could not be other than explicit, but yet it might be implicit. A desire of embracing the Christian religion in one who has yet heard nothing of baptism, would, according to De Lugo,[5] be sufficient for the validity.

428. To receive baptism, however, not only validly, but licitly and with fruit—in other words, to receive not only the character which it impresses on the soul, but the sanctifying and regenerating grace which it produces—certain dispositions are required besides the intention. What these are, we are taught in the following words of the Catechism of the Council of Trent: "Besides a will to be baptized, in order to obtain "the grace of the sacrament, faith also is, in like manner, most "necessary; for our Lord and Saviour has taught: 'He that "'believeth and is baptized, shall be saved' (*Mark*, xvi. 16). "Another necessary condition is compunction for past trans "gressions, and a fixed determination to refrain from all sins "for the future."[6]

---

[1] Pars ii. cap. ii. n. 38.   [2] St. Lig., lib. vi. n. 81 et n. 139.
[3] Supra, n. 137.   [4] St. Lig., l. c.
[5] *De Sacramentis*, Disp. ix. n. 130. *Valeret tamen.*   [6] Loc. cit. n. 40

429. The more perfect these dispositions are, the greater the grace that will be received in the sacrament;[1] and hence it is important that the candidates for baptism should be, as the rubric here directs, employed in pious exercises for some days previous to receiving it. According to the instructions drawn up for the use of the missionaries of the Propaganda, the time for the instruction and preparation of catechumens should not, as a general rule, be less than forty days.[2]

§ II.—At vero si quis, dum instruitur, in mortis periculum incidat, baptizarique voluerit, habita ratione periculi, vel necessitatis, baptizetur.

*430. This rubric provides for the case in which a catechumen is in danger of death before his instruction has been fully completed; and we are here led to inquire what articles he must know and believe, in order that baptism may be administered to him.

I. It is certain that he must believe "that God exists, "and is a rewarder to them that seek Him."[3] An explicit belief in this is necessary to the justification of an adult, *necessitate medii*, and without it baptism could not be administered to him in any circumstances.

431. II. He must believe in the doctrines of the Trinity and of the Incarnation. An explicit belief in these articles is held by many theologians to be, since the promulgation of the Gospel, equally necessary with the preceding. This opinion seems the more probable to St. Liguori, but he admits, as probable enough,[4] the opinion of others who maintain that the explicit belief of these articles is not necessary, *necessitate medii*, but only *necessitate præcepti.* Cardinal De Lugo discusses the question at great length;[5] and although he maintains this second opinion as more probable,[6] he concludes by saying that the explicit belief of these mysteries is necessary, *necessitate medii*, for the first justification of an adult, not indeed *in re*, but *in voto*, which he explains thus: To receive the grace of justification, it is required, *necessitate medii*, to have the desire (*votum*) of fulfilling all the precepts, and amongst the rest, of course, that of explicitly believing these mysteries. Now, in the law of grace, this belief is required, not simply as the fulfilment of another precept

[1] Vid. De Lugo. *De Sacramentis*, Disp. ix. sec. ii. n. 12.
[2] *Monita ad Missionarios* S. Congreg. De Propaganda Fide, cap. vii. art. i.   [3] Heb. xi. 6.   [4] Lib. iii. n. 2.
[5] *De Fide*, Disp. xii. sec. iv.   [6] Loc. cit. n. 91, et seq.

might be required, but as a positive disposition, at least for first justification; and, therefore, may be said, when it is not had *in re*, to be necessary *in voto*, just in the same way as baptism is necessary *in voto* when it is not actually received. "Unde," he says, "ultime addere possumus, cum Suarez, "fidem explicitam Trinitatis et Incarnationis esse in lege "gratiæ medium necessarium omnibus ad salutem, nam per "se loquendo, debet hæc fides præcedere susceptionem "baptismi; si autem aliquando non præcedit, hoc est propter "ignorantiam, vel impotentiam, et per accidens."[1] And again: "Cum fides illa per se præcedere debeat baptismum "nisi per accidens ignorantia vel inadvertentia, aut impotentia "excuset, consequens est ut sicut baptismus est necessarius, "sic et fides illa quæ baptismum præcedere debet, et sicut "votum baptismi supplet pro baptismo, ita et votum illius "fidei, quod includitur in voto baptismi, supplet pro eadem "fide explicita."[2]

*432. At all events, it is certain that baptism cannot be conferred on any one who does not explicitly believe the Trinity and Incarnation, unless in a case of extreme necessity. The Congregation of the Holy Office, being asked whether a missionary is bound, before administering baptism, to instruct in these mysteries an adult in danger of death, or whether it might not suffice to exact a promise that he would be instructed in them in case of recovery, decided: "Non "sufficere promissionem, sed missionarium teneri adulto etiam "moribundo, qui incapax omnino non sit, explicare fidei "mysteria, quæ sunt necessaria necessitate medii, ut sunt "præcipua mysteria Trinitatis et Incarnationis."[3] If he be at all capable of instruction, therefore, he must be taught these mysteries before he is baptized. But if we suppose the case of a convert from paganism, who explicitly believes in the existence of God and the rewards and punishments of the next life, and desires to embrace the Christian religion, but is suddenly seized with a fatal illness, that renders him incapable of being instructed, we think that baptism might and ought to be administered to him.

*433. III. He is required to know, at least in substance and according to his capacity, the Lord's Prayer, the Apostles' Creed, the precepts of the Decalogue, and the Christian

---

[1] Loc. cit. n. 106.   [2] Loc. cit. n 107.
[3] 10 Mai, 1703, cit. apud "Analecta Juris Pontificii," IIme Série, pag. 1805.

doctrine regarding the sacraments of Baptism Penance, and the Eucharist. Every Christian adult is bound to this under pain of grievous sin,[1] and no one should be baptized, unless in case of necessity, until he has learned them.[2]

*434. So much for what is of strict obligation. But we need scarcely add that every candidate for baptism should, as far as circumstances permit, be fully instructed in the Christian doctrine, as given in some approved catechism, and not only learn in substance, but carefully commit to memory, the Apostles' Creed, the Lord's Prayer, and the Angelical Salutation, as all the faithful are bound to do, at least *sub veniali*.[3]

These are the principles by which it may be decided how far, in any proposed case, the previous instruction may be dispensed with. There can be no doubt that, according to the ancient discipline of the Church, it was dispensed with in danger of death, not only in the case of catechumens, but even with regard to those who were not yet enrolled amongst the catechumens, provided they manifested, either by themselves or through others, a desire of receiving baptism.[4]

§ III—Adultorum Baptismus, ubi commode fieri potest, ad Episcopum deferatur, ut si illi placuerit, ab eo solemnius conferatur; alioquin Parochus ipse baptizet, stata cæremonia.

435. This rubric is a relic of the ancient discipline, according to which the solemn administration of baptism was usually confined to the bishop.[5] The Church desires to invest the baptism of adults with as much solemnity as possible, and hence the rubric directs that, if it be at all convenient, it should be reserved for the bishop himself; if not, that it be administered by the pastor with all the ceremonies hereafter prescribed.

§ IV.—Decet autem hujusmodi Baptismum, ex Apostolico instituto, in Sabbato Sancto Paschatis, vel Pentecostes solemniter celebrari.

Quare si circa hæc tempora Catechumeni sint baptizandi, in ipsos dies, si nihil impediat, baptismum differri convenit.

436. We have anticipated, in a preceding chapter, the explanation of this rubric.[6] Here we shall merely add that the delay of baptism, which it may not unfrequently require, is not always a sufficient reason for departing from it; since,

---

[1] St. Lig., lib. iii. n. 3.   De Lugo, *De Fide*, Disp. xiii. n. 63, et seq. 161, et seq.   [2] St. Lig. lib. vi. n. 139.
[3] St. Lig., lib. iii. n. 3.   De Lugo, l. c. n. 133.
[4] Catal., tit. ii. cap. iii. § ii. n. iv.   [5] Supra, n. 184,
[6] Vid. supra, chap iii. § xxix.

in the words of the Catechism of the Council of Trent, cited
by the "Monita ad Missionarios,"[1] "the delay is not attended
"with the danger already noticed in the case of infants; for,
"should any unforeseen accident render it impossible for
"adults to be baptized, their intention of receiving it, and
"their repentance for past sins, will avail them to grace and
"righteousness.   On the other hand, this delay seems to be
"attended with some advantages; for, in the first place, as
"the Church must take particular care that none approach
"this sacrament with dissimulation and hypocrisy, the inten-
"tions of such as solicit baptism are better explored and
"ascertained; and hence it is that we find it decreed in
"ancient councils that Jewish converts, before admission to
"baptism, should be some months in the ranks of the cate-
"chumens.   The candidate for baptism is also thus better in-
"structed in the faith which he is to profess, and in the practices
"of a Christian life; and the sacrament, when administered
"to adults with solemn ceremonies, on the appointed days of
"Easter and Pentecost only, is treated with more religious
"respect."[2]

§ V.—Verum si circa, seu post tempus Pentecostes aliqui conversi
fuerint, qui ægre ferant suum Baptismum in longum tempus differri, et
ad illud festinent, instructique ac rite parati esse noscantur, citius baptizari possunt.

437. It would be a long time to wait from Pentecost, or
soon after Pentecost, till Easter of the next year; and hence,
if there be any converted about this time, who would be unwilling to wait so long, the rubric permits them to be baptized
sooner, provided they be properly instructed and prepared.
"Sometimes," says the Catechism of the Council of Trent,
"when there exists a just and necessary cause to exclude
"delay, its administration is not to be deferred; as, for instance,
"when danger of death seems imminent, and particularly
"when the person to be baptized is already fully instructed
"in the mysteries of faith.   This we find to have been done
"by Philip and by the Prince of the Apostles, when the one
"baptized the eunuch of Queen Candace, the other Cornelius,
"without the intervention of any delay, as soon as they pro-
"fessed to embrace the faith (Acts, viii. 38, x. 48)."[3]

§ VI.—Catechumenus instructus baptizetur in Ecclesia, seu Baptisterio. Patrinus ei assistat, et ipse Catechumenus ad Sacerdotis interrogationes respondeat, nisi mutus fuerit, aut omnino surdus, vel ignotæ

---

[1] Cap. vii. art. i.   [2] Pars ii. cap. ii. n. 36.   [3] Loc. cit. n. 37

linguæ; quo casu vel per Patrinum, si illam intelligat, aut alium inter-pretem, vel nutu consensum explicet suum.

438. The rubric here repeats, with respect to adults, what is prescribed regarding the place for the solemn administration of baptism generally.[1] But the exception which is made in favor of the children of princes,[2] is not understood to extend to adults.[3] All that has before been said regarding the sponsors, their qualifications, duties, etc.,[4] applies to those who assist at the baptism of adults. The adult himself, how-ever, and not the sponsor, must reply to the interrogations of the priest, as the rubric directs, unless he is a deaf-mute or speaks a language which the priest cannot understand.

*439. A deaf-mute, if trained according to the method now adopted with so much success, can be easily instructed, and may answer to the interrogations in writing or by signs; but still we think the sponsor should answer for him as for an in-fant, and it would be obviously a great convenience if the sponsor selected were one who could interpret the signs and express them in words for the priest. If he has not been trained, since he cannot have received the necessary instruc-tion, the baptism must be deferred until he shall have been, in some way, trained and instructed. If there be no time for delay, or if it be found impossible to instruct him, some say he should not be baptized;[5] but others, whose opinion should be followed in practice, teach that one in such circumstances may be baptized. Either he is to be treated as one whose condition does not practically differ from that of children, or, at all events, he is not to be deprived of the chance which conditional baptism would give him.[6]

440. If he speaks a language which the priest cannot understand, the rubric directs that he should answer through an interpreter, if possible through the sponsor acting at the same time as interpreter. It must seldom happen that an in-terpreter cannot be found, if there be time to seek one; but, in case of necessity, baptism may be administered to any one who, even by signs, manifests a desire of receiving it.

§ VII.—Pro hujus autem veneratione Sacramenti, tam Sacerdotem qui adultos baptizabit, quam ipsos adultos qui sani sunt, convenit esse jejunos.

[1] Vid. supra, n. 238, et seq.   [2] Supra, n. 241.
[3] Baruff., tit. xii. n. 44. Fornici, pars iii. cap. viii.
[4] Supra, n. 218, et seq.
[5] Cfr. Ferraris, *V. Baptismus*, art. v. n. 132.
[6] Vid. La Truix, lib. vi. pars i. n. 291. Gousset, vol. ii. n. 92.

Quare non post epulas, aut prandia, sed ante meridiem, nisi ex rationabili causa aliter faciendum esset, eorum Baptisma celebretur.

441. According to the ancient usage, baptism was conferred, as we have seen,[1] only on the vigils of Easter and Pentecost, which were fast days; moreover, the neophytes were confirmed and received the holy eucharist immediately after baptism.[2] But it was not merely for these reasons that they, as well as the minister, were required to be fasting. This was prescribed also out of respect for the holy sacrament of baptism itself, as is plain from the fact that, when it became usual to administer it at other times, and without its being immediately followed by communion, fasting was still enjoined by several canons.[3] The present rubric recommends it, but is not understood to convey a strict precept. Of course, if the minister is to celebrate mass, and the neophytes to receive communion, according to what is said hereafter in the rubric,[4] all must be fasting. But, in other circumstances, what is here prescribed regarding the fast or the hour of the day, is rarely attended to, according to Baruffaldi[5] and Catalani.[6]

§ VIII.—Admonendus est Catechumenus ut peccatorum suorum pœniteat.

442. "The remission of all sin, original and actual," says the Catechism of the Council of Trent, "is the proper effect "of baptism; and that such was the object of its institution "by our Lord and Saviour is, to omit other testimonies, con"veyed in the clearest terms by the Prince of the Apostles, when "he says: 'Do penance, and be baptized every one of you "' in the name of Jesus Christ, for the remission of sins' (*Acts*, ii. 38)."[7]

443. For the remission of original sin no act of sorrow is necessary; and hence, if we suppose a catechumen never to have fallen into any actual sin, it is enough for him, in order to receive baptism with fruit, to have, besides faith and hope, the purpose of observing the precepts.[8] This, however, is a very rare case;[9] and it is certain that, if he has been guilty of grievous actual sin, he must have sorrow for it in order to obtain its remission.[10] The Council of Trent teaches that this

---

[1] Supra, n. 235.
[2] Baruff. tit. xii. n. 53. Vid. infra, chap. vi. § xlvi.
[3] Vid. Chardon, *Histoire des Sacrements*, liv. i[re] sect. i[re] part. 2[d] chap. ix. Marteue, lib. i. cap. i. art. iv. n. iv.
[4] Infra, chap. vi. § xlvi.
[5] Tit. xii. n. 55.
[6] Tit. ii. cap. iii. § ix. n. iii.
[7] Pars ii. cap. ii. n. 44.
[8] Suarez. *De Baptismo*, Disp. xxviii. sect. i. n. 5.
[9] Suarez, ibid
[10] St. Lig., lib. vi. n. 86.

sorrow has been at all times necessary for justification to all
who have defiled themselves by mortal sin, even to those who
seek to be cleansed by the sacrament of baptism: "Fuit
"quidem pœnitentia universis hominibus qui se mortali aliquo
"peccato inquinassent, quovis tempore ad gratiam et justitiam
"assequendam necessaria, illis etiam qui baptismi sacramento
"ablui petivissent, ut perversitate abjecta et emendata, tan-
"tam Dei offensionem cum peccati odio et pio animi dolore de-
"testarentur."[1] The catechumen then should be admonished,
as the rubric here directs, to repent of his sins.

*444. Unless we suppose the rare case in which baptism is
administered immediately after he comes to the use of reason,
it is certain that he is not free from all actual sin; and if, as
is commonly the case, he has been guilty of grievous sin, the
sacrament, though valid, will be without fruit, unless he has
at least attrition.[2] If he has committed only venial sins, it is
true the want of sorrow will not be an obstacle to the grace
of the sacrament and the remission of original sin; yet, since
no actual sin, however venial, is remitted without sorrow for
it, as theologians commonly teach with St. Augustine, these
venial sins will not be remitted, but will remain until he re-
pents of and retracts them.[3]

445. According to the ancient discipline, catechumens prepared themselves for baptism by a course of penitential
exercises.[4] They frequently even made a confession of their
sins;[5] but of course this cannot be understood of sacramental
confession, since no sacrament could be received before baptism.
It was an act of humiliation performed in a penitential spirit,
and, though not necessary as a preparation for baptism, was
most useful with the view of getting advice and direction as
to their future lives.

446. St. Thomas, for this reason, recommends that the
confession of those who desire it before baptism should be
heard. Having stated that, before baptism, there is no
obligation of making a particular confession of sins, such as
is required to obtain absolution in penance, but that it suffices
to make a confession in a general way, as is made by the
catechumen when he renounces Satan and his pomps, he concludes by adding: "Si qui tamen baptizandi, ex devotione,
"sua peccata confiteri vellent, esset eorum confessio audienda,

---

[1] Sess. xiv. cap. i.   [2] St. Lig., l. c. et n. 139.   [3] De Lugo, *De*
Sacramentis. Disp. ix. n. 36, et *De Pœnitentia*, Disp. ix. n. 13.
[4] Martene, lib. i. cap. i. art. x. n. ix. et seq.   [5] Ibid. n. xii.

"non ad hoc quod eis satisfactio imponeretur, sed ad hoc quod
"contra peccata consueta eis spiritualis informatio vitæ
"traderetur."[1]

447. "In baptism, not only are sins forgiven, but all the
"punishments due to sins and enormities are also benignantly
"remitted by God."[2]   Hence the exercises of penance
which precede baptism, are never undertaken or imposed as
works of satisfaction, but in order to correct evil habits, and
to prepare the catechumens to receive more abundant grace
in the sacrament.[3]   The only act of the virtue of penance that
is strictly required, is sorrow for the actual sins of which they
may have been guilty, with the purpose of avoiding sin for
the future.   Some theologians would require them to have
perfect contrition, but there can be no doubt that attrition is
sufficient.[4]

448. If any one, conscious of actual mortal sin, is baptized
without this sorrow, he does not receive the grace of the
sacrament.   He receives the character which it impresses on
the soul, and becomes subject to the laws of the Church;[5]
but his sins remain and will remain until he has the dispositions required, in order that the sacrament may produce its
effect.   As soon as these dispositions are present, the sacrament revives and produces those effects of grace, which it
would have produced the instant it was conferred, had the
dispositions been then present.[6]

449. If he has committed no grievous sin since his baptism, the same disposition, which would have sufficed for its
effect at the time of receiving it, will suffice still, that is to
say, attrition;[7] but if he has committed any grievous sin since
his baptism, either by knowingly receiving it without the requisite dispositions (which would be a sin continued and consummated after the moment of receiving the sacrament), or
by any other mortal transgression, it is necessary for him to
have either perfect contrition or attrition with the sacrament
of penance.

Baptism remits only original sin, with the actual sins committed before receiving it; and as these cannot be remitted
without the remission, at the same instant, of the grievous

---

[1] Pars 3, Quæst. lxviii. art. vi.   [2] Cat. Conc. Trid., l. c. n. 45.
[3] Vid. Billuart, *De Baptismo*, Diss. iii. art. v. *Petes* 4°.
[4] St. Lig., lib. vi. n. 139.
[5] Cfr. Collet, *De Bapt.*, cap. vii. art. ii. concl. 2 et 3.
[6] De Lugo, *De Sacramentis*, Disp. ix. sect. iii. n. 22.
[7] De Lugo, sect. iv. n. 52.

sins committed since receiving it, it follows that, in the present case, baptism cannot revive to produce its effect in remitting the former, unless there be concurrent with it the means of remitting the latter; and the only means for the remission of sin after baptism is, according to all, either perfect contrition or attrition with the sacrament of penance.[1]

450. It is not to be supposed that the sin committed after baptism must be remitted *before* baptism produces its effect; for in this supposition original sin would be remitted by the infusion of sanctifying grace *before* baptism could operate. We must here distinguish the presence of a cause from its operation. We can conceive the presence of contrition or of attrition with the sacrament of penance for an instant, *prioritate signi*, before the effect. Now this presence is enough for the reviviscence of baptism, for we have then not only the disposition which would have sufficed for its effect at the time it was conferred (or subsequently, if no grievous sin had been committed after it), but we have also present, and ready to coöperate with it, the means of remitting the sins committed since, and which it could not of itself remove. Both causes then operate simultaneously: baptism, in the remission of original sin and the actual sins committed before it; and penance, or perfect contrition, in the remission of those committed after it. All this is beautifully explained by De Lugo.[2] In like manner, if a person has received baptism without sufficient sorrow to obtain the remission of his venial sins, they will be afterwards remitted, both as to guilt and punishment, as soon as he has this sorrow.[3]

§ IX.—Amentes et furiosi non baptizentur, nisi tales a nativitate fuerint : tunc enim de iis idem judicium faciendum est, quod de infantibus, atque in Fide Ecclesiæ baptizari possunt.

Sed si dilucida habeant intervalla, dum mentis compotes sunt, baptizentur, si velint. Si vero, antequam insanirent, suscipiendi Baptismi desiderium ostenderint, ac vitæ periculum immineat, etiamsi non sint compotes mentis, baptizentur.

*451. We have already seen that the intention of receiving baptism is necessary in adults even for its validity, while other dispositions are required to receive it with fruit.[4] Now, in the present matter, all who have had at any time the use of reason are reckoned as adults, and it is on this principle the rubric here proceeds in its directions regarding the insane,

[1] De Lugo, sect. iv. n. 55, et seq.   [2] Sect. iii. n. 41, et seq.
[3] Ibid. u. 36.   [4] Supra, n. 427, et seq.

which are the same in substance as those given by the Catechism of the Council of Trent.[1] If they have been insane
from the time of their birth—in other words, if they have
never had the use of reason—they are to be treated as infants,
and baptized in the faith of the Church. If they have had
at any time the use of reason, then either the insanity under
which they labor is permanent, or it is broken by lucid intervals. If it be permanent, baptism is to be administered,
provided that, while they had the use of reason, they manifested any desire of receiving it, and in case of doubt it should
be administered conditionally; but if there be no ground for
supposing that they had any such desire, they are not to be
baptized. The same rule is to be followed if there be danger of death before any existing fit of insanity ceases. If it
be not permanent, however—if there be any hope that reason
will return—we should wait for the lucid interval, and then,
of course, baptize them like other adults if they desire it.[2]

§ X.—Idemque dicendum est de eo qui lethargo aut phrenesi laborat,
ut tantum vigilans et intelligens baptizetur, nisi periculum mortis impendeat, si in eo prius apparuerit Baptismi desiderium.

*452. What has just been said regarding the insane, is
equally applicable to those who are in a state of lethargy,
and therefore, for the time being, without the use of their
senses. They are not to be baptized until they recover from
that state, except when there is danger of death; and not
even then, unless there be some ground for supposing that
they had previously a desire of receiving baptism.

§ XI.—Sacerdos diligenter curet ut certior fiat de statu et conditione
eorum, qui baptizari petunt, præsertim exterorum: de quibus facta
diligenti inquisitione, num alias ac rite sint baptizati, caveat ne quis jam
baptizatus, imperitia, vel errore, aut ad quæstum, vel ob aliam causam,
fraude dolove iterum baptizari velit.

453. We have already dwelt on the obligation of the priest
to make careful inquiry, even in the case of infants, as to
whether they were previously baptized;[3] and the same obligation exists, *a fortiori*, in the case of adults, especially in
countries where there might be any reason to suspect that some
would ask for baptism through worldly motives, as has not
unfrequently happened, according to Baruffaldi[4] and Catalani.[5]
Instances of the kind can hardly occur, unless where there are

<hr>

[1] Pars ii. cap. ii. n. 39.   [2] Vid. St. Lig., lib. vi. n. 139,
et n. 81, in fine.   [3] Supra, n. 174.   [4] Tit. xii. n. 70,
[5] Tit. ii. cap. iii. § xiv. n. iii.

Jews or Pagans, who might hope to gain some temporal advantage by a pretended conversion to the faith.

§ XII.—Omnes autem de quibus, re diligenter investigata, probabilis dubitatio est an baptizati fuerint, si nihil aliud impediat, sub conditione baptizentur.

*454. When, after due inquiry, there remains any doubt as to whether a person has been baptized, the rubric directs that he be baptized conditionally, if there be nothing to prevent it, that is, if he be properly instructed and prepared. But the doubt must be a reasonable one, for every slight suspicion would not suffice.[1] In any case that may occur, therefore, it is necessary to weigh the reasons carefully; but, this being done, baptism should be administered conditionally, *unless there be a moral certainty that it was previously conferred.* This is the rule laid down by St. Liguori with regard to children that are exposed;[2] and being founded on the necessity of baptism, it manifestly applies to all about whose baptism any doubt is raised.

§ XIII.—Hæretici vero ad Catholicam Ecclesiam venientes, in quorum Baptismo debita forma aut materia servata non est, rite baptizandi sunt; sed prius errorum suorum pravitatem agnoscant et detestentur, et in Fide Catholica diligenter instruantur: ubi vero debita forma et materia servata est, omissa tantum suppleantur, nisi rationabili de causa aliter Episcopo videatur.

455. This rubric directs what is to be done with regard to the admission into the Church of converts from any heretical community. The chief difficulty in the matter is to ascertain whether they previously received a valid baptism. It was defined by the Church, on occasion of the controversy raised in the time of St. Cyprian, that baptism administered by heretics is not on that account invalid.[3] It was decided that, in receiving converts from heresy, a distinction should be made between those in whose sect baptism was administered with the proper matter and form, as the Novatians, and those in whose sect it was not so administered, as the Paulianists. The latter should be baptized, not the former.[4] The rule thus laid down has been always religiously observed in the Church.

456. In forming our judgment in any proposed case, we must be guided very much by the ritual, or the authorized

---

[1] St. Lig., lib. vi. n. 134.   [2] Lib. vi. n. 135, *Secunda sententia.*
[3] Denzinger, *Enchiridion,* n. 14, *Decr. Steph.* n. 16, *Conc. Arelat* n. 21, *Decret. Liber. et Siric.*   [4] Denzinger, nn. 16, 20, 21, 62, 63.

mode of baptizing in the sect from which the convert comes. This is clearly conveyed in the answer of the Sacred Congregation of the Inquisition[1] to a question regarding the valid ty of baptism amongst the Lutherans and Calvinists. If the essential matter and form are prescribed in the ritual as of necessity to be used, we are to assume the validity of the baptism, unless there be very grave reasons for questioning it. If not, further inquiry must be made into the circumstances of the case. Should it be ascertained that the convert of whom there is question, was, in point of fact, validly baptized, of course baptism is not to be repeated. Should it, on the other hand, be made clear that the baptism was invalid, he ought now to be baptized absolutely. But if, as is commonly the case, a reasonable doubt remains, he should be baptized conditionally.

457. The sectaries, then, may be divided into three classes; those who are certainly baptized, those who are certainly unbaptized, and those whose baptism is doubtful

I. At the present day no one, we believe, doubts that baptism is validly conferred, not only in the Greek Church, but amongst the Eutychians, Nestorians, and other Oriental sects; and the same is true, according to Bouvier,[2] of the sect known in France as "*La Petite Eglise.*" These sects not only use rituals which prescribe the essential matter and form, but also profess the Catholic doctrine regarding the efficacy and necessity of baptism, which is a sufficient guarantee of the care that is taken to have it properly administered. When a convert, therefore, from any of these sects is received into the Church, he is not to be baptized; but, as the rubric here directs, the ceremonies that may have been omitted are to be supplied, unless the bishop, to whom the matter should be referred, determines otherwise. A sufficient reason for omitting to supply the ceremonies would be the fear of exciting controversy regarding the validity of the previous baptism.[3]

II. Amongst the other sects that still retain baptism, there is not one, as far as we know, whose ritual does not prescribe the essential matter and form; so that, when there is not certainty, there is ground of probability that their baptism, if conferred at all, has been validly conferred. But in most

[1] 17 Nov. 1838, cit. apud. Falise. *Sac. Rit. Cong. Decreta,* etc. V. Baptisma, in nota, n. 7. Vid. Append.
[2] *De Baptismo,* cap. vi. art. 2, § 3.
[3] Cutal., tit. ii. cap. iii. § xvi. n. i.

of them may be found individuals who were never baptized, owing very often to the neglect of parents, who look upon the baptism of their children as a useless ceremony. When there is sufficient evidence of this in the case of any convert he is of course to be baptized absolutely.

Again, some sects reject baptism altogether, as the Quakers,[1] and converts from amongst them should, therefore, be baptized absolutely. The Baptists reject infant baptism, and baptize only adults who make a special profession of faith.[2] Converts from their sect are, therefore, to be baptized absolutely, unless it be known (as it may be, from their own testimony) that they were baptized in adult age, in which case they are, generally speaking, baptized conditionally, for the reason given below.

III. The class whose baptism is doubtful, embraces almost all the sects that go under the general name of Protestants. Most of them, it is true, in their rituals, prescribe all that is essential to baptism, and if we had sufficient security that it is always administered by them in exact accordance with their rituals, we should have no reason to doubt its validity. As a matter of fact, the validity of baptism by Protestants at first was generally admitted; and when a doubt was raised in France regarding that conferred by the Calvinists, St. Pius V decided in favor of its validity.[3] But their errors regarding the efficacy and necessity of the sacrament gradually led to habitual carelessness and frequent substantial defects in its administration, so as to leave reasonable ground for doubting in any given case whether it was rightly conferred. Hence the practice, now so extensively received, of baptizing *sub conditione* converts from the various sects of Protestantism,[4] though inquiry should be made in each case, as is done in Rome, according to a decree of the Inquisition.[5] Kenrick, who enters fully into this question in reference to the various sects in America, thinks that no doubt ought to be entertained about the validity of the sacrament as conferred by the Baptists; but yet, seeing that it is questioned by some whether they do not separate the immersion too much from the form, he does not quite condemn the practice of rebaptizing converts from amongst them. Having given his own opinion against it, he concludes by saying: "Rem sapientiorum judicio

· [1] Vid. Hook's *Church Dictionary*, v. Quakers.   [2] Ibid. v. Baptists.
[3] Cfr. Benedict XIV., *De Synod. Diœc.*, lib. vii. cap. vi. n. 9.
[4] Cfr. Perrone, *De Baptismo*, cap. v. in nota.
[5] Vid. "Decretum," prefixed to this volume.

relinquimus."[1] It is usual, then, and it is the safer course, to confer conditional baptism even on these converts, unless there be satisfactory evidence that the rite was duly performed.

458. If we could have sufficient certainty, about the baptism conferred in any Protestant sect at the present day, it would be about that conferred by the Anglicans, for the *Book of Common Prayer*, which contains their ritual, prescribes all that is essential to the sacrament, and, moreover, seems to convey the Catholic doctrine respecting its efficacy and necessity. Yet there is always sufficient reason to doubt, in any particular case, whether it has been actually conferred in the manner directed by the prayer-book.

A great many, probably the great majority, of the Anglican ministers repudiate the Catholic doctrine. A considerable authority amongst them, Whately, in his work on the *Book of Common Prayer*, denies the validity of baptism by laics, and says that the sanction given to it by the first reformers was founded on "the error they had imbibed in the Romish "Church concerning the impossibility of salvation without the "sacrament of baptism."[2] Many of them simply ridicule the supposition that the salvation of a child depends on whether or not it has been washed with water. The prevalence of this error amongst them was very clearly brought out by the Gorham controversy; and the decision of the privy council on that occasion leaves it free to every minister to maintain or reject the Catholic doctrine as he pleases.[3] Since, then, the validity of the rite depends on the application by the minister of the proper matter and form with the intention of doing what the Church does, it cannot be surprising that a doubt should be entertained whether it may not have been invalidly performed by men who confessedly think it of little importance.

Again, as a matter of fact, it is very often administered in a manner which leaves its validity doubtful. It is admitted that baptism by aspersion or sprinkling is valid;[4] but if the water which is sprinkled falls merely on the dress, it is certainly null;[5] if it falls only on the hair, and does not touch the skin, the baptism is at least doubtful,[6] and the same

[1] *De Baptismo*, cap. ii. n. 119.
[2] Appendix i. to chap. vii. sec. ii. pag. 356. Edition 1842.
[3] Vid. "Dub. Review," No. lv. March, 1850.
[4] Vid. supra, n. 178.   [5] St. Lig., lib. vi. n. 107, Quær. 3L.
[6] St. Lig., ibid.

is to be said if not more than a drop or two should touch the skin.[1] Now it is well known that very frequently the minister contents himself with dipping his finger in the water, and throwing one or two drops on the child, without much anxiety as to whether they may touch the skin, or merely fall on the dress. No doubt there are some ministers who are scrupulously exact in performing the ceremony as prescribed in their prayer-book; and if it could be ascertained in any particular case that a convert had been baptized by one of these, he certainly should not be again baptized; but as this can be very rarely known so as to leave no reasonable doubt, it is not surprising that, as a general rule, converts from the Anglican establishment, as well as those from other Protestant sects, are baptized conditionally.

*459. In this case, as well as when baptism is conferred absolutely, the ceremonies prescribed for the baptism of adults are to be observed; while those prescribed for infant baptism are to be supplied in the case of an adult Catholic who was baptized in infancy, but with the omission of the ceremonies. Both points have been decided by the Sacred Congregation.[2]

In the United States of America, until recently, the ceremonies prescribed for infant baptism were used in the baptism of adults also, in virtue of faculties granted by the Holy See. In 1852, these faculties were renewed only for five years, with an intimation that they should not be again renewed; and accordingly, since 1857, the American clergy are required to observe what is prescribed by the rubrics for adult baptism.[3]

460. In England, according to a decree of the first Synod of Westminster, adult converts are to be baptized privately with holy water, and without any of the ceremonies of solemn baptism: " Hujusmodi baptismus non fiat publice sed omnino " privatim, cum aqua lustrali et absque cæremoniis. Confessio " etiam Sacramentalis semper in tali casu est exigenda."[4]

461. In Ireland there is no indult, as far as we know, authorizing the omission of the ceremonies of adult baptism in the case of converts; or the substitution, for them, of those prescribed for infants. The provincial Synod of Dublin, in 1853, has the following decree on the subject: " Cum acath-" olici sub conditione sunt baptizandi, ritus in rituali pro bap-" tismate adultorum præscripti sunt adhibendi."[5]

---

[1] Ibid. *Quær.* vi. Vid. supra, n. 160.   [2] 27 Aug. 1836, in *Rhed. men.*, ad. 3 et 4, n. 4780.   [3] Cfr. Concil. Plenarium Baltimor., *Decretum* xxiii. et *Resp. Sac. Cong.*, in Appendice.
[4] Decr. xvi. 8°.   [5] Decr. 11.

*462. Before he is received into the Church, the convert must acknowledge and detest his errors, and be carefully instructed in the Catholic doctrine, as the rubric here prescribes; and hence some time is necessary for the due preparation. He should make a profession of faith publicly, or at least before some witnesses, as circumstances may determine. The form used is the Creed of Pius IV, translated into the vernacular; or at least an abridgment of it, such as is given in the ritual for the use of the American clergy. We have already seen that confession is not necessary as a preparation for baptism, though a private manifestation of conscience, with the view of obtaining advice and instruction, is very salutary,[1] and, therefore, may be recommended even to converts who are to receive baptism absolutely.

*463. Those who are certainly baptized, being already bound by the laws of the Church,[2] and coming to know, by their conversion, the obligation of confession, are clearly bound to comply with it like the other faithful, if they be conscious of grievous sin, and have not, as may be supposed, confessed within the year.[3] And even though the precept of confession might not, in strictness, urge at the exact time of their reception into the Church, yet this time is manifestly most suitable for confession, because they thus not only fulfil the precept, but have an opportunity of receiving that special direction which is just then so necessary for them, and is nowhere given with so much effect as in the tribunal of penance.

*464. Those whose previous baptism is doubtful, and who are to be baptized conditionally, are required to make a sacramental confession, as has been decided by a recent decree of the Holy Office.[4] Previous to this decision, converts in such circumstances were earnestly recommended, and, as a rule, even required, to confess, and were conditionally absolved. But many theologians held that they were not in strictness bound to confess, seeing that the doubt about their baptism makes it doubtful whether their sins could be the matter of sacramental confession.[5] It is true that sins after baptism, validly received, are not remitted without perfect contrition or sacramental absolution; and hence, the theologians who would exempt con-

---

[1] Supra, n. 445.
[2] Busembaum, apud St. Lig., lib. i. n. 154, et lib. vi. n. 665.
[3] Vid. St. Lig., lib. vi. n. 668.   [4] 17 Dec., 1868.
[5] Lacroix, lib. vi. pars i. n. 324. Vid. Gury, *De Pœnitentia*, n. 419 cum nota ibid. subjecta Edit. Ballerini.

verts, in the case supposed, from the obligation of confession, would require them nevertheless *either* to make an act of perfect contrition, *or* to make a sorrowful confession of some sin in order to get (conditional) absolution.[1]

Acting on this opinion, some confessors in England received converts into the Church without requiring from them a full confession of their sins, while the great majority required a full confession in accordance with the traditional practice, and the decree of the first Synod of Westminster.[2] In these circumstances, the matter was referred to the Holy See, and it was decided that a full sacramental confession should be exacted.[3]

465. The decree of the Holy Office, containing this decision, refers to and includes another on the same subject, issued on the 17th June, 1715, containing a similar decision, and prescribing also the order to be observed in conferring the baptism and giving the absolution. The same order is prescribed by the Holy Office in the form given in the ritual published for the use of the American clergy.[4] In receiving converts who are to be baptized conditionally, the order to be observed is,—first, the abjuration, or profession of faith; second, conditional baptism; third, sacramental confession with conditional absolution.[5] The absolution is to be given "sub conditione," on account of the doubt about the previous baptism; and, according to Gury,[6] it is of no great moment whether it be given before or after the conditional baptism. But the above order prescribed by the Holy Office directs that the conditional baptism shall precede the absolution.

*466. The same order seems to imply that the confession should be made only after the baptism. At least it clearly implies that the convert is not required to confess until he has been conditionally baptized. Yet there is no doubt that a confession before baptism, if the convert desires it or is willing to take it,[7] has many advantages. The priest is thereby better able to judge of his dispositions, and has also a better opportunity of giving him special instructions, of exciting him to sorrow, and preparing him to receive with greater fruit that sacrament, whichever it be, that he is now

---

[1] Gury, loc. cit. Vid St. Lig., lib. vi. n, 473, *Recte vero advertunt.*
[2] *De Baptismo*, n. 8°. [3] Vid. Decretum in Appendice.
[4] Editio tertia, Baltimori, 1860.
[5] Vid. "*Modus excipiendi*," etc. in Appendice.
[6] Loc. cit. n. 420. Cfr. Bouvier. *De Baptismo*, cap. vi. art ii. § iii. De Herdt,·pars vi. n. 8.
[7] Vid. supra, n. 445, 446.

capable of receiving. These considerations, it may be seen, are urged by the bishops of England in the preamble to the question which they submitted to the Holy See.[1] Hence the common practice hitherto has been: first, to hear the convert's confession and dispose him for the worthy reception of either sacrament; then, to baptize him conditionally; and lastly, having got him to repeat the confession, at least in general terms, and to supply whatever might be judged necessary to make it full and complete, to give him conditional absolution.[2] When, as is usually the case, the confession is made to the same priest, the penitent is not required to repeat the sins he has already confessed in detail, but merely to accuse himself of them in general terms.[3]

This practice may seem perhaps hardly in accordance with the order prescribed by the Holy Office; but we think it is not at variance with that order provided the confession before baptism be not exacted, but merely recommended. The order, we take it, is not to be understood as prohibiting all confession before the baptism, but simply as requiring that sacramental confession be made after the baptism; and this clearly is the case when the previous confession is repeated, in the manner supposed, before absolution.

467. It may be doubted how far special faculties are necessary, in this case, to absolve from the sin of heresy or the excommunication annexed to it. In the first place, the heresy may be only material, for it can hardly be doubted that amongst Protestants many are only material heretics. Reiffenstuel gives this as his opinion regarding great numbers amongst the mass of heretics.[4] The same is the opinion of Lacroix, and several other authors cited by him, with regard to the Protestants of Germany; and what is true of them is equally true of Protestants in other countries. "Some of "them," he says, "are so simple, or so prejudiced by the "teaching of their ministers, that they are persuaded of the "truth of their own religion; and at the same time so sincere "and conscientious, that, if they knew it to be false, they "would at once embrace ours. Such as these are not formal, "but only material, heretics; and that there are many such is "testified by numbers of confessors in Germany, and authors "of the greatest experience. What is most deplorable in "their case is, that, should they fall into any other mortal

[1] Vid. Decretum in Appendice.
[2] Cfr. St. Lig., lib. vi. n. 502.
[3] Vid. Gury, l. c. n. 420, in fine.
[4] Lib. v. *Decret.* tit. vii. n. 13.

"sin, as may very easily happen to such persons, they are
"deprived of the grace of the principal sacraments, and are
"commonly lost, not through want of faith (for I suppose
"them to believe what is necessary, *necessitate medii*), but on
"account of other sins they have committed, and from which
"they are not freed by the sacrament of penance, which does
"not exist amongst them; nor by an act of contrition or per-
"fect charity, which they commonly do not attend to, or
"think of eliciting (to say nothing of the very great difficulty
"such men would have in doing so), thinking they are justi-
"fied by faith alone and trust in Christ; and by this accursed
"confidence they are miserably lost." [1]

It may be assumed, then, that, amongst Protestants, there
are a great many whose heresy is only material; and it may
be added, that this is most likely to be the case with those
who are converted to the faith, the very fact of their conversion being, generally speaking, an evidence of the sincerity
with which they previously adhered to their errors. Now it
is *formal* heresy alone (*i. e.*, heresy to which one pertinaci-
ously adheres, though the true doctrine and the motives of its
credibility are clearly proposed to him) which is reserved to
the Pope, and not material heresy, even when the person is
guilty of grievous sin by his neglecting to inquire when
doubts occurred, or by his culpable ignorance, for this, though
it may be a grievous sin against faith, is not, after all, the
sin of formal heresy. It may easily happen, therefore, that
no special faculty is required for the absolution of these
converts.[2]

Again, since there is a doubt, as we suppose, whether they
have been really baptized, there must be a doubt whether
they could incur the censures of the Church. De Lugo discusses this question, and gives it as his opinion, that when,
after diligent inquiry, there remains a doubt as to the validity
of the baptism of one who is guilty of heresy, he is not to
be regarded as having incurred the censures attached to
heresy.[3] We look on it, then, as extremely probable that
the converts of whom there is question have not incurred the
excommunication annexed to heresy; and since the case is
reserved to the Pope dependently on the excommunication
annexed to it,[4] and since an ordinary confessor can absolve

---

[1] Lib. ii. n. 94.   [2] Vid. Lacroix, lib. vi. p. ii. n. 1613.   De Lugo,
De Pœnitentia Disp. xvi. n. 197.   *De Fide*, Disp. xx. n. 174, et seq.
[3] *De Fide*, Disp. xx. n. 143.   [4] St. Lig., lib. vi. n. 580.

from reserved cases when there is a doubt either as to law or fact,[1] it would seem to follow that no special faculty is required to absolve in the cases we are discussing, so far, at least, as the papal reservation is concerned.

*468. The practice is, however, to deal with all converts from heretical sects, as if they had incurred the reserved excommunication. Kenrick observes[2] that the Church does not acknowledge, *in foro externo*, the distinction between "material" and "formal," which would exempt from the reserved censure any one living in an heretical communion; and cites a decree of the Holy Office, reprehending one who, relying on that distinction, had absolved a Calvinist:—"Eo "quod ignarus hæresum et errorum Calvini non posset dici "hæreticus formalis sed tantum materialis."[3] The doubt whether a convert has incurred the reserved censure, may be expressed in the form of absolution, as is directed in the ritual for the use of the American clergy, by inserting the word *forsan* : ". . . . a vinculo excommunicationis quam *forsan* "incurristi," etc.[4]

Although bishops cannot by their ordinary power absolve from heresy,[5] they can do so in virtue of special faculties which they usually have from the Holy See. Besides, when any one who has publicly professed heresy solemnly abjures it, and penitently returns to the Church, the bishop is authorized, as delegate of the Apostolic See, to absolve him *pro foro externo*, after which he may be absolved by any confessor *pro foro interno* ;[6] or, after receiving his abjuration, he may remit him to a simple confessor, whose absolution, though only *in foro sacramentali*, avails also *pro foro externo*.[7] In these countries the bishops receive faculties to absolve from heresy, whether public or occult, and to communicate the same under certain restrictions to others.[8] When a convert from heresy, therefore, is to be received into the Church, the bishop should get notice of it, that he may himself receive him or send the necessary faculties to the priest who is to receive him.

§ XIV.—Cæterum legantur et serventur ea, quæ supra de Baptismo in communi præscripta sunt.

---

[1] Ibid., n. 600.   [2] *De Baptismo*, n. 243.   [3] Ibid., in nota.
[4] "*Modus excipiendi*," etc.   [5] St. Lig., lib. vii. n. 83.
[6] Reiffenstuel, lib. v. tit. vii. n. 369.   Bened. XIV, *De Synod. Diœc.*, lib. ix. cap. iv. n. 3.   [7] Bened. XIV, l. c.
[8] Formul. VI[a], 1° et 24°.

469. The rubrics that regard the matter, form, minister, the font, the holy oils, the vestments, and other requisites, of which we have treated in a preceding chapter,[1] apply to baptism generally, and must be attended to in the baptism of adults as well as in that of infants. The present rubric refers us to them, as they are supposed, though not repeated here.

[1] Chap. iii.

CHAPTER VI.

§ L.—In primis Sacerdos, paratis his quæ supra de observandis in administratione Sacramenti Baptismi Parvulorum dicuntur, indutus superpelliceo et stola, vel etiam pluviali violacei coloris, cum suis Clericis accedit ad gradus altaris, et genibus flexis, pia mente ad Deum preces effundit, ut tantum Sacramentum digne valeat ministrare, et ad implorandum divinum auxilium, surgens, se signat, et si temporis ratio ferat, dicit: ℣. *Deus in adjutorium*, etc.

Postea incipiat, prosequentibus Clericis, Antiphonam, *Effundam*, etc.

470. Everything being prepared, both in the baptistery and at the church porch, in the same way as for the baptism of infants,[1] the priest puts on a surplice and violet stole, and, if convenient, a cope of the same color. The Church wishes to have the ceremony performed with the greatest possible solemnity, and hence the rubric here recommends the use of a cope, even when it is performed by a simple priest.

471. The cope was originally a large cloak with a hood, used in processions, and designed as a protection from the rain: hence its name—*pluviale*. In shape it still bears a resemblance to such a garment; but it is usually made of rich material, and is worn in certain functions[2] to give them greater solemnity.

472. The words of the rubric, "vel etiam pluviale," might seem to imply that the stole may be dispensed with when the cope is used; but that such is not the meaning is clear from the general rubric regarding the administration of the sacraments,[3] and from the fact that, when the bishop officiates, both stole and cope are distinctly prescribed.[4] We take it that the "*vel*" is meant to convey that it would be becoming and proper for him, though he is not required, to wear the cope in addition to the stole. It is understood in this sense by Falise.[5]

---

[1] Supra, chap. iii. n. xlii. et seq.
[2] Vid. Baruff., tit. xiii. n. 3 et 4. Gav., pars i. tit. xix. lit. (d).
[3] Supra, chap. ii. § vii. [4] Infra, cap. viii. § iii.
[5] *Cours Abrégé*, pars 3ᵐᵒ sect. Iᵃ cap. Iʳᵒ § vi. n. 6.

473. The priest should be attended by at least two clerics vested in surplice, or a greater number, if possible.[1] When he wears a cope, he should be attended by three, and one should walk at each side holding the borders in front, while he is proceeding to the altar steps, and again while going from the altar to the porch. This is prescribed in the ceremonies to be observed in certain solemn functions in minor churches, where the priest is attended only by clerics.[2] And it seems to be a general rule that, when the priest is vested in cope, and is moving to or from the altar, or elsewhere, two attendants should accompany him, raising the borders of the cope on each side. This rule, we think, should be adhered to in the present ceremony.

474. All, then, having vested in the sacristy, the first clerk precedes with hands joined, and the priest, accompanied by the second and third raising the borders of his cope, goes to the altar, and, having uncovered, kneels on the lowest step, the clerks kneeling with him,[3] and there implores the divine assistance in the sacred function he is about to perform, saying the "*Veni, Sancte Spiritus,*" etc., or some other appropriate prayer. Then rising, he says, if time permits, "*Deus in "adjutorium,*" etc., making on himself the sign of the cross, and proceeds with the antiphon, psalms, and prayers, as in the ritual, still standing at the foot of the altar,[4] and reciting the verses of the psalms alternately with the clerks.[5] These are very appropriate to the occasion, as is shown by Catalani[6] and Baruffaldi,[7] but are not strictly prescribed, as appears from the words of the rubric itself.

§ II.—Si plures fuerint baptizandi, hæc tertia Oratio dicatur in numero plurali.

475. When two or more are baptized together the last prayer, "*Da quæsumus,*" etc., is said in the plural, that is, we say "*Electis nostris . . . . edocti,*" etc., in the masculine gender, unless *all* be females. This is expressly prescribed in the rubric which precedes the prayer in the ·Pontifical. The words are: "In plurali pro pluribus et in genere mascu-"lino nisi omnes sint fœminæ."[8] The same rule is to be followed in all the prayers.

---

[1] Baruff., tit. xiii. n. 6. Vid. supra, n. 126. et seq.
[2] *Memoriale Rituum*, jussu Benedicti XIII. in Festo Purific., Fer iv. Cin., Sabbat. Sanct., etc.   [3] Rit. Toul. tit. iiime § i. n. 1.
[4] Baruff., tit. xiii. n. 8.   [5] Rit. Toul., n. 2.
[6] Tit. ii. cap. iv. § i. n. ii.   [7] Loc. cit. n. 10.
[8] *Pontificalis Ritus pro Baptismo Adultorum.*

476. Those who are to be baptized are frequently, throughout the ceremony, called in the rubrics "Electi." We have already mentioned[1] the classes into which, according to Catalani, the catechumens were distributed. Those who, after the scrutinies, were judged sufficiently prepared to receive baptism, were called "Competentes," or "Electi;" but, according to Baruffaldi,[2] we must distinguish between the two, as they were not called "Electi" but on the very day on which they received baptism.

§ III.—Deinde Sacerdos procedit ad fores Ecclesiæ, et stat in limine, catechizandus vero extra limen. Et si sunt plures, mares et fœminæ, illi ad dexteram Sacerdotis, hæ vero ad sinistram statuantur. Sacerdos interrogat: *Quo nomine vocaris?* Catechumenus respondet: *N.* Sacerdos: *N. Quid petis ab Ecclesia Dei?* Respondet: *Fidem.* Sacerdos: *Fides quid tibi præstat?* Respondet: *Vitam æternam.* Sacerdos: *Si vis habere,* etc.

477. Having concluded the psalms and prayers at the foot of the altar, he takes his cap, and having made a profound inclination, or a genuflection if the Blessed Sacrament be present in the tabernacle, the clerks genuflecting in any case, he puts on his cap, and proceeds to the porch of the church, where the person or persons to be baptized should be already in waiting.[3]

478. If there should be males and females to be baptized at the same time, they ought to be placed so that the former be on the right, and the latter on the left of the priest, as the rubric here expressly directs.[4] The priest then puts the interrogations as they are in the ritual.[5] The answers are to be given, not by the sponsors, as in infant baptism, but by the catechumens themselves, who should be between the sponsors, each one having his or her godfather on the right, and godmother on the left.[6] The first question regards the name which he is now to take in baptism, and not that by which he may have been previously known.[7]

It may be seen that, in the address of the priest, "*Si vis habere vitam,*" etc., we have at the end an extract from the Athanasian Creed, which is not found in the order of infant baptism.

---

[1] Supra, n. 421. [2] Loc. cit. n. 13, 14.
[3] Rit. Toul., l. c. n. 5. Vid. supra, n. 288.
[4] Vid. infra, § viii. [5] Vid. supra, n. 297. et seq.
[6] Rit. Toul., tit. iiime § i. n. 5. [7] Vid. supra, n. 291, et seq.

§ IV.—Et rursus interrogat : N. Abrenuntias Satanæ ? etc.
Deinde Sacerdos interrogat de Symbolo Fidei, dicens: Credis in
Deum, etc.

479. We have already treated of the renunciation of Satan
and the interrogations on the Creed, in the order of infant
baptism.[1]

§ V.—Tunc Sacerdos exsufflet ter in faciem ejus, semel dicens:
Exi, etc.
Hic in modum Crucis halet in faciem ipsius, et dicat: N. Accipe, etc.

480. The great antiquity of the exsufflations used in
baptism, and their mystic meaning, have been already noticed.[2]
The rubrics here plainly distinguish between "exsufflet" and
"halet," the former signifying that he blows, the latter that
he breathes, on the face, having the mouth, in the one case,
nearly closed, and in the other wide open.

This ceremony of breathing on the face is not mentioned
in the order of infant baptism. As the cross should be formed
by the breath exhaled, the priest must move his head so as to
describe it. He cannot, of course, pronounce the words while
he is thus exhaling his breath ; and it would seem, from the
position of the cross as marked in the ritual after the word
"benedictionem," that he should first say the words, and then
perform the ceremony.

§ VI.—Deinde facit Crucem cum pollice in ejus fronte, et in pectore,
dicens: N. Accipe, etc.

481. The forehead and breast are signed in the manner
already explained in treating of infant baptism,[3] the ceremony
here being exactly the same, though the form of words is
much longer. The Ritual of Toulon[4] here observes that it
is not necessary to have the breast uncovered.

§ VII.—Et si Catechumenus venit de Gentilitatis errore sive de
Ethnicis et Idololatris, dicat: Horresce idola, respue simulacra.
Si ex Hebræis, dicat: Horresce Judaicam perfidiam, respue Hebraicam
superstitionem.
Si ex Mahumetanis, dicat: Horresce Mahumeticam perfidiam, respue
pravam sectam infidelitatis.
Si ex Hæreticis, et in ejus baptismo debita forma servata non sit,
dicat: Horresce hæreticam pravitatem, respue nefarias sectas impiorum.
N. Exprimens proprio nomine sectam, de qua venit. Inde prosequatur.
Cole Deum, etc.

482. The above is the form in which these rubrics are
given in the latest Propaganda edition of the ritual. In

[1] Vid. supra, n. 332, et n. 340.   [2] Supra, n. 302, et seq.
[3] Supra, n. 307.   [4] Loc. cit. n. 9. Vid. supra, n. 308.

many other additions, they are given in a somewhat different form, but what they prescribe is exactly the same.

The directions as to the change to be made in one clause, according to the errors which the catechumen renounces, are so clear as to require no explanation.

§ VIII.—Si plures sint Electi, omnia supradicta dicuntur singillatim super singulos.

483. Should there be a number baptized together, the priest must go through the preceding interrogations and ceremonies with each separately, commencing with the males.[1]

There is no doubt that the priest, having reached the door of the church, should stand facing the catechumens. If, therefore, we suppose that, while he is in that position, the males are on his right, and the females on his left, as a preceding rubric[2] might naturally enough be understood to require, he must either commence with the male on his extreme right, and proceed from right to left, which would be reversing the order usually observed in such circumstances, as, e. g., in giving Holy Communion, when he is expressly directed by the rubric to commence with those on the Epistle side;[3] or he must commence with the first male on his left, and proceed to the last on his right, and then pass to the females, commencing with the one on his extreme left. We would prefer the latter course, but it occurs to us that the rubric should rather be understood of the right and left of the priest, while he is standing, not opposite to, but in the same line with, or looking in the same direction as, the catechumens. We think this more probable; first, because of the inconvenience just mentioned as following from the other interpretation; and secondly, because, according to the other interpretation, the males would be on the left of the females, and therefore in the less honorable place, while the design of the rubric is, according to Catalani[4] and Baruffaldi,[5] to give them the more honorable place.

§ IX.—Si plures sint Electi, præcedens Oratio dicatur in numero plurali. Sequentes autem signationes fiant cum suis verbis singillatim super singulos.

484. The priest should be uncovered in saying the prayer, "*Te deprecor*," etc.[6] When there are more than one, it should

---

[1] Rit. Toul. n. 11.
[2] Merati, pars ii. tit. ix. Rub. 6, n. xxvi.   Vid. infra, cap. xii. § v.
[3] Supra, § iii. n. 478.
[4] Tit. ii. cap. iv. § v. n. iii.
[5] Tit. xiii. n. 19.
[6] Rit. Toul., tit. iiime § i. n. 11.

be said for all in common, and in the plural number. There is a change of gender only when all are females, according to what has been said above.[1]

At the end of the prayer the priest puts on his cap,[2] and proceeds to make the following signs of the cross, which are here directed to be made on each in case there be a number.

§ X.—Deinde signet Electum signo Crucis cum pollice in fronte, dicens: *Signo tibi*, etc. . . . In auribus. . . . In oculis. . . . In naribus. . . . In ore. . . . In pectore. . . . In scapulis. . . . In toto corpore, illud non tangens, manu producit signum Crucis, et dicit: *Signo te totum*, etc. . . . *Oremus. Preces nostras*, etc.

485. The signs of the cross here prescribed are not found in the order for infants, but they are prescribed in very ancient rituals.[3] The form used with each sign in the present ceremony explains its meaning and object. We may observe that the signs are made on each of the ears, eyes, and nostrils, in the same way as in anointing these parts in extreme unction.[4] The Ritual of Toulon not only directs this, but has two crosses marked at each, to show that they are double organs;[5] and the same authority[6] observes that the signs on the breast and shoulders may be made outside the dress. In signing the whole body, the cross should be formed with the hand in front of the catechumen, but not touching him, three times, as marked in the ritual, i. e., once at the name of each person of the Blessed Trinity. The first line should be drawn vertically from the person's head as low as convenient, and the second intersecting it across the breast, or from his right to his left shoulder.

§ XI.—Tunc imponit manum super caput Electi, et dicit: *Oremus. Omnipotens*, etc.
Si plures sint, hæc, et precedens Oratio, *Preces nostras*, etc.. dicantur in numero plurali.

486. After the signs of the cross made as directed in the preceding rubric, the priest uncovers.[7] Then follow three prayers, the first of which is the same as that used in infant baptism, except a slight change in one clause. Before reciting the third prayer (which is also the same as that used in infant baptism, with the addition of one clause at the end, "*ut idoneus*," etc.), he is directed to impose his hand on the

[1] Supra, n. 475.
[2] Cutal., tit. ii. cap. iv. § xii. n. i.
[4] Baruff., tit. xiii. n. 39.
[6] Ibid.
[2] Rit. Toul., l. c. n. 12.
Vid. supra. n. 305, et seq.
[5] Tit. iiime § i. n. 12.
[7] Rit. Toul., l. c. n. 13.

head of the catechumen; he should use his right hand, and it is enough that he hold it over, it is not required that he touch, the head.[1]

Should a number be baptized together, this prayer, and the prayer, "*Preces nostras*," etc., are ordered to be said in the plural. No mention is made of the second prayer, "*Deus qui humani generis*," etc., probably because it serves equally for one or more without any change. Also, if there be a number, the hand must be imposed on the head of each, as is here noted by Catalani,[2] and is expressly directed by the rubric of the Pontifical, which runs thus: "(Singulis) Tunc imponit manum super caput Electi et stans sine mitra dicit; (In plurali pro pluribus). *Oremus.* "*Omnipotens sempiterne*, etc.[3]

§ XII.—Deinde Sacerdos benedicit sal.

487. On this rubric see what has been said before.[4]

§ XIII.—Quod si Catechumenus fuerit Gentilis, sive ex Idololatria venerit ad Fidem; benedicto sale, antequam ejus medicinam gustet, Sacerdos addat sequentem Orationem, quæ tamen pro venientibus ex Hebræis vel aliis, ut supra, non dicitur. *Oremus. Domine Sancte,* etc.

488. When the catechumen is a convert from idolatry, this prayer is said immediately after the blessing of the salt, and before it is administered. When there are two or more such catechumens, the prayer is said in the plural; but should there be one or more of them amongst a number of others, we think the salt should be administered to the others first; then after this prayer, "*Domine sancte*," etc., to the converts from idolatry; and, lastly, when it has been administered to all, the following prayer, "*Deus Patrum nostrorum*," etc., should be said in the plural. By following this order, the prayer, "*Domine sancte*," etc., cannot even appear to have reference to any except those for whom it is specially intended.

§ XIV.—Tunc pollice et indice accipit de ipso sale, et immittit in os Catechumeni dicens: N. *Accipe sal,* etc., Sacerdos: *Pax tibi,* etc. *Oremus. Deus Patrum nostrorum,* etc.
Si plures sint dicatur singulis. N. *Accipe sal,* etc., et præcedentes Orationes, in numero plurali.

489. In some editions of the Roman Ritual this rubric immediately follows the blessing of the salt, and is placed be-

---

[1] Vid. supra, n. 310.
[2] Tit. ii. cap. iv. § xv. n. iii.
[3] *Pro Bapt. Adultorum.*
[4] Supra, n. 270, et seq. n. 311, et seq.

fore the preceding rubric, "Quod si Catechumenus," etc. It
is so placed by Baruffaldi and Catalani, in their commentaries.[1]

The quantity of blessed salt usually given to infants
suffices for adults also, but there need not be so much anxiety
about it, as there is less danger of doing injury to adults.
Even the rubric here has not the word "modicum," which it
has in speaking of the quantity to be given to infants.[2]

It is to be administered to each, in case there be a number
and then the prayer, "*Deus Patrum*," etc., is to be said in
the plural for all together.

§ XV. Si inter Catechumenos adsint fœminæ recedant ipsæ in partem
quousque tertio dicatur masculis: *Ora Electe*, etc., et hi signati fuerint
in fronte.

490. This rubric is not given in some editions of the ritual,
nor is it mentioned by Baruffaldi or Catalani; and the same
is to be said of the similar rubrics which occur afterwards.[3]
It is given, however, in the Propaganda edition,[4] as well as
in the Pontifical, and it is manifestly important for the decorous performance of the ceremonies that the females should
here be required to withdraw, as the ceremonies and prayers
which immediately follow are for males exclusively.

§ XVI.—Si plures sint Catechumeni hic et in sequentibus Sacerdos
dicat in numero plurali: *Orate Electi, flectite genua*, etc.
Deinde Sacerdos dicat super masculum tantum: *Ora Electe, flecte
genua, et dic: Pater Noster*. Et Electus genuflexus orat, et dicit:
Pater Noster. Et cum oraverit, et dixerit *Pater Noster* usque ad *sed
libera nos a malo* inclusive, Sacerdos subjungit: *Leva, comple orationem
tuam, et dic: Amen*. Et ille respondet: *Amen*. Et Sacerdos dicit
Patrino: *Signa eum*. Deinde Electo: *Accede*. Et Patrinus pollice
signat eum in fronte dicens: *In nomine Patris*, etc.

491. The first part of this rubric, "Si plures sint," etc.,
directing the change to be made when there are more than
one, is given in many editions, and in the commentaries of
Baruffaldi and Catalani, only after the prayer and exorcism,
but it is much more conveniently placed here.

The catechumen should kneel on both knees while reciting
the "Pater Noster." This is the obvious meaning of the
rubric, "flecte genua." Nor is there any instance of a prayer
directed to be said on one knee. The reasoning of Gavantus
on the words, "flectamus genua," of the missal,[5] does not

---

[1] Baruff., tit. xiii. § xiv. xv. Catal., tit. ii. cap. iv. § xviii. xix.
[2] Supra, n. 314.   [3] Infra, § xx. et § xxii.
[4] Rome, MDCCCXLVII.   [5] Pars ii. tit. v. Rub. 4, lit. (e).

apply in this case, as Baruffaldi justly observes.[1] Besides, in the Missal, the priest is directed to say the prayer only *after* the genuflection.[2] He rises up before saying "*Amen*," which he is to say only after the priest has directed him to do so. When the priest says "*Accede*," the catechumen should advance a step, and then the godfather makes the sign of the cross on his forehead, saying the words, "*In nomine Patris*," etc., as directed in the rubric. The signs of the cross here prescribed are made in the manner before explained.[3]

It is obviously necessary that the godfather and the catechumen himself be instructed beforehand in what they are required to do.

§ XVII.—Tum quoque Sacerdos facit Crucem in fronte ejus, ita dicendo: *In nomine*, etc. Et imponit manum super eum, et dicit: *Oremus. Deus Abraham*, etc.

492. Immediately after the godfather, the priest makes the sign of the cross on the catechumen's forehead, in the same manner and with the same words. Then he imposes his right hand on him, and says the prayer, "*Deus Abraham*," etc., and, having put on his cap,[4] the exorcism which immediately follows. The wording of the rubric here is to be carefully noted. It requires him to say "*In nomine Patris*," etc., while making the sign of the cross, but it does not require him to keep the hand imposed while saying the prayer, "*Deus Abraham*," etc. For the former it has "ita dicendo;" for the latter, "imponit . . . et dicit." It is not improbable that the difference of expression is intended to convey this difference of meaning, seeing that, if there be a number, the imposition of the hand must precede the prayer.[5]

493. When there are two or more male catechumens, he addresses them in the plural, *Orate*, etc , as has been directed above,[6] but the sign of the cross is made on them singly. Then he imposes his hand on each, and, having done this, he says the preceding prayer and exorcism in the plural, as is clearly directed in the Pontifical. It is to be observed, however, that at the words, *sanctæ crucis* ✠, in the exorcism, he makes the sign of the cross on the forehead of each, and then continues, as is also clearly prescribed in the Pontifical, which has the rubric, "Signat singulos," immediately before the words, "*Quod nos fronti*," etc.[7]

[1] Tit. xiii. n. 44.   [2] Missal. Rubr., l. c.   [3] Supra, n. 307.
[4] Rit. Toul., ti . iii. § i. n. 19.   [5] Vid. supra, n. 486.
[6] Supra, § xvi.   [7] Pontif. Rom., *Pro Baptismo Adultorum*.

§ XVIII.—Sacerdos dicit secundo Electo: *Ora Electe*, etc.

494. The same ceremony is repeated with a different prayer and exorcism. The signs of the cross and the imposition of the hand are to be "singulis," but the prayer and exorcism to be "in plurali pro pluribus," as is expressly prescribed by the rubric of the Pontifical.[1]

§ XIX.—Sacerdos tertio dicit Electo: *Ora*, etc.

495. The ceremony is performed for the third time with two exorcisms, the second being a repetition of the one given above, "*Ergo maledicte*," etc. In reciting the first, "*Exorciso te immunde*," etc., the sign of the cross is to be made over the catechumen three times, as marked in the ritual. Should there be a number, it can be made over all in common, as is clear from the Pontifical,[2] but the imposition of the hand, which precedes, must be "singulis," as before.[3]

The priest is uncovered except during the exorcisms, when he wears his cap.[4]

§ XX.—Si, ut supra, adsint fœminæ, retrahunt se masculi in partem, et accedunt fœminæ ante Sacerdotem et stant.

496. This rubric is not given in some editions of the ritual, as has been already noticed.[5]

§ XXI.—Si plures fuerint fœminæ Catechumenæ, hic et in sequentibus, Sacerdos dicat in numero plurali: *Orate, Electæ, Flectite genua*, etc. Sacerdos dicit Catechumenæ: *Ora, Electa, flecte genua*, etc.

497. The preceding ceremonies are prescribed also for females, but with prayers and exorcisms somewhat different. All that we have said above regarding the signs of the cross and the imposition of the hand, is equally applicable here. It is very convenient to have the prayers and exorcisms for the females given at length in their proper places, as they are in the Pontifical and in the Propaganda edition of the ritual. In many editions of the ritual we have here only the prayer and exorcism that are proper, and we are referred to the preceding for those that are the same for both males and females.

§ XXII.—Postmodum accedunt iterum masculi qui se retraxerant. et ipsi ad dexteram, fœminæ vero ad sinistram Sacerdotis, ut in principio, disponuntur.

498. This rubric is not found in the older editions of the ritual.[6] The male catechumens, who were before directed to

---

[1] Loc. cit.   [2] Rubr. in loc.   [3] Supra, n. 493.
[4] Rit. Toul., l. c. n. 20, 21.   [5] Supra, n. 490.
[6] Vid. supra, n. 490.

withdraw, are now invited to come forward, and are placed on the right, as at the commencement,[1] the rest of the ceremony being the same for all.

§ XXIII.—Sacerdos imponit manum super Electum, vel si sint plures, super singulos tam masculos, quam fœminas, et dicit: *Æternam ac justissimam*, etc.

Si plures fuerint Electi, sive mares, sive fœminæ, præcedens oratio dicatur in numero plurali, et in genere proprio, ut superius dictum est.

499. After the preceding ceremonies, if there be only one catechumen, whether male or female, the priest, having taken off his cap,[2] imposes his hand, and then says the prayer, "*Æternam*," etc. But if there be a number, they are arranged as above directed, and the priest imposes his hand on the head of each, and then says for all in common, in the plural number, but in the masculine gender, unless *all* be females, the prayer, "*Æternam*," etc.[3]

§ XXIV.—His peractis, Sacerdos sinistra manu apprehendens dexteram Electi prope brachium, vel ei porrigens extremam partem stolæ, introducit eum in Ecclesiam, dicens: N. *Ingredere*, etc.

500. Up to this time the catechumen is supposed to be outside the church, and he is now conducted inside with the ceremony here mentioned. The priest with his left hand takes him by the right, almost by the wrist—"prope bra-"chium," (brachium being the part of the arm between the elbow and the hand[4])—or he presents to him the extremity of the stole, to be held in his right hand, and in this manner leads him into the church, saying "N. *Ingredere*," etc. The priest is free to adopt either way; and Baruffaldi recommends that the extremity of the stole be used when females alone are baptized.[5] In the order for the baptism of infants, no choice of the kind is given, for it is prescribed, as we have seen,[6] that he put the extremity of the stole on the child.

501. The ritual nowhere states which extremity is meant, but the rubric of the Pontifical here distinctly says, it is that which hangs from the left shoulder. The reason why the priest uses the left hand, or the left side of the stole, is, according to Baruffaldi,[7] that he may have the right hand free, or that he himself may be at the right, which is the more honorable position.

[1] Vid. supra, n. 483.
[2] Vid. supra, n. 365.
[5] Tit. xiii. n. 51.
[7] Loc. cit. n. 53.
[3] Rit. Toul., l. c. n. 24.
[4] Smith's *Latin Dictionary*.
[6] Chap. iv. § ix.

§ XXV.—Si plures fuerint, dicat in numero plurali : *Ingredimini, etc.,* et introducat eos, ut supra.

502. When there are two or more together, he addresses them in the plural, "*Ingredimini,*" etc. If all are females, he presents the end of the stole, and if there be not more than two or three, each may take hold of it; otherwise the first takes it, the second takes the hand of the first, the third that of the second, and so on. If all are males, each may hold the stole in the same way, when there are only two or three; otherwise they hold each other's hands, while the priest, with his left hand, takes the first by the wrist, as above explained. If some are males and some females, they take each other's hands in line, while he takes with his left hand the first of the males. This is the manner recommended by Baruffaldi,[1] and implied, as we understand it, in the rubric of the Pontifical, which is as follows : "Si autem baptizandi "erint plures, Pontifex vel porrigit singulis extremam partem "stolæ, vel trahit illum quem manu tenet, et ille secundum, "et secundus tertium, etc., pariformiter ducat."[2]

It may be seen, on a little reflection, that, in the third case we have mentioned, *i. e.,* when there are persons of both sexes, the males should be on the right of the females, in order that the priest may·be on the right of all ;[3] and this confirms the view before expressed,[4] regarding their relative position.

§ XXVI.—Et ingressus Electus procumbit, seu prosternit se in pavimento, et adorat.

Deinde surgit, et Sacerdos imponit manum super caput ejus, et Electus cum eo recitat Symbolum Apostolorum, et Orationem Dominicam.

Ita etiam si plures fuerint, omnes surgunt et simul recitant : *Credo in Deum,* etc.

503. As soon as the catechumen has entered the church, he is directed to prostrate himself on the pavement, and in this posture to adore God, thanking Him for His mercy in having called him to the faith, and having now permitted him to enter His holy temple, to receive the grace of regeneration, etc.[5] The prostration is only for some seconds, when he rises, and the priest imposes his (right) hand on his head, and then both together recite the Apostles' Creed and the Lord's Prayer.

The same thing is required of each when there are more than one. All prostrate themselves and rise up at the same

---

[1] Loc. cit. n. 52.　　　　[2] *Pro Baptismo Adultorum.* Rub. in loc.
[3] Supra, n. 501.　　　　[4] Supra, n. 483.
[5] Catal., tit. ii. cap. iv. § xxxv.

time, and the priest imposes his hand on the head of each; after which all together, the priest included, say the Creed and Pater Noster.[1]

504. In the order for infants, it is prescribed that the priest and sponsors recite these in going to the font. This is not expressed here, but it seems to be implied in the rubric of the Pontifical, which says "Interim," that is, as we take it, while reciting the Creed and Pater Noster. "Interim Ponti- "fex accedit ad faldistorium extra Baptisterium, et versis "renibus ostio cancellorum, accepta mitra et adhuc stans "(singulis si plures) imponit rursus manum super caput "Electi et dicit: (In plurali pro pluribus). *Nec te latet,* "*Satana,* etc."

We think, then, that the ceremonies which immediately follow here are performed at the entrance of the baptistery. If the sponsors have not finished the Creed and Pater Noster before reaching it, they stand looking towards the high altar until they have concluded,[2] and then the priest, having put on his cap,[3] proceeds as is directed in the following rubric.

§ XXVII.—Tunc rursus Sacerdos imponat manum super caput Electi, et dicat: Exorcismus. *Nec te latet, Satana,* etc.
Similiter si plures fuerint. imponit manum super capita singulorum, et dicit eumdem Exorcismum in numero multitudinis, et genere suo.

505. When there are several, the hand is to be imposed on the head of each, and, this being done, the priest says the exorcism for all in the plural.

In this rubric, as given by Baruffaldi, the words, "in nu- "mero multitudinis, et genere suo," are omitted, and he observes that it requires the exorcism to be said for each in particular, and does not allow it to be said in general for all, adding reasons why this should be so.[4] He was probably led into this mistake by the omission of the last words in the ritual he had before him, and, therefore, may not deserve the censure passed on him by Catalani.[5] At all events, the words of the rubric, as we have it, make it clear enough that, in case there be a number, the exorcism should be said in the plural for all in common; and if there could be any doubt, it is removed by the very explicit rubric of the Pontifical, which we have cited above.[6]

[1] Pontif. Rom., *De Bapt. Adult.*
[2] Rit. Toul., tit. iiime § i. n. 27.
[3] Cap. iv. § xxxix. n. ii.
[4] Vid. supra, n. 326.
[5] Tit. xiii. n. 59.
[6] Supra, n. 504.

§ XXVIII.—Postea Sacerdos pollice accipit de saliva oris sui, et tangit aures et nares Electi; tangendo vero aurem dexteram et sinistram dicat: *Ephpheta, quod est, adaperire;* deinde tangendo nares, dicat: *In odorem suavitatis:* et subdit: *Tu autem,* etc.

506. The ceremony here prescribed is the very same as that prescribed for infants, and is performed in the same manner.[1]

§ XXIX.—Deinde interroget Electum: *Quis vocaris?* Et ipse respondet: N. Interroget: N. *Abrenuntias,* etc.

507. The interrogations here, except the first, are the same as in the order for infants.[2] Baruffaldi has several conjectural reasons[3] why the first question is put, though the priest was told the name at the commencement, and has just used it in the exorcism. One reason, which seems to him very probable, is, that sometimes the preceding ceremonies were all performed by inferior ministers, after which the bishop himself conferred the sacrament, commencing at this part by asking the name.[4] The renunciations, however, were also required before.[5] It may be that the repetition of all these questions is simply for the purpose of making sure of the catechumen's dispositions in embracing the Christian religion.[6]

§ XXX.—Tunc Sacerdos intingit pollicem dexteræ manus in Oleo sancto Catechumenorum, et inungit Electum, primum in pectore, deinde inter scapulas in modum Crucis, dicens: *Ego te linio,* etc.

Mox bombacio, vel re simili, tergit pollicem et loca inuncta, et sub jungit, dicens: *Exi immunde,* etc.

508. This ceremony has been fully explained before. We may observe that the reason there given for wiping the oil from the breast before anointing the back in the case of infants, does not apply here. The catechumen stands upright, having the breast and shoulders uncovered; and there is no reason why, in turning for the unction on the back, his breast should come in contact with anything to remove the oil.

Hic Sacerdos deponat stolam et pluviale violaceum et sumat aliud albi coloris.

§ XXXI.—Quando plures sunt Electi idem fit circa singulos eorum. Et ducitur Electus ad Baptisterium: ubi, si ob aliquam causam non habeatur, sive præparata non fuerit aqua Baptismalis, fiat benedictio Fontis, ut infra ponitur. Et cum fuerit prope Fontem, Sacerdos interrogat: *Quis vocaris,* etc.

509. The above ceremonies are performed at the entrance

---

[1] Supra, n. 327, et seq.   [2] Vid. supra, n. 332.
[3] Tit. xiii. n. 64.   [4] Vid. infra, chap. viii. § v.   [5] Supra, § iv.
Vid. supra, n. 333, et seq   [6] Cfr. Catal., § xli. n. 1.

to the baptistery, and the catechumen is then conducted within the rails[1] to the font. The present rubric directs that they be performed for each, should there be a number, but it is not easy to determine whether the exorcism, "*Exi immunde*," etc., is to be said for each individually, or for all in common. The words of our rubric, "*idem fit circa singulos*," leave a doubt, and the rubric of the Pontifical does not remove it. It merely gives in brackets the words [Singulos si plures], before *Ego te linio*, etc., and then the rubric, "*Mox bombacio*," etc., is inserted before the exorcism, just as we have it here; so that we cannot be sure whether the [Singulos si plures], any more than the words of our rubric, extend to the exorcism. We are inclined to the opinion that they do not, and that the exorcism may be said for a number in common. Our reasons are, first, because this is the case with all the exorcisms which precede: even those that are peculiar to one sex are said in common for all of that sex, if there be a number; and, secondly, because the rubric here directs him to wipe his thumb as well as the parts anointed, before he says the exorcism; and it is not probable that this would be required until he had anointed all. Nor is it any objection that the Pontifical, which is so very minute in this particular, gives no notice that the exorcism may be for a number in common; because this notice is given by words (In plurali pro pluribus), which would be out of place here, as the present exorcism admits no change of number.

Catalani,[2] however, understands the rubric as directing the exorcism to be applied to each; and as we have seen no other authority on the subject, we should be unwilling to depart from his view of it.

510. The rubric which here requires the stole and cope of violet to be exchanged for a stole and cope of white, is not found in the older editions of the ritual; but even in these it is understood from the order for infants,[3] and is comprehended under the general rubric placed at the commencement of the present order.[4] Should it happen, by any accident, that there is not a sufficient supply of baptismal water, even with the expedient permitted by the rubric,[5] the font must here be blessed in the manner afterwards directed.[6] In this case

---

[1] Vid. supra, n. 243.
[2] Chap. iv. § xv.
[3] Vid. supra, chap. iii. § v.

[4] Cap. iv. § xliv. n. i.
[5] Supra, § i.
[6] Infra, chap. ix.

the violet vestments are retained till after the benediction of the font.[1]

§ XXXII.—*Iterum interroget*, dicens: N. *Quid petis ?* etc.

511. The object of these interrogations, and of those that immediately precede, is, according to Baruffaldi,[2] to elicit anew from the catechumen a profession of his faith and a declaration of his desire to receive baptism, so that there might be no doubt about his dispositions at this solemn moment, when the sacrament is about being conferred.

§ XXXIII.—Tunc Patrino, vel Matrina, vel utroque (si ambo admittantur), admota manu, teneute seu tangente Electum (vel Electam) aperto capite, et laxatis a collo vestibus, inclinatum, Sacerdos vasculo vel urceolo hauriat aquam Baptismalem de fonte, et cum ea sub trina supra caput in modum Crucis infusione baptizet Electum (seu Electam) in nomine SS. Trinitatis, sic dicens: *Ego te baptizo*, etc.

512. On this rubric we have little to add to what has been said regarding the baptism of infants. The catechumen should be between his sponsors, the godfather on the right and the godmother on the left,[3] holding him by the arm or shoulder, or at least touching him. In this position he inclines forward, his head and neck uncovered, and his hands joined,[4] while the priest pours on the water in the manner explained in treating of infant baptism.[5] If the hair be thick, care should be taken to adopt the precaution before recommended.[6]

§ XXXIV.—Si aqua, quæ ex capite baptizati defluit, non dilabitur in sacrarium Baptisterii, recipiatur in subjecta aliqua pelvi, et in illud postmodum projiciatur.

513. If there be, adjoining the font, or forming one of its compartments, in the manner already explained,[7] a basin which serves as a sacrarium, the catechumen should keep his head inclined over it, so that the water poured on may fall into it; otherwise a vessel should be held under his head by one of the clerks, and its contents afterwards thrown into the sacrarium.[8]

514. Our rubric does not say whether the catechumen should stand or kneel. This, we think, must be determined by circumstances. The Pontifical directs that he be on his knees with his head bent forward; but this is probably be-

---

[1] Rit. Toul., tit. iii^ce § i. n. 31. Vid. infra, chap. ix. § ii.
[2] Tit. xiii. n. 64.   [3] Rit. Toul., l. c. n. 33.   [4] Ibid.
[5] Vid. supra, n. 343, et seq.   [6] Supra, n. 345.   [7] Supra, n. 245.
[8] Vid. supra, chap. iii. § xli.

cause the bishop is seated on the faldstool while pouring on the water.[1]　Baruffaldi[2] supposes him to stand; and this is, perhaps, the more convenient posture when the ceremony is performed by a priest.

§ XXXV.—Cum plures sunt Electi, singillatim singuli interrogantur, et baptizantur, ut supra.
Si sint mares et fœminæ, primum mares, deinde fœminæ.

515. This rubric appears to convey that, when there are more than one, the interrogations should immediately precede the baptism of each. It would not be in exact accordance with it to put the interrogations to each in the first place, and then baptize.

§ XXXVI.—Verum si probabiliter dubitetur an Electus fuerit alias baptizatus, dicat Sacerdos: *Si non es baptizatus*, etc.

516. We have already dwelt on the circumstances in which the conditional form is to be used.[3]

§ XXXVII.—Deinde Sacerdos intingat pollicem dexterum in sacrum Chrisma, et perungat verticem Electi in modum Crucis, dicens: *Deus Omnipotens*, etc.

517. This rubric has been explained in the order of infant baptism.[4]

§ XXXVIII.—Tunc bombacio, vel re simili pollicem tergit, et imponit capiti Electi Chrismale, seu candidum linteolum, et dat illi vestem candidam, dicens: *Accipe vestem*, etc.

518. The rubric here directs the priest to wipe his thumb, but does not tell him to wipe the part to which he has applied the chrism, as he is directed to do in the order for infants.[5]　Instead of this, he is directed to bind on the head of the neophyte a piece of white linen, which, being designed as a protection and a mark of respect for the holy chrism, is called "Chrismale," and, according to the ancient usage, was worn by the neophyte for seven days.[6]　This, though so clearly prescribed, is rarely attended to, the chrism being usually rubbed off in the same way as in the baptism of infants[7].　The Ritual of Toulon even directs that it be rubbed off by the priest, or by some one in holy orders, though it at the same time prescribes the "Chrismale."[8]　The priest then presents him with a white garment, saying, "*Accipe vestem*," etc.

---

[1] Vid. infra, chap. viii. § iv.　　[2] Tit. xiii. n. 70.
[3] Supra, n. 173, et seq.　　[4] Vid. chap. iv. § xxi.
[5] Supra, chap. iv. § xxii.　　[6] Cfr. Catalani, *Pontificale Romanum*, pars i. tit. i. § viii. n. 1.　[7] Vid. supra, n. 351.　[8] Tit. iii. § i. n. 36.

§ XXXIX.—Et Electus deponit priores vestes, et induitur novis albi coloris, vel saltem exteriore candida, quam a Sacerdote accepit.

519. On the white garments worn by the newly-baptized, see what has been said in a previous chapter.[1] The neophyte is here directed to take off the clothes he has worn up to the present, and put on white ones; or at least to put on as an outside garment that one which he has received from the priest. Of course, arrangements should be made for all this beforehand, and the sponsors should render assistance in this change of dress, but only to those of their own sex.[2] To avoid the trouble of this ceremony, the catechumens sometimes presented themselves clothed in white at the commencement. This practice, which prevailed even in Rome, was condemned as an abuse by a constitution of Benedict XIII, who ordered the strict observance of the rubric.[3] Baruffaldi says they sometimes presented themselves, as he himself was witness, having over the white garments a dark-colored cloak or veil, which was laid aside at this part, so that they at once appeared clothed in white; but he condemns this practice, and insists on a strict observance of the rubric, which requires a change of dress. He would be satisfied, however, with the change of the outside garments, at least in females.[4]

Notwithstanding all this, it would seem that in Rome the catechumens are still presented for baptism clothed in white. At least this was the case in the church of St. John Lateran, on Easter Saturday, 1855, according to the author of the "*Cérémonial des Evêques Expliqué.*"[5]

§ XL.—Postea dat ei Sacerdos cereum, seu candelam accensam in manu dextera, dicens: *Accipe lampadem*, etc.

520. On this ceremony see what has been said in the order of infant baptism.[6] The candle is here put into the hand of the neophyte himself, and not into that of the sponsor, as is usually done in the case of infants.

§ XLI.—Ipse vero Neophytus eumdem cereum accensum manibus teneat usque in finem, præterquam dum confirmatur.

521. The word "Neophytus" is here for the first time applied by the rubrics to the newly-baptized. Hitherto he has been called "Catechumenus," or "Electus;" but being now planted in Christ by baptism, he is said to be "Neophytus,"

---

[1] Supra, n. 352, et seq.   [2] Baruff., tit xiii. n. 76.
[3] Apud Baruff., n. 74.   [4] Loc. cit. n. 77, et seq.
[5] Lib. ii. cap. xxvii. n. 13 in nota.   [6] Supra, n. 354, et seq.

which, from its etymology (νεόφυτος), signifies "newly planted." He is to hold the lighted candle in his hands until the
conclusion of the ceremony, unless when he is receiving confirmation, if there be a bishop present to confer it.[1]

§ XLII.—In Ecclesiis autem ubi Baptismus fit per immersionem, sive
totius corporis, sive capitis tantum, Sacerdos accipiat Electum per
brachia prope humeros, ut superiore parte corporis nudatum, reliqua
honeste contectum, ter illum, vel caput ejus mergendo, et toties elevan-
do, baptizet sub trina immersione, sanctam Trinitatem semel tantum sic
invocando: *Ego te baptizo in nomine Patris* ✠ mergat semel: *et Filii* ✠,
mergat iterum: *et Spiritus Sancti* ✠, mergat tertio: Patrino, vel Matrina, vel utroque eum tenente, vel tangente.

522. We had occasion to say something of baptism by immersion in a preceding chapter.[2] There is much more difficulty
in performing the ceremony for adults than for infants, as is
plain from the present rubric. Hence St. Charles permitted
adults to be baptized by effusion, even in Milan, when the
Ambrosian rite requiring immersion could not conveniently
be carried out.[3] The words of his instruction on the subject
are inserted as a rubric in the edition of the Ambrosian Ritual
by Cardinal Cæsare Monte: "Baptizetur per immersionem
"ut ritus Ambrosianæ Ecclesiæ postulat, siquidem commode
"fieri possit: alioquin per infusionem."[4]
From the last words of our rubric it appears that the spon
sors are required to hold or touch the adult while he is being
immersed, though this is not required when infants are
baptized by immersion.[5]

§ XLIII.—Et cum Electus surrexerit de fonte, Patrinus vel Matrina
cum linteo in manibus suscipit eum de manu Sacerdotis: et Sacerdos,
intincto pollice dextero in sacro Chrismate, illum in vertice in modum Crucis perungit, dicens: *Deus omnipotens*, etc.
Deinde Sacerdos imponit capiti ejus linteolum seu Chrismale, et dat
ei vestem caudidam dicens: *Accipe vestem*, etc.

523. On coming out of the font, the neophyte is received
from the priest by the sponsor, holding in his hands a linen
cloth, which he immediately wraps around him. The priest
then applies the vertical unction, and presents the linen
garment.

§ XLIV.—Et statim prædicto linteo abstergitur, et in loco semoto
vestitur novis et albis vestibus, et exteriore candida, quam accepit.

---

[1] Baruff., n. 82, 83.   [2] Chap. iv. § xviii.
[3] *Act. Eccl. Mediol.*, pars iv. Instruct. Bapt. *De Baptismo Adultorum*,
pag. 419. Cfr. Baruff, l. c. n. 85. Catal., tit. ii. cap. iv. § lvi. n. ii.
[4] Apud Martene. lib. i. cap. i. art. xviii. ord. xxi. *De Bapt. Adult*
[5] Vid. supra, n. 347.

524. This rubric shows that the neophyte is expected to put on white garments which he had not worn before, as well as the exterior one which is presented to him by the priest.[1] But the rubric of the Pontifical has the words, "vel saltem '·exteriore candida," instead of "et exteriore candida," and would seem, therefore, in strictness, to require no more than that the neophyte put on the exterior white garment presented to him by the priest.

§ XLV.—Postea dat ei Sacerdos candelam accensam in manu dextera, dicens: *Accipe lampadem*, etc.
Eodem modo, si plures fuerint, fit pro singulis.
Postea dicat; N. *Vade in pace*, etc.

525. When two or more are to be baptized, the whole of this ceremony, commencing with the interrogations on the Creed, is performed for each separately. But it is not necessary that it be performed uninterruptedly. He first baptizes all, then applies the vertical unction to all, and having removed the chrism from his thumb, performs the rest of the ceremony.[2]

§ XLVI.—Si adsit Episcopus qui id legitime præstare possit, ab eo Neophyti Sacramento Confirmationis initiantur. Deinde si hora congruens fuerit, celebratur Missa, cui Neophyti intersunt, et Sanctissimam Eucharistiam devote suscipiunt.

526. If the preceding ceremony has been performed by the bishop, or if the bishop be present after it has been performed by a priest, he should forthwith confer on the neophyte the sacrament of confirmation. Every bishop can lawfully do so in his own diocese, but not in a strange diocese without the permission of the Ordinary, and hence the words of the rubric, "Qui id legitime præstare possit."[3]

Then, if the hour be suitable, mass ought to be celebrated, at which the neophytes should assist, and receive the Holy Communion. We have seen that, according to the ancient usage, even infants, immediately after baptism, were confirmed and received the Holy Eucharist;[4] and though this usage has been abolished with regard to infants, the rubrics here show that the Church wishes it to be continued when adults are baptized.

§ XLVII.—Si vero ob baptizandorum multitudinem, ut in India et novo Orbe quandoque contingit, in singulorum Baptismo præscripti ritus adhiberi non possunt, tunc vel pluribus simul adhibeantur, vel, si urget necessitas, omittantur.

[1] Baruff., n. 87.   [2] Vid. supra, n. 376, et seq.
[3] Cfr. St. Lig. lib. vi. n. 171. Concil. Trid. sess. vi. cap. v. *De Reform.*
[4] Vid. supra, n. 411, et seq.

527. This provides for the case in which time would not permit the observance of all the preceding ceremonies, on account of the great number to be baptized. We have seen from the preceding rubrics, that many of the prayers and exorcisms may be said for a number of catechumens together; but this rubric permits even those that are prescribed for each, to be applied in case of necessity to all in common; and, if the necessity be very pressing, it even permits the entire omission of all, except what is essential to the sacrament, that is, except the application of the matter and form. It can rarely happen that these cannot be applied to each in particular, no matter how great the number, or how pressing the necessity; but yet, in case of *extreme* necessity, as, *e. g.*, in case of an earthquake or an inundation, it would be lawful to apply the matter and form to a number together, sprinkling them with water, and pronouncing the words in the plural: "*Ego vos baptizo, in nomine,*" etc. This is clearly enough laid down in a preceding rubric, which, in reference to this form, "*Ego vos,*" etc., after permitting it in a certain case, says: "Quam tamen formam in iis solum, et in "aliis similibus mortis periculis ad plures simul baptizandos, "et ubi tempus non patitur ut singuli separatim baptizentur "alias nunquam, licet adhibere."[1]

---

[1] Supra, chap. iii. § xxiii.

CHAPTER VII.

ORDER FOR SUPPLYING THE CEREMONIES OMITTED IN BAPTISM: "ORDO SUPPLENDI OMISSA SUPER BAPTIZATUM."

§ I.—Cum, urgente mortis periculo, vel alia cogente necessitate, sive parvulus, sive adultus, sacris precibus ac cæremoniis prætermissis, fuerit baptizatus; ubi convaluerit, vel cessaverit periculum, et ad Ecclesiam delatus fuerit, omissa omnia suppleantur.

528. It is never lawful, unless in case of necessity, to separate the ceremonies used in baptism from the application of the matter and form;[1] and if they be separated, the ceremonies omitted are to be afterwards supplied in the church, when the infant or adult, as the case may be, can be presented there for the purpose. This obligation of supplying the ceremonies is "*sub mortali*," according to St. Liguori;[2] but there may be very often sufficient reason for dispensing with it in the case of adults, the matter being left to the discretion of the bishop.[3]

§ II.—Idemque ordo ac ritus servetur, qui in Baptismo Parvulorum (si fuerit parvulus), seu Adultorum (si fuerit adultus) præscriptus est. Excepto quod interrogatio: An velit baptizari, formaque Baptismi, et ablutio prætermittuntur, et quædam Orationes, et Exorcismi, suo quique loco immutati, ut infra, dicuntur.

529. The "Propaganda" edition of the ritual gives the "Ordo supplendi omissa" for infants, and also for adults, at full length. But many editions, including nearly all the older ones, as, *e. g.*, those used by Catalani and Baruffaldi, give only some of the prayers, noting, for the rest, in general terms, the changes to be made, as is done in the present rubric.

Whether all the ceremonies are to be supplied, or only those that precede the application of the matter and form, the priest goes vested in surplice and violet stole, and attended by his clerk, to the door of the church, where the sponsors with the infant or adult should be in waiting, and proceeds with the interrogations and the rest, exactly as if he were about to confer the sacrament, with the exceptions noted in the present rubric.

---

[1] St. Lig., lib. vi. n. 141.
[2] Loc. cit. n. 144, *in parenth.*
[3] Vid. supra, chap. v., § xlii.
[4] Vid. supra, n. 328.

530. Instead of this rubric, the "Propaganda" edition has the following in the "Ordo supplendi," etc., for infants: "Sacerdos itaque, lotis manibus, superpelliceo et stola violacea "indutus, accedat: Clericum unum, seu plures, si potest, "secum adhibeat, superpelliceo pariter indutos, qui sibi mi-"nistrent.

"Ita paratus accedat ad limen Ecclesiæ, extra quam ex-"pectant qui infantem, vel infantes detulerunt, illum proprio "nomine eidem imposito appellando et dicens: N. *Quid* "*petis ?* etc.   Patrinus Catechesis respondet: *Fidem,* etc."

It is remarkable that the sponsor is not here called simply "Patrinus," but "Patrinus Catechesis," as if to convey that, in the present case, he does not contract all the obligations of the sponsor.[1]   The edition of the ritual for the English clergy gives, like the "Propaganda" edition, the "Ordo supplendi omissa" for infants at full length, with all the necessary changes; and this is very convenient for priests who may be often required to supply the ceremonies in this way.

§ III.—Sacerdos igitur antequam immittat sal in os baptizati, manum super caput ejus imponens, dicat: *Oremus. Omnipotens sempiterne Deus,* etc.

531. If the "Ordo supplendi," etc., be not given *in extenso*, at least the prayers that are changed are given, and the priest must turn over to read them at the proper time, instead of those given in the usual "Ordo Baptismi."   By comparing them, it may seem that the changes are very few, being only such as are necessary to make the prayers refer to baptism *already received*.   In this prayer, "*Omnipotens,*" etc., the word '*dudum*" is inserted before "*ad rudimenta fidei ;*" and there is added, at the end, the entire clause: "*ut idoneus* (vel "*idonea*) *sit frui gratia Baptismi tui, quem suscepit, salis* "*percepta medicina.*"

§ IV.—Deinde posteaquam modicum salis immisit in os baptizati, dicens: *Accipe sal,* etc., dicit: *Oremus. Deus Patrum nostrorum,* etc.

532. This rubric, as it lies in most editions of the Roman Ritual, might be understood to direct that the prayer, "*Deus* "*Patrum nostrorum,* etc., should be said immediately after "*Accipe sal,*" etc., as if the "*Pax tibi,*" etc., were to be omitted. This would be a mistake, for it is here supposed (and indeed expressly ordered in the rubric above, "Idemque ordo ac "ritus," etc., given in those editions), that everything be done

---

[1] Vid. supra, n. 402, et seq.

and said as if the sacrament were to be conferred, simply substituting the prayers given here for the corresponding prayers in the ordinary ceremony. In this prayer, "*Deus Patrum*," etc., the words, "*et quem* (vel *quam*) *ad novæ* "*regenerationis lavacrum perduxisti*," are substituted for "*Per-* "*duc eum ad novæ regenerationis lavacrum.*"

§ V.—Post hæc, facto signo Crucis in fronte baptizati, dictisque illis verbis, *Et hoc signum Crucis* ✠ etc. . . . . manu super caput ejus imposita, dicit: *Oremus. Æternam ac justissimam*, etc.

533. The words "Post hæc" do not mean immediately after the prayer, "*Deus Patrum nostrorum*," etc., but after the exorcism which follows it, and of which the words, "*Et* "*hoc signum*," etc., are the conclusion. In this prayer, "*Æternam ac justissimam*," etc., we have the words, "*ut* "*dignus* (vel *digna*) *sit frui gratia Baptismi tui quem suscepit*," for "*ut dignus gratia Baptismi tui effectus ;*" and we have the last clause entirely added, "*ut aptus* (vel *apta*) *sit ad retinen-* "*dam gratiam Baptismi tui.*" These are the only changes made in supplying the ceremonies for infants. After the unction with oil of catechumens, the priest lays aside the violet, and puts on a white stole as usual for the remaining ceremonies, unless these have been already applied.[1]

§ VI.—In Baptismo autem adultorum, præter illa quæ supra notata sunt, quando supplentur omissa, hæc mutari debent. Primum in Exorcismo, *Audi maledicte Satana*, ubi dicitur (*habitaculum perficiat*). dicatur, *habitaculum perfecit :* Deinde in Exorcismo, *Nec te latet*, etc., ubi dicitur (*ut fiat*), dicatur, *ut fieret.*

534. On this rubric we shall merely observe that the ceremonies of adult baptism are very rarely supplied. If one has been baptized in infancy, and has been educated as a Catholic, the ceremonies to be supplied, even when he is an adult, are those assigned in the ritual for infants, as was decided by the Sacred Congregation.[2] Adult converts are usually baptized, on being received into the Church, with the ceremonies prescribed in the "Order for Adults." If the baptism be conferred conditionally, the ceremonies are often dispensed with ; but if performed at all, they are still the same, except that the form is made conditional.[3]

The case, then, can hardly occur unless when it is *certain* that an adult convert was baptized validly before his conver

---

[1] Vid. supra, n. 398.   [2] 27 Aug. 1836, *in Rhedonen.*, ad 3ᵐ, n. 4780.
[3] Sac. Cong. Rit. *Decr., cit.* ad 4ᵐ.

sion ; or was baptized on account of some urgent necessity, without the ceremonies, at the time when he was received into the Church. In such circumstances the ceremonies, unless the bishop thinks it expedient to omit them altogether, are to be supplied according to the form given for adults; and the priest who officiates must carefully note the changes to be made according to the present rubric. The "Propaganda" edition gives the "Ordo supplendi omissa super Baptizatun " adultum " at full length, and the use of a ritual which gives this " Ordo " would save a great deal of trouble, and prevent the danger of mistakes.

CHAPTER VIII.

RITE TO BE OBSERVED WHEN A BISHOP BAPTIZES: "RITUS SERVANDUS CUM EPISCOPUS BAPTIZAT."

§ 1.—Si Episcopus, vel S. R. E. Cardinalis parvulos vel adultos baptizare voluerit, parantur et servantur omnia, ut superius de ordine Baptismi dictum est, atque hæc præterea quæ infra notantur.

535. It is recommended in a previous rubric[1] that the baptism of adults in every diocese be left to the bishop, if he be pleased to confer it. At least, when he officiates on Holy Saturday, there should be some adults or infants to be baptized by him after the benediction of the font.[2] But at whatever time he may administer solemn baptism, everything should be prepared for the ceremony in the manner already prescribed by the ritual, both at the door of the church and at the font.[3] The whole rite is performed in the same way as when a priest is the minister, with the exceptions noted in the following rubrics.

§ II.—Adsint Capellani, vel alii Presbyteri, et Clerici superpelliceis induti; qui ei assistant ac ministrent.

536. If the ceremony be performed after the benediction of the font on Holy Saturday or Pentecost Eve, the bishop is, of course, attended by the ministers of the mass and by his assistant deacons, as is directed by the "Ceremoniale Episco-"porum."[4] At other times he should be attended by at least two priests vested in surplice, who put on and take off the mitre at the proper time, point out the place in the ritual or pontifical, hold the bugia, etc., etc., and not less than four clerics, who are required to act as ministers respectively, *de libro, de bugia, de mitra,* and *de baculo.* They should be vested in surplice, the two last wearing also light humeral veils, or using the sleeves of the surplice to cover their hands in holding the mitre and crosier.[5]

---

[1] Chap. v. § iii.
[2] Vid. supra, n. 237.
[3] Supra, chap. iii. § xlii. et seq.
[4] Lib. ii. cap. xxvii. n. 16.
[5] Cæremoniale Episcoporum, lib. i. cap. xi. n. 5 et 6.

§ III.—Ipse vero super rochetum, sive superpelliceum, si est Regularis, accipiat amictum, albam, et cingulum, et stolam, et pluviale violacei coloris, ac mitram.

537. The bishop may, if he pleases, perform the ceremony as a simple priest, putting on a stole over his rochet, and wearing his cap instead of the mitre;[1] but here we suppose him to perform it pontifically, and in this case he should vest as the rubric directs. He may take the vestments wherever he pleases, or wherever it is found most convenient,—in the sacristy, at the high altar, in the baptistery, or some side chapel: "in secretario vel alibi, ad ejus libitum," according to the rubric of the Pontifical.[2]

No mention is made of the amict in many editions of the ritual. It is expressly mentioned in our rubric, which is taken from the "Propaganda" edition; but even if it were not, there could be little doubt that it should be put on before the alb, as it is at vespers and high mass. There is no mention of the crosier in the rubric of the ritual, but it is mentioned in the rubric of the Pontifical, according to which the bishop uses it in the procession to the door of the church.

§ IV.—Atque ita paratus cum Ministris procedat ad Baptismi ministerium. Et dum interrogat: N. *Quid petis ab Ecclesia Dei?* ac dum facit reliquas interrogationes, sedet cum mitra: cum vero exsufflat, dicendo: *Exi ab eo, immunde spiritus,* surgit cum mitra. Rursus sedet, cum signat Catechumenum signo Crucis in fronte, et in pectore, vel dicit: *Accipe signum Crucis,* etc. Et cum dicit Orationes quæ præcedunt vel sequuntur benedictionem-salis, surgit deposita mitra, similiter cum ipsum sal benedicit. Cum autem sal benedictum immittit in os baptizandi, mitram accipit, et sedet. Cum vero legit Exorcismos, et dum saliva aures et nares Catechumeni tangens dicit: *Ephpheta,* ac dum introducit eum in ecclesiam, stat cum mitra. Cum autem dicit: *Credo in Deum Patrem,* etc., et *Pater noster* super Catechumenum, stat sine mitra. Sed cum nomen quærit, et interrogat: N. *Abrenuntias Satanæ?* etc., et baptizandum Oleo sacro in pectore et inter scapulas inungit, sedet cum mitra: quo facto, accipit stolam et pluviale album. Et cum rursus interrogat de fide: *Credis in Deum Patrem . . . . ?* etc. *Vis baptizari,* etc., et cum baptizat per infusionem. sedet cum mitram. Si vero baptizat per immersionem, mitram retinens stare debet.

Cum demum Chrismate verticem baptizati linit, et dat ei vestem candidam, et candelam accensam, ac dicit: *Vade in pace,* etc., sedet eum mitra.

538. The whole ceremony is given at length in the recent editions of the Pontificale Romanum, with the rubrics in their proper place, containing minute instructions on everything the bishop is required to do. It would save much trouble, there-

---

[1] Rit. Toul., *Baptême,* tit. iv‑‑‑.   [2] *Pro Baptismo Parvulorum.*

fore, to h. re a Pontifical in readiness, and to use it instead
of the ritual. But, for the convenience of those who might
be required to assist the bishop, and who might not have a
Pontifical at hand, we think it well to note the following,
taken partly from the Pontifical, and partly from what is
observed in analogous functions, according to the Ceremoniale
Episcoporum.

539. A faldstool with a violet cover should be placed on a
piece of carpet at the door, and be afterwards removed and
placed at the entrance of the baptistery, when the bishop and
sponsors enter the church. It may be removed by a clerk
when the bishop rises to recite the prayer, "*Deus Patrum
nostrorum*," etc.

When the bishop lays aside the violet, and puts on
white vestments, it would be well to change also the cover
of the faldstool; and it would be convenient, therefore,
to have a white cover under the violet one from the
commencement.

540. The Pontifical or Ritual, with the bugia, should be
in readiness on a small table or credence near the door.

The bishop uses the simple or plain mitre, with the violet
vestments, and puts on the cloth-of-gold mitre (*mitram au-
riphrygiatam*), with the white vestments, and continues to
wear it until the end. It would seem that the precious mitre
is not used at baptism, as the Pontifical makes no mention of
it. These different mitres and their use are treated of in the
Ceremoniale Episcoporum.[1]

541. The bishop, having vested, is accompanied by the
clerks and chaplains to the door or porch. Arrived there, he
lays aside the crozier, and takes his seat on the faldstool,
where, with the mitre on, he proceeds with the interrogations,
N. "*Quid petis ?*" etc., the clerk "de libro" kneeling and holding the book, while one of the chaplains holds the bugia, etc.
We may as well insert here the rubric of the Pontifical at
the commencement of the ceremony, as it gives very minute
instructions: "Pontifex infantem, vel infantes sive pueros,
"sacri Baptismatis unda immergere, seu perfundere volens,
"solitis indumentis in Secretario, vel alibi ad ejus libitum,
"pluvialique violacei coloris, et mitra simplici paratus, et
"baculo Pastorali accepto, Capellanis vel aliis Presbyteris,
"et Clericis, superpelliceis indutis, qui ei assistant ac minis-
"tren , præcedentibus, ad Ecclesiæ portam, extra quam ex-

---

[1] Vid. Ceremoniale Episcoporum, lib. i. cap. xvii.

"pectant, qui infantem vel infantes baptizandos detulerunt,
"procedit; ibique, deposito baculo, sedet cum mitra in faldis-
"torio, ad ejusdem portæ limen, cum strato et violacea veste
"præparato. Sicque sedens cum mitra, interrogat infantem
"positum super brachium dextrum illius, qui eum defert, illum
"nomine proprio, eidem imposito, appellando, et dicens (si
plures fuerint baptizandi dicat singulariter singulis): N.
"*Quid petis ?*" etc.

This rubric of the Pontifical seems to imply that the bishop
should be preceded by his chaplains as well as by the clerks
in the procession to the door of the church. , But, from the
general instructions of the Ceremoniale Episcoporum, regarding the attendance of a bishop when vested in cope, we are
inclined to think that two chaplains may accompany him, one
on each side, raising the borders of the cope, while during the
ceremony there is no doubt that one of them standing on the
bishop's right should raise the border of the cope whenever he
makes the sign of the cross.[1]

542. The bishop is seated or standing, and the mitre is
taken off and put on, as is directed in the above rubric of the
ritual.   If the ritual be used, it would be convenient to note
in the margin what is to be done in the several parts.   It
may be observed that the bishop wears the mitre not only at
those parts at which the priest may wear his cap, according
to the directions of the Ritual of Toulon, which we have
given in the notes to the rubrics of the "Ordo Baptismi ;"[2]
but also at the unction with the oil of catechumens, and the
rest of the ceremonies to the end, during which the priest
should be uncovered.

The words of the rubric, "Similiter dum ipsum sal bene-
"dicit," seem to imply that he does not wear the mitre at any
part of the "*Benedictio salus,*" but, in the Pontifical, he is
directed to wear the mitre until the words, "*ad effugandum
"inimicum,*" after which he lays it aside, and then proceeds,
"*Proinde te rogamus,*" etc., till the end.   To reconcile this
apparent opposition between the Ritual and the Pontifical, it
has occurred to us, that perhaps the first part, "*Exorcizo te
"creatura salis,*" is to be regarded as an exorcism, and that
the benediction, properly speaking, commences with the
words, "*Proinde te rogamus,*" etc., for in this interpretation
he should, even according to the ritual, wear the mitre during
the first part as being an exorcism.

[1] Ibid. lib. i. cap. viii. n. 2 3.   [2] Chap. iv. et chap. vi.

§ V.—Si autem Pontifex quempiam a Presbytero jam catechizatum, tantum baptizare voluerit, sic paratus vestibus albis incipiat, postquam ad Baptisterium deventum fuerit, dicens : *Quo nomine vocaris ?* R. N. Episcopus interrogat : N. *Credis in Deum Patrem Omnipotentem . . . ?* etc., et prosequitur usque in finem juxta ordinem Baptismi, ut supra.

543. The bishop may, if he pleases, merely confer the sacrament, and apply the ceremonies which follow, those which precede having been, immediately before, performed by a priest. This arrangement is not unfrequently adopted on Holy Saturday. It is followed in Rome on that day, according to the author of the "*Cérémonial Des Evêques Ex-* "*pliqué.*" [1] In this case, the bishop puts on white vestments at the commencement, and goes at once to the baptistery. He begins by the interrogations on the Creed, having first put the question, "*Quo nomine vocaris ?*" as here directed, and then proceeds as in the "Ordo."

The same privilege, however, is not allowed to a simple priest. If he confers baptism, he must also himself perform the ceremonies that precede, as was decided by the Sacred Congregation.[2]

[1] Lib. ii. chap. xxvii. 18, note.
[2] 19 Decr. 1665, in *Florentia.*, n. 2350.

CHAPTER IX.

BLESSING OF THE BAPTISMAL FONT WHEN THERE IS NO
CONSECRATED WATER, AT ANY TIME EXCEPT THE
SATURDAYS OF EASTER AND PENTECOST:—"BENE-
DICTIO FONTIS BAPTISMI EXTRA SABBATUM PASCHÆ
ET PENTECOSTES, CUM AQUA CONSECRATA NON HABE-
TUR."

544. We have seen before that the water used in the solemn
administration of baptism should be blessed on Holy Saturday or the Eve of Pentecost, according to the form given in
the Missal; and that, to keep up the supply, unblessed water
may be occasionally added to what is contained in the font.[1]
But when the font is exhausted, or what it contains becomes
unfit for use, a new supply must be blessed, according to the
form here given in the ritual.

§ I.—Primum lavatur et mundatur Vas Baptisterii, deinde limpida
aqua repletur.

545. In the first place, the font must be thoroughly
cleansed, the sediment being carefully removed and thrown
into the sacrarium, according to the instructions of St. Charles,[2]
and then a supply of pure clear water poured in. The rubrics
plainly suppose that the ceremony takes place in the baptistery, within or adjoining the church.[3] The words, "Vas
"Baptisterii," here, and in the next rubric, "Altare Baptisterii,"
and the very title of the present chapter, evidently imply this.
Nevertheless, in dioceses or districts where there are no
baptismal fonts, and where, on account of peculiar circumstances, baptism is conferred, with all the ceremonies, in
private houses, the water used should still be blessed according to the form here prescribed, unless there be permission
to use an abbreviated form.[4]

But, in any case, when water is to be blessed for baptism,
whether in the regular font or in a vessel temporarily used for

[1] Supra, n. 158, et seq.
[2] *Act. Eccl. Mediol.*, pars iv. *De Baptismi Administratione*, p. 410.
[3] Vid. supra, n. 239.
[4] Vid. supra, n. 384, et seq., n. 390, et seq.

the purpose, care should be taken to carry out what the present rubric directs, as regards the condition of the vessel and the quality of the water.

§ II.—Tunc Sacerdos cum suis Clericis, vel etiam aliis Presbyteris, Cruce et duobus cereis præcedentibus, ac thuribulo et incenso, et cum vasculis Chrismatis et Olei Catechumenorum descendit ad Fontem, et ibi, vel ante Altare Baptisterii dicit Litaniam ordinariam prout habetur infra post septem Psalmos Pœnitentiales. Et ante ℣. *Ut nos exaudire digneris*, dicat, et secundo repetat sequentem ℣. *Ut Fontem istum*, etc.

*546. The rubric here says nothing of the vestments to be worn, but there can be little doubt that the priest who is to bless the font should be vested in a stole, and, if possible, also a cope of violet over his surplice. These are the vestments expressly assigned to him by Catalani[1] and De Herdt.[2] He wears the same, having an alb instead of the surplice, on Holy Saturday.[3] But, at least, he must have on a surplice and stole, according to the general rubric for benedictions given hereafter in the ritual. The priests, if any, who assist him, and the clerks, are vested in surplice.

The procession from the vestry to the front is formed as follows: first, the thurifer, with thurible and incense; next, the cross-bearer between two acolytes with lighted candles; and, lastly, the officiating priest between two assistants (clerks, if there be no priests to act as such), who raise the borders of his cope. If there be others in surplice, they walk, two and two, immediately after the cross-bearer. This is the order of the procession to the font on Holy Saturday, except that the Paschal candle is carried instead of the thurible, and that the celebrant is attended by the deacon on his right, and the subdeacon on his left.[4]

For the proper performance of the function, there should be at least six clerks—viz., a thurifer, cross-bearer, two acolytes, and two assistants. Four would suffice for the blessing of the font on Holy Saturday in minor churches, according to what is prescribed in the "Memoriale Rituum."[5] But on Holy Saturday the thurible is not used, and the acolytes can be dispensed with, as one of the clerics carries the Paschal candle. If, in the case supposed by our rubric, the priest has only four clerks, either he must dispense with the assistants (and in this case it would, perhaps, be better that he should

---

[1] Tit. ii. cap. vii. § i. n. iii.   [2] Pars iv. n. 3, iv. in fine.
[3] Merati, pars iv. tit. x. n xxxv.
[4] Merati, loc. cit.   [5] Tit. vi. cap. ii. sec. 4.

not wear the cope),[1] or he should have two lighted candles
placed at the font, so that the cross-bearer could stand
between them.

*547. The rubric seems to direct that the holy oils be
carried by some one in the procession. This should be done
if there be any one in holy orders to carry them ;[2] otherwise
they should be in readiness on a table or credence covered
with a white cloth and placed near the font.[3]

Arrived at the baptistery, the cross-bearer takes his position
near the font, so as to be opposite the priest during the benediction, and stands there with the acolytes till the end of the
ceremony; but the exact arrangement depends so much on
the place in which the font is constructed, that it must be
left in each case to be determined by the master of ceremonies.[4]
The officiating priest, and all the rest, except the cross-bearer
and acolytes, kneel facing the altar of the baptistery, if it
have one, or facing the high altar.[5]

Then the priest recites the Litany of the Saints, the rest
answering ; and before the " *Ut nos exaudire digneris*," he
rises up, and, turning to the font, says twice, " *Ut fontem*
" *istum*," etc., making each time the sign of the cross with
his right hand over the font, at the words marked in the
ritual. After which he kneels again, until " *Dominus vobis-*
' *cum*," when he rises and recites the prayer " *Omnipotens*
" *sempiterne*," etc., at the end of which all rise.[6]

§ III.—Potest etiam dici Litania brevior, ut in Missali in Sabbato
Sancto.

*548. The priest may recite, as he pleases, either the
ordinary litany given in the ritual after the Seven Penitential
Psalms, or that which is given in the Missal for Holy Saturday. If he selects the latter, it may be asked, Should not
what he says be repeated in the responses? or, in other words,
should not the litany be doubled, as is the case on Holy
Saturday ?[7] We should say not, for, in this supposition, the
litany of the Missal could not well be called, as it is here,
" brevior," since it would take a much longer time to recite
it. It is even inserted in some editions of the ritual, as, *e. g.*,
that for the use of the English clergy, with the responses in
the ordinary way.

[1] Vid. supra, n. 473.   [2] Rit. Toul., tit. v. n. 1.
[3] Rit. Toul., ibid. Memoriale Rituum, tit. vi. cap. i. *De præparandis*
in Baptisterio si adsit.   [4] Cfr. Merati, l. c. n. xxxvi.
[5] Rit. Toul., l. c.   [6] Rit. Toul., tit. v. n. 1. et 2.
[7] Rub. Mis. in loc.   Mem. Rituum, tit. vi. cap. ii. sec. vi. n. 5.

§ IV.—Et dicto ultimo, *Kyrie eleison*, Sacerdos dicat: *Pater Noster*, *et Credo in Deum*, etc., omnia clara voce: quibus finitis, dicat: ℣ *Apud te, Domine*, etc.

*549. In the ordinary litany, after the last "*Kyrie*," the Pater Noster is said "secreto," according to the rubric, and then the psalm, "*Deus in adjutorium*," etc. Here it is directed that the Pater Noster and the Creed be recited "clara voce," after which the priest is to say the versicles, prayers, and exorcism, marked in the ritual.

Rising from his knees, he says "*Dominus vobiscum*," with the prayer which follows; and then taking his place at the font, if he be not in it already, proceeds with the exorcism, which he says with his hands joined, making the sign of the cross over the water at the words marked in the ritual, which is held before him by one of the clerks.[1]

§ V.—Hic manu aquam dividat, et deinde de ea effundat extra marginem Fontis versus quatuor Orbis partes, prosequens: *Et in* quatuor *fluminibus*, etc.

550. If the place of the font admits of such an arrangement, the priest, according to some, should stand, during the exorcism and the rest of the ceremony, with his face to the west or the door of the church, the cross-bearer being on the other side of the font opposite him. This is the position assigned to him by Bauldry[2] and Merati.[3] But De Herdt[4] says he should have his face to the east, and this we think the more convenient position, because he is thus turned towards the high altar, as he is required to be in reciting the litany when there is no altar in the baptistery, and also because in this position he can more easily perform the ceremony which is prescribed in the present rubric.

*551. He first divides the water, and this with his *hand*, as Baruffaldi here observes,[5] and not merely with his fingers. He does so by making the sign of the cross (for the division should be made in the form of a cross),[6] with his hand immersed in the water to the wrist, or at least as far as the thumb. Then with his hand he throws out a little, or causes a little to overflow the margin towards the four cardinal points, in the following order, as is expressly directed in the "Memoriale

[1] Rit. Toul., l. c. n. 2.
[2] Pars iv. cap. xi. *De Sabbato Sancto*, art. 4, n. iii.
[3] Pars iv. tit. x. n. xxxviii.   [4] Pars v. n. 16, vi.
[5] Tit. xvi. n. 16.   [6] Ibid. n. 18.

"Rituum."[1]　1° Towards the east; 2° towards the west; 3° towards the north; 4° towards the south, thus:

1 E.
3 N.　　　　4 S.
2 W.

Now this arrangement of the numbers, which is given in the "Memoriale Rituum," appears to suggest that the priest should stand facing the east, otherwise he should pour out the water first towards himself; secondly, opposite himself; thirdly, on his right hand; and lastly, on his left; which would be against the usual order in such circumstances.

This ceremony signifies, according to Baruffaldi,[2] the universality of baptism and its diffusion throughout the world.

Having dried his hand with a towel, which should be presented to him by one of the clerics,[3] he continues; "Et in "quatuor fluminibus," etc.

§ VI.—Tunc sufflet ter in aquam versus tres partes secundum hanc figuram Ψ: deinde imponit incensum in thuribulo, et Fontem incensat.

*552. There is some diversity of opinion as to the manner in which the insufflation should here be made, or as to the figure which should be described by it; and this diversity arises, in part at least, from the different forms found in different editions of the Ritual and Missal. In some we have Y, in others Ψ, in others T, in others ✠.[4]　The "Memoriale Rituum" says: "Ter sufflat in formam Tridentalem juxta figuram in missali."[5] Now this expression, we think, implies that it is not made simply in the form of a cross, as Catalani maintains,[6] otherwise it would say "in modum Crucis," but in some one of the other figures above given, most probably Ψ, because this is the form given in the most approved editions of the Missal and Ritual. It is made, according to the Ritual of Toulon,[7] by describing first the centre line, then the line towards the right, and lastly the line towards the left.

After the insufflation he puts incense into the thurible, and, according to the Ritual of Toulon,[8] blesses it with the usual form: "Ab illo benedicaris in cujus honore cremaberis." Baruffaldi also[9] supposes that the incense is blessed, and

[1] Tit. vi. cap. ii. sec. iv. n. 9.　　[2] Loc. cit.　[3] Rit. Toul., tit. v. n. 3
[4] Cfr. Baruff., n. 19, et seq.　　Rit. Toul., l. c. n. 4.　Catal., tit. ii
cap. vii. § iv. n. i.　　　　　　[5] De Sab. Sanct. cap. ii. sec. iv. n. iii
[6] Loc. cit.　　　[7] Loc. cit.　　[8] Loc. cit.　　[9] Loc. cit. n. 21.

observes that the incensation here prescribed supplies the
place of the immersion of the Paschal candle, which is part
of the ceremony on Holy Saturday.   He incenses the font
with three swings,[1] in the same manner as the candles on the
Feast of the Purification, or the ashes on Ash Wednesday,
one towards the centre, one towards his left, and one towards
his right,—for the *right* of any object in front of us is to our
left, and its *left* to our *right*.[2]

§ VII.—Postea infundens de Oleo Catechumenorum in aquam in
modum Crucis, clara voce dicit : *Sanctificetur*, etc.
  Deinde infundit de Chrismate, modo quo supra, dicens : *Infusio
Chrismatis*, etc.
  Postea accipit ambas ampullas dicti Olei sancti et Chrismatis, et de
utroque simul in modum Crucis infundendo, dicit : *Commixtio Chrismatis*, etc.

*553. He next pours in some of the Oil of Catechumens,
making a cross on the water three times with the stream as
it issues from the vessel containing it, saying, at the same
time, " *Sanctificetur et fœcundetur*," etc.
  Then he pours in chrism in the same manner, *i. e.*, three
times in the form of a cross,[3] saying, "*Infusio Chrismatis*," etc.
  Lastly, taking the two vessels (both together, if possible, in his right hand), he pours oil and chrism together,
likewise thrice in form of a cross, saying, " *Commixtio
" Chrismatis*," etc.
  554. These ceremonies are of very great antiquity, being
prescribed wholly, or in part, in the most ancient missals and
rituals extant.   In some there is mention only of chrism, but in
many others both oil and chrism are mentioned.   There is some
variety also in the prayers, but the same idea runs through all,
as may be seen in the extracts from these books given by
Martene.[4]   "When baptism is administered with solemn cere-
" monies," says the Catechism of the Council of Trent, "the
" Catholic Church, guided by apostolic tradition, has
" uniformly observed the practice of adding (to the water) holy
" chrism, by which it is clear the effect of baptism is more
" fully declared."[5]
  The whole ceremony, as here prescribed, or as it may have
been formerly observed, is designed to signify that the water

---

[1] Rit. Toul., l. c.
[2] Vid. Merati, pars iv. tit. vi. n. x. et xi. et pars ii. tit. vi. n. xxxi.
[3] Cfr. Merati, pars iv. tit. x. n. xliii.
[4] *De Ant. Eccl. Ritibus.*, lib. i. cap. i art. xvii.
[5] Pars ii. cap ii. n. 11.

is sanctified, and has imparted to it, by the Holy Ghost, the
virtue of sanctifying and regenerating those who are baptized,
according to the idea expressed by so many of the early
Fathers. "Aquæ sanctificatæ vim sanctificandi combibunt,"
says Tertullian, *De Baptismo*, cap. 4. "Quod est uterus
"embryoni, hoc est fideli aqua."—St. Chrys., *Hom.* 25 *in
Joan.* "Spiritûs efficacitate sensibilis aqua in divinam
"quamdam et ineffabilem vim transformatur, omnesque demum
"in quibus fuerit sanctificat."—St. Cyr. Alex., lib. 2 *in
Joan.*[1]

§ VIII.—Tum, deposita ampulla, dextera manu Oleum sanctum et
Chrisma infusum miscet cum aqua, et spargit per totum Fontem.
Deinde medulla panis manum tergit; et si quis baptizandus est, eum
baptizat, ut supra. Quod si neminem baptizat, statim manus abluat, et
ablutio effundatur in Sacrarium.

*555. This rubric requires little or no explanation. There
cannot be, properly speaking, a mixture of the oil and water,
which refuse to unite; but the priest is directed to mingle
them with his right hand, so as to make the oil and chrism be
diffused, for the moment at least, through the water of the
font, and not merely rest on its surface; the mystic signification of the ceremony being the union of the faithful, represented by the water, with Christ represented by the oil and
chrism, according to Durandus and Quarti.[2] A film will
afterwards be formed on the surface, but this can be removed,
as has been stated before.[3]

*556. The rubric clearly supposes that he has such a
supply of the oil and chrism that they can be *poured into* the
font.[4] But if he has not, the ritual published for the use of
the English Church directs him, in a parenthetic clause, to
make the signs of the cross on the surface of the water with
his thumb, or an instrument of silver, after having dipped it
into the oilstocks. To apply the oil and chrism together in
such a case, we think he might dip his thumb into one, and
the index finger into the other, and with both united make
the sign of the cross.

He then rubs his hands with crumbs of bread, or a little
meal, and if there be any one to be baptized, does not wash
them until he has conferred baptism. But if there be no one
to be baptized, having rubbed his hands as directed, in order

[1] Cit. apud Delahogue, *De Sacramentis in genere*, cap. iv. art. i.
[2] Cit. apud Catalani, cap. vii. § vii. n. i.   [3] Supra, n. 163.
[4] Vid. supra, n. 265.

to remove the oil, he immediately washes them, and throws the water into the sacrarium.

The water, towel, and crumbs of bread should have been placed, before the commencement of the ceremony, on a table near the font; and, of course, if there be any one to be baptized, care should be taken to make the preparations prescribed by the rubrics in a preceding chapter.[1]

[1] Chap. iii. § xlii. et seq.

CHAPTER X.

§ I.—Siqua puerpera post partum, juxta piam ac laudabilem consuetudinem, ad Ecclesiam venire voluerit pro incolumitate sua Deo
gratias actura, petieritque a Sacerdote benedictionem, ipse superpelliceo
et stola alba indutus, cum ministro aspergillum deferente, ad fores
Ecclesiæ accedat, ubi illam foris ad limina genuflectentem, et candelam
accensam in manu tenentem Aqua benedicta aspergat, deinde dicat:
Adjutorium nostrum, etc.

557. This ceremony of the blessing, or, as it is sometimes
called, the churching, sometimes the purification, of women
after childbirth, is of great antiquity in the Church. St.
Gregory the Great, in one of his letters to St. Augustine,
Apostle of England, refers to it in words which are adopted in
the text of the canon, *Dist.* 5, *Si mulier*, and in which he declares that Christian women after childbirth are not prohibited, under pain of sin, from entering the church at any time,
but are free to go without the least delay to give thanks to
God. "Si mulier eadem hora qua genuerit, actura gratias intrat
"Ecclesiam, nullo peccati pondere gravatur."[1] Innocent III
declares the same, stating that the provisions of the Mosaic law,
which fixed a time during which women after childbirth were
excluded from the Temple, ceased under the Gospel; but
he adds: "Si tamen ex veneratione voluerint aliquamdiu
abstinere, devotionem earum non credimus improbandam."[2]

558. The law of Leviticus[3] prohibited women after childbirth from entering the sanctuary, and from touching anything
sacred, for forty days, if the child born were a male, or for
eighty days, if it were a female. It is evident, from the
words of the law, that it could not apply to the Blessed Virgin,
in whom there were none of the effects of ordinary childbirth,
since not only in conceiving, but in giving birth to the divine
Infant, she still remained a pure and perfect virgin.[4] Yet we

---

[1] Cit. apud Catal., tit. vii. cap. iii. n. ii.
[2] Cap. i. lib. iii. *Decret.* tit. 47, *De purif. post partum*, cit. apud
Catal., ibid.   [3] Chap. xii.
[4] Vid. Benedict XIV., *De Festis B. V. M.*, cap. ii. n. ii.

know from St. Luke[1] that she did not avail herself of the
exemption, but humbly complied with the requirements of the
law. A desire of imitating this humility of the Blessed Virgin
induced the custom amongst Christian mothers of abstaining
from entering the church for some time after childbirth.
They then asked the blessing of the priest at the church door,
and made their first visit one of thanksgiving to God for their
safe delivery.[2]

559. In the Greek Church, the custom is looked on as
imposing a strict obligation: "Obedientiam illam," says
Goar, "ex debito requirunt Græci."[3] But the canons above
cited, and the words of our rubric, show clearly that, in the
Latin Church, the custom, although recommended as pious
and laudable, does not bind under pain of sin. De Herdt
states that the third Provincial Council of Mechlin proposes
to make this benediction a matter of precept, but the decree
on the subject was changed by the authorities at Rome.

The pastor, then, should exhort women to receive the
benediction, but must not insist on their receiving it, as if the
omission would be a sin.

*560. There is nothing in the rubric, nor in any general
law of the Church, to exclude from this benediction women
who have given birth to illegitimate children, but they are
excluded by many diocesan and provincial statutes.[5] In
some parts of Ireland they are excluded, in others they are,
at least with certain restrictions, admitted. Amongst the
statutes of Cashel and Emly, drawn up in 1782, we find the
following: "Nulla mulier quæ extra matrimonium pepererit
"ante mensem elapsum purificetur; si iterum et similiter
"pepererit ante duos menses elapsos non purificetur; ter extra
"matrimonium pariens nunquam purificetur."[6]

The Congregation of Rites having been consulted on the
subject, decided that none but those whose children are the
fruit of lawful wedlock can claim a right to this benediction.[7]
The pastor, therefore, may refuse it in any case in which the

---

[1] Cap. ii. v. 22, et seq.   [2] Vid. Baruff., tit. xliii. n. 8. Catal.,
l. c. n.iii. Caval., vol. iv. cap. xiii.

[3] ΕΥΧΟΛΟΓΙΟΝ, etc., In Orationem pro muliere puerpera post quadraginta dies Notæ, n. i. pag. 328.   [4] Pars. vi. n. 11, iii.

[5] De Herdt, l. c. i. Vid. Mélanges Théologiques, Vme Série, 3me
Cahier, pag. 375.

[6] Cap. ii. De Baptismo. Vid. Collections on Irish Church History,
etc., Appendix C, p. 475.

[7] 18 Jun. 1859, in Wratislavien., apud Falise, Sac. Rit. Cong. Decr.
V. Benedict., § i. n. 13.

birth is notoriously illegitimate, even when there is no diocesan or provincial statute requiring him to do so.

*561. The rubric clearly supposes that the ceremony is performed in the church, and, according to the discipline that generally prevails now, it should not be performed elsewhere. There is no doubt that in some places it was the custom to perform it in private houses, at least when asked for by those who were unable to go to the church. Martene gives an extract from the ancient ritual of Chalons, which directs the priest what to do in such circumstances.[1] Catalani gives another from the "Sacerdotale Romanum," published at Venice in 1567, which likewise prescribes what the priest should do in the case.[2] The prevalence of the practice may be inferred also from the many decrees prohibiting it, which are cited by Catalani.[3] St. Charles, in the third Provincial Council of Milan, prohibits it: "Etiamsi mulier ob adversam "valetudinem ecclesiam adire nequeat."[4]

The custom prevailed in Ireland in the times of persecution when there were no churches, and is still continued in some parts of the country. It appears to have prevailed in America also, for, in the first Provincial Council of Baltimore, the fathers express a desire, though they do not strictly order, that for the future the benediction be not given "extra Ec-"clesiam vel locum ubi sacrum fit."[5]

The decree in its first form contained a strict precept, but this was changed, by direction of the Sacred Congregation, into the expression of a wish. The reason assigned for the change shows what prudent caution is necessary, as has been before stated,[6] in dealing with an old custom at variance with the rubric: . . "Nam valde periculosum est," says the Sacred Congregation, "contrarium morem generali lege repente "mutare."[7]

In districts, then, where there are no churches, and where mass is celebrated in private houses, the benediction may be given to those who desire it; for, after all, the ritual, according to the instruction of the Sacred Congregation just cited, does not require that it be given in the church exclusively. Even where there is no want of churches, it may, in special

---

[1] *De Antiquis Ecclesiæ Ritibus*, lib. i. cap. ix. art. v. ordo xi.
[2] Tit. vii. cap. iii. n. viii.   [3] Loc. cit. n. ix. et x.   [4] *Act. Eccl. Mediolan.*, Conc. Prov. iii. ∮ *Quæ ad Sacramentalia et Sacramenta generatim spectant*, pag. 74.   [5] Decr. xix. q. v. in Append.
[6] Vid. supra, n 84, et seq.   [7] *Instructio circa Decr. a Syn. Prov. Balt.*, in Decr. 19°. Vid. Append.

cases, at least with the sanction of the bishop, be given " extra " ecclesiam." This is the conclusion of the "Melanges " Theologiques."[1]

562. But the ceremony, as we have seen, is not of obligation, and may be omitted without scruple.[2] It should, therefore, at least as a general rule, either be performed in exact accordance with the rubric, or be omitted altogether.[3]

563. There is nothing in the rubric to imply that the right of giving this benediction is reserved to the parish priest. The wording appears to leave the woman free to receive it in any church she may select. Hence it was commonly maintained that Religious might give it in their churches to any who presented themselves, and this view is supported by several decisions of the Congregation of the Council cited by Cavalieri.[4] But a decree of the Congregation of Rites,[5] and the latest decisions of the Congregation of the Council,[6] are in favor of the opinion more commonly held at present, which would reserve the right of giving the benediction to the parish priest.[7] The "Melanges Theologiques" regards these as decisive. So do De Herdt[8] and Falise.[9]

Cavalieri, however, contends that the decree of the Congregation of Rites applies only to the churches of certain confraternities, about which there was question in the case proposed;[10] and it is probable that the answers of the Congregation of the Council may be understood also as applying only in the cases proposed,[11] so that it is very doubtful whether there be any general law reserving this benediction to the parochial clergy, but there are many provincial and diocesan statutes reserving it.[12]

564. It is clear,[13] from what has been said above, that the benediction may be given at any time after childbirth that is found convenient. In the Greek Church it is given only after an interval of forty days.[14] But there is no obligation to wait for this, or for any other fixed time. It is even recommended *not* to do so, in order to avoid the

---

[1] Loc. cit. pag. 379.   [2] Supra, n. 559.
[3] Vid. Catal. l. c. n. x. Caval., vol. iv. cap. xiii. *De Benedictione Puerperarum*, in Decr. v. n. vi. De Herdt, l. c. vi.
[4] Loc. cit.   [5] 10 Decr. 1703, *Urbis et Orbis*, ad. 6, n. 3670.
[6] 31 Mar., 1759, et 26 April, 1788, cit. apud Melanges Théologiques, Vme Série, pag. 386.   [7] Loc. cit. p. 383, et seq.   [8] Pars vi. n. 11, v.
[9] IIIme Partie, sec. ii. chap. i. § i. n. i. note.   [10] Loc. cit. in Decr. iv.
[11] Vid. Ferraris, edit. Migne. *Supplementum*. Resolutiones Sac. Cong. Concilii, n. 340. *Celsonen.*, vol. viii. pag. 1109.   [12] Vid. De Herdt, l. c.
[13] Supra, n. 558.   [14] Goar, loc. cit. note 2, p. 383.

appearance of conforming to the old Jewish law, as if it were still in force.[1]

In some places it is usual for women not to leave the house for about six weeks after childbirth, and this custom, where it prevails, is sufficient, according to the common opinion, to excuse them from the obligation of hearing mass during that time.[2] But we have already seen[3] that they are free to go to the church as soon as they please; and though it is usual and even advisable, to ask for the benediction the first time they go, they may put it off without scruple till another time, which they may think more convenient.

565. Quarti, and others cited by Baruffaldi,[4] say that the mother, when about to receive the benediction, should bring her child with her and offer it to God, after the example of the Blessed Virgin, who offered the divine Infant in the temple on the day of her purification. This is the usage in the Greek Church. The Euchologium contains a prayer having special reference to the child, and directs this prayer to be omitted in case the child be dead, supposing thereby that this is the only case in which the child is not present with the mother.[5]

In the Latin Church, however, the usage, though recommended by some as pious and laudable, does not prevail. It is easily seen that the ceremony, as we have it in the Roman Ritual, regards only the mother, and contains nothing to imply that the child should be present.[6]

*566. The priest is directed by the rubric to vest for this ceremony in surplice and white stole. The stole should be white, because this is the color used by the Church on the feast of the Purification of the Blessed Virgin, with which, as has been said,[7] the present ceremony is closely connected.[8]

He should be attended by a clerk vested in surplice,[9] who precedes him from the vestry to the door of the church, carrying the "aspergillum," or brush for sprinkling the holy water, which is supposed to be, as usual, in a stoup at the door.

*567. The rubric requires that the woman be outside the door of the church, just at the threshold, "foris ad limina, as she thus acknowledges her unworthiness to enter until she

---

[1] Baruff., tit. xliii. n. 10. De Herdt, loc. cit. i.
[2] St. Lig., lib. iv. n. 330, in fine.   [3] Supra, n. 557.
[4] Loc. cit. n. 14.   [5] Vid. Catal., tit. vii. cap. iii. n. xxiii.
[6] Baruff., n. 15. Caval., l. c. De Herdt, l. c. iv.
[7] Supra, n. 558.   [8] Baruff., n. 22. De Herdt, loc. cit. vii.
[9] Vid. supra, n. 126.

receives the blessing of the priest and is introduced by him.
Hence the ceremony should not be performed elsewhere, *e. g.*,
in the sacristy, or at the door of the sacristy. This is an
abuse strongly censured by Baruffaldi[1] and Cavalieri,[2] who
say that the ceremony, being free, should be performed as the
rubric directs, or not at all. If there be a porch, she can
remain within it, as she is still "foris." But if there be not,
and if she cannot remain outside without danger to her
health, she may be allowed to remain just within the door,
according to De Herdt.[3]

The rubric prescribes that she be kneeling with a lighted
candle in her hand, when the priest comes to the door.

*568. Taking the "aspergillum," which is presented by
the clerk, he sprinkles her with holy water. This should be
done in form of a cross, according to De Herdt[4] and Falise,[5]
though the rubric does not explicitly prescribe this here as it
does below. Cavalieri[6] and Baruffaldi[7] recommend him to
say the usual words, "*Asperges me Domine*," etc., though the
rubric does not mention them.

Having returned the "aspergillum" to the clerk, he says,
"*Adjutorium nostrum*," etc. Falise[8] directs him, while saying these words, to make the sign of the cross on the woman,
but we think it is more in accordance with usage and analogy
to make it on himself.[9] He then says the antiphon and psalm,
"*Domini est terra*," etc.

§ II.—Deinde porrigens ad manum mulieris extremam partem stolæ,
eam introducit in Ecclesiam, dicens : *Ingredere*, etc.

*569. The priest then presents to her the extremity of the
stole that hangs on his left, which she takes in her right
hand ;[10] then, rising up, she enters the church, walking on the
left of the priest, when he says, "*Ingredere*," etc.

The commentators do not say what she is to do at this time
with the lighted candle. They are agreed that the reason
why it is required at all is, because lighted candles are car-

§ III.—Et ipsa ingressa genuflectit coram Altari, et orat, gratias
agens Deo de beneficiis sibi collatis ; et Sacerdos dicit, *Kyrie eleison*, etc.

---

[1] Tit. xliii. n. 23, 24.
[2] Cap. xiii. *De Benedictione Puerperarum*, Decr. v. n. vi.
[3] Pars vi. n. 11, vii. 2°. Vid. supra, n. 289.
[4] Loc. cit. 5°.   [5] *De la purif. des femmes*, etc., n. 2.
[6] Loc. cit.   [7] Loc. cit. n. 28.
[8] Loc. cit.   [9] Vid. infra, chap. xiv. § xvi.
[10] Baruff., n. 30. Caval., l. c. n. vii. De Herdt, l. c. 6°.

ried in the procession on the feast of the Purification of the
Blessed Virgin, which the present ceremony commemorates.
It would seem, therefore, that she should carry the candle
while entering the church; and as she can no longer hold it
in her right hand, she should have transferred it to her left
before taking hold of the priest's stole.

*570. The priest conducts her, in the manner explained,[1]
to the altar, before which she is directed to kneel down and
make her thanksgiving. This altar, according to Baruffaldi,[2]
should be that of the Blessed Sacrament or of the Blessed
Virgin. One of these is usually selected, but it may be any
other. Cavalieri recommends the one nearest the door, as
more conformable to the words of the rubric.[3] The prayers
she is to say are left to her own devotion. When she has
knelt down, the priest, having made the proper reverence,
ascends the predella, and turning towards her,[4] says the
prayers prescribed, "*Kyrie eleison,*" etc.

§ IV.—Deinde illam aspergit iterum Aqua benedicta in modum
Crucis, dicens: *Pax et benedictio*, etc.

*571. Having finished the prayers, he takes the asper-
gillum presented to him by the clerk, and again sprinkles
her with holy water. The rubric here directs that he do so in
form of a cross, saying the words, *Pax et benedictio*, etc.
When water is sprinkled in form of a cross, it should be
sprinkled first on the centre, then on the right, and lastly on
the left of the person or object.[5]

The holy water should have been previously left on the
credence, otherwise it should be carried by the clerk along
with the "aspergillum" from the door.

572. We find nothing in the commentators about the time
of extinguishing the candle. The woman usually holds it
lighted until the end of the ceremony, having transferred it
again to her right hand on kneeling down before the altar.
She then presents it to the priest, who hands it to the clerk
to be extinguished.

It is the custom in many places to present other offerings
as well as the candle. The manner in which these are disposed of is regulated by the statutes or approved usages of
the diocese.[6] In churches where there is no fund for the
altar requisites, the candles are usually set apart for the use of
the altar.

[1]Caval., l. c. n. viii.   [2] Loc. cit. n. 32.   [3] Loc. cit. in Decr. v.
[4] De Herdt, l. c. 7°. [5] Vid. De Herdt, vii. 5°. [6] Vid. De Herdt, l. c. 9°.

573. The priest, having concluded the ceremony, returns to the sacristy, preceded by the clerk, and leaves the woman to continue her thanksgiving according to her devotion.[1]

Should he be asked on this occasion to celebrate mass in honor of the Blessed Virgin, it was decided by the Sacred Congregation that he cannot say the mass of the Purification, but must take the votive mass assigned for the season, at the end of the Missal.[2] Moreover, the mass enjoys no privilege, and can be said only on the days on which votive masses are permitted by the rubric.[3]

If he be about to celebrate this votive mass, or any other for which the color is white, he may vest in alb and stole from the commencement, and at the conclusion of the foregoing ceremony put on the rest of the vestments for mass.

Should two or more present themselves together, the ceremony may, we think, be performed for them in common.[4] In this case the priest should use the plural number in the invitation to enter the church (saying " *Ingredimini*," etc., and presenting the stole, as in the baptism of adults),[5] in the versicles, the prayer, and the benediction.

---

[1] Baruff., n. 33. Caval., l. c. n. ix.
[2] 12 Mar. 1678, *in Mexican.* n. 2359, ad 8.   [3] De Herdt, 1 c. 10ᶜ
[4] Vid. infra, n. 949.   [5] Vid. supra n. 502.

CHAPTER XI.

§ I.—Omnibus quidem Ecclesiæ Catholicæ Sacramentis religiose sancteque tractandis, magna ac diligens cura adhibenda est; sed præcipue in administrando ac suscipiendo sanctissimo Eucharistiæ Sacramento, quo nihil dignius, nihil sanctius et admirabilius habet Ecclesia Dei; cum in eo contineatur præcipuum et maximum Dei donum, et ipsemet omnis gratiæ et sanctitatis fons auctorque Christus Dominus.

574. The object of all the ceremonies and observances prescribed by the Church in the administration of the Blessed Eucharist, is to secure that profound reverence which is due to this adorable mystery. What she here prescribes in her ritual, is in perfect accordance with what she elsewhere prescribes in her liturgy. In all, the same object is apparent; in all, there is shown the same firm and lively faith in the real presence of "the Word made flesh" under the sacramental veils. This faith is the very soul of her public worship. This it is which gathers round the altar and the tabernacle all that is most costly in material, and all that is most elaborate in art. This it is which directs the minutest ceremony, which surrounds the consecrated host, wherever it may be, whether on the altar or carried to the poorest dwelling, with all the outward marks of respect and reverence which the circumstances will permit.

575. In the instructions which the Church here gives to her pastors, she commences by putting before them the dignity and excellence of the Eucharist, as the greatest of all the sacraments, the greatest and most astonishing of all God's gifts, inasmuch as it contains not merely grace, like the other sacraments, but the author and source of all grace and sanctity, Christ our Lord Himself. "If any one denieth," says the Council of Trent, "that, in the sacrament of the most "holy Eucharist, are contained truly, really, and substantially, "the body and blood together with the soul and divinity of "our Lord Jesus Christ, and, consequently, the whole Christ, "but saith that He is only therein as in a sign, or in figure, "or in virtue: let him be anathema." [1]

[1] Sess. xiii. can. i. Waterworth's translation.

§ II.—Parochus igitur summum studium in eo ponat, ut cum ipse venerabile hoc Sacramentum, qua decet reverentia, debitoque cultu tractet, custodiat, et administret; tum etiam populus sibi commissus religiose colat, sancte frequenterque suscipiat, præsertim in majoribus anni solemnitatibus.

576. The pastor should show a great zeal for the honor of the Blessed Sacrament; in the first place, by taking care to provide, as far as he can, whatever is requisite in order to keep it and administer it in a manner suited to its dignity; and, secondly, by inspiring those who are committed to his charge with a great devotion towards it, inducing them to adore it reverently, and to receive it with the proper dispositions frequently, and especially on the more solemn festivals. Further on, the Rubrics treat of the manner in which it is to be kept and administered, but they first treat of its reception by the faithful. The pastor is to exhort them to communicate frequently. We cannot do better than give here what the Catechism of the Council of Trent has on this subject, for it presents us with a clear view of the teaching and practice of the Church from the earliest times.

577. After referring to the decree which obliges the faithful to receive the Eucharist at least once a year, it proceeds: "Let not the faithful, however, deem it enough to receive the "body of the Lord once a year only, in obedience to the "authority of this decree: they should approach oftener; but "whether monthly, weekly, or daily, can be decided by no "fixed universal rule. St. Augustine, however, lays down a "most certain standard: 'Live,' says he, 'in such a manner "'as to be able to receive daily'" (St. Aug., *de Verbis Do-* "*mini*, ser. 28, qui desumptus est ex Amb. lib. *5 de Sacram.*, c. "4). It will, therefore, be the part of the pastor frequently "to admonish the faithful, that as they think it necessary "every day to nurture the body, they should also not neglect "every day to feed and nourish the soul with this sacrament; "for the soul, it is clear, stands not less in need of spiritual, "than the body of corporal food. And here it will be most "useful to recapitulate the inestimable and divine advantages, "which, as we have already shown, flow from sacramental "communion. The pastor will also cite the figure of the "manna, which it was necessary to use every day in order to "repair the strength of the body (*Exod.* xvi. 21, 22); and "will add the authorities of the Fathers, which earnestly rec- "ommend the frequent participation of this sacrament, for "these words, 'Thou sinnest daily, receive daily,' '*Quotidie*

" '*peccas, quotidie sume,*' are not the sentiment of St. Augus-
" tine alone, but also, as diligent inquiry will easily discover,
" the sentiment of all the Fathers who wrote on this subject
" (St. Ignat. *in Ep. ad Eph.*, Basil *ad Cæsar. Patriar.*, Amb.,
" lib. *5 de Sacram.*, etc.).

" That there was once a time when the faithful received
" the Eucharist daily, we learn from the *Acts of the Apostles,*
" ii. 42, etc.; for all who then professed the faith of Christ
" burned with such true and sincere charity, that, devoting
" themselves, as they did unceasingly, to prayer and other
" works of piety, they were found prepared to receive every
" day the sacred mysteries of the Lord's body. This practice,
" which seems to have been interrupted, was again partially
" revived by St. Anacletus, Pope and Martyr, who com-
" manded that the ministers assisting at the sacrifice of the
" mass should communicate; an ordinance, declares the pon-
" tiff, of apostolic institution (S. Anacl., *Ep.* 2, et citatur *de*
" *Cons. dist.* 2, *c. Peracta*). It was also for a long time a
" practice in the Church, that as soon as the sacrifice was
" ended, the priest, turning to the congregation, invited the
" faithful to the holy table in these words: ' Venite fratres
" ' ad Communionem '—' Come, brothers, to the Communion ; '
" and those who were prepared then received the holy mys-
" teries with the greatest devotion (Dionys. *de Eccl. Hier.*, c.
" 3. Greg. *lib.* 2, *dial.* c. 23; *de Consec., dist.* 2, c. 13).
" But subsequently, when charity and devotion had grown so
" cold that the faithful very rarely approached the Commu-
" nion, it was decreed by Pope Fabian that all should com-
" municate, thrice every year, at Christmas, at Easter, and at
" Pentecost; a decree which was subsequently confirmed by
" many councils, particularly by the first of Agatha (S. Fab.,
" *Epis.* 3, *ad Hilar. Ep.*, cit. *de Consecr., dist.* 2, cap. *Etsi.*,
" Concil. Turon., iii. c. 50; Conc. Agath., c. 38). When, at
" length, such was the decay of piety, that not only was this
" holy and salutary ordinance unobserved, but communion
" was deferred even for years, it was decreed in the Council
" of Lateran that all the faithful should communicate at least
" once a year, at Easter, and that those who might have
" neglected to do so should be prohibited access to the Church
" (Conc Later., can. 1, cit. *de pœn. et remiss.*, c. *Omnis.*, et
" Trid., Sess. 13, can. 9)."[1]

578. On the advantages of frequent communion, and the

---

[1] *Pars.* ii. cap. iv. n. 60 et 61.

dispositions to be required by the confessor in those who are
admitted to it, we must refer to St. Liguori, whose authority
is the great guide of confessors at the present day. He treats
the subject at length in his "*Praxis Confessarii.*"[1] What he
there teaches regarding the dispositions required, appears to
be pretty fairly summed up in the following passage, from
which it will be seen that by frequent communion he means
communion at least several times in the week. It may be
found in the chapter on communion, printed with the translation
of his "*Visits to the Blessed Sacrament.*" "A soul that
" commits deliberate venial sins by telling wilful lies, by
" vanity of dress, by feelings of rancor, or by inordinate
" attachments, or who is guilty of any other similar faults
" which she knows to be an obstacle to her advancement in
" perfection, and who does not endeavor to correct these
" defects, cannot be permitted to communicate more frequently
" than once a week. To receive strength to preserve her
" from falling into mortal sins, she may be allowed commu-
" nion every eight days. For my part, I should have great
" difficulty in allowing frequent communion to persons dis-
" posed to persevere in any defect which, though not clearly
" a venial sin, would be certainly contrary to perfection,
" particularly if it were a defect against humility or obedience.
" But if a soul has no affection for any venial sin, if she
" abstains from deliberate venial sins, and attends to prayer
" and the mortification of her passions and senses, the con-
" fessor may permit her to communicate three, four, or even
" five times in the week. And when a soul has attained a
" considerable degree of perfection, when she spends several
" hours in the day at prayer, and has moreover conquered the
" greater part of her evil inclinations, she may, according
" to St. Francis de Sales (*Introd. to a Devout Life,* chap. 20),
" be allowed communion every day. For, as St. Prosper
" says, this is the perfection which a person subject to human
" frailty can attain in this life."[2]

§ III.—Ideo populum sæpius admonebit, qua præparatione, et quanta
animi religione ac pietate, et humili etiam corporis habitu ad tam divinum Sacramentum debeat accedere, ut præmissa Sacramentali Confessione, omnes saltem a media nocte jejuni, et utroque genuflexo Sacramentum humiliter adorent, ac reverenter suscipiant, viris quantum fieri
potest a mulieribus separatis.

579. The faithful are to be carefully instructed as to the
preparation they must make when about to receive the Holy

[1] Cap. 9, § iv. u. 148, et seq.   [2] *On Communion,* n. 7.

Communion.   Certain dispositions both of soul and body are
required.   These dispositions are very fully explained in the
Catechism of the Council of Trent.   "The first preparation,"
it says, "which the faithful should make, is to distinguish
"table from table, this sacred table from profane tables, this
"celestial bread from common bread.   This we do when we
"firmly believe that the Eucharist really and truly contains
"the body and blood of the Lord, of Him whom the angels
"adore in heaven (*Psal.* xcvi. 8; *Heb.* i. 6), at whose nod
"the pillars of heaven fear and tremble (*Job*, xxvi. 2),
"of whose glory the heavens and earth are full (*Isaias*, vi. 3).
"This is to discern the body of the Lord, in accordance with
"the admonition of the Apostle (1 *Cor.* xi. 29), venerating
"rather, as we ought, the greatness of the mystery, than too
"curiously and disputatiously investigating its truth."[1]

580. If a person be conscious of mortal sin, he cannot
approach the holy table until he has purified his soul by the
sacrament of penance.   "We should next carefully examine
"our consciences," says the Catechism,[2] "lest perhaps they
"be defiled by some mortal sin, of which it is necessary to
"repent, in order to be cleansed from its defilement by the
"salutary medicine of contrition and confession; for the
"Council of Trent has declared that no one conscious of
"mortal sin, and having an opportunity of a confessor, how-
"ever contrite he may deem himself, is to receive the Holy
"Eucharist until he has been purified by sacramental con-
"fession" (Sess. xii. can. 11).

The Council teaches[3] that this obligation of confession for
such as are conscious of mortal sin, is included in the probation required by the Apostle,[4] and theologians commonly
teach that it is imposed even by divine precept.[5]   To receive
any other sacrament, it is enough that the sinner be contrite,
or that he *bona fide* believe himself to be contrite; but he
cannot receive the Eucharist, however contrite he may think
himself, until he has gone to confession, if he has an opportunity.[6]   That any one conscious of mortal sin may lawfully
communicate without previous confession, these two things
must concur: there must be no opportunity of confessing,
and there must be a moral necessity of communicating.[7]

*581. The words of the rubric here seem to extend the

---

[1] Pars ii. cap. iv. n. 57.   [2] Loc. cit.
[3] Cap. vii.   [4] 1 Cor. xi. 28.
[5] St. Lig., lib. vi. n. 256.   [6] Vid. supra, n. 108, et seq.
[7] St. Lig., n. 255, in parenth.   Vid. etiam, n. 250, et seq.

obligation of confession as a preparation for communion to
all the faithful. In strictness it applies only to those who
are conscious of mortal sin. But confession is recommended
even to those who are not, that they may approach with
greater purity of soul and greater fervor; and in practice it
may be said that it is required of all who communicate only
seldom. The pastor, then, is perfectly justified in laying it
down, as a general rule, that confession is a necessary preparation for communion; but he should explain that only
those who are conscious of mortal sin would be guilty of sacrilege by communicating without previous confession.

582. He would do well, also, in giving instructions on
this subject, to state, in order to prevent the perplexity which
may easily happen to some, that if a person, when just about
to communicate, so that he cannot retire without risk of injury
to his character, remembers a sin which he inculpably omitted
in his confession, he may, nevertheless, receive communion,
and is merely required to mention that sin in his next confession. All theologians are agreed on this decision.[1] Collet[2] and some others go further, and would give the same
decision even when the person could abstain from communion
without any injury to his character, and could even go to confession without inconvenience. Because that sin, they say,
has been remitted, though indirectly, by the confession already made; and the Council of Trent merely requires that
no one conscious of mortal sin, however contrite he may
think himself, shall approach without being purified by previous sacramental confession. He is still bound, no doubt,
to confess that sin, but he is not bound till the precept of
confession urges. St. Liguori regards this opinion as very
probable.[3]

*583. We have already seen[4] what are the dispositions
required in those who are allowed frequent communion. It
is not required, nor even recommended, that they should go
to confession before every communion. "Some persons,"
says St. Liguori, "of very delicate consciences, have been
"in the habit of going to confession every day. But, for the
"generality of spiritual souls, and particularly for the scru-
"pulous, it will be sufficient to confess their sins once, or, at
"most, twice a week. In his treatise on communion, Father

---

[1] St. Lig., n. 257, Prima Sententia *Excipiunt tamen.*
[2] *De Eucharistia,* cap. vi. art. iii. Concl. iv. Quær. 2.
[3] Ibid. *Secunda Sententia.*   [4] Supra, n. 578.

"Barisoni, resting on the authority of St. Ambrose and of
"many other authors, says, that when a spiritual soul feels
"her conscience burdened with a venial sin which she has
"not an opportunity of confessing, she ought not to abstain
"from the Holy Communion. St. Francis de Sales gives
"the same advice in one of his letters. The holy Council
"of Trent teaches that, for the remission of venial sins, there
"are other means, such as acts of contrition or of charity.
"It is better to employ these means to purify the soul from a
"venial sin, than to be deprived of communion in conse-
"quence of not having an opportunity of going to confession.
"And a learned director has said, that it is sometimes more
"profitable to a timorous soul to prepare for the Holy Com-
"munion by her own acts than by confession, because she
"then makes more fervent acts of sorrow, of humility, and
"confidence." [1]

*584. So much for the dispositions of the soul. But the
body also must be prepared, as we are here admonished by
the rubric. The exterior should be humble and modest; no
pomp or vanity in the dress or manner. St. Charles, in his
"Instructions,"[2] directs pastors to admonish the faithful, and
especially women, that they must present themselves for
communion in a modest dress, and to refuse communion to
those who do not. St. Liguori also teaches that communion
should be refused to one who "nimis immodeste accedat."[3]
The dress, however, should be decent, according to one's condition, and particular attention should be paid to cleanliness.[4]
Martene shows that in the early ages the faithful never approached without having carefully washed their hands and
face.[5]

St. Charles[6] would require men to lay aside their arms.
St. Liguori says it is congruous that they should; but he
excepts the military knights of St. John of Jerusalem, who
should wear their swords.[7]

Priests, when they communicate, "more laicorum," should
wear a surplice and stole.[8]

585. "The dignity of so great a sacrament also demands,"
says the Catechism of the Council of Trent, "that for some
"days previous to communion, married persons abstain from

[1] *Praxis Conf.*, n. 148.
[2] *Act. Eccl. Mediol.*, pars iv. *Instruct. Sacr. Com.* pag. 611.
[3] Lib. vi. n. 275.   [4] St. Lig., ibid.
[5] *De Ant. Eccl. Rit.*, lib. i. cap. iv. art. x. n. vii.
[6] Loc. cit.   [7] Ibid.   [8] Vid. infra, chap. xii. § vi.

"the marriage debt."[1] Theologians, however, commonly teach that the obligation of abstaining, even on the day of communion, is only *sub levi ;* and, if the act be free from sin, there is no obligation, it is only of counsel, to abstain.[2]

586. The disposition of body most strictly required is, that the communicant be fasting from the previous midnight. The Blessed Eucharist was instituted by our Lord after supper, and for a short time was celebrated and administered only after supper. Martene shows that for the first three centuries, and even much later, it was still in many places celebrated after supper.[3] But there is little doubt that in others the custom of receiving communion, fasting, prevailed from the very time of the Apostles, though it is not quite certain at what date it became obligatory throughout the whole Church.[4] The Catechism of the Council of Trent says that "the practice of receiving it fasting, introduced, as ancient "writers record, by the Apostles, has always been retained "and observed."[5]

*587. The fast required is to be understood of the natural fast, or entire abstinence from anything in the way of meat or drink. The Catechism of the Council of Trent says: "We are to approach the holy table fasting, having not at "all eaten or drunk at least from the preceding midnight up "to the very moment of receiving the Holy Eucharist."[6]

St. Charles, in his "Instructions," recommends the communicant to fast also the previous day, or at least to sup sparingly. The fast thus recommended, however, is to be understood of an ecclesiastical fast, that is, of a fast on a single meal and collation, according to the law of the Church. This may serve to explain what is meant by saying that the communicant should be fasting *at least* from the preceding midnight, "saltem a media nocte," for it was the practice of many to observe an ecclesiastical fast on the previous day.

588. The smallest quantity in the way of food or drink is sufficient to violate this natural fast. No "levitas materiæ" is admitted here, as it is when there is question of violating the ecclesiastical fast.[7] But then what is taken must be, according to the common opinion of theologians, in the first place, something external, "ab extrinseco." Hence, to

---

[1] Loc. cit. n. 58.   [2] St. Lig. n. 273.
[3] De Ant. Eccl. Rit., lib. i. cap. iii. art. iv.
[4] Cfr. Chardon, His. des Sacrem., liv. i^{er}, sec. iiime, cap. vii.
[5] Pars ii. cap. iv. n. 6.   [6] Pars ii. cap. iv. n. 58.
[7] St. Lig., n. 278.

swallow one's saliva, or blood proceeding from the gums or teeth, etc., is no violation of the natural fast.

Secondly, it must be taken as food or drink. Hence it is not a violation of the fast to snuff, or smoke tobacco, though some particles may reach the stomach, nor to swallow along with the saliva some drops of the water used in washing the mouth, or particles of the food taken on the previous day that may have adhered to the gums, or may have been fastened in the teeth.[1] Here something depends on the intention. If any of these things be swallowed purposely, the fast, according to a very probable opinion, is violated; but it is not, if they be inhaled with the breath or get mixed with the saliva, and thus pass into the stomach unintentionally. St. Liguori observes that one should not be scrupulous in this matter.

Thirdly, it must be something which affords nutriment, or is capable of being digested. Hence, to swallow a bit of metal, a small pebble, or the like, does not violate the fast.[2]

589. There are certain cases, however, in which the Holy Eucharist may be received by those who are not fasting. 1° When it is administered to those who are in danger of death, as we shall see in treating of the viaticum.[3] 2° When it is received in order to protect it from irreverence. 3° When it is received in order to avoid scandal, as, e. g., if a priest, after having commenced mass, remembers that he has broken the fast; but if he remembers it before commencing, he can almost always remove the scandal by simply stating what has happened. 4° When it is received in order to complete the sacrifice in the various cases mentioned in the rubrics of the Missal.[4]

590. The communicant should kneel on both knees and adore the Blessed Sacrament before receiving it, according to that of St. Augustine: "Nemo illam carnem manducat nisi "prius adoraverit" (in Psal. xcviii.).[5] In the early ages the communicants received standing, and this is still the custom in the Oriental Church,[6] but in the Western Church they are required to be kneeling.

---

[1] Vid Rub. Missalis, De Defectibus, § ix. n. 3.
[2] St. Lig., n. 279, et seq.　　　[3] Infra, chap. xiv. § vi.
[4] De Defectibus, § iii. n. 5; § iv. n. 5 et 6; § x. n. 3. Vid. St. Lig., n. 287, et seq.
[5] Cit. apud Bellarmine, De Eucharistia, lib. ii. cap. xxiv.
[6] Cfr. Martene, lib. i. cap. iv. art. x. n. vii.

591. Care must be taken also that men and women communicate apart from each other, at different hours, or at different places in the church.

St. Charles directs the pastor to prepare two altars, one for men and the other for women, especially if there be a great concourse of communicants.[1] In this country the arrangements to be made for the purpose will, of course, depend on the accommodation which the church affords, the number of communicants, the number of masses celebrated, and other circumstances, which the prudent pastor will take into account. The rubric is clearly an important one, and he should make provision, as best he can, for carrying out what it prescribes.

§ IV.—Moneantur præterea communicantes, ut sumpto Sacramento non statim ab Ecclesia discedant, aut colloquantur, ne statim vagis oculis circumspiciant, aut expuant neque de libro statim orationes recitent, ne Sacramenti species de ore decidant; sed, qua par est devotione, aliquantisper in oratione permaneant, gratias agentes Deo de tam singulari beneficio, atque etiam de sanctissima Passione Dominica, in cujus memoriam hoc mysterium celebratur et sumitur.

592. This rubric, as Baruffaldi observes,[2] recommends rather than prescribes. But it contains a great deal of important instruction as to what should be done immediately after communion; and the pastor should be careful to convey this instruction to his flock. To look about one, or to converse with others just after receiving, could hardly be excused from a positive irreverence to our Lord in the Blessed Sacrament. To spit out, or to recite prayers, especially with considerable action of the organs, while the sacred species is still in the mouth, would be manifestly attended with the danger of allowing some particles to drop from the mouth. The communicant, then, is to be warned against all this, and to be advised, before using his prayer-book, to spend a few moments in mental prayer and thanksgiving to God for the incomparable gift he has received, devoutly calling to mind our Saviour's passion and death, of which the Blessed Eucharist is the perpetual memorial.

593. St. Charles gives several most useful instructions on this subject. According to these instructions, the communicant, in receiving the Blessed Sacrament, should hold the communion cloth with both hands under the chin. He should keep the face somewhat elevated, and open the mouth,

[1] Act. pars iv. Inst. Euch. § *De Preparatione quam adhibebit Parochus*, etc., pag. 426.   [2] Tit. xxiii. n. 45.

so that the priest, in placing the Sacred Host on the tongue, may not be obliged to touch the beard, lips, or teeth.

The extremity of the tongue should rest on the lower teeth, and not protrude beyond them; nor should the tongue be moved from that position until the priest has withdrawn his hand after placing the sacred particle on it.

He should abstain from sighing or breathing in such a way that the breath might reach any of the sacred particles.

When the priest has withdrawn his hand, he should incline his head a little, and reverently swallow the Sacred Host, taking care, if possible, not to raise the tongue to the palate. Having remained in the same place for about the space of a " Pater " and " Ave," he should go to receive the purification,[1] unless it be administered where he is, and then withdraw to some quiet spot in the church, where he will make his thanksgiving on his knees, turned towards the high altar.

He should not spit out for at least a quarter of an hour; but if he cannot avoid it, he ought to do so in a place where people do not tread.

He should not take food for half an hour, or at least a quarter of an hour after communion, and he should endeavor to keep himself recollected, and employ himself in exercises of piety during the day.[2]

594. In giving instructions on this matter, the pastor must be careful to distinguish what is only recommended as becoming, from what is of strict obligation. Though it is meet that the communicant abstain from spitting immediately after communion, theologians commonly say it is no sin, provided no fragment or particle remains in the mouth.[3]

According to an ancient canon, the communicant was obliged to continue his fast till the hour of sext.[4] This observance had fallen into disuse long before the time of St. Thomas, and some say it is now no sin to take food immediately after communion. But, according to the more probable opinion, it cannot be excused from venial sin, unless there be some reasonable cause, as, e. g., if a member of a religious community were obliged to go to the refectory at a fixed hour. The reason is, that there is a certain irreverence in taking

---

[1] Not now in use.—Vid. infra, cap. xii. § i.
[2] *Acta Eccl. Mediol.*, pars. iv. De Sacramento Sanctissimo Eucharistiæ. § *De Præparatione Corporis.* pag. 425. § *Quæ observentur post Communionem,* pag. 426; *et Instructiones Civitatis et Diœceseos Pastoribus pro administranda in suis Ecclesiis Eucharistia,* pag. 600, et seq.
[3] St. Lig., lib. vi. n. 283.   [4] Cit. apud St. Lig., l. c.

food while the consecrated species is still unaltered in the
stomach.[1] It remains unaltered, however, only a very short
time, not more, probably, than one or two minutes in laics,
nor more than eight or nine minutes in priests, who receive a
large host as well as the chalice; certainly not more than
a quarter of an hour in any one, provided the stomach be
healthy.[2]

§ V.—Curare porro debet, ut perpetuo aliquot Particulæ consecratæ
eo numero, qui usui infirmorum et aliorum fidelium communioni satis
esse possit, conserventur in pyxide ex solida decentique materia, eaque
munda, et suo operculo bene clausa, albo velo cooperta, et quantum res
feret, ornato in tabernaculo clave obserato.

595. In the first ages the faithful were permitted to carry
the Blessed Eucharist to their houses and retain it there, that
they might receive it themselves when they were unable to
assist at the celebration of the holy mysteries. It was often
sent to them also by the hands of deacons or acolytes. This
was the case particularly during the fury of the persecutions,
when they were in constant danger of being seized and
dragged to prison or execution, and when it was therefore
important that they should not be deprived of the consolation
and the strength to be derived from the Holy Eucharist. The
solitaries of the deserts were not, it is true, so far removed
from priests and churches as is commonly supposed;[3] but
many of them were at a great distance, and there is no doubt
that these were allowed to keep the Blessed Sacrament by
them, and communicate with their own hands.[4]

This usage was manifestly open to many abuses, and was
therefore abolished in many places soon after peace was given
to the Church. Commencing in Spain, the abolition was
gradually extended to other places, though not completed
everywhere until about the twelfth century.[5]

596. Even while this usage prevailed, the Blessed Sacrament was at the same time kept in the churches or places
where the sacred mysteries were celebrated. It was enclosed
in dove-shaped vessels of gold or silver, which were suspended
over the altar. These "Columbæ aureæ" and "Columbæ

---

[1] St. Lig., ibid.
[2] St. Lig., n. 225. Vid. De Lugo, Disp. x. sec. iii. n. 54.
[3] Cfr. Dalgairns on *Holy Communion*. cap. vi. pag. 153, et seq.
[4] Martene, *De Antiquis Ecclesiæ Ritibus*. lib. i. cap. v. art. i. Caval.,
vol. iv. cap. vi. *De Asserv. SS. Sacramenti*.
[5] Martene, l. c. Caval., l. c. Vid. Mélanges Théologiques, IV
Série, IIme Cahier, pag. 210, et seq.

argenteæ" are frequently mentioned in ecclesiastical writers after the fourth century. Some had the form of a turret, and were hence called "Turres."[1]

As the permission to keep the Blessed Sacrament in their houses was gradually withdrawn from the faithful, the right of reserving it, of course, became more and more confined to the churches, until at length, by a general law, it became exclusively confined to them, as it has been, at least since the Fourth Council of Lateran.[2]

*597. It is not permitted, however, to keep it in every church. Its administration properly belongs to the pastor, and, therefore, the right of keeping it is confined to cathedral and parochial churches,[3] and is not allowed in others without the permission of the Holy See. This has been declared in several answers of the Sacred Congregation.[4] The only exception is the case of a non-parochial church, where it has been kept from time immemorial. But this immemorial usage, according to Benedict XIV, founds a presumption that the church had received at one time the requisite permission.[5]

The Blessed Sacrament not only may be kept, but ought to be kept in every parochial church.[6] The bishop is even directed to provide for the necessary expense, if the parish cannot defray it, by having alms collected for the purpose.[7]

The churches of Regulars usually have the privilege of keeping the Blessed Sacrament, and the Sacred Congregation has declared that it ought to be kept in them.[8] In fact, they may be regarded as in a manner parochial churches with respect to the members of the religious community.[9]

When a convent of nuns is canonically erected, the Blessed Sacrament may be kept in the church of the convent.[10] It must, however, be a public church, for the Council of Trent forbids the Blessed Sacrament to be kept in the choir, or within the enclosure of the religious.[11] That the convent be

---

[1] Vid. Catal., tit. iv. cap. i. § v. per totum.
[2] Cfr. Mél. Théol., l. c.   [3] Baruff., n. 12. Vid. infra. chap. xiii. § 1.   [4] Cong. Epis. 15 Jan. 1610. Cong. Conc. 3 Mar. 1668, et 3 Jan. 1683, cit. apud Falise, *Decr. Authent.*, etc. V. *De Asserv. SS. Euch.* in notis.   [5] Constit. *Quamvis justo*, 30 Apr. 1749, § 24.   [6] Congr. Episcop., 28 Jan. 1603, apud Caval., tom. iv. cap. vi. *De Asserv. SS. Sacram.*, Decr. i.
[7] Cong. Epis., 14 Mar. 1614, et Cong. Conc., 22 Mar. 1594, apud Caval., loc. cit.   [8] Cong. Epis., 25 Maii, 1635, cit. ibid.
[9] Cfr. Caval., l. c. n. ii.   [10] S. R. C., 16 April, 1644, in Marianen., n. 1496.   [11] Sess. xxv. cap. 10. *De Reg. et Monial.*

canonically erected, it is necessary that the nuns make solemn vows, and observe strict enclosure,[1] and that the house be established with the consent of the Holy See.[2] These are the churches in which the Blessed Sacrament may be kept without any special indult.

But in other churches, or in private oratories, even for the use of religious, or in any other place whatever, it can be kept only with the permission of the Holy See. The Ordinary can give permission in particular cases and for a short time; but, without special faculties from the Holy See, he cannot give permission to have it kept permanently.[3]

*598. In Ireland, and in other countries similarly circumstanced, there are many parish churches in which the Blessed Sacrament cannot be permanently kept, on account of the danger of sacrilege. Besides, the priest sometimes lives at so great a distance from the church, that he could not, without very great inconvenience, go to the church for it as often as he is required to bring it to the sick. To provide for such cases, special faculties are granted by the Holy See. Amongst the faculties received by the Irish bishops, and which they can communicate to others, is the following: "Deferendi Sanc-"tissimum Sacramentum occulte ad Infirmos sine lumine, "illudque sine eodem retinendi pro iisdem infirmis, in loco "tamen decenti, si ab hæreticis aut infidelibus sit periculum "sacrilegii."[4] Hence, generally speaking, in this country, priests have permission to keep the Blessed Sacrament in their houses. It ought to be, however, "in loco decenti." The Synod of Thurles earnestly recommends that a room be set apart, or at least that a tabernacle be provided for the purpose.[5] There is no one who cannot provide a little tabernacle; of late years many have been constructed expressly for this purpose; and it may be hoped that very soon every priest who keeps the Blessed Sacrament in his house will have one.

599. The rubric here directs the pastor to have at all times such a number of consecrated particles as may suffice for the communion of the sick, and also of the other faithful, who may require to receive " extra missam." St. Charles directed that at least five should be so kept.[6] The vessel in

[1] Cfr. Mélanges Théologiques, l. c. p. 219.
[2] Bened. XIV. De Synod. Diœces., lib. ix. cap. i. n. 9.
[3] Vid. Caval., cap. vi. Decr. iv.
[4] Formula VIta n. 31.   [5] De Eucharistia, n. 23.
[6] Instruc. Euchar. § De custodia Sanctissimæ Eucharistiæ, pag. 424.

which they are kept is called a "pyxis." It is often called
also a "ciborium." In every parochial church there ought
to be two, a larger one for communion in the church, and a
smaller one for communion of the sick.[1] With us the larger
one is usually called a "ciborium," and the smaller one a
"pyxis." Writers on the rubrics, however, make no distinction between these words, as applied to vessels containing the
Blessed Eucharist, but they sometimes use the word
"ciborium" to signify the tabernacle in which the pyxis is
kept,[2] and also to signify a press or safe, such as that in
which the holy oils are kept in the baptistery.[3]

600. The rubric does not determine the material of which
the ciborium should be made, further than that it should be
solid and suitable, "ex solida decentique materia." It should
not, then, be of glass or any fragile substance. A decree of
the Sacred Congregation of Bishops is more explicit. It declares that the material should not be ivory, but silver, gilt
within.[4] It is usually made of the same material as the
chalice, sometimes of gold, but mostly of silver, gilt inside.

St. Charles gives minute instructions both as to the material and shape. "The pyxis," he says,[5] "should be of gold,
"or at least of pure silver, gilt inside, if not both inside and
"outside. The foot or stem should be six inches in length, so
"that it may be easy to hold it firmly in the hand. The
"'nodus,' or knob in the centre of the stem, may be suitably
"enchased, but should not be embossed in such a way as to
"make it inconvenient for the hand in holding it. The cup
"may be in shape either circular or oval, the depth and width
"being correctly proportioned to each other. It should have
"a slight orbicular eminence in the centre of the bottom, and
"near the edge a rim on which the cover may rest. The
"cover, at the lowest part, must correspond to the shape of
"the pyxis, and should have a little hook at each side to
"fasten it on. It should taper upwards like a cone, and be
"surmounted by a cross, or by the figure of our Lord crucified,
"or rising from the dead." He concludes by adding that,
where poverty will allow no better, the bishop may permit
the pyxis and cover to be of brass or tin gilt.

We may observe that the "uncia" of St. Charles is only
about three-fourths of our inch, so that the six inches men-

---

[1] Baruff., tit. xxiii. n. 54. 　　　[2] Catal., tit. iv. cap. i. § v. n. v
[3] Vid. supra, n. 266. 　　　[4] 26 Jul. 1588, cit. apud Caval., cap. .
decr. x. n. iv. 　　　[5] *Act. Eccl. Mediol.*, pars iv. Instruct. supell. Eccl.
lib. ii. § *De pyxide*, pag. 528.

tioned as the length of the stem, are equal only to four and
one-half of our inches.   The reason of having the bottom
raised at the centre, is to enable the priest the more easily to
take up the last particles, which it would be otherwise
difficult to get hold of with the thumb and index.   The books
for fastening the cover are now generally dispensed with, as
the cover is easily made fast enough without them.

601. The rubric directs that the pyxis be covered with a
white veil.   This veil should be of silk or satin, and richly
embroidered.   According to St. Charles,[1] it should be embroidered with gold or silver, or, better still, it should be of
gold or silver cloth, with fringes of the same material.   It is
usually attached to the top of the cover, being sometimes
fastened to the foot of the cross or figure which surmounts it,
and thus hangs in loose folds around the pyxis.   Great care
must be taken, in covering and uncovering the pyxis, that
the veil do not come in contact with the corporal before the
corporal is purified, as the folds of the veil might easily take up
minute fragments.   The difficulty of guarding against this is
probably the reason why in some places the veil is not in use

*602. The pyxis does not require to be consecrated.[2] It
is blessed by the bishop, or by a priest having the requisite
faculties, according to the form given in the Ritual or in the
Missal, and entitled "Benedictio Tabernaculi seu vasculi pro
"sacrosancta Eucharistia conservanda."   Some hold that
this blessing, though laudable, is not of precept, and that
consequently the pyxis may be used without it.   This is the
opinion of Suarez, De Lugo, and other great authorities, cited
by St. Liguori.[3]   There is no evidence, they say, of a precept.   The fact that a form of benediction for it is given in
the Ritual or Missal, is not enough; for benedictions are
given there, which, though it be pious and laudable to use
them, are certainly not of precept.   But St. Liguori himself
adopts as more probable the opinion of Benedict XIV,
Collet, and others, who maintain that this benediction is of
precept.   The rubric of the Missal favors this opinion,
when it directs the priest who is about to consecrate a number of particles, to place them "in aliquo calice consecrato
"vel in vase mundo benedicto."[4]   St. Liguori seems, however, to imply that the precept does not bind sub gravi.[5]

---

[1] Loc. cit. § De velis pyxidis.   [2] St. Lig., n. 384.
[3] Lib. vi. n. 335.   [4] Ritus servandus in Celebratione Missæ,
tit. ii. n. 3.   [5] Vid. St. Lig., l. c.

A priest who has faculties to bless vestments, corporals, etc., can also bless the pyxis. This is the common opinion of rubricists,[1] and is implied, if not expressly decided, by an answer of the Sacred Congregation.[2]

What has been said of the pyxis may be said also of the lunette of a remonstrance, and it would be laudable to have even the remonstrance itself blessed, the same form of benediction being used for all.[3]

603. "The Church," says the Catechism of the Council of Trent, "has prohibited by a law any but consecrated persons, "unless in some case of great necessity, to dare handle or "touch the sacred vessels, the linen, or other instruments "necessary to its completion."[4] Hence, no one, who is not in deacon's orders, is permitted to touch a sacred vessel of any kind while it actually contains the Holy Eucharist. He would be guilty of grievous sin by doing so.[5]

When it does not actually contain the Holy Eucharist, it may be handled by laics, according to St. Liguori, "si adsit "rationabilis causa, secluso scandalo et contemptu," but not otherwise without venial sin, although some authors, whom he cites, make no restriction in this case, and say that it may be freely handled by any one, when it does not contain the Blessed Eucharist.[6] Benedict XIV says[7] that all who are in orders, even those who have received only the first tonsure, are, by custom, allowed to handle the sacred vessels when empty, if they have any reason for doing so . . . . "si aliqua causa intercedat." The same privilege is extended also, according to St. Liguori,[8] to lay-brothers, nuns, and in general to all who perform the duties of sacristan.[9]

This question is discussed at some length in the "Mélan-"ges Théologiques."[10] The writer distinguishes vessels that are consecrated, as the chalice, from those that are merely blessed, as the ciborium. According to him, theologians speak only of the former, and he maintains that the latter may be handled by any one after they have been purified, just as corporals may be handled by any one after they have

---

[1] Gavan., pars ii. tit. ii. n. 3, lit. (p). Baruff., tit. xxiii. n. 56. Collet, *Traité des Saints Mystères*, chap. ix. n. 7. De Herdt, pars i. n. 55, ii.
[2] 17 Maii, 1760, *in Calagur. et Calceat.*, n. 4290.
[3] Vid. De Herdt, l. c.   [4] Pars ii. cap. iv. n. 67.
[5] St. Lig., lib. vi. n. 382.   [6] St. Lig., l. c.
[7] *Inst.* xxxiv. n. 18.   [8] Loc. cit.
[9] Cfr. Bouvier, *De Eucharistia*, cap. vi. art. vi. § i. 12, et seq.
[10] IVᵐ Série, IIIᵐˢ Cahier, p. 376, etc.

been washed. He concludes, therefore, that they may be
cleansed or repaired by laics without the least scruple, and
that any custom to the contrary is founded on error. There
is good reason, no doubt, for this distinction, and we believe
it is recognized to some extent—at least so far, that in many
places a laic would have less scruple in handling a ciborium
than in handling a chalice. It is admitted also that corporals,
after having been washed by a person in holy orders, may
be freely handled by laics;[1] and it is difficult to get over the
par'ty urged by the "Mélanges," between the ciborium after
it is purified, and the corporal after it is washed, for all seem
to be agreed that in this matter the corporal and the ciborium
are to be treated alike; "Idem quod dictum est," says St.
Liguori, "de tactu sacrorum vasorum dicendum est de tactu
"corporalium."[2]

At the same time, we think, custom does not acknowledge
the parity in the precise point urged by the "Mélanges."
It is plain from his words, that St. Liguori, in the place cited,
includes all vessels, whether consecrated or merely blessed,
that are used for containing the eucharistic species, and that
the decision he gives applies to the ciborium and the lunette,
as well as to the chalice. Bouvier says that the ciborium,
though blessed, may be handled by any one *before* it has
been used to contain the Blessed Sacrament, but afterwards
only by those who are allowed to handle the chalice. The
remonstrance, however, he would permit to be handled by
any one, when the lunette is removed.[3]

The custom above-mentioned, in favor of all who are in
tonsure, and of all laics who perform the duties of sacristan,
is not recognized everywhere. In France, in the time of
Collet,[4] the law above referred to by the Catechism of the
Council of Trent, was still in force, so that only those in
holy orders were permitted to handle the sacred vessels; and
although it would appear from Bouvier,[5] that, by the present
usage, inferior clerics are permitted to do so, it is still usual,
he says,[6] for laics who may require to touch the sacred
vessels, to get leave from the bishop or his vicar-general.
The decision of St. Liguori clearly implies that a sacred
vessel might be handled by a laic for the purpose of repair-
ing it, for then there is a "rationabilis causa." Yet even in

---

[1] Merati, pars ii. tit. i. rub. i. n. xvi. Lacroix, lib. vi. pars ii. n. 358.
Collet, *De Eucharistia*, pars ii. cap. ix. art. ii. sect. viii. Quær. 8.
  [2] Loc. cit.   [3] Loc. cit. § ii. 6°.
  [4] Vid. loc. cit.   [5] Loc. cit. § i. 12°.   [6] Loc. cit. n. 14°.

this case, if the vessel still retains its consecration, e. g., a chalice, requiring merely to have the gilding renewed, Gardellini would have the workmen get leave from the Ordinary.[1]

In Ireland, the law of the Church in this matter has suffered no relaxation, and with us, therefore, no one who is not in holy orders ventures to handle the sacred vessels without the leave of the Ordinary.

604. The pyxis is kept in the tabernacle, which is treated of in the next rubric. Here it is merely stated that it must be carefully locked. The keys of the tabernacle, of which there ought to be two,[2] should be kept by the parish priest, or priest who has charge of the church, and by no other.[3] Many recommend that they be gilt or plated.[4]

§ VI.—Hoc autem tabernaculum conopeo decenter opertum, atque ab omni alia re vacuum, in Altari majori, vel in alio, quod venerationi et cultui tanti Sacramenti commodius ac decentius videatur, sit collocatum, ita ut nullum aliis sacris functionibus, aut Ecclesiasticis officiis impedimentum afferatur.

605. According to a decree of the Congregation of Bishops, the tabernacle ought, generally speaking, to be of wood, gilt on the outside, and suitably lined inside with silk : " Taber-"naculum regulariter debet esse ligneum, extra deauratum, "intus vero aliquo panno serico decenter contectum."[5] Cavalieri[6] observes that this decree, as is plain from the word, regulariter, does not hinder the tabernacle from being made of a material stronger and more precious than wood. St. Charles recommends that in the principal churches it be of silver or brass gilt, or of precious marble, but having the interior lined with wood as a protection against damp.[7] Amongst those recently constructed in Ireland and England, a considerable number are of wrought iron, being in fact safes, encased in gilt wood or sculptured stone. These are very much approved of by the parochial clergy, on account of their great strength, and the consequent security they give against the depredation of thieves and against fire.

---

[1] Annotat., in Decr. S. R. C. 20 Apr. 1822, n. 4588.
[2] De Herdt, pars vi. n. 14, ii. 5°.
[3] Sac. Cong. Concil. 14 Nov. 1693, cit. apud Falise, Dec. Authen., etc. V. De Asserv. SS. Euch. note 14. Vid. Ferraris, V. Tabernaculum, n. 4. et seq. [4] Baruff. tit. xxiii. n. 62. De Herdt, l. c.
[5] Cong. Episcop. 26 Oct. 1575, apud Falise, loc. cit. note 9.
[6] Tom. iv. cap. vi. De Asservatione SS. Sacramenti, Decr. x.
[7] Instruct. Fabric. Eccl. lib. i. cap. xiii. De Tabernaculo SS. Eucharistiæ, pag. 472.

*606. The form of the tabernacle is not precisely fixed by
any authority. It may be round, square, hexagonal, etc.,
according to taste or convenience. Whatever be the shape,
however, it should be surmounted by a cross. This is not
prescribed in the rubric, but writers on the rubrics, treating
of the tabernacle, either expressly say, or clearly suppose,
that there is at least a small cross placed over it, or fixed on
its summit.[1]

607. It has been decided by the Sacred Congregation,[2]
that the tabernacle cannot be made the base or support of a
sacred picture or relic, even a relic of the true cross, or of
some of the other instruments of our Lord's passion. Gardellini observes[3] that there would be a certain want of reverence
in making it serve as such, or indeed in making it serve any
other purpose than that of containing the Blessed Sacrament,
as the rubric here requires that it be " ab omni alia re vacuum."
Besides, he says, the top of the tabernacle should not be a flat
surface, but round. A writer in the " Mélanges Théologiques "[4] likewise maintains that the top should be spherical
or conical, and should form one solid piece, with the cross
surmounting it.

It certainly does seem more in accordance with the spirit
of the rubric and of the decrees of the Sacred Congregation
just cited, to have the tabernacle so constructed and placed
that it would be unnecessary, in any circumstances, to make
it serve as a support. At the same time, there is nothing in
the rubric, nor in any decision we have seen, which would
make it unlawful to put on the tabernacle, as on a support,
the crucifix which the rubric of the Missal requires to be
placed between the candles at mass.[5] It is true that a small
cross or crucifix placed over the tabernacle has been declared
insufficient to satisfy the rubric of the Missal.[6] But it is
evident from Merati,[7] Cavalieri,[8] Benedict XIV,[9] and

[1] De Herdt, pars vi. n. 14, ii. 3°. Benedict XIV. Encycl. *Accepi-
mus*, 16 Jul. 1746, *De retinenda Crucifixi imagine*. etc. Cfr. Gardellini,
Annotat. in Decr. generale, S. R. C. 3 April, 1821, ad 6, n. 4578, et in
Decr. 17 Sept. 1822, ad 8, n. 4590.
[2] 3 April, 1821, *Decr. gen.*, ad 6, n. 4578; 12 Mar. 1836, *in Trident.*,
ad 1. n. 4777.   [3] *Annot. in Decr. gen.*, ad 6, 3 April, 1821, n. 4778
[4] IVme Série, 3me Cahier, p. 360.   [5] Pars i. tit. xx.
[6] S. R. C. 16 June, 1663, *in Rossanen.*, ad 1, n. 2231, 17 Sept. 1822,
ad 8, n. 4590. Benedict XIV., *Encyc. cit.*
[7] Pars i. tit. xx. *Novæ observationes*, n. vi. in fine.
[8] Tom. iv. cap. xviii. *De cruce in altari*, etc., in Decr. ii.
[9] *Encycl. cit.*

Gardellini himself,[1] that this is solely and entirely on the sup-position that the cross so placed is too small, for it should be such, "ut sacerdos celebrans ac populus sacrificio assistens eum-"dem crucifixum facile et commode intueri possint."[2] Again, there is an obvious difference between an image or a relic of any kind exposed to public veneration, and the cross; otherwise, no cross, fixed or movable, should be allowed to surmount the tabernacle.

We conclude, therefore, that where necessity or notable convenience requires it, the tabernacle may be surmounted by a crucifix distinct from, but resting on, the top, and large enough to satisfy the rubric of the Missal. St. Charles clearly supposes that it may, at least in churches where the place occupied by the tabernacle is the only suitable place for the cross required by the Missal: "In summo taber-"naculo," he says, "sit imago Christi gloriose resurgentis, vel "sacra vulnera exhibentis, vel si in altari exiguae alicujus "ecclesiae per tabernaculi occupationem congruus locus cruci "(quae alias super eo collocaretur) esse non potest, ea pro alia "sacra imagine in tabernaculi summitate vel perpetuo affiga-"tur, vel processionum causa aliquando amovenda, decore "constituatur, affixa Christi crucifixi sacra effigie."[3]

608. What is said of the crucifix may be said also, and perhaps *a fortiori*, of the throne, or the remonstrance used for the exposition of the Blessed Sacrament in the ceremony of benediction. This ceremony is now very frequent even in poor churches, and in many of these the top of the tabernacle is a flat surface, and is made to serve (the crucifix being removed for the time) as a throne for the remonstrance. It is true a different provision for the purpose can be made, and is made in many churches, but this one is so common and so convenient, that it should not be condemned without an authoritative decision against it.

609. The door of the tabernacle should be large enough to allow the ciboriums to be put in and taken out easily. It may be highly ornamented, but the figures carved or painted on it should have reference to the mystery of the Eucharist, or to the Passion or Resurrection, as, *e. g.*, a representation of the chalice and host, a representation of our Lord crucified, or rising from the dead, or showing the wound in his sacred side, etc.[4]

[1] *Annot. in Decr.*, 17 Sept. 1822, ad 8.
[2] Bened. XIV., *Encycl. cit.* in fine.   [3] Act., pars iv. l. c. pag. 472.
[4] St. Carol., l. c. p. 472. De Herdt, pars vi. n. 14, ii. 3°.

It is strictly prohibited, by a decree of the Sacred Congregation, to place a vase of flowers, or anything of the kind, immediately in front of the door.[1] It is also prohibited, by another decree,[2] to have the tabernacle so constructed or placed that the ciborium containing the Blessed Sacrament could be seen within it. If the door or sides be of precious stone that is transparent, it must be covered with the veil in such a way that the ciborium cannot be seen.

610. The veil which covers the exterior should be of precious material. It is usually of brocade or rich silk. It is used, according to St. Charles, not only for ornamenting the tabernacle, but also for protecting it from dust, and, on more solemn occasions, if the pastor thinks proper, it may be removed altogether.[3] According to De Herdt,[4] the tabernacles in the churches of Belgium are rarely covered in this manner.

Where the Ambrosian rite is followed, as in Milan, the color of the veil is red.[5] Elsewhere the color should be that which is suited to the office of the day. This is, at least, the more common opinion. It is that of Gavantus,[6] Cavalieri,[7] Bauldry,[8] De Herdt.[9] Baruffaldi insists, on the other hand, that it should be white, as white is the color which properly belongs to the Blessed Sacrament.[10] This, however, must not be urged too far, for, as we shall see, the Sacred Congregation has decided that the color of the stole used in administering the Eucharist should be that of the office of the day. Besides, the veil clearly belongs to the "para-"menta altaris," which the rubric requires to be of the color suited to the office of the day: "Paramenta altaris, celebran-"tis et ministrorum debent esse coloris convenientis officio et "missæ diei," etc.[11]

An exception is made, however, when the office requires black. In this case, Cavalieri says that the color of the veil should be violet.[12] So also Gavantus.[13]

By a recent decree of the Congregation of Rites,[14] it has been decided that the opinion of Baruffaldi, as to the color

[1] 22 Jan. 1701, *in una Cong. Montis Coron.*, n. 3575.
[2] 20 Sep. 1806, *in Toletan.*, ad 2, n. 4505.
[3] *Act. Eccl. Mediol.*, pars iv. *Instruct. variæ*, pag. 703.
[4] Loc. cit. 6°.
[5] Caval., vol. iv. cap. vi. *De Asserv. SS. Sacram.*, Decr. xiii. n. iii.
[6] Pars i. tit. xx.   [7] Loc cit. n. ii.
[8] Pars iii. cap. 7, tit. xv. n. 1.   [9] Loc. cit.
[10] Tit. xxxiii. n. 65.   [11] *Rub. Gen. Miss.*, xviii. n. 1,
[12] Loc. cit. n. iii.   [13] Pars i. tit. xx. V. *Tabernaculum.*
[14] 21 Jul. 1855, *in Briocen*, ad 12, n. 5221.

of the tabernacle veil, may be followed, although that of Gavantus is preferred, as having the usage of Rome in its favor. The "Mélanges Théologiques,"[1] suggests that in churches which do not provide veils of all the colors, there ought to be at least two white ones: one for ordinary use, and the other of richer material for the more solemn festivals.

611. In the decree above cited,[2] it is prescribed that the interior of the tabernacle be lined with silk. The color is not mentioned, but authors generally say it should be white, and the material very rich.[3] On the bottom of the tabernacle there should be spread a clean corporal, on which the ciborium may rest.[4] It would be desirable to have the corporal fitted to the shape of the tabernacle, and reserved for this purpose alone. But any corporal will do. Even a pall may be used, for the pall is regarded as a part of the corporal, the blessing for both being the same.[5]

*612. The tabernacle must contain nothing else than the Holy Eucharist. It must be "ab omni alia re vacuum," according to our rubric. A decree of the Congregation of Bishops prohibits the holy oils, relics, or anything else, however sacred, from being placed in it.[6] But, according to Cavalieri,[7] this does not exclude the pyxis, or other sacred vessel destined to hold the Blessed Sacrament, though not actually containing it.

*613. The tabernacle is blessed with the same form of benediction as that which is used for the pyxis.[8] Some deny that it requires to be blessed, as the "Mélanges Théologi-"ques,"[9] and "Cavalieri,"[10] who observes that the word *vasculum*, in the prayer of the benediction, could not well be applied to a large tabernacle. Most authors, however, maintain either that it should be blessed, or at least that it is laudable to have it blessed.[11] Cavalieri suggests that, if it be blessed, the word *tabernaculum* be substituted for *vasculum* in the prayer, although in the end he admits that the words may be used as they are.[12]

---

[1] IVme Série, 3me Cahier, p. 364.   [2] Supra, n. 605.
[3] De Herdt. l. c. 2°. *Act. Eccl. Med.*, pars iv. *Instr. Fab. Eccl.*, lib. .. cap. xiii. pag. 472.   [4] De Herdt, l. c. 7°. Mél. Théol., l. c.
[5] De Herdt. l. c. St. Lig., lib. vi. n. 388.
[6] 3 Maii. 1693, apud Caval., *De Asserv. SS. Sacramenti*, Decr. xiii.
[7] Loc. cit.   [8] Baruff., tit. lxviii. n. i. Catal., tit. viii. cap. xxv n. iv. De Herdt, l. c. 8°.   [9] Loc. cit.. pag. 365.
[10] Vol. iv. cap xi. *De Benedict. Sac. Sup.*, Decr. i. n. viii.
[11] Vid. De Herdt, loc. cit.   [12] Loc. cit., n. ix.

614. Generally speaking, the tabernacle should be placed on the high altar or principal altar of the church, as the place that is most conspicuous, and best suited to the dignity of the Holy Sacrament. This is what the rubric here prescribes. In cathedrals, however, the tabernacle containing the Blessed Sacrament should be placed on a side altar, because the ceremonies to be observed in pontifical functions at the high altar would be interfered with by those which reverence for the Blessed Sacrament would require at the same time. The question was formally decided by the Congregation of Bishops: "Tabernaculum SS. Sacramenti in Cathedralibus "non debet esse in altari majore, propter functiones Pontifi- "cales quæ fiunt versis renibus ad altare; in parochialibus et "regularibus debet esse regulariter in altari majori tanquam "digniori."[1] The Blessed Sacrament can be kept only on one altar, which, when there is any doubt, should be designated by the bishop, according to a decision of the Sacred Congregation.[2] Our rubric, as may be observed, does not fix on the high altar exclusively, but says, the high altar or another altar that may be better accommodated to the worship and veneration of the Holy Sacrament, so as not to interfere with the sacred functions. Hence, when there is a tabernacle containing the Blessed Sacrament on an altar, at which one of these solemn functions is about to take place, the "Cære- "moniale Episcoporum" prescribes that the Blessed Sacrament be removed, for the time, to another altar.[3]

§ VII.—Lampades coram eo plures, vel saltem una, die noctuque perpetuo colluceat; curabitque Parochus, ut omnia ad ipsius Sacramenti cultum ordinata, integra, mundaque sint, et conserventur.

*615. At least one lamp should be kept constantly burning before the tabernacle. The rubric implies that it would be desirable to have more, but at least there should be one. It was usual to have lamps constantly burning in the churches from the very earliest times. It is certain that lights were used at the celebration of the sacred mysteries, not only in the catacombs and other dark places, but in the full light of day, and, therefore, not merely to dispel the darkness, but as a symbol of the light of Christ. In some churches they were kept constantly burning; and, though it cannot be

[1] Febr. 10, 1579, et Nov 29, 1594, apud Caval., De. Asserv. SS. Sacram., Decr. xii.
[2] 21 Jul., 1696, in Augusta Prætoriæ, ad 3, n. 3392.
[3] Vid. lib. i. cap. xii. n. 8.

clearly proved, it is highly probable that they were, in most instances, designed to honor the Blessed Sacrament.[1]

At all events, for several centuries, by a universal custom, having the force of law, acknowledged and enforced by numberless decrees, there is an obligation of having a lamp constantly burning before it, as a mark of respect and reverence towards Him who is "the true light," and also as a sign to the faithful of the place where He is present.[2] The pastor or rector of the church is specially charged with this obligation; and, according to the common opinion, to leave the Blessed Sacrament, through negligence, for a notable time, as, e. g., for an entire day, without a light before it, would be a mortal sin.[3]

The oil used should be oil of olives; but in places where it cannot easily be procured, other oil may be used.[4] A recent decree of the Congregation of Rites has decided the point, but requires that what is substituted be, if possible, a vegetable oil.[5]

616. This is the general law, which should be, as far as possible, strictly observed. The poverty of a parish is not admitted as a sufficient reason for a dispensation from it. It was decided that, in the case of a poor parish, one should be appointed to collect alms for the purpose;[6] or two or three such parishes, if near each other, should be made to contribute towards the lamp and the other requisites, in one church selected by the bishop, in which the Blessed Sacrament might be reserved for the use of all.[7]

We believe there are few parishes in Ireland that could claim an exemption on the score of poverty; few in which the faithful, if called on, would not readily contribute the necessary funds. The Synod of Thurles directs pastors to endeavor, as far as they can, to give the faithful an opportunity of visiting and adoring our Lord in the Blessed Sacrament, and, with this view, to leave the doors of their churches

---

[1] Vid. Mél. Théol., IVme Série, 4me Cahier, p. 501, et seq.

[2] Baruff., tit. xxiii. n. 69, et seq. S. R. C. 22 Aug. 1699, in una Ord. Capucin.. n. 3525. Cfr. Mél. Théol., l. c.

[3] De Herdt, pars vi. n 14, iv. Busemb. apud St. Lig., lib. vi. n. 248.

[4] Baruff., n. 73. Caval., cap. vi. De Asserv. SS. Sacram., Decr. xv. n. ii.

[5] 9 Jul. 1864, cit. apud "The Irish Ecclesiastical Record," No. ii. November, 1864.

[6] Congreg. Epis., 14 Martii, 1844, et Congreg. Concil., 22 Martii, 1594, apud Falise, Decret. Authen., etc. V. De Asserv. SS. Euch., in nota.   [7] S. C. Conc. 17 Aug 1697, apud Falise, loc. cit.

open, at least for some hours every day, where they can conveniently do so.[1] This may be easily done in towns, and
wherever the priest lives near the church.   Moreover, if a
confraternity of the Blessed Sacrament were established in
the parish, the members would provide everything necessary
for the tabernacle, lamp, etc.   There are some churches
however, in which this could not well be done, and there are
some also in which the lamp could not be kept burning
during the night without exposing the Blessed Sacrament to
the danger of irreverence or even sacrilege.   Hence, the
Synod of Thurles, in its decree on the subject, requires the
lamp to be kept lighted during the night only in those
churches where this can be done with safety.[2]   A similar
state of things exists in parts of Belgium, and is provided
for in the same way.[3]

617. The priest is often permitted to keep the Blessed
Sacrament in his house, and in some cases is not required to
have a light before it.[4]   There is no doubt, however, that it
would be highly laudable in him to have the tabernacle, if
possible, so placed that he could have a little lamp constantly burning before it.   This would present no difficulty, if he
can afford to have a small oratory, or a room set apart for
the purpose, as the Synod of Thurles recommends.[5]

. It would seem from the first Synod of Westminster,[6] that
in England permission is not given to keep the Blessed Sacrament anywhere without a light.   It would be impossible
to observe the same strictness in Ireland, where the priest is,
in some places, so badly lodged.   At the same time, no one
doubts that every priest who has permission to keep the
Blessed Sacrament in his house, should aim at providing, as
far as circumstances permit, and on a scale commensurate
with the place in which he keeps it, everything that the
rubrics prescribe for its custody in parish churches.

§ VIII.—Sanctissimæ Eucharistiæ particulas frequenter renovabit.
Hostiæ vero, seu particulæ consecrandæ sint recentes; et ubi eas conse-
craverit, veteres primo distribuat, vel sumat.

618. The rubric prescribes that the sacred species be frequently renewed, but it does not say how often, or does not
exactly determine after what interval they ought to be renewed.   Accordingly, this interval has not been the same

---

[1] *De Eucharistia*, n. 20.   [2] Ibid., n. 19.
[3] De Herdt, n. 14, iv.   [4] Synod. Thurl., loc. cit. n. 23.
[5] Loc. cit.   [6] *De SS. Euch. Sacramento*, 6°.

everywhere, but has been different in different places, having been determined by particular rituals or synodal statutes. It was pretty generally fixed at eight days, or at most fifteen days, being extended in only one or two instances to a month.[1]

*619. St. Charles ordered the renewal at least every eight days,[2] and this interval is fixed by Gavantus,[3] and by the authority of two decrees: one of the Congregation of Bishops,[4] and the other of the Congregation of Rites.[5] Th same is fixed also by the Synod of Thurles, which says: " Ne " autem diutius asservatæ corrumpantur particulæ, a parochis " et aliis sacerdotibus ad quos spectat renovandæ sunt octavo " quolibet die."[6] In Ireland, therefore, there can be no doubt as to the time within which the particles ought to be renewed.

In Belgium, however, according to the " Mélanges Théo- " logiques," even by recent statutes that have received the sanction of the Holy See, an interval of fifteen days is per- mitted, unless in case of rainy weather, or great damp, when the renewal is required to be more frequent.[7] Of course such a permission cannot be acted on in other places where it has not been given, especially seeing that, in one of the decrees cited above, the Sacred Congregation expressly declares that the renewal of the particles should not be deferred for fifteen days.[8]

620. Speaking of the obligation generally, no one can have a doubt that it binds " sub gravi," since it is imposed by the Church in a matter that intimately concerns the honor and reverence due to our Lord in the Holy Sacrament.[9] But if it be asked what delay would amount to a mortal sin, we should answer in accordance with the opinion of Romsée,[10] which is cited and adopted by De Herdt.[11] 1° To defer the renewal of the particles for fifteen days would not, we think, exceed a venial sin, unless in case of great damp, or some other cause that would accelerate the corruption. We say, " would not exceed a venial sin," because, although, of course, it is no sin where this interval is permitted, as in Belgium, we

[1] Cfr. Martene, De Antiquis Ecclesiæ Ritibus, lib. i. cap. v. art. iii. n. ix.
[2] Act. Eccl. Med., pars iv. Instruct. Euch. § De custodia, pag. 424.
[3] Pars ii. tit. x. n. 5, lit. (t).
[4] 5 April, 1573, apud Caval., De Asserv. SS. Sacram., Decr. xvii.
[5] 3 Sep. 1672, in Conchen., n. 2602.   [6] De Eucharistia, n. 17.
[7] IVme Série, 4me Cahier, p. 527.
[8] 5 April, 1573. Vid. Decr. in Appendice.
[9] Cfr. De Herdt, pars ii. n. 30, i.
[10] Tom. i. pars i. cap. ii. art. xiv. n. 8.   [11] Loc. cit.

would not say that to do so without cause is free from all sin
where, as in Ireland, the renewal every eight days is prescribed by a synodal decree.   But any reasonable cause would
justify a delay of this renewal for a few days longer, *e. g.*,
the convenience of having a number of communicants to
whom the particles might be distributed, the convenience of
using the same host for benediction during the nine days of a
Novena, etc.   In a word, we think it is plain, from the
Belgian statutes above referred to, that a delay, which does
not put off the renewal for more than fifteen days, cannot be
regarded as, *per se*, a " materia gravis;" otherwise, these
statutes would not have been approved at Rome.   Besides,
Gardellini, or his continuator, commenting on the decree
which prohibits the consecration of bread that has been made
three months, takes occasion to observe regarding the renewal:
" Quod si ad quindecim dies protrahatur renovatio non id
" reprobandum culpæque vertendum, quia hoc intra breve
" tempus haud formido quod sacræ species corrumpantur."[1]

2° Te defer the renewal for more than a month, above all
in damp weather, cannot be excused from mortal sin.   This
may be justly inferred from the decrees and declarations
already cited.   It may be added, that when the statutes of
the Provincial Council of Mechlin, held in 1607, were submitted for approval at Rome, the words, " *singulis mensibus*
" *renoventur*," which were in the statute regarding this subject,
were struck out, and the words, " *singulis saltem hebdomadis*,"
inserted in place of them.[2]   It is no excuse that the
species might remain unaltered for even a much longer time
than a month, for the law is founded on a general presumption of danger, and, therefore, does not cease to bind even
in cases where it is known that no danger exists.[3]   Besides,
the object of the law is not only to guard against this danger,
but to secure that reverence for the holy mystery which is
implied in the frequent renewal of the sacred species.[4]

*621. The rubric requires not only that the consecrated
particles be frequently renewed, but also, and for the same
reason, that the particles to be consecrated shall have been
recently made.   But how recently, it does not determine.   It
is certain, from an answer of the Sacred Congregation,[5]

[1] *Annot. in Decr.*, S. R. C., 16 Dec. 1826, *in Gandaven.*, *Quær.* i. ad
1 et 2, n. 4623.   [2] Mél. Théol., l. c. p. 526.
[3] Suarez, *De Legibus*, lib. iii. cap. xxiii. n. 6.
[4] Mél. Théol., l. c. p. 528.
[5] 16 Decr., 1826, *in Gandav.*, *Quær.* i. n. 4623.

that it is not lawful to consecrate particles that have been made three months, and the annotator holds that to act against this decree would be a grievous sin.[1] Within this limit nothing is strictly defined on the subject. St. Charles prescribes that the hosts to be consecrated be not older than twenty days at most,[2] and we think it would be well to adopt this rule in practice. On the one hand, it would not be too difficult for the priest in any circumstances to get his supply of altar breads renewed every third week; and on the other, by doing so, and renewing the species every eight days, he would be pretty sure to guard against all danger of irreverence.[3]

622. When new hosts are consecrated, the old ones, according to the rubric, are to be distributed to the faithful who may be for communion at the time, or to be consumed by the priest himself. The ciborium, or pyxis, ought to be purified at the same time. The same reason which requires the renewal of the sacred species, holds also, as is plain, for the removal of the minute particles that may remain in the ciborium.

Various methods are suggested for purifying the ciborium, which is done by the priest at mass.

I. Having collected the fragments as carefully as possible, with the index finger of the right hand, he receives them by applying the finger to his tongue, or by bringing the fragments close to the edge, and then putting the ciborium to his mouth. He afterwards pours in some wine, which he makes pass round the interior with his index finger, and having received this, dries the ciborium with the purificator. This is the method of Gavantus,[4] but it is commonly rejected as inconvenient.

II. Having distributed the large particles or consumed them, he collects the fragments in the ciborium as above, and holding it with his left hand over the chalice, makes them fall into it with the index of his right; he then takes the wine for the first ablution in the ciborium, and having carefully passed it round the interior with his finger, he pours it into the chalice, after previously drying the finger. This is the method of Merati.[5]

III. In the preceding methods, the priest is supposed to

<hr>

[1] *Annotat. in Decr. cit.*
[2] *Act. Eccl. Med.*, pars iv. Instruc. Euch. § *De custodia SS. Eucha-istiæ*, pag. 424.
[3] Cfr. Mél. Théol., l. c. pag. 530.   [4] Pars ii. tit. x. n. 7, lit. (b).
[5] In Gav., l. c. n. xxxii.

have received the Precious Blood, for he is supposed to distribute or to consume the larger particles before collecting the fragments in the ciborium. But some suggest that he should collect the fragments and allow them to fall into the chalice *before* he receives the Precious Blood, so that he may receive them along with it. This is the method of Quarti and Coninck, cited by the "Mélanges Théologiques,"[1] and is there preferred to any other. We think this method, however, is liable to serious objections. In the first place, it cannot be adopted when the priest has to distribute or to consume any large particles before collecting the fragments, because the rubric of the Missal plainly requires that he should receive the Precious Blood before doing so, and the decree already cited still more clearly requires the same, since it says these particles are to be consumed "post sumptionem "sanguinis ante purificationem."[2] To meet this, it may be said that the priest could take out the larger particles, and put them aside on the corporal, or in another ciborium, until he has received the Precious Blood. But this would be an additional trouble, and even still he would have to dispose of the minute fragments that might be left by those particles on the corporal or in the other ciborium. The method then could be adopted only in the case which is rather the exception than the rule, that is, when there are no large particles in the ciborium to be purified. Even in this case, though we would not condemn its adoption on account of the authority in favor of it, we would not recommend it, for we think it more in accordance with the rubric, that the priest should consummate the sacrifice by receiving the Precious Blood, before receiving even the minute fragments that had been consecrated at another time.

IV. Having received the Precious Blood, and consumed or distributed the larger particles, he gets a little wine in the chalice, collects the fragments in the ciborium, and makes them fall into the chalice as above. He then gets wine in the ciborium, and after carefully passing it round the interior, pours it into the chalice; if he thinks it necessary, he may repeat this a second or a third time, or he may use his index finger in applying the wine to any part of the interior. He next dries the ciborium with a purificator, if he have new consecrated particles to be put into it; and having put them in, collects and puts into the chalice the fragments they may have

---

[1] Loc. cit. p. 534.   [2] 3 Sept. 1672, in *Conchen.*, n. 2602.

left on the corporal. He then takes the contents of the chalice as the first ablution, and proceeds as usual. If he have no particles to put in, he need not dry the ciborium until after the second ablution, which, like the first, he may take in the ciborium, to be poured out of it into the chalice. In this case he first dries the chalice and then the ciborium.

623. We prefer this last mode to any other we have seen, and we know it is found in practice very convenient and very effective. It agrees in substance with that proposed by Merati, and putting together what De Herdt states on the subject,[1] we think it is the method recommended by him. But it has one suggestion that is not made by either, viz., that a little wine be poured into the chalice before the fragments are made to fall into it. The object of this is to prevent the fragments from adhering to the bottom, or from being dispersed round the sides of the chalice by the wine that is afterwards poured in out of the ciborium.[2] Again we think that, generally speaking, the wine poured into the ciborium may be made to pass over the whole interior surface, and take up the minute particles, without applying the finger, and hence we have said, *if he thinks it necessary*. But if he uses the finger, he should dry it with the purificator before emptying the ciborium into the chalice, otherwise a drop from it may fall on the altar-cloth or on the corporal.

624. M. Caron[3] observes that very often the ciborium may be purified sufficiently well with the finger, without pouring in wine, if only a little more time and pains be taken. Any one who makes the trial, will find that this is so; and when newly consecrated particles are to be put into the ciborium immediately after it is purified, it is a great matter to be able to do without pouring in wine, as it is difficult to dry the interior so perfectly as to prevent the danger of particles adhering to it.

§ IX.—Fideles omnes ad sacram Communionem admittendi sunt, exceptis iis qui justa ratione prohibentur. Arcendi autem sunt publice indigni, quales sunt excommunicati, interdicti, manifesteque infames, ut meretrices. concubinarii, fœneratores, magi, sortilegi, blasphemi. et alii ejus generis publici peccatores, nisi de eorum pœnitentia et emendatione constet, et publico scandalo prius satisfecerint.

625. According to this rubric, all the faithful have a right

[1] Pars ii. n. 30, iv.
[2] Cfr Vavasseur, part iv. sect. i. chap. ii. art. i., *Manière de donner la Sainte Communion*, n 121, in nota.
[3] *Les Cérémonies de la Messe Basse*, art. xiv. § i. n. 129, *note.*

to be admitted to Holy Communion, except such as are for
just reasons excluded. It is the common opinion of theo
logians, that the pastor is bound to give communion to the
members of his flock, not only when the precept of receiving
it actually urges, but as often as they reasonably ask for it:
"Quoties rationabiliter et opportune petunt."[1] It is for the
pastor himself to judge when the demand is reasonable, taking all the circumstances into account, the condition of the
person, the preparation required, etc.

626. It may be laid down as a general rule, that when a
priest administers communion in public, he should administer
it to all who present themselves to receive it. But there are
some to whom, even in these circumstances, it is to be refused.
Such are those whom the rubric here points out,—those,
namely, who are *publicly known to be unworthy.* They are not
to be admitted to Holy Communion in any circumstances, until
they have given proof of their repentance and amendment.
They have no claim to be admitted. By their exclusion they are
merely prevented from consummating an act of sacrilege;
and even their reputation cannot suffer, since they are, by
supposition, public sinners; and on the other hand, great
scandal would arise from admitting them. The priest, therefore, is bound to exclude them. According to some theologians, he might administer the sacrament to save his own
life, provided he were not required to do so in contempt of
religion. St. Lignori for a time thought this opinion probable,
but he afterwards rejected it, and maintains that the priest
must refuse the sacrament to the notoriously unworthy, at
the risk of his life, even when contempt is not intended.[2]

627. The chief difficulty here is in determining what kind
of publicity is required in order that a person be a "public sin-
"ner" in the sense of the rubric. According to the usual distinction of theologians and canonists, a crime may be public in
three ways. 1° By publicity "of law" (*publicitate juris*)—
when a person juridically accused of any crime confesses it, or
is convicted of it. 2° By publicity "of fact" (*publicitate facti*)
—when the crime has been committed before so many, that no
subterfuge or evasion can conceal it. 3° By publicity "of
"fame" (*publicitate famæ*)—when the crime is already known
to the greater part of any community, or to so many that it is
morally certain to come to the knowledge of the community.[3]

---

[1] St. Lig., lib. vi. n. 253.   [2] Lib. vi. n. 49. Dub. 5.
[3] Vid. Carrière, *De Justitia et Jure*, n. 891.

Various rules are given as to the number who should know it, according to the different communities, of which there may be question. We need not seek for mathematical accuracy in a matter of this kind, and Carrière concludes that a crime may be looked on as public in any community when, considering the crime itself, the persons to whom it is known, and the community of which there is question, the knowledge of it is morally certain to spread.[1]

In practice, therefore, the priest, in his parish or district, must take all the circumstances into account, and decide according to the best of his judgment. If, all things considered, a doubt still remains as to whether a crime has been committed, communion is not to be refused.[2] It is a well-known principle of canon-law, that one is presumed to be innocent unless he is proved to be guilty : " Nemo præsumitur malus, nisi probetur malus."[3] When the doubt regards, not the commission, but the publicity, of a crime, the sacrament should not be refused in public, according to Lacroix.[4] In truth, the reasons to be presently stated, why the sacrament is not to be refused in public to an occult sinner, may be applied with almost equal force here.

628. With regard to the proof of amendment that is to be required, it is enough if it be publicly known that the person has gone to confession, has abandoned the occasion of sin, has made restitution or satisfaction where due, etc. Here also much must be left to the prudent judgment of the priest. But it may be observed that if a person has been living in the occasion of sin, theologians insist that he shall have actually given up the occasion : no other proof of amendment can be accepted.[5] In doubt about the amendment, the sacrament is to be refused ; for the crime being once certain, the amendment must be clearly proved.[6]

629. If one, who has been a public sinner, has amended and done penance in private, he may be admitted to Holy Communion in private.[7] This, however, must be understood of one who is prepared to make public reparation as soon as he can, but may be unable for a time ; otherwise it is plain he would not have the requisite dispositions.[8]

---

[1] Loc. cit.   [2] St. Lig., lib. vi. n. 48. Lacroix, lib. vi. pars i. n. 142.
[3] C. *Mandata*, 6 apud Reiffenst., lib. ii. *Decretal.*, tit. xxii. *De Præsumptionibus*, n. 42.   [4] Loc. cit.   [5] St. Lig., n. 47. Lacroix, l. c. n. 141.   [6] St. Lig., n. 48.   [7] St. Lig., n. 47.
[8] Cfr. Bouvier, *Tract. de Deca.*, cap. i. a. t. iii. § iii. punct. ii. in fine.

§ X.—Occultos vero peccatores, si occulte petant, et non eos emendatos agnoverit, repellat, non autem si publice petant, et sine scandalo ipsos præterire nequeat.

630. By "occult sinners" are here understood those whose sins are not public in any of the ways above explained.[1] If one of these asks for Holy Communion in private, the priest should refuse. We suppose, of course, that the priest has certain knowledge that the person has been guilty of grievous sin, and has no evidence of his repentance. The reason is obvious. The priest, as a general rule, is bound not to administer the sacrament to one whom he knows to be unworthy, according to the words of our Lord: "Nolite dare sanctum canibus."[2] In the present case he prevents an act of sacrilege, and does not even hurt the person's character.

631. If the priest has his knowledge only through the confessional, he cannot make use of it, he cannot allow it to influence his conduct in any way towards the penitent. He cannot admonish him, or refuse him communion on some other pretext, however specious; in a word, outside the confessional he must treat him exactly as he would *if that knowledge did not exist.* If he knows it from another source as well as from the confessional, his knowledge from that other source must be morally certain, otherwise he cannot act on it.[3] If the knowledge be derived from the confession, not of the person who asks for communion, but of another, the confessor cannot directly use the knowledge without the express permission of that other. He may use it so far as to ask some general questions regarding the preparation made, etc., just as he might use it in interrogations in the confessional. Great prudence and caution, however, are necessary in this case. It is better to tolerate the sacrilege than expose one's self to the least danger of breaking the seal of confession.[4]

632. If an occult sinner presents himself for Holy Communion in public, so that he cannot be passed over without the circumstance being observed by others, and, therefore, without scandal, the rubric here directs, and theologians are unanimous in teaching, that the sacrament is to be administered to him. One reason commonly assigned is, the injury which his character would otherwise suffer. This reason of itself

---

[1] Supra, n. 627.   [2] Matt. vii. 6.   Vid. St. Lig., n 43.
[3] St. Lig., lib. vi. n. 50, in fine, n. 51, et n. 658.
[4] Vid. S. Lig., n. 631, *Si autem.*

would scarcely suffice, for it is hard to believe that we are bound to consult for the reverence due to our Lord in the sacrament less than for the character of a wretch who would outrage Him by an unworthy communion. But very serious evils might follow from allowing the priest to refuse communion in public to one whose unworthiness he knows only by private information. A power of this kind would be liable to great abuse. The priest, after all, is but a man, liable to be deceived, to be influenced by passion, prejudice, ill-will, etc., and thus, under the plea of private knowledge, he might publicly refuse the sacrament to those who are really worthy. The fear of being thus excluded might deter many from approaching, and great spiritual injury would result. Again, the obligation of discriminating, weighing the evidence, etc., would be an almost intolerable onus on the priest, and a source of endless scruples and anxieties.

It is for these reasons chiefly, according to St. Lignori,[1] and not merely to save the character of the occult sinner, that our Lord has been pleased to yield His right, and allow His sacred body to be profaned by the unworthy communicant, as it was by Judas, to whom He Himself administered the Eucharist at the Last Supper. If the priest, by private remonstrance, or by general exhortation before administering communion, can prevent such a one from approaching, he ought to do so, but he cannot go beyond this.[2]

It is not permitted to administer in such circumstances an unconsecrated particle; for although this might prevent the sacrilege, it would be the cause of material idolatry.[3]

633. If a person be guilty of a crime which is not public where he presents himself for communion, though it is public in another place, it is a disputed question whether he is to be regarded as an occult, or as a public sinner. Many hold that he should be regarded as a public sinner, and be refused the sacrament. St. Liguori, however, holds that he is to be treated as an occult sinner, unless when it is certain that his crime will soon be known in the place where he is.[4]

634. A person might, through mere ignorance or simplicity, go to receive communion with others, though not prepared, e. g., without having gone to confession, though conscious of grievous sin; and we may conceive circumstances in which

[1] Loc. cit. n. 49, in fine, et n. 50.
[2] Bened. XIV., Syn. Dioec. lib. vii. cap. xi. n. 4.
[3] St. Lig., n. 59–61. De Lugo, De Sacramentis, Disp. viii. n. 187.
[4] Lib. vi. n. 46.

the priest could, without any danger of scandal, pass by such a one, or gently convey to him that he should withdraw.

If the priest be in any case perfectly certain that he can do so, we see no reason why he should not; for the rubric here directs communion to be given to the occult sinner who presents himself in public, only in case he cannot be passed over without scandal. The case is a rare one, no doubt, but we have been told that it has occurred sometimes at stations for confession in remote country districts, where communion is given at intervals during the day.

§ XI.—Amentibus præterea, seu phreneticis communicare non licet licebit tamen, si quando habeant lucida intervalla, devotionem ostendant, dum in eo statu manent, si nullum indignitatis periculum adsit.

*635. Communion is not to be given, in any circumstances, to those who are insane and who have never had the use of reason.[1] If they have lucid intervals, and if, during these intervals, they desire communion, there is no reason why it may not then be administered to them, since, by supposition, they have the use of reason, and may, therefore, be disposed like any of the other faithful. But if, after such a lucid interval, in which a desire of communion is expressed, the insanity returns before the sacrament is administered, can it still be administered provided there be no danger of irreverence? The words of the present rubric leave its meaning somewhat ambiguous; but all doubt as to what should be done in practice, is removed by the common teaching of theologians, that communion can be given to the actually insane only "in articulo mortis."[2] The Catechism of the Council of Trent says: "To persons "laboring under insanity, and at the time incapable of "sentiments of piety, the sacrament is on no account to be "given. If, however, before they become insane, they evinced "pious and religious sentiments, they, according to the de-"cree of the Council of Carthage, may be admitted to its "participation at the close of life, provided there be no "danger to be apprehended of discharging the stomach, or of "other indignity and inconvenience."[3]

*636. Those who are not quite bereft of reason, but whose reason is feeble, who are simpletons or half fools, should be admitted to communion when the precept urges, as well as "in articulo mortis," provided they have sufficient intelligence to distinguish it from ordinary food, but not oftener.[4]

[1] St. Lig., lib. vi. n. 302.   [2] St. Lig., n. 302. in fine.
[3] Pars ii. cap. vi. n. 64.   [4] St. Lig., n. 303.

§ XII.—Ita etiam iis, qui propter ætatis imbecillitatem nondum hujus Sacramenti cognitionem et gustum habent, administrari non debet.

637. According to the usage which prevailed in the early ages of the Church, the Eucharist was administered to infants immediately after baptism, and frequently besides before they attained the use of reason.[1] There is no doubt that they are capable of receiving it, and that it would confer on them an increase of grace; and the same is true of baptized adults, who have never had the use of reason.[2] This custom was gradually given up, and for more than five centuries has ceased in the Latin Church, although it still exists, to some extent, in the Greek Church.[3]

*638. According to the present law, which is expressed in this rubric, communion is not to be administered to children who have not yet attained the use of reason, for till then it is plain they cannot have a sufficient knowledge of this divine sacrament. They would seem to be bound by the precept of communion, as expressed in the decree of Lateran, "*Omnis* "*utriusque*,"[4] as soon as they attain the use of reason. The words, "*postquam ad annos discretionis pervenerit*," are understood to impose the obligation of confession on those who are capable of committing mortal sin. "It may be laid "down as a general principle," says the Catechism of the Council of Trent, "that children are bound to go to con- "fession as soon as they are able to discern good from evil, "and are capable of malice."[5] Now, the words of the canon evidently apply to communion as well as to confession. Hence, St. Antoninus and other theologians, cited by St. Liguori,[6] maintain that children are bound by both precepts at the same age, though the communion may be deferred for some time, as the decree itself expressly permits, if the confessor judges it expedient. This view is strongly urged by a writer in the "Analecta Juris Pontificii."[7]

But the more probable opinion, and that which agrees best with the practice of the Church, does not bind them to communion as early as they are bound by the precept of confession, but gives them a longer time to prepare, and

---

[1] Martene, *De Ant. Eccl. Rit.*, lib. i. cap. i. art. xv. n. xi. xii. Bened. XIV, *De Synod. Diœc.*, lib. vii. cap. xii. n. 1.

[2] St. Lig., n. 301. Vid. de Lugo, *De Eucharistia*, Disp. xiii. sect. ii.

[3] Bened. XIV, l. c.   [4] Infra, cap. xiii. § i.

[5] Pars ii. cap. v. n. 44.

[6] Loc. cit.   [7] Vme Série, pag. 352, *Communion des enfants*.

would thus interpret the "annos discretionis" for communion as later than the "annos discretionis" for confession.[1]

*639. No precise age is fixed for the obligation, but it is laid down as a general rule that children are not bound before the age of nine or ten, and that their communion should not be deferred beyond the age of twelve, or, at most, fourteen. It is said, "*as a general rule,*" for some may show so much intelligence, and be so well instructed, as to be bound, or at least to be admissible at an earlier age; and, therefore, those pastors are reprehensible, who refuse communion indiscriminately to all children under a certain age.[2] "The age "at which children should be admitted to communion," says the Catechism of the Council of Trent, "no one can better deter-"mine than the father and confessor, for it is theirs to examine "and to inquire from the children whether they have acquired "any knowledge of, and experience a relish for, this admira-ble sacrament."[3]

*640. There is no doubt, however, that, in danger of death, the Eucharist is to be administered to children who have attained the use of reason, though they may not yet have reached the age at which they would, in the ordinary course, make their first communion.[4] They are bound by divine precept to receive the viaticum if they have sense enough to distinguish the Eucharist from other food.[5] According to Benedict XIV, it is to be administered to children in danger of death, if they have sufficient maturity of judgment to distinguish it from common and material food—or, as he afterwards expresses it, if they have sufficient intelligence to believe and adore our Lord under the sacramental species. The bishop, he says, may compel pastors to administer it to them . . . . "Si eos compererint tantam assecutos judicii "maturitatem ut cibum istum cœlestem et supernum a com-"muni et materiali discernant;"[6] or to those . . . "quos "iidem parochi diligenti præmisso examine, tantâ compere-"rint pollere ingenii perspicaciâ ut latentem sub speciebus "sacramentalibus Christum et firmiter credant et reverenter "adorent."[7]

[1] St. Lig., n. 301. *Secunda Sententia.* Billuart, *De Eucharistia,* Dissert. vi. art. i. § iii.   [2] St. Lig., ibid., *Sed hic dubitatur.* Vid. Benedict XIV, *De Syn. Diœc.,* lib. vii. cap. xii. n. 2.
[3] Pars ii. cap. iv. n. 63.
[4] Benedict XIV, l. c. n. 3.   De Lugo, Disp. xiii. sec. iv. n. 37.   St. Lig., l. c. Dub. 2, in fine.   [5] De Lugo, loc. cit. n. 39.
[6] Loc cit. n. 1.   [7] Loc. cit. n. 3.

*641. By comparing these two sentences, it may be seen that, in the mind of Benedict XIV, to distinguish the Eucharist from common food, is to believe in the real presence of our Lord, and adore Him under the sacramental species. De Lugo[1] also conveys clearly enough that this is the sense in which he uses the expression; and the Catechism of the Council of Trent, in the passage already cited,[2] plainly teaches that this is the sense in which the expression ought to be understood. In doubt about the capacity of a child, theologians are not agreed as to whether the viaticum should be administered or withheld. De Lugo thinks it may 'be administered, but that there is no obligation of administering it.[3] Bouvier would be in favor of administering it.[4]

642. There is no more important duty of the pastor than that of preparing the children of his parish for their first communion. A fervent first communion is often followed by frequent participation of the sacraments and a steady perseverance in virtue; while, on the other hand, it is hardly possible that those who do not receive communion till long after the age when the passions are fully developed, or who receive it without due preparation, should persevere amidst the temptations to which youth is exposed.[5] The Council of Trent teaches that this spiritual food is given to us "as an "antidote, whereby we may be freed from daily faults, and "be preserved from mortal sins."[6] Hence, there are numberless decrees of provincial and diocesan synods, in which the attention of pastors is specially directed to this important duty. The "Mélanges Théologiques"[7] cites several decrees of synods held in France and Belgium; and a decree of the Synod of Thurles also directs special attention to it.[8]

643. We have already seen that the age at which children may be admitted to first communion is not fixed, and depends very much on the degree of intelligence and the state of preparation shown in each case.[9] But, at least it is certain that no child who has attained the use of reason should be excluded from the preparatory instructions. The time and manner of giving these instructions must depend, to some extent, on local circumstances. The Synod of Thurles[10]

[1] Loc. cit. n. 36.   [2] Supra, n. 579.   [3] Loc. cit. n. 43, 44.
[4] De Eucharistia, cap. vi. art. i. Notanda circa Viaticum, n. 2°.
[5] Vid. St. Lig., lib. vi. n. 193.   [6] Sess. xiii. cap. ii. Waterworth's translation.   [7] I⁰ Série, 3ᵐᵉ Cahier, p. 293 et seq., et iiᵐᵉ Série, 2ᵐᵉ Cahier, p. 266, et seq.
[8] De Eucharistia, n. 22.   [9] Supra, n. 639.   [10] Loc. cit.

directs that some days be devoted to them every year during
the summer season. In the country parishes of Ireland, the
children could hardly attend at any other time, on account
of the distance of many of them from the church, and the
general severity of the weather.

644. There ought to be, in every parish, a confraternity
of the Christian doctrine, the members of which are charged
with the duty of catechising children. This confraternity is
earnestly recommended to the bishops of the Church by Pope
Innocent XI, in an encyclical letter, 16 Junii, 1686. It is
enriched with many indulgences; and special facilities are
granted for its establishment in every parochial church.[1]
Such a confraternity, properly organized and directed, would
lighten very much the labor of the priest, and enable him,
without much difficulty, to ascertain those who might be
admitted to first communion. It would be easy to form these
into a separate class, or into two or more classes, according
to their degrees of proficiency. Select members of the confraternity could be charged with the care of these classes,
and a few instructions from the priest would then suffice to
complete the preparation of the more advanced. It is only
by adopting some such plan that the priest, in a populous
parish, can at all perform the duty.

645. It is well to give as much solemnity as possible to
the ceremony of first communion. This exterior solemnity is
not only a help to devotion at the time, but serves to fix the
event in the memory; and there can be no doubt that the
remembrance of the day of one's first communion often produces a most salutary effect in after life. The Synod of
Thurles expressly directs[2] that the mass at which first communion is administered, be celebrated with the greatest
possible solemnity.

It must, of course, be left to the zeal and prudence of the
pastor to regulate the details according to circumstances. The
decorations of the altar, the vestments, the number of lights,
etc., etc., may be such as are used on great festivals. The
communicants should be dressed in their best attire. In
many places, according to a laudable custom, the female
children are dressed in white. Provision must be made, also,
for carrying out the separation of the sexes prescribed in a
preceding rubric.[3]

---

[1] Vid. Bouvier, *Traité des Indulgences*, IIme Partie, cap. i. art. ii. § 1
except. 2°.   [2] Loc. cit.   [3] Supra, n. 591.

646. The first communion of children is usually fixed to
take place within the Paschal time. Though many of them,
according to what has been said,[1] may not, in strictness, be
bound by the Paschal precept, there is always a considerable
number who are so bound, and who have thus an opportunity
of complying with the obligation. Hence, in many of those
synods cited by the " Mélanges Théologiqúes,"[2] it is expressly
directed that the first communion should take place in
Paschal time.

When this first communion is, at the same time, the fulfilment of the Paschal precept, it can be administered only by
the parish priest, or with his consent.[3] In some of the
statutes referred to, as, e. g., those of Ghent,[4] it is forbidden,
in general terms, and without any limitation, to admit a
child to first communion without the leave of the parish priest
or the ordinary. In dioceses where such regulations exist,
they should, of course, be observed. But, according to the
common usage at present, the leave of the parish priest or
ordinary is not required for first communion, or for any other,
unless it be the Paschal communion, or the viaticum.[5]

[1] Supra, n. 638.   [2] Loc. cit.   [3] Vid. infra, cap. xiii.
[4] Apud Mélanges Théol.. IIme Série, p. 267.
[5] Vid. St. Lig., n. 235, 236.

CHAPTER XII.

ORDER OF ADMINISTERING HOLY COMMUNION: "ORDO ADMINISTRANDI SACRAM COMMUNIONEM."

§ I.—Sacerdos igitur Sanctissimam Eucharistiam ministraturus, Hostiis, seu Particulis pro populi multitudine consecratis, vasculoque uno vel pluribus, decenti et commodo loco expositis, cum vino et aqua ad purificationem eorum qui Communionem sumpserint, et ante eos linteo mundo extenso, lotis prius manibus, et superpelliceo indutus, ac desuper stola coloris Officio illius diei convenientis, præcedente Clerico seu alio ministro, procedit ad Altare manibus junctis, et accensis cereis, facta prius et postea genuflexione, extrahit pyxidem, et illam super corporale depositam discooperit.

647. Priests alone are the ordinary ministers of the Eucharist. According to the ancient discipline of the Church, and while holy communion was administered under both species, deacons also acted as ministers, and they are in fact, by their ordination, "comministri et co-operatores corporis et "sanguinis Domini."[1] They usually assisted the bishop or priest who administered the host, while they immediately after presented the chalice; but they sometimes administered both.[2]

According to the present discipline, deacons can administer the Eucharist only in case of necessity.[3] They may be commissioned to do so by the bishop or parish priest, when no priest can be conveniently had; or, if there be question of the viaticum, they can administer it in the absence of a priest, without any commission.[4] These cases, however, must be of rare occurrence, for, as De Lugo observes,[5] a deacon is seldom found where there is no priest.

*648. When the sacrament is about to be administered, care must be taken in the first place that there be a sufficient number of consecrated particles for all who are to communicate. The particles should be round, not square, or of any

---

[1] Pontif. Rom., *De Ord. Diaconi.* [2] Catal., tit. iv. cap. ii. § i. r. vii. viii. [3] Sac. Rit. Cong., 25 Febr. 1777, *in Ord Min. Observ.*, n. 4379.
[4] St. Lig., lib. vi. n. 237. De Lugo, Disp. xviii. § i. n. 27.
[5] Loc. cit.

other shape.[1] In size they should be, at the very least, an inch in diameter, as a particle of less size can hardly be administered without bringing the fingers into contact with the tongue of the communicant.[2] There is a very convenient instrument by which they are cut at once to the proper form, and which no sacristy should be without. It is a useful precaution, after cutting them, to shake them gently on a piece of linen or white paper, so as to free them from the minute fragments that often adhere loosely to the edges. De Herdt[3] recommends the use of a sieve or some other such instrument for the purpose.

649. The rubric here directs that there be prepared, in a convenient place, one or more vessels containing wine and water for the purification of the communicants. The rubric of the Missal also directs how the purification is to be administered to those who receive communion "intra missam:" "Minister autem dextra manu tenens vas cum vino et aqua, "sinistra vero mappulam aliquanto post Sacerdotem eis "porrigit purificationem et mappulam ad os abstergendum."[4]

We have seen, above, the instructions of St. Charles regarding this purification.[5] Baruffaldi,[6] also, supposes that it takes place, and observes that there should be two vessels, one of water, the other of wine, so that the communicants may have a choice, as some of them might not wish to take wine. Benedict XIV supposes the same, and shows that it was introduced to enable the communicant more easily and more effectually to swallow the least fragment of the Sacred Host that might remain in the mouth, and not, as was maintained by De Vert, by way of substitute for the chalice when it was withdrawn.[7]

650. There are few places, however, in which it has not completely fallen into disuse. De Herdt testifies for Belgium. Citing Janssens, he says it has been given up for many just reasons—the danger of effusion, the poverty of the churches, the difficulty of presenting it to each when there is a crowd of communicants, the nausea some would feel, etc., etc.[8] M. Caron testifies the same for France;[9] and it is

[1] St. Lig., n. 205. De Herdt, pars iii. n. 4. l. Cfr. Synod. Thurl., De Euch. n. 32.   [2] Vid. infra, n. 687.
[3] Pars ii. n. 30, iv. in fine.   [4] Rit. Cel. Miss., tit. x. n. 6, in fine.
[5] Supra, n. 593.   [6] Tit. xxiv. n. 13, et seq.
[7] De Sacrif. Miss., lib. ii. cap. xii. 4, 5.   [8] Pars ii. n. 28, i. in fine
[9] Cérémonies de la Messe Basse, art. xiv. n. 137.

entirely unknown in Ireland, England, and America. Merati, in his commentary on the rubric of the Missal above cited, states that the custom is observed only in some churches.[1] It would seem from a note in the "Cérémonial des Evêques "Expliqué," that at present the custom is not observed even in Rome,[2] and the same may be inferred from the fact that Baldeschi, in his instructions on the ceremonies to be observed in administering communion,[3] is entirely silent on the subject. In many places, however, the rubric is still observed at a mass of ordination—the purification being presented immediately after communion to those who have received orders.[4]

There is nothing, it must be confessed, in the wording of the rubric, to imply that it is not as binding as any other, nor can it be maintained that a contrary custom suffices of itself to remove the obligation of a rubric.[5] Yet it seems as if an exception must be admitted in regard to the present rubric. It is hard to conceive that the contrary custom could have prevailed, as it has prevailed, without at least that constructive consent of the legislator, which would suffice to remove the obligation.[6] In fact, this consent appears to be implied in a recent answer of the Sacred Congregation.[7] Being asked whether it would be expedient to introduce into the diocese of Luçon the observance, at least at the communion of the clergy, of what is prescribed in the rubrics regarding the purification, the Sacred Congregation answered so as to allow the existing usage, according to which there was no purification, to be retained.[8] At all events, the reasons above mentioned by De Herdt show that it would be inexpedient to revive its observance, where it has already fallen into disuse.[9]

651. The linen cloth which the rubric here directs to be extended before the communicants, is for the purpose of receiving any particle or fragment which might accidentally fall while the priest is administering the sacrament.[10] It is usually attached to the altar rails, and is held by the communicant in both hands, while the priest puts the Sacred Host into his

---

[1] *Nov. Obs. et Addit.*, etc., n. xxxiv.
[2] Lib. ii. cap. xxix. n. 3, note (3).
[3] *Esposizione delle Sacre Ceremonie, etc.*, parte ia, capo iii.
[4] In Rome, according to present usage, there is no purification even at a mass of ordination.   [5] Vid. chap. i. n. 55, et seq.
[6] Chap. i. n. 51, 52.
[7] 12 Aug., 1854, *in Lucionen.*, ad 20 et ad 24.
[8] Vid. Decr. in Appendice.
[9] Vid. Mél. Théol., VIme Série, 4me Cahier, pp. 544, et seq.
[10] Baruff., tit. xxiv. n. 16. Catal., cap. ii. § i. n. iii.

mouth. It is evident from the purpose for which it is intend
ed, that it should be held extended horizontally under the
chin. St. Charles, in his instructions, directs that it be held,
not by the communicant, but by two clerics, and held so that
it may extend under the ciborium and the priest's hands, as
well as under the chin of the communicant.[1] There is certainly good reason for this precaution, for particles may easily
fall outside the communion cloth when it does not extend
under the pyxis.

But as it is unusual for clerics to hold the cloth unless for
the communion of the clergy, other expedients have been suggested. One is to hold the patena between the index and
middle finger of the left hand, which holds the ciborium.
This is recommended by Possevin and Corsetti.[2] But the
Sacred Congregation, being consulted on the subject, forbade
this use of the patena.[3] It allows a priest, however, to hold
it under the chin at a general communion given by dignitaries.[4] Merati would permit it to be held in like manner by
the deacon when communion is given at solemn mass.[5]
Cavalieri disapproves of this opinion of Merati, and would
confine the use of the patena strictly to a general communion
administered by a dignitary, as, e. g., on a great festival in
cathedral or collegiate churches, where both clergy and laity
communicate.[6] The Sacred Congregation having been consulted, decided that the opinion of Merati may be followed.[7]
It also sanctions the use of a silver plate or dish placed on
the communion cloth at the grating in giving communion to
nuns.[8]

Quarti recommends the priest to hold the ciborium itself
under the chin of the communicant,[9] but this would be to
avoid one danger by incurring another and a greater one, for
the particles would be thus exposed to the breath of the person receiving. Besides, as is observed by the "Mélanges
Théologiques,"[10] it would be hardly possible to hold the ciborium in this way on account of its shape and the usual position
of the communicant.

*652. We must, then, be satisfied in ordinary cases with the

---

[1] *Act. Eccl. Med.*, pars iv. *Instr. de Sac. Com.*, p. 606.
[2] Apud. Mél. Théol., l. c. p. 532.
[3] 12 Aug., 1854, *in Lucionen.*, ad 21.
[4] 3 Sept., 1661, *in Andrien.*, n. 2127.   [5] Pars ii. tit. x. n. liv.
[6] Cap. iv. *De Comm. Fidel.*, Decr. viii. n. 1.
[7] 12 Aug. 1854, *in Lucionen.*, ad 20.   [8] Decr. cit. ad 23.
[9] Cit. apnd Caval., l c. n. ii.   [10] Loc. cit. pag. 533.

provisions of the rubric; and it is for the priest to take care
that they be carried out, so as to guard, as far as possible,
against the danger of allowing the minutest fragment to fall
on the ground. This is, in substance, what the Sacred Congregation tells us in answer to a question on the subject.[1]
Some recommend that the top of the altar rails be of considerable width, so that the communion cloth may rest extended
on it There is no doubt that, by this arrangement, a fragment that may fall is more easily recovered than when each
one, after receiving, allows the cloth to drop towards the
ground.[2] At least the communicants should be instructed to
keep the cloth properly extended, and the priest should be careful, in administering each particle, to adopt the precautions
recommended below.[3]

When there is a great number of communicants, as on the
occasion of a Jubilee, a Mission, or the like, benches furnished with communion cloths may, according to a decision of the
Sacred Congregation,[4] be placed outside the sanctuary, on
each side of the altar rails. They may be arranged in rows,
straight or circular, as is found convenient, but, besides the
lights on the altar, there should be, at the ends of the space
thus occupied, at least two candelabra lighted while communion is being distributed.[5]

653. Notwithstanding the precautions taken, it may still
happen that a whole particle or a minute fragment will fall
on the floor or on the dress of one of the communicants. The
rubric of the Missal provides for the case in which it falls on
the floor. It is to be reverently taken up, and the place
where it fell to be washed and scraped a little: what is thus
scraped off being afterwards thrown into the sacrarium.[6]
Collet[7] observes that the place where it fell should be marked, and covered with something clean, that it may not be
trodden on until it can be scraped as directed.[8] The rubric[9]
also prescribes that, if it falls outside the corporal, on the altar
cloth, or any other linen, the linen should be carefully washed,
and the water thrown into the sacrarium. If, therefore, the
priest, in giving communion, observes that any fragment has

[1] Decr. citat., ad. 22.   [2] Vid. Mél. Théol., l. c. pag. 536.
[3] Vid. infra, § vii.   [4] 26 Mar., 1859, in Tarnovien., n. 5285.
[5] Vid. Decr. cit. in Append.
[6] Pars iii. tit. x. rub. 15. De Defectibus.
[7] Traité des Saints Mystères, chap. xiv. n. 15.
[8] Cfr. St. Lig., lib. vi. n. 250.   [9] Loc. cit..

fallen on the cloth, he should immediately take it up, and, at the same time, note, as well as he can, the spot where it fell, so that it may be washed as the rubric directs.[1]

654. Should a particle fall on the dress of one of the communicants, the priest ought at once to take it up; but should it fall inside the dress of a female, he ought to direct herself to take it up.[2] He must take care, however, to avoid anything that would excite disturbance or alarm. If the particle cannot easily be found, or if it be a minute fragment that is not easily seen, he may direct the person to withdraw quietly to the sacristy, or some other private place, and search for it and having found it, either consume it or bring it to the church. These are the instructions of Collet,[3] who discusses several cases that may arise.

655. He observes that if the priest alone notices the fall of a minute fragment, and has reason to think that the search would be fruitless, or would be, in the circumstances, attended with very great inconvenience, he may be silent about the matter, and leave all to Providence. It may be added, that there is nearly always reason to apprehend such inconvenience when there is a great number of communicants; and, therefore, in such circumstances, it is better, at least as a general rule, not to call attention to the matter. It is evident that, in neglecting what is prescribed by the rubric of the Missal above cited,[4] there is risk of leaving a minute fragment to be trampled on the floor. Yet, St. Liguori,[5] speaking of this rubric, says that it does not bind *sub gravi*; and also that, as a general rule, the washing of the dress or beard (on which a particle might have fallen) may be omitted, "ad evitandam turbationem populi."

In fact, the loss of minute fragments in this way, as well as of others that fall unobserved by any one, when there is a great number of communicants, may be looked on as an unavoidable accessory of the mystery itself; and, therefore, one should not be over-anxious about the matter, when he has taken the ordinary precautions against irreverence. The objections of the heretics to the doctrine of the Real Presence, founded on the supposed indignity to our Lord in this and other like cases, are refuted by Bellarmine.[6]

656. When there are only a few to receive communion,

[1] Collet, l. c.   [2] St. Lig., l. c.   Collet, *Traité des Saints Mystères*, l. c., et *De Eucharistia*, cap. v. in fine Quær. 6.   [3] Loc. cit.
[4] Supra, n. 651.   [5] Lib. vi. n. 250.   [6] *De Eucharistia* lib. iii. cap. x.

there is less danger that a particle or fragment may fall. In this case the cloth used is commonly a short one, presented by the clerk to the first of the communicants, and given by him to the next, and so on. A piece of cardboard, covered with linen, somewhat like the pall,[1] but much larger, is sometimes used for the purpose, and is found very convenient. It is recommended by Cavalieri,[2] in his commentary on a decree of the Apostolic Visitation, which expressly prohibits the use of the chalice veil, or finger towel, as a communion cloth. The same decree is cited by Merati.[3] It is not right to use the purificator,[4] or any part of the priest's vestments, as, *e.g.*, the extremity of the surplice, chasuble, stole, etc.[5] In a word, the cloth used should be appropriated to that use exclusively, as is ordered by the decree of the Apostolic Visitation just cited.

657. The priest should wash his hands as directed by the rubric, even though they be perfectly clean, because the words make no exception, and because the washing of the hands here, as well as that which is prescribed before mass, has a mystic meaning, being suggestive of the purity required for the sacred function he is about to be engaged in.[6] Cavalieri thinks it may be omitted without any fault if the hands be already clean, though he still recommends a compliance with the letter of the rubric.[7]

*658. Having washed his hands, he vests in surplice and stole. Nothing short of strict necessity can dispense him from the obligation of wearing these vestments in giving communion;[8] but there can be no difficulty in complying with the rubric in the present case, for it is supposed that communion is administered in the church.[9]

The color of the stole should be that which is suited to the office of the day, in other words, that of the vestments used in the mass of the day. Baruffaldi,[10] Merati,[11] Bal-

---

[1] Vid. Vavasseur, part. i. sec. iii. chap. iii. art. i. *Des Linges Sacrés*, in nota.   [2] Cap. iv *De Communione Fidelium*, Decr. xiv. n. iv.
[3] Pars ii. tit. x. n. xxix.   [4] Merati, l. c. n. lvi.   [5] Cavalieri, l. c.
[6] Cfr. Gavan., pars ii. tit. i. rub. i. lit. (e).
[7] Cap. iv. Decr. xiii. n. xv.   [8] Vid. infra, chap. xiv. § xii.
[9] Even canons who have the use of the rochet must wear the surplice in the administration of the sacraments, as we have seen. (Supra, n. 121.) But according to a recent decision of the Sacred Congregation the surplice may be put on over the rochet. (31 Aug., 1867, *in Ambianen.* ad. 4, q. v. in Append.)   [10] Tit. xxiv. n. 23-27.
[11] Pars ii. tit. x. n. xxxi.

deschi,[1] and others, are of opinion that white, as the color appropriated specially to the Blessed Eucharist, may be used on any day. But the question being referred to the Sacred Congregation, it was decided that the color should be that of the office of the day, according to the literal meaning of the rubric.[2]

It may be observed that, on the 2d November, the office of the day is not the office for the dead, but the festive office which is recited with the office of the dead.[3] On Good Friday, communion cannot be administered unless as the viaticum.[4] And when communion is administered as the viaticum, the color of the stole should be white.[5]

659. The clerk, or minister who attends the priest, should be already vested in soutane and surplice,[6] and in readiness to go before him from the sacristy, where we suppose him to vest, to the altar where the Blessed Sacrament is kept.

The clerk should have previously gone to this altar to prepare it, by removing the cover, lighting the candles, etc. He should also place on the altar a small vessel of water and a purificator, for the ablution of the priest's fingers.[7]

*660. It is enough to light two candles, according to Baruffaldi;[8] but Merati would have, besides, a torch, lighted at the epistle side, and, on festival days, one at the gospel side also.[9] Torches, however, are seldom used at communion, unless when it is given "intra missam solemnem." It has been already stated that additional lights are required when, on the occasion of a great concourse of communicants, benches are placed for them outside the altar rails.[10] At solemn mass, acolytes, with lighted candles, are permitted to accompany the priest in giving communion, but the same is not permitted at low mass.[11]

661. The rubric directs him to proceed with his hands joined, from which it would seem that the burse, containing the corporal, should be carried by the clerk, as is expressly directed by the rubric regarding communion of the sick.[12] Baruffaldi[13] and Cavalieri[14] approve of this, if the attendant be

---

[1] *Esposizione*, etc., pars i. cap. iii. art. ii. n. 10.
[2] 12 Mar. 1836, *in una Trident.*, ad 13, n. 4777.
[3] Vid. De Herdt, pars v. n. 32.　　　　[4] Infra, § xii.
[5] Chap. xiv. § xii.　　　　　　　　　　[6] Vid. supra, n. 126.
[7] Merati, n. xxxiv. Baruff., l. c. n. 73.　[8] Tit. xxiv. n. 34.
[9] Loc. cit. n. xxxiv.　　　　　　　　[10] Vid. supra, n. 652.
[11] Sac. Rit. Cong., 12 Aug. 1854, *in Lucion.*, ad 72 et 73.
[12] Infra, chap. xiv. § xiii.　　　　　　[13] Loc. cit. n. 37.
[14] *De Communione Fidelium*, Decr. xiii. n. xx. et n. xlii.

really a "clericus;" but, if not, they would have it carried by
the priest himself. Merati[1] and Catalani[2] would have the
burse and the key of the tabernacle previously placed on the
altar by the sacristan. The Sacred Congregation, however,
without precisely condemning what is sanctioned by these
high authorities, has declared that it is becoming (decere)
that the burse be carried by the priest himself.[3] It has also
declared that the burse, containing the corporal, should be
used whenever communion is given "extra missam," and that
the rubric requiring it is preceptive.[4] From these decisions
it is not unreasonable to infer that the priest may be said to
proceed "manibus junctis," while carrying the burse; for it
is hard to suppose that the Sacred Congregation would
recommend what is incompatible with the observance of a
clear rubric of the ritual.

*662. All things, then, being ready, the priest, vested in
surplice and stole, puts on his cap, takes the burse, holding
it horizontally, with his left hand under and his right over it,
the opening being turned towards him; and having saluted
the cross of the sacristy, goes, preceded by the clerk or clerks,
to the altar, where, having uncovered and given his cap to
the clerk, he genuflects in plano, and ascends to the predella.

The manner of carrying the burse is not prescribed by any
authority we have seen, but the above is suggested by the
way in which it is carried over the chalice for mass.[5] The
rest is in exact accordance with the instructions of Merati,[6]
and of Vavasseur, who gives a number of authorities for
them.[7]

According to Merati,[8] Bauldry,[9] and Catalani,[10] he should
say a short prayer on his knees before ascending the altar.
Other writers are silent on this, as the rubric does not
mention it; but it appears to be implicitly recommended in a
previous rubric regarding the administration of the sacraments
generally.[11]

*663. Having ascended the altar, he takes the corporal
out of the burse (which he places on the gospel side as at
the commencement of mass), unfolds and spreads it out

---

[1] Loc. cit. n. xxxiv.   [3] Cap. ii. § i. n. xiv.
[2] 24 Sept. 1842, in Neapol., ad 3, n. 4950.
[4] 27 Feb. 1847, Cong. Cler. Reg. Sanct. Crucis, n. 5068.
[5] Baldeschi, Esposizione, cap. i. art. i. n. 6.   [6] Loc. cit.
[7] Part iv. chap. ii. Manière de donner la Sainte Communion, art. ii.
[8] Loc. cit.   [9] Pars iii. cap. 8, n. ii.
[10] Loc. cit. n. xiii.   [11] Supra, chap. ii. § vi.

on the middle of the altar, opens the tabernacle, and genuflects; takes out the ciborium and places it on the corporal, shuts the door of the tabernacle, uncovers the ciborium, putting the lid on the corporal, but the veil, if it have one, outside the corporal, and then genuflects a second time.[1]

There is an obvious reason why the veil of the ciborium should not be placed on the corporal, viz., because minute fragments might easily adhere to it. On the other hand, the lid or cover of the ciborium should be placed on the corporal.[2] It would seem, therefore, that the veil should be fastened to the lid in such a way as to be very easily removed. Catalani, however, supposes that it is fastened in such a way as to be inseparable from the cover.[3] When it is so fastened, the cover, we think, should be placed with it outside the corporal.

664. The corporal is so called, because it is the linen on which the body of our Lord is laid. On it the host is consecrated at mass, and on it the pyxis or vessel containing the Blessed Sacrament should always repose unless when carried by the priest. This is the practice everywhere. It is either expressly prescribed by the rubric, as in the present instance, or it is required by the common teaching of rubricists.[4]

The corporal should be of fine linen, and blessed by the bishop, or one having the requisite faculties.[5] The edges may be trimmed with lace, but no ornament of any kind is permitted in the centre.[6] The pall may be used, if necessary, instead of the corporal. In fact, it was formerly a part of the corporal, and is still regarded as such, being blessed with the very same benediction.[7]

The burse, containing the corporal, should be of the same color as the stole, i. e., the color suited to the office of the day.[8]

§ II.—Minister genibus flexis nomine populi ad cornu Epistolæ facit Confessionem generalem, dicens: *Confiteor Deo*, etc.

665. The minister or clerk having genuflected with the priest, but a little behind,[9] on first coming to the altar, remains on his knees at the epistle side (if there be two, one

---

[1] Vavass., loc. cit. art. i. n. 122.
[2] Ibid., l. c.   Baruff., n. 40.   [3] Loc. cit. n. xiii. in fine.
[4] Cfr. Mél. Théol., IVme Série, 3me Cahier, pag. 375.
[5] Rub. Miss. *Ritus Servandus*, etc., n. 1.
[6] Romsée, pars i. cap. i. art. iv. n. viii.
[7] Merati, pars ii. tit. i. n. xv.   St. Lig., lib. vi. n. 388.
[8] Catal., loc cit. n. xiv.   [9] Merati, pars ii. tit. x. n. xxxiv.

is at the gospel side also), and commences the "*Confiteor*," etc. He makes this confession in the name of the communicants, as is prescribed both here and in the rubric of the Missal.[1] The ceremony was introduced first in the communion of monks and religious, and then gradually extended to all the faithful.[2] At the words, "*et tibi Pater*," the clerk turn his head a little towards the priest. At the words, "*mea culpa*," etc., he strikes his breast three times with the right hand, placing the left at the same time under his breast.[3]

Before, or immediately after, the "*Confiteor*," he will present the communion cloth, unless it be already prepared at the rails. And should the priest require the use of a step to reach the tabernacle, he will be careful to place it on the predella, and remove it at the proper time.[4]

§ III.—Tum Sacerdos iterum genuflectit, et manibus junctis ante pectus vertit se ad populum, advertens ne terga vertat Sacramento, et in cornu Evangelii dicit: *Misereatur vestri*, etc.

Dicens: *Indulgentiam*, etc., manu dextera in formam Crucis signat communicandos.

666. The priest is supposed to have made two genuflections already, one before, and the other after, taking out the pyxis.[5] The rubric here prescribes a third, immediately before the "*Misereatur*," etc. But should it happen, as it generally does, that the "*Confiteor*" is finished before the priest has made the second genuflection on uncovering the ciborium, the second would coincide with the one here prescribed, and a third would, therefore, be unnecessary. This is clearly implied by Merati[6] and De Herdt.[7]

*667. Having genuflected in the centre, he joins his hands before his breast, and turns so as to stand a little on the gospel side, facing partly the communicants, and partly the epistle corner.[8] In this position he says "*Misereatur vestri*," etc., then "*Indulgentiam absolutionem*," etc., making the sign of the cross with his right hand, the left being placed under his breast. He makes the first line of the cross by raising his hand as high as his forehead and then lowering it to his breast, saying at the same time, "*Indulgentiam, absolutionem;*" and the second line by moving it from his left

[1] *Rit. Celeb. Missam.*, tit. x. n. 6.   [2] Catal., tit. iv. cap. ii. § ii. n. ii
[3] Vavass., part iv. sec. ii. *Du Serrant de la Messe Basse*, n. 239 et 258.
[4] Ibid., l. c.   [5] Supra, n. 663.   [6] Loc. cit. n. xxiv.
[7] Pars ii. n. 28, v.   [8] Merati, pars ii. tit. x. n. xxiv.

shoulder to his right, pronouncing the words, "*et remissionem peccatorum vestrorum*," then joining his hands, he continues, "*tribuat vobis*," etc.[1] He keeps the fingers joined and extended, for the thumb and index are not required to be joined as in giving communion "intra missam."

The hand, while forming the cross, should be always in a vertical plane at right angles to his breast; and before drawing the second or transverse line, it should he raised as high as the shoulder in the same plane in which it was lowered.[2]

*668. The words, "*vestri*," "*vos*," "*vestrorum*," "*vobis*," are used even when there is but one communicant as they are addressed to all, even to those who communicate only spiritually.[3] The words should be pronounced in a clear, distinct voice, and the clerk should answer "*Amen*" at the end of each, as he does at the beginning of mass.[4]

§ IV.—Deinde ad Altare se convertit, genuflectit, manu sinistra pyxidem prehendit; et duobus digitis, pollice et indice, Sacramentum accipit, et elevat; conversusque ad populum in medio Altaris dicit clara voce: *Ecce Agnus Dei, ecce qui tollit peccata mundi.* Mox subdit: *Domine, non sum dignus ut intres sub tectum meum, sed tantum dic verbo et sanabitur anima mea;* quod iterum ac tertio repetit: qua formula etiam utendum est, cum fœminæ Communio administratur.

*669. Having pronounced the "*Indulgentiam*," etc., he turns to the centre of the altar, and genuflects, separating his hands and resting them on the altar outside the corporal.[5] At communion "intra missam," he places his hands on the corporal, having the thumb and index of each joined, as they have touched the Blessed Sacrament. Then he takes the ciborium in his left hand by the knob or centre of the stem, and with the thumb and index of the right hand (the other three fingers being joined and extended) he takes one of the consecrated particles, and holds it elevated a little over the centre of the ciborium, so that it may be seen above it, keeping the hand at the same time resting on the edge of the ciborium; then turning by his right, he faces the people, leaving his back to the centre of the altar.[6]

670. He takes this position though all the communicants

---

[1] De Herdt, l. c. i.
[2] Cfr. Carön, *Les Cérémonies de la Messe Basse*, art. i. n. 11, et art. xiii. n. 114.
[3] Baruff., n. 47. Gavant., pars. ii. tit. x. Rub. 6, lit. (f).
[4] De Herdt, l. c.   [5] Ibid., pars ii. n. 28, v.
[6] Ibid. l. c. i.

be at the epistle or gospel side, and even though there be another pyxis containing the Blessed Sacrament on the altar.[1] De Herdt[2] would except the case in which the Blessed Sacrament is exposed, and would have him then stand a little to the gospel side; but Merati says, expressly, that he stands with his back to the centre of the altar, "etiamsi esset "sacramentum expositum."[3] So does Cavalieri.[4] It appears, however, from a recent decision of the Sacred Congregation, that it is not allowed to give communion at an altar where the Blessed Sacrament is exposed.[5] At least it is not allowed unless in case of necessity, as e. g., when there is no other altar in the church, etc.[6]

*671. In this position he says, in a clear distinct voice, his eyes fixed on the Blessed Sacrament, "Ecce Agnus Dei," etc.; and in the same voice, still holding the Sacred Host in the same way, he says three times, "Domine, non sum dignus," etc. He pronounces these words exactly as they are in the ritual, without any change of number or gender, no matter how many communicate, or even though all should be females.

Gavantus observes[7] that the use of the words, "Ecce Agnus," etc., taken from the gospel,[8] is not very ancient, though extremely appropriate. The words, "Domine, non sum dignus," etc., are said in the name of the communicants, and were formerly said, not by the priest, but by themselves.[9] St. Charles prescribed that they be said in their name by the deacon or a clerk, in a clear voice.[10] Both the missal and the ritual, however, clearly prescribe that they be said by the priest. But the communicants may say them at the same time, "submissa voce." The rubric[11] even prescribes this in communion of the sick.[12] They may also strike their breasts in the usual way, according to Falise,[13] although Merati says this should be done only by the clerk on behalf of all.[14]

*672. In some places it was usual for the priest to repeat in the vernacular the "Ecce Agnus," etc., and "Domine, non "sum," etc. Cavalieri[15] cites a ritual in which the priest is even

[1] Baruff., n. 52. Merati, pars ii. tit. x. n. xxv.
[2] Loc. cit. [3] Loc. cit.
[4] Cap. iv. De Commun. Fidelium, Decr. xi. n. xiii.
[5] 12 Nov. 1831. in Tarent., n. 4677.
[6] Cfr. Annotat. in Decr. cit., in Collect. Gardell.
[7] Loc. cit., litera (g). [8] John, i. 29. [9] Catal., § iv. n. ii.
[10] Act. Eccl. Med., pars. iv. Instruct. Euch., p. 427.
[11] Infra, chap. xiv. § xix. [12] Vid. Caval., cap. iv. Decr. ix. n. vi.
[13] Part iiime, chap. iii. § ii. n. 4. [14] Pars ii. tit. x. n. xxvi.
[15] Loc. cit.

directed to invite the communicants to join with him in saying the "*Domine, non sum dignus,*" etc., which he is to say the second and third time, not in Latin, but in the vernacular. The Sacred Congregation, however, having been consulted on the subject, decided that the practice should be discontinued.[1] But he is permitted to give an instruction immediately before administering the sacrament, in accordance with what is prescribed in a preceding rubric;[2] and it was decided that, at mass, he may give this instruction after his own communion.[3]

§ V.—Postea ad communicandum accedit, incipiens ab iis qui sunt ad partem Epistolæ.

*673. Having said "*Domine, non sum,*" etc., the third time, he descends by the middle of the front steps, even though the communicants be entirely at the gospel or entirely at the epistle side—as is often the case in convent chapels. This was decided by the Sacred Congregation.[4] Having reached the floor, he may then go straight to the place where he commences the distribution. This should be at the epistle side, as is' here directed by the rubric, or, at least, at what corresponds with the epistle side ; so that he always commences with the communicant on his extreme left, moving from left to right ; and, when he has finished one row, returning, and commencing the next in the same place, and so on.[5]

§ VI.—Sed primo, si Sacerdotibus, vel aliis ex Clero danda sit Communio, iis ad gradus Altaris genuflexis præbeatur, vel si commode fieri potest, intra sepimentum Altaris sint a laicis distincti. Sacerdotes vero cum stola communicent.

*674. Members of the clergy are admitted to Holy Communion at the altar steps, or, at least, within the sanctuary ; and hence, when any of them are for communion, the priest administers it to them before he leaves the predella, or, at least, between the altar and the rails.

*675. A priest cannot receive communion from his own hand "extra missam," if there be another to administer it : " Si "tamen desit alterius sacerdotis copia," says Cavalieri, " haud "dubito posse licite seipsum communicare, nedum in casu

[1] 23 Maii, 1835, *in una Capucinorum,* ad 5, n. 4748.　　[2] Cap. ii. § x.
[3] Sac. Rit. Cong., 16 April, 1853, *in una Ord. Min.,* ad 24, n. 5183. 12 Sept. 1857, *in Molinen.,* ad 10.
[4] 15 Sept. 1736, *in Tolet.,* ad 8, n. 4055.
[5] Baruff , n. 56.　De Herdt, pars ii. n. 28. i.

" necessitatis, puta in articulo mortis, sed etiam causa solus
" devotionis."[1]

*676. Priests, in receiving communion, should always wear
a stole. Its color should be suited to the office of the day,[2]
and it should be worn hanging from the neck, as is expressly
prescribed by the "Cæremoniale Episcoporum."[3] But religious are permitted to wear it crossed on the breast, and
fastened with the cincture of the habit.[4]

The rubric here says nothing of the surplice, which, however, the " Cæremoniale Episcoporum"[5] supposes to be worn.
In private communions it probably may be dispensed with,
according to Cavalieri;[6] but on public solemn occasions there
is no doubt it should be worn. Catalani[7] mentions, seemingly
with approval, the practice of some churches, according to
which deacons, in communicating, wear the stole on the left
shoulder. But both the ritual and the " Cæremoniale Episco-
" porum" are silent about deacons; and hence it is justly
concluded by Cavalieri[8] that priests alone should wear the stole,
the rest of the clergy, deacons included, communicating simply
in surplice.

§ VII.—Sacerdos unicuique porrigens Sacramentum, et faciens cum
eo signum Crucis super pyxidem, simul dicit: *Corpus Domini,* etc.

677. In the early ages of the Church, the Blessed Eucharist was put into the hand of the communicant, the right
hand being presented resting on the left in form of a cross.[9]
The men received it in the naked hand, the women in a linen
cloth, which was called "Dominicale."[10] This usage was
general throughout the Church until the seventh century.
Afterwards, the present mode of administering the sacrament,
which had been in use in Rome as early as the middle of the
sixth century, was gradually introduced and adopted everywhere throughout the Western Church.[11]

678. Although the sacrament was, from the very beginning,
often administered under the species of bread alone, and its
administration under the species of wine in the communion of
the laity gradually fell into disuse, and was for good reasons

---

[1] Tom. iv. cap. iv. Decr. xiii. n. viii. Cfr. St. Lig., n. 238 *in parenth.*
[2] Caval., tom. iv. cap. i. Decr. v. n. vii.
[3] Lib. ii. cap. xxiii. n. 6.
[4] Suc. Cong. Rit., 3 Sept. 1679, *in una Capucin.*, ad 9, n. 2903. Cfr.
Caval., l. c., n. iv.   [5] Loc. cit.   [6] Loc. cit. n. v.
[7] Tit. iv. cap. ii. § v. n. vi.   [8] Loc. cit. n. v.
[9] Martène, *De Antiq. Eccl. Ritib.*, lib. i. cap. iv. art. x. n. viii.
[10] Ibid   [11] Ibid.

abolished in the Western Church,[1] there is no doubt that it
was for many centuries usually administered under both species, as it still is in the Greek and other Eastern Churches.

679. In giving communion under both species, it was, at
first, the universal practice, after the administration of the
host, to present the chalice to the communicant, who drank
out of it in the ordinary way; but very soon recourse was had
to various expedients, in order to lessen the danger of effusion.
In some churches the communicants sucked a portion of the
contents through a reed or pipe. In others, the consecrated
bread was dipped into the chalice, and was put, thus moistened
with the precious blood, into the mouth of the communicant
This practice was very commonly adopted.[2]

680. In some of the Eastern Churches, according to Renaudot, a little was taken out of the chalice and given to the
communicant with a spoon, the use of the reed being unknown
amongst them. But the "Communio intincta," just described
was everywhere adopted by them in the communion of the
laity, and even of the inferior clergy, when not actually
serving at the altar. "Quod igitur Ecclesiis omnibus com-
"mune est, Sacerdos primus accipit Corpus Christi, tum ex
"calice bibit sanguinem Christi. Deinde sacerdotibus qui
"sacrificio interfuerunt sacram particulam ipse porrigit:
"calicem quoque dat ipse, vel diaconus, ut ex eo bibant. Ita
"etiam alicubi observatum fuit ad communionem diaconi
"ministrantis; vulgo tamen, tam ipsi quam diaconis et
"reliquis ex clero, particula intincta cochleari distribuitur,
"postea tandem laicis. Communis est Græcis, ut omnibus
"Ecclesiis orientalibus, hæc disciplina."[3]

681. The details are not given in the Euchologium, but
there is no doubt that the two consecrated species are usually
mixed in the chalice, and with a spoon are put both together,
in a very small quantity, into the mouth of the communicant.
Goar, describing the ceremony in the Greek Church, says:[4]
"Particulam quamlibet sanguine perfusam (junctas enim panis
"et vini species ille ritus ostendit, ubi supra diaconus sacrum
"discum spongia tersit et cuncta fragmenta panis in calicem
"mersit) μαργαρίτην quasi unionem pretiosissimam vocant,
"eumque cochleari parvulo (cujus manubrium, tenue et ob

[1] Vid. Bellarmine, De Eucharistia, lib. iv. cap. xxviii.
[2] Martène, loc. cit. n. xiii.
[3] Renaudot, Liturgiarum Orientalium Collectio, vol. ii. pag. 118. Vid.
seq. ibid. et vol. i. pag. 261, et seq.
[4] ΕΥΧΟΛΟΓΙΟΝ, etc., in S. Chrysost. Missam Notæ, n. 179, pag. 151.

" longum crucicula in extremitate ornatum est) pro communione
" e calice educit."

682. The same author tells us that what is reserved by
the Greeks for the communion of the sick, is consecrated only
on Holy Thursday. The consecrated bread, having been
dipped in the precious blood, is carefully and reverently dried
over a fire. It is afterwards moistened with ordinary wine
before it is administered. This, of course, cannot be looked
on as communion under both species, for, as Goar observes,
the species of wine is no longer there; yet the Greeks seem
to regard it as such, for their object in dipping the consecrated
bread, prepared as described, into ordinary wine, before
administering it, is " ut sopitæ et exsiccatæ sanguinis species
" quasi de novo exsuscitari et emergere videantur."[1]

The practice, thus described by Renaudot and Goar, still
continues throughout the East, as we have been assured by a
priest formerly a member of the Russo-Greek Church, and as
we have learned also from a Syrian priest intimately acquainted with the existing discipline in the Churches of the Levant.

*683. The manner of giving communion throughout the
Western Church, is that which is directed by the present rubric.
The priest, holding the Sacred Host over the ciborium, makes
the sign of the cross by raising it about three or four inches
in a vertical line, and then lowering it as far in the same line,
raising it again about half the height, and then drawing the
transverse line (thus signing the communicant, according to
Baldeschi),[2] taking care not to pass the limits of the ciborium. He says, at the same time, " Corpus Domini," etc.,
concluding the words as he places the Sacred Host on the
tongue of the communicant.[3]

In taking each particle out of the ciborium, he would do
well to cause the minute fragments that may adhere to
it to fall back, as he may do, by gently striking his finger
and thumb on the edge of the ciborium before making the
sign of the cross.[4]

684. According to the usage of the early Church, the form
in administering the sacrament was simply, " Corpus Christi,
" Sanguis Christi," to which the communicant answered "Amen,"

---

[1] ΕΥΧΟΛΟΓΙΟΝ, etc., in S. Chrysost. Missam Notæ, not. 180, pag.
153. Vid. not. 32, In Præsanctif. Notæ, pag. 208.
[2] Esposizione, etc., tom. i. par. i. cap. iii. art. i. n. 8.
[3] Baruff., tit. xxiv. n. 66. De Herdt, pars ii. n. 28, i.
[4] De Herdt, loc. cit.

as appears from St. Augustine, *Serm.* 272, and St. Jerome, *Ep. ad Pammachium,* cited by Martène.[1] In conformity with this ancient usage, St. Charles directs the priest to pronounce the words only as far as "*vitam æternam,*" and give time to the communicant to answer "*Amen,*" before receiving the host.[2] But the rubric here, as well as that of the Missal,[3] plainly requires that the word "*Amen*" be said by the priest, not by the communicant.

At a mass of ordination, however, the bishop, in giving communion to the newly-ordained, uses the form, "*Corpus* "*Domini nostri Jesu Christi custodiat te in vitam æternam,*" and the rubric of the Pontifical directs each to answer "*Amen.*" But he is not permitted to use this form in giving communion at any other time.[4]

685. In the rubrics of the Missal[5] it is prescribed that, when the sacred name occurs in the prayers, the head be inclined towards the cross. It was decided also by the Sacred Congregation,[6] that the priest at his own communion, when signing himself with the host and chalice, should incline his head at the sacred name, "juxta rubricas." Hence it might be concluded by analogy that he should do so, also, every time he pronounces it, when giving communion to others; and in fact Vavasseur states it as the common teaching of authors that he should.[7] But we have not seen it prescribed by any author except himself, and we are, therefore, disposed to adopt the opinion of Romsée, who is in favor of omitting it, at least when there is a considerable number of communicants. . . . "Quia in diuturnâ Eucharistiæ distributione "frequens et, ut ita dicam, continua inclinationis renovatio "aliquid indecori habet. Ideoque circa debitum hujus incli-"nationis silent auctores ususque generalis eam negligit."[8]

It is hardly necessary to say, however, that he should show all possible attention and devotion in this holy function, keeping his eyes during the entire time fixed on the Blessed Sacrament.

686. A bishop, in giving communion, presents his hand to

---

[1] Lib. i. cap. iv. art. x. n. ix.
[2] Pars iv. *Instruct. Euch.*, § *Ordo ministrandi Sacram Communionem,* pag. 427.   [3] *Rit. Celeb. Missam,* tit. x. rub. 6
[4] Sac. Rit. Cong., Maii, 1853, in *Grossetan.*, ad 3, n. 5186.
[5] *Rit. Cel. Miss.*, tit. v. n. 2.
[6] 24 Sept. 1842, in *Neapol.*, ad i. n. 4950.
[7] Pars iv. chap. ii. *Manière de donner,* etc., n. 121.
[8] Pars i. cap. i'. art. xiv. *De Communione Fidelium,* n. vii.

be kissed, according to what is prescribed in the "Cære-
"moniale Episcoporum,"[1] and Bauldry observes that the
communicant should kiss the hand, and *not* the ring.[2]
A priest, however, is not allowed to present his hand to be
kissed by the communicant, as was decided by the Sacred
Congregation[3]

*687. In placing the host on the tongue of the communi-
cant, he must be careful to avoid touching the face; and
hence it is recommended that the three fingers, which are
extended while he takes each particle out of the ciborium and
makes the sign of the cross, be closed under the index and
thumb, in the act of putting it on the tongue.[4] He must
also endeavor, as far as possible, not to allow his fingers to
be moistened by contact with the tongue. He should, therefore, take each particle, not by the middle, but by the edge,
and present it so that the opposite edge may first come in
contact with the tongue; then, by withdrawing a little the
index finger, which is under the host, he is likely to avoid all
contact, especially if the communicants are instructed as to
the manner of presenting themselves.[5]

688. It is very often, however, impossible to prevent the
fingers from being moistened. Writers on the rubrics are
not agreed as to what should be done in this case. When
the fingers are moist, the particles adhere to them, and it is
difficult to continue the distribution. Besides, many have,
very naturally, an objection to receive from the priest while
his fingers are in this state.

For these reasons, several authors, Merati,[6] Lacroix,[7] De
Herdt,[8] with Vinitor, Pavone, Lohner, cited by the "Mélanges
"Théologiques,"[9] recommend him to have in his left hand,
under the ciborium or patena, a purificator, in which he may
dry his fingers.

They say, however, that he should first carefully rub them
against each other over the ciborium, so that any fragment
adhering to them may fall into it, and then, joining them as
before, press them on the purificator.

In giving communion at mass, this purificator should be

---

[1] Lib. ii. cap. xxix. n. 5.
[2] *Manuale Sac. Cær.*, pars v. ex 2º Lib. Cær. Epis., cap. 29, n. iv.
[3] 22 Nov. 1659, in *Matherana*, n. 2008.   [4] De Herdt, l. c ii. 3ᶜ.
[5] Ibid., l. c. 4º.   Baldeschi, pars iᵃ, cap.iii. art. i. n. 8, in nota.
[6] Pars. ii tit x. n. xxvi.   [7] Lib vi. pars i. n. 481.
[8] Loc. cit. i. et ii. 4º.   [9] VIᵐᵉ Série, 4ᵐᵉ Cahier, p. 529.

different from that which is used with the chalice.[1] It is
most conveniently held by passing it over the middle finger,
and allowing it to hang loosely.[2]

689. Baldeschi,[3] and Vavasseur who cites him,[4] are altogether opposed to the use of the purificator in this way; but
they manifestly go too far, when they assert that it is not approved of by any author of note. Cavalieri,[5] no doubt, is
opposed to it, but he recommends what St. Charles prescribes,[6] viz., that the priest return to the altar, and there
wash his fingers in a vessel prepared for the purpose, and dry
them with a purificator; or, without returning to the altar,
have the vessel and purificator brought by a clerk. This, of
course, would be a most effectual way of obviating all irreverence; but there are few, if any, places in which it is adopted,
probably on account of the great interruption it would cause,
and the inconvenience of going to the altar as often as would
be required. On the other hand, the use of the purificator,
in the manner already explained, is common enough, and, with
the precautions recommended, appears to be free from any
danger of irreverence.

On the whole, therefore, in the case of a priest who finds
from experience that in administering communion he cannot
keep his fingers free from saliva, we would subscribe to the
opinion of Merati, who, after citing the recommendation of
Quarti and Diana to keep the fingers free, adds: " Verum
" quia difficile est hoc inconveniens evitare: ideo absque
" ullo scrupulo introducendi novam rubricam, in sententia
" sum illorum qui tale purificatorium adhibendum esse
" approbant."[7]

690. Should it happen that the host he has in his fingers
when saying " Ecce Agnus Dei," etc., adheres to them on
account of perspiration in very warm weather or the like, he
may put it back into the ciborium, and take another to give
to the first communicant.[8]

*691. The rubric directs that care be taken to have as
many particles as will suffice for the number of communicants;[9]
but should it be observed near the close that there are not
enough, the priest may divide them, so as to be able to give

---

[1] A. A. cit.   [2] De Herdt, l. c.   [3] Loc. cit.   [4] Loc. cit. note (1).
[5] Cap. iv. Decr. xiii. n. xxxiv.   [6] Instructiones Eucharistiæ, loc. cit.
[7] Loc. cit.   Vid. Mél. Théol., l. c.
[8] Baruff., tit. xxiv. n. 55.   De Herdt, n. 28, ii. 6.
[9] Vid. supra, chap. xi. § v.

communion to all.[1] He should return to the altar to make
this division,[2] and it is recommended that, if possible,
the parts thus broken be given to the better-instructed,
for some ignorant persons might suppose that there is an
important difference between one of these and a whole
particle.[3]

692. It is a question whether, in the same circumstances,
the host that has been used for Benediction of the Blessed
Sacrament may be broken and distributed.   There is no
doubt that, as a general rule, the priest should consume this
host, as is directed in the "Instructions for the Forty Hours."[4]
Besides, it is expressly prohibited, by a decree of the Sacred
Congregation of the Council, to give two or more particles together, or one larger than usual, or indeed any but a single
particle of the ordinary size.[5]   Hence Cavalieri, commenting
on this decree, infers that it is not permitted to break and
distribute a large host, and he would not allow it, except to
give communion to one in danger of death, when there is no
other host consecrated.[6]   In this case he would even permit
the priest to give a portion of the large host which be has
consecrated at mass, if he got notice before communion, and
had no other; but he would not permit it when there is
question merely of not disappointing persons who present
themselves for communion.

St. Liguori, however,[7] clearly implies that it may be done
if the parties presenting themselves cannot wait without inconvenience. Collet[8] teaches the same.[9] We think the decision may apply in the same circumstances to the distribution of the host used at Benediction.

693. If another priest be celebrating mass at the altar
where he is giving communion, or at an altar beside it, he
does not genuflect at the elevation, but merely turns to the
altar, holding the ciborium in his hands, and waits in that
position till the elevation is over.[10]

[1] Sac. Rit. Cong., 16 Maii, 1833, in Veronen., ad i. n. 4707.
[2] Caron, Les Cérémonies de la Messe Basse, art. xiv. n. 125.   Rit.
Toul., cit. apud Mél. Théol., l. c. p. 539.
[3] De Herdt, l. c. 7°.   [4] Instr. Clement., § xxi
[5] 12 Febr. 1679, apud Caval., cap. iv. De Communione Fidelium,
Decr. ii.   [6] Loc. cit. n. viii. et ix.
[7] Lib. vi. n. 245, Sufficit autem in parenth.
[8] Traité des Saints Mystères, chap. xiv. n. 17.
[9] Cfr. De Lugo, Disp. xx. n. 69.
[10] De Herdt, l. c. 5.

§ VIII.—Ubi vero ɔmnes communicaverint, Sacerdos reversus ad Altare dicere poterit : *O Sacrum*, etc.

Tempore Paschali additur, *Alleluia*. Mox Sacerdos dicit : ℣ *Domine exaudi*, etc.

Tempore Paschali dicitur Oratio : *Spiritum nobis*, etc.

*694. When all have communicated, the priest returns to the altar, but always by the middle of the front step.[1] He keeps the thumb and index united over the ciborium, the other fingers being extended.[2] Having reached the altar, he rubs the thumb and index against each other so as to make any minute fragment adhering to them fall into the ciborium, and genuflects.[3] He then washes his fingers in the vessel prepared, and dries them with the purificator, and with the hand thus perfectly free he covers the ciborium.[4] Then, and not sooner, according to Cavalieri,[5] he says the antiphon, " *O Sacrum*, " etc., with the versicles and prayer, which he should say " alta voce et manibus junctis, " according to De Herdt.[6] It is plain from the word, " reversus," that he should not say them until he has returned to the altar; but Baldeschi[7] would permit him to say them while washing the fingers, etc. There is nothing in the rubric to prevent this, and we believe it is generally done.

*695. " *Alleluia* " is to be added to the antiphon, as well as to the ℣. *Panem*, etc., according to Cavalieri[8] and Merati,[9] in Paschal time and during the octave of " Corpus Christi. " The prayer, " *Deus qui nobis*," etc., should have the long conclusion, while the prayer substituted for it in Paschal time, " *Spiritum nobis*," etc., should have the short conclusion, as appears by the " Propaganda" edition of the Ritual. Baruffaldi[10] and Merati[11] teach that " *Dominus vobiscum* " should here be omitted; but they were deceived by the terms of a decree which they refer to, but which regarded the prayers before Benediction of the Blessed Sacrament, at the close of the solemn procession on Corpus Christi, or at the close of the " Quarant' Ore."[12] The Sacred Congregation, having been consulted as to whether it should be said, replied: " Affirmative ut præscribitur in Rituali Romano."[13]

· Cava.., vol. iv. cap. iv. Decr. xi. n. xvii. De Herdt, pars ii. n. 2ϲ, i.   [2] De Herdt, l. c.   [3] Vid. infra, § x.
[4] Caval., cap. iv. Decr. xiii. n. xl. De Herdt, l. c. v. Falise, pars iii. chap. iii. § ii. n. 6.   [5] Loc. cit. n. xxviii.   [6] Loc. cit.
[7] Pars i. cap. iii. art. ii. n. 11.   [8] Loc. cit. n. xxx.
[9] Pars ii. tit. x. n. xxxiii.   [10] Tit. xxiv. n. 70.   [11] Loc. cit.
[12] Martii, 1761, *in Aquen.*, ad 7, n. 4299. Vid. infra, chap. xiv. § xxiv.
[13] 24 Sept. 1842, *in una 3ii Ord. Sti. Franc.*, ad 3, n. 4947.

He is to say all aloud, according to De Herdt,[1] and as may be inferred from the rubric, which requires the minister to respond.

*696. The words, "dicere poterit," imply that there is no obligation, but that it is merely of counsel to say the antiphon, "O Sacrum," etc.[2] De Herdt[3] seems to extend this to the versicles and prayer also. But Cavalieri thinks that it cannot be so extended, and that the versicles and prayer are obligatory, for the rubric regarding communion of the sick, saying nothing of the antiphon, prescribes the versicles and prayer, when the priest has returned to the church, and has placed the Blessed Sacrament on the altar, "deinde dicit," ℣ "Panem de cælo," etc.,[4] and here also the rubric has "mox "dicit," not "dicere poterit," ℣. "Domine exaudi," etc.[5] And this view of Cavalieri is sustained by the word, "præscribitur," in the above answer of the Sacred Congregation.

§ IX.—Antequam reponat Sacramentum, diligenter advertat ut, si fragmentum aliquod digitis adhæserit, illud in pyxidem deponat; et eosdem digitos, quibus tetigit Sacramentum, abluat, et abstergat purificatorio: ablutionem vero sumat, si celebraverit, aut iis qui tunc communicarunt sumendam tradat, aut saltem in sacrarium injiciat.

*697. The ablution of the fingers takes place before he covers the ciborium, according to the authorities above cited.[6] But according to others it takes place after.[7] The priest may follow either order, but we should prefer that which enables him to have the fingers free in covering the ciborium, when it is possible for him to follow it. He cannot follow it when he gives communion at mass, for then he does not purify the fingers until the second ablution, as is plain from the order prescribed by the rubric of the Missal.[8]

The wording of the Rubrics does not define minutely the order that is to be followed in the several acts, and hence it is differently laid down in different authors. We may observe, however, that the "Antequam reponat," in the present rubric, may be fairly understood to imply "before he even covers the ciborium," since he evidently should examine the fingers before covering it; and it is not improbable that the words may be understood in the same sense as qualifying the second clause also, regarding the ablution of the fingers.

[1] Loc. cit.   [2] Baruff., n. 68.   [3] Pars ii. n. 28, v.
[4] Infra, chap. xiv. § xxvi.   [5] Caval., cap. iv. Decr. xiii. n. xxix.
[6] Supra, n. 694.   [7] Merati, l. c. xxxiv. in fine. Baldeschi, l. c.
[8] Pars ii. tit. x. n. 6. Vid. Merati, in loc. n. xxvii.

But we would not extend it to the third clause, since no one would require him to leave the ciborium uncovered until he has first disposed of the ablution.

*698. The priest himself may take this ablution if he has already said mass (for if he have yet to say mass, he cannot take it, as it would break his fast), or he may give it to one of the communicants. But as he might have a repugnance to take it on account of the probable contact of his fingers with the saliva of the communicants, and as any of the communicants might have a similar repugnance, he is permitted to throw it into the sacrarium.[1] And this is what is usually done, according to Baruffaldi[2] and Merati,[3] who further observe that it need not be done every time, but only when the water in the vessel, placed on the altar for the purpose, requires to be renewed.

§ X.—Postea genuflectens reponit Sacramentum in tabernaculo, et clave obserat.

*699. Having done all that is required by the preceding rubric, he opens the tabernacle, places the ciborium in it with his right hand, his left being supported on the altar,[4] makes a genuflection, and then shuts and locks the door of the tabernacle. The genuflection here marked is the only one that the ritual expressly prescribes after the priest returns to the altar. Hence Falise,[5] and the " Mélanges Théologiques,"[6] contended that it is the only one required. The rubric, they said, is so precise regarding the genuflections to be made before distributing the communion,[7] that it would be equally so here if more than one were required. But all the other commentators we have seen, prescribed at least two. Cavalieri,[8] Merati,[9] Romsée,[10] Baldeschi,[11] De Herdt,[12] prescribed one immediately on the priest's return to the altar, after he has placed the ciborium on the corporal. Merati[13] and De Herdt[14] prescribed another on opening the tabernacle, immediately before putting in the ciborium. Cavalieri would require this only when there is another ciborium containing the Blessed Sacrament in the tabernacle.[15] The others made no mention

---

[1] Caval., cap. iv, Decr. xiii. n. xxxvii.   [2] Tit. xxiv. n. 74.
[3] Loc. cit. n. xxxiii.   [4] Merati, l. c.   De Herdt, pars ii. n. 28, v.
[5] Cours Abrégé, etc., IIIme part. cap. iii. § ii. n. 6. in nota.
[6] IVme Série, 4me Cahier, pag. 543.   [7] Supra, § i. et § iii.
[8] Loc. cit. n. xxviii.   [9] Loc. cit. n. xxxiii.
[10] Pars i. cap. ii. art. xiv. n. v.   [11] Pars i. cap. iii. art. ii. n. 11.
[12] Loc. cit.   [13] Loc. cit.   [14] Ibid.   [15] Ibid. n. xl.

of this genuflection.   But all, without exception, were agreed
that one is to be made after placing the ciborium in the tabernacle.

All controversy on the subject, however, has been set at
rest.   The question was submitted to the Sacred Congregation
of Rites, which decided[1] that the priest, on returning to the
altar, should make two genuflections—one before covering
the ciborium, and another after placing it in the tabernacle,
before closing the door.   This decision, as we learn from the
decree,[2] is founded on what the rubrics prescribe as to the genuflections to be made on taking the ciborium out of the
tabernacle immediately before giving communion.[3]

§ XI.—Deinde extenta manu dextera, benedicit iis qui communicarunt,
dicens : *Benedictio Dei*, etc.

*700.   Having locked the tabernacle, standing in the centre
with his face to the altar, he raises his eyes to the crucifix,
extends his hands, and elevates them to the height of his
shoulders; then lowers the eyes, joins the hands, and inclines
the head while saying " *Benedictio Dei Omnipotentis ;* " after
which, turning to the communicants, he continues, " *Patris et*
" *Filii et Spiritus Sancti,*" making over them the sign of the
cross with the right hand, the left being placed on his breast ;
then joining his hands, he continues, " *Descendat super vos et*
" *maneat semper.*"   To which the clerk answers " *Amen.*"
This is the manner of giving the benediction, according to
Merati,[4] Cavalieri,[5] Baldeschi,[6] De Herdt,[7] Vavasseur.[8]   The
Sacred Congregation decided that the hands are to be elevated,
etc., as in the Benediction at mass,[9] but that the altar is not to
be kissed.[10]

*701.   He then turns again to the altar by the same way,
not completing the circle as he does at mass,[11] folds the corporal, and puts it into the burse, which he carries himself, or
leaves to be carried by the clerk,[12] inclines to the cross, and
descends to the floor, where, having received his cap, he
genuflects, puts on his cap, and returns to the sacristy, preceded by the clerk.[13]

[1] 23 Dec. 1862.   [2] Vid. Decr. in Append.
[3] Vid. supra, § i. in fine, et n. 663.   [4] Loc. cit.
[5] Ibid. n. xli.   [6] Ibid. n. 12.   [7] Ibid.   [8] Part. iv. n. 196
[9] 12 Aug. 1854, *in Lucionen.*, ad 76.
[10] 16 March, 1833, *in Veronen.*, ad 6. n. 4707.
[11] Caval., n. xlii.   Vavass., loc. cit.   Baldeschi, loc. cit.
[12] Vid. supra, n. 661.
[13] Caval., l. c.   Baldeschi, l. c.   Vavasseur, l. c.

According to Cavalieri,[1] the clerk extinguishes the lights while the priest folds the corporal, etc.; but, as the priest would be too long delayed by this, the clerk generally returns to extinguish the lights, and put the usual covering on the altar.

§ XII.—Communio autem populi intra Missam statim post communionem Sacerdotis celebrantis fieri debet (nisi quandoque ex rationabili causa post Missam sit facienda) cum Orationes, quæ in Missa post Communionem dicuntur, non solum ad Sacerdotem, sed etiam ad alios communicantes spectent.

702. According to the ancient usage, Holy Communion was given during mass to all the faithful who assisted at it.[2] The Council of Trent also expresses a wish that, at every mass, the faithful who are present should communicate, that they may thus receive more abundant fruit from the holy sacrifice.[3] The proper time, then, for distributing Holy Communion is at mass, and immediately after the communion of the celebrant. This is the time marked for it in the ancient liturgies, one of which is cited in the extract already given from the Catechism of the Council of Trent;[4] and it is plain from the present rubric, that this is the time at which the Church still wishes it to be distributed, in order that those who receive it may have all the advantage of the prayers which follow, and which refer to the communion of the faithful, as well as to that of the priest.

703. It is admitted, however, that there may be a sufficient reason for giving communion "extra missam." It is the common teaching of theologians, according to St. Liguori,[5] that it may be administered at any hour except late in the evening or at night. But an answer of the Sacred Congregation restricts it to the same hours of the day as the celebration of mass, that is, from the aurora till mid-day, unless where there is an indult extending the time.[6] The rubric here supposes that there may be a reasonable cause for deferring communion till after mass. One reason commonly assigned as sufficient is, that the congregation may not be kept too long waiting for the conclusion of mass.[7] When there is a great

---

[1] Loc. cit.   [2] Bened. XIV., De Sac. Missæ, lib. ii. cap. xxii. n. 10.
[3] Sess. xxii. cap. vi.
[4] Supra, n. 577. Cfr. Martène, De Antiquis Ecclesiæ Ritibus, lib. i. cap. iv. art. x. n. vi.   [5] Lib. vi. n. 252.   [6] 7 Sept. 1816, in Tuden., ad 37, n. 4526. Cfr. Gury, De Eucharistia, n. 297.
[7] Gavant.. pars ii. tit. x. n. 6. lit. (d). Baruff., tit. xxiv. n. 80. Benedict XIV., De Sac. Miss., lib. iii. cap. xviii. n. 9.

number for communion, the distribution occupies a consider
able time, and there may be, amongst the rest of the congregation, many unwilling, many perhaps unable without great
inconvenience, to wait so long.

704. There are other reasons, also, on account of which it
may be deferred in the same way. The state of the celebrant's health might require him to leave the altar as soon as
possible, or might render him unable to get through the work
of distributing communion to great numbers.[1] All the preparations for its distribution may not be completed.[2] Some
who wish to go to communion may not have had an opportunity of confessing till after mass.[3] In short, it may be said
that whatever would make the distribution of communion
after, instead of during, mass notably more convenient to the
celebrant, to the communicants, or to the others who are present, may be regarded as a sufficient reason for deferring it.

705. The rubric does not contemplate the giving communion before mass, and Merati cites a decree of the Congregation
of the Apostolic Visitation under Urban VIII, which expressly forbids it unless when there is great necessity.[4] It
would seem, therefore, that a stronger reason is required for it
than for deferring communion till after mass. But there may
be sufficient reason to justify it, as is plain from Merati himself, who prescribes what is to be done in the case.[5] According to Cavalieri, in his commentary on this decree of the
Apostolic Visitation, there would be sufficient reason if the
communicant could not wait till the communion of the
priest, on account of some pressing business, or could not fast
so long.[6] Baldeschi,[7] De Herdt,[8] and Vavasseur,[9] do not require a more urgent reason in one case than in the other; and
we believe that, in practice, what has just been said about
communion after mass, may be applied also to communion
before mass.

706. Until recently, communion could not be given at a
requiem mass with pre-consecrated particles, unless in places
where there was an established usage in favor of so administering it. But now it may be everywhere so administered
according to a recent decree of the Sacred Congregation
of Rites.[10]

[1] Catal., tit. iv. cap. ii. § x. n. vi.
[3] Supra, n. 581.
[5] Loc. cit. n. xxx iii.
[7] Pars i. cap iii. n. 13.
[9] *Manière de donner*, etc., n. 127.

[2] Baruff., l. c.
[4] Pars i. tit. x. n. xxix. in fine
[6] Cap. iv. Decr. x. n. i
[8] Pars ii. n. 28, v
[10] 23 Julii, 1868

707. Previous to this decree it had been ordered that, pending the determination of the question by the Sacred Congregation, the received practice in each diocese should be followed.[1] But the long-continued controversy on this matter[2] has been finally settled by a general decree. It is unnecessary now to touch upon the history of that controversy as we did in the preceding editions of this work. The reader will find in the decree itself a reference to the more important of the decrees previously issued on the subject.[3]

708. Although the rubric of the Missal[4] prescribes black as the color to be used in masses for the dead, it was the common opinion of rubricists that, for any reasonable cause, a requiem mass might be celebrated in violet.[5] This was inferred from a decree of the Sacred Congregation declaring that masses for the dead cannot be celebrated "nisi cum colore "nigro aut saltem violaceo."[6] Cavalieri, in his commentary on this decree,[7] would allow the use of violet if, e. g., on any occasion a number of priests together wished to say mass for the dead in a church not having a sufficient supply of black vestments. But, in the general decree already cited,[8] it has been decided that violet vestments cannot be used at a requiem mass, unless on the second of November, in a church in which the Blessed Sacrament is exposed for the devotion of the Forty Hours.

709. It is strictly prohibited to give communion at the midnight mass of Christmas, or at any other time during the night. Nor can the other two masses be celebrated immediately after the midnight mass. The priest must wait for the aurora before he can celebrate the second. All this has been decided by decrees of the Sacred Congregation;[9] also by a decree of Clement XI;[10] but in some cases special indults have been granted, permitting communion at this midnight mass. Such was that granted to the Ursuline Nuns of Goritia.[11] Others, of a recent date, are mentioned in the "Analecta Juris Pontificii."[12]

---

[1] Vid. Decretum, 14 Feb., 1868, prefixed to this volume.
[2] Vid. St. Lig., lib. vi. n. 249, Dub. 2.
[3] Vid. Decretum in Appendice.   [4] Pars i. tit. xviii. Rub. 6
[5] Cfr. St. Lig., loc. cit.   [6] 21 Junii, 1670, in Oritana, n. 2504.
[7] Tom. iii. cap. xii. Decr. i. n. iii.   [8] Supra, n. 706.
[9] 20 April, 1641, in Pisauren., n. 1319; 7 Dec. 1641, Trium Miss. in Natal. Domini, n. 1360; 16 Feb. 1781, in Una Ordinis Carm. Excalc. Cong. Hisp., ad 7 et 8, n. 4401.   [10] 18 Dec. 1702, cit. ap. Merati, pars iv. tit. iii. De Natal. Domini, n. xiii. q. v.
[11] 27 Jul 1720, in Aquileien., n. 3940.   [12] IIme Série, pag. 1801, etc.

710. The rubric of the Missal for Holy Thursday,[1] by directing that some consecrated particles be reserved, if necessary, *for the sick*, clearly implies that communion is to be administered to no others after the mass of Holy Thursday.[2] It cannot, then, be administered on Good Friday, except as the viaticum, not even when the feast of the Annunciation falls on that day.[3]

711. According to the ancient discipline, communion was administered at the mass of Holy Saturday to the newly baptized, as has been said in treating of Baptism,[4] and not only to them, but to the faithful generally, according to Merati.[5] An opposite custom, however, was pretty generally introduced, and some authors maintained that communion should not be administered, except to the sick, on Holy Saturday. Benedict XIV,[6] amongst others, inclined to this opinion, but it was decided by the Sacred Congregation that it might be administered.

712. There are several decrees on the subject. One of 22d March, 1806,[7] decided that Holy Communion might be administered during mass, and that the communion then received suffices for the fulfilment of the Paschal precept. Another, of the 23d September, 1837,[8] decided that it cannot be administered during mass, unless there be a custom in favor of its being then administered : while another, yet more recent, September 7, 1850,[9] not found in Gardellini, but given amongst the " Decreta Authentica," etc., by Falise,[10] declares that it is not to be administered during mass, but may be after mass. To reconcile these decrees, we must suppose that the answer of 1806 is restricted to the case in which there is a custom, such as is mentioned in the question to which the answer is given.[11]

It would seem, therefore, that communion may be freely administered on Holy Saturday after mass, but not during mass, unless there be custom in favor of it. It cannot, however, be administered before mass, as the permission does not extend to this, and the rubrics of the Missal clearly

---

[1] Gavant., pars iv. tit. viii. rub. 6.
[2] Benedict XIV, *De Sac. Missæ*, lib. iii. cap. xviii. n. 14.
[3] Benedict XIV, l. c. Merati, pars iv. tit. ix. n. lxxviii.
[4] Vid. supra, n. 441.
[5] Pars iv. tit. x. *De Sab. Sancto*, n. lvii.
[6] Loc. cit.   [7] *In Tiphernen.*, n. 4499.
[8] *In Mutinen.*, Dub. ii. n. 4815.   [9] *In Veronen.*, ad 15.
[10] V. *Communio*, § i. n. 3   [11] Vid. Decr. in Appendice.

suppose that before mass there are no particles consecrated, except those reserved for the sick.   Nor is the ciborium brought back to the tabernacle until after mass.[1]

§ XIII.—Itaque Sacerdos, sumpto sacratissimo Sanguine, antequam se purificet, ponat Particulas consecratas in pyxide, vel, si pauci sint communicandi, super patenam, nisi in principio positæ fuerint in pyxide, et genuflectit, ministro interim faciente confessionem ut supra

*713. The ceremonies to be observed in giving communion during mass, differ only in a few particulars from those already described.   In receiving the precious blood, the priest must be careful that the least drop do not remain near the edge of the chalice, lest it come in contact with the pall, for, having received the precious blood, he immediately covers the chalice with the pall.[2]   Then, if the consecrated particles he is to distribute be on the corporal, he genuflects, and puts them into the pyxis, or, if there be only a few, on the patena; and keeping the thumb and index of each hand joined, he again genuflects, and (the clerk having in the meantime said the "*Confiteor*," etc.) turns towards the communicants to say the "*Misereatur vestri*," etc., as before.   These two genuflections are distinctly prescribed in the Missal,[3] though the ritual here seems to prescribe only one.

*714. If the particles have been from the commencement in a pyxis beside the chalice, he uncovers the pyxis and genuflects only when he turns to say the "*Misereatur*," etc.[4]

*715. If he has consecrated no particles, but has to take the ciborium out of the tabernacle; having placed the chalice a little towards the gospel side and covered it with the pall,[5] he removes, if necessary, the chart or canon, and opens the tabernacle; then genuflects, takes out the ciborium, and places it on the middle of the corporal, shuts the tabernacle, uncovers the ciborium and (the clerk having finished the "*Confiteor*," etc.) genuflects, and turns to say the "*Misereatur*," etc., as before.[6]

§ XIV.—Postea vertens se ad populum, in cornu Evangelii dicit: *Misereatur vestri*, etc., et eo, quo supra dictum est, modo, porrigit communicandis Eucharistiam, incipiens a ministris Altaris, si velint communicare.

---

[1] Merati, l. c. n. lxiii.   [2] De Herdt, pars ii. n. 28, i.
[3] Pars ii. tit. x. n. 6.   [4] Caval., vol. v. cap. xxiv. n. xxviii.
Baldeschi, pars i. cap. iii. art. i. n. 6.
[5] Vavass., pars iv. *Manière de donner*, etc., n. 122.
[6] Vavass., ibid.   De Herdt, l. c.

*716. He proceeds here exactly as in giving communion "extra missam," except that he must keep the thumb and index of each hand joined, and touch nothing with them except the host, until the ablution. Hence, in making the sign of the cross at "*Indulgentiam,*" etc., he places the left hand on his breast, so as to have the little finger in contact with it, and the palm horizontal.[1] He also holds the patena or the ciborium " per nodum," between the thumb and index joined, and the other fingers.[2]

*717. But if there be a great number of communicants, and if the priest finds it difficult to hold the ciborium with his fingers in this way, he may separate the thumb and index of the left hand, having previously removed the fragments from them with the tongue, or washed them and dried them with the purificator in the manner before prescribed.[3] This is the opinion of Falise, who cites Lohner and Vinitor in favor of it.[4]

*718. It is here directed that in giving communion the celebrant is to begin with those who serve at the altar, if they wish to communicate. At a private mass he gives it first to the server,[5] who should present himself on the predella.[6] At the solemn mass he administers it first to the deacon and subdeacon, then to the priests, and, after the priests, to the acolytes.[7]

719. The order to be observed by the clergy in going to communion at solemn mass, is as follows. After the " Pax," the clergy who are to receive communion go, two and two. with heads uncovered and hands joined, to the centre of the choir, and there kneel,[8] forming a double line from the altar steps down the centre of the choir.[9] During the " *Confiteor*," which is either sung or said, " alta voce," by the deacon,[10] they incline and strike the breast,[11] and remain kneeling till the priest has said the third time " *Domine, non sum dignus*," etc. Immediately after the " *Confiteor*," the two acolytes ascend and kneel on the edge of the predella, directly facing each

---

[1] De Herdt, l. c. [2] Baldeschi, l. c. n. 7. De Herdt, l. c.
[3] Supra, § ix.
[4] *Cours Abrégé*, etc.. iiime partie, chap. iii. § ii. n. 7.
[5] Sac. Rit. Cong., 13 July, 1668, n. 1907.
[6] De Herdt, pars ii. n. 28, vi. Vid. supra, n. 656.
[7] Vavass., par. v. sect. ii. chap. v. n. 135.
[8] Baldeschi, tom. ii. parte 1a cap. i. art. iv. n. 15.
[9] *Manuel des Cérémonies Romaines*, tom. 1re par. 4me art. viii. n. 1.
[10] Merati, pars. ii. tit. x. n. lii. De Herdt, pars ii. n. 54, ii.
[11] Baldeschi, ibid.

other—one on the epistle and the other on the gospel side—
and in this position they hold the communion cloth by the
four corners, thus keeping it extended with both hands.[1] At
the same time the deacon and subdeacon, being the first to
receive communion, kneel on the edge of the predella in front,
and it is only when they have taken this position that the
acolytes extend the cloth.[2] After receiving communion, the
deacon goes to the celebrant's right, and the subdeacon to his
left.[3] For this purpose both, after communicating, rise ;
then the subdeacon descends to the floor, while the deacon
moves to the centre of the step on which he is ; and both
genuflect at the same time, one behind the other.[4] The
deacon then ascends to the predella on the gospel side, taking
the end of the communion cloth from the hands of the acolyte
as he passes, and immediately returning it, the subdeacon
doing the same as he ascends on the epistle side.[5] The
purification after communion being no longer in use,[6] the
sacred ministers remain at the sides of the celebrant, the
deacon holding the patena under the chin of each communicant, and the subdeacon keeping his hands joined.[7]

720. When the celebrant is giving communion to the
deacon, the clergy rise from their knees, and the first two
genuflect on the floor, at the same time that the deacon and
subdeacon genuflect before going to the sides of the celebrant.
They then ascend and kneel on the edge of the predella.
Having communicated, they rise up and separate, each
making a single step, one towards the gospel, and the other
towards the epistle corner. Then turning round, one by his
right, and the other by his left, so as not to turn their backs
to the Blessed Sacrament, they both descend to the floor,
while the two next, having previously genuflected, ascend
between them to the predella. According to the "Manuel,"[8]
the second two genuflect at the same time with the first two,
and are thus ready to ascend at once as the others descend.

Having reached the floor, the first two again turn to the
altar, and genuflect at the same time, and in the same line,
with the third two, and then retire to their places. The
second two act in like manner, genuflecting with the fourth
two, and so on.[9]

: Cær. Epis., lib. ii. cap. xxix. n. 3.　Baldeschi, tom. iv. cap. vi.
art. ii. n. 13.　　　[2] Baldeschi, ibid.　　[3] Baldeschi, l. c. n. 14.
　[4] Cfr. Merati, l. c. n. li.　　　　　[5] Manuel, l. c. n. viii.
　[6] Vid. supra, n. 650.　　[7] Merati, l. c. n. liv.　　[8] Loc. cit.
　[9] Bald., tom. ii. cap. i. art. iv. n. 15.

The priests communicate immediately after the sacred ministers, and are required to wear stoles, as explained in a preceding rubric.[1] If there be not a sufficient number of stoles of the proper color to allow each priest to have one, there should be at least four. Then the first two could give theirs to the third two after genuflecting with them, the second two to the fourth, and so on.

Should there be more than form the double line from the altar to the limits of the choir, the rest should remain in their places until some have communicated, when they can go and join the line at the end.[2]

721. When there is a general communion at low mass, the ceremonies to be observed are nearly the same. The "Pax" not being given, the clergy take their places in the centre as soon as the priest has said the "Domine, non sum dignus," etc., before his own communion. The first two rise and ascend to kneel on the edge of the predella, at the same time that the clerks spread the communion cloth; but the rest remain on their knees till the priest has said the third time "Domine, non sum dignus," etc., when they rise, and the ceremony proceeds as above.

722. After communion, each one returns to his place in choir, and there, according to Baldeschi,[3] conforms in posture to the rest of the clergy. This posture should be kneeling as long as the celebrant is giving communion. The "Cæremoniale Episcoporum"[4] says that those of the clergy who do not communicate remain standing during the "Confiteor." But even they should go on their knees when the priest, after the "Indulgentiam," etc., turns to the communicants, saying "Ecce Agnus Dei," and should remain on their knees while he is giving communion, as may be inferred from the same authority,[5] and as was decided by the Sacred Congregation.[6]

723. If the "Communio" be sung while the priest is still administering the sacrament, as it may be according to the rubric of the Missal,[7] the clergy rise and stand when the singing commences. Another rubric[8] allows them to sit during the singing of the antiphon. But this is to be understood, according to Gavantus,[9] not of the case in which the

---

[1] Supra, n. 676.   [2] Manuel, l. c. n. i.   [3] Loc. cit.
[4] Lib. ii. cap. xxix. n. 3.   [5] Chap. xxx. n. 5 in fine.
[6] 9 Mar. 1711, in Catanien., ad 3, n. 3834. Vid. Baldes., tom. i. cap. i. art. ii. n. 5 in nota.   [7] Pars ii. tit. x. n. 9.
[8] Pars i. tit. xvii. n. 7.
[9] In loc. litera (c).

antiphon is sung while the priest is still giving communion, for then they should stand out of reverence for the Blessed Sacrament; but of the case in which it is sung, as it usually is, while the celebrant is taking the ablutions. The "Manuel "des Cérémonies Romaines"[1] recommends that the antiphon be not commenced until the celebrant is *nearly* done giving communion, so that it may not be concluded before the Blessed Sacrament is put into the tabernacle, otherwise th clergy would be obliged again to kneel.

§ XV.—Finita Communione, revertitur ad Altare, nihil dicens: non dat eis benedictionem, quia illam dabit in fine Missæ. Deinde dicit secreto: *Quod ore sumpsimus*, etc., ut in Missali, se purificat, et Missam absolvit.

*724. He returns to the altar, observing what is before directed,[2] but he does not say the "*O Sacrum*," etc., or any other prayer, except "*Quod ore sumpsimus*," etc., as marked in the Missal. If no particles remain, he does not genuflect on returning; but, if any remain, he immediately genuflects, placing his hands on the corporal; and, if they are not to be reserved, he consumes them reverently:[3] if they are to be put into the tabernacle, he covers the pyxis (keeping the thumb and index, however, still united), puts it into the tabernacle, genuflects, and then closes the tabernacle.[4]

If there be no tabernacle on the altar, so that the pyxis must be left on the corporal, to be afterwards removed, the priest should be careful to observe the reverences prescribed by the Missal for the case in which the pyxis containing the Blessed Sacrament remains on the altar till the end of mass.[5]

Should the particles have been placed on the corporal, and administered from the patena, he must now carefully collect with the patena the fragments that may remain on the corporal, and put them into the chalice, as is directed by the rubric of the Missal.[6]

If he has to purify the ciborium, he will do so in the manner before explained.[7]

*725. He gives no benediction here, as he is to give it at the end of mass, before the last gospel. The words of the rubric, "quia illam dabit," seem to imply that in no case should the communicants be allowed to depart without the

---

[1] Loc. cit. n. x.   [2] Supra, n. 694.
[3] De Herdt, pars. ii. n. 28, i.   [4] Ibid.
[5] Pars ii. tit. x. n. ".   Vid. Gav., in loc. lit. (b).
[6] Loc cit. n. 6.   [7] Supra, n. 622, iv.

benediction; and this was the chief ground on which Gavantus,[1] who is here followed by Baruffaldi,[2] maintained that communion should not be given at a requiem mass, since there is no benediction at the end of it, as in other masses. We have already seen, however, that communion may be given at a requiem mass;[3] but no benediction is to be given, as the rubric does not permit it.[4]

§ XVI.—Quod si contingat, absoluta Missa, statim aliquos interdum communicare, tunc Sacerdos adhuc planeta indutus sacram Communionem eo modo, quo supra dictum est, ministrabit.

*726. When communion is administered immediately after mass, and before the priest returns to the sacristy, he retains all the vestments; not only the chasuble, as is here expressly stated, but the maniple also.[5] After purifying the chalice, he places it on the corporal, which he leaves on the centre of the altar, merely turning up the first fold. Having finished mass, he returns to the centre, removes the chalice, covered with its veil, from the corporal, and places it on the gospel side, spreads out the corporal, opens the tabernacle, and proceeds, as before directed, in giving communion "extra "missam."[6]

After the benediction, which he gives in the manner above explained,[7] although the communicants have already received the benediction at mass,[8] he folds the corporal, and puts it into the burse, which he places over the veil of the chalice, and carrying all in the usual way, returns to the sacristy.

*727. It was the more common opinion that communion could not be given in black vestments, unless strictly "intra "missam."[9] The present rubric was, therefore, understood not to apply to the case of a requiem mass. But it has been recently decided by the Sacred Congregation that communion may be given in black vestments, immediately after, or immediately before, a requiem mass; the benediction, however, in either case, being omitted.[10]

*728. If communion be given immediately before mass, the priest comes from the sacristy fully vested, and carrying the

---

[1] Pars ii. tit. x. n. 6, lit. (n).   [2] Tit. xxiv. n. 86.
[3] Supra, n. 706, et seq.   [4] Rub. Miss. pars ii. tit. xii. n. 4.
[5] Catal., tit. iv. cap. ii. § xi. n. iv.   Baruff., n. 87.   Caval., cap. iv.
Decr. xiii. n. i.   [6] Ibid., l. c. n. ii.   [7] Supra, n. 700.
[8] Caval., l. c.   Merati, pars ii. tit. x. n. xxxiii.
[9] Merati, l. c. n. xxxi.   De Herdt, pars ii. n. 28, v.   St. Lig., lib. vi.
n. 249, Dub. 3.
[10] Vid. Decretum Generale, 23 Julii, 1868, in Appendice.

chalice as usual.[1] Having ascended to the middle of the altar, he puts the chalice a little to the gospel side, and spreads out the corporal on the centre, then opens the tabernacle, etc., etc., proceeding exactly as before directed.[2] If he be in black vestments, he omits the benediction in accordance with the decree above cited; otherwise he gives the benediction, unless it be certain that all the communicants will remain till the end of mass.[3]

*729. If the tabernacle containing the Blessed Sacrament be on an altar different from that at which the mass is celebrated; and if the priest be required, for a just reason, to give communion in any church, immediately before or immediately after mass, he may stop for the purpose on his way from or to the sacristy, at the altar of the Blessed Sacrament, and retaining all the vestments, proceed as above, provided there be a custom of doing so in that church. It was expressly decided by the Sacred Congregation[4] that a usage of this kind might be tolerated.

When there is no such usage, the priest may find it convenient, in the circumstances, to give communion vested in alb and stole. The answer of the Sacred Congregation just referred to, taken in connection with the question proposed, seems to imply that he may do so.[5] If before mass, he should, of course, return to the sacristy to put on the maniple and chasuble, and bring the chalice. If after mass, he should have returned to lay aside these vestments and to leave the chalice.

---

[1] Merati, l. c. n. xxxiii. Caval., cap. iv. Decr. x. n. ii. De Herdt, pars ii. n. 28, v. Vid. Decretum 31 Aug. 1867, *in Ambianen* , ad 5.

[2] Supra, n. 663, et seq.

[3] De Herdt, l. c. Caval., in Decr. x. n. iii.

[4] 12 Mart. 1836, *in Trident.*, ad 12, n. 4777.

[5] Vid. Decret. cit. in Appendice. From the answer of the Sacred Congregation, 31 Aug. 1867, *in Ambianen.*, it may be inferred that, when there is a reasonable cause, the alb with the stole crossed on the breast, may be used in any function instead of the surplice and stole. But when mass immediately follows, the answer requires that the priest put on the chasuble also. This, however, we are inclined to think, applies only when the function takes place at the altar, as in giving communion, or performing the marriage ceremony (both these being expressly mentioned in the question proposed to the Sacred Congregation); but not when the function is performed at a distance from the altar, as, *e. g.*, the blessing after childbirth in the case supposed in a preceding chapter.—Supra, n. 573. It is not improbable that even the words of the answer, "*Si immediate sequitur missa,*" imply the supposition that the function is performed at the altar.

CHAPTER XIII.

ON THE PASCHAL COMMUNION: "DE COMMUNIONE PASCHALI."

§ I.—Curet autem Parochus, ut in quadragesima per se, vel per alios concionatores populo opportune denuntietur Constitutio Concilii Lateranensis sub Innocentio III, quæ sic habet:

Omnis utriusque sexus Fidelis, postquam ad annos discre- tionis pervenerit, omnia sua peccata confiteatur fideliter, saltem semel in anno, proprio Sacerdoti, et injunctam sibi pœnitentiam studeat pro viribus adimplere, suscipiens reverenter, ad minus in Pascha, Eucharistiæ Sacramentum, nisi forte de consilio proprii Sacerdotis ob aliquam rationabilem causam ad tempus ab ejus perceptione duxerit abstinendum: alioquin et vivens ad ingressu Ecclesiæ arceatur, et moriens Christiana careat sepultura.

730. It is the duty of the pastor to take care, as he is here directed, that the law of the Church regarding annual com- munion, expressed in the decree of the Council of Lateran, be promulgated to his flock. The time of Lent is here mentioned as the time when it ought to be announced to them, because it is the usual time of preparation for complying with the law; and it is, therefore, a suitable time for the pastor himself, or some other preacher under his direction, to address the faithful on the subject.

We have already seen that the pastor must not content himself with urging on his flock the observance of the decree of Lateran; but should exhort them to receive the Holy Eucharist frequently, and especially on the principal festivals of the year. The Catechism of the Council of Trent, in the passage before cited,[1] gives the practice of the faithful and the laws of the Church with regard to communion from the very earliest times. It remains for us here to consider the meaning and extent of the law which is at present in force, and what precisely is required for its fulfilment. We shall understand this best by considering: 1° Who are those who

[1] Supra, n. 577.

are bound to receive communion ? 2° From whom, or in
what place, they are bound to receive it ? 3° Within what
time they are bound to receive it ?

731. I. The terms of the decree appear to be sufficiently
explicit on the first question. Every one of the faithful,
male or female, who has reached the years of discretion, is
bound not only to go to confession, but also to receive Holy
Communion. The sole difficulty is in determining what is
meant by the years of discretion; but this has been already
discussed under a preceding rubric.[1]

732. II. It is necessary to receive the Paschal Communion
from one's own pastor, or with his permission; otherwise the
precept of the Church is not fulfilled.[2] This condition is
frequently expressed by saying that each one must communicate in his own parish; but it is always understood that one
can satisfy the precept by communicating elsewhere, provided
he has the leave of his parish priest.[3]

By the common law, no sacrament can be licitly administered unless by the pastor, or with the consent of the pastor
of the person who receives it. This was the case with regard
to the Eucharist, as well as the other sacraments, from the
earliest times down to the fifteenth century. Though the
regular clergy were allowed to open their churches to the
faithful, they were not allowed to administer the Eucharist
to them without the consent of the parochial clergy. Sometimes this consent was not asked; sometimes it was
unreasonably refused; and, as might be supposed, there were
many disputes on the subject. Sixtus IV granted to the
Dominicans the privilege of administering the Eucharist to
such of the faithful as were unjustly refused it by their parish
priest; and from this time various privileges and exemptions
were conferred on the religious orders, so that they gradually
acquired the right, which they now everywhere enjoy, of
administering communion in their churches independently of
the parochial clergy.[4]

Moreover, by the custom now universally prevailing, it is
understood that any priest who is permitted to say mass, is
permitted also to give communion,[5] unless in private oratories,
in which, according to a constitution of Benedict XIV,[6] the

---

[1] Vid. supra, n. 638 et seq.   [2] St. Lig., lib. vi. n. 300.
[3] Baruff., tit. xxv. n. 32.   St. Lig., l. c.
[4] Vid. Mél. Théolog IIme Série, 2me Cahier, p. 227-233.
[5] St. Lig n. 235.   [6] 2 Junii, 1751, *Magne cum*, § 23.

celebrant cannot give communion without the leave of the bishop.[1]

733. All this, however, must be understood of communion received through devotion ; for the communion that is of precept—that is to say, the Paschal Communion and the Viaticum —can be lawfully administered only by the parish priest or with his permission.[2] So strictly is the right of administering the Paschal Communion reserved to the parochial clergy, that communion, even on Easter day, received without their consent, would not fulfil the precept of the Church.[3] The opposite doctrine, maintained by some authors, is called by Benedict XIV, "falsa nec certe toleranda,"[4] being, as he adds, plainly contrary to the decree of Lateran, and to the apostolic constitutions, which, in conferring privileges on regulars respecting the administration of the Eucharist, have expressly excepted the Paschal Communion.

It is true that regulars, in virtue of their privileges, can administer communion in their churches even during Paschal time, except Easter Sunday alone ; but the communion thus administered does not satisfy the precept. Both points have been expressly decided by the Sacred Congregation of the Council,[5] in two decrees cited by Benedict XIV.[6] It is certain, then, that the communion by which the precept is fulfilled, must be received in the parochial church, or, if elsewhere, with the consent of the pastor. It does not suffice to receive it even in the cathedral for those who do not belong to the cathedral parish, unless they receive it from the hand, or with the consent, of their own parish priest, or of the bishop.[7]

734. It is to be observed, however, that to have the consent required, in order to fulfil the precept out of one's own parish, it is not necessary to ask it for every year, or for every individual case. A well-known and recognized custom in any parish or diocese would be sufficient evidence of it. It may be sometimes also presumed, and Bouvier[8] holds as certain the opinion of St. Liguori, who, with Suarez, Lugo, and others whom he cites, teaches that it suffices if the consent can be presumed with moral certainty.[9]

---

[1] Vid. St. Lig., n. 359, versus finem, *Quæres hic.* Bouix, *De Parocho*, pars iv[ta] cap. v. n. vii. [2] St. Lig., n. 240 et n. 300.
[3] St. Lig., n. 300. [4] *De Syn. Diœc.*, lib. ix. cap. xvi. n. 5.
[5] 11 Junii, 1650, et 31 Jan. 1682. [6] Loc. cit. n. 3.
[7] Benedict XIV, *Instit.* xviii. n. 11. St. Lig., n. 300, *Sed opinio*, in parenth. Bouvier, *De Eucharistia*, cap. vi. art. ii., *Observanda circa Com. Pasch.*, 14°. [8] Loc. cit. 15°.
[9] Lib. vi. n. 300, 4, *Modo adsit* in parenth.

It is, of course, to be understood that the consent of the bishop, or his vicar-general, suffices as well as that of the parish priest.[1] Under the general name of "pastor," in truth, we are to understand the Pope in the Universal Church, and the bishop in his diocese, as well as the parish priest in his parish.[2]

735. There is a special difficulty about strangers, which we shall discuss below under the rubric referring to them;[3] but we may here say a word regarding one or two classes about whom doubts may occur.

1° Priests satisfy the precept, wherever they may be, by celebrating mass. But if a secular priest make the Paschal Communion "more laicorum," he must, like others, communicate in the parish where he resides, or with the leave of the pastor.[4]

2° Servants in monasteries and religious houses share, according to the Council of Trent, in the privilege which exempts the religious from the jurisdiction of the ordinary, provided they be in actual service, residing in the houses of the religious, and living under obedience to them ... "qui "actu serviunt, et intra eorum septa ac domos resident, subque "eorum obedientiâ vivunt,"[5] These, then, can satisfy the Paschal precept in the churches of the religious, as well as the religious themselves, without any reference to the parish priest. But other secular servants, though they may reside in religious houses, cannot, unless in virtue of some special privilege, such as, according to Lacroix,[6] was granted to the Society of the Jesuits.[7]

3° Students, in houses of education conducted by religious, cannot fulfil the Paschal precept in those houses without the consent of the parish priest. This is the opinion of Cardinal De Lugo,[8] and the same may be inferred from a decision of the Sacred Congregation of the Council, which expressly excepts the Paschal Communion in the permission given to certain religious to administer sacraments to the boarders in a house of education opened by them.[9] According to another decision of the same Congregation,[10] what is said

[1] Busemb. apud St. Lig., n. 300.   [2] Vid. supra, n. 102.
[3] Infra, § iv.   [4] St. Lig., n. 300. Bouvier, l. c. 12°.
[5] Sess xxiv. cap. xi. De Reform.   [6] Lib. vi. pars i. n. 624.
[7] Vid. St. Lig., n. 240-10.
[8] Resp. Moral., lib. iv. Dub. xxxiii. n. 9.
[9] Thesaur. Resol., tom. i. pag. 71, cit. apud Mél. Théol., IImᵉ Série,
pag. 262.   [10] Cit. apud Mél. Théol., l c. pag. 272.

of students may be applied also to seculars who choose to reside permanently in religious houses as in places of retreat.[1]

It may be observed, with regard to all these, that the requisite permission is usually granted without difficulty, and in most places is understood almost as a matter of course.[2]

736. III. The time within which communion must be received, in order to satisfy the precept of the Church, is the " Paschal time." This is plain enough from the terms of the decree, but all doubt is removed by the practice of the Church herself, as well as by the teaching of her theologians. Any one, then, who wilfully, and without any sufficient reason, neglects to communicate during Paschal time, is guilty of violating the ecclesiastical precept, no matter how often he may have gone to communion before its commencement, or after its close. Even if he went before the commencement of the Paschal time, believing that he should be unable to go during the time, and if it turns out afterwards that he can go, he is still bound to go.[3] In a word, the obligation is annexed to the Paschal time, although, as we shall see, it is not strictly confined to it.

737. The Paschal time, according to the declaration of Eugene IV, in the bull, "*Fide digna*," commences on Palm Sunday and terminates on Low Sunday, both included; but the time for fulfilling the precept may be extended by necessity, custom, or privilege.[4] The time in Ireland, by a special indult of the Holy See,[5] extends from Ash Wednesday until the octave of the Feast of SS. Peter and Paul;[6] in England, by a similar indult,[7] from Ash Wednesday till Low Sunday;[8] and in America, from the first Sunday in Lent till Trinity Sunday.[9]

738. It is a question amongst theologians, whether one, who has not communicated during the Paschal time, is bound to communicate as soon as possible afterwards, or, at least, bound to communicate within that year.

St. Antonine, Soto, Sylvius, and others cited by St. Liguori,[10] maintain that the obligation in each year is annexed to the

---

[1] Cfr. Bouix, *De Parocho*, pars iv. cap. v. n. iv.
[2] Cfr. Bouvier, l c. n. 13°.   Gousset, vol. ii. n. 223.
[3] St. Lig., n. 297, in fine.   Bouvier, l. c. 10°.
[4] Ibid. n. 296.   [5] 4 May, 1851.
[6] Syn. Thurl., Appendix i.   [7] 14 May, 1853.
[8] Synod. Westm. I^m Appendix, pars i. n. xiii.
[9] Indult, 16 Oct., 1830.   Concil. Prov. I^m Baltimor., pag. 92.
[10] Lib. vi. n. 297, *Tertia Sententia*.

Paschal time, in the same way as the obligation of hearing mass is annexed to Sunday; and that. therefore, the obligation ceases as soon as the time to which it is annexed is past. They deny, therefore, that one who has not communicated during Paschal time this year, is bound by the law of the Church to communicate sooner than Paschal time next year, any more than one who has neglected to hear mass on a Sunday, is bound to hear mass sooner than the next Sunday or festival. St. Liguori[1] thinks this opinion not quite im probable, "non contemnendam." Of course, even in this opinion, the case of one who defers his communion by the advice of his confessor is to be excepted, for, according to the terms of the Lateran decree, he is plainly bound to communicate at the time which his confessor may determine.[2]

739. The more common opinion—that which is held by Suarez, De Lugo, Benedict XIV, and others cited and followed by St. Liguori[3]—maintains that the precept of the Church is, in reality, twofold—imposing the obligation, 1° of communicating in Paschal time; and 2° of communicating, at least, once within the year, as is inferred from the words of the Council of Trent.[4] The fulfilment of the first obligation is necessarily a fulfilment of the second, as is plain; but if one fails to comply with the first, he is still, they say, bound by the second.

740. The ecclesiastical precept, by requiring communion at least once a year, only determines, according to many, how often it must be received in order to comply with the divine precept, Christ having left this to be determined by the Church.[5] Now, if this be assumed, it is plain that one who does not communicate in Paschal time, is still bound by the divine precept, as well as by the ecclesiastical precept which determines it, to communicate within the year. But all do not admit that the ecclesiastical precept is thus a determination of the divine. It is, indeed, admitted by all, that one who complies with the ecclesiastical precept is sure of communicating as often as he is required by the divine,[6] but many deny that the divine precept requires annual communion. It is denied by those who maintain the above

---

[1] Loc. cit. [2] St. Lig., ibid. Billuart, *De Eucharistia*, Dissert. vi. art. i. § iii. Petes 2°. Bouvier, l. c. 7°.

[3] Loc. cit. *Prima Sententia.*

[4] Sess. xiii. can. 9. Vid. St. Lig., l. c.

[5] St. Lig., n. 297. De Lugo, Disp. xvi. sect. ii. n. 28.

Ibid. n. 295. Billuart, l. c. § ii. Petes 2°.

opinion of St. Antonine, and who are cited by St. Liguori.[1] Suarez also, who appears to be cited by St. Liguori in favor of his own opinion, says that the divine precept *per se* requires communion only "aliquoties in vita, saltem tertio, vel quarto "quoque anno."[2]

But the precept of the Church, whether it be looked on as in any sense a determination of the divine precept or not, is almost universally regarded as imposing the twofold obligation above mentioned, and, therefore, as requiring one who has not communicated in Paschal time to communicate at least within the year. There still, however, remains a question of great importance in practice, viz.: Is he bound to communicate *as soon as possible* after the Paschal time?

741. For sake of greater precision in treating this question, it must be observed that there are three modes of computing the year of obligation. According to the first, it coincides with the civil year, commencing with January and ending with December. According to the second, it is to be reckoned simply from the last communion. According to the third, and most common, it is reckoned from the commencement of the Paschal time in one year to the commencement of the Paschal time in the next year.[3]

If the first mode of reckoning, which is that of De Lugo,[4] be adopted, and if we suppose that the person has communicated between the first of January and the commencement of the Paschal time, the question proposed must, we think, be answered in the negative, for there is no reason or authority requiring him to communicate again within the year, unless in the Paschal time, which the question supposes to be now past. The reasoning of St. Liguori, and of the authorities he cites,[5] proceeds on the supposition that the person has not yet complied with the obligation of annual communion. If we suppose that he has not communicated between the 1st of January and the commencement of the Paschal time, even still De Lugo[6] answers the question in the negative, and maintains that when the Paschal time is elapsed, there remains no other obligation than that of communicating before the end of the year.

742. According to the second mode of computation, to

---

[1] St. Lig., lib. vi. n. 297. *Tertia Sententia.*
[2] Disp. lxix. sect. iii. n. 6.
[3] Bouvier, l. c. *Observanda circa Com. Pasch.* 1°.
[4] Disp. xv. sect. 4, n. 69.
    Loc. cit. *Prima Sententia.*   [5] Loc. cit.

answer the question, we have only to inquire how long it is since his last communion. If it be less than a year—if, *e. g.,* he has received communion on the feast of All Saints last preceding—he is not bound to receive again until the feast of All Saints next succeeding. The Paschal time being past, he cannot comply with the obligation annexed to it; and the only obligation that remains is, that he shall not defer his next communion beyond a year from his last. This is the opinion of Billuart[1] and of Cardinal Gousset.[2] But if a year or more has elapsed since his last communion, he is now bound to communicate as soon as possible, and is guilty of grievous sin as often as he deliberately neglects an opportunity of doing so.[3]

743. The third is the most correct mode of computing, according to the common opinion of theologians, and according to the custom now generally received.[4] This being supposed, it is plain that one who has not communicated during Paschal time has not yet complied with the obligation of receiving within the year, which commences with Paschal time. The sole question then is, whether the precept of the Church binds him to receive as soon as possible, in order to comply with this obligation, so that he would be guilty of grievous sin as often as he deliberately omits to avail himself of an opportunity of receiving that may be presented to him. The more common and the more probable opinion, according to St. Liguori, who cites Suarez, Vasquez, Lacroix, etc., in favor of it,[5] affirms that the precept of the Church *does* so bind. The precept, they say, imposes the obligation of communicating in Paschal time, not intending to affix the obligation to the time, so that it would cease when the time expires, but intending, by determining a certain time, to stimulate the faithful to comply with the obligation within that time, and not defer it longer: "non ad "finiendam sed ad solicitandam obligationem."[6]

744. Cardinal De Lugo, however, denies that the precept of the Church binds in this manner, and contends that one who has omitted to communicate in Paschal time, is not bound to communicate as soon as possible, but merely to

---

[1] Loc. cit. § iii. Petes 2°. *Supponit responsio.*
[2] Vol. ii. n. 222.
[3] Gousset, ibid.   Billuart, ibid.   [4] St. Lig., n. 296.
[5] Lib. ii. n. 297.   *Prima Sententia.*
[6] St. Lig., l. c.   Suarez, Disp. lxx. sect. ii. n. 6.

communicate before the close of the year. Of the two obligations imposed by the precept, the first has been violated, and cannot now be fulfilled; and there remains only the second, which, according to him, is fulfilled by communicating any time before the close of the year, that is, in his reckoning, before the end of December.[1] Hence, *e. g.*, if a person omits to go to communion in Paschal time, 1872, he would still satisfy the annual precept by communicating on the 31st December, even though he had not been at communion since Paschal time, 1871. Cavalieri adopts the very same view, only that he reckons the year of obligation from Pasch to Pasch. According to him, if one, *e. g.*, omits to go to communion in Paschal time, 1872, he would still comply with the annual precept by going before the end of Paschal time, 1873, which would allow a still greater interval.[2]

745. In practice we should not like to recede from the opinion of St. Liguori, and the other great authorities whom he cites, especially as this opinion seems to be sustained by the next rubric.[3] At the same time it can hardly be doubted that the opinion of Billuart and Gousset[4] is solidly probable; and hence, if, *e. g.*, a person went to communion immediately before the commencement of Paschal time, and (culpably or inculpably) omitted to receive during Paschal time, we would not pronounce him guilty of violating the precept of the Church as often as, after Paschal time, he would decline an opportunity offered him of receiving, *provided he does not defer his communion beyond a year from the last.* In favor of this opinion, besides the authority of those who hold it in distinct terms, we have the authority of De Lugo and Cavalieri,[5] who go further, since they would allow him to defer his communion till the end of the year of obligation, no matter how long it may have been since his last; and we have also the authority of those who go yet further, and deny all obligation for the year when the Paschal time is once past.[6]

The advantage of adhering in practice to the opinion of St. Liguori is, that it tends to prevent in any case the interval between two communions from exceeding a year. Thus, for example, if a person who omits to communicate this year in Paschal time, has not communicated since Paschal time last

---

[1] Disp. xvi. sect. iv. n. 69.
[2] Vol. iv. cap. ii. in Decr. xviii. n. viii. et ix.
[3] Infra, § ii. Cfr. Gury, vol. i. n. 481.
[4] Supra, n. 742.   [5] Ibid., n. 744.   [6] Vid. Ibid., n. 738.

year, he is now required, according to this opinion, to communicate "quam primum," while, according to the opinion
of De Lugo and Cavalieri, he might now defer his communion
till the end of this year, and thus allow an interval of nearly
two years to elapse since his last.   It is true that St. Liguor;'s
opinion would require him now to communicate "quam
"primum," even though he had communicated shortly before
the beginning of Paschal time.   In this we would follow it
only so far as earnestly to exhort him to communicate without
delay; but we would not bind him under pain of grievous
sin, because, for the reasons already stated, we think the
obligation in this case is not sufficiently certain.

746. It may be asked whether one, who foresees that he
shall be unable to communicate during Paschal time, is bound
to anticipate.   If Paschal time has already begun, and if he
foresees that, unless she communicates, e. g., on the second
or third day, he shall be unable to communicate at all
during Paschal time, he is certainly bound;[1] just as one on a
Sunday morning is bound to hear mass, e. g., at eight
o'clock, if he foresees that he shall be unable to hear mass
at a later hour.

If Paschal time has not yet begun, the answer depends on
the mode of reckoning the year of obligation.   According to
the ordinary mode,[2] he would not be bound to anticipate,
because, in reality, neither of the two obligations imposed by
the precept yet exists, and, consequently, his communion
would not be a fulfilment of either.   This is the decision
of St. Liguori;[3] but he says the decision should be different
if the manner of computing the year were different.

If the year were supposed to commence on the 1st January,
or if it were reckoned from the last communion, one would be
bound to anticipate who foresees that he cannot receive communion either during Paschal time or after it, before the end
of the current civil year, or till beyond a year from his last,
respectively.   Because, though by anticipating he cannot
fulfil the obligation of communicating in Paschal time, he can
fulfil, and is therefore bound to fulfil, the obligation of
communicating within the year.   But he is not bound to
anticipate, if he foresees that, although prevented during
Paschal time, he shall still be able to communicate at some
time within the year.   This is the decision of Gousset,[4]

---

[1] St. Lig., n 298, in fine.   [2] Supra, n. 743.
[3] Loc. cit.   [4] Vol. ii. n. 221.

Billuart,[1] and seemingly of Lacroix.[2] St. Liguori[3] also
approves of it for the hypothesis in which it is given.

747. Many theologians held that the precept of the Church
requires, in strictness, no more than the act of receiving the
Eucharist sacramentally. Whatever the Church may intend
or desire, her precept, they maintained, does not reach the
internal dispositions. But it is certain that, to satisfy the
precept, communion must be received worthily. A proposition in the following terms was condemned by Innocent XI:
" Præcepto communionis annuæ satisfit per sacrilegam Domini
" manducationem."[4] It is, more probably, not enough, according to Lacroix,[5] that the communicant be excused from
formal sacrilege, as he might be by invincible ignorance, but
he must have the dispositions necessary to receive the grace
of the sacrament.

§ II.—Ut igitur hoc salutare Concilii decretum inviolabiliter servetur,
descripta Parochus habeat nomina suorum Parochianorum; et qui dicto
tempore non communicaverint, et post Octavam Paschæ eos qui propriæ
salutis immemores sæpius admoniti non obtemperaverint, Ordinario suo
denuntiet.

748. The pastor is supposed to have the names of all his
parishioners inscribed, according to the form given at the end
of the ritual, in the " Liber status animarum." He should
see to the accuracy of this book or register every year, about
the beginning of Paschal time, that he may be able to
ascertain those who fail to comply with the Paschal precept.
St. Charles required pastors to visit the families of their
parishioners during Lent, and make out an accurate list of
those who are bound by the precept.[6]

Various means have been employed for ascertaining those
who do not comply with the obligation. The faithful were
required to present a certificate of confession before they
would be admitted to communion,[7] or the pastor gave a
certificate to each one at the time of receiving communion, and
after Paschal time went round to the houses of the parishioners
to collect these certificates.[8] Such means are no longer in use
in France;[9] and we believe that, at present, those certificates

---

[1] Dissert. vi. art. i. § iii. Petes 2°.   [2] Lib. vi. par. i. n. 631.
[3] Loc. cit.   [4] Apud St. Lig., n. 294, in parenth. [5] Loc. cit. n. 618.
[6] Act. Eccl. Mediol., pars iv. Instruct. Euchar., § Quæ Parocho servanda sunt in Paschali Communione, pag. 428.
[7] Bouvier, cap. vi. art. ii. Observanda circa Com. Pasch. 17°. Gousset, vol. ii. n. 225.   [8] Baruff., tit. xxv. n. 17.
[9] Bouvier, loc. cit. Gousset, loc. cit.

ot communion are employed in very few, if any, places out of Italy, where they are still continued.[1] But the pastor is everywhere bound to use such means as prudence may suggest in his circumstances, to ascertain the defaulters, and induce them to comply with their obligation.

749. A public exhortation, in general terms, just before the close of the Paschal time, might have the desired effect. If this fails, he should have recourse to private remonstrance. And it is only after such remonstrance has been two or three times repeated without effect, that the rubric requires him to denounce the parties to the ordinary.

But the parish priest cannot go further than this.[2] The penalties mentioned in the decree are only "ferendæ senten-"tiæ," and the parish priest cannot inflict them of his own authority. They can be inflicted only by the authority of the ordinary.[3] Bouvier[4] seems to say that even the denunciation to the ordinary, here mentioned, is no longer in use. It is plainly a matter for the consideration of the bishop, whether it be expedient to insist on it in his diocese or not.

750. The fact that those who do not communicate in Paschal time are, immediately after the expiration of it, urged to communicate under a threat of such severe penalties, appears to be a strong confirmation of the opinion of St. Liguori given above.[5] But De Lugo replies to this argument that the censures are inflicted, not on account of the refusal to comply with an obligation still urging, but on account of the violation of the precept already committed, the prelate agreeing *not* to inflict the censure (which he might inflict at once according to the words of the decree), provided the person, when admonished, goes to communion.[6] Cavalieri replies to it in the same way.[7]

§ III.—Dabit quoque operam Parochus, quoad fieri potest, ut in ipso die sanctissimo Paschæ communicent; quo die ipse per se, nisi legitime impediatur, parochiæ suæ Fidelibus hoc Sacramentum ministrabit.

751. The Paschal time, as above stated,[8] is of fifteen days' duration, and by necessity, privilege, etc., generally much longer. But it is the desire of the Church that the faithful receive Holy Communion on the very day of the Paschal

---

[1] Analecta, etc., IVme Série, pag. 2276.   [2] Baruff., n. 21.
[3] St. Lig., n. 295, in fine, et lib. vii. n. 11.   Scavini, *De Euch.*, cap. i. art. 3, Quær. 2.   [4] Loc. cit.
[5] Supra, n. 743.   [6] Disp. xvi. n. 70–73.
[7] Vol. iv. cap. ii. Decr. xviii. n. vii.   [8] Supra, n. 737.

solemnity, that is to say, on Easter Sunday, and that the parish priest himself administer it on that day, unless there be a just reason to prevent him.   In populous parishes, where the number of clergy is small, it would be impossible to give all an opportunity of confessing, so that they might be able to communicate on Easter Sunday.   Other reasons, too, might make it inconvenient for some to receive communion on that day, and, of course, there may be sufficient reasons to prevent the pastor himself from administering it.   The rubric, accordingly, is not preceptive, but merely expresses a desire that the pastor will do what he can to administer communion to his flock on this great solemnity.

752. The more effectually to guard against any interference with him, the Holy See, in the privileges by which religious are permitted to give communion during Paschal time, always excepts Easter day,[1] so that on Easter day they cannot distribute communion to the people in their churches unless by the permission of the parish priest or the ordinary.   Not only, then, are the faithful bound to communicate in their own parish, in order to fulfil the Paschal precept, but it seems to be the wish of the Church that on Easter day they should not, even through devotion, communicate elsewhere.

§ IV.—Alienæ vero parochiæ Fideles ad proprium Parochum remittet, præter peregrinos et advenas, et qui certum domicilium non habent, quibus ipse sacram præbebit Communionem, si accesserint rite parati ; vel ubi est ea consuetudo, eos ad Cathedralis Ecclesiæ Parochos remittet.

753. The rubric here directs that strangers are not to be admitted to Holy Communion, but are to be sent or referred to their own pastors.   This applies not only to Easter day, but to the whole Paschal time, because, as we have seen,[2] each one must communicate in his own parish, or at least have the leave of his parish priest, in order to fulfil the Paschal precept.   St. Charles[3] ordered that in Paschal time, as often as communion is administered, notice be given of this obligation, so that strangers who might be present would know what is required of them in order to fulfil the precept of the Church.   This is the proper course, and in populous parishes the only effectual course, for the parish priest could hardly know personally who the strangers are amongst so

[1] Cfr. Benedict XIV., *De Syn. Diœc.*, lib. ix. cap. xvi. n. 3.
[2] Supra, n. 732.
[3] *Act. Eccl. Mediol.*, Concil. Prov. ii. tit. i. Decr. xii. pag. 53.

many. Besides, it would be extremely inconvenient, and, considering present usages, we doubt if it would be allowable, to exclude individuals who might present themselves at the rails, on the ground that they are strangers to the parish.

754. Bouvier[1] and Gousset[2] observe that at present communion is freely administered to strangers as well as the rest, because it is presumed that they have already complied with the Paschal precept in their own parish, or that they intend yet to do so, or that they have the permission of their own pastor. This may be very justly presumed in places where the people are sufficiently instructed in the obligation of the Paschal precept, or where there is an understanding about the matter amongst the parochial clergy.

755. But, independently of all custom or arrangement on the subject, there are certain classes here mentioned by the rubric to whom the parish priest can give communion, and who satisfy the precept by this communion, though they do not belong to his parish. These are "peregrini," "advenæ," and those who have no fixed domicile, usually called "vagi." The words "peregrini" and "advenæ" are used by most authors in the very same signification, viz., as meaning those who are absent from the place of their domicile, without determining how long or how short a time. They are so used by Suarez,[3] Ferraris,[4] St. Liguori,[5] etc.

756. Some, however, distinguish them. By a "peregrinus" they understand one who has a fixed domicile and intends to return to it, but is for the present living in another place, where he intends to stay only a short time, less than half a year at the utmost. By "advena" they understand one who, having left the place of his domicile, if he has one, comes to another with the intention of remaining there for at least the greater part of the year. This appears to be the distinction made by Bouvier[6] and Scavini.[7] According to this distinction, an "advena" is one who has acquired at least a quasi-domicile in the place where he is.[8] By "vagi" all understand those who have no fixed domicile, but go from place to place.

757. Baruffaldi[9] seems to suppose that the words, "qui "certum domicilium non habent," qualify "peregrinos et

---

[1] *De Eucharistia*, Observanda circa Com. Pasch., n. 17.
[2] Vol. ii. n. 224.　　　　[3] *De Legibus*, lib. iii. cap. xxxiii.
[4] Verb. *Lex.*, art. iii. n. 28, et seq.　　　　[5] Lib. i. n. 156.
[6] *De Legibus*, cap. v. art. v.　　　　[7] Ibid., cap. v. art. ii. Qu. 3.
[8] Vid. St. Lig. l. c., *Ille autem acquirit*, etc.　　　　[9] Tit. xxv. n. 36.

"advenas," and understands the rubric therefore to speak
here of "vagi" exclusively, as, in the first clause, it directs
that strangers who have a domicile be sent to their own
parish. This, however, restricts the meaning too much.
The rubric, according to this explanation, would make no
provision for those who are at a great distance from the place
of their domicile, and who could not therefore, without great
inconvenience, or perhaps could not at all, go back to it,
during the Paschal time.

Besides, the "et" shows that the "qui certum domicilium
"non habent" are distinct from those mentioned before. By
"peregrinos et advenas," then, are most probably meant
strangers from a distant place. Those from a neighboring
parish would hardly be called by these names, and at all
events are manifestly to be understood as comprehended in
the first clause, which directs them to be sent back to their
own parish priest.

758. If those strangers acquire a quasi-domicile in the
parish, or if they be "advenæ" in the sense above explained,[1]
they not only are at liberty to make their Paschal communion
in the parish, but, according to a general principle of law,[2]
they are bound to make it there like the rest of the inhabitants, unless they choose to go back and make it in the parish
of their domicile.[3]

759. If they have not acquired a quasi-domicile, in other
words, if they be "peregrini" in the sense above explained,[4]
but cannot conveniently go to the place of their domicile, they
can satisfy the precept by receiving in the parish where they
are. This we think is plainly implied in the present rubric,
and at all events it is the common doctrine of theologians.[5]
The same is to be said of "vagi," or those who have no
domicile.[6] But it may still be a question whether or not both
these classes are bound like the other inhabitants to receive
communion from the parish priest, or with his permission.
Many authors cited by St. Liguori maintain that they are:
but St. Liguori himself gives it as the most common opinion
that they are not, and that they can satisfy the precept by
communicating in the churches of religious.[7] This decision
of St. Liguori is combated by the "Mélanges Théologiques;"[8]

[1] Supra, n. 756.   [2] St. Lig., lib. i. n. 156, *Dubit.* L
[3] Vid. Mél. Théol., IIme Série, 2me Cahier, pag. 273.
[4] Supra, n. 756.   [5] St. Lig., n. 300 . . . 2 in parenth.   [6] St. Lig., ibid.
[7] Lib. vi. n. 240, v. 9.   [8] Loc. cit.

but whatever may be said of the grounds on which it rests, it is sufficient to justify any one who resolves to act on it, for, after all, there is question merely of interpreting a positive law of the Church.

760. In some places these " peregrini " and " vagi " may be required to go to communion during the Paschal time in the cathedral church. By the decree of St. Charles above cited,[1] they were required to do so in the city of Milan, but not in other parts of the diocese. Where such a custom exists, the rubric here wishes it to be respected, but the words do not convey that a compliance with the custom is necessary to fulfil the Paschal precept.[2]

§ V.—In cæteris vero servabit ea, quæ in libro de statu animarum, ut infra, præscribuntur.

761. He must carefully observe what is prescribed as to the manner of entering the names and noting the sacraments received in the " Liber de statu animarum." It should contain the names of all his parishioners, divided into families, the names of the members of each family being written together, as is directed in the ritual hereafter. He should note after each name whether the person has received Holy Communion. The sacraments, of which the reception is to be marked in this book, are Confirmation and the Eucharist. The reception of the other sacraments is noted in other books.

The ritual does not require him to enter the names of strangers in the " Liber status animarum," unless when they live in the family of a parishioner. But it would be well to note in it, or in some other book, if he can conveniently, the names of strangers to whom he gives communion in Paschal time, as they may wish him to certify that they received it.

§ VI.—Ægrotis quoque parochialibus, etiamsi Communionem extra præscriptos Paschales dies sumpserint, in Paschalibus diebus illam deferet ac ministrabit.

762. The sick who are unable to go to the Parish church are still bound to comply with the Paschal precept, if the opportunity be given them;[3] and the pastor is here directed to give them the opportunity, by bringing the Blessed Sacrament to them within the Paschal time. The rubric directs this to be done, even though they may have received communion shortly before the beginning of the Paschal time, for

---

[1] Supra, n. 753.   Baruff., n. 41.   [2] Ibid., n. 52.

that communion does not fulfil the precept.[1] But if the priest has reason to believe that a sick person will be able shortly after the close of the Paschal time to receive communion in the church, he can extend the time for him.[2]

763. One who receives the viaticum during Paschal time, does not, according to Cavalieri,[3] thereby fulfil the Paschal precept, which is distinct from that of the viaticum. But it is much more probable that by the same communion he satisfies both precepts.[4]

[1] Vid. supra, n. 736.
[2] Catal., tit. iv. cap. iii. § v. n. ii. Gousset, vol. ii. n. 290.
[3] Vol. iv. cap. ii. in Decr. xxxiv. n. vi.
[4] Gousset, l. c. Gury, pars i. n. 484, Quær. 9°.

CHAPTER XIV.

ON COMMUNION OF THE SICK: "DE COMMUNIONE INFIRMORUM."

§ L—Viaticum sacratissimi Corporis Domini nostri Jesu Christi summo studio ac diligentia ægrotantibus, opportuno tempore, procurandum est, ne forte contingat illos tanto bono, Parochi incuria, privatos decedere.

764. Whatever contributes to give spiritual strength or comfort to the dying, was, by many of the holy Fathers and other ancient writers, called a "viaticum," since it prepares them for the passage out of this world into the next, and enables them to make it with greater confidence and security. Hence, not only the Blessed Eucharist, but the other sacraments administered to the dying, and even the prayers offered up, or the good works performed by themselves or by others on their behalf, came under this general designation. But in course of time, the Holy Eucharist came to be regarded as the "Viaticum" by excellence, and, according to present use, is exclusively meant by the word.[1] "Sacred writers," says the Catechism of the Council of Trent, "call it the 'Viaticum,' "as well because it is the spiritual food by which we are sup- "ported in our mortal pilgrimage, as also because it prepares "for us a passage to eternal glory and happiness."[2]

*765. All are bound by divine precept to receive it when in danger of death, as a protection against the assaults of the enemy in the last struggle; and this, according to the more probable opinion, even though one may have communicated a few days before through devotion.[3]

*766. It is a question amongst theologians whether one who has communicated in the morning through devotion, is bound to receive again "per modum viatici," if danger of death supervenes that day. Some affirm that he is; others, that he is not. Of the latter, some say he is free to receive, though not bound; others, that he not only is not bound, but

---

[1] Vid. Caval., vol. iv. cap. v. *De Com. Infirm.* Catal., tit. iv. cap. iv. § i. n. i. et seq.　　[2] Pars ii. cap. iv. n. 5.
[3] St. Lig., lib. vi. n. 285, Dub. 2, *Secunda Sententia.*

is not permitted, to receive a second time on the same day. Benedict XIV gives these several opinions, and says the pastor is free to act on any of them.[1]   St. Liguori[2] thinks it more probable that one in the circumstances is bound to receive the viaticum if the danger comes from an external cause, as a fall, a violent assault, or the like, for he has not yet complied with the obligation of receiving "in periculo "mortis;" but not if he were already sick, nor if the danger already existed in some internal though unknown cause, as might be presumed in case of sudden illness, *e. g.*, an attack of apoplexy.

767. The rubric here requires the pastor to take all possible care that the sick may have an opportunity of receiving Holy Communion in due time, that is, according to Baruffaldi,[3] while they have still the use of their faculties, and can, therefore, receive it with greater fruit.   He should prepare them for it, and exhort them to receive it, even when there is no imminent danger of death, because it is the great means of imparting strength and vigor to the soul in the trials and temptations incident to sickness, and because he thus makes sure that they shall not be without this great succor, should the illness suddenly take a fatal turn.

§ II.—Cavendum autem in primis est, ne ad indignos cum aliorum scandalo deferatur, quales sunt publici usurarii, concubinarii, notorie criminosi, nominatim excommunicati, aut denuntiati, nisi sese prius sacra Confessione purgaverint, et publicæ offensioni, prout de jure, satisfecerint.

768. Public sinners, such as are here mentioned, must give proofs of sincere conversion before they are admitted to Holy Communion even in sickness; otherwise great scandal would arise, especially in places where the Blessed Sacrament is carried to the sick in solemn procession, and where, consequently, their communion becomes known to the whole neighborhood.   When one of this class is visited by the pastor, it is not enough that he goes to confession; he must be required to repair the injuries and scandals of which he has been the cause, as far as his present circumstances permit.   It is for the prudent confessor to decide in each case the nature and extent of this obligation.   We shall merely observe, that where restitution is to be made, or where the

---

[1] *De Syn. Diœc.*, lib. vii. cap. xi. n. 2.   [2] Loc.
[3] Tit. xvi. n. 10.

proximate voluntary occasion of sin is to be removed, and
where it is possible that this can be done by the sick man
immediately, he should not be absolved, nor consequently
admitted to Holy Communion, until it has been done. This
is the doctrine of St. Liguori, laid down or supposed by him
in several places.[1] In the "Praxis Confessarii,"[2] he speaks
specially of the sick, but he does not except them anywhere; and it is evident that what he says applies to them as
much as to others, when they have it in their power to make
the restitution, or to remove the occasion.

769. Of course, if death seems imminent, and there is
reason to fear that they may not have time, nothing more can
be exacted than a firm purpose of doing what is required of
them, should they recover. In the "Modo Pratico di Assistere
"A'Moribondi," etc., a little book highly prized by the parochial clergy in Italy, it is suggested[3] that one who has to
make reparation for public scandal, should be induced to ask
pardon of those who may be present in the room after having
accompanied the Blessed Sacrament, and to request them to
publish the retractation. Where the priest brings the viaticum
privately, he can easily introduce a few persons for the purpose, if he thinks it expedient to act on this suggestion.

§ III.—Hortetur Parochus infirmum, ut sacram Communionem sumat,
etiamsi graviter non ægrotet, aut mortis periculum non immineat,
maxime si Festi alicujus celebritas id suadeat; neque ipse illam ministrare recusabit.

*770. The rubric everywhere supposes that the viaticum
is administered by the parish priest. No other can lawfully
administer it without his sanction, except in case of necessity.[4]
The pastor, as has been said,[5] should exhort the sick to receive
Holy Communion, even when there is no immediate danger
of death. The celebration of some festival affords a good
opportunity of doing so without exciting fears that might
aggravate the disease. He must take care, above all, not to
refuse it to those who are anxious to receive it, especially
those who, when in good health, were wont to communicate
often.[6]

[1] Lib. iv. n. 436 et n. 682. Lib. vi. n. 454. *Praxis Conf.*, ns. 43, 66,
et 105.   [2] Cap. vii. n. 105.
[3] Cap. vii. Edit. Roma, 1818.
[4] Vid. St. Lig., lib. vi. n. 235, et seq.   [5] Supra, n. 767.
[6] Cfr. *Act. Eccl. Mediol.*, pars iv. Instruct. De Visitatione et Cura
Infirmorum, § *De Communione*, pag. 445.

771. Where the decree of St. Pius V, "*Supra gregem*," etc., is in force, physicians are bound at once to admonish their patients to go to confession, and are obliged to withhold their services after the third day, unless there be proof that they have confessed.[1] At all events, they, and indeed all who are in attendance on the sick, are clearly bound in charity to give them notice, when it is ascertained that the disease is likely to be fatal, that they may prepare to receive the last sacraments. The obligation of the pastor to give this notice is strongest of all, since he is bound, *ex-officio*, to consult for their spiritual welfare. The notice, however, should be conveyed so as to excite as little alarm as possible, and be accompanied by words of consolation and encouragement.[2]

§ IV.—Pro Viatico autem ministrabit, cum probabile est quod eam amplius sumere non poterit.

*772. Communion is to be administered as the viaticum, when, as is here stated, it is probable that the sick person shall be unable to receive it any more, that is, according to Cavalieri, when he is in probable danger of death. The priest in administering the Eucharist, "pro viatico," or "per "modum viatici," uses the form "*Accipe frater*," etc., instead of the ordinary form, "*Corpus Domini*," etc.[3] On the words of the present rubric, Cavalieri observes: "Verba sunt per "quæ instruimur nonnisi in probabili mortis periculo Eucha-"ristiam per modum viatici administrandam esse, nempe per "illa verba, '*Accipe frater, Viaticum*,' etc., extra vero tale "periculum, semper per consueta '*Corpus Domini*.'" etc.[4] This, then, is the rule by which the priest is to be guided as to the form he should use in giving communion to the sick. If the danger be such as to make it probable that the person cannot receive it again, it is to be administered with the form, "*Accipe frater*."

773. It matters not whether he be fasting or not. Cavalieri altogether rejects the opinion of those who say that it is to be administered "per modum viatici" only to those who are not fasting: "Sive ægrotus jejunus sit vel non, semper "communicat per modum viatici quando ei administratur "Eucharistia in articulo mortis constituto."[5] It is true that those who are not fasting can receive communion only "per

[1] Vid. St. Lig., lib. vi. n. 664.
[2] Ibid., *Praxis Confessarii*, cap. xi. n. 227, et seq.
[3] Vid. infra, § xx.   [4] Cap. v. *De Com. Inf.*, Decr i. n. iv.
[5] Loc. cit. Decr. x. n. xiv. Cfr. etiam Ferraris, verb. *Viaticum*, n 6, Edition Migne.

"modum viatici;"[1] but it does not follow, nor is it true, that they alone can receive it "per modum viatici." On the contrary, the rubric itself, as we shall see,[2] clearly implies that it is desirable that those who receive the viaticum should be fasting.

In a word, it appears from the present rubric that the form to be used is to be determined entirely by the consideration, whether or not the person be at the time in probable danger of death. If he be, then the form should be "*Accipe frater*," etc.; if not, then the form should be the ordinary one. Hence, *e. g.*, a criminal about to be executed should receive communion "per modum viatici," and it should, therefore, be administered with the form, "*Accipe*," etc. This is expressly taught by Cavalieri,[3] and the "Modo Pratico,"[4] which adds that it is to be administered to him with this form, even though he be fasting.

§ V.—Quod si æger, sumpto Viatico, dies aliquot vixerit, vel periculum mortis evaserit, et communicare veluerit, ejus pio desiderio Parochus non deerit.

774. If the sick person, after having received the viaticum, recovers from the danger, or even if he only survives some days, and desires to communicate again, the priest should endeavor to gratify this pious desire. There can be no difficulty about the matter, if he has so far recovered as to be able to receive it in the ordinary way, or at least to receive fasting. Clericati observes that the rubric here supposes him to be able to receive fasting, for it includes the case in which he may have recovered from the danger of death, as is plain from the words, "vel periculum mortis "evaserit," and it does not treat till the next sentence of those to whom it may be administered after having broken the fast.[5] Cavalieri says, and it seems more probable, that the rubric here altogether prescinds from the question of fasting.[6]

*775. If he be unable to receive fasting, theologians commonly require an interval of about eight days before they would permit him again to communicate. But it is a very probable opinion, maintained by many, that communion may be administered the next day, and even every day. "Est "sententia valde probabilis et pia," says Cavalieri,[7] using the

---

[1] Vid. infra, § vii.
[2] Infra, § vi.
[3] Loc. cit. Decr. ii. n. iii.
[4] Cap. xiv.
[5] *De Eucharistia*, Decis. xix. Ad Aprilis casum ii. n. 13.
[6] *De Com. Inf.*, Decr. i. n. x.
[7] Loc. cit. n. ix.

words of Clericati,[1] whom he cites, "quod altera die sacro "viatico per non jejunum infirmum recepto, si duret idem "mortis periculum, possit idem infirmus, etiam non jejunus, "sacram Eucharistiam suscipere; et sic quod liceat parocho "etiam quotidie infirmum prædictum, licet non jejunum per "viaticum communicare."

Some extend the favor to all who are in danger of death; others restrict it to those who are accustomed to communicate often, and have a great desire of communion.[2] Gury[3] cites St. Liguori for allowing it to these only twice in the week, but we could not find this restriction in St. Liguori. On the contrary, he seems to us, in the place referred to,[4] to admit as probable that they may be allowed it every day. It is justly observed that this may be more readily permitted whenever the Blessed Sacrament can be brought to the sick without a public procession, as is usually the case, e. g., in convents, colleges, etc.[5] Cavalieri thinks there should be no difficulty in allowing it in such cases. He says[6] that the expression of the rubric, "dies aliquot" (which is one of the chief grounds for requiring an interval of some days), is intended to limit, not the communion of the sick, but the obligation of the pastor to carry the Blessed Sacrament from the church.

776. With regard to the form to be used, if the danger of death be past, the communion should not be given "per "modum viatici," and, therefore, should be administered with the ordinary form, "Corpus Domini," etc. But if the danger still continues, authorities are divided on the point. Some say the form to be used is "Corpus Domini," etc., because, during the same illness, communion, they say, should be administered only once as the viaticum, and, therefore, only once with the form "Accipe frater," etc. St. Charles lays down this very distinctly, while recommending what the rubric here prescribes. He says: . . . . "Ejus pio desiderio "Parochus non deerit, sed pro viatico illam iterum in eodem "morbo non ministrabit ideoque ministrando utetur illis "verbis, Corpus," etc.[7] Catalani cites and adopts these words.[8] The same is taught by Billuart[9] and De Herdt.[10]

[1] Loc. cit. n. 11.   [2] Vid. Caval., loc. cit.
[3] Vol. ii. n. 335.   [4] Lib. vi. n. 285.
[5] Gury, loc. cit.   [6] Loc. cit. n. x.
[7] Instruct. Visitat. Inf., De Communione, pag. 445.
[8] Cap. iv. § iv. n. ii.   [9] Diss. vi. art. iv. § ii. Dixi, 4°.
[10] Pars vi. n. 17, ii.

Bouvier also maintains this opinion : " Ubi infirmitas protra-
"hitur et periculum mortis perseverat, Sacra Eucharistia
"iterum moribundo etiam non jejuno . . . . dari potest, non
"per modum viatici, quod semel tantum in eadem infirmitate
"administratur, sed modo consueto, ad satisfaciendum devo-
"tioni."[1]   This weight of authority is plainly sufficient to
justify any one who chooses to act on it.

*777. But we think it more probable that while the danger
continues, the form should always be "*Accipe frater,*" etc.
The words of the rubric are very general : " Pro viatico
"ministrabit cum probabile est quod eam amplius sumere non
"poterit." Now, the probability of his being unable to
receive it again, which made it be administered as the viaticum
the first time, must evidently still continue while the same
danger continues. Benedict XIV clearly supposes this, at
least for the case in which the sick person is unable to observe the fast.   He says : " Potest et interdum debet Episco-
"pus constituere ne parochi renuant SS. Eucharistiam iterato
"deferre ad ægrotos qui, etiam perseverante eodem morbi
"periculo, illam sæpius *per modum viatici* cum naturale jeju-
"nium servare nequeant, percipere cupiant."[2]   There is no
reason to suppose that the Pontiff here restricts the administration, "*per modum viatici,*" to the case in which the fast has
been broken. He mentions this case, probably because it is
of frequent occurrence, and because it is precisely the case in
which priests might have a difficulty about administering it
more than once. Besides, we have seen that the form to be
used is not determined by the fact that the person is fasting
or not fasting.[3]   The " Modo Pratico," having stated that the
viaticum may be administered more than once in the same
illness, adds that the formula, "*Accipe frater,*" is always to be
used.[4]   Cavalieri evidently conveys the same in the passage
above cited ;[5] for the expression, " per viaticum," or its equivalent, is always understood by him to imply the use of the
words, "*Accipe frater,*" etc.[5]

778. Some theologians taught that the precept of receiving
'he viaticum is fulfilled even by a sacrilegious communion.[7]
But we have seen before[8] that a similar opinion regarding the
precept of annual communion was condemned by Innocent XI

De Euch., cap. v. art. ii. § ii.
[2] *De Synod. Diœc.*, lib. vii. cap. xii. n. 4.   [3] Supra, n. 773.
[4] Cap. vii.   [5] Supra, n. 775.   [6] Vid. supra, n. 772.
[7] De Lugo, Disp. xvi. sect. ii. n. 45.   [8] Supra, n. 747.

It is quite certain, therefore, that the precept of receiving the viaticum is not fulfilled by receiving it unworthily.[1] But if one who has received the viaticum with the proper dispositions, should fall into mortal sin, he is not, according to the more probable opinion, bound to receive it again. It is enough that he goes to confession.[2]

§ VI.—Potest quidem Viaticum brevi morituris dari non jejunis : id tamen diligenter curandum est, ne iis tribuatur, a quibus ob phrenesim, sive ob assiduam tussim, aliumve similem morbum, aliqua indecentia cum injuria tanti Sacramenti timeri potest.

*779. If one who is about to receive the viaticum can receive it fasting, he should do so. But if abstinence from food or medicine be in the least inconvenient to him, it is not required, and there should be no scruple or hesitation about acting on this decision.[3]

780. By a usage formerly existing in some places, and especially in Spain, criminals condemned to death were altogether excluded from Holy Communion. But this usage was condemned as contrary to Christian charity in the Council of Mayence, in 847, and afterwards by St. Pius V, in 1569.[4] Many other Councils and Popes are cited by Gousset.[5] Benedict XIV, without formally prohibiting it in places where it may have existed in his time, urges the bishops to introduce the opposite custom.[6] We believe there are now few places where the viaticum is not administered to such persons, as well as to those who are in danger of death from sickness. By a decree of the Congregation of Bishops,[7] it was decided that it may be administered to them on the very day on which they are executed. According to the common opinion of theologians, these, and in general all to whom the Eucharist is administered by way of viaticum, are exempt from the obligation of receiving it fasting, when the fasting is attended with any inconvenience.[8]

*781. It is not to be administered in any case in which there is danger of irreverence to the sacrament; and it is for

---

[1] Cfr. Lacroix, lib. ii. pars i. n. 610 et 617. Bouvier, *De Eucharistia*, cap. vi. art. i. *Notanda circa Viaticum*, 10°.
[2] St. Lig., n. 293.   [3] Ibid., n. 285, *Hic autem sedulo.*
[4] Cfr. Baruff., tit. xxvi. n. 35 et seq. Caval., *De Comm. Infirm ,* Decr. ii. n. i. et seq.   [5] Vol. ii. n. 230.
[6] *De Synod. Diœc.*, lib. vii. cap. xi. n. 3.
[7] 16 Jun. 1590, apud Caval., l. c. n. ii.
[8] Baruff., n. 43, 44. Caval., l. c. n. iii. St. Lig., l. c. De Lugo, Disp. xv. sec. iii. n. 58, et Disp xvi. sect. ii. n. 46, in fine.

the priest to judge, from the circumstances in each case, of the danger that exists. It generally arises from some of the causes here mentioned in the rubric.

We have seen that communion cannot be given to one who has never had the use of reason.[1]

If loss of reason be caused by disease, as in fever, or if the person be subject to passing fits of insanity, the priest should await the return of reason, and be prepared to avail himself of the first favorable moment to administer the sacrament. It may happen, however, that the use of reason is not recovered, or, at least, is not recovered until the patient is dying and unable to receive communion. If this be apprehended, the viaticum may be administered even during the delirium to those who have led a good Christian life, provided there be no danger of irreverence. This is the common teaching of theologians,[2] and is clearly enough conveyed in the passage before cited[3] from the Catechism of the Council of Trent.

Some would restrict the decision to the case in which the sick person has had the use of his faculties a short time before. But, according to De Lugo, there is no reason why it should be thus restricted. No matter what be the duration of the insanity, if, when in full possession of his faculties, he has lived as a pious Christian, and if there be now no danger of irreverence, the viaticum should be administered to him.[4] It is not, however, to be administered to one who has lost his senses in an evidently impenitent state.[5]

We may observe that, in all diseases where there is any reason to apprehend delirium, the priest should endeavor to administer the last sacraments as early as possible.

*782. The danger of irreverence may arise from incessant coughing, from difficulty of breathing, from difficulty of swallowing, or from frequent vomiting. In all these cases, a little food or drink may be given first, to try whether the person can receive without danger of rejecting the Sacred Host. The same may be done in case of delirium also. Many recommend the trial to be made with an unconsecrated particle.[6] This undoubtedly would be a very secure test, but notice should be given lest it might be mistaken for the sacrament.

With regard to cough, it may be observed that, if it be not

---

[1] Supra, n. 635.   [2] St. Lig., n. 302. Modo Pratico, cap. vii.
[3] Supra, L. 635.   [4] *De Eucharistia*, Disp. xiii. sec. iii. n. 24, et seq
[5] St. Lig., l. c.   Modo Pratico, l. c.
[6] Ibid., n. 292, et Busemb., ibid.   De Herdt, pars vi. n. 15. Bouvier *Notanda circa Viaticum*, 4°.

so continuous as to prevent swallowing, the viaticum may be given; for although expectoration may immediately follow, the phlegm thrown off does not come from the œsophagus or passage to the stomach, but from the trachea or passage to the lungs, and there is, consequently, no danger of the Sacred Host being rejected.[1] If it be ascertained that, from the parched state of the palate, or from any other cause, the sick person might have a difficulty in swallowing the Sacred Host, a little wine or water may be given immediately before or after, or, if necessary, a very small particle may be put into a little wine or water, and administered in this way.[2]

In case of vomit, the sacrament may be administered if there is reason to believe, by trial as recommended, that he will have no attack for about half an hour after receiving. This is the rule laid down by the "Modo Pratico,"[3] probably because within this time, in any state of the stomach, the species would be altered so that there could be no danger of irreverence.[4] If the vomit, however, is not provoked by food, but is frequent independently of any food, he should be free from it for at least six hours before the sacrament is administered.[5]

If, after all, a doubt still remains as to whether the Sacred Host can be received without the irreverence against which the present rubric is designed to guard, the more common and the more probable opinion is, that it ought not to be administered.[6] In such circumstances, the sick person should be exhorted to make a spiritual communion[7].

783. Should the Sacred Host be rejected by vomit, if it still appears entire, or is easily discernible, it should be reverently taken up and carried in a clean vessel to the church, to be kept there till it corrupts, when it is to be thrown into the sacrarium. If it cannot be distinguished from the rest of what is thrown off, all should be carefully taken up and burned, and the ashes thrown into the sacrarium. This is what is recommended by Bouvier,[8] and it is in accordance with what is prescribed by the rubric of the Missal.[9]

---

[1] St. Lig., n. 292.   [2] Ibid., n. 288, *Dicunt Suarez*, etc. Modo Pratico, cap. vii. Benedict XIV, *De Syn. Diœc.*, lib. xiii. cap. xix. n. 25. Caval., cap. v. Decr. vi. n. vi. De Herdt, l. c.
[3] Loc. cit.   [4] Vid. supra, n. 594.
[5] Busemb., apud St. Lig., n. 292. Gury, ii. n. 320. Modo Pratico, l. a.
[6] St. Lig., l. c.   [7] Modo Pratico, cap. vii. in fine.
[8] Loc. cit., 5°.   [9] *De Defectibus*, tit. x. n. 14.

We have already touched on the difficulties that regard the administration of the viaticum to children.[1]

§ VII.—Ceteris autem infirmis, qui ob devotionem in ægritudine communicant, danda est Eucharistia ante omnem cibum et potum, non aliter ac ceteris Fidelibus, quibus nec etiam per modum medicinæ ante aliquid sumere licet.

*784. Sickness of itself, unless when there is danger of death, does not exempt from the general law which requires those who receive the Holy Eucharist to be fasting from midnight. Hence, the sick who communicate through devotion, must observe the law like the other faithful, by an entire abstinence from food or drink, or anything even by way of medicine.

785. But it may be asked whether a sick person, who, though not in danger of death, is yet unable to fast till a convenient hour in the morning, and who continues in this state for a long time, may be permitted to receive Holy Communion after having broken his fast.

The question is discussed at great length in the "Mélanges "Théologiques."[2] Amongst the authors there cited, some, as Elbel and Witasse, expressly affirm that he may be permitted occasionally; others, as Toletus and Tournely, plainly imply that he may be permitted when there is any urgent cause. The writer himself strongly insists that one in the circumstances may be permitted to receive Holy Communion, at least in order to fulfil the Paschal precept; and he labors hard to refute a Latin dissertation, maintaining the opposite view, which he gives at full length.[3] He relies very much on the argument that the Paschal precept, or the precept of annual communion, which is probably the determination of the divine precept,[4] ought to prevail over the law which requires the Eucharist to be received fasting, just as the precept of receiving it in danger of death prevails over the same law. He contends that, as the faithful, in order to fulfil the latter precept, are exempt from the obligation of fasting when it is attended with inconvenience, so should they be, and so it is to be presumed they are, in like manner exempt, when they are required to fulfil the former. When it is objected that a parity of reasoning would prove the exemption, not only for the fulfilment of the Paschal precept,

[1] Vid. supra, n. 640.
[2] Ibid., pag. 422, et seq.
[3] Ire Série, pag. 400, et seq.
[4] Vid. St. Lig., n. 297.

but at least for several communions in the year, just as the exemption in favor of those in danger of death is extended to a repetition of the viaticum, he replies by virtually admitting the parity and the inference; he sees no inconvenience in it, but he would not insist on it.[1] This opinion seems not improbable, and we should be slow to condemn one who would make up his mind to act on it.

786. But, on the other hand, the interpretation of the law which requires the Eucharist to be received fasting, and the nature and extent of the exemption granted to the sick, can be ascertained only by the practice of the Church made known to us by the testimony of her doctors and theologians.[2] Mere reasoning from analogy will avail us little. A priest, for example, most probably could not celebrate without sacred vestments, or without an altar, in order to receive the viaticum, though the vestments and the altar are required only by the law of the Church, while he is bound to receive the viaticum by divine precept.[3] Now, the great bulk of theologians, though they do not discuss the present question in precise terms, either suppose or expressly assert that the sick, in order to have the privilege of communicating without being fasting, must be in danger of death. It is true, therefore, as Gury says,[4] that the common opinion of theologians is against the permission of communion in the case proposed. The present rubric is also against it, at least when there is question of communion "ob devotionem," and we think it means to embrace all communions of the sick who are not in danger of death, the "ceteris infirmis" being all who are not "brevi morituri." A strong argument is also furnished against it by the Papal indults, which have been granted to certain individuals laboring under infirmities of this kind, and in virtue of which they were permitted to receive after having broken the fast. One of these was granted by Benedict XIV to the son of James II, King of England, and the brief contains the following words, which appear to be decisive: "Cum generali lege caveatur ut nonnisi jejuno universim "sacra ministretur communio . . . ut alicui expressis casibus "(exceptis) non comprehenso liceat, etsi non jejuno, sacra "participare mysteria, necesse erit eundem expressa dispensa-

---

[1] Pag. 425, n. 12.　　　[2] Vid. De Lugo, Disp. xv. sec. iii. n 68.
[3] De Lugo, ibid., n. 61, et Disp. xiv. sec. v. n. 108.
[4] Vol. ii. n. 334, Qu. 11º.

" tione juvari, quæ porro dispensatio, a nemine præter
" Romanum Pontificem potest indulgeri."[1]

787. The case seemingly can but very rarely occur; for if
one be unable to fast from midnight until an early hour in
the morning, his infirmity is generally such as to justify communion " per modum viatici." The writer in the " Mélanges,"
however, testifies that it occurs often enough, especially
amongst those who are affected with asthma. In practice,
then, we think the most that can be done without a Papal
dispensation is, to administer communion to one in the
circumstances soon after midnight. Gury[2] thinks this may
be done several times in the year, or at least in order that he
may fulfil the Paschal precept. So does the author of the
Latin dissertation already referred to.[3] The general prohibition against carrying the Blessed Sacrament to the sick at
night, would not extend to a case of this kind, which might
be fairly regarded as a case of necessity. At all events,
there is little difficulty about the matter in countries where
the Blessed Sacrament cannot be carried in procession, or
when there is question of one sick in a college, convent, or
other religious house in which the Blessed Sacrament is kept.[4]
Should it happen, however, that the Blessed Sacrament cannot
conveniently be brought during the night, one in the circumstances supposed would be exempt from the precept of Paschal
communion while the infirmity continues.[5]

§ VIII.—Sed alicui ad adorandum solum seu devotionis, seu cujusvis
rei prætextu ad ostendendum non deferatur.

788. The Blessed Sacrament is never to be brought to any
one merely that he may satisfy his devotion by adoring it,
or remaining in presence of it. It is to be brought to the
sick to be administered to them, and for no other purpose.
But should the priest, on coming to the house, find that the
sick person is unable to receive communion, St. Charles
directs him to place the Blessed Sacrament on the table
prepared, and kneel down and pray for some time before it
with those who are present, so that the sick person may join
in this act of devotion. He adds that, if the sick person
earnestly desires it, the priest may even uncover the pyxis,

---

[1] Constit. *Quadam de more*, 24 Mar. 1756, § 4.
[2] Loc. cit.   [3] Supra, n. 785.
[4] Cfr. Gury, " *Casus Conscientiæ*," De Eucharistia, casus xix. vol. ii
p. 298.   [5] Bouvier, *De Eucharistia*, cap. v. art. ii. § ii.

and allow him to adore the Blessed Sacrament exposed. And on leaving he is to give the benediction with the pyxis.[1]

§ IX.—Deferri autem debet hoc Sanctum Sacramentum ab Ecclesia ad privatas ægrotantium domos decenti habitu, superposito mundo velamine, manifeste atque honorifice, ante pectus cum omni reverentia et timore, semper lumine præcedente.

789. Where, as in Ireland, the Blessed Sacrament cannot be carried in the manner here prescribed, the priest should, at least, endeavor to comply with the spirit of the rubrics, by showing towards it all the marks of reverence which circumstances permit, as often as he carries it to the sick. The words of this rubric regarding the manner of carrying the Blessed Sacrament, are taken from a decretal of Honorius III, in the thirteenth century,[2] and are fully explained in the rubrics that follow.

§ X.—Parochus igitur processurus ad communicandum infirmum aliquot campanæ ictibus jubeat convocari Parochianos, seu Confraterni tatem Sanctissimi Sacramenti, ubi fuerit instituta, seu alios pios Christi fideles, qui sacram Eucharistiam cum cereis seu intorticiis comitentur, et umbellam, seu baldachinum, ubi haberi potest, deferant.

790. In countries where the Blessed Sacrament can be carried to the sick publicly and in solemn procession, the church bell should be rung so as to give notice to those who may desire to accompany it, by the number of strokes, or the manner of tolling the bell.[3] The members of the Confraternity of the Blessed Sacrament are bound by one of their rules to attend and carry lights in these processions, or send one of their family to do so; and hence they are specially mentioned in the rubric. The chief object of this confraternity is to honor our Lord in the sacrament of His love, and to repair the many outrages He has there to suffer. It may be established anywhere by the authority of the ordinary of the diocese, and the members become entitled at once to all the privileges and indulgences that have been granted, or may hereafter be granted, to the confraternity at Rome.[4]

791. The " baldachinum " is the large and richly-decorated canopy used in processions of the Blessed Sacrament. It is

---

[1] *Act. Eccl. Mediol.*, pars i. Conc. Prov. V. *Quæ ad Sanctiss. Euch. Sacramentum pertinent*, pag. 180; pars iv. *De Visitat. Infirm.*, § *De Communione*, pag. 446.

[2] Apud Catal., tit. iv. cap. iv. § vii. n. i.

[3] Barruff., tit. xxvi. n. 82.

[4] Cfr. Bouvier, *Traité des Indulgences*, iiime part. chap. ii. see ii. art. i.

supported by long staves, which it is the highest honor to be permitted to carry.[1] The "umbella" is a small canopy which opens like an umbrella, but flat, not conical. It is supported on a single staff, and carried by one person, and is consequently much more convenient than the "baldachinum" for carrying the viaticum, as it is often necessary to pass through narrow streets and entrances.[2] Both are used for the processions of Holy Thursday and Corpus Christi.[3]

§ XL.—Præmonest, ut ægri cubiculum mundetur, et in eo paretur mensa linteo mundo cooperta, in quo Sanctissimum Sacramentum decenter deponatur. Parentur luminaria, ac duo vascula, alterum cum vino, alterum cum aqua. Præterea linteum mundum ante pectus communicandi ponatur, atque alia ad ornatum loci pro cujusque facultate.

*792. The chamber of the sick person ought to be as clean as possible, and suitably ornamented according to his means and circumstances. In it there should be prepared a table covered with a clean white napkin, on which the priest may place the pyxis. St. Charles prescribes that there be on the table a crucifix, and, at least, two wax-candles.[4]

793. If the sick man be a priest, there should be in readiness a surplice and a white stole, to be put on when he is receiving the viaticum.[5] If a cleric, but not a priest, there should be a surplice.[6] It might be inconvenient, in many cases, on account of the condition of the patient, to put on the surplice; but it can rarely happen that there would be any inconvenience in putting on the stole. The ceremony of administering the viaticum to a priest differs in no other respect from what is observed in administering it to laics. The Sacred Congregation forbade the use of any rite not prescribed in the ritual.[7]

794. Although the rubric here directs that there be two little vessels prepared for the purification of the priest's fingers, one containing wine and the other water, Baruffaldi[8] observes that it is sufficient to have one containing water, as wine is seldom or never used. St. Charles prescribes only a single

[1] Vid. Cæremoniale Episcoporum, lib. ii. cap. xxxiii. n. 21.
[2] Baruff., n. 93.
[3] Vid. Merati, pars iv. tit. viii. n. x., et tit. xii. n. xiv. Baldeschi, tom. iv. cap. vi. art. iii. n. 23.
[4] *Act. Eccl. Mediol.*, Concil. Prov. V. *Quæ ad SS. Euch. Sacr. perti nent*, pag. 180.   [5] De Herdt, pars vi. n. 17, i. 20º.
[6] Ibid, ibid. Vid. supra, n. 676.
[7] 21 Jul. 1855, *in Briocen..* 1 d 10, n. 5221
[8] Tit. xxvi. n 102 et n. 184.

vessel of glass.[1] There should be also in readiness a clean linen cloth, to be placed under the chin, and serve as a communion cloth. This is specially necessary in giving communion to the sick, lest a sudden fit of coughing or some other accident might cause the Sacred Host to be rejected.[2]

*795. To have these preparations made, it is necessary that the priest give notice beforehand—"præmoneat," as the rubric directs him. It is not enough, however, that he give notice immediately before he goes to the house. In his instructions regarding the sacrament of the Eucharist, he should take occasion to speak of the communion of the sick, and explain in detail the preparations required, having due regard, of course, to the circumstances of his people. He might get established in his parish a Confraternity of the Blessed Sacrament, or induce the members of some other pious confraternity, as, e. g., that of Our Lady of Mount Carmel, to coöperate with him in carrying out, as far as cir cumstances permit, what is prescribed by the ritual.

In Catholic countries on the Continent, the members of the Confraternity of the Blessed Sacrament undertake this charitable office, and even supply themselves whatever is necessary in the houses of the poor.[3] We have no doubt that in Ireland many would be found in almost every parish, who, if asked, would willingly do the same.

*796. Of course, cases will often occur in which the preparations here mentioned must be dispensed with, either from want of time, or from the impossibility of procuring what is required in the place where the sick person is lying. To meet such cases, it would be desirable to have a small box containing all the requisites, which the priest could bring with him or send before him. This is strongly recommended by the first Synod of Westminster[4] to priests on the English mission. We have seen a box of this kind, not larger than a good-sized duodecimo volume, constructed so as to contain a corporal, a communion cloth, a vessel for ablution, a purificator, two wax-candles, a crucifix, and a vessel of holy water.

§ XII.—Ubi vero convenerint qui Eucharistiam comitaturi sunt, Sacerdos indutus superpelliceo et stola, et, si haberi potest, pluviali albi coloris, Acolythis seu Clericis, aut etiam Presbyteris si locus feret, sui er-

---

[1] Acta Eccl. Med., l. c.   [2] Vid. supra, n. 783.
[3] Baruff., n. 103. Vid. Acta Eccl. Med., il. cc.
[4] Decr. xviii. 12°.

pelliceo pariter indutis comitatus, decenter, et de more acceptas aliquot Particulas consecratas, vel unam tantum (si longius aut difficilius iter sit faciendum) ponat in pxyide, seu parva custodia, quam proprio suo operculo cooperit, et velum sericum superimponit; ipse vero Sacerdos, imposito sibi prius ab utroque humero oblongo velo decenti, utraque manu accipiat vas cum Sacramento, et deinde umbellam seu baldachinum subeat, nudo capite processurus.

797. These instructions as to the manner of carrying the Blessed Sacrament, have reference for the most part, as is evident, to those solemn processions which cannot take place with us. We shall content ourselves, therefore, with noticing those points that may serve in some way to guide the priest in the circumstances in which he is placed in these countries. In the first place he is supposed, in carrying the Blessed Sacrament, to be vested in surplice and stole, and even, if convenient, a cope; and he retains these vestments, at least the surplice and stole, in administering the viaticum. With us the priest goes to the house of the sick person in his ordinary dress; but he should bring with him, or contrive to send before him, the vestments which the rubric requires him to wear.

*798. St. Liguori says: "Ministrare (Eucharistiam), sine "stola et superpelliceo communiter censent Doctores esse "mortale ex genere suo;"[1] and the Sacred Congregation, being asked whether the custom prevailing in some places of administering communion to the sick with a stole alone, "super vestem communem," and without the surplice, might be allowed, answered: "Negative, et eliminata consuetudine "servetur Ritualis Romani præscriptum."[2] Some theologians go so far as to say that the priest should rather permit one to die without the viaticum, than administer it without the sacred vestments prescribed by the rubric. But it is more commonly admitted that, in case of necessity, the viaticum may be administered without any sacred vestments.[3]

*799. The color of the stole should be white, as is plain from the rubric, and this, no matter on what day the Blessed Sacrament is brought to the sick, even though it be Good Friday.[4] In the Ambrosian rite the color used is red.[5]

---

[1] Lib. vi. n. 241.   [2] 16 Dec. 1826, in una Gandaren., ad 1 Quæ-siti ii. n. 4623. Vid. Gardellini, Annotat. in hoc. decret.
[3] Vid. St. Lig., l. c. Caval., tom. iv. cap. v. De Com. Infirm., in Decr. vii. n. v.
[4] Sac. Rit. Cong., 15 Maii, 1745, in Lucana, n. 4170.
[5] Act. Eccl. Mediol., pars iv. § Ordo Minist. Euch. Sacram. Infirmis, p. 447.

800. The Blessed Sacrament is supposed to be kept in the church, where consequently the priest and his attendants meet and vest as here prescribed. The priest then takes some particles out of the pyxis or ciborium in the tabernacle, and puts them into the small pyxis or "custodia," which is to be carefully closed and covered with a silk veil. Besides the large pyxis or ciborium which is kept in the tabernacle, there ought to be in every parochial church a smaller pyxis for carrying the Blessed Sacrament to the sick.[1] The "custodia" here mentioned differs in form from the pyxis, and is used as more convenient and more secure when the journey is long, or must be made on horseback.[2] Barufialdi[3] and Cavalieri[4] seem to suppose that the silk veil which the rubric directs to be placed over it, is no other than the humeral veil which the priest puts on before he takes the Blessed Sacrament in his hands when the procession is starting. The rubric, however, appears to distinguish them, and to require here for the "pyxis" or "custodia" a small veil, such as is prescribed in a preceding chapter.[5]

The priest, having taken the pyxis in his hands, covers it with the extremities of the humeral veil, and carries it before his breast, the left hand holding the "nodus," and the right resting on the lid, at the same time keeping over it the ends of the veil.[6]

*801. In these countries the priest is, generally speaking, permitted to keep the Blessed Sacrament in his house.[7] He would do well to have the small pyxis which he carries to the sick always in readiness, so that it may be unnecessary for him to transfer any particles to it when he is required to attend a call. As he goes in his ordinary dress, and without attendants, we would not require him to vest in order to take the pyxis out of the tabernacle. It is enough that, having opened the door, he genuflect and adore the Blessed Sacrament. He may then take out the pyxis and fasten it, as directed below.[8] Should it be necessary, however, to transfer particles from a larger pyxis or ciborium, whether in his private oratory or in the church, we think he ought to vest

[1] *Act. Eccl. Mediol.*, pars i. § *Quæ ad SS. Euch. Sacram. pertinent*, pag. 110.
[2] Catal., cap. iv. § x. n. iv.   Baruff., n. 121.   Vid. infra, § xiv.
[3] Loc. cit.   [4] *De Com. Inf.*, Decr. vii. n. viii.
[5] Vid. supra, n. 601.
[6] Vid. Gavant., pars iv. tit. viii. *De Feria V. in Cœna Dom.*, rub. 9 lit (o).   [7] Vid. supra, n. 598.   [8] Infra, § xiv.

in surplice and stole, for nothing short of strict necessity could
justify him in thus handling the Blessed Sacrament without
the vestments prescribed by the rubric.

§ XIII.—Præcedat semper Acolythus, vel alius Minister deferens
laternam (noctu autem hoc Sacramentum deferri non debet, nisi necessitas
urgeat); sequantur duo Clerici, vel qui illorum vices suppleant, quorum
alter aquam benedictam cum aspersorio, et bursam cum corporali quod
supponendum erit vasculo Sanctissimi Sacramenti super mensa in
cubiculo infirmi, et cum linteolo purificatorio ad digitos Sacerdotis
abstergendos; alter hunc librum Ritualem deferat, et campanulam
jugiter pulset.   Succedant deinde deferentes intorticia.   Postremo
Sacerdos Sacramentum gestans elevatum ante pectus sub umbella, dicens
Psalmum *Miserere*, et alios Psalmos et Cantica.

802. This rubric contains the instructions regarding the
solemn procession. They are very clear and very minute.
It may be seen that great pains are taken to have the Blessed
Sacrament always accompanied with lights, no matter what
be the state of the weather.   Hence, it is prescribed that a
lantern be always carried, as the light it contains is protected
from the wind, and will serve to re-light the others that may
happen to be blown out.[1]   And although, according to a
decree of Benedict XIII,[2] there should be four lanterns, two
on each side of the priest, when he carries the Blessed Sacrament outside the church, the lantern here prescribed should
still be carried at the head of the procession, for the convenience of lighting the torches if required.[3]

803. The Blessed Sacrament should not be brought to the
sick at night, unless in case of necessity. The reason assigned
is, because it cannot then be carried with so much solemnity
and reverence.[4]   This reason does not apply where, as in
these countries, it is never carried to the sick in public
procession.   At all events, the case of necessity—that is,
when there is danger that the person might otherwise be
unable to receive the viaticum—is excepted.   We have
already mentioned another case, which, though not strictly
one of necessity, may be regarded as an exception.[5]

*804. It remains to say a word about the way of providing,
in these countries, the requisites which are here supposed to
be carried by clerks in the procession.   The holy water
should be already in the chamber of the sick person, and may

---

[1] Baruff., n. 131.   [2] Conc. Rom., 1725, tit. xv. cap. vii.   Labbe,
tom. xxi. pag. 1876.   [3] Catal., cap. iv. § xi. n. ii.
[4] *Act. Eccl. Mediol.*, Conc. V. § *Quæ ad SS. Euchar Sacram. pertinent*, pag. 180.   Catal., l. c.   Baruff., n. 133.
[5] Vid. supra, n. 787.

be placed on or beside the table before mentioned.[1] Even
when the Blessed Sacrament is brought in procession, if the
priest knows that there is holy water in the house he is going
to, he need not bring any with him.[2]

A feather, a little brush, or something similar, may be
easily found in the house, and will serve as an "aspersorium,"
which, as Baruffaldi observes,[3] may be of any material.

The corporal to be spread out under the pyxis when it is
placed on the table, must be brought by the priest. If not
carried in a box with the other requisites,[4] it is usually folded
up, and with it a small purificator, in the case which contains
the pyxis.

The burse in which the corporal is carried when a procession
is formed, is, of course, dispensed with; so also is the bell, the
use of which is to give notice to the people along the way,
that they may adore the Blessed Sacrament as it passes.

805. The priest is directed to say the psalm, "*Miserere,*"
and other psalms and canticles. In processions, the Penitential Psalms, with appropriate hymns and canticles, are recited
alternately by the ecclesiastics. This was ordered by several
provincial councils; amongst the rest, the fifth Council of
Milan, under St. Charles.[5] The "*Miserere*" is the only psalm
distinctly prescribed; but the other Penitential Psalms are
recommended when there is time, and with them the canticles,
"*Benedicite,*" "*Magnificat,*" etc.[6] If there be none to chant
these, or recite them alternately with the priest, he says them
himself "submissa voce," and the rest may say the rosary, the
litanies, or other prayers, the object of all being to implore
the divine mercy for the sick. In reciting the litanies, the
response should be "*Ora pro eo,*" or "*Ora pro eâ.*"[7] The
priest, reciting alone, may say, with the "*Miserere,*" any other
psalms or canticles, as, *e. g.*, the "*Benedictus,*" or the "*Magnificat,*" which he may know by heart.[8]

§ XIV.—Quod si longius aut difficilius iter obeundum sit, et fortasse
etiam equitandum, necesse erit vas, in quo Sacramentum defertur, bursa
decenter ornata, et ad collum appensa, apte includere, et ita ad pectus
alligare atque adstringere, ut neque decidere, neque pyxide excuti
Sacramentum queat.

[1] Supra, n. 792.   [2] Baruff., n. 136.   [3] Loc. cit. n. 137.
[4] Vid. supra, n. 796.   [5] *Act. Eccl. Mediol.*, pars i. Conc. Prov.
§ *Quæ ad. SS. Euch. pertinent*, pag. 180.
[6] Baruff., n. 151, et seq. Caval., *De Com. Inf.*, Decr. xi. n. iv.
[7] Caval., l. c. n. v. De Herdt, pars vi. n. 17, i. 4to.
[8] Catal., l. c. § xii. n. vi. De Herdt, l. c.

*806. In country parishes in Ireland, the priest must go a considerable distance, and is very often obliged to ride to the houses of the sick. He must carefully attend, therefore, to what is here prescribed by the rubric for the greater security of the Blessed Sacrament in such circumstances. The "bursa" here mentioned is different from that referred to in the preceding rubric, which is for holding the corporal. This is generally a kind of loose bag, of a suitable size and shape, for holding the pyxis.[1]

It should be securely closed and fastened round the neck by a cord or chain, so as to prevent the danger of the pyxis falling, or of any of the particles being shaken out. The pyxis, or custodia, is sometimes provided with a handle or hook, to which the chain may be attached; and in this way it is more secure than when merely the "bursa" containing it is fastened to the neck. A leathern case, lined with silk, may be used as the "bursa," and many prefer it to the loose bag, as being a better protection to the pyxis.

*807. Whatever it be made of, it should not be permitted to hang loosely from the neck, but be made fast on the breast, as the rubric here directs, so as to prevent the danger of the pyxis falling, or of the Blessed Sacrament being shaken out. This may be done, as the words of the rubric—"alligare," "adstringere"—would seem to suggest, by means of strings attached to the case or "bursa." In our first edition we said that it might be done also by putting the pyxis with its covering into a pocket made in the vest for this purpose, and used for no other. But the Sacred Congregation of Rites, referring to this matter, requires that, when the Blessed Eucharist is carried privately, what the Rubric prescribes be observed in every particular—"In hoc casu adamussim servetur quod præscribit Rubrica."[2]

§ XV.—*Ingrediens vero locum ubi jacet infirmus, dicat:* ℣ *Pax huic domini,* etc.

*808. The salutation here prescribed in the ritual is that which our Lord Himself prescribed in His instructions to the seventy-two disciples: "Into whatsoever house you enter, "first say, 'Peace be to this house.'"[3] The priest is, in nearly every case, directed to use these words on his first entrance into any house or place where he is about to perform a duty

---

[1] Baruff., n. 157.   [2] "Decretum" prefixed to this volume.
[3] Luke, x. 5.

of his sacred ministry. But should he perform several dis
tinct duties before leaving—should he, *e. g.*, administer the
Viaticum and Extreme Unction, and give the benediction
"in articulo mortis," as very often happens—he is not required to repeat the words at the commencement of each.
The ritual gives them, it is true, but the ritual clearly
supposes that the functions take place separately, and that
the priest comes to the house for each.[1]

§ XVI.—Tum depositum Sacramentum super mensa, supposito
corporali, genuflexus adorat, omnibus in genua procumbentibus ; et mox
accepta aqua benedicta, aspergit infirmium, et cubiculum, dicens Antiphonam : *Asperges me*, etc., et primum versum Psalmi, *Miserere mei,
Deus*, cum *Gloria Patri*, etc.
    Deinde repetitur Antiphona : *Asperges me*, etc.
    Postea : ℣ *Adjutorium nostrum*, etc.

809. Having entered the chamber with the preceding salutation, he places the Blessed Sacrament on the table, on
which he has been careful first to spread out the corporal, for
the pyxis should be laid down nowhere, if possible, without
a corporal under it.[2]   Then the priest, and all who are present,
adore the Blessed Sacrament, genuflecting on both knees,
according to Baruffaldi[3] and Catalani ;[4] but Cavalieri[5] thinks
the priest should genuflect only on one knee.

810. He sprinkles the holy water on the sick person in the
form of a cross.[6]   The rubric prescribes this in similar
circumstances elsewhere, from which it is inferred that here
also the sprinkling should be in the form of a cross.[7]   Standing as nearly as possible opposite to the sick person, but so
as not to turn his back to the Blessed Sacrament, he sprinkles
the water first in the centre, *i. e.*, in front of himself, then on
his (own) left, then on his (own) right, thus forming the cross
with the water over the sick person.[8]   He then sprinkles
some around him, on the floors or walls of the chamber, and
on those who are present, taking care that none may fall
on the pyxis,[9] and saying, while he sprinkles, the antiphon,
"*Asperges me*," etc., as directed by the rubric.

---

[1] Vid. Revue Théologique, 1856, 1re Série, pag. 615.
[2] Sac. Rit. Cong., 27 Feb. 1847, *in Cong. Cler. Reg. S. Crucis*, n.
5068. Vid. supra, n. 804.
[2] Tit. xxvi. n. 160.   [4] Tit. iv. cap. iv. § xiii. n. ii.
[5] *De Com. Infirmorum*, Decr. xi. n. vii.
[6] De Herdt, pars vi. n. 17, i. 8°.
[7] Vid. Cavalieri, *De Agone Infirm.*, Decr. ii. n. xi.
[8] Vid infra, chap. xvi. § v. in fine.   [9] De Herdt, l. c.

In the ordinary aspersion before mass, the antiphon during Paschal time is, "*Vidi aquam egredientem*," etc.[1] But the Sacred Congregation decided that, in administering the viaticum, no change should be made, so that the antiphon, "*Asperges*," etc., and the first verse of the Psalm, "*Miserere*," are to be used at all times.[2]

811. While saying "*Adjutorium nostrum*," etc., he makes on himself the sign of the cross. This is not prescribed by any rubric of the ritual, as it is by the rubric of the Missal at the commencement of mass.[3] Nor is it mentioned by any of the commentators we have seen. But in treating of the general rubrics, given hereafter in the ritual, to be observed in benedictions, many authors distinctly say that the priest signs himself in pronouncing these words.[4] Thus, then, although it does not appear that he is bound, he is certainly recommended, to do so here, since the present ceremony, as far as the prayer, "*Exaudi nos*," etc., inclusive, is like that which is assigned for the "Benedictio Domorum" in another part of the ritual. At all events, there is a general custom in favor of his making the sign of the cross on himself at these words.[5] The proper way of making it is to put the hand to the forehead at "*Adjutorium;*" to the breast, at "*nostrum;*" to the left shoulder, at "*in nomine;*" and to the right, at "*Domini.*"[6]

§ XVII.—His dictis, accedat ad infirmum, ut cognoscat num sit bene dispositus ad accipiendum sacrum Viaticum, et utrum velit aliqua peccata confiteri ; et illum audiat, atque absolvat: quamvis prius deberet esse rite confessus, nisi necessitas aliter urgeat.

*812. As a general rule, the Blessed Sacrament is not to be brought to the sick person until he has been previously visited by the priest, and has made his confession, because he might not be in a condition to receive communion, or even to be absolved, on the first visit of the priest.[7] If the case be urgent, however, and the distance considerable, the priest may bring it with him on his first visit. In Ireland, and other countries where it cannot be carried in procession, he usually

---

[1] Rub. Missalis, "*De Benedictione Aquæ.*"
[2] 11 Feb. 1702, *in Lerien.*, ad 7, n. 3614.
[3] *Ritus Servandus*, etc., § iii. n. 7.
[4] St. Carol., *Act. Eccl. Mediol.*, pars iv. *Instruct. gener. pro Benedictionibus*, pag. 462. Catal., vol. ii. tit. viii. cap. i. § iv. De Herdt, pars v. n. 37, vii. 5°.
[5] Cfr. Revue Théologique, loc. cit. pag. 616.
[6] Merati, pars ii. tit. iii. n. xvi.　　[7] Vid. supra, n. 768.

does so whenever he gets a sick call.   In such circumstances, before he takes the pyxis out of its covering, or lets it be known that he has it with him, he takes care to hear the person's confession, and thus be able to decide whether he should administer the viaticum.

But even though he may have made a previous visit, and heard the confession, he should not administer the viaticum until he has given an opportunity of confessing again if the person desires it.   The sick man's conscience may be still burdened with some sin, which he previously concealed or forgot, and which he now wishes to confess.   Besides, by approaching for this purpose, the priest has also an opportunity of ascertaining whether the sick person be in a physical condition to receive, for even a few hours may have produced a notable change in this respect.[1]

*813. If, in these circumstances, he has a long confession to make, and if there be reason to fear that, by a tedious confession just then, he may incur grave suspicions injurious to his character, or that, after making it, he may not have time, or may be unable, to receive the viaticum, the priest should be satisfied with hearing a few sins.   He can then absolve, reminding him of the obligation of completing the confession, should he be afterwards able.[2]   The words of the rubric, "nisi necessitas aliter urgeat," imply, according to Baruffaldi[3] and Cavalieri,[4] that in such circumstances the priest need not hear the entire confession.

The penance to be imposed should be very light: a short prayer, a single ejaculation, an act of resignation made mentally would suffice, with a general exhortation to submit patiently to his present sufferings, and to do penance if he recovers.[5]

§ XVIII.—Postea facta de more Confessione generali, sive ab infirmo, sive ejus nomine ab alio, Sacerdos dicit: *Misereatur*, etc., *Indulgentiam*, etc.

*814. The priest then goes to the table where the Blessed Sacrament is placed (or where he now places it[6]), and having genuflected, uncovers the pyxis.   Meantime the communion cloth should be adjusted under the chin, and the stole, if the person be a priest, around the neck.[7]   The "*Confiteor*" is

---

[1] Vid. Baruff., n. 162, et seq. Caval., *De Com. Inf.*, Decr. xi. v. ix. et x.   [2] St. Lig., lib. vi. n. 260, in parenth.   Caval., l. c.
[3] Loc. cit. n. 167.   [4] Loc. cit.
[5] St. Lig., n. 507, ii.   [6] Supra, n. 812.   [7] Baruff., n. 206.

said as is prescribed for the ordinary communion in the church. It is to be said by the sick person, if he be able; if not, it is to be said in his name by the clerk or minister in attendance, or by any one present; or if there be no one else, by the priest himself.[1]

*815. After the "Confiteor," the priest again genuflects, and turns towards the sick person, taking care, however, not to turn his back to the Blessed Sacrament. In this position he says "Misereatur," etc., "Indulgentiam," etc., using the words "tui," "tuis," in the singular, but observing the very same ceremonies as before directed for communion in the church.[2] The text of the Roman ritual has simply "Misereatur," etc., "Indulgentiam," etc., and does not, therefore, expressly prescribe the use of "tui," "tuis," in the singular; on the contrary, it seems rather to imply that the form should be "vestri," "vestris," in the plural, as this is the form given in full before for communion in the church, and to be used, according to all, even when there is but one communicant.[3]

To this, however, it may be replied, that the "Confiteor" is there expressly directed to be said "nomine populi," whereas here it is to be said "ab infirmo sive ejus nomine ab "alio," and that, therefore, the "Misereatur," etc., should be directed in the former case to the people, and in the latter to the sick person alone. But, at all events, the commentators are unanimous in teaching that the form here should be in the singular.[4] The most probable reason for using the singular is, according to Cavalieri,[5] that the Church wishes our prayers on this occasion to be offered specially on behalf of the sick person, just as in reciting the litanies for the dying, we are directed by the ritual to say in the singular, "Ora pro eo (eâ)," and to suggest to the dying person the prayer, "Sancta "Maria, ora pro me," etc., although in other circumstances, one reciting these, even when alone, would say "Ora pro nobis."

§ XIX.—Deinde facta genuflexione, accipit Sacramentum de vasculo, atque illud elevans ostendit infirmo, dicens: *Ecce Agnus Dei,* etc., et more solito ter dicat: *Domine, non sum dignus,* etc.

Et infirmus simul cum Sacerdote dicat eadem verba, saltem semel, submissa voce.

*816. He then turns to the Blessed Sacrament, and again genuflects; and holding the pyxis in his left hand, he takes

---

[1] Vid. De Herdt, n. 22, 5°.   [2] Chap. xii. § iii.
[3] Supra. n. 668.
[4] Baruff., n. 170. Caval. cap. v. in Decr. xi. n. xi. De Herdt, pars vi. n. 17, 10°.   [5] Loc. cit.

the host, and holds it with the thumb and index of his right, proceeding exactly as directed before,[1] except that here he turns towards the sick person,[2] while saying "*Ecce Agnus,*" etc. He is required to let him see the host, and it is plain, therefore, that he should turn towards him, no matter what be the position of the table, which, however, should, if possible, be placed so that the crucifix on the centre of it could be easily seen by the sick person.

*817. It is here directed that the "*Domine, non sum* "*dignus,*" etc., be said by the sick person at the same time with the priest, at least that it be said once by him, but in a low tone. He should be previously instructed to do this. The priest could remind him of it in the little exhortation which he ought to address to him immediately before uncovering the pyxis. If he cannot say it in Latin, he may say it in the vernacular, but the priest is not at liberty to repeat it in the vernacular, just before presenting the host, by way of suggesting it to him at that moment.[3]

§ XX.—Tum Sacerdos dans infirmo Eucharistiam, dicat: *Accipe frater* (vel *soror*), *Viaticum,* etc.

*818. This is the form to be used whenever the Blessed Sacrament is administered "per modum viatici." And we have seen under a preceding rubric,[4] that it is to be so administered, whenever it is probable that the person will be unable to receive again.

According to Clericati,[5] Baruffaldi,[6] and others, this formula, being prescribed by the Church, has a certain efficacy attached to it, and, therefore, should always be used when the Eucharist is given as the viaticum. According to St. Liguori, however, the rubric does not bind *sub gravi*, and the substitution of the words, "*Corpus Domini,*" etc., would not exceed a venial sin. And hence, if the sick person would be greatly distressed by hearing the words "*Accipe,*" etc., the priest would be justified in omitting them, and using the ordinary form, "*Corpus,*" etc.[7] The case must be a very rare one in which it would be found necessary or expedient to act on this decision; for, as has been before stated,[8] the priest is, at least generally speaking, bound to give him notice of his danger, and cannot, therefore, be justified in departing from

[1] Supra, chap. xii. § iv.
[2] Vid. supra, n. 672.
[5] *De Eucharistia*, Decis. xix. n. 12.
[7] Lib. vi. n. 285, Dub. 4.
[3] Caval., l. c. n. xii.
[4] Supra, § iv.
[6] Tit. xxvi. n. 173.
[8] Supra, n. 771.

the rubric to conceal that danger, or avoid any allusion to it in administering the sacrament. We may, however, conceive a case in which the person is in the state of grace, and, therefore, not unprepared for death, however suddenly it may come, while, at the same time, his danger would be notably aggravated by any warning of it. In such a case the decision might be acted on, but hardly, we think, in any other.

§ XXI.—Si vero communio non datur per modum Viatici, dicat more ordinario: *Corpus Domini*, etc.

*819. If the communion be not administered " per modum " viatici," the ordinary form, " *Corpus Domini*," etc., is used. This, taken in connection with the preceding rubric, shows plainly that to administer the Eucharist " pro viatico," " per " modum viatici," etc., is understood to imply the use of the form, " *Accipe frater*," etc. The expressions are used constantly in this sense.[1]

*820. The change here marked is the only one mentioned in the ritual, for the case in which the sick communicate in the ordinary way. According to Cavalieri,[2] " *Misereatur* " *vestri*," etc., is to be said, and not, as in giving the viaticum, " *Misereatur tui*," etc. But the other prayers and ceremonies prescribed in this chapter are to remain unaltered.[3]

§ XXII.—Quod si mors immineat, et periculum sit in mora, tunc dicto *Misereatur*, etc., prædictis precibus omnibus vel ex parte omissis, ei statim Viaticum præbeatur.

*821. If there be reason to fear that the sick person would be unable to receive the sacrament unless it be administered immediately, and without waiting to say the preceding prayers, short as they are, the rubric here directs that the prayers be omitted, in whole or in part, as may be judged necessary, and the viaticum be given at once The words appear to imply that in no case should the " *Misereatur*," etc., be omitted; but there is no doubt that, in urgent necessity, whatever precedes the administration of the host may be omitted;[4] nor are the prayers thus omitted to be afterwards supplied.[5]

822. It might seem that such a case can hardly occur in practice; for if the priest believes that death is so very

---

[1] Vid. supra, § iv. et § v.   [2] Cap. v. Decr. xi. n. xi.
[3] Vid. De Herdt, pars vi. n. 17, ii.
[4] Caval., *De Communione Infirmorum*, Decr. xi. n. xv. De Herdt, n. 17, 13°.   [5] De Herdt, ibid.

imminent, he should also believe that the person would be
unable to receive the communion, or at least to consume the
Sacred Host.   Baruffaldi[1] and Cavalieri[2] notice this difficulty,
but say that, notwithstanding the risk, the practice of the
Church and the sacred canons sanction the administration in
the circumstances.   The canon, *Is qui*, 8, c. 26, q. 6,[3] which
regards the administration of the sacraments to the dying, says:
".. et si continuo creditur moriturus, reconcilietur per manus
"impositionem et infundatur ori ejus Eucharistia."   In
accordance with the ancient discipline, these words suppose
that the Eucharist might be administered under the species
of wine, but they show the intention of the Church ; and it
may be inferred from them that every effort should be made
to administer the viaticum in the only way permitted by the
present discipline, that is, under the species of bread.[4]   We
have seen that, if necessary, a very small particle may be
put into a little wine or water, and administered in that way.[5]

823. Of course, the administration is not to be attempted,
if it be evident that the person is unable to swallow, and that
the Blessed Sacrament, therefore, would not pass into the
stomach.[6]   But the apprehension that death will occur before
it is consumed or altered in the stomach, is not a sufficient
reason why it should be withheld.

If it be observed that, in point of fact, the Sacred Host
has not been swallowed, but remains in the mouth after death,
it should be taken out reverently and brought to the sacrarium,
in some vessel distinct from the pyxis, or in the corporal.[7]
But if it be not visible in the mouth, and there be a doubt
whether it has been swallowed, nothing further is to be done.[8]
There is no irreverence in allowing it, in such circumstances,
to be buried with the dead body.   There is reason to believe
that, in the early ages, it was not unusual in some places to
put a consecrated host on the breast of the dead body, and
bury it with it.[9]

824. It may be asked, whether, in time of pestilence, it
would be lawful to administer the viaticum by means of an
instrument, or to place it so that the sick person could receive
it, without its being necessary for the priest to administer it
with his hand in the usual way.   St. Charles expressly

[1] Tit. xxvi. n. 177, et seq.   [2] Loc. cit.
[3] Cit. apud Caval., l. c.   [4] Vid. supra, n. 677, et seq.
[5] Vid. supra, n. 782.   [6] Vid. De Lugo, Disp. xii. sect. ii. n. 28. 29.
[7] De Herdt, n. 17, 18°.   Vid. supra, n. 783.   [8] De Herdt, ibid.
[9] Vid. Caval., *De Com. Fidelium*, in Decr. i. n. viii. in fine.

forbade this.[1] St. Liguori, however, thinks it not improbable
that it is lawful.[2] The "Modo Pratico" also would allow
it.[3] Benedict XIV discusses the question at great length,
citing authorities on both sides.[4] He is of opinion that some
such mode of administering the viaticum in time of pestilence
may be sanctioned by the bishop.[5] A priest in Ireland
could hardly act on this opinion without giving scandal. At
all events, we never heard of one who had recourse to any
such expedient, in order to guard himself against infection.

§ XXIII.—Postea Sacerdos abluat digitos, nihil dicens, et infirmo
detur ablutio.

*825. Having administered the viaticum, he returns to the
table, places the pyxis on the corporal, and (if he has brought
more than one particle) genuflects.[6] He then rubs his thumb
and index against each other, to make any little fragments
that might adhere to them fall into the pyxis, washes them
in the vessel prepared for the purpose, and dries them with
the purificator, and then covers the pyxis.[7] The words, "nihil
"dicens," admonish him that there are no prayers prescribed
during the ablution of the fingers here, as there are at mass,
when he is required to say "*Corpus tuum*," etc.[8]

*826. The ablution is to be given to the sick person if he
can conveniently take it, and on this account the quantity of
water in the vessel should be very small. The priest himself
is not required to administer it. It may be given by one of
the attendants.[9] If the sick person, however, would suffer the
slightest inconvenience from taking it, it should not be given
to him, but either be brought to the church, and thrown into
the sacrarium, or thrown into the fire in the house of the sick
person.[10] Baruffaldi[11] suggests that, in these circumstances,
the priest need not dip his fingers into the vessel, but may dip
a part of the purificator into it, and with the part thus
moistened wipe his fingers, and dry them with the remainder.
Falise seems to approve of this suggestion.[12] It would be

[1] *Act. Eccl. Mediol.*, pars i. Conc. Prov. v. § *Cautio in Sacerdote
ministrante*, pag. 195.   [2] Lib. vi. n. 244, in parenth.
[3] Cap. vii.   [4] *De Syn. Diœc.*, lib. xiii. cap. xix. n. 20, et seq.
[5] Loc. cit. n. 27, in fine.   [6] Caval., *De Com. Infirm.*, Decr.
xi. n. xvi. De Herdt, pars vi. n. 17, i. 14°.
[7] Vid. supra, n. 697.   [8] Baruff., n. 181. Caval., l. c.
[9] Caval., ibid. De Herdt, l. c. 15.°
[10] Caval., ibid. Baruff., n. 186. De Herdt, ibid.   [11] Loc. cit.
[12] IIIme Partie, sect. i. chap. iii. § iii. n. 8.

convenient to act on it, if there be no fire into which the ablution could be thrown. We would add, that if the purificator has been used before, it should not be dipped into the vessel, but a part should be moistened by carefully pouring a little water on it.

§ XXIV —Deinde dicat: ℣. *Dominus vobiscum*, etc.

827. According to some, "*Dominus vobiscum*" should here be omitted, unless when only a single particle has been brought in the pyxis.[1] Cavalieri lays it down as a general rule, that it should be omitted whenever benediction of the Blessed Sacrament immediately follows, as it does here, and again after returning to the church.[2] Gardellini[3] and De Herdt[4] also adopt the same view. But the Sacred Congregation, being consulted on the question, replied that the ritual is to be strictly followed.[5]

The clerk or attendant should give the response, and also say "*Amen*," at the close of the prayer.

§ XXV.—His expletis, si altera particula Sacramenti superfuerit (superesse autem semper debet, præterquam in casu jam dicto), genuflectit, surgit, et accipiens vas cum Sacramento, facit cum eo signum Crucis super infirmum, nihil dicens, et reverenter illud deferens, ordine quo venerat, revertitur ad Ecclesiam dicendo Psalmum *Laudate Dominum de cælis*, etc., et alios Psalmos et Hymnos, prout tempus feret.

828. In countries where it is possible to carry the Blessed Sacrament in procession, as prescribed in the preceding rubrics, there should be at least two consecrated particles in the pyxis, so that at least one may remain after the communion of the sick, to be carried in procession back to the church, as it was carried from it. The case of exception has been mentioned before,[6] and is again noticed with the directions to be followed when it occurs.[7]

According to the general rule, the priest, having said the prayer, "*Domine sancte*," etc., puts on the humeral veil, genuflects, and having taken the pyxis, and covered it with the extremities of the veil, in the manner before directed,[8] turns to the sick person, and makes over him the sign of the cross in this manner:—He first raises the pyxis to the height of his eyes, then lowers it under his breast, raises it again in

[1] Caval., l. c. n. xvii. De Herdt, l. c. 18°.
[2] Vol. iv. cap. ix. in Decr. iii. n. iv.
[3] *Comment. ad Instr. Clement.*, § xxxi. n. 6 et 7.   [4] Loc. cit.
[5] 24 Sept. 1842, in una 3ll *Ord. Sti. Franc.*, ad 3, n. 4947. Vid. supra, n. 695.   [6] Supra, § xii.   [7] Infra, § xxix
[8] Baruff., n. 188. Caval., cap. v. Decr. xi. n. xviii.

the same vertical line, to the height of his shoulders, and then crosses this line by moving it horizontally, first towards his left shoulder, and then towards his right. This is the way of forming the cross in giving Benediction of the Blessed Sacrament, whether in the remonstrance[1] or in the pyxis.[2] But here, after moving the pyxis to his right, he does not complete the circle as he does in giving benediction at the altar,[3] but brings it back before his breast to the position in which he should hold it in the procession.

While giving the benediction, he says nothing, according to the present rubric, and this is to be always observed in the act of giving benediction with the Blessed Sacrament.[4]

829. The procession is now formed as before, and he carries it back to the church in the same manner as he carried it from it.[5] The prayers and canticles prescribed on leaving the church, are directed to implore the divine mercy in favor of the sick to whom the Blessed Sacrament is carried.[6] Those here prescribed on returning are different, being recited in praise and thanksgiving for the immense favor conferred.[7] The "*Laudate Dominum de cœlis*," etc., is the only one expressly mentioned here, as the "*Miserere*," etc., is the only one expressly mentioned before;[8] but not only the two psalms which are usually joined with it, but the other psalms of lauds may be added, and with them the canticles, "*Benedicite*" and "*Benedictus*," and the hymns, "*Te Deum*," "*Pange lingua*," etc., according to the circumstances of time, distance, etc.[9]

830. The rubric supposes a priest, when carrying the Blessed Sacrament, never to be alone. The Sacred Congregation would require him, even when on horseback, to have, if possible, at least one attendant bearing a light.[10] But in Ireland, and other countries similarly circumstanced, he is often without any one to accompany him, and, in this case, he would do well to recite such of those psalms and canticles as he knows by heart.[11]

§ XXVI.—Cum pervenerit ad Ecclesiam, ponit Sacramentum super Altare, adorat, deinde dicit: *Panem de cœlo*, etc.

[1] Baldeschi, *Esposizione*, etc., tom. iv. Appendice i. art. vii. n. 58. Syn. Thurl., Appendice ii.
[2] Baldeschi, Appendice ii. n. 5.
[3] Baldeschi. Synod. Thurl., ll. cc.   [4] Caval., l. c. Baruff., n. 189.
[5] Baruff., n. 193.   [6] Supra, n. 805.
[7] Baruff., n. 194. Catal., l. c. n. xix.   [8] Supra, § xiii.
[9] Baruff., l. c. Caval., l. c. Catal., tit. iv. cap. iv. § xxi. n. ii.
[10] 23 Mai', 1846, *Birinian.*, n. 5036.   [11] Vid. supra, n. 580.

831. Having returned to the church, he ascends the altar, spreads the corporal on the centre, and places the pyxis on it. He then genuflects and descends to the lowest step, on which he kneels in adoration, still retaining the humeral veil, and keeping his hands joined before his breast, until all the people have entered the church.[1] He then rises and says the versicle, "*Panem de cœlo*," etc. In some places, according to Cavalieri[2] and Baruffaldi,[3] "*Tantum ergo*," etc., is previously sung; but Cavalieri shows that the custom is unauthorized and opposed to the rubric, which makes no mention of it, as it does on the return of the procession of Corpus Christi, but directs the versicle to be said at once after the adoration.[4] We have before seen that "*Dominus vobiscum*" is to be said, as marked in the ritual.[5]

§ XXVII.—Deinde annuntiat Indulgentias a Summis Pontificibus concessas Sanctissimum Sacramentum comitantibus.

832. Having finished the prayer, he genuflects, and turning to the people, but taking care not to turn his back to the pyxis, he announces the indulgences granted to those who accompany the Blessed Sacrament. These are: " 1° An indulgence of seven years and seven quarantines to those who accompany it with a lighted taper, or any other light. 2° An indulgence of five years and five quarantines to those who accompany it without a light. 3° An indulgence of three years and three quarantines to those who, being lawfully hindered from going themselves, send some one in their stead to carry a light in attendance upon the Holy Viaticum. 4° An indulgence of one hundred days to those who cannot go themselves with the Blessed Sacrament, provided they say one 'Pater Noster' and one 'Ave Maria' for the intention of the Pope, when they see it carried to the sick."[6]

It is not necessary for the priest to mention all these in detail. It is enough for him to announce them in general terms, saying that all who accompanied the Blessed Sacrament with the proper dispositions, have gained the indulgences granted by the Pontiffs.[7]

§ XXVIII.—Postea cum Sacramento in pyxide velo cooperta faciat signum Crucis super populum, nihil dicens. Postremo illud in loco suo reponat.

[1] Baruff., n. 195.   Caval., cap. v. Decr. xii. n. i.   De Herdt, n. 17, i. 18°.   [2] Loc. cit.   [3] Loc. cit.   [4] Caval., l. c.   [5] Supra, n. 827.
[6] "The Raccolta," *authorized translation*, n. 51.   Cfr. Bouvier, *Traité des Indulgences*, iime par. chap. x. § ix.
[7] Bar ff., n. 200.   Caval., l. c. n. iii.   De Herdt, n. 17, i. 18°.

833. Having announced the indulgences, he genuflects on the lowest step, and ascends to the predella, where he again genuflects, and taking the pyxis, which he covers with the humeral veil,[1] he gives the benediction, making the sign of the cross in the manner before explained.[2] On this occasion, however, after moving the pyxis from the left to the right shoulder, he immediately turns to the altar, and (carefully withdrawing the extremities of the humeral veil) places it on the corporal, and then puts it into the tabernacle, genuflecting as before directed.[3] No genuflections are here expressly prescribed by the rubric, but there can be no doubt that they are understood, and they are directed to be made as a matter of course by all the commentators.[4]

In addition to the two benedictions prescribed by the ritual, others are permitted by custom in some places, or even ordered by the rituals used in particular dioceses.[5] The Sacred Congregation has allowed such customs, where they exist, to be retained.[6]

§ XXIX.—Quod si ob difficultatem aut longitudinem itineris, vel quia ea qua decet veneratione Sacramentum ad Ecclesiam commode reportari non potest, sumpta fuerit una tantum Particula consecrata, ut dictum est, tunc ea infirmo administrata, Sacerdos prædictis precibus recitatis, eum manu benedicit, et una cum aliis privato habitu, extinctis luminibus, umbella demissa, latente pyxide, ad Ecclesiam, vel domum quisque suam revertatur.

*834. When the journey is long or difficult, or when the priest has to go on horseback, only one particle is to be brought, according to a previous rubric.[7] Many other cases are mentioned by authors, in which the same rule is to be followed; as, when it must be brought at night, when the weather is rainy, or the like.[8] Indeed, the present rubric seems to include every case in which the Blessed Sacrament cannot be carried in public with suitable marks of reverence. St. Charles adds also the case in which it is foreseen that Extreme Unction must be administered immediately after the viaticum.[9]

835. When only a single particle is brought, the priest is here instructed, after administering the communion, to recite

[1] Baruff., n. 201. Caval., l. c. n. iv. [2] Supra, n. 828.
[3] Supra, cap. xii. § x. [4] Caval., l. c. Baruff., l. c., etc., etc.
[5] Vid. De Herdt, pars vi. n. 17, i. 19°.
[6] 7 April, 1832, Massæ et Popul., ad 2, n. 4685. [7] Supra, § xii.
[8] Baruff., n. 116. Cavalieri, cap. v. Decr. vii. n. vii. De Herdt, n. 18, iii. [9] Act. Eccl. Mediol., pars iv Instruct. Visit. Inf., § De Communione, pag. 445.

the preceding versicles and prayers, and give the benediction with his hand. He should give the benediction in the same manner as after communion in the church,[1] raising his eyes, extending his hands, etc.[2] The form there prescribed is, *"Benedictio . . . descendat super vos"*. . . and no commentator that we have seen suggests a change of number here. Cavalieri[3] even gives the form here in full, with the plural *"super vos."* We have no authority, then, for a change of number, but it appears to us that the reasons why the form, *"Misereatur tui,"* etc., is used instead of *"Misereatur vestri,"* etc., in administering the viaticum, would require or justify here the use of the form, *"Benedictio . . . descendat super te"* . . .[4]

836. Having given the benediction, the priest takes off his sacred vestments, and, with his attendants, returns to the church, or each may go to his own house. The lights are extinguished, the canopy lowered or folded up, and the pyxis concealed, so as to avoid anything which might indicate that the priest is carrying the Blessed Sacrament.

*837. When the priest brings only one particle, he may purify the pyxis immediately after giving communion, and he will often find it very convenient to do so.[5] He may proceed thus:—Holding it with his left hand over the vessel prepared for the ablution of his fingers, he collects, with the index of his right, any fragments he may perceive, and makes them fall into the vessel. Then, if necessary, he pours a little water into the pyxis, and, having made it pass round the interior, pours it into the vessel. He then washes his fingers, and dries them with the purificator. If the pyxis be large enough, he may hold his thumb and index over it, and wash them with the water which he pours into it. The ablution is then given to the sick person, as directed before.[6]

*838. The rubric makes no provision for the case in which the priest must carry the Blessed Sacrament privately and without attendants, as in Ireland, and is at the same time called on, as may easily happen in time of pestilence, to administer the viaticum to several sick persons in different houses, before he returns to the church or to his own house.[7]

---

[1] Baruff., n. 202. Caval., Decr. xii. n. v. De Herdt, n. 18, iii.
[2] Vid. supra, n. 700.   [3] Loc. cit.   [4] Vid. supra, n. 815.
[5] Vid. St. Lig., lib. vi. n. 251. *Hic autem.*   [6] Supra, n. 268.
[7] It is only when he is thus *called on* that he can bring the Blessed Sacrament in the manner supposed. See the "Decretum" prefixed to this volume; also the "Letter of the Cardinal Prefect of Propaganda," in Appendix.

Having, in this case, brought more than one particle in the pyxis, is he, after giving communion, to give Benediction of the Blessed Sacrament, as above directed?[1] We have not seen the case discussed anywhere, but we think he should. The rubric seems to prescribe it in every case in which a particle remains in the pyxis, "si altera particula Sacramenti "superfuerit." In these circumstances, we think the priest should put the pyxis into its case or covering, and give the benediction with it thus covered. He should then fasten it round his neck, as before directed;[2] and, after this, but not sooner, he may lay aside the stole and surplice.

When he returns to the place where he keeps the Blessed Sacrament,[3] he should say the versicle and the prayer, "Deus "qui nobis," etc., prescribed in the rubric. It is unnecessary for him to place the pyxis on the altar if he can put it at once into the tabernacle, but he must be careful to genuflect before closing the door.[4]

839. In Holy Week, from the mass of Holy Thursday till the mass of Holy Saturday, communion can be administered only "per modum viatici."[5] If the Blessed Sacrament be brought to the sick during this time, the following rules should be observed, according to a decree of the Sacred Congregation.[6] 1° The color of the stole should be white. 2° The psalms may be recited with the "Gloria Patri," etc., at the end, but they are to be recited in a very low tone. 3° Benediction is not to be given in the church, nor is the Blessed Sacrament to be brought back to the altar of the church, but to be placed elsewhere.[7] The benediction with the pyxis, however, in the chamber of the sick person, may be given.[8]

*840. The viaticum can seldom be administered "intra "missam," for it has been decided by the Sacred Congregation[9] that the priest cannot give communion "intra missam," if he has to go to a place from which the altar is not visible. It may happen, however, that a person who is to receive the viaticum is in good health, and able to assist at mass, as, e. g., a criminal about to be executed;[10] or, it may be, in a hospital

[1] Supra, § xxv.   [2] Supra, n. 807.   [3] Vid. supra, n. 598.
[4] Vid. supra, cap. xii. § x.   [5] Vid. supra, n. 711.
[6] 15 Maii, 1745, Lucana, n. 4170.
[7] Vid. Caval., vol. iv. cap. i. De Feria V. in Cœna Domini, Decr. ix.
t. i. et cap. v. De Com. Infr.. Decr. xii. n. vii.
[8] De Herdt. pars vi. n. 18. i.
[9] 19 Decr. 1829. in una Florentin., ad 1, n. 4651.
[10] Vid. supra, n. 773.

or in a private house where mass is allowed to be celebrated, that the sick person is within view of the altar. In this case communion may be administered to him "intra missam." The ceremonies to be observed are exactly the same as those prescribed for communion in the church "intra missam,"[1] with the sole exception of the formula, which should be "*Ac-*"*cipe frater*," etc., if the communion be administered as a viaticum.[2] The color of the vestments is, of course, that which is suited to the mass, and may be even black.[3] This is the only case in which communion is given to the sick in a stole of any other color than white.[4]

841. If the viaticum be administered to two or more at the same time, as may happen in a hospital, or even in a private house, where several members of the family may be prostrated by fever or some other infectious disease, it may be administered to them successively, just as communion is administered in the church, provided they be in the same apartment, or even in adjoining apartments opening into each other. This is the opinion of De Herdt,[5] and of the "Mélanges Théolo-"giques;"[6] and there seems no reason why it may not be acted on.

In this case, the salutation at entrance, the sprinkling of holy water, the versicles and prayer, "*Exaudi*," etc., may serve for all in common.

After the "*Confiteor*," "*Misereatur vestri*," etc., should be said in the plural.

The ablution of the fingers may be given to any one of them, and need not be divided.

In the prayer, "*Domine sancte*," etc., "*fratri nostro*" (*vel*, "*sorori nostræ*") should be changed into "*fratribus nostris*," or, if all be females, "*sororibus nostris*."[7]

Lastly, the benediction with the pyxis may be given to all together.

---

[1] Supra, cap. xii. § xiii.　　　[2] De Herdt, n. 18, ii.
[3] S. C. R., Decr. cit. *in una Florentin.*, ad 2.　De Herdt, ibid.
[4] Vid. supra, n. 727 et n. 799.　　[5] Pars vi. n. 24, ii.
[6] VIme Série, 3me Cahier, pag. 503.　　[7] Vid. supra, n. 365.

CHAPTER XV.

§ I.—Extremæ Unctionis Sacramentum a Christo Domino institutum, tanquam cœlestis medicina non animæ solum, sed etiam corpori salutaris, omni studio ac di igentia periculose ægrotantibus adhibendum est, et eo quidem tempore, si fieri possit, cum illis adhuc integra mens et ratio viget, ut ad uberiorem Sacramenti gratiam percipiendam ipsi etiam suam fidem ac piam animi voluntatem conferre possint, dum sacro liniuntur Oleo.

842. This sacrament, according to the Catechism of the Council of Trent,[1] is called "Extreme Unction," because, amongst the other sacred unctions which are used in the Church, this is the last to be administered. The other unc tions are those used in Baptism, Confirmation, Ordination, and certain Consecrations.[2] Another reason why it is so called may be, because it is administered to the faithful only when they are laboring under some bodily infirmity which warns them that they may have nearly reached the *extreme* term of life. Hence it is called by the Council of Trent "Unctio infir- "morum,"[3] and "Sacramentum exeuntium."[4] It is called by the Greeks Εὐχέλαιον, i. e., (from Εὐχῆ, and Ἔλαιον), unction with prayer, and also τὸ Ἅγιον Ἔλαιον, i. e., the Holy Oil.

843. The Council of Trent has defined that Extreme Unction is a true sacrament instituted by Christ our Lord, and promulgated by the Apostle St. James.[5] The proof of the Catholic doctrine from the well-known text of this Apostle, "Infirmatur quis in vobis," etc.,[6] is fully developed by Bellarmine,[7] who shows that the unction there mentioned has all the conditions necessary to a true sacrament, and refutes the objections of the heretics.

844. The rubic here states that Extreme Unction has been instituted by our Lord as a celestial medicine for the health,

---

[1] Pars ii. cap. vi. n. 2.   [2] Catal., tit. v. n. i.
[3] Sess. xiv. *De Ext. Unct.*, cap. i.
[4] Ibid., xiv. *De Ext. Unct.*, cap. iii.
[5] Ibid., can. i.   [6] Cap. v. 14, 15.
[7] *De Extrema Unctione,* cap. ii. et iii.

not only of the soul, but of the body also. It is certain that it produces sanctifying grace like the other sacraments, and has, at the same time, like each of them, certain effects peculiar to itself.[1] Of these the principal, according to St. Liguori,[2] resting on the authority of St. Thomas, is to remove the spiritual torpor and weakness which are the result of actual sin, and which are most probably meant by the "reli-"quias peccati," mentioned by the Council of Trent.[3] This effect, so explained, is closely connected with the other spiritual effects mentioned by the council. Indeed, they may be said in some degree to suppose each other, for the grace of the sacrament, we are there taught, ... "raises up and "strengthens the soul of the sick person, by exciting in him "a great confidence in the divine mercy; whereby the sick "being supported bears more easily the inconveniences and "pains of his sickness, and more readily resists the tempta-"tions of the devil, ' who lies in wait for his heel ' (*Gen.*, iii. "15)."[4] All these may be regarded as constituting the primary effect intended in the institution of the sacrament.[5] Many hold that this effect supposes a spiritual infirmity resulting from actual sin, and that, therefore, no one who has not committed actual sin can validly receive the sacrament. This is the opinion of St. Thomas, who says that Extreme Unction cannot be administered to infants, because . . . . "non datur "contra reliquias originalis peccati nisi secundum quod "sunt per actualia peccata quodam modo confortatæ."[6] It is maintained, however, by Suarez and many others, that, to be a fit subject for the sacrament, it is enough that one be capable of sinning, and have that spiritual infirmity which results from original sin.[7] Suarez even holds that one, by nature liable to contract original sin, though by a special privilege exempted from it, could receive the primary effect of the sacrament; and that, therefore, the Blessed Virgin could receive, and more probably did receive, Extreme Unction, as well as Baptism.[8]

845. The second effect is the remission of sin; not only venial, but mortal sin, if the person be properly disposed.

---

[1] St. Lig., lib. vi. n. 6, not. v.
[2] Lib. vi. n. 731, *Secunda Sententia.* in fine.
[3] Sess. xiv. *De Ext. Unct.*, cap. ii.
[4] Loc. cit. Waterworth's translation.
[5] Vid. Suarez, *De Ext. Unct.*, Disp. xli: sec. i. n. 11, et seq.
[6] *Supplem.*, Quæs. 32, art. 4, ad 2.
[7] Disp. xlii. sect. ii. n. 7, et seq.　　[8] Loc. cit. n. 10 et 11.

It is true that, being one of the "sacramenta vivorum," it is not instituted primarily for the remission of sin, like Baptism or Penance.[1] Hence it requires that the recipient be in the state of grace. The rubric even directs[2] that, as a general rule, he should have already received the sacrament of Penance and the Viaticum. But should it happen, from any cause, that he is still in the state of sin, being invincibly ignorant of it, this sacrament received with attrition will restore him to the state of grace, as is clearly inferred from the words of St. James: "Et si in peccatis sit remittentur ei."[3] This effect of remitting sin it has, not merely *per accidens*, like the Eucharist or the other "sacramenta vivorum," but *per se*, as being directly intended in its institution, though not as its principal effect.[4]

846. A third effect which it sometimes has, is to restore the health of the body. The first effect, already explained, includes a certain alleviation of the bodily infirmity, which is often very perceptible, as many priests can attest from experience; but, besides, the sick person, by virtue of this sacrament, "at times obtains bodily health when expedient for the "welfare of the soul."[5] When and how far it *is* expedient in any particular case, can be known only to God; but it is not implied that one who is restored to health by virtue of this sacrament, will persevere and be saved; or that one who is not so restored, would not acquire greater merit and a higher degree of glory, if he were permitted to live longer. The nature of the resulting spiritual advantage on which the restoration of bodily health depends, is altogether determined by the order of God's wisdom and providence, and does not necessarily imply final perseverance.[6]

It is observed by St. Liguori that this effect, though due to the supernatural virtue of the sacrament, is not produced "per "modum miraculi," but by the operation of natural causes assisted by the sacrament.[7]

*847. It is to be administered only to those who are in danger of death from sickness—"periculose ægrotantibus," but, if possible, while they have the perfect use of their faculties, for, as the rubric here states, their own good dispositions

---

[1] Vid. St. Lig., lib. vi. n. �, not. 1.   [2] Infra, § ii.
[3] St. Lig., lib. vi. n. 731, *Commune est*.
[4] St. Lig., l. c. *Secunda Sententia*.   Vid. Suarez, Disp. xli. sect. 1.
Assertio II* n. 14. et seq.
[5] Conc. Trid., l. c.   [9] Vid. Suarez, l. c. sec. lv.
[7] Lib. vi. n. 714, *Advertendum autem*, 1.

make them receive more abundant grace from the sacrament.
Besides, as St. Liguori observes,[1] if administered in time, it
might restore the sick person to health, whereas it cannot have
this effect when the powers of nature are completely exhausted, since it does not operate " per modum miraculi." " It is
" a very grievous sin," says the Catechism of the Council of
Trent, " to defer the holy unction until, all hope of recovery
" now lost, life begins to ebb, and the sick person is sinking
" into insensibility. It is obvious that if administered whilst
" the mental faculties are yet unimpaired, and the sick man can
" bring to its reception sentiments of faith and devotion, this
" circumstance must contribute very much to enable him to
" partake more abundantly of the graces of the sacrament."[2]
It is an important duty of the pastor, then, to instruct the
faithful on this subject, and to remove the senseless fear which
many of them entertain of receiving Extreme Unction, as if
it cut off all hope of recovery.[3]

§ II.—In quo illud in primis ex generali Ecclesiæ consuetudine
observandum est, ut si tempus, et infirmi conditio permittat, ante
Extremam Unctionem, Pœnitentiæ et Eucharistiæ Sacramenta infirmis
præbeantur.

*848. It is here directed that, if circumstances permit, the
sick person should receive the sacraments of Penance and the
Holy Eucharist before Extreme Unction. It may easily happen that he is not in a condition to receive the viaticum, as,
e. g., if he be afflicted with vomit.[4] In this case, Extreme
Unction may be administered before the viaticum, which he
may be able to receive afterwards. In fact, Martène shows,
by abundant testimonies, that, according to the ancient
discipline of the Church, Extreme Unction was usually administered before the viaticum,[5] and, according to St. Liguori, it
would hardly be even a venial sin to follow the same order
at present.[6]

*849. But it is very hard to conceive a case in which the
sacrament of Penance may not be administered first. Extreme
Unction can be administered only by a priest; and it is
certain that any priest can hear and absolve one who is a fit

---

[1] Loc. cit. [2] Pars ii. cap. vi. n. 9.
[3] Vid. Benedict XIV, *De Syn. Diœc.*, lib. viii cap. vii. n. 2.
[4] Vid. supra, n. 782.
[5] *De Ant. Eccl. Rit.*, lib. i. cap. vii. art. ii. n. iii.
[6] Lib. vi. n. 716. Cfr. Benedict XIV, *De Synod. Diœc.*, lib. viii. cap.
viii. n. 1 et 2.

subject for Extreme Unction; for, to be a fit subject for Extreme Unction, he must be "in periculo mortis,"[1] and any priest can absolve one who is "in periculo mortis."[2] If the sick person, therefore, has the use of his faculties, there is plainly nothing to prevent him from receiving Penance when it is possible for him to receive Extreme Unction. There *can* be nothing, unless we fancy an almost incredible amount of ignorance or perversity on the part of the priest.[3]

850. Nay more, if he be conscious of mortal sin, he cannot licitly receive Extreme Unction, as being one of the "sacra-"menta vivorum," until he has recovered the state of grace either by perfect contrition or by receiving the sacrament of Penance.[4] In strictness, no doubt, it suffices that he elicit an act of contrition before Extreme Unction; but being in danger of death, and having the opportunity, he is certainly bound to confess either before or immediately after, and bound too, even by the divine precept, which urges precisely in his circumstances.[5] Hence, if he had reason to fear that he would not have time, or would be unable, to confess after receiving Extreme Unction, he would be bound to go to confession first. According to Suarez,[6] he would not be justified in even abridging his confession, or leaving it incomplete, in order that he might have time to receive Extreme Unction. Penance is necessary to him, "*necessitate medii*,"[7] and in his present state the divine precept of confession actually urges,[8] whereas Extreme Unction is necessary at most "*necessitate præcepti*," and, according to many theologians, the precept *of itself* does not bind *sub gravi*.[9] One in his circumstances, then, is sometimes strictly bound, and should, in every case, be earnestly recommended to receive Penance first.[10]

If he be not conscious of mortal sin, he is not, it is true, bound to go to confession; but if he desires to go, the priest is certainly bound to hear him; and as there are few Christians who, at the hour of death, have not this desire, even though they be not conscious of mortal sin, the rule for the priest is, to administer the sacrament of Penance, or at least to give the sick person an opportunity of receiving it, before he administers Extreme Unction.

---

[1] Vid. infra, § vi. [2] St. Lig., lib. vi. n. 561.
[3] Vid. Suarez, Disp. xliv. sect. i. n. 7.
[4] Lacroix. lib. vi. pars ii. n. 1108.
[5] De Lugo, *De Pænitentia*, Disp. xv. sec. iii. n. 37.
[6] Loc. cit. n. 9. [7] Con. Trid., Sess. xiv. cap. fl.
[8] De Lugo l. c. [9] St. Lig., n. 733. [10] Vid. Suarez, l. c. n. 9-11.

851. If he has not the use of his faculties, it is indeed possible that he might receive Extreme Unction validly and with fruit, although absolution in the same circumstances would be null. We may conceive a person in the state of mortal sin, and having attrition, which still morally continues, but who is now unconscious, and utterly unable to make any sign that would be a manifestation of sorrow or an acknowledgment of sin. If he were absolved in these circumstances, the absolution would be null, perhaps for want of the necessary intention,[1] but at all events "ex defectu materiæ sacramenti."[2] This is certain according to the Thomist theory regarding the matter of the sacrament, which is the theory now almost universally adopted; and it can hardly be denied even in the Scotist theory, which requires confession of some kind, not indeed as an essential part of the sacrament, but as a condition absolutely indispensable to its effect.[3] Such a one, however, could receive Extreme Unction validly,[4] and being attrite, would be restored by it to the state of grace.[5]

All this is perfectly true, and if the priest could be certain that any one is precisely in these circumstances, he should not absolve him, but at once administer Extreme Unction. But we believe he can never be certain of this; and in the doubt he not only may give, but he ought to give, absolution *sub conditione.*[6]

We conclude, therefore, that in practice there is no case in which Penance may not be administered absolutely or conditionally before Extreme Unction.

§ III.—Habeat igitur Parochus loco nitido et decenter ornato, in vase argenteo seu stanneo, diligenter custoditum sacrum Oleum infirmorum, quod singulis annis Feria V. in Cœna Domini ab Episcopo benedictum, veteri combusto, renovandum est.

852. The matter of this sacrament, according to the Council of Trent,[7] is "oil blessed by the bishop." The oil is understood to be "oil of olives," for the word used simply and without any qualification has this meaning; and besides,

---

[1] St. Lig., lib. vi. n. 447.
[2] De Lugo, *De Sacramentis*, Disp. ix. sect. vii. n. 124, et *De Pœnitentia*, Disp. xvii. sec. iii. n. 39.   Suarez, Disp. xxiii. sec. i. n. 13. Lacroix, lib. vi. par. ii. n. 1161. St. Lig., n. 482.
[3] Vid. Billuart, *De Pœnitentia*, Dissert. i. art. ii. *Dico* 5° et seq.
[4] Vid. infra, § vii.   [5] St. Lig., n. 731, *Commune est.*
[6] Ibid., l. c.   Lacroix, l. c. n. 1162.
[7] Sess. xiv. *De Ext. Unct.*, cap. i.

in the decree of Eugene IV, "Pro Armenis," the matter is said to be "oleum olivæ per episcopum benedictum."[1]

It is the common opinion of theologians, founded on the words of the councils, that the benediction is not merely required by precept, but is essential to the sacrament.[2] They are not, however, agreed as to the necessity of a special benediction. Some eminent theologians, amongst others Suarez,[3] maintain that oil blessed in any way by the bishop is sufficient for the validity of the sacrament, because it is still true to say that it is "oleum ab episcopo benedictum;" while others, no less eminent, maintain that it is not sufficient, unless it be specially blessed for this sacrament.[4]

*853. Hence, in case of necessity, but not otherwise, Extreme Unction might be administered conditionally with Chrism or Oil of Catechumens; and if the proper oil can afterwards be had, the sacrament should again be conferred.[5] St. Liguori says nothing of a condition in this repetition of the ceremony. Neither does St. Charles, in ordering a repetition in case of mistake as to the oil, even though the oil used had been Chrism or Oil of Catechumens.[6] Lacroix, however, says that the sacrament should be repeated in this case *sub conditione*,[7] and we think there should be a condition, at least implied in the intention, unless the state of the disease has changed in the meantime, so that the sacrament might be simply repeated.[8]

854. In the Latin Church the oil is always blessed by a bishop; and it was decided by a decree of the Congregation of the Inquisition, approved by Gregory XVI,[9] that, even in case of necessity, a priest cannot use for Extreme Unction oil blessed by himself.

In the Greek Church, however, it is blessed by simple priests; and there can be no doubt that this benediction suffices. It is certain, therefore, notwithstanding the contrary opinion of some theologians, that a simple priest, when expressly or tacitly commissioned by the Pope, can validly bless the oil for this sacrament. . . . "Res videtur explora-

---

[1] Denzinger, *Enchiridion*, lxxiii. n. 595.   St. Lig., lib. vi. n. 709, *Certum est.*
[2] St. Lig., n. 709.   [3] Disp. xl. sect. i. n. 9.
[4] St. Lig., ibid. *Dub.* 2.   [5] Ibid., ibid.
[6] *Act. Eccl. Mediol.*, para iv. Instruct.   Extr. Unct. § *De Diligentia in ministrando*, pag. 450.
[7] Lib. vi. pars ii. n. 2090.   [8] Vid. infra, § xiv.
[9] 14 Sept. 1842, Denzinger, *Enchiridion*, cxxv.

"tissima, quam nemini liceat in questionem adducere," are the
words of Benedict XIV.[1]

The holy oils are blessed by the bishop on Holy Thursday,
and should be renewed every year, what remains of the old
oils being burned in the manner before explained.[2]

855. The present rubric directs that the "Oleum infirmo-
"rum" be kept in a silver or tin vessel, in a place perfectly
clean and suitably ornamented. Baruffaldi[3] recommends that
it be kept in a press or safe placed in the wall of the church
on the gospel side of the high altar, or altar where the Blessed
Sacrament is kept, so that a lamp may be always burning
before it; and that the door of the press have on it, in legible
characters, "SANCTUM OLEUM INFIRMORUM." The
first Synod of Westminster ordered that, in the erection of
new churches, provision should be made for keeping it in this
manner;[4] and it is the most suitable provision where it can
be effected.[5] The rubrics undoubtedly suppose that, at least
as a general rule, it is kept in the church; and the Sacred
Congregation, having been consulted on the subject, decided[6]
that a priest is not justified by any existing custom in keeping it in his house, unless when he lives at a great distance
from the church.[7]

*856. In Ireland, however, and in other countries similarly
circumstanced, the priest is, generally speaking, obliged to
keep it in his house; but he is certainly bound, as the Sacred
Congregation adds, in the decision just referred to, to observe
what the rubric prescribes, "quoad honestam et decentem
"tutamque custodiam." Should he have permission to keep
the Blessed Sacrament in his house, as he usually has,[8] he is
not permitted to put the holy oil in the tabernacle with the
Blessed Sacrament, this being prohibited by a decree of the
Sacred Congregation of Bishops;[9] but he can easily provide a
suitable place for it in the room or oratory where he keeps the
Blessed Sacrament. He might have a small drawer for the
purpose immediately beside the tabernacle. We think the
drawer might be put even in the framework of the tabernacle,
under or at either side, without any infringement of the decree.

---

[1] *De Synod. Diœc.*, lib. viii. cap. i. n. 4.
[2] Vid. supra, chap. iii. § xxxiii. et seq.
[3] Tit. xxvii. n. 40, et seq.   [4] Decr. xx. *De Sac. Ext. Unct.*, 4º.
[5] Vid. supra, cap. iii. § xxxix.
[6] 16 Dec. 1826, *in una Gandaven.*, ad Quæs. iii. n. 4623.
[7] Vid. *Annotationem*, in Decr. cit.
[8] Vid. supra, n. 598.   [9] Vid. supra, n. 612.

§ IV.—Id tamen si forte infra annum aliquo modo ita deficiat, ut suf-ficere non posse videatur, neque aliud benedictum haberi queat, modico oleo non benedicto in minori quantitate superinfuso, reparari potest.

857. What was said in a preceding chapter[1] regarding the oil and chrism used in Baptism, may be repeated here regarding the "Oleum infirmorum." If, during the year, the supply becomes nearly exhausted, and a further supply cannot easily be procured, unblessed oil may be added, but in less quantity; and this, too, as often as may be necessary, although what is thus added, taking all the additions together, may exceed in quantity what was first blessed.[2]

Should there be any delay in procuring the new oil blessed on Holy Thursday, the old oil may be used but only in case of necessity.[3] We have already dwelt on the obligation of the pastor to procure a timely supply of the holy oils after their consecration,[4] and it is enough to observe here, that Benedict XIV,[5] and the continuator of Gardellini,[6] urge this obligation as strictly with reference to the "Oleum infirmorum," as with reference to the oils required in Baptism.

§ V.—Oleum porro ipsum vel per se solum, vel in bombacio seu re simili servari potest; sed ad evitandum effusionis periculum multo com-modius ad infirmos defertur in bombacio.

858. Besides the vessel for containing the annual supply, there should be another smaller one of silver, and legibly marked, to contain what is immediately required for use, absorbed in a little cotton or other like material, as here recommended by the rubric.[7]

§ VI.—Debet autem hoc Sacramentum infirmis praeberi, qui cum ad usum rationis pervenerint, tam graviter laborant, ut mortis periculum imminere videatur; et iis qui prae senio deficiunt, et in diem videntur morituri etiam sine alia infirmitate.

*859. This rubric determines the subject of Extreme Unction. It is to be administered only to those who are in danger of death from disease already affecting the body. The words of St. James, Ἀσθενεῖ τις and καμνοντα,[8] imply that the person is laboring under a dangerous illness.

[1] Chap. iii. § xxxiv. et seq.　　[2] Supra, n. 257, 258.
[3] Gavant., Manuale Episcoporum, V. Ext. Unct., n. 10.
[4] Supra, n. 251, et seq.　　[5] Instit., lxxx. n. 3.
[6] Annot. in Decr. 16 Dec. 1826, in una Gandaven., ad iv. n. 4693.
[7] Vid. chap. iii. n. 261, et seq.　　[8] Cap. v. 14, 15.

Such is their usual acceptation,[1] and so they are interpreted
by the unanimous consent of theologians.[2] Hence its
administration to one in sound health, or to one but slightly
indisposed, would be, according to the common opinion, not
only illicit, but invalid. The practice observed in the Greek
Church of anointing all who are present when the oils are
blessed on Holy Thursday, is sometimes urged as an objection; but this practice is to be understood as merely a pious
ceremony, and not as a sacramental unction.[3]

It is enough, however, that a person is prudently judged,
from the apparent symptoms, to be in danger, even though
the danger does not really exist. This appears to be con
veyed in the present rubric, which requires only that one be so
ill, "ut mortis periculum imminere videatur."[4]

As soon, then, as it can be prudently pronounced that one
is in danger of death from sickness, even though the danger
be not proximate, even though there be a hope of recovery,
the sacrament may be administered; and there is a strict
obligation, as we have seen,[5] of not deferring it till the last
moment.[6]

* 860. It is to be administered only to those who have
had the use of reason. It cannot be administered even
validly to children who have not yet attained the use of
reason; for as they are incapable of yielding to temptation,
it could not have, with regard to them, the primary effect
before explained;[7] nor, failing this, any of its secondary
effects.[8] But it may be administered to children who have
attained the use of reason, although it be judged inexpedient
as yet to admit them to Holy Communion.[9] Benedict XIV
lays it down as a principle, that when children are considered capable of receiving the sacrament of Penance, they
may be also considered capable of receiving Extreme Unction :
"Quandocumque censentur capaces Sacramenti Pœnitentiæ,
"sunt pariter idonei reputandi ad Extremam Unctionem, quæ
"est illius complementum, quamvis nondum tantâ polleant
"judicii maturitate ut videantur apti ad rite participandam

[1] Vid. Estium in loc.
[2] Bened. XIV, De Syn. Diœc., lib. viii. cap. v. n. 5.
[3] St. Lig., lib. vi. n. 713.   Bened. XIV., l. c.
[4] Vid. St. Lig., n. 714.   [5] Supra, n. 847.
[6] Vid. St. Lig., l. c. Advertendum, 1 et 2.
[7] Supra, n. 844.   [8] St. Lig., n. 718.
[9] Ibid., n. 720.

"Eucharistiam, de cujus ineffabili excellentiâ et sanctitate
"non ita facile edoceri queunt."[1]

Hence, although the viaticum, as has been said in a
previous chapter,[2] should be sometimes administered to
children sooner than they would be, in the ordinary course,
admitted to first communion, it would appear that Extreme
Unction may be administered to them at a still earlier age
than the viaticum. When it is doubted whether a child has
attained the use of reason, the sacrament should be conferred
conditionally.[3]

*861. It should be administered to those who are sinking
from old age, although they may have no other infirmity, for
this is, in itself, an infirmity sufficiently comprehended under
the terms used by the Apostle.

§ VII.—Infirmis autem, qui dum sana mente et integris sensibus
essent illud petierint, seu verisimiliter petiissent, seu dederint signa
contritionis, etiamsi deinde loquelam amiserint, vel amentes effecti sint,
vel delirent, aut non sentiant, nihilominus præbeatur.

*862. The different kinds of intention distinguished by
theologians, have been already noticed.[4] It appears from
the present rubric that, for Extreme Unction, it is sufficient
that the sick person have an *interpretative* intention; in other
words, that he *would have* the intention of receiving it if he
had now the use of his faculties, though, in point of fact, he
has not and may never have had, formally and explicitly,
such intention.[5] An intention or disposition of this kind is
rightly presumed in all who have lived as Catholics, unless
there be evidence to the contrary;[6] and hence it is to be
administered to those who have fallen into delirium, not only
when it is known that they desired it, or desired the assistance of a priest before falling into that state, but also when it
is ascertained that they lived as Catholics.

It is in such circumstances—when the person is unable to
make any sign of sorrow or acknowledgment of sin—that the
case already discussed may arise : that, namely, in which Extreme Unction can be validly administered while Penance
cannot, and in which, therefore, the salvation of one who is
dying may depend on his receiving Extreme Unction.[7]

[1] *De Syn. Diœc.*, lib. viii. cap. vi. n. 2.   [2] Chap. xi. n. 640.
[3] St. Lig., n. 719.   Baruff., tit. xxvii. n. 62.
[4] Chap. ii. n. 137.   [5] St. Lig., lib. vi. n. 82.
[6] Baruff., n. 67.   Lacroix, lib. vi. pars i. n. 172.
[7] Vid. supra, n. 851.

§ VIII.—Sed si Infirmus, dum phrenesi aut amentia laborat, verisimiliter posset quidquam facere contra reverentiam Sacramenti, non inungatur, nisi periculum tollatur omnino.

*863. Those who have been insane from infancy, are incapable of receiving this sacrament, for the reason already assigned in the case of infants.[1] But if they have had at any time a lucid interval, it is to be administered if it can be without danger of irreverence. To prevent this danger, they may be held or bound, at least in circumstances in which the sacrament may be judged necessary.[2] If there be a doubt as to whether the person has ever had a lucid interval, it should be administered, but, according to St. Liguori, "sub con-"ditione."[3]

§ IX.—Impœnitentibus vero, et qui in manifesto peccato mortali moriuntur, et excommunicatis, et nondum baptizatis penitus denegetur.

*864. The rubric here enumerates certain classes to whom the sacrament cannot be administered. By the impenitent, are understood those who are known to have been guilty of grievous sin, and who give no reason to think that they have since repented.[4] It is not to be administered to one who is manifestly dying in mortal sin—to a murderer, for example, who is seized with a fatal illness, or receives a mortal wound in the act of killing his victim.

If such a one, however, survives even for a short time, and gives signs of repentance, he may be absolved,[5] and there is no reason why he may not be anointed also, for it cannot be said of him that he is dying "in manifesto peccato mortali." But if he be deprived of his senses in the very act of sin, though he may be absolved conditionally, according to St. Liguori,[6] the present rubric would seem to deny him Extreme Unction. Some theologians, however, would permit him to be anointed.[7] Bouvier[8] and Scavini[9] say that the same rule is to be followed in administering Extreme Unction as in giving absolution. In practice we should act on this opinion, and anoint, as well as absolve, unless there be evident signs of impenitence.

---

[1] Supra, n. 860. Benedict XIV, lib. viii. cap. vi. n. 3.
[2] Baruff, n. 70. Lacroix, lib. vi. pars ii. n. 2110.
[3] Lib. vi. n. 732, in parenth.
[4] Baruff., n. 76.   [5] Vid. St. Lig., n. 483.   [6] Loc. cit.
[7] Vid. Baruff., n. 76. Cleric., De Ext. Unct., Decis. lxxx. n. 6.
[8] De Ext. Unct., cap. vii. art. iii. 7°.
[9] De Ext. Unct., Disp. ii. cap. iv. Quær. 2, Impœnitentibus, etc.

865. It cannot be conferred on one who is excommunicated, until he is first absolved from the excommunication; but this cannot, we think, present much difficulty in practice, if the person be otherwise disposed and prepared to receive the sacrament; for if so, he must have sorrow for the offence by which he incurred excommunication, and be anxious to be reconciled to the Church, and being also, as must be supposed, " in periculo mortis," he can be absolved from the censure by any priest.[1]

866. The rubric says nothing of interdict, but we may observe that, if it be *personal*, what has just been said of excommunication may be applied to it. If it be *local*, however, Extreme Unction cannot be administered to any in the place except in case of necessity, according to Collet;[2] but St. Liguori gives it as the common opinion, that it may be administered to religious, and cites, without disapproval, the opinion of some who maintain that it may be administered generally.[3]

*867. Those who are not yet baptized are incapable of receiving this or any other sacrament.[4] But if an adult be baptized in a dangerous illness, or fall into a dangerous illness immediately after receiving Baptism, Extreme Unction should be administered to him; for though Baptism remits all sin both as to guilt and punishment,[5] it does not produce what is the primary effect of Extreme Unction, for it does not remove the torpor and weakness which are the result of sin, nor give a special strength against the temptations of the devil in the last agony.[6]

§ X.—Non ministretur etiam prælium inituris, aut navigationem, aut peregrinationem, aut alia pericula subituris, aut reis ultimo supplicio mox afficiendis, aut pueris rationis usum non habentibus.

*868. It has been already stated, that the subject of Extreme Unction must be in danger of death from some infirmity actually affecting the person to whom it is administered.[7] It is not enough that he be in danger of death, or even certain of suffering death, by violence or from any external cause. Hence it cannot be administered to those mentioned in the present rubric: to soldiers entering the field of battle, to

---

[1] Vid. Gury, *De Censuris*, cap. i. art. iv. n. 952.
[2] *De Censuris*, cap. iii. art. ii.   [3] Lib. vii. n. 334, in parenth.
[4] St. Lig., lib. vi. n. 79.
[5] Conc. Trid., Sess. v. *Decr. de Peccat. Origin.*, § v.
[6] St. Lig., n. 721. Vid. supra, n. 844.
[7] Supra, n. 859.

persons undertaking a perilous voyage or journey, or to crim
inals about to be executed.   But if any of these has already
suffered what is sufficient to cause death—if a soldier, for instance, is mortally wounded, or if a criminal, after hearing
his sentence, gets into a fever, or if he is mortally injured by
a fall from the scaffold, or if, being condemned to die by slow
torture, he has already suffered enough to cause death—in
any such case Extreme Unction may be administered if there
be an opportunity, since there is then a dangerous ailment
actually affecting the body.[1]

*869. Women cannot be anointed on account of the ordi-
nary pains of childbirth; but if these be very severe, and
such as to endanger life, the sacrament may be ad ministered.[2]

We have seen under a preceding rubric that it cannot be
administered to children who have not the use of reason.[3]

§ XI.—Si quis autem laborat in extremis, et periculum immineat, ne
'ecedat antequam finiantur Unctiones, cito ungatur, incipiendo ab eo
seo: *Per istam sanctam Unctionem*, etc., ut infra: deinde, si adhuc
supervivat, dicantur Orationes prætermissæ suo loco positæ.

870. Several questions of great importance in practice are
suggested under this rubric.   When there is reason to apprehend that the sick person may die before the whole ceremony
as given in the ritual can be performed, the priest is here
directed to omit what precedes, and commence with the application of the matter and form, and afterwards, if the person
survives, to supply what has been omitted.   There is no
difficulty, if time permits the unction of the five organs of
sense,[4] with the form appropriate to each; but if there is not
time, or, what comes to the same, if it is feared there will not
be time for this, how is the priest to act?   It would seem
from the rubrics that he should proceed with the usual
unctions as far as he can, and cease if death takes place
before he has completed them.

*871. But theologians commonly teach that, in this case,
he should apply a single unction, with the form expressing
all the senses.   St. Liguori recommends him to pronounce the
form as follows: "*Per istam sanctam Unctionem et suam
"piissimam misericordiam indulgeat tibi Dominus quidquid*

[1] Baruff., n. 83, 84.   Cleric., Decis. lxxix. n. 34, et seq.
[2] St. Lig., n. 713, Dub. 3.
[3] Vid. supra, n. 869.
[4] Vid. infra, § xv.

"*deliquisti per sensus,—visum, auditum, gustum, odoratum, et*
"*tactum,*" putting the word "*deliquisti*" before the expression
of the senses; for should the person expire before it is pronounced, the sacrament would be null.[1]   Benedict XIV,
speaking of this case, says: " Parochos monebit (episcopus) ut
"cum prudenter timent ægrotum decessurum priusquam omnes
"absolvantur quinque sensuum unctiones, unicum sensum
"inungant formam universalem pronuntiando; . . . . quinimo
"in prædicto eventu consultius esse ut caput, e quo omnium
"sensuum nervi descendunt, sub eâdem formâ universali inun-
"gatur, non immerito advertit Coninck (*De Sacram.*, disp. 19,
"dub. iii. n. 2).   Ne veró parochi hac libertate abutantur, ex-
"pedit ut episcopus simul serio eosdem admoneat a gravis
"culpæ reatu non excusari qui extra casum veræ necessitatis
"vel unam ex quinque sensuum unctionibus prætermittit."[2]
St. Liguori says: " Tempore pestis, vel alia urgente necessi-
"tate, poterit adhiberi sub conditione una unctio in aliquo
"sensu (et consultius in capite)."[3]

*872. It is not stated by either of these authorities to what
part of the head this single unction should be applied; but
they seem to convey that the part is not one of the organs, as,
e. g., an eye or an ear, since the head is distinguished in the
above extracts from any particular organ.   The " Modo
" Piatico" directs that it be applied to the forehead, " nella
" fronte."[4]   Baruffaldi appears to recommend the same,[5] and so
does Falise.[6]   It would be well, we think, to follow this in
practice.   But, after applying the thumb to the forehead, we
would instantly, and without making the sign of the cross,[7]
pass it over one eye, over the nose and lips, and then apply it
to one ear.   We should thus have the unction of all the
organs, the forehead holding the place of the hand.   We are
convinced this could be done as quickly as the words of the
form above given could be pronounced.   In most cases, even
the hand, after the ear, could be anointed within the time.
The reasons for preferring this mode are given hereafter.[8]   If,
however, this mode be impossible, on account of the position
of the head, or from some other cause, any organ, or, if all
else fails, any part of the body that can be reached, may be
anointed.[9]

[1] Lib. vi. n. 710.   Vid. Baruffaldi. tit. xxvii. n. 125.
[2] *De Synod. Diœc.*, lib. viii. cap. iii. n. 5.   [3] Loc. cit.
[4] IIIme Partie, sect. i. chap. iv. n. 4.   [5] Cap. ix.
[6] Vid. infra, cap. xvi. § x.   [7] Tit. xxvii. n. 125.
[8] Infra, § xv. n. 888.   [9] Cleric., *De Ext. Unct.*, Decis. lxvi. n. 8.

*873. In the words above cited, St. Liguori supposes that the unction takes place "sub conditione." Neither Benedict XIV, nor the "Modo Pratico," makes mention of a condition; but they, perhaps, suppose it, as the validity of the sacrament, though highly probable, is not quite certain.[1]

We have nowhere seen the words to be used, if a person chooses to express the condition; but we think it may be accurately expressed thus: "*Si hæc materia sit sufficiens*: "*Per istam sanctam*," etc. In all cases of this kind, it is enough that the condition be such as, if actually placed, must remove the existing doubt regarding the validity of the sacrament. When a form of words expressing the condition is prescribed by the rubric, of course it should be used; but where no form is prescribed, the condition need not be expressed in words: it is enough that it be formed in the mind.[2]

If the person survives, the organs are to be anointed in the usual way,[3] with the form appropriate to each, but conditionally.[4] The condition here expressed, or mentally formed, would be, "*Si non valeat unctio facta*," or one equivalent.

*874. Nothing but a case of real necessity can justify the priest in omitting even one of the five unctions, as is clearly laid down in the above extract from Benedict XIV.[5] The case in which it is feared that the person may die before they are completed, is, undoubtedly, such a case of necessity. But is there any other, it may be asked, in which the priest is justified in applying a single unction in the manner explained? The "Modo Pratico"[6] mentions two others. The first is the case of pestilence. This is commonly admitted by theologians,[7] and seems to be included by St. Liguori in the words above cited, "tempore pestis," which may be taken to mean, "when "there is danger of catching the infection," for it cannot be implied that in pestilence there is always danger of death before the unctions can be completed.

The second case is that in which the sacrament is to be administered to a number of sick, and in which there is danger that, if the five unctions are applied to each, there will not be time to administer the sacrament to all.[8] This case must be of frequent occurrence in time of epidemic, and

---

[1] Vid. infra, § xv.
[2] Gury, ii. n. 206, Quær. 7°.   Vid. supra, cap. iii. § x.
[3] Lacroix, lib. vi. pars ii. n. 2121.   [4] Modo Pratico, cap. ix.
[5] Supra, n. 871.   [6] Loc. cit.
[7] Vid. Cleric., Decis. lxvi. n. 9.   Bened. XIV., *De Syn. Diœc*, lib xiii. cap. xix. n. 29.   [8] Modo Pratico, l. c.

must, no doubt, be often dealt with by military chaplains in time of war, when they have to administer the last sacraments to a number of wounded men together.

§ XII.—Si vero dum inungitur, infirmus decedat, Presbyter ultra non procedat, et prædictas Orationes omittat.

Quod si dubitet an vivat adhuc, unctionem prosequatur, sub conditione pronuntiando formam dicens : *Si vivis, per istam sanctam Unctionem,* etc., ut infra.

*875. If the priest be sure that the person is dead before he has completed the unctions, he is to proceed no further : he is not even to supply the prayers that may have been omitted. The whole rite supposes the person to be living, and should therefore cease the instant it is known that he is dead. The priest should in this case read the prayers for a soul just departed, commencing, " *Subvenite Sancti Dei,*" etc.[1]

But if he be in doubt, as is usually the case in practice, for it is very difficult to ascertain the exact moment of death, he is to proceed with the unctions, using the conditional form here prescribed, " *Si vivis, per istam,*" etc. The rubric clearly supposes that the priest is administering the sacrament by anointing the organs in the usual way. But from what has been said above,[2] it may be inferred that as soon as the doubt, whether the person be alive, occurs, he should instantly apply a single unction with the general form, and then proceed with the separate unctions, resuming where he left off, and using in all the condition, " *Si vivis,*" etc.

§ XIII.—Si autem acciderit infirmum post peccatorum suorum Confessionem ad exitum vitæ properare, tunc cum sacro Viatico poterit et Oleum Infirmorum ad eum deferri per ipsum Sacerdotem qui defert sacram Eucharistiam. Si tamen alius Presbyter, vel Diaconus, qui Oleum sanctum deferat, haberi possit, per ipsum deferatur, qui superpelliceo indutus, cum Oleo sacro occulte delato sequatur Sacerdotem Viaticum portantem ; et postquam infirmus Viaticum sumpserit, inungatur a Sacerdote.

876. In countries where the Blessed Sacrament is carried to the sick in solemn procession, the priest is not allowed to carry the " oleum infirmorum " along with it, unless in the case here mentioned by the rubric, i. e., the case in which both the Viaticum and Extreme Unction must be administered at the same time, while there is no other priest, nor even a deacon, to carry the holy oil. In this case, the rubric permits the

---

[1] De Herdt, n. 23, i. 3°.   [2] Supra, n. 871.

priest to carry the holy oil as well as the Blessed Sacrament, but it does not explain in what manner.   De Herdt says the vessel of oil should be fastened round the neck, and carried under the surplice, so as not to appear; because if the rubric directs that even another priest, or a deacon carrying it after him, should carry it secretly, much more should this be required of the priest himself, who is publicly carrying the Blessed Sacrament.[1]

*877. But what the rubric regards as exceptional, is, in Ireland, and other countries similarly circumstanced, the general rule.   On account of the scarcity of priests, and the distance in most cases of the houses of the faithful from the church or parochial residence, the priest, when called on to attend a sick person, usually goes prepared to administer both the Viaticum and Extreme Unction, before he leaves him. He is, moreover, obliged to carry the Blessed Sacrament, as well as the oil, privately.[2]

In case of very urgent necessity, the holy oil might be carried by a laic, according to De Herdt[3] and the continuator of Gardellini[4]   Hence, if a priest, attending one that is dying, had not the holy oil with him, he might send a laic to bring it, while he himself is engaged hearing the dying man's confession.[5]

§ XIV.—In eadem infirmitate hoc Sacramentum iterari non debet, nisi diuturna sit, ut si, cum infirmus convaluerit, iterum in periculum mortis inciderit.

* 878. Extreme Unction can be administered only to those who are in danger of death, as we have seen.[6]   When once administered, it cannot be repeated *while the same danger continues*.   Benedict XIV mentions some strange opinions which were held on this subject.   One of these was, that a person could receive Extreme Unction only once during his life.   Another, that it could be received only after an interval of three years from the last.   In the opposite extreme, he cites some ancient rituals which prescribed a repetition of the unctions, as well as the administration of the viaticum, every day for seven successive days.[7]

[1] De Herdt, pars vi. n. 24, l.   [2] Vid. infra, chap. xvi. § 11.
[3] Loc. cit. n. 20, i.
[4] *Annotat.* in Decr. 16 Dec. 1826, in *Gandaven.*, ad 2 Quæs. 1 2.
1623.   [6] Vid. *Annotat.* cit.   [6] Supra, § vi.
[7] *De Synod. Diœc.*, lib. viii. cap. viii. n. 3 et 4.

But these opinions and practices were confined to a few. The doctrine commonly received and acted on at all times is that which is conveyed in the present rubric. It is the doctrine taught by St. Thomas, and after him by all theologians, viz., that in the same sickness, and while the same danger of death continues, the sacrament cannot be administered a second time (according to many, not even validly),[1] but that it may be repeated as often as a person, having recovered from the danger, again falls into it, even during the same sickness.[2]

879. The great difficulty in practice sometimes is, to ascertain when a person during the same illness has so far recovered that it should be again administered in case of relapse. In an illness of very short duration, it is never administered a second time, for in such a case the recovery is either complete or merely apparent. Hence the rubric says, "cum diuturna sit."

880. But a mere continuance of life, no matter how long, does not of itself justify the administration of the sacrament a second time. All theologians seem to be agreed that a recovery of some kind is required. St. Lignori, after citing the words of our rubric, says: "Unde adverte quod in morbo "diuturno, si infirmus post unctionem certe manserit in eodem "periculo mortis, non poterit rursus ungi."[3] Generally speaking, however, changes for the better do take place in diseases of lengthened duration, as consumption or dropsy. In one of these, a person in manifest danger of death at present may be over this danger in a few days, and be tolerably well for several weeks or months, although it is known that the disease still continues, and is even likely to end fatally. In such a case, when the disease takes another turn, and the person is again in similar danger, Extreme Unction may be again administered, for, though the disease is the same, the *state* of the disease is different.

We cannot do better than give here the words of St Thomas on the subject, quoted by Benedict XIV:[4] "Hoc "sacramentum non respicit tantum infirmitatem sed etiam "infirmitatis statum; quia non debet dari nisi infirmis qui "secundum humanam æstimationem videntur morti appro "pinquare. Quædam ergo infirmitates non sunt diuturnæ;

[1] Vid. Lacroix, lib. vi. p. ii. n. 2103.
[2] Benedict XIV, l. c. St. Lig., u. 715.
[3] Loc. cit. [4] Ibid.

"unde si in iis datur hoc sacramentum, tunc cum homo ad illum
"statum perveniat, quod sit in periculo mortis, non recedit
"a statu illo, nisi infirmitate curatâ : et ita iterum non debet
"inungi ; sed si recidivum patiatur, erit alia infirmitas, et
"poterit fieri alia inunctio.   Quædam vero sunt ægritudines
"diuturnæ, ut hectica et hydropisis, et hujusmodi ; et in talibus
"non debet fieri inunctio, nisi quando videntur perducere ad
"periculum mortis ; et si homo illum articulum evadat, eâdem
"infirmitate durante, et iterum ad similem statum per illam
"infirmitatem reducatur, iterum potest inungi ; quia jam est
"quasi alius infirmitatis status, quamvis non sit alia infirmitas
"simpliciter."[1]

881. To verify the condition of the rubric, "si convaluerit,"
it is not enough that the patient appears to be out of danger
for a few days.   There must be probable ground for believing
that he has really got out of danger, and there must, therefore,
be an improvement that continues for a considerable time.[2]

It is the practice of some, in all cases of tedious illness, to
repeat Extreme Unction after the interval of a month.   It
would be hard to reconcile this practice with the rubric and
the words of St. Liguori above cited,[3] when it is certain that
the same danger has continued all the time.   But it often
happens that, all things considered, there is a doubt whether
the state of the disease has really changed—whether the
danger has at any time ceased, or has all along continued ;
and in this case of doubt the priest is recommended to administer the sacrament again, as more in accordance with the
ancient practice of the Church.[4]   Now, it may be contended
that there is, generally speaking, ground for such a doubt in
the case of any one who lives a month after receiving Extreme
Unction, and is still in danger of death ; and that, therefore,
in a tedious illness, the sacrament should, as a general rule,
be repeated after the lapse of a month.

882. If one has received Extreme Unction without the
necessary dispositions, and therefore without fruit, though
validly, the sacrament cannot, on this account, be repeated
during the same danger.   But theologians commonly teach
that, in such circumstances, the sacrament would revive and
produce its effect, as soon as the requisite dispositions are
present.[5]   If the want of these dispositions at the time was

[1] In Supplem., 3ᵗⁱˢ partis, Quæs. 33, art. ii.
[2] St. Lig., l. c. in fine.   [3] Supra, n. 880
[4] Bened. XIV.; l. c.   St. Lig., l. c.   [5] St. Lig., n. 707, · Quær. ii

not culpable, and if no mortal sin has been committed in the meantime, attrition would suffice for the reviviscence: otherwise, perfect contrition or the sacrament of Penance would be necessary, just as in the case of the reviviscence of Baptism.[1]

883. Should one who has received Extreme Unction with the proper dispositions, fall into grievous sin while the same danger still continues, he would lose, from that moment, the right to those special helps that are the effect of the sacrament but that right would be restored to him, along with sanctifying grace, on his making an act of perfect contrition, or receiving sacramental absolution.[2]

§ XV.—Quinque vero corporis partes præcipue ungi debent, quas veluti sensuum instrumenta homini natura tribuit, nempe oculi, aures, nares, os et manus: attamen pedes etiam et renes ungendi sunt; sed renum unctio in mulieribus, honestatis gratia, semper omittitur; atque etiam in viris quando infirmus commode moveri non potest. Sed sive in mulieribus sive in viris, alia corporis pars pro renibus ungi non debet.

884. "The sacred unction," says the Catechism of the Council of Trent, " is to be applied, not to the entire body, "but to the organs of sense only: to the eyes, because the "organs of sight; to the ears, because the organs of hearing; "to the nostrils, because the organs of smelling; to the "mouth, because the organ of taste and speech; to the hands, "because the organs of touch. True, the sense of touch is "diffused alike throughout the body, but the hands are its "principal seat. This manner of administering Extreme "Unction is observed throughout the universal Church, and "admirably accords with the medicinal nature of this sacra- "ment. As in corporal infirmity, although it affects the "entire body, the cure is applied to that part only which is "the source and origin of the disease; so is this sacrament "applied, not to the entire body, but to those members which "are preëminently the organs of sense, and also to the loins, ·which are, as it were, the seat of concupiscence; and to the "feet, by which we move from one place to another."[3]

*885. It is certain that the unction of the feet, as well as that of the loins, may be omitted, without affecting the validity of the sacrament. It is also certain that when the organ is double, it is enough for the validity to anoint one,

---

[1] Vid. supra, n. 449.
[2] Vid De Lugo, *De Sac. Pœnitent.*, Disp. xi. sect. iii. n. 49.
[3] Pars i. cap. vi. n. 10.

as, e. g., one eye for the sense of sight. · Nor is it necessary to the validity to observe the order of the parts anointed.[1]

*886. But theologians are not agreed whether or not the unction simply of the five organs of sense be necessary. The more common opinion, according to St. Liguori,[2] affirms that it is; and since there is here question of the validity of the sacrament, this opinion, as the safer, must be followed in practice.[3] It is probable, however, that a single unction suffices, and we have already seen how this opinion is to be acted on in case of necessity.[4]

887. The several opinions that are or might be held on this subject, are expressed in the following propositions:—

1° The unction of the five organs of sense, with the form appropriate to each, is essential.

2° The unction of the five organs, with one general form expressing all the senses, is sufficient.

3° The unction of the forehead for all the organs, with the general form, is sufficient.

4° The unction of one organ, with the general form, is sufficient.

5° The unction of any part of the body, with the general form, is sufficient.

6° The unction of one organ of sense, with the form appropriate to that sense, is sufficient.

Now those who maintain that the unction of the five organs of sense is necessary, may hold either the first or the second of these opinions; and from the way in which some authors speak on the subject, it is difficult to determine which of the two they do hold. Generally speaking, they seem to hold the first. At all events, the first opinion is the one which St. Liguori says is "communior et tutior."[5] It is manifestly the "tutior," and since there is here question of the validity of the sacrament, this is the opinion which must be followed in practice, unless when necessity may require one to act on some of the others.[6]

888. The second opinion appears to be somewhat more probable than any of those which follow. It is sustained by all that can be alleged in favor of any of them, and has, besides, the advantage of approximating more to the first, for in it there is really the unction of the five organs, and the

[1] St. Lig., n. 710, *Certum est.*
[2] Vid. St. Lig., lib. i. n. 48
[3] Loc. cit. n. 710.
[4] Loc. cit. *Secunda sententia.*
[5] Supra, n. 872.
[6] Vid. St. Lig., lib. vi. n. 57.

sole doubt is regarding the sufficiency of the form. Hence, in case of necessity, several theologians recommend the priest to follow it if he can.[1] Suarez, after explaining this opinion, says: "Hanc sententiam hoc modo explicatam improbare non "possum," and seemingly would allow it and no other to be acted on, when the unctions cannot be applied in the usual way.[2] Coninck appears to adopt the same view, and, since his authority is referred to approvingly by Benedict XIV,[3] we give his words. After stating that, in case of necessity, the Pastoral of Mechlin directs a single unction to be applied with the general form (which is the form above cited from St. Liguori), he proceeds: "Securius tamen esset in dicto casu "ungere celeriter quinque organa sensuum in capite, pronunti- "ando formam ibi præscriptam, quod videtur fere æque celeriter "posse fieri; et tunc ipsæ unctiones responderent ipsi formæ "qua videtur significari omnium sensuum organa inungi."[4]

889. It is hard to say that the third opinion is more prob- able than the fourth, while the fourth cannot be said to differ in reality from the fifth, since the sense of touch is "diffused "alike throughout the body," as stated by the Catechism of the Council of Trent, in the extract given above.[5]

Those who prefer the unction of the head to the unction of any particular organ, do not express this preference in a very decided way. They merely say, it is more advisable. "Consultius" is the word used by Benedict XIV[6] and St. Liguori, and this word certainly does not convey the idea of notably greater security. At the same time the reason assigned for the preference seems to be its greater security, inasmuch as the unction of the head, in which all the organs of sense are united by the nerves, is a better substitute for the unction of all the organs, than the unction of any one organ could be.[7]

890. It is highly probable that either one or other is sufficient for the validity; nay more, that the unction of any part of the body with the general form, as asserted in the fifth opinion, is quite sufficient.[8] Benedict XIV, after citing a great many authorities in favor of this view, observes that it is powerfully sustained by the variety of usage in different

---

[1] Busembaum, qui citat. Laym. et Diana, apud St. Lig., n. 710.
[2] Disp. xli. sect. iii. n. 8, in fine. [3] Supra, n. 871
[4] De Extrema Unctione, Disp. xix. Dub. iii. n. 12.
[5] Supra, n. 884. [6] Vid. supra, n. 871.
[7] Bened. XIV. cit. supra, n. 871.
[8] De Synod. Diœc., lib. viii. cap. iii. n. 3 et 4.

parts of the Church, both as to the number of unctions and
the particular parts anointed; and still more by the authority
of the many rituals, which expressly permit the use of a
single unction with the general form, when all the unctions
cannot be applied.[1]

891. We do not know that the sixth opinion is held by
any one, although it might, perhaps, be deduced from opinions
that are held.[2] One great objection to it is, that, if it be true,
it would follow that, in the ordinary manner of anointing,
a complete sacrament is conferred in every unction, which, we
think, would not be admitted by any one.

So much for the speculative question. In practice, we have
already seen what is to be done in case of necessity; but in
ordinary cases the unctions are to be applied as directed
in the present rubric, and more fully explained hereafter.[3]

892. The usage regarding the parts anointed has not been
invariable. In the Greek Church, at present, the unction is
applied to the forehead, chin, and both cheeks (thus forming
a cross in the unction of the head), then to the breast, to the
two hands, and to the two feet.[4] But, in the commencement of the ninth century, only three unctions, it is said,
were in use in the Eastern Church.[5]

In the Western Church, the custom of anointing the five
organs of sense appears to have prevailed everywhere, and
from the earliest times; but there was a great diversity of
usage, and there still is considerable diversity in different
places, as to the parts anointed *in addition to these*. In
several ancient rituals, the unction of one or more of the following parts is prescribed—in some, of one part, in others, of
another—the neck, the throat, the breast, the loins, the knees,
the calves, the feet, between the shoulders, the navel, the
place of greatest pain.[6]

In many rituals used in Belgium, the unction of the breast
is prescribed, but that of the loins is omitted.[7] The same
is also true of many rituals used in France.[8]

*893. In the ritual published for the use of the clergy in
England,[9] the unction of the loins is not mentioned, but

---

[1] Vid. infra, § xix.   [2] Supra, n. 872.   [3] Chap. xvi.
[4] Martène, *De Ant. Eccl. Ritibus*, lib. i. cap. vii. art. iii. n. viii.
[5] Martène, ibid.
[6] Martène, l. c. et art. iv. per totum.   Cfr. Benedict XIV, l. c. n. 3.
[7] De Herdt, pars vi. n. 21, iii. et iv.
[8] Dictionnaire des Rites Sacrés, art. *Ext. Unct.: Résumé d'un grand
nombre de R tuels*, par Beuvelet.'   [9] Richardson, Derby, MDCCCLVI.

the other unctions are prescribed, as in the Roman ritual. In
the "Excerpta ex Rituali," etc., for the use of the clergy of
the United States of America,[1] it is observed in a note that
the usage throughout the States is, always to omit the unction
of the loins.[2]

Wherever the Roman ritual is ordered to be observed, as it
is in Ireland,[3] the unction of the loins is not to be omitted in
men, unless in the case here excepted by the rubric itself;
but in no case is it permitted to anoint another part (e. g., the
breast) instead of the loins, that is, as we take it, with the
form, . . . "*quicquid per lumborum delectationem deliquisti.*"
Nor is it permitted to add these words while anointing
another part; e. g., to use, while anointing the feet, the form,
. . . "*quicquid per gressum et lumborum delectationem deli-
"quisti.*" The present rubric clearly forbids any substitution
for the unction of the loins, and will have it simply omitted
when it cannot be properly applied, although, when any of
the other parts mentioned cannot be anointed, the unction
may be applied to the part nearest, according to what is
directed below.[4]

§ XVI.—Manus vero, quæ reliquis infirmis interius ungi debent,
Presbyteris exterius ungantur.

*894. Two reasons are assigned for this provision of the
rubric, but they are reasons of mere congruity; the validity
of the sacrament is nowise involved. One is, that the priest's
hands are anointed on the palms at his ordination; another,
that the priest, if he still retains his consciousness, may be
thus reminded of his dignity, and excited to compunction for
the sins of which his hands, though consecrated, may have
been the instruments.[5]

The distinction here made between priests and others is
mentioned by very few of the ancient rituals given by
Martène,[6] and by none of them earlier than the twelfth century.

---

[1] Baltimori, 1860.
[2] The Sacred Congregation having been consulted on a similar usage
in the diocese of Utrecht, answered that it might be tolerated; but at
the same time expressed an earnest desire (*ardentissimum votum*) that
this unction as prescribed in the Roman Ritual should be gradually introduced. In the same answer the Sacred Congregation refused to allow
any change or suppression in the text of the Ritual—14 Aug., 1858, *in
Ultrajecten.*, q. v. in Appendice.
[3] Syn. Thurl., *De Ext. Unct.*, n. 51.
[4] Infra, § xviii.   [5] Baruff., n. 113.   De Herdt, l. c. iv.
[6] Loc. cit. art. iv.

Some of them are silent about the part of the hand to be anointed, while many of them expressly direct that the exterior be anointed, without any distinction of persons. But the Ritual of Fleury, in the twelfth century, at the unction of the hands, has the rubric, "*Si fuerit sacerdos solummodo* "*deforis,*"[1] and from that date we find the practice here fixed by the Roman ritual, commonly established.

§ XVII.—Dum oculos, aures, et alia corporis membra, quæ paria sunt, Sacerdos ungit, caveat, ne alterum ipsorum inungendo, Sacramenti formam prius absolvat, quam ambo hujusmodi paria membra perunxerit.

*895. The right eye or ear, etc., is always anointed first. What is here prescribed is required, not for the validity of the sacrament, as may be inferred from what has been said elsewhere,[2] but merely for the exact and decorous performance of the ceremony. The precise distribution of the words is not fixed, but we believe it is the usual practice to anoint, *e. g.*, the right eye while pronouncing the words, "*Per istam* "*sanctam unctionem,*" and then the left, while pronouncing the remaining words of the form, "*et suam piissimam,*" etc.

§ XVIII.—Si quis autem sit aliquo membro mutilatus, pars loco illi proxima inungatur, eadem verborum forma.

*896. If one has lost a member, the part nearest to it is to be anointed as here directed. If it be a member of which he once had the use, it is easy to understand how the words of the form can be verified. But the unction is to be applied, although he may have wanted the member, or its use, from his birth; *e. g.*, the eyes of one who has been born blind, are to be anointed with the usual form, "*quicquid per visum* "*deliquisti.*" Theologians explain this, with St. Thomas, by saying that, though the person has been, of course, incapable of sinning like others by the external organs, he may have sinned by analogous internal desires, or by those internal powers or faculties which correspond to, and are immediately exercised through, the external organs.[3]

Should the person have redundant members, *c. g.*, a third hand, then those are to be anointed that have been most in use, or that are nearest to the natural position.[4]

---

[1] Martène, l. c.   Ord. xxiv.
[3] Supra, n. 134, et n. 885.
[2] St. Lig., n. 732, in fine.   Baruff., tit. xxvii. n. 120.
[4] Baruff., n. 119.   De Herdt, pars vi. n. 21, iii. 7°.

§ XIX.—Hujus autem Sacramenti forma, qua Sancta Romana Ecclesia utitur, solemnis illa precatio est quam Sacerdos ad singulas unctiones adhibet, cum ait: *Per istam Sanctam Unctionem, et suam piissimam misericordiam, indulgeat tibi Dominus quidquid per visum, sive per auditum,* etc., *deliquisti.*

*897. "The form of the sacrament," says the Catechism of the Council of Trent, "is the word and that solemn prayer " used by the priest at each anointing : '*Per istam sanctam* " '*unctionem,*' etc. That such is the true and proper form of " this sacrament, the Apostle St. James intimates, when he " says, 'et orent super eum et oratio fidei salvabit infirmum ;' " words from which we may infer that the form is to be " pronounced by way of prayer, although the Apostle does " not say of what particular words that prayer is to consist; " but this has reached us by the faithful tradition of the " Fathers, so that all the churches retain that form observed " by the holy Church of Rome, the mother and mistress of " all churches. Some, it is true, alter a few words, as when " for '*Indulgeat tibi Deus,*' they say, '*Remittat,*' or '*Parcat,*' " and sometimes, '*Sanet quicquid commisisti ;*' but, as the " sense is the same, it is clear that the same form is religiously " observed by all."[1]

It is certain, therefore, that the priest is bound to use the deprecative form, which is the only one used at present in the Eastern, as well as in the Western Church. Many theologians maintain, with St. Thomas,[2] that it is essential to the validity of the sacrament, and that the indicative form would not suffice. This they infer from the words of St. James, using the argument just given by the Catechism of the Council.[3]

898. Others, however, maintain[4] that the indicative form is valid, and they give one argument which appears to be very strong, viz., that, in many of the ancient rituals, the form is indicative—"*Ungo te,*" etc.,—as may be seen in those given by Martène.[5] Many of them, no doubt, may be interpreted in a deprecative sense, as, *e. g.*, that of Cambray, which has, "*Ungo oculos tuos de oleo sanctificato* UT *quicquid illicito* "*visu deliquisti hujus olei unctione expietur, per,*" etc.; and so of the other senses.[6] The particle "*ut*" may be understood to give a deprecative sense to this and other similar forms in

---

[1] Pars ii. cap. vi. n. 6.
[2] 3 par. *Sum. Theolog. Supplem.*, Q. xxix. art. viii.
[3] St. Lig., n. 711, Dub. i. Suarez, Disp. xl. sec. iii. n. 7.
[4] Apud St. Lig., l. c.
[5] Lib. i. cap. vii. art. iv.　　　[6] Martène, l. c. Ordo xix.

which it occurs. But there are some ancient forms, as that of Narbonne,[1] in which no word occurs to insinuate a deprecative sense, and which do not admit of it without violence, as is observed by Benedict XIV.[2] It cannot be denied, then, that the opinion of those who maintain the validity of the indicative form is probable, but of course it can never be used in practice.[3]

899. The form here given is that prescribed by the decree of Eugene IV.[4] The priest must be careful to pronounce it according to the instructions of the ritual, otherwise he is certainly guilty of sin.[5] But the variety of the ancient forms is such, that it is difficult to determine what words are essential, or what could be omitted without affecting the validity. It is certain that the form of this sacrament has not been determined by Christ *in specie infimâ*, that is to say, the words have not been fixed by Him like those in the forms of Baptism, and the Eucharist. "Formam sacramenti extremæ "unctionis," says Benedict XIV, "non esse a Christo Domino "institutam *in specie infimâ*, ut aiunt, hoc est, certis verbis "præscriptam, theologi omnes admittunt, atque ex diversis "formulis etiam in Ecclesia Latina in illius administratione "usurpatis evidenter demonstratur."[6]

900. It is agreed that the word, "*sanctam*," is not essential; and it is most probable that the words, "*et suam piissimam "misericordiam*," are not essential.[7] Hence the form expressed thus would be valid: "*Per istam unctionem indulgeat tibi "Dominus quicquid deliquisti per visum, auditum*," etc. It is commonly admitted that the word, "*deliquisti*," or some other of the same import, is essential.[8] But it is not equally certain that the expression of the senses is essential. We have seen that when, in case of necessity, a single form is used, it should contain an expression of each sense after the word, "*deliquisti*,"[9] but many are of opinion that it suffices for the validity to express them in general, . . . *quicquid deliquisti per sensus*."[10]

Some go still further, and contend that it is not necessary to express the senses at all, and that the words, "*Indulgeat tibi "Deus*," alone are essential; for the act of anointing, they say, precludes the necessity of using the words, "*per istam "unctionem*," while the word, "*indulgeat*," sufficiently implies

---

Ordo xiii.   [2] *De Synod. Diœc.*, lib. viii. cap. ii. in fine.
[3] St. Lig., lib. i. n. 48.
[4] *Pro Armenis*, apud Denzinger, *Enchiridion*, etc., n. 595.
[5] St. Lig., n. 711.   [6] *De Syn. Diœc.*, lib. viii. cap. ii.
[7] St. Lig., n. 711.   [8] St. Lig., ibid.   [9] Supra, n. 871.
[10] Vid. Collet, *De Extrema Unctione*, cap. iv. Quær. i.

"*quicquid deliquisti.*"[1] To this opinion it may be objected
that from it, especially if combined with that which asserts
the sufficiency of a single unction, the conclusion seems to
follow that, in the ordinary administration, the sacrament is
conferred not once, but six or seven times. It may be
answered, however, that the words, "*per visum,*" "*per audi-*
"*tum,*" etc., restrict and determine the meaning of the form,
so as to make the unction of each sense only a part of the
sacrament, for even the addition of a word to those that are
essential can affect the meaning of a sacramental form.[2]

901. It is disputed amongst theologians whether a distinct
grace is produced by each unction, or the whole grace is
conferred only when the last unction with its form is completed.[3] Some maintain the former opinion, and illustrate it
by the example of "Orders," which, though only one sacrament, contains under it several partial sacraments, each with
its own matter and form; and by the example of the
Eucharist, in which a distinct grace is perhaps received by
the reception of each species, or even, in many cases, of each
of several particles successively, although "the sacrament"
is received only once at a single refection. Suarez says this
opinion is probable, but he himself holds the latter, which is
the opinion of St. Thomas. He explains the last unction to
be, not the last which may be actually conferred, but the
unction of the last of the five organs of sense.[4] St. Liguori[5]
seems to regard the two opinions as equally probable.

---

[1] Jnenin, apud Catal., tit. v. cap. i. § xix. n. ix.
[2] Vid. De Lugo, *De Sacramentis*, Disp. ii. sect. vi. n. 127.
[3] St. Lig., lib. vi. n. 707.
[4] Vid. Disp. xli. sec. ii. [5] Loc. cit.

CHAPTER XVI.

ORDER OF ADMINISTERING THE SACRAMENT OF EXTREME UNCTION: "ORDO MINISTRANDI SACRAMENTUM EX TREMÆ UNCTIONIS."

§ I.—Sacerdos igitur Sacramentum ministraturus, quatenus fieri poterit, parari curet apud infirmum mensam mappa candida coopertam; itemque vas, in quo sit bombacium. seu quid simile in septem globulos distinctum, ad abstergendas partes inunctas; medullam panis ad detergendos digitos, et aquam ad abluendas Sacerdotis manus; ceream item candelam. quæ deinde accensa ipsi ungenti lumen præbeat. Denique operam dabit ut quanta poterit munditia ac nitore hoc Sacramentum ministretur.

902. The Council of Trent has defined that a priest alone is the minister of Extreme Unction, and that the "Presbyteri "Ecclesiæ," mentioned by St. James,[1] are not the elders in each community, as the heretics maintain, but priests ordained by a bishop.[2] This interpretation was never doubted in antiquity. The very name given to them, "Presbyteri "Ecclesiæ," the function assigned to them, and the effects attributed to their ministry by the Apostle, show clearly that he did not mean simply persons advanced in years.[3]

903. Any priest can confer the sacrament validly, but its administration is reserved to the ordinary pastor. Another who would confer it without his leave, expressed or implied, or at least reasonably presumed, would be guilty of grievous sin.[4] A religious incurs excommunication if he administers it, without this leave, to any except members of his community, or others to whom he may be privileged to administer it.[5] But in case of necessity it may be administered by any priest, at least by any priest who is not excommunicated.[6]

*904. A table should be prepared in the chamber of the sick person in the manner already directed for the case in which the Viaticum is about to be administered.[7] The same

---

[1] Cap. v. 14.   [2] Sess. xiv. *De Sac. Extr. Unct.*, can
[3] Vid. Estium, in loc.   [4] St. Lig., n. 722.   [5] Ibid., l
[3] Ibid., n. 723. Vid Bened. XIV, *De Synod Diœc.*, lib. viii. ca
1 . n. 7.   [7] Vid. supra, n. 792.

that has been prepared for the Viaticum serves also for Extreme Unction, which is so often administered immediately after.[1] There should be placed on it, besides the crucifix and candles, a plate containing cotton or flax, divided into seven, or, for a female, six little balls or pellets, to be used in wiping the parts anointed, and also some crumbs of bread, or a little dry meal, with a basin of water for the priest's hands. Should the table be prepared for Extreme Unction alone, it suffices to have one wax-candle, to be lighted and held by a clerk, when the priest is anointing. If it be prepared for the Viaticum, two candles are lighted from the commencement, and one of these may be held at the proper time by the minister. Out of reverence for the sacrament, it is recommended, also that the parts to be anointed be washed immediately before the priest comes.[2]

905. The last clause of this rubric shows the object of the Church in all these preliminary arrangements. It is that thus due regard may be had to cleanliness and propriety, and that the whole ceremony may be performed in a manner to conciliate the respect and veneration of the faithful. The rubric says, "quatenus fieri poterit, parari curet" . . . . "operam dabit." It does not then require the priest himself to do these things. It simply requires him to do what he can, in the circumstances in which he may find himself, to have these preparations made. In giving instructions to the people regarding this sacrament, he may very easily take occasion to tell them how the chamber of the sick person should be prepared for the visit of the priest when he is sent for.

There is no cabin so poor that it may not be made clean, at least around the bed of the sick ; none in which a table with a clean white cover may not be prepared, at least by borrowing from some charitable neighbor. There might be some pious confraternity, the members of which would undertake to have the necessary preparations made.[3] There would be rarely wanting at least some pious person in the townland or district who would see to the arrangement of everything as prescribed by the rubric, were the priest only to suggest this, and to show what is to be done. The only expensive requisite is the wax-candle. Even this costs very little, and would be supplied, we have no doubt, by the charity of others, to the few who might be unable themselves to procure it. The same

[1] De Herdt. n. 24, i. 3°.   [2] De Herdt. n. 21, ii.
[3] Vid. supra, n. 795.

candles could be taken from house to house, as they might be required, until consumed; and, if necessary, they could be purchased by the priest himself, and some given to one in each district, who would be charitable enough to take charge of them for the purpose. In this way, we believe, a few shillings anually would suffice to supply the poor of an entire parish.

Of course there are cases so urgent as to leave no time for preparation, but in ordinary cases there is rarely a sufficient reason for not complying with what the rubric prescribes.

§ II.—Deinde convocatis Clericis seu ministris, vel saltem uno Clerico qui Crucem sine hasta, Aquam benedictam cum aspersorio, et librum Ritualem deferat, ipse Parochus decenter accipit vas sacri Olei infirmorum, sacculo serico violacei coloris inclusum, illudque caute deferat, ne effundi possit.

906. For many centuries this sacrament was usually administered by a number of priests together. This practice is still continued in the Greek Church, and it prevailed in the Latin Church down to the thirteenth century, although from the earliest times instances are recorded of its being administered by a single priest, and no doubt was entertained of its validity when thus conferred. All this is stated by Benedict XIV,[1] and is very clearly shown by Martène.[2] According to the Greek Euchologium, the number of priests should be seven; but all admit that, in case of necessity, it may be administered by three.[3]

907. The Greeks insist on a plurality of ministers on account of the words of St. James: ... "inducat presbyteros;" but this expression of the Apostle is fairly interpreted to signify, "one of the priests;" at least it cannot be shown that in strictness it requires the presence of more than one.[4] The Greeks who are united to the Church are allowed to retain their usage, but they are required to acknowledge that the sacrament can be validly conferred by a single priest.[5]

According to the Greek usage the ceremony is very long. The priests bless the oil with several prayers and canticles; they recite seven epistles, seven gospels, and seven long prayers. Each of them anoints the sick person, reciting,

[1] De Syn. Diœc., lib. viii. cap. iv. n. 6.
[2] De Rit. Ant. Eccl., lib. i. cap. vii. art. iii. n. ii. iii. et v.
[3] Benedict XIV, l. c. n. 8.   Martène, l. c.
[4] Vid. Cornelium A Lapide, in loc.   Suarez, Disp. xliii. sect. ii. n. 1.
[5] Benedict XIV, loc. cit.

while he anoints, the prayer, Πατερ °Αγιε ιατρὲ τῶν ψυχῶν και τῶν σωμάτων, etc.　This prayer, according to the common opinion, constitutes the form of the sacrament.[1] The book of the Gospels is placed on the sick man's head, and all the priests impose hands on him, while the principal priest, called in the rubric ὁ προϊστάμενος, recites a prayer. We may observe that the oil is blessed each time, and the ceremony is performed in the church if the sick person can be brought to it, otherwise in his house.

The extract given by Martène[2] is an exact translation of the Ἀκολουθία του °Αγιου °Ελαιου, given in the ΕΥΧΟΛΟΓΙΟΝ ΜΕΓΑ used at present in the Greek Church.　The rubric regarding the unctions is not very clear.　It simply says that the priest anoints, saying the prayer, "Pater Sancte," etc., . . . and then, that this same prayer is said by each priest while he anoints.　All the parts, however, are anointed by each priest, not one by one priest, and another by another.

908. Although, as has been said, the same usage as to a plurality of priests prevailed in the Western Church, there was a diversity of practice, according to Martène, as to the part taken by each priest in the administration.　Sometimes each priest anointed all the parts with the appropriate forms; sometimes one anointed one part, and another another, with the form appropriate to each; and some instances are mentioned in which it would seem that one applied the unctions while another pronounced the form.[3]　This last mode is, most probably, invalid; but the others are, undoubtedly, valid.[4]　Benedict XIV says there can be no doubt of the validity of the sacrament when the organs of sense are anointed by different priests, each pronouncing the form appropriate to that which he anoints.[5]

909. According to the present usage, the unctions are applied by a single priest, and it is not lawful to depart from this usage, at least if we except the case of necessity;[6] and we doubt if it would be expedient even then, for the case of necessity is otherwise provided for.[7]　But should the priest be prevented by a sudden attack, or by any accident, from completing the unctions, another should supply what has been omitted.　The second priest in this case should not repeat the

---

[1] Sylvester, Compendium Theologiæ Classicum pro Græcis, cap. lxiii.
§ 5.　Collet, De Ext. Unct, cap. iv. concl. ii.　[2] Art. iv. ordo xxxiii
[3] Art. iii. n. iv.　　　　　[4] Suarez, Disp. xliii. sect. ii.
[5] Lib. viii. cap. iv. n. 5.　　[6] St. Lig., n. 724, in parenth.
[7] Vid. supra, n. 871.

unctions performed by the first, but commence where he left off, unless there be a notable delay. If there be a delay of even a quarter of an hour, he should repeat the previous unctions "sub conditione."[1]

910. It is not only permitted, however, but even recommended, that the priest who administers the sacrament be assisted by other priests, when they can be easily had, who may act as his ministers in the ceremonies, and join in the prayers.[2] Hence, St. Charles directed that he should have with him as many priests and clerics as he conveniently can.[3] According to our present rubric, the parish priest, when about to administer the sacrament, convenes them, or a few of them (supposing, of course, that there is a sufficient number attached to the parish church), or, at least, gets one to accompany him and carry the cross, etc., as here prescribed, while he himself carries the holy oil from the church. It is unnecessary to bring the holy water if it be certain that there is some already in the chamber of the sick person.[4] A procession may be formed, but the cross is carried "sine hasta," that is, without the long staff or pole on which it is usually fixed in processions; and this, according to Baruffaldi,[5] very probably for the convenience of passing through doors, ascending stairs, etc., to reach the chamber of the sick. A decree of the Sacred Congregation[6] appears to prohibit the carrying of lights in this procession, though, according to Baruffaldi, they may be carried.[7] It is certain, however, that the bell is not to be rung, lest the faithful might think that the priest is carrying the Viaticum, and kneel down to adore.[8] Hence the rubric[9] expressly prohibits the ringing of the bell.

*911. This, however, regards countries where there is nothing to prevent such processions. With us the priest usually has the oil of Extreme Unction in his house,[10] and carries it unattended by any one when he is going to administer the sacrament. He should always bring with him a small crucifix and a little holy water, unless he has reason to believe that he will find both before him in the sick chamber. If he cannot otherwise have a supply of holy water, he

---

[1] St. Lig., n. 724, in parenth.
[3] Act. Eccl. Mediol., pars iv. Min'strando, pag. 450.
[5] Tit. xxviii. n. 32.
[7] Tit. xxviii. n. 29.
[9] Infra, § iii.

[2] Benedict XIV, l. c.
Inst. Ext. Unct. § De diligentia in
[4] Vid. supra. n. 804.
[6] 28 Jan. 1606, in Baren., n. 289.
[8] Baruff., n. 40, 41.
[10] Supra, n. 856.

should bless some in the house before the commencement of the ceremony, or at least before he takes his leave.[1]

912. The vessel containing the "Oleum Infirmorum" should be apart from those which contain the oils used in baptism. The necessity which justifies the priest in keeping the "Oleum Infirmorum" in his house, does not justify him in keeping the others also in his house, still less in carrying them along with it whenever he goes to administer Extreme Unction.[2]

The oil should be absorbed in a little cotton, as is directed by a previous rubric,[3] and the silver vessel containing it should be put into a case made of silk (or, better, perhaps, made of leather lined with silk), of a violet color. It would be well also to have always in the case a little loose cotton, lest on any occasion none might be found where he has to administer the sacrament.

§ III.—Quod si longius iter peragendum, aut etiam equitandum sit, vel alias adsit periculum effusionis, vas Olei sacculo aut bursa inclusum, ut dictum est, ad collum appendat, ut commodius et securius perferat. Procedat autem sine sonitu campanulæ.

*913. The case contemplated in this rubric is of ordinary occurrence in these countries, and the precautions here recommended should be carefully attended to. We have already seen how the pyxis containing the Blessed Sacrament is to be carried in these circumstances.[4] When the holy oil is carried at the same time, the vessel containing it must not be joined to, or form part of, the pyxis.[5] But we think it may be fastened to the same chain or guard round the neck by which the pyxis is secured. For this it is not necessary that it be carried beside the pyxis; it may be put by itself in an inside pocket. A second ring or a second spring-hook would suffice for the purpose. Both would thus be carried with great security, and, as nearly as the circumstances allow, in accordance with what is prescribed in the rubric. The reason for proceeding without sound of bell has been already noticed.[6]

§ IV.—Cum perventum fuerit ad locum ubi jacet infirmus, Sacerdos intrans cubiculum dicit : Pax huic domui. R. Et omnibus, etc.

*914. The salutation here mentioned is pronounced by the priest also before administering the Viaticum.[7] The rubric

[1] Vid. Baruff., n. 94.   [2] Vid. supra, n. 267.   [3] Chap. xv. § v.
[4] Supra, n. 807.   [5] Vid. Decr. S. R. C., 26 Mar., 1859, in Tarnovien., ad 6.   [6] Supra, n. 910, in fine.   [7] Supra, n. 808.

supposes that the sick person has received the Viaticum some
time previously, and that the priest now comes to administer
Extreme Unction alone. In this case, entering the chamber
he is to say again, "*Pax huic*," etc., as here directed. But
if he administers Extreme Unction immediately after the
Viaticum, he need not repeat it.[1] According to the words
of the rubric, he is to say it "intrans cubiculum." But if he
has said it "ingrediens locum ubi jacet infirmus," as directed
by the rubric just before administering the Viaticum,[2] and
has not since left the chamber or place where the sick person
is, it is evident that he has done all that the present rubric
requires.

§ V.—Deinde deposito Oleo super mensam, superpelliceo stolaque
violacea indutus, ægroto Crucem pie deosculandam porrigit; mox in
modum crucis eum aqua benedicta, et cubiculum et circumstantes aspergit,
dicens Antiphonam: *Asperges me, Domine*, etc.

*915. Having entered the sick chamber, he places the holy
oil on the table prepared as already stated, and then vests in
surplice and violet stole. The rubric here supposes the priest
to come for the purpose of administering Extreme Unction
alone; for if he has but just administered the Viaticum, he is
already vested in surplice, and requires only to lay aside the
white stole, and put on a violet one.

St. Liguori discusses the question whether the priest would
be guilty of grievous sin, by administering this sacrament
without the surplice and stole; and he says: "Si non urgeat
"necessitas, certum est graviter peccare."[3] He cites Suarez
and others who would not even except the case of necessity,
on account of the reverence due to the sacrament, which
should, they say, be preferred to the advantage of the
individual.[4] Bouvier maintains the same opinion, and says it
should be followed in practice unless there be a dispensation,
as there is, according to him, in England, where it may be
administered without the surplice and stole.[5] St. Liguori,
however, inclines to the opinion which would except the case
of necessity.[6]

It is to be observed that the case of necessity, here
considered, is the case in which the sick person is otherwise in
danger of dying without Extreme Unction, not the case in
which Extreme Unction might be itself necessary, as when he

[1] De Herdt, n. 24, i. 4o.   [2] Supra, chap. xiv. § xv.
[3] Lib. vi. n. 726.   [4] St. Lig., l. c.
[5] *De Ext. Unct.*, cap. viii. 1°.   [6] Loc. cit.

could receive no other sacrament;[1] for in such a case, we believe, no theologian would hold that it could not be administered without the sacred vestments.

916. It is, then, the general law of the Church that the priest, in administering this sacrament, be vested in surplice and stole; and nothing but *bona fide* necessity can excuse him from complying with this law. Such necessity existed in these countries during the operation of the penal code, when the priest could administer the sacraments only by stealth. But this necessity exists no longer. There is nothing now, generally speaking, to prevent him from complying with what the rubric requires. We say *generally speaking*, for it may be useful here to discuss the question how far the inconvenience of bringing a soutane and surplice with him to sick calls may justify the priest in dispensing with them We have no doubt it is often so great as to justify him. But we do not think it is always, or even generally so.

917. In the first place, the surplice used on these occasions may be such as can be put into very small bulk, and easily carried. Then, it may be very often given to be carried by the messenger who comes for the priest, and who usually returns immediately to the house of the sick person.

There is a greater difficulty about the cassock or soutane over which the surplice is worn, for it should not be worn over a secular coat. The rubric makes no mention of the soutane, simply because it supposes that this is the ordinary dress of the priest, and it makes no provision for the case in which the priest, as in these countries, can wear out of doors no other than a secular coat, or, at all events, a coat with short skirts. We have not seen the case discussed in any author, nor are we aware of any decision regarding it by a diocesan or provincial synod. To determine the obligation of the priest, then, we must have recourse to general principles.

Now it cannot, we think, be doubted, that the priest is bound to wear the soutane, or what is called the "vestis "talaris" in the canons, in the performance of every sacred function, *if he can do so without notable inconvenience.* From this principle we infer that, even in these countries, the priest is bound to wear the soutane when he administers a sacrament, or performs any religious ceremony *in the church,* for there is no law of the state, no danger of insult, nor any other like reason, to prevent his wearing it while

[1] Vid. supra, n. 851

there. If his house be near the church, there is usually
nothing to prevent him, if he chooses, from wearing it while
passing from the one to the other; but at least he may
easily have a soutane in the sacristy, which he can put on
after going there.

He is bound to wear it also when he administers a sacrament outside the church, provided he can, without inconvenience, bring or send a soutane to the place where he is
required to administer it. No doubt, the inconvenience of
bringing it is, as we have said, often so great, as to justify
the priest in dispensing with it. But surely it is not always
so. For example, there can be no great inconvenience if he
goes to the place on a car or other vehicle, or if he is
accompanied by the messenger who came for him.

If he has to go a considerable distance alone, whether on
foot or on horseback, he could not easily bring his soutane
with him; but even in such circumstances a great deal might
still, we think, be done to carry out the spirit, if not to comply
with the letter, of the rubric. The soutane, for instance,
might be of very light material, made without sleeves, and sc
as to fit easily over the ordinary coat; it could thus be
carried without much inconvenience along with the surplice,
both being, as we suppose, compressible into very small
bulk.

918. We saw before[1] that the Sacred Congregation—being
asked whether the practice existing in some places of giving
the Viaticum without the surplice, but with a stole alone,
could be permitted—answered: "Negative et eliminata
"consuetudine servetur Ritualis Romani præscriptum." On
the same occasion, and under the very same head, it was
further asked: 2° "An saltem sacramentum Extremæ
"Unctionis cum stolâ tantum administrari potest?" and the
answer was: "Negative ut ad proximum."[2] The continuato
of Gardellini, in his note on this decree, would not admit that
even a long or difficult journey is a sufficient reason for dispensing with the vestments required by the rubric; he excepts
only the case of positive necessity.

In all that we say, however, regarding the obligation of
this rubric, and the possibility of complying with it more
frequently than is usual in these countries, we would not, and
we trust we shall not, be understood as implying a censure

[1] Supra, n. 798.
[2] 16 Dec., 1826, in una Gandaven., ad 2, Quæsiti ii. n. 4623.

on any priest who conforms to existing customs, as long as these are not abolished by the proper authority.[1]

*919. The stole used in administering Extreme Unction should be of a violet color. This is the color adopted by the Church to express sorrow and affliction, and used by her in the sacrament of Penance, and in all her offices during the penitential seasons.[2] It is prescribed for Extreme Unction also, which is regarded as the completion of Penance.[3] The priest can rarely, if ever, be obliged to administer the sacrament without at least the stole, as it is so easily carried. Baruffaldi observes[4] that sometimes the sick person might be alarmed if the priest presented himself at once clothed in the sacred vestments, and recommends, therefore, that he should first appear in his ordinary dress, and prepare the sick person for what is to follow. The wording of the rubric appears to convey that the priest puts on the surplice and stole only after he has placed the holy oil on the table, though St. Charles,[5] Catalani,[6] and others, would have him vested in these while carrying the oil to the house.

*920. Being vested, he first presents the cross to be kissed by the sick person, who thus declares his faith and his hope in Christ crucified. The ritual, as we have seen, supposes the priest to have a cross with him, but if there be one already, as there ought to be,[7] in the room, it will do equally well. Then he sprinkles with holy water the sick person, the room, and all who are present, saying the usual antiphon, "*Asperges me,*" etc. He sprinkles the sick person, as here directed, "in "modum crucis," that is, he sprinkles, 1° in front (of himself); 2° on his (own) left; 3° on his right.[8] If he has done so, however, before administering the Viaticum, he is not required to do so again when Extreme Unction immediately follows.[9]

§ VI.—Quod si ægrotus voluerit confiteri, audiat illum, et absolvat Deinde piis verbis illum consoletur, et de hujus Sacramenti vi atque efficacia, si tempus ferat, breviter admoneat; et quantum opus sit, ejus animum confirmet, et in spem erigat vitæ æternæ.

*921. The priest should give the sick person an opportunity

---

[1] Vid. chap. i. n. 84, et seq.

[2] Baruffaldi, tit. xviii. n. 19. Gavant., pars i. tit. xviii. *De Coloribus Paramentorum,* rub. 5.

[3] Conc. Trid., Sess. xiv. *De Ext. Unct.*   [4] Tit. xxviii. n. 43.

[5] *Act. Med. Eccl.,* pars iv. Instr. Ext. Unct. § *Ordo ministrandi,* page 451.   [6] Tit v. cap. ii. § iv. n. iii.

[7] Supra, n. 904.   [8] De Herdt, n. 22, 2°. Vid. supra, n. 810.

[9] De Herdt, n. 24, i. 4°.

of confessing immediately before Extreme Unction; and
hence, if any interval elapses between the Viaticum and Extreme Unction, he should, before he proceeds to anoint, ask
him whether he desires to go to confession.   This is, of course,
unnecessary if Extreme Unction immediately follows the
Viaticum;[1] but for greater security he may ask him to renew
his sorrow, and make a fresh act of contrition.

In any case, he should say a few words to console and encourage him, and, if time permits, explain briefly the advantages and effects of the sacrament.   He may do so in his own
words, or he may read the instruction or exhortation on the
subject, which is usually found in an appendix to the ritual.
In his general instructions on this matter, he should be careful
to impress on the faithful the importance of receiving the
sacrament in time, and to remove from their minds the senseless notion that whoever receives it must give up all hope of
recovery.[2]

§ VII.—Postea dicat: ℣. *Adjutorium nostrum,* etc.

*922. In the ancient rituals given by Martène,[3] a consider-
able variety may be observed in the prayers to be recited
before administering the sacrament, but all have the same
object, and express nearly the same sentiments, as those here
given.   The first and third are found in some of the most
ancient, as in the Ritual of Beauvais,[4] and that of the Monastery of Pontlevoy, as old as the twelfth century.[5]   The latter
contains also the prayer, "*Oremus et deprecamur,*" etc., but
not in the same part of the ceremony.

Saying "*Adjutorium,*" etc., the priest makes the sign of
the cross on himself.[6]   It is not stated in what manner he is
to make the sign of the cross at the words "*benedic* ✠ *nostræ*
"*conversationi,*". . . and again, *benedicat* ✠ *hoc tabernaculum.*"[7]
The words seem to imply that the blessing is intended for the
house or chamber which the priest has entered, and we think,
therefore, the sign should be made over the place in front of
him without being directed to any special object.   According
to the Ritual of Toulon, these prayers are to be said by the
priest standing, uncovered, and turned partly towards the bed
of the sick person, and partly towards the crucifix on the table.[7]

[1] Vid. supra, n. 812.   [2] Vid. supra, n. 847.
[3] Lib. i. cap. vii. art. iv.   [4] Loc. cit. ord. xx.
[5] Ord. xxv.   [6] Vid. supra, n. 811.
[7] Apud Dictionnaire des Cérémonies, etc., Art. *Ext. Unct.,* n. 23.

§ VIII.—Quæ Orationes, si tempus non patiatur, ex parte, vel in totum poterunt omitti.   Tum de more facta Confessione generali, latino vel vulgari sermone, Sacerdos dicat: *Misereatur*, etc., *Indulgentiam*, etc.

*923. When the case is so urgent as to justify the omission of these prayers, they are afterwards to be supplied if the person survives, as is directed by a preceding rubric.[1] The "*Confiteor*" is said by the sick person himself, if he is able, the rubric expressly permitting it to be said either in Latin or in the vernacular, as in going to confession. If he is unable, it may be said by the clerk or assistant, or even by the priest himself.[2] Then the priest says "*Misereatur tui*," etc., "*Indulgentiam*," etc., in the singular, as in administering the Viaticum.[3]

It was decided by the Sacred Congregation of Indulgences that the "*Confiteor*" is here to be said, although it may have been said a few minutes before, as when the Viaticum immediately precedes; and is to be said even a third time if the indulgence "in articulo mortis" is given immediately after Extreme Unction.[4]

§ IX.—Antequam Parochus incipiat ungere infirmum, moneat adstantes, ut pro illo orent; ut ubi commodum fuerit, pro loco et tempore, et adstantium numero vel qualitate recitent Septem Psalmos Pœnitentiales-cum Litaniis, vel alias Preces dum ipse Unctionis Sacramentum administrat.   Mox dicat: *In nomine Patris*, ✠ *et Filii*, etc.

*924. "There is no sacrament," says the Catechism of the Council of Trent, "the administration of which is accom-
"panied with more prayers; and with good reason, for then
"most particularly the faithful require the assistance of pious
"prayers, and, therefore, all who may be present, but the
"pastor in particular, should pour out their fervent aspira-
"tions to God in behalf of the sick person, most earnestly
"recommending his life and salvation to the divine mercy."[5]

Hence the ritual here directs the priest to invite all who are present to pray for the sick person. The prayers specially recommended are the Penitential Psalms and the Litanies, these being most appropriate; but it is plain from the rubric that any others, as, *e. g.*, the Rosary, may be selected; and the priest would do well to suggest those that he thinks most suitable for the persons present. These prayers should be

---

[1] Chap. xv. § xi.   [2] De Herdt, pars vi. n. xxii. 5°.
[3] Ibid., l. c.   Rit. Toul., l. c. n. 24.   Vid. supra, n. 815.
[4] 5 Feb. 1841. in *Valentinen.*, ad 6, n. dvi.   Decreta Authentica, etc., a Prinzivalli, Bruxellis, 1862.   [5] Pars ii. cap. vi. n. 7.

continued while the priest is administering the sacrament, but, of course, in so low a tone as not to distract or disturb him. The prayers are to be said kneeling, according to the "Instructiones" of St. Charles.[1] At least the Penitential Psalms and the Litanies should be recited "flexis genibus," as is apparent from the very title prefixed to them in the ritual.

*925. Immediately before applying the unction, the priest says: "*In nomine Patris ✠ et Filii ✠ et Spiritus ✠ Sancti* "*extinguatur*," etc., making the sign of the cross three times over the sick person, as he pronounces the words. The ritual does not say explicitly how the sign is here to be made, but is understood as implying that it should be over the sick person.[2] The words, "*in te*," indeed convey clearly enough that the priest is then turned towards the sick person, and the words, "*per impositionem manuum nostrarum*," that he puts or raises his hand over him. It is enough, however, that he make the sign of the cross in the manner explained, for, as Baruffaldi observes,[3] this is here called an "impositio manuum." Certainly no imposition of hands, distinct from this, is prescribed by the rubric, nor by any commentator we have seen, except, perhaps, Catalani,[4] whose words are not very clear on the subject.

§ X.—Deinde intincto pollice in Oleo sancto, in modum Crucis ungit infirmum in Partibus hic subscriptis, aptando proprio loco verba formæ in hunc modum.

*926. Those present being engaged in praying devoutly for the sick person, the priest dips his thumb into the vessel of oil, pressing, not the nail, but the fleshy part on the cotton in which the oil is absorbed, and makes with it the sign of the cross on the several parts, pronouncing at the same time the words of the form as the rubric directs. A clerk should hold the ritual in a convenient position before him. Another should hold the candle, and the same may also hold the plate or salver containing the pellets of cotton. If there be a third, he may hold the vessel of oil,[5] otherwise the priest himself holds it, and, indeed, generally he will find it most convenient to hold it himself in his left hand. Baruffaldi[6] suggests that in this case there should be a purificator round

¹ *Inst. Ext. Unct.,* § *Ordo ministrandi,* etc., pag. 451.
² Baruff., tit. xxviii. n. 60. De Herdt, n. 22, 7°. Rit. Toul., 1 ᴠ
n. 24.   ³ Loc. cit.   ⁴ Tit. v. cap. ii. § vii. n. iv.
⁵ Baruff., tit. xxviii. n. 64, et seq.   ⁶ Loc. cit. r 65.

the vessel to guard against effusion, but there is not much danger of effusion when the oil is absorbed in cotton.

Nearly all the ancient rituals cited by Martène[1] direct the unctions to be applied in the form of a cross. Our rubric prescribes the same, and a neglect of this in ordinary cases cannot be excused from venial sin.[2] It is not essential, however, and in case of necessity, need not be attended to.[3] What is here prescribed regards the usual administration of the sacrament.

927. We have already discussed what is to be done in case of necessity.[4] Here we may add, that in time of pestilence, if the priest apprehends danger from using his thumb, he may apply the oil by means of an instrument.[5] To preserve the oil from being tainted, the instrument, which may be of any material, ought to be wiped with cotton after each unction, before it is again dipped into the vessel of oil; or, if it be of wood, a different piece may be used for each unction, and burned immediately after use. The mouth may be anointed in this way in case of hydrophobia, or any other disease in which there might be danger from contact with the saliva of the patient, but in such circumstances it is enough to anoint the cheek or part near the mouth.[6] If there be no other instrument at hand, the priest might use a little cotton dipped in the oil, being careful to burn it after the unction. We have already seen that, in these cases of extraordinary danger, the priest, according to a highly probable opinion, may apply only a single unction with the general form.[7]

§ XI.—Ad Oculos. *Per istam sanctam Unctionem* ✠ *et suam*, etc.

*928. The unctions commence with the eyes, which should be closed. The oil is applied to the eyelids,[8] and the words of the form are distributed, so that he will have made the cross on the right eyelid when he has pronounced the word *unctionem*, and on the left before he has completed the remaining words. The same is to be observed in anointing the other double organs.[9] It may be noted that the word "*Amen*" here is not a response, but belongs to the form, and should be said by the priest himself.[10]

When the organ is double, the unction always begins with

: *De Ant. Eccl. Rit.*, lib. i. cap. vii. art. iv. [2] St. Lig., n. 728.
[3] Baruff., n. 68. [4] Supra, n. 871, et seq.
[5] St. Lig., n. 710, in parenth. De Herdt, n. 23, iii. Benedict XIV, *De Syn. Diœc.*, lib. xiii. cap. xix. n. 30. [6] Vid. De Herdt, l. c.
[7] Supra, n. 874. [8] Baruff.. tit. xxviii. n. 71.
[9] Vid. supra, chap. xv. § xvii. [10] Modo Pratico, cap. ix.

the right.[1] The cross is formed by drawing, first, a line
downwards, as, *e. g.*, in the present instance, from the eyebrow
towards the cheek, and then one across it from left to right
(of the priest).[2] In the Roman Ritual only one cross is
marked, though each of the unctions is to be made in the form
of a cross. Two crosses are marked in some rituals, as in
that of Liége.[3]

§ XII.—Minister vero, si est in Sacris, vel ipsemet Sacerdos post
quamlibet unctionem tergat loca inuncta novo globulo bombacii, vel rei
similis, eumque in vase mundo reponat, et ad Ecclesiam postea deferat,
comburat, cineresque projiciat in Sacrarium.

*929. It seldom happens in these countries that the priest
is accompanied by another person in holy orders, and consequently he himself is usually obliged to do what is here prescribed. He should use a fresh pellet for each unction, but
one suffices, even when the organ is double, as may be inferred
from the number prepared according to the rubric.[4] He is to
wipe the part anointed as here directed after each unction; but
where there are two unctions for a single sense, he need not
wipe the parts until he has completed both.[5]

There is danger sometimes, however, that the organ first
anointed may come in contact with the dress or bedclothes,
while the second is being anointed. This is the case with
regard to the ears especially. Indeed it is hardly possible,
when the head is resting on a soft pillow, that the lobe of one
ear would not touch the pillow when the lobe of the other is
being anointed. Hence the Ritual of Toulon prescribes that
the oil be wiped from the right ear before the left is anointed.[6]
Falise recommends the same,[7] and it is, we think, a very
laudable practice.

930. After use the pellet should not be put back on the
plate or salver from which it was taken, but on another, or,
better still, into a little pocket or bag, in which all can be
conveniently carried to the church, where they are to be
burned, and the ashes thrown into the sacrarium. Such a
pocket is sometimes made in the case which contains the holy
oil. If so, it should be well closed, so as to prevent the
cotton from touching the vessel. The priest is to put into the
same place the crumbs of bread with which he has rubbed his

[1] St. Lig., n. 711.   [2] De Herdt, n. 21, iii. 3°.
[3] Apud Ibid., n. 21, iv.   [4] Supra, § i.
[5] De Herdt, n. 21, iii. 6.   [6] Dictionnaire des Cérémonies. Art. *Ext*
Unct., n. 25.   [7] Part IIIme sec. i. cap. iv. n. 8.

fingers.[1] But generally in this country he is obliged to throw all into the fire.[2]

§ XIII.—Ad Aures.

*931. The ears are to be anointed on the lobes or lower extremities.[3] This is the universal practice now, though some ancient rituals prescribe that the unction be applied to the hollow of the ear—"*deintus*"—as that of Troyes used in the tenth century,[4] that of Tours in the same century,[5] and that of Cambray in the thirteenth.[6]

*932. The distribution of the words in applying the unctions here may be the same as in anointing the eyes. He may have the right ear anointed when he has completed the word *unctionem ;* and the left, before he has got to the end. The rubric merely requires that the form be not completed until the second unction is applied,[7] but prescribes no particular distribution of the words. The ritual, indeed, has a cross marked after the word *unctionem,* but it does not imply that after this word the priest is to make a pause, during which the unction is to take place, and then complete the form. A pause of this kind might be sometimes inconveniently long. It is best, then, to adopt some distribution of the words in applying the unctions, and to adhere to it as far as possible. We believe the one we have mentioned is that which is commonly adopted in practice. By pronouncing the words slowly, the priest would have time enough to wipe the oil from the right ear before anointing the left, without being obliged to make any notable pause.

§ XIV.—Ad Nares.

933. Commentators are not agreed whether there should be two unctions here, one for each of the nostrils, or only one on the extremity of the nose for both. De Herdt[8] maintains that there should be only one, because, he says, the rituals do not mention "the nostrils" when speaking of the double organs, and because in the Ritual of Liége only one cross is marked for the unction of the nostrils, while two are marked for the unction of the eyes, ears, hands, and feet. Hence he concludes that, though in strictness the organ is double, a

---

[1] Baruff., n. 77.
[2] Baruff., n. 78. De Herdt, n. 21, iv. 2°.
[4] Apud Martène, lib. i. cap. vii. art. iv. ord. iii.
[6] Ibid. ord. xix.   [7] Supra, chap. xv. § xviii.
[3] Vid. infra, § xix.
[5] Ibid ord. iv.
[8] Loc cit. iv. 3°.

single unction at the extremity of the nose suffices for the unction of the two nostrils.

*934. The other opinion, however, which requires two unctions, is the more common, and is the one usually followed. Baruffaldi does not say expressly there should be two unctions here, but he evidently implies it, by saying, "*Ad nares* nempe "ad narices quæ sunt nasi alæ laterales," and then, observing on the next words, "*Ad os, compressis labiis,*" that here there is only one unction, by which both lips are touched ; thus clearly supposing that at the preceding organs, including the "*nares,*" there are two unctions.[1]   Two crosses are marked in the "Instructiones" of St. Charles, "*Ad nares,*" just as "*Ad oculos,*" from which it is plain that according to him there should be two unctions here.[2]   Two are prescribed also by the Ritual of Toulon,[3] and by Falise.[4]

§ XV.—Ad Os, compressis Labiis.

*935. Here there can be no doubt that there is only one unction by which both lips are anointed together, the mouth being firmly closed.   But if the sick person have a difficulty of breathing, or if he cannot hear when told to close the mouth, or if there be any other inconvenience in requiring the mouth to be closed, it is enough to apply the unction to the upper or under lip alone.[5]

§ XVI.—Ad Manus.
Et adverte quod Sacerdotibus, ut dictum est, manus non inunguntur interius, sed exterius.

*936. The hands are to be anointed on the palms, first the right, and then the left.   This applies to all, except such as are in priest's orders.   Deacons and other clerics inferior to priests, have the hands anointed in the same way as laics.[6] The hands of a priest are anointed on the back.   We have before mentioned the reasons of congruity which are commonly assigned for this direction of the rubric.[7]

§ XVII.—Ad pedes.

*937. We have already seen[8] that the unction of the feet is not essential.   In some places it is altogether omitted, accord-

---

[1] Tit. xxviii. n. 79, 80.
[2] *Act. Ecrl. Med.*, pars iv., Instruct. Ext. Unct. § *Ordo Ministrandi,* etc., pag 452.   [3] Dictionnaire des Cérémonies, l. c. n. 25.
[4] *Cours Abrégé,* etc., iiime partie, sect. i. chap. iv. n. 8.
[5] Baruff., n. 80.   De Herdt, l. c. 4°.   Falise, l. c.
[6] De Herdt, l. c. 5°.   [7] Supra, n 894.   [8] Supra, n. 895.

ing to De Herdt;[1] and St. Liguori seems to convey that, as regards this unction, the custom of each church may be followed.[2]

There is a diversity of usage as to the part of the foot to which the unction is applied. According to Baruffaldi[3] it should be applied to the upper part of the foot, the instep, or metatarsus. The same is taught by Billuart,[4] and is prescribed by the Ritual of Liége.[5] The ritual used in England also directs the upper part to be anointed. It has the rubric: "*Ad pedes, in parte superiore.*"

According to St. Liguori, the unction should be applied to the under part, or the sole, "*in plantis.*"[6] The same is prescribed by St. Charles,[7] who is cited and followed by Catalani.[8] In Ireland, generally speaking, the practice is conformable to this second opinion, which also seems to accord better with the words of the form, "*quidquid per "gressum deliquisti,*" the sole being the part that touches the ground in walking. The Sacred Congregation, being consulted on the subject, decided that each one may follow the local usage.[9]

All are agreed that, if there be any difficulty in getting at the part usually anointed, *e. g.*, the sole, then the upper, or, indeed, any other part of the foot, may be anointed in its stead.[10]

§ XVIII.—Ad Lumbos sive Renes.

Hæc autem unctio ad lumbos, ut dictum est, omittitur semper in fœminis, et etiam in viris, qui ob infirmitatem vix, aut sine periculo moveri non possunt.

*938. The unction is applied to the loins, immediately above the " os ischion," or prominent hip bone.[11] It is applied only on one side, as appears from the " Instructiones" of St. Charles,[12] in which only one cross is marked at this unction.

939. The loins, as the rubric here tells us, are never anointed in females. According to the usage of many places, they are not anointed in males either, insomuch that the

[1] N. 21, iii. 9º. [2] Lib. vi. n. 710, *Unctio vero pedum.*
[3] Loc. cit. n. 84. [4] *De Ext. Unct.*, art. ii. *Observanda*, 6º.
[5] Apud De Herdt, n. 21, iv. 6º. [6] Lib. vi. n. 711.
[7] *Act. Med. Eccl.*, pars iv. Instruct. Ext. Unct. § *Ordo ministrandi*, pag. 452. [8] Tit. v. cap. ii. § xiv. n. i.
[9] 27 Aug. 1836, *in Rhedonen.*, ad 1, n. 4780. Vid. subjectam annotationem Contin. Gardell.
[10] Baruff., n. 85. De Herdt, l. c. [11] Baruff., n. 86.
[12] Loc. cit. pag. 452.

rituals published for use in these places omit altogether the rubric which refers to this unction.[1]

It is plain, however, that, according to the Roman Ritual, the unction of the loins is not to be omitted in anointing males, unless in the cases here mentioned. If there be any danger, or any serious inconvenience to the sick person, or any reasonable apprehension of such inconvenience, the priest is to omit it without scruple, but not otherwise.

§ XIX.—Quibus omnibus peractis Sacerdos dicit : *Kyrie eleison,* etc.

* 940. Having completed the unctions, the priest puts the vessel of holy oil on the table, rubs his thumb, and any other finger that may have touched the oil, with the crumbs of bread, then washes his hands and dries them with a towel, and afterwards proceeds with the prayers. This is the order prescribed by St. Charles,[2] Baruffaldi,[3] Catalani,[4] De Herdt,[5] Falise,[6] etc. The rubric here says nothing of it, but seems rather to suppose that he proceeds immediately with the prayers. It is plain, however, from the preparations ordered in a previous rubric,[7] that he is to rub and wash the fingers after the unctions, and this seems to be the proper time, as otherwise there is danger that, with the oil still on them, they may come in contact with the book or with his vestments. If everything be in readiness, there need be only a slight interruption. But if the priest fears that the interruption might be too long, and especially if the sick person be on the point of dying, he may continue the prayers, taking care that the fingers used in the unction shall touch nothing until the end.[8]

941. The prayers here prescribed are found in the most ancient rituals, but not in the same part of the ceremony. The first, " *Domine Deus qui,*" is found at the commencement, and the prayer, " *Respice quæsumus,*" towards the end, in the Pontifical of the Monastery of Joumieges of the ninth century.[9] In the Sacramentary of Tours of the tenth century, both these prayers are placed at the commencement, and the prayer, " *Domine Sancte Pater,*" etc., is amongst those at the end.[10]

---

[1] Vid. supra. n. 892.
[2] Pars iv. Instruct. Ext. Unct., § *Ordo ministrandi,* pag. 452.
[3] Tit. xxviii. n. 89.   [4] Ibid., v. cap. ii. § xvi. u. ii.
[5] Pars vi. n. 22, 9°.   [6] IIIme partie, sec. i. chap. iv. n. 8.
[7] Supra. § i.   [8] Baruff. n. 90. De Herdt, l. c. Falise, l. c.
[9] Martène, lib. i. cap. vii. art. iv. Ordo i.   [10] Ibid. Ord. iv.

It may be seen that in these prayers God is earnestly besought to grant to the sick person health of body as well as of soul, the restoration of corporal health being, as already stated, one of the effects of the sacrament. A knowledge that such is the purport of those prayers, would help to remove that fear which some have of receiving the sacrament, and to which we have before adverted.[1]

It was decided by the Sacred Congregation[2] that, when the person anointed is a female, there should be a change of gender in the versicles and prayers. The priest should say, " *V. Salvam fac ancillam tuam,*" instead of " *Salvum fac* " *servum tuum,*" etc.

*942. The prayers being concluded, the priest puts the vessel of holy oil into its case or cover, and puts the crumbs of bread he has used into the little bag or pocket, with the pellets of cotton, so that they may be carried to the church and burned together with them.[3] Some would require that even the water in which he has washed his hands, be carried to the church and thrown into the sacrarium.[4] This, however, would be, generally speaking, impracticable, and hence many authorities, as the " Modo Pratico,"[5] the Ritual of Toulon,[6] De Herdt,[7] etc., expressly state that the water may be thrown into the fire. De Herdt adds that this should be done by the priest himself or his assistant, and not by any of the domestics.

The same authorities also permit him to throw into the fire the piece of bread and the cotton which he has used.[8] With us, indeed, the priest is, for the most part, obliged to do so, as he cannot conveniently carry them back to the church; and in all such cases the fire is the best substitute for the sacrarium, as may be inferred from a rubric of the Roman Pontifical, which directs that the crumbs of bread, etc., used in removing the chrism from a chalice, after its consecration, be thrown *either* into the fire *or* into the sacrarium ... " Deinde extersiones projiciuntur in ignem vel sacrarium."[9]

§ XX.—Ad extremum, pro personæ qualitate, salutaria monita breviter præbere poterit quibus infirmus ad moriendum in Domino confirmetur, et ad fugandas dæmonum tentationes roboretur.

[1] Supra, n. 847. [2] 12 Aug. 1854, *in Lucionen.* ad 63.
[3] Baruff., n. 77, et n. 90. [4] *Act. Eccl. Med.*, loc. cit.
[5] Cap. ix. § *Rito di amministrare l'estrema unzione.*
[6] Dictionnaire des Cérémonies, etc., Art. *Ext. Unct.*, n. 26.
[7] Loc. cit. [8] Locis cit.
[9] *De Consecratione Patenæ et Calicis* in fine.

943. Before he leaves, the priest should address to the sick person a few words of consolation and instruction, as here directed. In most rituals a brief exhortation to be used for the purpose is given in an appendix. It is, of course, very general, and such as might be addressed to one in any condition of life; but it at least suggests what the priest himself may easily adapt to the special circumstances of the individual, " pro personæ qualitate." His own knowledge and piety will direct him better than any rule in what he should say, in order to inspire courage in resisting the temptations of the enemy, and resignation to the holy will of God, these being the dispositions most necessary to a Christian in danger of death.

§ XXI.—Denique Aquam benedictam, et Crucem, nisi aliam habeat, coram eo relinquet, ut illam frequenter aspiciat, et pro sua devotione osculetur et amplectatur.

*944. The rubric supposes that the priest is accompanied by a minister who carries holy water and a crucifix to the house of the sick person. He is now directed to leave them there, and to have the crucifix so placed that the sick person may often look at it, and even embrace and kiss it. If there be another crucifix, it is unnecessary to leave that which the priest brought with him, as the rubric here clearly conveys. It has been already stated that there ought to be a crucifix and holy water on the table prepared in the sick room,[2] and the present rubric shows that this is the more necessary when the priest comes unattended by any one, and, therefore, very often unable to have these requisites with him.

945. We need not dwell on the importance of having a crucifix placed before the eyes of the dying Christian. It speaks to him more eloquently than words of the mercy and love of God. It suggests to him those acts which are then most necessary for him : acts of sorrow for his sins, of faith in the great mysteries of redemption, of hope through the infinite merits of his Saviour, of love and of resignation to the will of Him who has done and suffered so much for him, etc.

§ XXII.—Admoneat etiam domesticos, et ministros infirmi, ut si morbus ingravescat, vel infirmus incipiat agonizare, statim ipsum Parochum accersant, ut morientem adjuvet, ejusque animam Deo commendet : sed si mors immineat, priusquam discedat, Sacerdos animam Deo rite commendabit.

Quæ autem pertinent ad visitationem curamque infirmorum, et ad juvandos morientes, ad Commendationem Animæ et ad Exequias, infra suis locis præscribuntur.

[1] Vid. supra, § ii.   [2] Supra, n. 904.

*946. It is of the greatest importance that the priest be present to assist the dying in the last agony, and he should, therefore, warn the attendants, as he is here directed, to give him notice, that he may be present if possible. We know that it is not possible for him, as a general rule, in large and populous parishes, where the number of priests is small; but he may be very often present, and there are cases in which he should strive to be present to assist the dying, in preference to any other duty that might be pressing at the time. At all events, if the sick person survives some days after receiving Extreme Unction, and expresses a desire to see the priest again, the priest would be guilty of a grievous violation of duty if he failed to visit him.

947. Should the agony commence before the priest leaves the house, he ought to remain by the bedside and assist until the soul has departed, as directed in the "Ordo com-"mendationis animæ," and "In expiratione." The rubric here refers him for further instruction to those parts of the ritual which treat of the visitation and care of the sick and dying.

In returning to the church or to his house, he should carry the holy oil as before directed.[1]

§ XXIII.—Additamentum.

948. Before concluding this chapter, it may be useful to say a few words on the case in which Extreme Unction is to be administered to two or more at the same time. This may easily happen in a hospital, or in time of pestilence, or even of prevalent sickness, though not pestilential. We have already seen what may be done as to the application of the matter and form in cases of urgent necessity or of very great danger.[2] But we now speak of cases that are not so urgent, and in which there is time enough to administer the sacrament in the ordinary way to each; and we may inquire whether in these it be lawful to recite any of the prayers or perform any of the ceremonies in common for all, as is done in administering Baptism to a number together.[3]

949. The ritual makes no provision for this case, nor is it touched on in any authority we have seen except in De Herdt,[4] and in an answer to a correspondent in the

---

[1] Supra, § iii.

[3] Supra, chap. iv. § xxv.

[2] Supra, n. 871, et seq.

[4] Pars vi. n. 24, ii.

"Mélanges Théologiques."[1]   In both it is decided that some
of the prayers may be recited for a number in common.   In
fact, the case may be regarded as analogous to that of Baptism or Orders administered to a number; and, from what is
prescribed in the ritual and the pontifical regarding these
sacraments, it may be inferred that, in administering Extreme
Unction, the prayers which are accompanied by no actions or
ceremonies, may be recited for a number in common.   This
view is confirmed by the ritual itself, in the last of the rubrics
regarding the visitation of the sick, which prescribes that the
prayers be said in the plural, should there be a number
together in the same apartment; and it is further confirmed
by an answer of the Sacred Congregation of the Inquisition,
regarding the case in which two or more marriages are celebrated together.   The priest having received the consent,
and pronounced for each the words, "*Ego vos,*" etc., may bless
the rings, and read the benedictions for all in common.[2]

950. If the priest, then, chooses to act on this opinion, he
may proceed thus:—Having entered the sick chamber with
the usual salutation, "*Pax huic,*" etc., he places the holy oil
on the table, sprinkles the holy water, and after this presents
the crucifix to be kissed by each, giving him at the same time
an opportunity of confessing.   The rubric prescribes that the
crucifix be presented before the sprinkling of holy water,[3]
but we think the order may be changed for greater convenience, should there be a number in different parts of the same
room; otherwise the priest would be obliged to go round them
all to present the crucifix, and afterwards to give each an opportunity of confessing.

He may then address the exhortation to all in common, and
recite for all in common the three prayers, "*Introeat,*" etc.,
which require no change of number, as is plain from reading
them.   The "*Confiteor*" is then said by each of them if he
is able, otherwise by an assistant, or even by the priest himself for all.[4]   The priest says the "*Misereatur vestri,*" etc.,
and gives notice to those who are present to pray while he is
administering the sacrament.

Judging from the exorcism in Baptism,[5] we are inclined to
think that he may say the prayer "*In nomine Patris* ✠,"
etc., for all in common, making the signs of the cross over

[1] VIme Série, pag. 503.   [2] 1 Sept. 1841, cit. apud Mél. Théol.,
l. c. et apud Falise, *Sac. Rit. Cong. Decr.,* V. Bened. Nup. in nota, 7.
[3] Supra, § v.   [4] Supra, n. 928.   [5] Supra, n. 370.

all, and changing "*te*" into "*vobis.*" But in the absence of
any clear authority on the point, it is better to say it for each
just before commencing to anoint him. The unctions, of
course, are applied to each individually. These finished,
the priest washes his hands,[1] and says the versicles and
prayers to the end for all in common, making the necessary
changes in number, and, if all be females,[2] in gender.

A priest, who may be called on to administer the sacrament
in this way to a number together, would do well to mark the
necessary changes in the margin of his ritual.

951. It has been before observed that in Ireland, and other
countries similarly circumstanced, the priest, when called to
attend the sick, finds it expedient, as a general rule, to go
prepared to administer both the Viaticum and Extreme
Unction. We have already stated how, in these circumstances, he is to carry with him the Blessed Sacrament and the
holy oil.[3] And it may be useful to state briefly here how he
should proceed so as to conform, as nearly as he can, to what
the rubrics require.

952. Having entered the chamber with the salutation,
"*Pax huic,*" etc., he sprinkles the holy water, saying, "*Asper-*
"*ges,*" etc., and says the versicles and the prayer, "*Exaudi*
"*nos,*" etc.

He then approaches the sick person, addresses to him a few
words of instruction or exhortation suited to his condition, and
hears his confession.[4]

953. If now he judges it expedient to administer the
Viaticum and Extreme Unction, he lays aside the violet
stole, and puts on the surplice and white stole.[5] He will find
it convenient, in these circumstances, to have a double stole,
such as has been before described.[6]

He then takes out the pyxis and places it on the table.
He may place the holy oil on the table at the same time, not
on the corporal, but to one side.[7] The reason why he does
not place the pyxis on the table on first entering the house,

---

[1] Supra, n. 940.   [2] Vid. supra, n. 365.   [3] Supra, n. 807, et 913.
[4] Supra, n. 809, et seq.   [5] Supra, n. 798-913.
[6] Chap. iii. n. 279. The use of this double stole is expressly permitted by the Sacred Congregation of Rites—26 Mar. 1859, *in Tar-*
novien., ad 7—in the ceremonies of Baptism, although these ceremonies,
as a rule, are performed only in the church (Vid. supra, n. 382), where
it is easy to have distinct stoles of the prescribed colors. There can be
no doubt, therefore, about the lawfulness of using it in the circumstances here supposed.   [7] Supra, n. 809, et n. 915.

has been intimated before.[1] He visits now, for the first time, as we suppose, and he does not know, until he has heard the person's confession, whether he is in a condition to receive the Viaticum. It may be that he is not. It may be that he cannot be absolved.[2] If, in such a case, the pyxis had been placed publicly on the table, either he should administer the sacrament, though knowing that it would be received unworthily (and he would be even bound to do so if the sick person demanded it),[3] or those present might take occasion to suspect that the sick person could not be absolved, etc. He effectually guards against this danger by not placing the pyxis on the table, until he has first heard the confession.

The " *Confiteor*," etc., is said, and the sacrament administered with the ceremonies before explained.[4] But if he has brought more than one particle,[5] he leaves the pyxis on the table, and does not give benediction with it until he has finished all.[6]

954. After the prayer, " *Domine Sancte*," etc., he changes the white stole for a violet one, and proceeds to administer Extreme Unction.

Omitting the salutation and the sprinkling of holy water,[7] he may, if time permits, say a few words to the sick person on the nature and effects of the sacrament. Then, having given him the crucifix to kiss, he says the versicles and prayers, " *Introeat Domine*," etc., and the " *Confiteor* " is repeated with the " *Misereatur tui*," etc.[8]

Those present having been on their knees during the administration of the Viaticum, should be requested to continue kneeling, and pray for the sick person before the Blessed Sacrament,[9] while he administers Extreme Unction, as before directed,[10] taking care, in going to or leaving the table, to genuflect, and also to avoid, as far as possible, turning his back to the pyxis.[11]

955. Having said the prayers, " *Domine Deus*," etc. . . . . " *Respice quæsumus*," etc., " *Domine Sancte*," etc., he may give the benediction " in articulo mortis," if he has the faculty.[12]

Omitting the " *Pax huic*," etc., and the " *Asperges*,"[13] he

[1] Supra, n. 812.   [2] Supra, n. 76ª.
[3] Vid. supra, n. 631.   [4] Supra, n. 814. et seq.
[5] Vid. supra, n. 838.   [6] De Herdt, n. 24. i. 4º.   [7] Supra, n 914.
[8] Supra, n. 920, 921, 923.   [9] Supra, n. 924.
[10] Supra, n. 926, et seq.   [11] De Herdt, l. c. 5º.
[12] Vid. infra, chap. xvii. § ii.   [13] Vid. infra, n. 968.

says a word or two on the efficacy of the benediction, invites the sick person to renew his sorrow by an act of contrition, and exhorts him to patience and resignation.[1]

He then says the versicles and the prayers, " *Clementissime* " *Deus*," etc. The " *Confiteor* " is said the third time, and he proceeds as below directed.[2]

956. Having given the Apostolic Benediction, he may say a word of advice and instruction, as recommended in a preceding rubric.[3]

Lastly, just before leaving, he gives the benediction with the pyxis, and puts it up securely as before.[4]

957. It is hardly necessary to observe that, in case of very urgent necessity, he should omit in each of the three functions all that he is allowed to omit, confining himself to the parts that are essential, according to what has been said in treating of each.

---

[1] Infra, n. 972.
[2] Supra, § xxi.
[3] Vid. chap. xvii. § v. et § vi.
[4] Vid. supra, n. 838.

CHAPTER XVII.

RITE TO BE OBSERVED BY PRIESTS DELEGATED TO GIVE THE APOSTOLIC BENEDICTION "IN ARTICULO MORTIS:" "RITUS BENEDICTIONIS APOSTOLICÆ IN ARTICULO MORTIS A SACERDOTIBUS AD ID DELEGATIS IMPERTIENDÆ."

958. This title or chapter is not found in any of the rituals published before the time of Benedict XIV, for it was he who prescribed the present formula. From the earliest ages of the Church bishops were invited, from time to time, to give their blessing to the dying,[1] and when given by the popes, or those specially delegated by them, it was, no doubt, very often accompanied by a plenary indulgence. We have, most probably, an instance of this in the indulgence granted to St. Clare by Innocent IV, as we read in her life given in the Roman Breviary.[2] At all events, it is certain that the popes have power to grant such indulgences, and that this power has been frequently used in the Church.[3]

959. Before the time of Benedict XIV, they readily granted to bishops the faculty of giving, by themselves, or by priests, whom they were permitted to delegate in special cases, a benediction with plenary indulgence to the sick " in articulo " mortis." But this great pope, in the bull, " *Pia mater*," etc., extended the faculty very considerably. According to the analysis of the bull given by Bouvier,[4] he decreed:

1° That though previously granted to bishops for only three years, it should thenceforth continue as long as they held their sees.

2° That they might delegate one or more priests, secular or regular, to impart this indulgence in the city or other parts of the diocese, as the good of souls might seem to require, with power to withdraw this faculty from those to whom they granted it, and substitute others according to their discretion.

3° That titular bishops who are transferred to other sees, or are newly instituted, should not have this faculty until they

---

[1] Catalani, tit. v. cap. vi. n. ii.   [2] Catal., l. c.
[3] Vid. Bouvier, *Traité des Indulgences*, part. iime cap. ii.   [4] Loc. cit.

ask and obtain it from the Holy See, but that they should obtain it when asked, not for three years only, but as long as they retain their sees.

4° He would have the same favor granted to inferior prelates, who have an independent territory and jurisdiction over the clergy and people, provided they visit, at stated times, the "limina apostolorum," and give an account of the state of their churches to the Holy See.

5° He declares that this faculty does not cease by the death of the pope who granted it, since it belongs to gracious jurisdiction delegated indefinitely, to subsist until it is revoked, or until the death of the person delegated. It does not cease, even for the priests who have obtained it, by the death or the translation to another see of the prelate who delegated them.

6° That in permitting bishops and other prelates to delegate as many priests as they may think necessary to apply this indulgence to the dying, he does not mean to exempt them from going themselves, when they can, to administer this consolation, above all to the poor and those who are most abandoned.

7° That care be taken in catechisms and public in. tructions to explain to the people the doctrine of the Church with regard to the temporal punishment due to sin ; the obligation of satisfying God's justice, by fasting, alms, prayers, and other good works; and the danger of presumptuously relying on the efficacy of the sacrament of Penance and a plenary indulgence at the hour of death ; for, he says, it is uncertain what kind our death may be, whether we shall receive the plenary indulgence at that last moment, whether, even in case the external rite be applied, we shall reap the fruit of it, or to what extent we shall be benefited by it.

8° He prescribes that all priests who have to assist the dying, and apply to them this indulgence "in articulo "mortis," shall excite them to sorrow for their sins, and inspire them with sentiments of fervent love of God and perfect resignation to His holy will, so as to accept death from His hand in punishment for their sins. It is this disposition especially which he requires in order that they may gain the fruit of the indulgence. "Hoc enim præcipue opus in hujus-"modi articulo constitutis imponimus et injungimus, quo se ad "indulgentiæ plenariæ fructum consequendum, præparent atque "disponant."

9° Lastly, to leave nothing undecided, he prescribed the formula here given in the ritual to be used in the application of the indulgence.

§ I.—Benedictio in articulo ·nortis cum soleat impertiri post Sacra·
menta Pœnitentiæ, Euchari~t'æ, et Extremæ Unctionis, illis Infirmis
qui vel illam petierint, dum sana mente et integris sensibus erant, seu
verisimiliter petiissent, vel dederint signa coutritionis; impertienda
iisdem est, etiamsi postea linguæ, cæterorumque sensuum usu sint des-
tituti, aut in delirium, vel amentiam inciderent. Excommunicatis vero,
impœnitentibus, et qui in manife~to peccato mortali moriuntur, est omnino deneganda.

*960. The circumstances in which the benediction is to be
given or refused, as here stated, are evidently the same as
those in which Extreme Unction is to be given or refused,
and have been considered in a preceding chapter.[1] It may be
doubted, however, whether the benediction is restricted, like
Extreme Unction, to such as are in danger of death from
bodily sickness, whether it may not be given to one who is in
danger of death from any other cause, *e. g.*, to a convict about
to be executed.[2] The words of the bull, "*Pia mater*," as
well as of the rubrics here, undoubtedly seem to suppose that
the person receiving the benediction is "ægrotus, infirmus,"
etc. Now it may be that this is supposed or required
strictly *as a condition ;* and it may be that the words are used,
not to express a condition, but simply to describe the case
that usually occurs. It is quite uncertain, and depends altogether on the intention of the pontiff. But in the absence
of any authority against it, the benediction may be given at
least conditionally.[3]

*961. The Sacred Congregation decided that this benedic-
tion should be given to children who are thought too young
to be admitted to Holy Communion.[4] This decision is in
perfect accordance with what has been said regarding the
administration of Extreme Unction to children in the same
circumstances.[5]

The question of course regards children who have attained
the use of reason; otherwise, being incapable of sinning,
they would be also incapable of receiving an indulgence.[6]

*962. It is certain that the benediction may be repeated in
the circumstances in which Extreme Unction may be repeated;
that is, when the sick person, having partially recovered,
relapses, and is again in danger of death.[7] But in a case of

---

· Supra, chap. xv. § vii. et ix.   [2] Vid. supra, n. 868.
[3] Vid. "Analecta Juris Pontificii," VIme Série, pag. 2010.
[4] 16 December, 1826, *in una Gandaven.*, ad Dub. 4, Quæs. v. n. 4623.
[5] Supra, n. 860.
[6] Vid. *Annotationem*, Contin. Gardellini in Decr. cit.
[7] Vid. supra, chap. xv. § xiv.

protracted illness, where the same danger still continues, it cannot be repeated.   Both points have been expressly decided by the Sacred Congregation of Indulgences.[1]

It had been long before decided by the same Congregation, that a plenary indulgence "in articulo mortis," given simply and without any other declaration, should be understood strictly, as gained only when death actually occurs.[2] It would be different, of course, if the terms of the brief contained the clause, "*etiamsi mors non sequatur*," which is contained in some referred to by Bouvier in his discussion of this matter.[3]

963. If the person, however, be not in a state of grace when the benediction is given, it is of no avail, and should be repeated when he recovers the state of grace.

But should he, after having received it in the state of grace, again fall into mortal sin, he would receive the fruit of the indulgence at the moment of death, provided he had, in the meantime, recovered the state of grace ; and, therefore, in this case, the benediction should not be repeated.[4]

964. Bouvier observes that, in the diocese of Mans, it is usual to give the benediction immediately after Extreme Unction. This, undoubtedly, should be the ordinary rule. It is evident from what is said regarding the dispositions required,[5] that the priest should give it, if possible, while the person has still the full use of his faculties, and should not, therefore, wait till the last moment. If there be no immediate danger, however, and if the priest can conveniently return, it may be sometimes expedient to defer it for another visit.[6]

§ II.—Habens prædictam facultatem, ingrediendo cubiculum, ubi jacet infirmus, dicat : *Pax huic domui*, etc., ac deinde ægrotum, cubiculum, et circumstantes aspergat Aqua benedicta, dicendo Antiphonam : *Asperges me*, etc.

965. There are few, if any, bishops who fail to obtain this important faculty, which is so readily granted by the Holy See ; and as they can delegate the same to as many priests as the good of souls may seem to them to require, they usually grant it to all the parochial clergy, and to all whom they approve for hearing confessions, since there is not one of

---

[1] 20 Sept. 1775, *Vindana in Britannia Minori*, ad 6ᵐ n. ccclvii. 12 Feb. 1842, *Gandaren.*, n. dxxix.   [2] 23 April, 1675. ad 1ᵐ n. xᵉ
[3] *Traité des Indulgences*, part ii. chap. ii. Qu. 3ᵐᵉ.
[4] Vid. Bouvier, l. c.   [5] Supra, n. 959—8°.   [6] Vid. Bouvier, l. c.

these who may not at some time be called on to assist the dying.

966. An answer of the Sacred Congregation of Indulgences,[1] declares that a bishop cannot delegate the faculty to *all* the confessors of his diocese. But this answer, interpreted by the one which immediately follows,[2] as well as by the words of the bull, *" Pia Mater,"* already referred to,[3] must, we think, be understood with this limitation, "unless the " bishop may, in the circumstances of his diocese, judge it " expedient for the good of souls to delegate it to all." It is certain at all events that many bishops do delegate the faculty to all whom they approve for hearing confessions, and no one doubts the licitness or the validity of such delegation.[4]

967. This delegation, according to Bouvier,[5] ought to be express and positive, and, for greater security, though not necessarily, in writing. At least a priest cannot regard it as included in the approval he may have received to hear confessions, unless it be formally expressed. The bishop may have intended to convey it at the same time, but the intention does not suffice, unless it be expressed.

*968. The rubric supposes that the priest comes for the purpose of giving the benediction; and in this case, on entering the room he says, *" Pax huic domui,"* and sprinkles the holy water as here directed.[6] De Herdt[7] recommends for greater security that he do so even when he gives the benediction immediately after Extreme Unction, because the rubric occurs in the formula of Benedict XIV, and may therefore express a strict condition of the indulgence. But there can hardly, we think, be a reasonable doubt that in that case, having already said the *" Pax huic domui,"* and sprinkled the water on entering the room, he may safely omit the repetition.[8]

*969. He should be vested in surplice and violet stole,[9] and therefore should retain the vestments he has used in giving Extreme Unction, if he gives the benediction immediately after.

[1] 20 Sept. 1775, *Vindana*, ad 2m partem, Dub. 8vi n. ccclvii.
[2] Ad 3m partem ejusdem Dub.   [3] Supra, n. 959—2°.
[4] Cfr. Bouvier, part. iime chap. iime.   "Mélanges Théologiques," IIIme Série, 2me Cahier, pag. 324.   [5] Loc. cit.
[6] Vid. supra, n. 920.   [7] Pars vi. n. 25, vi.   [8] Vid. supra, n. 914.
[9] Caval., vol. iv. cap. xxvii. *De Benedictione in vita et mortis articulo*, Decr. vii. in fine. De Herdt, l. c.

§ III.—Quod si ægrotus voluerit confiteri, audiat illum, et absolvat. Si confessionem non petat, excitet illum ad eliciendum actum contritionis; de hujus Benedictionis efficacia ac virtute, si tempus ferat, breviter admoneat; tum instruat, atque hortetur, ut morbi incommoda ac dolores in anteactae vitae expiationem libenter perferat Deoque sese paratum offerat ad ultro acceptandum quicquid ei placuerit, et mortem ipsam patienter obeundam in satisfactionem poenarum, quas peccando promeruit.

970. The Church, anxious about the spiritual welfare of her children at every period of their lives, becomes more and more solicitous about them as death approaches, knowing that their salvation depends on their dying in the state of grace. Hence she is ready to administer to them over and over again the holy sacrament of Penance, instituted by her Divine Founder as the sovereign remedy for sin. She directs the priest, as often as he visits the sick, to ascertain whether they desire to confess, and if so, to hear and absolve them; and it is her wish that, if possible, he should be present with them in the last agony.

971. St. Liguori recommends confessors who assist the dying to give them absolution frequently while they have the use of their senses: " Dum infirmus adhuc sensibus viget, " absolutionem pluries ei conferri post brevem reconcilia- " tionem juvabit, ut ita ille magis circa statum gratiae securus " reddatur, si forsan praeteritae confessiones invalidae fuissent, " aut saltem gratiae augmentum recipiat, necnon purgatorii " poenae ei minuantur."[1]

" Juxta praescriptum et mentem Ritualis Romani," says the Council of Baltimore, " sedulus sit Pastor animarum in " visitandis infirmis et agonizantibus etiam postquam ultima " receperunt sacramenta; et illos exhortetur, consoletur, ad- "juvet; et elicito ab iis, si possint, novo confessionis et " contritionis actu, nova identidem donet absolutione."[2]

*972. In the present case, if the sick person does not confess, the priest should endeavor to excite him to contrition, as is directed not only by the rubric here, but in the bull itself, according to the analysis already given.[3] It does not appear, however, that this is rigorously required as a condition of the indulgence, but it gives greater security that the person is in the state of grace, which is absolutely necessary to gain any indulgence. He should then simply explain to him, if time permits, the efficacy of the benediction he is about to impart, and especially he should exhort him to be

[1] *Praxis Confess.*, n. 276.   [2] Prov. v. Decr. xi.   [3] Supra, n. 969—8°.

patient and resigned to the will of God in his sufferings, and
to be ready to accept death itself in satisfaction for his sins,
and as a punishment deserved by them. This is the disposition on which the Pontiff chiefly insists, as we have
already seen.[1]

§ IV.—Tum piis ipsum verbis consoletur, in spem erigens, fore. ut
ex divinæ munificentiæ largitate eam poenarum remissiouem, et vitam
sit consecuturus æternam.

973. He should then console and encourage him, inspiring
him with a confident hope of obtaining, through the mercy
and goodness of God, a full remission of all his sins, and
eternal happiness in the next life. He may use any words
which his piety may suggest, but it would be difficult to find
any more appropriate than those short sentences given in the
ritual itself, in its instructions to the pastor on the mode of
assisting the dying.

§ V.—Sacerdos dicat: *Adjutorium nostrum,* etc.
Tum dicto ab uno ex Clericis adstantibus *Confiteor,* Sacerdos dicat,
Misereatur, etc., Deinde: *Dominus noster,* etc.

*974. The form here given is that prescribed by Benedict
XIV, and of course should be adhered to in every particular
when circumstances permit.   It was doubted whether the
" *Confiteor* " should be said if the benediction be given immediately after Extreme Unction, since it has been said just before
the administration of that sacrament; but the Sacred Congregation of Indulgences decided that it should again be said,
the question proposed being, whether it should be recited
thrice when the Viaticum, Extreme Unction, and this benediction follow in immediate succession.[2]

*975. The priest says " *Misereatur tui,* " etc , as in administering the Viaticum, and makes the sign of the cross over
the sick person when saying " *In nomine Patris,*" etc., an
also at the end, while saying " *Pater, Filius,*" etc.[3]

§ VI.—Si vero infirmus sit adeo morti proximus, ut neque Confessionis
generalis faciendæ, neque præmissarum precum recitandarum tempus
suppetat, statim Sacerdos Benedictionem ei impertiatur.

*976. It is difficult to determine what part of the form
given is essential in order to apply the indulgence. Nothing
is decided here by the ritual, which gives the form prescribed
by the bull of Benedict XIV. It is certainly sufficient to

---

[1] Supra, n. 959—8°.   [2] 5 Feb. 1841, *in Valentinen.*, ad 6ᵐ n. dvi.
[3] De Herdt, n. 25, vi.

commence with the words "*Dominus noster,*" etc., but is it necessary to commence with them? Falise seems to think it is.[1] Cavalieri would have the priest commence in the case here supposed with the words, "*Ego facultate mihi ab Apostolica* "*Sede tributa Indulgentiam,*" etc.[2] Catalani maintains that the form to be used is given in the last words, "*Benedicat* "*te omnipotens Deus,*" etc.[3]

*977. The formula is given in many editions of the Roman Breviary, as well as in the ritual; but the rubric in the Breviary is more explicit, for it says, "Si vero infirmus sit . . . "statim ei benedictionem impertiatur dicens: *Dominus nos-* "*ter,*" etc., which would seem to favor the opinions of Falise. But then it adds: "Et si mors proxime urgeat, dicat: *In-* "*dulgentiam plenariam et remissionem omnium peccatorum tibi* "*concedo in Nomine Patris et Filii et Spiritus Sancti.*" This last form is given in the ritual only as part of the prayer, "*Dominus noster,*" etc., but there is no reason to doubt its validity, since it is given in breviaries printed in Rome. Tak ing, then, the rubric of the Breviary to be the best interprete of the ritual, we would follow it in practice, commencing with "*Dominus noster,*" etc., unless when the person is just expir- ing, in which case we would at once say, "*Indulgentiam,*" etc.[4]

978. It may be observed that this is not the only plenary indulgence that can be obtained at the hour of death. A great many have been granted for this hour to the faithful who are members of certain pious confraternities, who practise certain devotions, or who have rosaries, crosses, medals, etc., to which the indulgences are attached, provided they comply with the requisite conditions.[5] The titles on which these indul- gences are granted are altogether distinct, and the conditions are not incompatible. It has been decided by the Sacred Congregation of Indulgences that, when communion is re- quired as a condition of the indulgence, the same communion may suffice for several plenary indulgences.[6]

979. The conditions required for those granted "in articulo "mortis" are very easy. They are, for the most part, those acts which should, in any event, be frequently elicited by the Christian in danger of death: acts of contrition, acts of the love of God, and of perfect resignation to His holy will, and

[1] Part. iii. sec. ii. cap. i. § iii.
[2] Vol. iv. cap. xxvii. Decr. v. n. iii.   [3] Tit. v. cap. vi. § vii.
[4] Cfr. "Analecta," IVme Série, pag. 2010.
[5] Bouvier, *Traité des Indulgences,* partie iime chap. iime Qu. 4me.
[6] 29 Maii, 1841, *Briocen.,* ad 1^m n. dxi.

the invocation of the sacred name with the heart, if not with the lips.

To gain the indulgences attached to rosaries, crosses, medals, etc., it is enough to take the blessed object in the hand, or to have it about or near the person, while making the acts prescribed, which are usually those just mentioned. The ministry of a priest is not necessary, though it is of course very useful in assisting the sick person to make the acts required.[1] It is probable that, even by virtue of a single concession, the indulgence may by gained as often as the prescribed acts are repeated,[2] but there is no reason to doubt that several may be gained when the titles are distinct.[3]

With respect to the intention, it is sufficient that one have that of gaining all the indulgences he can by the acts he performs. It is not necessary to think of them in particular, nor even to know that they are attached to the acts.[4] It is even probable that an intention of gaining the indulgences is not required at all, provided the work to which it is attached be done. St. Liguori seems to think that, at all events, it is enough to have an interpretative intention.[5]

980. The priest, then, should not fail to suggest to the sick person this easy yet powerful means of satisfying the divine justice. It is true that if he had the happiness of gaining one plenary indulgence, he could not gain a second for himself at the same time, for even one includes a complete remission of all the temporal punishment due to his sins; but it is hard to reckon in any instance on the presence of all those conditions, and especially of those perfect dispositions which are necessary to gain a plenary indulgence in its full extent.[6] But, although it be not gained in its whole extent, it may be gained partially;[7] and if many be gained in this way, the effect of all united may come very near, and, when there is a complete renunciation of all venial sins, may be equal to the full effect of a plenary indulgence.[8]

[1] Bouvier, loc. cit. Qu. 5ᵐᵉ.
[2] Busemb., apud St. Lig., lib. vi. n. 534—4.
[3] Ibid. 5. Vid. Bouvier, l. c. Qu. 4ᵐᵉ.
[4] Bouv., par. i. chap. vii. art. i. § ii.   [5] Lib. vi. n. 534—14.
[6] Vid. Bouv., chap. vii. art. i. § i. St. Lig., n. 534. *Certum est.*
[7] St. Lig., ibid.   [8] Vid. De Lugo, *De Pœnitentia*, Disp. xxvii. sec. vi. n. 11.

APPENDIX.

DECREES OF THE SACRED CONGREGATION OF RITES.

The following are the decrees referred to in the present volume. They are here given with their numbers and dates as they are found, in chronological order, in the third edition of Gardellini (vid. Introduction, n. 37). The few not found in Gardellini are added under a distinct heading. At the end of each decree will be found the number or numbers under which it is referred to in the volume.

289. *Baren.*, 28 Jan., 1606. "In civitate Baren., solere presbyteros Ecclesiæ S. Nicolai ejusdem civitatis dum mannam ejusdem S. Nicolai ad infirmos d. ferunt, illam deferre superpelliceo indutos solemniter, cum luminaribus et lanternis, ac si Sacramentum Extremæ Unctionis ad infirmos deferrent, et S. R. C. pro parte Archiepiscopi dictæ civitatis expositum fuit, et petitum, an conveniat?

"Eadem S. R. C. non modo mannam S. Nicolai, sed neque Extremæ Unctionis Oleum solemniter cum superpelliceo, ac lanternis ad infirmos deferendum esse." respondit et declaravit. 910.

629. *Manilien.*, 2 Maii, 1626. "Archiepiscopus Manilien. petiit declarari: An Episcopi Philippinarum possint astringere Parochos Regulares ad observandum in praxi caput Ritualis Romani de Sacramento Pœnitentiæ in eo, quod dicit 'quod si confitendi desiderium suum per se, sive per alios ostenderit infirmus, absolvendus?'

"Et S. C. respon 'it: Placere sibi quod si non est introducta observatio Ritualis Romani, introducatur." 64.

753. *Dub. Urbis.*, 12 Jul., 1628. "1. An Canonicis usum Cappæ et Rochetti habentibus liceat sacramenta administrare cum solo Rochetto et deposita Cappa?

"Resp. : Ad 1. Sacramenta esse administranda cum superpelliceo et Stola juxta Rituale Romanum." 121.

1319. *Pisauren.*, 20 April., 1641. "Patres S. Caroli Congregationis Clericorum regularium petierunt respouderi: An liceat in nocte Nativitatis Domini, post cantatam primam missam, alias duas immediate celebrare, et communicare fideles ?

"Et S. R. C. respondit: Nullo modo licere, sed omnino prohibendum." 710.

1360. *Trium Missarum*, etc., 7 Dec., 1641. "Cum superioribus diebus consulta hæc S. R. C. an esset permittendum celebrari, in media nocte Nativitatis Domini, post missam decantatam successive alias duas missas, et in eis sacram communionem exhiberi fidelibus eam deposcentibus ?

"Et respondisset: 'Non esse permittendum sed omnino utrumque prohibendum;' nihilominus nonnulli Regulares asserentes id licere supplicarunt audiri:

"Et S. C. ipsis auditis cum procuratoribus et advocatis, ad relationem Em. Palloti, stetit in decretis, et respondit: Iterum prohibendum tam sacerdotibus celebrare volentibus, quam confluentibus media nocte ad ecclesias et communionem deposcentibus." 710.

1496. *Marianen.*, 16 Ap., 1644. "Moniales SS. Annunciationis de Bastia supplicarunt pro facultate asservandi in earum Ecclesia SS. Eucharistiam.

"Et S. C. respondit: Aut monasterium est canonice erectum, et non indiget: aut non, et non est approbandum." 597.

1907. *Galliarum*, 13 Jul., 1658. "Regularibus regni Galliæ declarare petentibus: An in communione quæ inter Missæ sacrificium peragitur, sit prius ministrandum SS. Eucharistiæ Sacramentum ministro Missæ inservienti, an vero monialibus vel cæteris ibidem præsentibus.

"S. R. C. responderi mandavit: In casu prædicto ministrum sacrificii, non ratione præeminentiæ, sed ministerii, præferendum esse cæteris quamvis dignioribus." 718.

2008. *Matherana*, 22 Nov., 1659. "Petrus Antonius Gallus cantor Ecclesiæ loci Lattezzæ Matheranæ diœcesis, declarari postulavit: An Archipresbytero ejusdem loci liceat in administrando populis SS. Sacramento, manum porrigere osculandum ?

"Resp. : Non licere et contrariam consuetudinem esse abusum omnino tollendum." 686.

2127. *Andrien.*, 3 Sept., 1661. Ad dirimendas controversias .... declaravit S. R. C. "Patenæ suppositionem per sacerdotem cotta indutum in Communione generali, quæ per Dignitates agitur, retinendam esse." 651.

2350. *Florentin.*, 19 Dec., 1665. "S. R. C. ad preces Laurentii Vanni præpositi S. Joannis Florentiarum, declaravit: 'Tam actum baptizandi, quam alias functiones præparatorias pro baptizandis Turcis, et aliis ad fidem venientibus, esse faciendas per eundem sacerdotem baptizantem, et consequenter ipsum præpositum, prout in Rituali disponitur, et usque adhuc servatum fuit, a quo solito recedendum non esse, censuit' : et ita decrevit, et servari mandavit." 543.

2504. *Oritana*, 21 Jun., 1670. S. R. C. censuit: "Servandum esse decretum Vicarii in Ecclesia Cathedrali, ne in posterum celebrentur Missæ Defunctorum nisi cum colore nigro vel saltem violaceo. Quo vero ad alias Ecclesias, Planetas hujusmodi facere non valentes, et proinde quolibet colore uti solitas, audiendum esse eundem Vicarium." 708.

2602. *Conchen.*, 3 Sept., 1672. "In renovatione, quæ quolibet octavo die fieri debet de Aug. Eucharistiæ Sacramento, consumi debet tum Hostia, tum etiam particulæ, quæ existunt in tabernaculo, post sumptionem Sanguinis ante purificationem; illa vero verba, quæ habentur in Missali cap. 10, num. 5, nempe: *Si vero adsint hostiæ consecratæ, etc.*, possunt intelligi de hac renovatione, æque ac de nova confectione Sacramenti reservandi pro alia die." Et ita censuit S. R. C. 619. 622.

2859. *Mexicana.*, 12 Mar., 1678. "VIII. In multis Ecclesiis solent celebrari Missæ de festivitatibus B. M. V. cum solemnitate pro re gravi, et concursu populi. Quæritur: An, quando celebratur Missa de Annunciatione modo dicto, sit faciendum ad *Incarnatus*, quod fit in ipsa die Annunciationis?

"Resp. Ad viii.: Missas proprias de festivitatibus B. M. V. non esse celebrandas, nisi diebus in quibus dictæ solemnitates occurrunt, et per eorum octavas, quas habent; cæteris temporibus earum loco celebrandam unam ex votivis B. M. V. in fine Missalis positis, juxta distributionem temporis in eo factam, cum intentione ad honorem Annunciationis, Assumptionis," etc. 573.

2903. *Ord. Min. Capuc.*, 30 Sept., 1679. "IX. Solent Capuccini Sacerdotes in die Cœnæ Domini Sanctum Corpus Christi sumentes, deferre stolam ante pectus in formam Crucis accommodatam; quæritur, an debeant observare consuetudinem introductam, vel deferre stolam a collo pendentem?

"Resp. Ad ix.: Posse utrumque observari." 676.

3025. *Albinganen.*, 24 Jul., 1683. "II. Utrum in Missa *de Requiem* conveniat Communionem fidelibus ministrare, vel post illam, et in casu convenientis administrationis post Missam cum paramentis nigris, conveniat dari benedictionem, an vero benedictio omittenda?

"Resp. Ad ii.: Non esse contra ritum, si tamen administretur communio post Missam, omittendam esse benedictionem." 727. (Vid. infra, *Decret. Gen.*. 23 Jul., 1868.)

3392. *Augustæ Prætoriæ*, 21 Jul., 1696. "Cum Episcopus Augustanus S. R. C. exposuerit: III. Quod SSmum. Eucharistiæ Sacramentum continuo retinetur in eadem Ecclesia super duplici altari, nimirum super altare chori, et super alio S. Joannis Baptistæ ratione parochiæ eidem cathedrali unitæ.

"Resp. Ad iii.: Sacratissimam Eucharistiam servandam esse in uno tantum altari designando ab Episcopo." 614.

3525. *Ord. Capuc.*, 22 Aug., 1699. "Exposito humiliter S. R. C. per Procuratorem generalem Ordinis Capuccinorum in nonnullis provinciis, in quibus chori Ecclesiarum suæ religionis, supra valvas earumdem Ecclesiarum diametraliter altari SSmæ. Eucharistiæ oppositas existunt, consuetudinem obrepsisse in iisdem choris tempore nocturno, tam ad lumine afficiendum altare SSmi. Sacramenti, quam dormitorium, unicam lampadem in arcellula ex tela constructa retinendi, ex qua quidem situatione lampadis, cum ex maxima distantia chori ab altari SSmi. Sacramenti, hoc nihil, vel pauxillum lumen recipiat. S. R. C. supplicavit declarari: An in Ecclesiis suæ religionis prædictis, juxta recensitam consuetudinem, retentio lampadis ante altare SSmi. Sacramenti nocturno tempore, modo superius expresso sufficiat, vel potius sit retinenda lampas intra, et ante altare SSmi. Sacramenti semper accensa, prout de die retinetur ?

"Et eadem S. R. C. respondit: Negative, et omnino lampadem esse retinendam intra, et ante altare SSmi. Sacramenti, ut continuo ardeat." 615.

3575. *Cong. Mont. Coronæ.*, 22 Jan., 1701. "X. An ante ostiolum tabernaculi SSmi. Sacramenti, retineri possit vas florum, vel quid simile, quod prædictum occupet ostiolum cum imagine Dni. N. in eodem insculpta ?

"Resp. Ad x. : Negative. Posse tamen in humiliori, et decentiori loco." 609.

3614. *Lerien.*, 11 Feb., 1702. "VII. Utrum a Parocho Viaticum ad infirmos deferente, antiphona *Asperges me.* aut *Vidi aquam* tempore paschali sit recitanda, et ab ipso quoque ad Ecclesiam redito, dicenda oratio *Deus qui nobis*, aut *Spiritum nobis. Domine*, etc. ?

"Resp. Ad vii. : Servandum esse omnino Rituale, nulla habita ratione temporis paschalis." 910.

3670. *Urbis et Orbis*, 10 Dec., 1703. "VI. An benedictiones mulierum post partum, Fontis Baptismalis, ignis, seminis, ovorum et similium sint de juribus mere parochialibus ?

"Resp. Ad vi.: Negative, sed Benedictiones Mulierum et Fontis Baptismalis fieri debere a Parochis." 563.

3834. *Catanien.*, 9 Mar., 1711. "III. An canonicus post sumptionem Corporis et Sanguinis, dispensans Corpus Christi clericis qualibet prima Dominica mensis (ut moris est), debeant canonici stare, an vero genuflecti, ut observatum est ?

"Resp. Ad iii. : Affirmative." 722.

4055. *Toletana*, 15 Sept., 1736. "VIII. An possit tolerari conversio super humerum sinistrum, communicando moniales habentes fenestellam ni parte evangelii ?

"Resp. Ad viii. : Debere descendere, et reverti per gradus anteriores, et non laterales altaris." 673.

4170. *Lucana*, 15 Maii, 1745. "An sit laudandus Parochus, qui in feria vi. in Parasceve, dum defert SS. Sacramentum ad domum sui parochiani infirmi pro ministrando ei Viatico, per vias publicas recitat suetos psalmos, sed in fine illorum omittit *Gloria Putri*, et ingressus Ecclesiam, statim reponit sacram pyxidem, et dimittit populum absque benedictione ?

"Et S. R. C. audito prius voto unius ex Apostolicarum cæremoniarum magistris, rescribendum censuit: Non est reprobandus Parochus, qui defert SS. Viaticum infirmo feria vi. in Parasceve, dummodo private, et submissa, quinimo submississima voce recitet psalmos consuetos per vias publicas, etiamsi dicat *Gloria Patri*, etc., quia in tali circumstantia, actio talis nihil habet esse cum functionibus Ecclesiæ hujus diei; et considerandum est, quod defert cum stola et pluviali albi coloris, quando in feria supradicta color paramentorum est niger pro Ecclesiæ functionibus: Ideoque, si defert privatim pro aliqua necessitate, non est reprobandus, si populum sine benedictione dimittąt feria vi. in Parasceve, quia in publica Ecclesia non debet recondi." 799, 839.

4252. *Lucana*, 12 April, 1755. III. "An fas sit Parochis uti in collatione Sacramenti Baptismatis Aqua in Ecclesia Matrice aut Plebenali benedicta cui privatim et separatim et non ipso actu Benedictionis Baptismalis infusa fuerint olea sacra?

"Resp. Ad iii.: Parochi ex Matricis fonte aquam, cui sacra olea jam fuerint commixta suscipere debent, quam adhibeant in Baptismi collatione. Qui vero ante fontis benedictionem, olea sacra recipere non potuerunt, illa subinde privatim, ac separatim in aquam mittere poterunt." 253.

4290. *Calagur. et Calceat.*, 17 Maii, 1760. "Indulta a S. R. C., die 7 Julii, 1759. Rmo. Episcopo Calagur. et Calceat., facultate subdelegandi ejus Vicarios aliosque sacerdotes pro benedictione sacræ supellectilis, in qua sacra unctio non adhibetur: dubitatum fuit ab eodem Rmo. Epis. An illi quibus dicta facultas delegata fuit, benedicere possint imagines Domini Nostri J. C. . . . Tabernaculum in quo asservatur SS. Eu ·h. Sacramen-

tum, Pyxidem, et generaliter omne illud, in quo sacra unctio non adhibetur?

Propterea idem Rmus. Episc. iterum S. R. C. supplicavit quatenus ad omnem scrupulum amovendum, declarare dignetur. An in indulto jam sibi concesso comprehenderetur facultas subdelegandi prædictarum rerum benedictionem? Sin minus nova facultas ad hunc effectum sibi necessaria concederetur.

"Et S. C. eidem Rmo. Epis. indulsit 'per viam novæ declarationis eandem facultatem subdelegandi benedictionem omnium quorumcumque ad Divinum Cultum spectantium in quibus sacra unctio non adhibetur.'" 602.

4299. *Aquen.*, 8 Mar., 1761. VII. "Extatne aliquod decretum prohibens ne in benedictione SSmi. Sacramenti ante orationem dicatur: *Dominus vobiscum?* Asserunt multi: Rituale tamen etiam nuper a Benedicto XIV editum id præscribit in festivitate Corporis Christi post reditum processionis.

"Resp. Ad vii.: In Benedictione SSmi. Sacramenti ante orationem, non debet dici *Dominus vobiscum*, juxta decretum S. R. C. in Granaten., 16 Junii, 1663, et in Salernitana 28 Septemb., 1675, quod ita se habet: In festo SSmi. Corporis Christi servanda est dispositio Cæremonialis Episcoporum. lib. 2, cap. 33, de re ponendo SSmo. Sacramento, ubi nulla fit mentio de *V̇. Dominus vobiscum*, non vero Rituale Romanum, ubi dicitur addi *Dominus vobiscum*: et sic servat in urbe Summus Pontifex, et servatur ab omnibus." 695

4879. *Ord. Min. Observ.*, 25 Feb., 1777. "An Diaconus in ordine tantum diaconatus constitutus, extra casum necessitatis, possit distribuere fidelibus communionem ?

"Resp.: Negative." 647.

4401. *Ord. Carm. Excalc.*, 16 Feb., 1781. VII. "Utrum sub prohibitione celebrandi Missas privatas post solemnem decantatam, et administrandi fidelibus sacram Eucharistiam in nocte Nativitatis, comprehendantur Carmelitæ utriusque sexus, maxime cum apud illos cantetur Missa solemnis non in media nocte (hoc enim tempore incipit matutinum), sed circiter horam tertiam ? Et quatenus Affirmative.

"VIII. An consuetudo contraria immemorabilis valeat sustentari saltem quoad moniales, religiosos, choristas, et laicos ?

"Resp. Ad vii.: Affirmative. Ad viii.: Negative." 710.

4477. *Romana*, 16 Sept., 1801. I. "An in Ecclesiis in quibus expositum manet SS. Sacramentum fidelium adorationi in turno perpetuæ adorationis, quæ dicitur quadraginta horarum, occurrente die Commemorationis omnium fidelium defunctorum, liceat recitare officium defunctorum, et celebrare Missam solemnem, et etiam Missas privatas itidem defunctorum ?

"II. Et quatenus affirmative. An adhiberi debeant paramenta coloris violacei potius quam coloris nigri ?

III. An in eodem casu excipiendum sit altare, in quo habetur expositum SS. Sacramentum ?

"Resp. Ad i.: Affirmative. Ad ii.: Arbitrio Superioris localis.

Ad. iii.: Affirmative.' 708. (Vid. *Decr. Gen.*, 28 Julii, 1868.)

4499. *Tiphernen.*, 23 Mar., 1806. "Cum sacerdos I. B. Berni, recenter Archipresbyteratu Ecclesiæ Parochialis, titulo SS. Cosmæ et Damiani, Diœces. Tiphernen. potitus, antiquam consuetudinem in eadem Ecclesia invenerit Sacrosanctam Eucharistiam impertiendi fidelibus in Sabbato Sancto pro satisfactione etiam Paschalis præcepti, et anceps hæserit: Num eadem consuetudo servanda foret, sive utpote abusiva removenda ? Ut omnem anxietatem deponeret, supplex fuit apud S. R. C. pro declaratione sequentis dubii; videlicet:

"An liceat in Sabbato Sancto inter Missarum solemnia sacram Eucharistiam fidelibus distribuere, et num per eandem sumptionem sacræ Communionis præceptum Paschale adimpleatur ?

"Resp. Affirmative in utroque." 712.

4505. *Toletana*, 20 Sep., 1606. II. "In Ecclesia Regalis Monasterii S. Laurentii Excurialensis adest in Altari majore Tabernaculum ex lapide pretioso, in quo continetur alia capsula eximior, in qua asservatur SSmum. Sacramentum, sed cum in pariete post Tabernaculum sit una fenestra, quæ illuminat dou Tabernacula prædicta, et ista habeant ante et retro fenestellas cum cristallo taliter, quod ex qualibet parte ecclesiæ videatur clare et distincte vas in quo est inclusum SSmum. Sacramentum; et cum hoc videatur inconveniens, quæritur. Utrum prædictum vas debeat permanere ut dictum est supra, vel debeat cooperiri aliquo velo at non videatur?

"Resp. Ad ii.: Negative ad primam partem. Affirmative ad secundam, atque ita obtegendum esse Tabernaculum, ut vas in quo SS. Sacramentum asservatur, a circumstantibus nullo modo videri possit." 609.

4526. *Tuden.*, 7 Sept., 1816. XXXVII. "An die magni concursus ad indulgentiam plenariam vel jubilæum, possit ministrari sacra Eucharistia fidelibus aliqua hora ante auroram, et post meridiem?

"Resp. Ad xxxvii.: In casu de quo agitur, Affirmative a tempore ad tempus quo in illa Ecclesia Missæ celebrantur, vel ad formam rubricæ, vel ad formam indulti eidem Ecclesiæ concessi." 703.

4536. *Dub. Addit.* 31 Maii, 1817. I. "An Canonici Cathedralis in administratione Sacramentorum tam intra quam extra Cathedralem Ecclesiam teneantur deponere cappam, atque uti superpelliceo et stola juxta Rituale Romanum?

"Resp. Ad i.: Affirmative." 121.

4572. *Calagur. et Calceat.*, 23 Sept. 1820. "Parochus in casu necessitatis periclitantem puerum stola violacea indutus domi baptizavit, eique sacrum chrisma et oleum sacrum quod secum detulit, imposuit, prout in Rit. Romano. Quæritur an bene, vel male se gesserit in casu unctionis extra Ecclesiam?

"Et S. R. C. . . . respondendum censuit: Juxta votum, nimirum parochum male se gessisse, baptizando cum stola violacea, et liniendo puerum periclitantem, extra Ecclesiam, oleo etiam catechumenorum. In casu enim necessitatis, juxta Ritualis præscriptum, omnia sunt omittenda quæ baptismum præcedunt, quæque post modum supplenda sunt in Ecclesia, ad quam præsentandus est puer cum convalescit." 382.

4578. *Decretum generale*, 8 Ap., 1821. VI. "An toleranda, vel eliminanda sit consuetudo, quæ in dies invalescit, superimponendi sacras reliquias, pictasque imagines tabernaculo, in quo augustissimum Sacramentum asservatur, ita ut idem tabernaculum pro basi inserviat?

"Resp. Ad. vi.: Assertam consuetudinem tanquam abusum eliminandam omnino esse." 607.

4594. *Panormit.*, 12 Ap., 1823. IX. "Quæstio sæpe exorta est, utrum in Missa *de Requiem* cum paramentis nigris celebrata, post communionem celebrantis, administrari possit fidelibus adstantibus Eucharistia cum particulis præconsecratis, asserentibus nonnullis posse: 1o Quia in operibus Ferdinandi Tetani decretum S. C. die 2 Sept., 1741, tanquam apocryphum habendum esse dicitur. 2o Quia affirmativum fuit responsum Josephi Dini apostolicarum cæremoniarum magistri, sententiæ innixi Benedicti XIV, in suo opere *De Sacrificio Missæ:* ut autem omnis hac de re tollatur scrupulus quæsitum fuit:

"An pro certa tenenda sit sententia affirmativa Benedicti XIV et Tetami, vel supradictum decretum sub die 2 Sept., 1741?

"Resp. Ad ix.: Dilata, et videatur particulariter ex officio," 85, 707. (Vid. infra, *Decr. Gen.*, 23 Jul., 1868.)

4623. *Gandaven.*, 16 Dec. 1826. I. "Facti species—Rector Ecclesiæ reperit in sua Ecclesia consuetudinem renovandi panem pro sacrificio Missæ, et communione fidelium, singulis tribus mensibus tempore hyemis tempore vero æstivo, solitum confici pro sex mensibus. Hinc quæritur: 1º An, attenta consuetudine, rector licite consecrare possit species a tribus mensibus tempore hyemis, vel a sex mensibus in æstate confectas ? 2. An casu, quo rector, sive pastor Ecclesiæ praxim illam approbet, nec velit eam relinquere, alii sacerdotes in eadem Ecclesia inservientes possint tuta conscientia in hoc ei obsecundare, utendo præfatis specibus ?

"II. Facti species—in Parochiis ruralibus, ubi longum faciendum est iter, plerumque portatur SSmum. Sacramentum Eucharistiæ ad ægrotos, eisque administratur cum stola super vestem communem absque cotta, sive superpelliceo. Quæritur propterea. 1. An praxis illa ubi invaluit, et Ordinarii locorum non contradicunt, retineri possit ? 2. An saltem Sacramentum Extremæ Unctionis cum stola tantum administrari possit ?

"III. Facti species—Sacerdotes curam animarum exercentes, pro sua commoditate, apud se in domibus suis retinent Sanctum Oleum infirmorum. Quæritur: An, attenta consuetudine, hanc praxim licite retinere valeant ?

"IV. Facti species—Sacra Olea, in Cœna Domini bene dicta, transmittuntur ad decanos foraneos, qui ea distribuant pastoribus suorum districtuum: Quæritur, an decani distributionem differre possint usque post Dominicam in Albis ?

"V. Facti species—Multi pastores accepta Sacra Olea apud se deponunt in domibus suis, usque in sequentem diem Dominicam ; et tunc cum solemni processione, videlicet cum cruce, cum candelis ardentibus sub baldachino a toto clero in habitu, portantur ad ecclesiam, exponunturque in aliquo altari cum hymnis, et eadem solemnitate portant. r ad fontem baptismalem eique infunduntur: Quæritur 1º An pastores recte retineant Sacra Olea in domibus suis, usque in Dominicam receptionem eorum subsequentem ? 2º An Sacra Olea cum tali solemnitate introduci possint in ecclesiam ? 3º An cum tali solemnitate infundi possint fonti baptismali, cui non potuerunt infundi in vigilia Paschatis, cum tunc necdum haberi potuissent ?

"Tandem Quæritur, An benedictio cum indulgentia plenaria, juxta Constitutionem Benedicti XIV. *Pia Mater*, 5 *Aprilis*, 1747, impertinenda sit pueris qui, defectu ætatis, primam communionem necdum instituerunt ?

"Resp. Ad 1 Quæs. i.—Negative et eliminata consuetudine servetur Rubrica. Ad 2—Negative.

"Ad 1 Quæs. ii.—Negative et eliminata consuetudine servetur Ritualis Romani præscriptum. Ad 2. ejusdem Quæs.—Negative ut ad proximum.

"Ad dub. unic. Quæs. iii. —Negative, et servetur Rituale Romanum, excepto tamen casu magnæ distantiæ ab Ecclesia; quo in casu omnino servetur etiam domi, rubrica quoad honestam et decentem, tutamque custodiam.

"Ad dub. unic. Quæs. iv.—Negative.

"Ad 1 Quæs. v.—Jam provisum in responsione ad Quæs. iii. Ad 2 ejusdem Quæs.—Tollendam esse inductam consuetudinem, et servandas Ritualis Rubricas. Ad 3 ejusdem—Jam provisum in præcedenti. Ad postremum—Affirmative." 251, 267, 621, 798, 855, 918, 961.

4651. *Florentin.*, 19 Dec., 1829. I. "An tempore SS. Missæ sacrificii in administratione Viatici præsertim in Xenodochiis, liceat ab Altare recedere usque ad ægrotorum lectum recitando interim psalmum *Miserere*, ut fieri solet extra Missam ?

"II. Utrum tempore etiam sacrificii Missæ administrari possit SSmum. Viaticum in paramentis nigris ?

"Resp. Ad i.: Negative, quoad psalmum *Miserere* recitandum; insuper animadvertendum, quod si Celebrans pro Viatici administratione *intra Missam*, altare e conspectu suo amittat, hanc administrationem non licere.

"Ad ii.: Affirmative." 840.

4677. *Tarentina*, 12 Nov., 1831. "Ex pio quodam legato tenentur moniales ordinis S. Claræ in propria Ecclesia ad altare majus, publicæ fidelium venerationi SS. Eucharistiæ Sacramentum exponere tribus postremis diebus carnis prævii. Ne vero in sacro audiendo ipsarum pietas fraudetur, humillimas S. R. C. preces porrexerunt, pro facultate celebrandi Missam conventualem sine cantu ad altare ubi expositio, ut supra, peragitur dictis tribus diebus.

"Resp.: Pro gratia, dummodo sacra Eucharistia in Missa non distribuatur." 670.

4685. *Massæ, et Popul.*, 7 Ap., 1832. "An servandum sit Rituale Romanum, seu potius consuetudo benedicendi nimirum cum SS. retrocedentem populum extra portas civitatis, regionis, sive domus infirmi, quando fertur Viaticum agrariis ?

"Resp.: Ex speciali gratia servari posse consuetudinem." 833.

4707. *Veronen.*, 16 M r., 1833. "I. Utrum tuto sequi valeat regula Ritualis Parisiensis sic expressa: Si quando Communio danda est, inventus non fuerit sufficiens numerus hostiarum, poterunt aliquot hostiæ dividi in plures particulas, quæ singulis distribuantur: Et quatenus non sit sequenda, utrum quibusdam saltem in circumstantiis, temporis, locorum, et personæ sequi possit ?

"VI. Utrum in Communione fidelium extra missam. sacerdos antequam populo benedicat, osculari debeat altare ut præcipit Pontificale Rom. de visitatione, vel non, ut Rituale Romanum innuere videtur ?

"Resp. Ad i.: Servetur consuetudo dividendi consecratas particulas, si adsit necessitas.

"Ad vi.: Servetur dispositio Ritualis Romani nihil præscribentis." 691, 700.

4748. *Ord. Min. Capuccin.*, 28 Maii, 1835. "I. An consuetudo benedicendi populum cum sacra Pyxide quoties Eucharistia distribuitur, sit servanda vel potius an benedicendus sit populus manu dextra tantum, uti habetur in Rituali Romano, et in una Urbinaten., 16 Jan., 1793 ?

"II. Et quatenus affirmative ad primam partem an tunc dicendum sit: *Benedicat vos*, etc.?

"V. An consuetudo dicendi in Communione Fidelium: *Ecce Agnus Dei*, et *Domine non sum dignus* idiomate vulgari, sit sustinenda, vel potius eliminanda utpote contraria Rituali et Missali Romano?

"Resp. Ad i.—Negative ad primam partem, affirmative ad secundam, juxta Rituale Romanum, et Decret. Urbinaten., die 16 Jan., 1793.

"Ad ii.—Provisum in primo.

"Ad v.—Consuetudinem esse eliminandam." 672.

4777. *Trident.*, 12 Mar., 1836. XII. "An toleranda sit, vel eliminanda consuetudo inveterata, sacerdotem, qui ad altare aliquod ad celebrandum accedit, vel ab eo recedit, sic sacris vestibus sacrificii indutum, et jam præ manibus calicem tenentem, ascendere in transitu altare, in quo adest SSma. Eucharistia, ut ibi sacram Communionem fidelibus distribuat? Et quatenus non sit toleranda, utrum depositis planeta, et manipulo in sacristia, accedere possit cum alba, et stola?

"XIII. An stola, pro ministranda sanctissima Eucharistia extra Missam, semper esse debeat coloris officio illius diei convenientis, ut præscribit Rituale Romanum, vel potius esse debeat alba prout valde conveniens Sacramento Eucharistiæ, ut multi censent doctores?

"Resp. Ad xii.—Si adsit necessitas posse tolerari.

"Ad xiii. Juxta Ritualis Romani rubricam, debet esse coloris officio convenientis " 69, **658, 729.**

4780. *Rhedonen.*, 27 Aug., 1836. I. "Utra pedum pars, superior ne an inferior, ungenda sit in Sacramento Extremæ Unctionis?

"III. Quænam servari debent cæremoniæ, et preces quæ supplendæ sunt adulto catholico valide post nativitatem baptizato, sed omissis cæremoniis, quæ juxta Rituale baptismum præcedere vel sequi debent: An illæ, quæ in Rituali assignantur pro baptismo adultorum, vel quæ pro baptismo infantium?

"IV. Quæ ex his cærem niis servari debent, quum adultus ab hæresi ad fidem catholicam conversus baptizandus est sub conditione, ob dubium fundatum de validitate baptismi a ministro hæretico collati?

"Resp. Ad i.—Nihil innovandum.

"Ad iii.—Cæremoniæ et preces serventur, quæ in Rituali assignantur pro baptismo infantium.

"Ad iv.—Quatenus supplendæ sint, et supplendæ credantur cæremoniæ, ut in dubio, illæ supplendæ sunt, quæ pro adultorum baptismo sunt præscriptæ." 459, 534, 937.

4815. *Mutinen.*, 23 Sept., 1837. II. "Quum orationes tam præcedentes quam subsequentes communionem Missæ Sabbati Sancti loquantur in numero plurali: hinc quæritur, utrum liceat in eadem Missa post Communionem celebrantis, Eucharistiam ministrare fidelibus, et præsertim cum particulis in eadem Missa consecratis?

"III. Perdurat adhuc in quibusdam Ecclesiis mos communicandi in Missa defunctorum cum particulis præconsecratis, propterea quod Decreta Sacra

Congregationis hac super re edita non censentur a multis authentica, aut saltem revocata. Hinc quæritur 1º An idem mos possit permitti vel saltem ab Episcopo prohibendus, adeo ut solum liceat communicare in dictis Missis, cum particulis in ipsis consecratis ? 2º An saltem toleranda consuetudo celebrandi prædictas Missas in paramentis violaceis, ad hoc ut possit præberi sacra Communio cum particulis præconsecratis ?

"Resp. Ad ii.—Negative, nisi adsit consuetudo.

"Ad iii.—Quoad 1. Dilata. et servetur Rescriptum in Panormitana diei 12 Aprilis, 1823, ad Dub. 9. Quoad 2. Serventur rubricæ." 707, 708, 712. (Vid. infra, *Decr. Gen.*, 23 Jul., 1868.)

4820. *Oriolen.*, 23 Sept., 1837. "Perdurantibus-belli civilis calamitatibus in Regno Hispaniarum, accidit ut Reverendissimus Oriolen. Episcopus, superiori anno 1836, olea sacra, feria quinta in Cœna Domini, consecrare nequiverit pro solemni benedictione Fontium Baptismalium parochialibus in ecclesiis peragenda in sequente Sabbato Sancto, neque eadem olea a vicinioribus Episcopis parochi habere potuerint, siquidem ob communia incommoda, pene omnes episcopales sedes proprio sunt viduatæ pastore, ita ut communicationibus interceptis, grex a pastore. filius a parente, Ecclesia ab Episcopis non sine magno animarum salutis detrimento separentur.

" Hujusmodi in angustiis constituti, parochi præbendati Oriolen. Diœcesis diversas inter se protulere sententias, et, nonnullis negantibus, bene multi opinabantur benedictionem solemnem Fontium Baptismalium perfici posse, adhibitis oleis superiori anno consecratis. In qua opinionum et sententiarum varietate, id sumpsere consilii, ut Sacram hanc Rituum Congregationem requirerent, ut certam sequerentur regulam, in re tanti momenti, ac propterea sequentia dubia enodanda humillime proposuerunt, nimirum:

"I. An talis Benedictio (Fontis Baptismalis in Sabbato Sancto) fieri debeat cum chrismate et oleo præcedentis anni, an potius omittenda sit infusio chrismatis et olei, usque dum accipiantur recenter consecrata?

"II. An in baptismo solemni infantium utendum sit hujusmodi aqua, benedicta quidem cum reliquis cæremoniis Missalis, sed absque consecratione seu mixtione sacrorum chrismatis et olei: an vero aqua consecrata præcedenti anno, quæ ad hunc finem conservetur ?

"III. An supposito quod aqua baptismalis benedicta sit cum veteribus oleis, eo quod recenter consecrata non habeantur, infundi debeat in piscinam, simul ac nova recipiuntur olea, et iterum cum his alia benedicenda sit aqua juxta cæremonias Ritualis Romani: an vero illa conservari et uti debeat, usque ad benedictionem in vigilia Pentecostes prout in Missali?

"IV. An in baptismo solemni, ungendi sunt infantes oleo et chrismate præcedentis anni, dum recenter consecrata non habentur; an vero omittenda hæc sit cæremonia, et postea supplenda quum novum oleum et novum chrisma recipiantur?

"S. R. C. rescripsit: Ad i.: Affirmative ad primam partem, Negative ad secundam.

"Ad ii.: Negative ad utrumque, sed fieri debet nova fontis benedictio cum oleis anni precedentis, seu provisum in prima parte superioris dubii.

"Ad iii.: Negative ad primam partem. Affirmative ad secundam.

"Ad iv.: Affirmative ad primam partem. Negative ad secundum." 253, 255.

4947. *Tertii Ord. Sti. Francisci.* 24 Sept., 1842. "III. An in Communione fidelibus ministranda, post versum. *Panem de cœlo*, etc., dici omnino debeant ante orationem alii versus, *Domine exaudi*, et *Dominus vobiscum?*

"Resp. Ad. iii.—Affirmative, ut prescribitur in Rituali Romano." 695, 827.

4950. *Neapol.*, 24 Sept., 1842. "I. An sacerdos seipsum signans cum hostia, et calice consecratis, ante sumptionem Sanctissimi Sacramenti ad verba,— *Jesu Christi,*—debeat caput inclinare?

"III. An sacerdos pergens ad explendam communionem extra missam debeat per se, vel per ministrum deferre bursam, in qua corporale recluditur?

"Resp. Ad i.—Affirmative, juxta Rubricas.

"Ad iii.—Decere ut a Sacerdote deferatur." 661, 685.

5000. *Patavina*, 7 Dec., 1844. "IV. An præter casum a Rituali Romano prævisum. *Tit. De Sacram. Ext. Unct.* in quo de Sacro Oleo adhibendo in hoc Sacramento hæc habentur—'Id tamen si forte intra annum aliquo modo ita deficiat, ut suffi-

cere non posse videatur, neque aliud benedictum haberi queat, modico oleo non benedicto, in minori quantitate superinfusa reparari potest,' liceat unquam Sacris Oleis Feria V. in Cœna Domini benedictis aliam Olei non benedicti quantitatem addere? An hæc additio saltem fieri possit eadem Feria V. in Cœna Domini, adeo ut pars tantum Olei subjiciatur benedictioni et immediate misceatur cum Oleo non benedicto?

"Resp. Ad iv.—Negative, sed in casu tantum necessitatis fieri potest additio, uti in Rituali præscribitur." 258.

5036. *Bisinianen.*, 23 Maii, 1846. "Quum ea sit positio Parochialis Ecclesiæ Acri in Diœcesi Bisinianen, ut ad Fideles ut plurimum per agros dissitos ac ad plura milliaria distentos, Sacrum Viaticum, dum ipsi infirmantur, deferri nequeat nisi summa cum difficultate ob viarum asperitatem, ac ventorum, nivium, glacierumque incommoda, inde fit ut animarum dispendia necessario eveniant, et semper majora timeri debeant.

"Queis incommodis occurrere, quoad fieri potest, exoptantes hodierni Parochus et Œconomi oppidi ipsius invectæ in enunciata parœcia consuetudini hujusmodi in casibus deferendi SSmum. Sacramentum capite pileo cooperto, et equitando, amplius se conformare formidant quia nulla usque nunc intercessit Apostolica venia. S. R. C. proinde enixis precibus adeuntes consuetudinis ipsius confirmationem instanter rogarunt, quod et ipse Rmus. Episcopus pro informatione et voto requisitus *exhibuit* ex propria notione, in sacra visitatione quæ enunciantur incommoda expertus.

"Et S. C., omnibus perpensis, rescribendum censuit '*Detur decretum in Lauden., dici 23 Jan.*, 1740,' nimirum commisit Rmo. Episcopo ut pro suo arbitrio et prudentia indulgeat, quod deinceps hujusmodi in circumstantiis equitantes ac capite pileo cooperto sacrum viaticum deferre valeant, comitante saltem uno homine, si fieri potest, accensam laternam deferente." 880.

5068. *Cong. Cler. Regul. St. Crucis*, 27 Feb., 1847. "I. An semper adhibenda sit bursa cum corporali, supra quod reponenda sit sacra pyxis, toties quoties administratur Communio Christifidelibus extra Missam, uti innuitur in Ritualis Romani rubrica, et clare docetur a Gavanto aliisque sacrorum rituum expositoribus ?

"II. An Rituale Romanum prout in casu, intelligendum sit, quod assumi debeat bursa cum corporali tantum quando Sacrum Viaticum defertur ad infirmos, an toties quoties extra Missam Sacra præbetur Synaxis ?

"III. An Rubrica Ritualis Romani sit, prout in casu, præceptiva, vel tantum directiva, et ad libitum ?

"Resp. Ad i.—Affirmative juxta Rituale.

"Ad ii.—In administranda Eucharistia intelligendum.

"Ad iii.—Præceptivam esse." 661. 809.

5102. *Angelop.*, 11 Sept..1847. "XVI. An Decreta Sac. Rituum Congregationis, dum eduntur, derogent cuicumque contrariæ invectæ consuetudini etiam immemorabili, et in casu affirmativo obligent etiam quoad conscientiam ?

"Resp. Ad xvi. : Affirmative, sed recurrendum in particulari." 40.

5132. *Ord. Carm.* 22 Jul., 1848. "V. An Ecclesia parochialis omnino adigatur ad functiones Sabbati Sancti, juxta parvum Cæremoniale Sa. Me. Benedicti XIII, si sufficienti clero destituatur; et an hujusmodi in casu Missa ordinanda sit, ut in præcedentibus dubiis tertio et quarto ?

"Resp. Ad. v.—Affirmative, et servetur in omnibus solitum, juxta parvum Cæremoniale Benedicti Papæ XIII." 251.

5165. *Cenomanen.*, 10 Jan., 1852. "IV. Etiamsi Ecclesia Cenomanensis sibi de Breviario et Missali iterum atque iterum, ut libuerit, providere queat, an istiusmodi facultas extendenda sit ad Pontificale, Cæremoniale Episcoporum, Martyrologium, et Rituale Romanum, ita videlicet ut præceptivas prædictorum librorum regulas, tolerante nempe aut permittente, aut etiam aliter quidpiam statuente Rvmo. Episcopo, canonici, aliive sacerdotes possint illæsa conscientia infringere aut omittere, atque Reverendissimi Episcopi voluntas his in casibus sit pro ipsis sufficiens dispensatio ?

"V. Utrum possint et ipsi canonici qui, ex antiquo more, mozetta et rochetto insigniti sunt, uti rochetto in administratione, seu confectione sacramentorum et sacramentalium, quum Reverendissimus Episcopus usum rochetti generaliter, et pro majori seminario, recenter præceperit, seu saltem probaverit, et pro omnibus insuper suæ diœcesis presbyteria, etiam in sacramentorum administratione, se toleraturum esse voce et scripto declaraverit, quidquid in contrarium faciant Cæremoniale Episcoporum, Rituale Romanum, Missale et Pontificale, licetque nulla in diœcesi Cenomanensi antiqua, aut usque dum generalis pro ea sacræ liturgiæ derogatione exstiterit consuetudo?

"Resp. Ad iv.—Negative et amplius.

"Ad v.—Rochettum non esse vestem sacram adhibendam in administratione sacramentorum, ac proinde tum ad ea administranda, tum ad suscipiendam primam tonsuram, et minores ordines necessario superpelliceo utendum." 71, 121. (Vid. infra, Decr. 81. Aug., 1867, in Ambianen., ad 4.)

5183. *Ord. Min. Sti. Francisci*, 16 April., 1853. "XXIV. Possunt ne in Missa post sumptionem haberi breves sermones, dum vel ad Sacram Synaxim prima vice adolescentes admittuntur, vel alia quacumque ex causa, qui quidem sermones *Fervorini* nuncupantur?

"Resp. Ad xxiv.—Affirmative." 872.

5186. *Grossetan.*, 7 Maii, 1853. "III. Utrum formula illa, quæ in Pontificali Romano adhibenda edicitur dum ordinatis SS. Eucharistiam administrat Episcopus ordinans, adhiberi possit ab Episcopo quotiescumque fidelibus Eucharistiam administrat, seu an extra communionem ordinatorum adhibere debeat communem formulam, prout jacet in Rituali Romano?

"Resp. Ad iii.—Formulam in Pontificali præscriptam dum ad Sacram Synaxim Episcopus ordinatos admittit extra casum illum non esse adhibendam; seu quoad primam, Negative—quoad secundam, Affirmative." 684.

5188. *Cochin.*, 9 Jun., 1853. "II. Plures Theologi, inter quos S. Alphonsus Maria de Ligorio, sentiunt veniale esse omittere vocem *Amen* in fine formœ Baptismi, quæ tamen vox non reperitur in Rituali Romano: quæritur ergo utrum adhibenda sit vel omittenda?

"Resp. Ad ii.—Strictim in casu servetur Rituale Romanum." 168.

5202. *Romana*, 8 Ap., 1854. "I. Quum in declaratione S. R. C. lata die 23 Maii, 1846, sancitum fuerit Decreta et Responsiones ab ipsa emanatas, dummodo scripto formiter editæ fuerint eandem auctoritatem habere, ac si immediate ab ipso Summo Pontifice promanarent, quæritur an per verba *dummodo formiter scripto editæ fuerint*, sufficiat quod sint subscriptæ a S. R. C. Præfecto ac Secretario, ac ejusdem sigillo munitæ, seu potius requiratur, ut sint vel Romæ, vel ab Episcopis in suis diœcesibus promulgatæ?

"II. Et quatenus affirmative ad 1 partem, negative ad 2. An tamquam formiter editæ habendæ sint Decreta, et Responsiones in Gardelliniana authentica collectione insertæ?

"Et sacra eadem Congregatio, post diligens examen omnium, respondere rata est. Ad 1—Affirmative ad primam partem, Negative ad secundam.

"Ad ii.—Affirmative uti patet ex adjecta declaratione." 26.

5221. *Briocen.*, 21 Jul., 1855. "X. Quæritur an in administrando Viatico Sacro ægrotanti

Sacerdoti aliquis sit ritus specialis diversus a ritu præscripto a Rituali Romano—'De Communione Infirmorum,' ut innuere videtur Cæremoniale Episcoporum, lib. ii. cap. xxxviii. n. 8 et 5, dicens, 'Profiteatur *Episcopus ægrotus* Catholicam fidem, ex formula ab Apostolica Sede præscripta ?' Et quatenus affirmative, utrum servari possit sequens ritus qui legitur in quodam Rituali ? (*Ritus describitur.*)

"XII. Utrum Tabernaculum in quo reconditur SSmum. Sacramentum Conopeo cooperiri debeat, ut fert Rituale, et quatenus affirmative. 2. Utrum Conopeum istud confici possit ex panno, sive gossypio, sive lana, sive cannabo contexto.

3. Cujusmam coloris esse debeat ? aliis opinantibus, ut Barruffaldus, Conopeum debere esse coloris albi, utpote convenientis SSmo. Sacramento; aliis autem, ut Gavantus, ejusdem coloris cujus sunt pallium Altaris et cætera paramenta pro temporis festique ratione, præter colorem nigrum, qui mutatur in colore violaceo in exequiis defunctorum.

"Resp. Ad x.—Negative in omnibus.

"Ad xii.—Quoad 1am questionem, Affirmative: quoad 2um pariter Affirmative: quoad 3um utramque sententiam posse in praxim deduci, maxime vero sententiam Gavanti quæ pro se habet usum Ecclesiarum urbis." 610, 793.

The following decrees are not found in Gardellini, although some have an earlier date than decrees given in the last edition of his work (vid. n. 253). They are taken from the *Decreta Authentica*, etc., by Falise; from the *Analecta Juris Pontificii;* or from the *Acta ex iis decerpta quæ apud Sanctam Sedem geruntur.*

Trecen., 22 Maii, 1841. "Precibus sacerdotis P. N. Parochi civitatis Bar-sur-Aube, diœcesis Trecen. queis expetebat sequentium dubiorum solutionem quoad usum Breviarii Romani, quod recitat ab anno 1828, nimirum.

"I. An non obstante prohibitione RR. Episcopi, possit tuta conscientia perseverare in recitando Breviario Romano, sicque oneri divini officii facere satis?

"III. An in administrandis sacramentis Rituali Romano uti queat ?

"Resp. Ad i.—Sine speciali indulto non posse.

"Ad iii.—In casu : Affirmative." 71.

Veronen., 7 Sept., 1850. "XV. Utrum intra Missæ actionem Sabb. S. Clerus et populus possint sumere Eucharistiam ? Insuper num expleta Missa possint fideles cum particulis præconsecratis, seu per modum Sacramenti communicari ?

"Resp. Ad xv.: Negative ad primum, affirmative ad secundum." 712.

Lucionen., 12 Aug. 1854.

"**XX.** Adsunt dispositiones Cæremonialis Eipscoporum, lib. ii. cap. xxxix. n. 3, de patena a diacono tenenda sub mento communicantium, quando Communio in Missa solemni ab Episcopo administratur : adest etiam decretum diei 3 Septembris, 1661, in Adrien. declarans licitam esse patenæ suppositionem per sacerdotem cotta indutum in communione generali, quæ per dignitates agitur.

" Sed quæritur utrum in aliis casibus liceat, ubi talis est consuetudo, dum celebrans ministrat sacram Communionem, patenam a diacono supponi sub mento communicantium, prout suadetur a nonnullis præclaris liturgistis, Merati et Bauldry—experientia enim, ut dicunt, necessitatem hujus ritus evidenter probat.—Et revera quoties pluribus administratur sacra Communio ex particulis consecratis parva fragmenta decidunt, quæ, si in linteum ante communicantes extensum cadant, in terram postea labentur dum hoc linteum movebitur per fideles successive ad sacram mensam accedentes, et præsertim quum, finita communione, aufertur linteum : itaque quum non appareant, pretiosissima fragmenta disperdentur. Ad hæc præcavenda, prælaudati auctores prædictam praxim de cujus legitimitate inquirimus, commendant. Vel potius eo tempore, quo distribuitur sacra Communio, diaconus debeat ministrare clericis purificationem, prout indicat rubrica Missalis, part ii. tit. x. n. 9 ?

"**XXI.** Propter eadem motiva ad præcavendum sacrorum fragmentorum perditionem, potestne sacerdos sanctam Communionem sive intra Missam, sive extra Missam administrans, tenere patenam inter digitos manus sinistræ, quæ sacram pyxidem gestat, ut eam sic mento communicantium supponat quamvis rubrica sileat de hoc ritu ?

"**XXII.** Quatenus autem suppositio patenæ de qua in duobus dubiis præcedentibus agitur non liceat, quæritur quodnam medium adhiberi debeat, ut præcaveatur sacrorum fragmentorum disperditio, dum sancta Communio administratur ?

"**XXIII.** Quando sacra Communio ministratur monialibus ad fenestellam clausuræ, muri crassitudo impedit quin sacerdos prope os communicantium pyxidem admovere possit ad præcavendum ne fragmenta cadant extra ipsam ; licetne in hoc casu servare consuetudinem apponendi, supra linteum ante communicantes extensum, laminam argenteam deauratam, seu bacile ejusdem materiæ ad recipienda fragmenta, quæ decidere possint, et unde a sacerdote, postquam ad altare regressus fuerit, colligentur ?

"**XXIV.** Purificatio post communionem de qua loquuntur rubricæ Missalis, part ii. tit. x. n. 9, et Cæremoniale Episcoporum, lib. ii. c. xxix. n. 4, non est in usu apud nos : quæritur utrum instaurationis liturgiæ Romanæ occasione in diœcesi nostra expediat hanc praxim inducere, saltem pro communione cleri sive generali sive particulari in Missa solemni ?

"**LXIII.** Utrum in vere. et

resp. qui in administratione Extremæ Unctionis post unctiones factas dicuntur, et in tribus orationibus quæ sequuntur, facienda sit variatio generis quando recitantur pro muliere, dicendo ℣. *Salvam fac ancillam tuam*, et similiter de aliis, sicuti variatio generis indicatur a Rituali in ritu Benedictionis Apostolicæ in articulo mortis, et a Pontificali in confirmatione unius?

"LXXII. An in Missa privata dum celebrans administrat sacram Communionem, minister debeat eum comitari cum cereo accenso, sicut aliqui putant, quamvis Rubrica taceat de hoc ritu? vel, quum purificationem quæ pro populi non est in usu non præbeat, nec mappam communionis utpote cancellis affixam ante communicantes sustineat, tunc debeat manere genuflexus in latere Epistolæ?

"LXXIII. An in Missa solemni a simplici sacerdote celebrata, dum administratur populo sacra Communio, duo Acolythi si non sustineant mappam ante communicantes, debeant comitari celebrantem cum suis candelabris, et cereis accensis; vel manere ad credentiam genuflexi, ita ut diaconus et subdiaconus tunc comitentur celebrantem? An saltem in Missa absque ministris sacris cantata Acolythi debeant assistere celebranti tempore communionis populi sive cum candelabris sive cum facibus?

"LXXVI. An sacerdos in fine administrationis communionis extra Missam, proferens verba: *Benedictio Dei Omnipotentis*, debent extendere manus eodem ritu ac dum dicit in fine Missæ:

Benedicat vos Omnipotens Deus, sicuti docent Cavalieri, tom. 4, cap. 4, dec. 13, n. 41, et alii, aliis contradicentibus, et Rituali hunc ritum non indicante, vel dicendo hæc verba, tenere manus junctas et tantum inclinare caput?

"LXXIX. In Diœcesi Lucionensi et in aliis, multi parochi ob distantiam locorum olea sacra feria quinta in Cœna Domini benedicta tempestive habere non possunt, ut ea in benedictione fontis baptismalis Sabbato Sancto facienda, adhibeant, sed paucos post dies accipiunt. Habetur quidem decretum *diei* 23 *Sept.*, 1837. At forsan sanctio hujus decreti spectabat casum particularem, in quo versabantur diœceses Hispaniæ in quibus benedictio oleorum facta non fuerat, et nesciebatur quonam tempore accipi possent nova olea sacra.

Hinc quæritur an in prædicta nostra circumstantia benedictio fontis baptismalis fieri debeat cum chrismate et oleo præcedentis anni, et sic tali casui applicanda sit responsio data in *Oriolen.*? vel potius omittenda sit tunc infusio chrismatis et olei, usque dum accipiantur recenter consecrata, prout innuere videtur decretum die 12 Aprilis, 1755, in *Lucana*, ad iii.?

"LXXX. Posito quod in prædicto casu benedictio fontis facienda sit cum chrismate et oleo præcedentis anni quæritur etiam utrum accepta nova olea infundi debeant in hanc aquam quæ cum infusione veterum oleorum fuit benedicta? An potius ad infundenda hæc nova olea expectandum sit usque ad aliam benedictionem fontis quæ fit in vigilia Pentecostes?

"Resp. Ad xx.—Quoad primam partem, licere. Quoad secundam, juxta consuetudinem, sed purificationem etiam clericos subministrare posse.

"Ad xxi.—Negative.

"Ad xxii.—Quoad communiones solemnes provisum in xx.; quoad alias curam et solertiam sacerdotis supplere debere.

"Ad xxiii.—Affirmative.

"Ad xxiv.—Provisum in xx.

"Ad lxiii.—Affirmative.

"Ad lxxii.—Negative ad primam partem, affirmative ad secundam.

"Ad lxxiii.—Servari posse consuetudinem laudabilem astandi cum facibus.

"Ad lxxvi.—Affirmative ad primam partem, negative ad secundam.

"Ad lxxix.—Pro diversitate circumstantiarum in praxi utrumque decretum servari posse, nam in *Lucana* supponitur quod ex aliquo fortuito casu olea sacra ad breve tempus retardentur; et in *Oriolen.* loquitur de omnimoda impossibilitate habendi olea sacra a propria cathedrali vel a vicinioribus diœcesibus.

"Ad lxxx.—In sensu præcedentis responsionis, Negative ad primam partem, Affirmative ad secundam." 258, 650, 651, 652, 660, 700, 941.

Molinen., 12 Sept., 1857. "X. Utrum sacerdos in Missa, postquam se communicaverit, priusquam communionem adstantibus distribuat, possit sermonem ad populum habere?

"XVII. Utrum in collatione Baptismi interrogationes possint fieri vernacule, vel saltem vernacule iterari, postquam latine factæ fuerint?

"Resp. Ad x.—Affirmative

ab altari et de consensu ordinarii.

"Ad xvii.—Quoad interrogationes quæ Baptismi ordinem præcedunt vel sequuntur, ac pro quibus Rituale nullam exhibet formulam, affirmative. Quoad interrogationes quæ in ipsomet Baptismi ordine occurrunt, ac pro quibus formulæ in Rituali extant, negative ad utramque partem." 298, 672.

Ultrajecten., 14 Aug., 1858. "Perillustrᵐᵉ et Revᵐᵉ Domine uti Frater. Quum in Ordinariis Comitiis S. R. C. hodierna die ad Vaticanum habitis subscriptus Secretarius retulerit Literas ab Amplitudine Tua SSmo. D. N. Pio Papæ IX. die 4 Martii vertentis anni datas, Emi. et Rmi. Patres Sacris tuendis Ritibus præpositi saluberrimum Amplitudinis Tuæ consilium adoptandi in ista Diœcesi Ultrajectensi Rituale Romanum, exclusis quibuscunque aliis Ritualibus libris summopere commendarunt, et quin illud quamprimum eadem Amplitudo Tua executioni demandatura sit dubitare minime potuerunt.

"Quod vero attinet ad renum unctionem, quam in administrando sacramento Extremæ Unctionis nunquam in ista Diœcesi Amplitudo Tua adhibitam fuisse testatur, et quam idcirco postulat ut in Rituali Romano omitti permittatur, visum est S. Congregationi nullam prorsus sive in hac sive in alia quacumque re suppressionem vel immutationem in Rituali induci oportere, sed illud voluit integre et fideliter imprimi prout a Paulo V. editum, et a Benedicto XIV. recognitum et castigatum fuit. Quod si unctio renum inusitata istic hactenus fuit, declaravit S. Congregatio patienter se quidem laturam si singularia istius Dioecesis adjuncta impediant quominus illico et universim ad praxim unctio isthæc deducatur, insimul tamen ardentissimum votum suum expressit, ut curante Amplitudine Tua et docentibus parochis, paulatim et sensim sine sensu disponantur fideles ad istam quoque specialem unctionem in extremo agone recipiendam juxta Ritualis Romani præscriptiones. Perill^mo et R^mo D^no uti Fratri, Archiepiscopo Ultrajectensi." 893.

Tarnovien., 26 Mar., 1859. "II. Utrum occasione Indulgentiarum, vel simili, qua fide-.es magna cum frequentia ad sacram Synaxim accedere solent, ne sese penes Altaris cancellos turmatim obtrudant, possit iisdem, sive per Ecclesiam sive extra illam, in genua provolutis Eucharisticus panis distribui, an potius debeat tantummodo distribui penes cancellos linteo mundo contectos sive ad gladus Altaris?

"VI. Ob distantiam et consuetudinem invaluit in his regionibus, ut sacrum Viaticum non in pyxide ad infirmos defe-.atur, sed in vase patenæ simili, quod operculo munitur, et cui pro sancto Oleo aliud vasculum adnexum est. Hoc autem vas linteo obvolutum reponi solet in bursa stolæ consuta, in qua præterea mos est Rituale, bombacium, candelas et crucem asportandi. Quæritur ergo qualis color conveniat huic bursæ, ubi defertur Sacrum Viaticum ad infirmos cum sancto Oleo?

"VII. Utrum in administrando sacramento Baptismi

licite Sacerdos uti possit stola bicolori, ex una parte violacea et ex altera alba, juxta opportunitatem ex ea parte invertenda quæ colorem præferat a Rituali præscriptum?

"Resp. Ad. II.—Præstare in casu ut plura genuflexoria sive scamna linteo mundo contecta hinc inde a cancellis circulatim seu in quadrum intra Ecclesiam ordinentur, et in extremitatibus interjecti spatii duo saltem candelabra disponantur, quæ perpetuo colluceant dum fidelibus circum adgeniculatis sacra Communio distribuitur.

"Ad vi.—Prædictum usum tolerari omnino non posse, et curandum ab Episcopo ut serventur præscriptiones Ritualis Romani.

"Ad vii.—Affirmative." 279, 652. 913, 953.

Wratislavien, 18 Jun., 1859. "An possit tolerari ut præfata benedictio post partum illegitimum denegetur?

"Resp.: Ad benedictionem post partum jus tantum habent mulieres quæ ex matrimonio legitimo pepererunt." 560.

"Quum Rubricæ nec Missalis, nec Ritualis determinent numerum genuflexionum quæ a Sacerdote fieri debent dum ad altare revertitur cum Sanctissimo Sacramento post distributam Fidelibus sacram Communionem, alter ex Apostolicarum Cæremoniarum magistris, de sententia desuper requisitus, post accuratum examen censuit, regulam in casu desumendam a Rubricis determinantibus duplicem genuflexionem antequam Sacerdos Communionem ipsam administret, nimirum primum antequam extrahat a tabernaculo pyxidem, alteram vero post discoopertam super altare eandem pyxidem. Cum enim agatur de culto debito Sanctissimæ Eucharistiæ, congruum profecto est ut eodem prorsus modo iste cultus præstetur a Sacerdote ad altare redeunte, nimirum genuflectendo primo antequam pyxidem cooperiat, et iterum postquam illam in tabernaculo recondidit, antequam tabernaculi ostiolum claudat.

Hanc porro sententiam cum infrascriptus SS. Rituum Congregationis Secretarius retulerit in Ordinario cœtu SS. Rituum subsignata die ad Vaticanum coadunata; Eminentissimi et Reverendissimi Patres Sacris tuendis Ritibus præpositi rescribendum censuerunt—*Placere seu, juxta votum Magistri cæremoniarum*—ac proinde de creverunt a Sacerdote redeunte ad altare post Fidelium Communionem genuflectendum, antequam cooperiat sacram pyxidem et iterum genuflectendum, antequam pyxide in tabernaculo reposita, ipsius tabernaculi ostiolum claudat. Atque ita ubique servandum mandarunt. Die 23 Decembris, 1862."

Plurium Diœcesum., 9 Jul., 1864. "Nonnulli Reverendissimi Galliarum Antistites serio perpendentes in multis suarum Diœceseum Ecclesiis difficile admodum et nonnisi magnis sumptibus comparari posse oleum olivarum ad nutriendam diu noctuque saltem unam lampadem ante Sanctissimum Eucharistiæ Sacramentum, ab Apostolica Sede declarari petierunt utrum in casu, attentis difficultatibus et Ecclesiarum paupertate, oleo olivarum substitui possint alia olea quæ ex vegetabilibus habentur, ipso non excluso petroleo.

"Sacra porro Rituum Congregatio, et si semper sollicita ut etiam in hac parte quod usque ab Ecclesiæ primordiis circa usum olei ex olivis inductum est, ob mysticas significationes retineatur; attamen silentio præterire minime censuit rationes ab iisdem Episcopis prolatas; ac proinde exquisito prius Voto alterius ex Apostolicarum Cæremoniarum Magistris, subscriptus Cardinalis Præfectus ejusdem Sacræ Congregationis rem omnem proposuit in Ordinariis Comitiis ad Vaticanum hodierna die habitis. Eminentissimi autem et Reverendissimi Patres Sacris tuendis Ritibus præpositi, omnibus accurate perpensis ac diligentissime examinatis, rescribendum censuerunt: *Generatim utendum esse oleo olivarum: ubi vero haberi nequeat, remittendum prudentiæ Episcoporum ut lampades nutriantur ex aliis oleis quantum fieri possit vegetabilibus.*" 615.

Ambianen., 31 Aug., 1867. "IV. Utrum Canonicus habens usum rochetti et cappæ vel mozettæ, teneatur ea insignia deponere, et induere superpelliceum: 1. Ad Sac. am Communionem ministrandam fidelibus extra Missam. 2. Ad celebrandum Matrimonium. 3. Ad impertiendam benedictionem nuptialem, si aliquando detur extra Missam. 4. In omni benedictione extra Missam.

"V. Utrum pro superpelliceo uti valeat Sacerdos alba cum stola in pectus transversa in casibus præfatis, præsertim in celebrando Matrimonio, cum immediate post absolutionem ritus Matrimonii Missam pro sponso et sponsa celebraturus sit?

"Resp. Ad iv.—Ex Decretis ejusdem S. Congregationis sacramenta administranda sunt cum cotta et stola, depositis cappa aut mozet a: potest tamen cotta superimponi rochetto, ideoque ad primam Dubii partem, Affirmative.— Ad secundam pariter, Affirmative.—Ad tertiam: Benedictio nuptialis dari non potest extra Missam, adeoque non esse locum Dubio.—Ad quartam, Affirmative.

"Ad v.—Si immediate sequitur Missa, sacerdos præter albam et stolam induere debet etiam planetam." 658, 729.

Decretum Generale, 23 Julii, 1868. "Post Liturgicas recentiores leges a Summis Pontificibus Pio V., Clemente VIII., Paulo V., et Urbano VIII. conditas, gravis exarsit controversia inter Doctores et Rubricistas 'An in Missis defunctorum aperiri possit tabernaculum ad Fideles pane Eucharistico reficiendos.' Sacrorum Rituum Congregatio prima vice interrogata, in una Albinganen. 24 Julii, 1683, ad IV. respondit. "*Non esse contra ritum ministrare communionem in Missa de Requiem, vel post illam cum paramentis nigris, omissa benedictione, si administraretur post missam.*"

Verum controversia nondum composita identidem Sacra Rituum Congregatio peculiaribus in casibus responsa dedit, quin unquam ad generale Decretum deveniret. Interea ex nonnullorum doctorum placitis, tum pervasit opinio, posse nempe fidelibus Sanctam Eucharistiam ministrari particulis tantum in Missa pro defunctis consecratis; tum in aliquibus locis mos invaluit missas defunctorum celebrandi in paramentis violaceis, ut non solum intra Missam, sed etiam ante vel post eandem pietati fidelium Sacra Eucharistia refici cupientium satisfieret.

Quapropter Episcopis præsertim Sacrorum Rituum Congregationem sæpissime rogantibus ut per generale Decretum quid hac in re faciendum sit statueret, Sacra eadem Congregatio die 12 Aprilis anni 1823, in una Panormitana edixit ut gravis hæc questio *videretur peculiariter et ex Officio*. Quod iterum obtinuit anno 1837, in una Mutinen., ubi ad III. Dubium "*An mos qui perdurat adhuc communicandi in Missis defunctorum cum particulis præconsecratis, possit permitti, vel, etc.*," responsum est: "*Dilata, et servetur rescriptum in Panormitana, 12 Aprilis, 1823.*"

Nihilominus ob temporum ac rerum circumstantias isthæc peculiaris negotii hujusmodi salebrosi disquisitio ad ætatem usque nostram dilata fuit; siquidem in Conventu die 16 Septembris, anni 1865, collecto, cum ageretur de usu coloris violacei in Missis defunctorum in altari ubi Sanctissimum Euchatistiæ Sacramentum asservatur, responsum fuit tertio: "*Dilata, et reproponatur una cum alio dubio, an Sacerdos possit aperire ciborium ad communicandos fideles cum paramentis nigris.*"

Tandem novis supervenientibus Sacrorum Antistitum precibus die 8 Martii, anni 1866, in Ordinariis Sacrorum Rituum Congregationis Comitiis **propo-**

situa: fuit Dubium una cum sententia quam ex officio aperuit alter e Consultoribus "*An sacerdos possit aperire Ciborium ad communicandos Fideles in paramentis nigris?*" Verum Emi. et Rmi. Patres Cardinales responderunt: "*Dilata, et scribat alter Consultor, nec non Assessor, reassumptis omnibus ad rem facientibus; habita praesertim ratione relate ad opportunitatem.*"

Typis traditis communicatisque hisce sententiis tum Rmi. Assessoris tum alterius ex Apostolicarum Caeremoniarum Magistris specialiter deputati, Sacrorum Rituum Congregatio in Ordinario Coetu hodierna die ad Vaticanum coadunata est: ubi Emus. et Rmus. D. Cardinalis Nicolaus Clarelli-Paracciani loco et vice Emi. et Rmi. Cardinalis Constantini Patrizi Praefecti absentis idem proposuit Dubium, et Emi. ac Rmi. Patres Sacris tuendis Ritibus praepositi, re mature accurateque perpensa etiam quoad opportunitatem, responderunt:

Affirmative seu posse in Missis defunctorum, cum paramentis nigris, Sacram Communionem Fidelibus ministrari, etiam ex particulis praeconsecratis, extrahendo pyxidem a tabernaculo.

Posse item in paramentis nigris ministrari Communionem immediate post Missam defunctorum; data autem rationabili causa, immediate quoque ante eandem Missam; in utroque tamen casu omittendam esse benedictionem. Missas vero defunctorum celebrandas esse omnino in paramentis nigris, adeo ut violacea adhiberi nequeant, nisi in casu quo die 2 Novembris Sanctissimae Eucharistiae Sacramentum publicae Fidelium adorationi sit expositum pro solemni Oratione Quadraginta Horarum prout cautum est in Decreto Sacrae hujus Congregationis diei 16 Septembris anni 1801. Et ita decreverunt, ac ubique locorum si Sanctissimo Domino Nostro placuerit, servari mandarunt die 27 Junii, 1868.

Facta autem per me Secretarium Sanctissimo Domino Nostro Pio Papae IX. relatione, Sanctitas Sua Decretum Sacrae Congregationis approbavit et confirmavit die 23 Julii anni ejusdem.

C. EPISCOPUS PORTUEN. ET S. RUFINAE CARD. PATRIZI,
S. R. C. PRAEFECTUS.

Loco + Sigilli.

DOMINICUS BARTOLINI, S.R.C.,
Secretarius.

The following decrees of the Sacred Congregations of th Council, of the Inquisition, and of Bishops, regarding Baptism and the Eucharist, bear on several of the important questions which we have had occasion to treat, many of them being expressly referred to. They are collected by Falise, and subjoined by him to the decrees of the S.C.R., under the heads, "Baptisma" and "Eucharistia."

1. Infantes sive domi sive ab haereticis baptizati, non sunt iterum sub conditione baptizandi, si non adsit probabile dubium invaliditatis baptismi. S. C. Conc. 27 Mart. 1688

(ZAMB.) S.C. Inq. 17 Nov. 1830, et 20 Julii, 1840 (MISC. THEOL.) v. n. 7 et 8.

2. Pueri expositi etiamsi habeant schedulam de baptismo testantem, baptizentur sub conditione. nisi schedula habeat certitudinem. S. C. C. 5 Jan., 1724. (ZAMB.)

3. Baptismus non est sub conditione conferendus puellæ quæ christiane vixit et ad confirmationem admissa, licet parentes sint incerti. 2 Martii, 1765. (ZAMB.)

4. Fœtus in utero supra verticem baptizatus, post ortum denuo sub conditione baptizetur. S. C. C. 12 Julii, 1794. (ZAMB).

5. Ad probandum validum baptisma sufficit unus fide dignus. S. C. C. 1769 (THES. tom. 80) et Bened. XIV. Bull. 1747.

6. Anno 1781 in Firmana, eadem dispensavit in irregularitate contracta ob reiteratum sub conditione baptismum. (THES. tom. 50.)

7. An Calvinistæ et Lutherani in illis partibus degentes, quorum baptisma dubium et suspectum est infideles habendi sint, ita ut inter eos et Catholicos disparitatis cultus impedimentum dirimens adesse censeatur?

Feria IV. die 17 Novembris, 1830.

In Congregatione generali S.

Romanæ et Universalis Inquisitionis in conventu S. Mariæ supra Minervam, coram Emin. et Rever. DD. S. Rom. Ecclesiæ Cardinalibus Inquisitoribus generalibus, proposito suprascripto dubio, iidem Emin. et Rever. DD., auditis DD. consultorum suffragiis decreverunt respondendum:

I. Quoad hæreticos quorum sectæ Ritualia præscribunt collationem baptismi absque necessario usu materiæ et formæ essentialis, debet examinari casus particularis.

II. Quoad alios, qui juxta eorum Ritualia, baptizant valide, validum censendum est baptisma. Quod si dubium persistat etiam in primo casu, censendum est validum baptismum in ordine ad validitatem matrimonii.

III. Si autem certe cognoscatur nullum baptisma ex consuetudine actuali illius sectæ, nullum est matrimonium.

Eadem die et feria, Sanctissimus D. N. Gregorius divina providentia PP. XVI. in solita audientia R. P. Assessori S. Officii impertita, resolutionem prædictam ab Eminentissimis datam approbavit.[1]

ANGELUS ARGENTI,
S. Rom. et Univ. Inquis.
Notarius.

8. Vir quidam Protestans Anglicanæ ecclesiæ vult amplecti Catholicam religionem. In An-

---

[1] "Sanctissimus, in audientia habita die 20 Decembris, 1837. Audita relatione dubii, utrum scilicet, in præsumptione Baptismi invalide collati parti hæreticæ, Matrimonium cum parte Catholica a Sede Apostolica dispensata inire cupienti, conferre debeat iterum Baptisma sub conditione, dixit:—

"Detur Decretum latum, etc. . . . . [Decretum supradictum] . . . . . et SSmus superaddi mandavit:—In tertio casu præfati decreti respiciente nullitatem certam Baptismi in parte hæretica, recurratur in casibus particularibus."—Append. n. xvi. ad. "Acta et Decreta Concilii Plenarii Baltimoren. IIdi."

glia matrimonium. fecit cum muliere, quæ ad sectam Anabaptistarum pertinebat, et quæ, prout ipse affirmat, nunquam baptizata fuit. Quum vir ipse baptismum a ministro Protestante Anglicano receperit, de validitate ejus proprii baptismatis ratio quoque gravis dubitandi existit. Propter jurgia continua mulierem Anabaptistam vir præfatus deseruit, venitque N. ubi matrimonium iterum fecit, sed cum muliere Lutherana. Quænam ex istis mulieribus tanquam ejus uxor vera haberi debet?

Feria IV., die 20 Julii, 1840.

Sanctissimus D. N. Gregorius divina providentia Pf. XVI. in solita audientia R. P. Assessori S. Officii impertita, audita relatione suprascripti dubii una cum Emin. et Rever. DD. Cardinalium Generalium Inquisitorum suffragiis, rescribi mandavit, quod dummodo constet de non collatione baptismi mulieris Anabaptistæ, primum matrimonium fuisse nullum; secundum vero, dummodo nullum aliud obstet impedimentum, fuisse validum. Ad dubium autem validitatis baptismi viri, standum esse decreto feriæ IV. 17 Novembris, 1830, nempe, etc., ut supra.

Angelus Argenti,
S. Rom. et Univ. Inquis.
Notarius

1. Sanctissimum Sacramentum conservandum est in qualibet parochiali. Congr. Episc. 28 Jan. 1608, quantumvis paupere; quod si redditus et societas non sufficiant, instituatur quæstor vel eleemosynarum collector. Eadem, 14 Martii, 1614, et Cong. Conc. 22 Martii, 1594.

2. Eucharistiæ Sacramentum quando in omnibus parochialibus Montanæ regionis asservari pro tenuitate redituum nequit, Episcopus decernere debet ut in singulas, ternas, quaternasque vicinas parochiales id onus distribuatur, ut in una ex eis habeatur Augustissimum Sacramentum, et ad impensum lampadis et hujusmodi, cæteræ vicinæ contribuant, et ubi se casus obtulerit, perinde uti rectores possint, ac si in propria parochiali illud asservaretur. 17 Aug., 1697, S. C. C. ap Petra, tom. 3, p. 166.

3. Debet quoque asservari in Regularium Ecclesiis quæ de hoc habent privilegium. Congr. Episc. 25 Maii, 1635.

4. Extra parochiales Ecclesias non conceditur retineri assidue Eucharistia. Eadem, 15 Jan., 1610.

5. Episcopus concedere non potest Ecclesiæ non parochiali, ut in ea retineatur SS. Sacramentum Eucharistiæ, sed requiritur licentia Sedis Apostolicæ. Cong. Conc. 8 Martii, 1668, et 8 Jan., 1683.

6. In Ecclesiis confraternitatum neque parochialibus neque regularibus, retineri non potest SS. Eucharistia sine speciali indulto Sedis Apostolicæ. 10 Dec., 1703, et 12 Jan., 1704, S. R. C.

7. SS. Eucharistiæ Sacramentum conservari potest in Ecclesiis etiam non parochialibus, si ab immemorabili fuerit in iisdem asservatum. Congr. Conc. 27 April., 1709.

8. SS. Eucharistiæ Sacramentum asservandum est uno tantum in loco cujuscumque Ecclesiæ, in qua custodiri debet, potest, aut solet. Congr. Episc. 18 Oct., 1620.

9. Tabernaculum regulariter debet esse ligneum, extra deauratum, intus vero aliquo panno serico decenter contectum. Ead. 26 Oct., 1575.

10. SS. Sacramentum teneri non debet in vasculis eburneis, sed in pyxide argentea intus deaurata. Ead. 26 Jul., 1588.

11. Tabernaculum SS. Sacramenti in cathedralibus non debet esse in altari majori, propter functiones pontificales, quæ fiunt versis renibus ad altare; in parochialibus et regularibus debet esse regulariter in altari majori tamquam digniori. Eadem, 10 Febr., 1579, et 20 Nov., 1594.

12. In tabernaculo SS. Sacramenti esse non debent vasa sacrorum oleorum, vel reliquiæ, vel aliud. Eadem, 3 Maii, 1693.

13. Legato de lampade ardente ante SS. Sacramentum satisfaciunt hæredes, per subministrationem olei; apud ecclesiæ rectorum remanente cura ut continuo ardeat. Eadem, 25 April, 1599.

14. Ad parochum privative competit jus retinendi clavem tabernaculi in quo reconditur SS. Sacramentum. S. C. C. 14 Nov., 1693. Petra, tom. 3, p. 168.

15. Renovatio SS. Sacramenti debet fieri qualibet Dominica non autem differri ad quindecim dies. Eadem, 00 April., 1573.

The following letter from the Cardinal Prefect of Propaganda to the Bishops of Ireland, concerning the Blessed Eucharist, is taken from the *Irish Ecclesiastical Record* (February, 1865, vol. i, page 242). The same letter is given in the Appendix [n. ix] to the "*Acta et Decreta Concilii Plenarii Baltimorensis IIdi*." It is there given under the title: "Literæ Encycl* S.C. De Prop. Fide *de SS. Eucharistia deferenda*," and addressed to the Archbishop of Baltimore.

ILLUSTRISSIME ET REVERENDISSIME DOMINE,

Etsi sancta omnia sancte tractanda sint, propterea quod ad Deum pertineant qui essentialiter sanctus est, attamen augustissimum Eucharistiæ sacramentum sicut sacris mysteriis omnibus absque ulla comparatione sanctitate præeminet, it a maxima præ ceteris veneratione est pertractandum. Nil itaque mirum si tot Ecclesia diversis temporibus ediderit decreta, quibus Sanctissimæ Eucharistiæ delatio pro adjunctorum varietate vel denegaretur omnino, vel ea qua par esset reverentia admitteretur;* cum nihil antiquius fuerit Ecclesiæ Dei quam ut animarum profectum atque ædificationem debito cum honore divinorum omnium divinissimi mysterii consociaret.

Hæc porro præ oculis habens Sacrum hoc Consilium Christiano Nomini Propagando, cum primum intellexit in quibusdam istius regionis Diœcesibus consuetudinem seu potius abu-

* Vid' quæ in rem proferuntur in subjecta pagina.

sum invaluisse, ut Sacerdotes Sanctissimum Sacramentum a mane usque ad vesperam secum deferrent ea tantum de causa quod in aliquem forte aegrotum incidere possent, ad Metropolitanos censuit scribendum, tum ut consuetudinem illam ab Ecclesiae praxi omnino abhorrere declararet, tum etiam ut ejus extensionem accuratius deprehenderet. Responsa Archiepiscoporum brevi ad Sacram Congregationem pervenerunt, ex quibus innotuit, multis in locis de abusu illo gravem admirationem exortam esse, cum aliqua in Dioecesi ne credibilis quidem videretur. Verum non defuerunt Antistites qui illius existentiam ejusque causas ingenue confessi sunt.

Quare Eminentissimis Patribus Sacri hujus Consilii in generalibus comitiis die 28 Septembris elapsi anni habitis omnia quae ad hanc rem referebantur exhibita sunt perpendenda, ut quid Sanctissimi Sacramenti debitus honor ac veneratio postularent in Domino decerneretur. Omnibus igitur maturo examini subjectis, statuerunt Eminentissimi Patres literas encyclicas ad Archiepiscopos atque Episcopos istius regionis dandas esse, quibus constans Ecclesiae rigor circa Eucharistiae delationem commemoraretur. Voluit insuper S. C. ut singuli Antistites excitarentur, quemadmodum praesentium tenore excitantur, ad communem Ecclesiae disciplinam hac in re custodiendam, quantum temporis ac locorum adjuncta nec non inductarum consuetudinum ratio patiantur, ita tamen ut sedulam navent operam ad veros abusus corrigendos atque elimi-

nandos. Quam quidem in rem censuerunt Patres Eminentissimi apprime conferre frequentem celebrationem sacrificii Missae, quo videlicet Sacerdotes facile necessitati occurrere possunt Sanctissimam Eucharistiam secum per multos dies retinendi.

Quae cum ita sint hortor Amplitudinem Tuam ut in eum finem rurales aediculas multiplicandas cures, atque talia edas decreta ex quibus delatio Sanctissimi Sacramenti ad urgentes tantum causas, atque ad actuale ministerii sacerdotalis exercitium coarctetur, injuncta vero presbyteris stricta obligatione semper in hisce casibus Sanctam Hostiam super pectus deferendi.

Denique decreverunt Eminentissimi Patres ut de negotio isto gravissimo in Provincialibus Conciliis agatur, quo nimirum Antistites eam in suis dioecesibus communem normam inducere satagant, quam augustissimum Eucharistiae mysterium decere existimaverint. Tandem Amplitudini Tuae significare non praetermitto omnia et singula quae superius decreta sunt Sanctissimo D. N. Pio PP. IX. per me relata fuisse in audientia diei 3 Octobris elapsi anni, eaque a Sanctitate Sua in omnibus adprobata fuisse atque Apostolica auctoritate confirmata.

Datum Romae ex Aedibus S. Congregationis de Propaganda Fide die 25 Februarii, 1859.

Amplitudinis Tuae
    Ad officia paratissimus.
AL. C. BARNABO, Praef.
CAJET. ARCHIEP. THEBAR.
        Secretarius.
R. P. D. PAULO CULLEN,
    Archiepiscopo Dublinensi

1. *Ex dubiis propositis pro christianis Sinensibus.* Ad propositum'dubium "An sacerdotibus Sinensibus liceat in itineribus quæ longissima sunt secum deferre Eucharistiam ne ea priventur?" Resp. Non licere. Qualificatores S. O. die 27 Martii, 1665, et Eminentissimi approbarunt die 15 April. 1665.

2. Pro Gubernatoribus navium Lusitaniæ qui singulis annis in Indias orientales navigant, petentibus licentiam deferendi sacramentum Eucharistiæ, ne nautæ et Rectores sine Viatico decedaut. Lecto memoriali et auditis votis Sanctissimus supradictam petitionem omnino rejecit; ita quod nec in posterum ullo modo de ea tractetur. S. C. S. O. die 13 Julii, 1660.

3. Bened. XIV. *Inter omnigenai* "pro Incolis Regni Serviæ et finitimarum Regionum." "At ubi (sicuti ibidem legitur) Turcarum vis prævalet et iniquitas, sacerdos stolam semper habeat coopertam vestibus; in sacculo seu bursa pyxidem recondat quam per funiculos collo appensam in sinu reponat et nunquam solus procedat, sed uno saltem fideli, in defectu Clerici, associetur."

4. Honorius III. in cap. *Sane* de celebratione Miss. expresse habet de delatione Eucharistiæ quod si "in partibus infidelium ob necessitatem S. Viatici permitti ur, tamen extra necessitatem permittenda non est, cum hodie Ecclesiastica lege absolute prohibitum sit ut occulte deferatur. Occulte deferre in itinere, nequit moraliter fieri absque irreverentia tanti sacramenti."

5. Verricelli de Apostolicis Missionibus, Tit. 8, pag. 186, expendit, "An liceat in novo Orbe Missionariis S. Eucharistiam collo appensam secum in itinere occulte deferre, etc., et quidquid sit de veteri disciplina concludit hodie universalis Ecclesiæ consuetudine et plurimorum Conciliorum decretis prohibitum est deferre occulte S. Eucharistiam in itinere, nisi pro communicando infirmo, ubi esset timor et periculum infidelium, et dummodo ad infirmum non sit nimis longum iter sed modicum et unius diei."

6. Thomas a Jesu de procur. salut. omnium gentium lib. 7, "non auderem Evangelii ministros qui in illis regionibus aut aliis infidelium provinciis conversantes, si imminente mortis periculo secum Viaticum, occulte tamen, deferrent, condemnare." 838.

The following letter, with the decree of the Holy Office in reply, is taken from the *Acta ex iis decerpta quæ apud Sanctam Sedem geruntur,* vol. iv, page 320.

"BEATISSIME PATER,

"Inter decreta primæ Synodi Provincialis Westmonasteriensis sub C. XVI. n. 8, ubi sermo est de abjuratione Protestantium adultorum, et de baptismate sub conditione eis conferendo, additur 'Confessio etiam sacramentalis semper in tali casu est exigenda.' In adnotationibus, quas adjecit Pater Ballerini Editioni Romanæ

Theologiæ Moralis P. Gury, dicitur hanc confessionem esse conformiorem Instructioni a Suprema S. Officii Congregatione super modo reconciliandi hæreticos editæ, ex qua Instructione deducitur, opportunam esse integram peccatorum confessionem. In textu P. Gury tenetur eam esse suadendam in praxi.

"Quum vero hic Auctor tam in Theologia, quam in casibus Conscientiæ citaverit opinionem aliorum Auctorum docentium propter existentiam dubide primo baptismate a neoconversis tempore infantiæ susce to (adeo ut si nullum id fuerit, vera baptismi susceptio sit ea. quæ occasione abjurationis sub conditione traditur) dubiam esse obligationem peccata integre confitendi ante hoc baptisma conditionatum, nonnulli Confessarii in Anglia censuerunt, eos auctores secuti, dubiam confessionis integræ obligationem esse nullam obligationem: ac propter repugnantiam conversorum ad eam faciendam, et propter periculum confessionis imperfectæ, vel etiam sacrilegæ, omnino expedire, ut conversi aliqua tantum peccata Confessario exponant, ut ab eo absolutionis sacramentalis, si forsan ea opus sit, beneficium impetrent.

"Ex alia parte habetur praxis constans maximæ partis Confessariorum Regni integram confessionem tam ante, quam post approbationem Concilii Provincialis non modo suadentium, sed etiam exigentium; habetur difficultas conversorum, intellectum ad obsequium fidei ipsius captivandi, nisi per animi humilitatem et submissionem, quas in Sacramento Pœnitentiæ Christus Dominus reponere dignatus est; habetur etiam impossibilitas sciendi, nisi per integram peccatorum manifestationem, utrum neo-conversus rite sit ad ipsum baptisma dispositus, velitque, ex. gr., restitutionem famæ vel bonorum (si ad eam teneri contigerit) facere, occasionem proximam peccandi vitare, a matrimonio nulliter contracto resilire etiamsi per S. Sedis dispensationem (uti in casibus quotidie frequentioribus matrimonii post divortium civile contracti) illud sanari nequeat; habetur insuper necessitas suæ saluti per justificationem in Sacramento Pœnitentiæ prospiciendi, a cujus integritate nemo in infantia semel baptizatus possit eximi; attenta præsertim diligentia juniorum e Clero Anglicano circa ritum baptizandi fideliter servandum, et attento proinde majori numero eorum, de quorum baptismatis infantilis valore non licet dubitare.

"Quum vero certum sit, quod post plures annos confessionis integræ obligatio vim suam omnino sit amissura, si in praxi sequivaleant Theologi uti tutam opinionem Auctorum præfatorum, Archiepiscopus Westmonasteriensis, et Episcopi Angliæ enixe rogant, ut Sanctitas Vestra, pro sua in Missiones Angliæ benignitate, dignetur declarare hac super quæstione gravissima mentem Ecclesiæ:

"An debeat, juxta Synodi Provincialis Decretum a S. Sede probatum, confessio Sacramentalis a neo-conversis in Anglia exigi, et an ea debeat esse integra?"

DECRETUM.

Feria V. loco IV. die 17 Decembris, 1868.

"In Congregatione generali S. R. et U. Inquisitionis habita in Conventu S. Mariæ supra Minervam coram Emis. ac Rmis. DD. Cardinalibus contra hæreticam pravitatem generalibus inquisitoribus proposito suprascripto dubio præhabitisque DD. Consultorum suffragiis, iidem Emi. ac Rmi. Patres ad utramque dubii partem censuerunt respondendum esse: *Affirmative; et dandum esse Decretum latum sub feria quinta die decimaseptima Junii anni millesimi septingentesimi decimi quinti.*"

Eadem die ac Feria.

"SSmus. D. N. D. Pius divina providentia Papa IX. in solita audientia R. P. D. Adsessori Sancti Officii concessa Resolutionem Emorum. Patrum ad probare ac confirmare dignatus est, eamque una cum memorato Decreto mandavit remitti R. P. D. Archiepiscopo Westmonasteriensi."

ANGELUS ARGENTI
S. R. et U. I. Notarius.

ALIUD ALLEGATUM DECRETUM.
Feria V. die 17 Junii, 1715.
DUBIUM.
"An plena fides sit adhibenda

Carolo Wipperman de Rostoch in ducatu Mechlemb. rgh prædicanti et Lectori theologiæ Lutheranæ quietisticæ superintendenti et doctori primario sectæ Lutheranorum Quietistarum. S. Fidei catholicæ reconciliato in S. O. Parmæ, et circa nonnullos errores detectos in ejus Baptismo; an ipsi credendum sit circa ea quæ enarrat, et quatenus affirmative, tum ut ipsius saluti, tum etiam ut cæterorum illius sectæ seu Regionis, præsertim si fuerint ignorantes, saluti pariter consulatur.

"Quæritur, an dictus Wipperman sit rebaptizandus, et quatenus affirmative, an absolute vel sub conditione; et quatenus affirmative, an teneatur confiteri omnia peccata præteritæ vitæ; et quatenus affirmative, an confessio præponenda sit, vel postponenda Baptismo conferendo sub conditione.

"SSmus. auditis votis Emorum. dixit: Carolum Ferdinandum esse rebaptizandum sub conditione, et collato Baptismo, ejus præteritæ vitæ peccata confiteatur, et ab iis sub conditione absolvatur."

Præsens Copia concordat cum suo Originali.

Ita est, ANGELUS ARGENTI,
S. R. et U. I. Notarius.

464.

The following decrees of the Sacred Congregation of Indulgences are taken from the *Decreta Authentica*, etc., by Prinzivalli.

CCCLVII. *Vindana in Britannia Minore*, 20 Sept., 1775. *Dub.* 6 Benedictio in articulo mortis potestne bis aut amplius in eodem morbo qui insperate protrahitur, impertiri, etiamsi non convaluerit ægrotus ? Si possit iterari hæc benedictio, quodn m requiritur intervallum inter ejus largitiones ?

Dub. 7m Invocatio saltem mentalis, de qua fit mentio in Brevibus ad Episcopos de hac benedictione missis præscribiturne, quamdiu ægrotus suæ mentis est compos, ut conditio sine qua non, ad Indulgentiam vi istius benedictionis lucrandam ?

Dub. 8m Episcopus ad supradictam benedictionem impertiendam delegatus cum facultate subdelegandi: *primo* debetne per paucos subdelegare Sacerdotes, ut majus sit benedictionis istius et Indulgentiæ huic adnexæ desiderium, simul et major utrique concilietur reverentia ? *secundo:* potestne omnes suæ Diœcesis subdelegare Confessarios, ne etiam una si fieri possit ex uis ovibus tanta privetur gra ia? *tertio* potestne subdelegare omnes directe et speciatim Parochos sive plurimos Sacerdotes in dignitate constitutos, et indirecte et confuse omnes Confessarios hisce verbis. *"Dilecto nobis in Christo, etc., te delegamus, eligimus et deputamus quatenus valeas, etc., insuper quemcumque Confessarium a te ad tui libitum semel vel pluries, et quandocumque opus fuerit, eligendum pariter eligimus et deputamus ad eandem gratiam conferendam,"* hic subdelegandi modus estne validus ?

" Resp. Ad 6m —Semel in eodem statu morbi. Ad 7m —Affirmative. Ad 8m —Affirmative ad primam partem. Negative, ad secundam. Affirmative ad tertiam partem quoad parochos speci tim ruri degentes." 962, 966.

DVI *Valentinen.,* 5 Feb.,

1841. "5° Utrum sufficiat recita io Confessionis, idest *Confiteor,* etc., in Sacramento Pœnitentiæ habita, pro recitatione illius præscripta quando impertjenda sit benedictio cum Indulgentia in Mortis Articulo ?

"Respondetur — Negative juxta praxim, et Rubricas, nisi necessitas urgeat.

"6° Utrum ne esse sit tribus vicibus recitare *Confiteor,* etc., quando administratur Sacrum Viaticum, Extrema Unctio. ac Indulgentia in Mortis Articulo impertitur ?

" Respondetur — Affirmative juxta praxim, et Rubricas.

"7° Utrum infirmus lucrari possit, Indulgentiam Plenariam in Mortis Articulo a pluribus Sacerdotibus facultatem habentibus impertiendam ?

" Respondetur—Negative in eodem Mortis Articulo.

"8° Utrum Sacerdos valide conferat Indulgentiam Plenariam in Mortis Articulo, omissa formula a summo Pontifice præscripta, ob libri deficientiam ?

" Respondetur — Negative, quia formula non est tantum directiva, sed præceptiva." 923, 974.

DXI. *Briocen.,* 29 Maii, 1841. "An eodem die lucrari possint plures indulgentiæ plenariæ, quando pro unaquaque præscripta est perceptio divinæ Eucharistiæ ?

" Resp.—Affirmative. servatis tamen respective aliis appositis conditionibus." 978.

DXXIX. *Gandaven.,* 12 Feb., 1842. "1° Utrum Benedictio in articulo mortis juxta formulam Benedicti XIV in Constitutione, *Pia Mater,* reiterari possit in eodem morbi statu ?

" 2° Quatenus affirmative an

ea toties iterari possit quoties aegrotus in peccata saltem venialia relapsus ab eis absolvetur?"

Sac. Congregatio in una *Veronen.*, die 24 Septembris, 1838, responsum dedit cuidam Dubio illius Episcopi. "An scilicet Benedictio Apostolica pluries impertiri posset novo mortis periculo redeunte?" et responsum fuit: "Negative, permanente infirmitate etsi diuturna; Affirmative vero si infirmus convaluerit, ac deinde quacumque de causa in novum mortis periculum redeat." Et ita Sac. Congr. respondit Episcopo Gandavensi. 962.

As the decrees of the Synod of Thurles are in the hands of nearly every priest on the Irish mission, we think it useless to give here those that are referred to in the volume. The following are the decrees of the Synods of Westminster and of Baltimore to which reference is made, besides those of which the words are cited.

EX DECRETIS CONCIL. WESTMON. PROV.I^{mi}.

XVI. *De Baptismo.*

1º In unaquaque ecclesia, cui annexa est cura animarum, sit fons baptismalis nisi ad tempus dispensaverit episcopus, in loco conspicuo et conveniente positus; in quo aqua baptismalis jugiter servetur.

2º Oleum catechumenorum et sanctum chrisma, necnon, si placet, sal, et alia ad baptismi administrationem requisita, in baptisterio, vel saltem in sacrario, seorsim et cum omni reverentia, et summa cum munditie, asserventur. In novis ecclesiis aedificandis, praeparetur locus in quo recondantur, in ipso baptisterio.

4º Baptismus in sola ecclesia debet administrari, nisi in casibus in Rituali exceptis; et quidem, secluso casu periculi, vel gravis incommodi, non sine episcopi permissu. Excipiuntur baptismata quae in stationibus a principali ecclesia seu sacello remotis administrantur, quando eas sacerdos, statutis quibusdam temporibus, vel vocatus, invisit.

7º Cum magis invaluerint causae quae animos Vicariorum Apostolicorum, ineunte hoc saeculo, impulerunt ut decernerent omnes post annum 1773, natos et inter Protestantes baptizatos, conversos ad fidem esse baptizandos sub conditione; hanc regulam absolute innovamus praecipientes, omnes a Protestantismo conversos esse baptizandos conditionate, nisi ex indubiis probationibus certissime constet in ipsorum baptismo omnia rite fuisse peracta quoad materiae et formae applicationem.

8º Hujusmodi baptismus non fiat publice sed omnino privatim, cum aqua lustrali et absque caeremoniis. Confessio etiam sacramentalis semper in tali casu est exigenda.

XVIII. *De SS. Eucharistiae Sacramento.*

5º Ante S. Eucharistiam in tabernaculo repositam lampas

diu noctuque luceat. Pyxis velo serico albo, vel aureo cooperiatur.

6o Si vero ob periculum sacrilegii S. Sacramentum in altari vel etiam in ecclesia tuto servari non possit, præparandus est locus decens et semotus, ab episcopo approbandus; in quo conservetur, cum lampade semper accensa, ut in Decreto 5o.

12o Quamvis, ob locorum circumstantias, non liceat absque sacrilegii et scandali periculo, Sanctissimum Viaticum ægrotis publice et solemniter deferre, et ideo a S. Sede nobis permissum jam sit sine lumine ac occulte illud portare, nunquam tamen non advertere sacerdos debet, se Deum absconditum sibi adhærentem habere, et secum ad suorum solatium ferre. Reverenter igitur, imo devote, et veluti in contemplatione defixus, Sanctissimum Sacramentum in sacculo decenter vel pretiose ornato, ad collum appenso, ad ægroti domum deferat. Et cum sæpe miserrimæ sint pauperum nostrorum habitationes, ita ut vix decore administrari in iis possit S. Viaticum, magnopere laudandum usum declaramus, et omnibus commendatum volumus, deferendi secum, vel præmittendi, capsulam omnibus requisitis instructam, ad decentem sancti sacramenti administrationem. Quamprimum fieri possit, pyxis post communionem infirmorum ad ecclesiam deferatur, et usque ad purificationem in Tabernaculo reponatur.

XX. *De Sacramento Extremæ Unctionis.*

4o Ad custodiam olei infirmorum habeat locum decentem, clave obseratum, si fieri potest in ecclesia, vel in sacrar o: aut etiam, juxta præscriptum in Concilio prov. Mediolanensi IV, "in ipsa domo, loco decenti ac tuto." In novis ecclesiis ædificandis, paretur fenestella prope altare majus, cui inscribatur *Oleum Infirmorum*, cum suo ostiolo clave munito.

EX DECRETIS CONCILIORUM BALTIMORENSIUM.

PROVINCIALIS Imi.

XIII. Quando diversa tum Sanctorum, tum familiæ nomina in baptismo infantibus tribuuntur, si Sacerdos censuerit expedire, in prima interrogatione omnia nomina exprimat: in sequentibus tamen formis et precibus, nomina vulgo dicta Christiana tantum repetat. In libro autem baptismatum, omnia nomina recenseantur.

XV. Meminerint etiam Missionarii Rituale Romanum, et universalem Ecclesiæ consuetudinem exigere ut aqua, in baptismo adhibita, fuerit benedicta in eum finem, vel Sabbato sancto Paschæ, vel Sabbato Pentecostes, vel alio saltem tempore ante baptismi administrationem, forma in ipso Rituali præscripta. Curandum iis idcirco, ut Fontes baptismales, *sub clavi*, in unaquaque Ecclesia, ubi baptismi sacramentum ordinarie ministratur, quamprimum erigantur; prope quos, omnia quæ ad administrationem hujus Sacramenti pertinent, nitide serventur.

XVI. Ex præteritorum temporum difficultate, invaluit in his regionibus consuetudo baptismum privatis in domibus administrandi. Cum igitur magnæ gravitatis sit generalem legem in illis regionibus servandam statim ferre, cui contraria est consuetudo; etsi censemus curandum esse, quoad fieri potest, ut hoc Sacramentum in Ecclesia conferatur, tamen Episcoporum et Missionariorum judicio relinquimus, ut statuant quando sint urgendi Fideles ut infantes ad Ecclesiam deferant, ut baptismus iis conferatur. *

XIX. Op ant Praesules hujus Provinciae ut benedictio mulieris post partum, non promiscue, atque nulla ratione habita puerperae dispositionis, neque extra Ecclesiam, vel locum ubi Sacrum fit, in posterum conferatur.

XXXII. Quoniam uniformitas etiam in rebus minimis maxime optanda Ecclesia semper visa est, statuimus Superpelliceum esse debere modestum, decorum, et sacris functionibus conveniens. Statuimus etiam ut Biretum, cum Episcopis singulis visum fuerit morem illud gestandi in suas Dioeceses inducere, Romano Bireto sit conforme.

[The decrees XVI, XIX, and XXXII, had been framed somewhat differently, but were altered in accordance with the *Instructio circa decreta a Synodo Provinciali Baltimorensi edita*, by the Sacred Congregation of the Propaganda, which, in reference to those decrees in their first form, has the following:

In directo decimo sexto statuitur: *In oppidis ubi Ecclesia est, extra eam Baptismus non con-*

feratur. S. Congregatio intelligens cujus gravitatis sit generalem legem in regionibus illis servandam statim ferre, cui contraria est consuetudo: prae oculis habens domiciliorum magnam distantiam ab Ecclesia, etiam in oppidis ubi Ecclesia est, Episcopis commendat Decretum, de quo serm est, in hunc modum immutare, ut appareat, habita ratione magni spatii quo saepe Ecclesia distare solet a locis ubi incolarum domicilia sunt, licere posse Baptismum extra Ecclesiam conferre; curandum tamen esse, quoad fieri potest, ut hoc Sacramentum in Ecclesia conferatur; Episcoporum denique et Missionariorum prudentiae relinquendum esse ut statuant quando sint urgendi fideles, ut infantes ad Ecclesiam deferant, ut baptismus eis conferatur.

In decimo nono Synodi Decreto, in quo statuitur puerperam in Ecclesia benedicendam esse, vel in locis ubi Sacrum fit, adhiberi tantum debent verba ejusmodi, quae insinuationem contineant, et Episcopos ita optare ostendant: nam valde periculosum est contrarium morem generali lege repente mutare. Praeterea, Rituale Romanum non praescribit ejusmodi benedictionem in Ecclesia fieri; multoque minus vetat benedictionem hanc iis puerperis conferri, quae Paschale praeceptum non impleverint, vel Sacramentalem confessionem paulo ante non fecerint, prout in memorato decimo nono Baltimorensi Decreto continetur.

In Decreto trigesimo secundo, in quo agitur de forma Super-

---

* Vid. infra, *Conc. Plen. Baltimoren.* II^{di} *Decreta*, n. 623 et n. 237.

pellicei adhibendi a Clericis, videtur satis esse affirmare *Superpelliceum esse debere modestum, decorum, et sacris functionibus conveniens*. In eo Decreto describitur quædam superpellicei forma, et dicitur eam esse in S. Romana Ecclesia usitatam: affirmari tamen non potest eam solam superpellicei formam in Urbe Roma usitatam esse.]

CONCIL. BALTIMOREN., PROV. II Decr. VII. Revmis. Episcopis S. Ludovici et Bostoniensi munus a Patribus demandatum est concinnandi, et hujus Concilii nomine et auctoritate, in lucem edendi Ritualis Romani accuratam editionem, necnon ejusdem breve exemplar in usum Missionariorum ; atque utrisque editionibus. in modum appendicis, adjungendi modificationes hucusque a S. Sede concessas, una cum versione, vernacula lingua. eorum quæ prædictis Præsulibus vertenda esse visa fuerint.

CONCIL. BALTIMOREN., PROV. III⁰ Decr. V. Placuit ut Rituale editatur Romano conforme, adjectis in appendice quæ ad ædificationem Fidelium conducere visa fuerint, quod Baltimori edatur. auctoritate Illmi. et Revmi. Archiepiscopi, et ubique per Fœderatas Provincias servetur. Ne autem peculiares ritus cujusque arbitrio inducantur, districte vetamus ne Sacerdotes a forma sibi in rituali præscripta, consuetudinis obtentu vel alio quocumque prætextu, discedant.

CONCIL. BALTIMOREN., PROV. IV⁰ In quinta Congregatione privata. Primo Concilio Balti-

morensi inhærentes censuerunt patres, in Ritualis editione, interrogationum et precum quarumdam, Archiepiscopi judicio, versionem lingua vernacula, ad paginæ calcem inserendam, ut adhiberi possit quandocumque videatur expedire in Fidelium ædificationem, latina formula precum nunquam omissa.

CONCIL. BALTIMOREN., PROV. V⁰ Decr. VIII. Patres unanimi voce probarunt Rituale Romanum editum auctoritate Conciliorum Provincialium secundi et quarti, curante Episcopo S. Ludovici, sed permiserunt ut Appendix fieret amplior, precibus quibusdam vernacula lingua redditis, judicio Archiepiscopi, prout in Concilio quarto decretum est. Districte tamen præceperunt Sacerdotibus omnibus latinam formam precum nunquam omittere.

CONCIL. BALTIMOREN. PLENARII DECRETA.

II. Quæ in Septem Conciliis Baltimorensibus decreta sunt, ad omnes diœceses Fœderatorum Statuum, et regionum omnium generali Gubernio subditarum, extendi statuimus, eaque ubique vim obtinere.

III. Rituale Romanum, jam adoptatum a Concilio primo Baltimorensi, accurate servandum in sacris muneribus peragendis ubique in diœcesibus Statuum Fœderatorum decernimus, vetantes districte ne consuetudines ritusve a Romanis alieni introducantur. Ritus Ecclesiasticos nolumus adhiberi in sepultura fidelium, quandocumque eorum corpora s peliuntur in cœmeteriis sectarum; vel etiam in cœmeteriis profanis, quando adsunt cœmeteria catholica.

XXIII. Quoniam gravissimæ Rationes a Patribus Concilii primi Baltimorensis Provincialis, A. S. 1829, allatæ, dum a SSmo. Patre peterent ut pro baptizandis adultis ea in hisce Provinciis uti liceret forma quæ in Rituali Romano pro baptismate parvulorum invenitur, adhuc vigent, immo in dies graviores evasuræ videntur; statuunt Patres S. Sedi supplicandum esse, ut privilegium tunc ad viginti annos juxta Patrum preces concessum, nunc perpetuum fiat, vel saltem ad viginti annos iterum concedatur.

Decretum quo prorogatur facultas adultos eadem ac parvulos forma baptizandi.

ARCHIEPISCOPI et Episcopi Plenarii Concilii Baltimorensis SSmum. Dnum. Nostrum PIUM PP. IX. obsecrandum censuerunt ut, permanentibus adhuc causis ob quas sa. me. decessor ejus PIUS PP. VIII., decretum S. Congregationis de Propag. Fide approbans die 26 Septembris anni 1830, annuit ut in baptismate adultorum is brevior cæremoniarum ordo adhiberi ad viginti annos posset, qui in Rituali Romano ad baptizandos pueros præscribitur, indultum hujusmodi rursus prorogare dignaretur. Precibus istis relatis ab Emo. ac Revmo. D. RAPHAELE Cardinali FORNARI in generali S. Congregationis conventu habito die 30 Augusti, 1852, Emi Patres censuerunt supplicandum SSmo. pro indulti prorogatione ad quinquennium, atque ita ut interim Episcopi paulatim ad observantiam ritus descripti pro adultorum baptismate in Rituali Romano accedere satagant.

Hanc vero S. Congregationis sententiam SSmo. Dno. Nostro PIO PP. IX. ab infrascripto Secretario relatam in Audientia diei 5 Septembris. Sancitas Sua benigne in omnibus probavit, ratamque habuit, contrariis qui buscumque haud obstantibus.[1]

Datum Romæ. ex Ædibus dictæ S. C. de Propag. Fide, die 26 Septembris, 1852.

J. PH. H. CARD. FRANSONI,
Præf.

AL. BARNABDO, *a Secretis.*

CONCIL. PLENARII BALTIMOREN. IIᵈⁱ DECRETA.

236. De more, qui olim in hac regione invaluerat, neque adhuc omni ex parte sublatus est, Baptismum in privatis domibus conferendi, hæc in supra commemorato Baltimorensi Concilio habentur:

"Ex præteritorum, etc. . . . ut supra," n. XVI. PROV. Iⁱ.

237. Verum, rebus plerisque in locis in melius mutatis, præcipimus ne unquam Sacerdotes extra ecclesiam hoc Sacramentum conferre audeant, præter mortis imminentem casum, in urbibus unam aut plures ecclesias habentibus. Qui ruri degunt, aut in pagis et oppidulis ubi nulla est ecclesia, infantes ad ecclesiam propinquiorem vel

---

[1] From this answer we inferred, as stated n. 459, that the indult was not renewed since 1857. It was, however, renewed, at least for several of the American dioceses, as appears from a decree of the Second Council of Baltimore, n. 243, given below.

stationem, in qua Sacrum fieri solet, baptizandos adducant. Quod si ob aeris intemperiem, itineris difficultatem, parentum inopiam, vel alias graves causas hoc fieri nequeat, tunc missionarii prudentiæ et conscientiæ relinquimus, ut eos domi cum omnibus Ecclesiæ cæremoniis baptizet.

288. Quum Baptismus privatus, ob mortis periculum, domi conferendus est, Sacerdos, stola alba indutus, omissis omnibus ante Baptismum dicendis vel agendis, "Catechumenum statim trina vel etiam una aquæ infusione rite baptizet; postea vero si tempus adhuc suppetat, et Chrisma secum habeat, liniat eum in vertice, et linteolum candidum imponat, candelamque accensam ei porrigat, sicut in Ordine baptizandi traditur."[1]

242. In conversis ab hæresi ad fidem excipiendis, volumus ut adamussim servetur modus ille qui in Forma a Sacr. Congr. S. Officii die 20 Julii, 1859, tradita habetur, et jam in quibusdam libris ritualibus typis impressus invenitur. Hanc, ut neminem lateat, in Appendicem referendam curabimus. Ibi enim explicite declaratur, quando Baptismus absolute, quando sub conditione, quando denique nullo modo sit iterandus.[2]

248. Concilii Baltimorensis Plenarii primi vestigiis inhæ-

rentes censuerunt Patres supplicandum esse S. Sedi ut privilegium olim quibusdam hujus regionis Diœcesibus ad annum usque 1870 concessum, quo liceat pro adultis baptizandis formulam breviorem pro parvulis constitutam adhibere, Summus Pontifex ad decem vel viginti annos omnibus extendere dignaretur.[3]

244. Sanctæ Sedi supplicandum pariter censemus, uti apud nos morem inducere liceat, qui apud Anglos viget et a Romano Pontifice probatus fuit, baptizandi scilicet privatim, cum aqua tantum lustrali, et absque cæremoniis, adultos ab hæresi ad Ecclesiam conversos, de quorum baptismate prudenter dubitatur.[4]

---

[5] *Formula brevis conficiendæ aquæ Baptismalis, præscripta a Concilio Baltimorensi Provinciali primo, et a Pio Papa VIII. approbata, ad usum Missionariorum Americæ Septentrionalis.*

BENEDICTIO FONTIS,

SEU AQUÆ BAPTISMALIS.

Exorcizo te, creatura aquæ, in nomine Dei Patris omnipotentis ✠, et in nomine Jesu Christi ✠ Filii ejus Domini nostri, et in virtute Spiritus ✠ Sancti. Exorcizo te, omnis virtus adversarii diaboli; ut

[1] Verba sunt Constitutionis a Sacra Rit. Cong. probatæ, et in Philadelphiensi Synodo sexta nuper promulgatæ.

[2] Vid. infra. *Modus excipiendi*, etc.

[3] Ad hanc supplicationem S. C. respondit: "Porro S. Cong. censuit Episcopos recurrere debere expleto tempore postremæ concessionis."

[4] "Quoad hoc postulatum S. Cong. censuit respondendum: pro nunc non expedire."

[5] Taken from the Ritual published for the use of the American clergy, Baltimori, 1860.

omnis phantasia eradicetur, ac effugetur ab hac creatura aquæ et fiat fons aquæ salientis in vitam æternam, ut qui ex ea baptizati fuerint, fiant templum Dei vivi. et Spiritus Sanctus habitet in eis in remissionem peccatorum: in nomine Domini nostri Jesu Christi, qui venturus est judicare vivos et mortuos, et sæculum per ignem. ℞. Amen.

OREMUS.

Domine sancte, Pater omnipotens, æterne Deus, aquarum spiritualium sanctificator te suppliciter deprecamur ut hoc ministerium humilitatis nostræ respicere digneris, et super has aquas, abluendis et vivificandis hominibus præparatas, Angelum sanctitatis emittas, ut peccatis prioris vitæ ablutis, reatuque deterso, purum sacrato Spiritui habitaculum regerationibus procuret. Per Christum Dominum nostrum. ℞. Amen.

Infundat deinceps Sanctum Oleum in aquam, in modum crucis, dicens:

Conjunctio olei unctionis, et aquæ baptismatis, sanctificetur et fœcundetur. In nomine Patris ✠, et Filii ✠, et Spiritus ✠ Sancti. ℞. Amen.

Deinde Chrisma aquæ infundat, in modum crucis et dicat:

Conjunctio Chrismatis sanctificationis, et Olei unctionis, et aquæ baptismatis. sanctificetur et fœcundetur. In nomine Patris ✠, et Filii ✠, et Spiritus ✠ Sancti. ℞. Amen.

Denique dicat benedicens ipsam aquam:

Sanctificetur et fœcundetur, Fons iste, et ex eo renascentes. In nomine Patris ✠, et Filii ✠, et Spiritus ✠ Sancti. ℞. Amen.

[1] *Modus excipiendi professionem fidei Catholicæ a Neo-conversis juxta formam a S. Congregatione S. Officii, die 2C Julii, 1859, præscriptum.*

In conversione hæreticorum inquirendum est primo de validitate baptismi in hæresi suscepti. Instituto igitur diligenti examine, si compertum fuerit, aut nullum, aut nulliter collatum fuisse, baptizandi erunt absolute. Si autem, investigatione peracta, adhuc probabile dubium de baptismi validitate supersit, tunc sub conditione iteratur, juxta ordinem baptismi Adultorum. Demum, si constiterit validum fuisse, recipiendi erunt tantummodo ad abjurationem, seu professionem fidei. Triplex igitur in conciliandis hæreticis distinguitur procedendi methodus:

I. Si baptismus absolute conferatur nulla sequitur abjuratio, nec absolutio, eo quod omnia abluit sacramentum regenerationis.

II. Si baptismus sit sub conditione iterandus, hoc ordine procedendum erit: 1º Abjuratio, seu fidei professio; 2º Baptismus conditionalis; 3º Confessio sacramentalis cum absolutione conditionata.

III. Quando denique validum judicatum fuerit baptisma, sola recipitur abjuratio, seu fidei professio, quam absolutio a censuris sequitur. Si tamen nonnunquam ejusmodi Neo-con-

---

[1] Taken from the Ritual published for the use of the American **lergy Baltimori 1860.**

versus valde desideret ut ritus in ejus baptismo olim omissi, hac occasione suppleantur, Sacerdos huic pio ejus voto morem gerere utique liberum habet.

Debebit tamen in tali casu adhibere ordinem baptismi Adultorum, et mutare mutanda ob baptismum jam valide susceptum.

The authors who have written *ex professo* on the rubrics of the Ritual are few in number, compared with those who have written on the rubrics of the Missal and Breviary. But the rubrics of the Ritual and those of the Missal sometimes regard the same matter, *e. g.*, the administration of the Eucharist. and then the same commentary to a great extent serves for both. Besides, many of the important questions involved are treated by the theologians generally (*Vid. introduction*, n. 9–10, 93).

The first complete commentary on the rubrics of the Ritual, and still one of the best, is that of Baruffaldi, "*Ad Rituale Romanum Commentaria*, Auctore HIERONYMO BARUFFALDO, Ferrariensi, Sacræ Inquisitionis Consultore, et insignis Collegiatæ Centensis Archipresbytero" (1 vol. 4to, Venetiis, 1792).

Baruffaldi has done for the Ritual what Gavantus had previously done for the Missal. He gives the entire text of the rubric divided into "Titles," and subdivided into sections, under which he gives his commentary. This is, undoubtedly, the most satisfactory plan for a work of the kind. The advantage to the reader of having under his eye the words of the rubric, more than compensates for the increased size of the book. On questions connected with the rubrics of the Ritual, even to the present day, no author is referred to more frequently, or with greater respect, by the consultors of the Sacred Congregation, than Baruffaldi.

Catalani, also, wrote a complete commentary on the Ritual. He follows the general plan of Baruffaldi, but attends less to the manner of performing the ceremonies, than to their symbolical meaning, origin, and history. The title of his work explains the object which the author proposed to himself: *Rituale Romanum, Benedicti Papæ XIV jussu editum et auctum, perpetuis Commentariis exornatum ac in duos Tomos divisum, quibus vetus ac nova Sacrorum Rituum Disciplina Sanctorum Patrum ac insignium Ritualium Testimoniis, Romanorum Pontificum et Conciliorum Decretis, Sacrarum S. R. E. Cardinulium Congregationum. Responsis, ac variarum Ecclesiarum Praxi recensetur atque explicatur. Eidem SSmo. Patri dicatum.* Auctore JOSEPHO CATALANO, presbytero Oratorii S. Hieronymi Charitatis" (2 vols. folio, Patavii, 1770). He wrote also a commentary on the Roman Pontifical, to which we refer in one ♥ two places.

"R. P. JOANNIS MICHÆLIS CAVALIERI, Bergomatis, Ord. Eremit. Sti. Augustini Cong. Observ. Lomb. S. Theologiæ lectoris emeriti *Opera omnia liturgica seu Commentaria in authentica Sac. Rit. Cong. Decreta, ad Romanum præsertim Breviarium, Missale et Rituale quomodolibet attinentia Quinque Tomis comprehensa.*" (5 vols. folio, Augustæ Vindelicorum, 1764.)

The liturgical works of Cavalieri, though professedly only commentaries on the decrees of the S. C. R., contain a commentary on a good part of the rubrics of the Ritual, which are cited and explained under the decrees that regard the same matter. He not only explains the ceremonies, but enters, sometimes at considerable length, into the questions of theology and canon law that arise out of the rubrics. He is highly esteemed for his learning and accuracy, and is cited as a standard authority by subsequent writers, especially by Gardellini.

"*Acta Ecclesiæ Mediolanensis a* SANCTO CAROLO, Cardinali S. Praxedis Archiep. Mediolanen. *condita*" (2 vols. folio, Lugduni, 1683). This great work by St. Charles Borromeo, called by Baruffaldi "vere aureum opus" (Tit. x. n. 45), has been always regarded as of the highest authority on the ceremonies of the Ritual. In fact, most of the rubrics of the present Roman Ritual are taken from it.

"*De antiquis Ecclesiæ Ritibus,*

Libri Tres, ex variis insigniorum Ecclesiarum Pontificalibus, Sacramentariis, Missalibus, Breviariis, Ritualibus sive Manualibus, Ordinariis seu Consuetudinariis, cum manuscriptis tum editis; ex diversis Conciliorum Decretis, Episcoporum Statutis, aliisque probatis Auctoribus permultis, collecti atque exornati a R. P. EDMUNDO MARTÈNE, presbytero et monacho Benedictino e Congreg. S. Mauri" (4 vols. in folio, Venetiis, 1788.) This work is looked on by all as the great authority on the history and antiquity of ecclesiastical ceremonies, and their variety in different parts of the Church. Nearly all that Catalani has on these subjects in his commentary, is taken from Martène.

"CATECHISMUS *ex decreto* SS. CONCILII TRIDENTINI, *ad Parochos Pii V. Pont. Max. jussu editus. Translated into English and published with the original Latin text by J. Donovan, D.D.*" (2 vols. 8vo, Rome, 1839.) The Catechism of the Council of Trent supplies, in many instances, the best explanation of the text of the rubric, while its authority is not much less than that of the rubric itself (vid. n. 132).

Many important questions regarding the administration of the sacraments are treated by BENEDICT XIV, "*De Synodo Diœcesana Libri Tredecim*" (given *in extenso* in vol. 25th of the "*Theologiæ Cursus Completus,*" Parisiis, 1840). References are made also to his "*De SS. Missæ Sacrificio*" and "*De Festis*" (the former in vol.

28d, the latter in vol. 26th of the "*Cursus*"), his "*Institutiones*" (being vol. 10th, "*Lambertini Opera*," Typographia Bassanensi, 1767), and his "*Bullarium*" (Venetiis, 1778).

The RITUAL OF TOULON may be looked on as a kind of commentary on the Roman Ritual. The parts of it that regard Baptism and Extreme Unction, are given in the "*Dictionnaire des Cérémonies et des Rites Sacrés*" (3 vols. imp. 8vo, Migne, Paris, 1846). It is often found to touch on minute details that others do not notice.

Amongst modern works the "*Sacræ Liturgiæ Praxis juxta Ritum Romanum, in Missæ celebratione, Officii recitatione et Sacramentorum administratione servanda*, cura P. J. B. DE HERDT, Archidiœcesis Mechlinensis presbyteri" (Editio tertia, 3 vols. 8vo. Lovanii, 1855), contains a pretty full explanation of the rubrics of the Ritual. It emb dies nearly all the text, and gives minute instructions on the manner of performing the ceremonies. The work is in high repute for its clearness and general accuracy.

The "*Cours Abrégé de Liturgie Pratique, comprenant l'explication du Missel, du Bréviaire, et du Rituel, à l'usage des Églises qui suivent le Rite Romain*, par M. L'ABBÉ FALISE" (seconde édition, 1 vol. 8vo, Paris, 1855), has a brief, but clear and comprehensive commentary on the rubrics of the Ritual. It often gives, in a single sentence, the various opinions that are held, as well as the practical decision, on a disputed question.

The "*Modo Pratico di assistere a' Moribondi, di dirigerli nel fare il testamento, di amministrare loro i Sacramenti, e diaiutare a ben morire i giustiziati, diretto a' Rev. Parrochi ed a' Sacerdoti*, dal P. M. ANTONIO BRANDIMARTE, Min. Conv. e Parroco Romano" (1 vol. 12mo, Roma, 1818), contains important instructions on the administration of the Viaticum and Extreme Unction, and is of great value as an evidence of the actual practice in the city of Rome.

The "MÉLANGES THÉOLOGIQUES, par une Société d'Ecclésiastiques" (Nouvelle Édition revue et corrigée, 6 vols. 8vo, Paris, Tournay, 1859); the "REVUE THÉOLOGIQUE *faisant suite aux Mélanges Théologiques* par une Société de Prêtres Belges et Français" (Paris, 1856 et seq.); the "ANALECTA JURIS PONTIFICII" (Rome, 1855 et seq.); and the "ACTA EX IIS DECERPTA QUÆ APUD SANCTAM SEDEM GERUNTUR" (Romæ, 1865 et seq.), contain a great many important decisions and valuable dissertations on matters appertaining to the Ritual. The "ACTA EX IIS DECERPTA, &c.," gives nearly all the decrees of the Sacred Congregation of Rites issued since the publication of the third edition of Gardellini.

On questions of moral

theology, ST. LIGUORI is by common consent the great authority (the references are to the edition in 10 vols., small 8vo, Mechliniæ, 1845). Where he speaks clearly, we seldom refer to any other. But on many points involved in the rubric, he is either silent, or touches but slightly and without giving any decided opinion. On these we refer to other authors well known to students of theology.

On many of the rubrics that regard the Eucharist, the principal authority is the "*Thesaurus Sacrorum Rituum*, Auctore Rev. Patre D. BARTHOLOMÆO GAVANTO, Cong. Cler. Reg. S. Pauli, S. R. C. Consultore, etc., *Cum novis Observationibus et Additionibus* R. P. D. CAJETANI-MARIÆ MERATI, Cler. Reg. ejusdem S. R. C. Consultoris" (4 vols. 4to, Venetiis, 1823); but recent writers on the ceremonies of the Missal are also cited.

For the fuller and more satisfactory explanation of a few points, we have had occasion to refer to the works of some of the great Scholastics; and on various incidental questions we have made use of any works within our reach, that seemed to us to throw light on the particular question treated. For the satisfaction of the reader, we subjoin the titles and editions of those, which (besides the works already noticed) have been used in compiling the volume.

A LAPIDE. *Comment. in Sac. Script.* Folio, Lugduni 1690.

Annals of the Propagation of the Faith. 8vo. Dublin.

BALDESCHI. *Esposizione delle Sacre Ceremonie, etc.* 3 vols. 12mo, Roma, 1857.

BAULDRY. *Manuale Sacrarum Cæremoniarum, etc.* 1 vol. 4to, Venetiis, 1743.

BELLARMINE. *De Controversiis adversus Hæreticos.* 4 vols. folio, Mediolani, 1721.

BILLUART. *Cursus Theologiæ juxta mentem D. Thomæ.* 10 vols. 8vo, Parisiis, 1839.

BONA. *Rerum Liturgicarum, Libri Duo.* 1 vol. 4to, Romæ, 1671.

BOUIX. *De Jure Liturgico.* 1 vol. 8vo, Atrebati, 1860. *De Parocho.* 1 vol. 8vo, Parisiis, 1855.

BOUVIER. *Institutiones Theologicæ.* Editio nova, 6 vols. 12mo, Parisiis, 1856. *Abrégé d'Embryologie* in *Supplemento ad Tract. de Matrim.* 12mo, Parisiis, 1846. *Traité des Indulgences.* 10ᵐᵉ édit., 1 vol. 12mo, Paris, 1855.

Bullarium Romanum. Edit. Car. Coquelenes. Roma, 1739 et seq.

Cæremoniale Episcoporum. 1 vol. 8vo, Romæ, 1848.

CARDENAS. *Crisis Theologica.* Venetiis, 1694.

CARON. *Les Cérémonies de la Messe Basse. Appendice au Traité des SS. Mystères par Collet.* Paris 1848.

CARRIÈRE. *De Matrimonio.* 2 vols. 8vo, Parisiis, 1837. *De Justitia et Jure,* 3 vols. 8vo, Lovanii, 1845.

Cérémonial des Évêques commenté et expliqué par un Évêque Suffragant de Québec. 1 vol. 8vo, Paris, 1856.

CHARDON. *Histoire des Sacrements,* in *Theologiæ Cursu*

Completo. Vol. XX^mo Parisiis, 1840.

CLERICATI. *Decisiones Sacramentales.* 8 vols. folio, Anconæ, 1757.

Collections on Irish Church History, from the MSS. of the late V. Rev. LAURENCE F. RENEHAN, D.D., President of Maynooth College, edited by the Rev. DANIEL MCCARTHY. Vol. 1, 8vo, Dublin, 1861.

COLLET. *Prælect. Theol. Honorati Tournely Continuatio, sive Tractatus de Universa Theologia Morali.* 8 vols. 4to, Venetiis, 1746-58. *Traité des Saints Mystères.* 12me édition, 1 vol. 8vo, Paris, 1848.

Concilii Tridentini, Canones et Decreta. 1 vol. 32mo, Parisiis, 1837.

Concilia Provincialia Baltimori habita ab anno 1829 ad annum 1849. 8vo, Baltimori, 1851.

Concilium Plenarium Totius Americæ Septentrionalis Fœderatæ Baltimori habitum anno 1852. 8vo, Baltimori, 1853.

Concilii Plenarii Ealtimorensis II^di, in Ecclesia Metropolitana Baltimorensi, A.D. MDCCCLXVI. habiti et a Sede Apostolica recogniti, Acta et Decreta. 8vo, Baltimori, 1868.

Concilii Primi Provincialis Westmonasteriensis habiti 1852, apud Oscott. 8vo, ex typis J. P. Migne, 1853.

CONINCK. *De Sacramentis et Censuris.* Folio, Rhotomagi, 1680.

DALGAIRNS. *The Holy Communion, its Philosophy, Theology, and Practice.* 1 vol. 8vo, Dublin, 1861.

DEBREYNE. *Traité Pratique d'Embryologie Sacrée; ou Théologique.* 12mo, Bruxelles, 1853.

Decreta Authentica Cong. Sac.

Rit. ex Actis ejusdem collecta cura et studio ALOISII GARDELLINI. 4 vols. 4to, Romæ, 1856 (vid. n. 37, 38).

Decreta Authentica Sac. Rit. Cong. alphabetico ordine disposita, cura M. FALISE. Editio 4ta, 1 vol. 8vo, Parisiis, 1862 (vid. n. 37-39).

Decreta Authentica Sacræ Congregationis Indulgentiis sacrisque Reliquiis præpositæ accurate collecta ab ALOISIO PRINZIVALLI, Suffecto ab actis ejusdem Sac. Cong. 1 vol. 8vo, Bruxellis, 1862.

DELAHOGUE. *Tractatus de Sacramentis in genere.* 1 vol. 12mo, Dublinii, 1828.

DE LUGO. *Opera Omnia.* 7 vols. folio. Venetiis, 1718.

DENS. *Theologia ad usum Seminariorum.* 8 vols. 8vo, Mechliniæ, 1830.

DENZINGER. *Enchiridion Symbolorum et Definitionum quæ de Rebus Fidei et Morum a Conciliis Œcumenicis et Summis Pontificibus emanarunt.* 1 vol. 12mo, Wirceburgi, 1865.

DEVOTI. *Institutionem Canonicarum Libri Quatuor.* 2 vols. 8vo, Gandæ, 1836.

DROUIN. *De Sacramentis in genere in Theologiæ Cursu Completo.* Vol. XX^mo. Parisiis, 1840.

DU CANGE. *Glossarium, med. et inf. Latinitatis.* 10 vols. folio, Parisiis, 1733-66.

ΕΥΧΟΛΟΓΙΟΝ ΤΟ ΜΕΓΑ. 1 vol. royal 8vo, *EN BENETIA,* 1854.

ESTIUS. *Comment. in Epistolas.* 8vo., Moguntiæ, 1841.

FERRARIS. *Prompta Bibliotheca.* 8vols. 4to, edit. Migne. Parisiis, 1860.

FORNICI. *Institutiones Liturgicæ ad usum Seminarii Romani.* 1 vol. 8vo, Parisiis, 1859.

GOAR. *EYXOΛOΓION* sive *Rituale Græcorum Illustratum.* 1 vol. folio, Lutetiæ Parisiorum, 1647.

GOUSSET. *Théologie Morale.* 3me édition, 2 vols. 8vo, Bruxelles, 1846.

GURY. *Compendium Theologiæ Moralis.* 12ma editio, 2 vols. 12mo, Paris, 1861.

HOOK. *A Church Dictionary,* 6th edition. 1 vol. 8vo, London, 1852.

JANSSENS. *Explanation Rubricarum Missalis Romani.* 2 vols. 8vo, Antverpiæ, 1757.

KENRICK. *Theologia Dogmatica.* 3 vols. 8vo, Mechliniæ, 1858.

LABBE, curante Coleti. *Sacrosancta Concilia.* Venetiis, 1728–33.

LACROIX. *Theologia Moralis.* 8 vols. folio, Venetiis, 1753.

LINGARD. *History and Antiquities of the Anglo-Saxon Church.* 2 vols. 8vo, London, 1845.

MABILLON. *De Liturgia Gallicana Libri Tres.* 4to, 1685.

MACRI. *Hierolexicon sive Sacrum Dictionarium.* Venetiis, 1735.

MASKELL. *Monumenta Ritualia Ecclesiæ Anglicanæ.* 3 vols. 8vo, London, 1846.

Manuel des Cérémonies Romaines. Nouvelle édition, 3 vols. 12mo, Paris, 1858.

Memoriale Rituum jussu Benedicti XIII. edit. in *Manuali Sacrarum Cæremoniarum.* 1 vol. 4to, Dublinii, 1856.

MELCHIOR CANUS. *De Locis Theologicis* edit. in *Theologiæ Cursu completc.* Vol. Imo, Parisiis, 1839.

Monita ad Missionarios S. Cong. De Propaganda Fide. 1 vol. 12mo. Roma, 1853.

MURRAY. *Tractatus de Eccle-*

sia Christi. 8vo, Dublinii, 1860.

PALEY. *Illustration of Baptismal Fonts.* 1 vol. 8vo, London, 1845.

PALMER. *Origines Liturgicæ.* 2 vols. 8vo, London, 1845.

PASQUALIGI. *Theoria et Praxis in qua Jura, Obligationes et Privilegia eorum qui in Periculo aut Articulo Mortis constituuntur, atque alia plura Dubia ad utrumque Forum pertinentia ex Theologicis principiis atque sacris et civilibus Legibus breviter et dilucide explicantur. Opus posthumum.* 1 vol. 4to, Romæ, 1672.

PERRONE. *Prælectiones Theologicæ.* 2 vols. imp. 8vo, Parisiis, 1842.

Pontificale Romanum. Mechliniæ, 1845.

Raccolta, or *Collection of Indulgenced Prayers.* Authorized Translation. 16mo, London, 1859.

REIFFENSTUEL. *Jus Canonicum Universum.* 6 vols. folio, Romæ, 1831.

RENAUDOT. *Liturgiarum Orientalium Collectio.* 2 vols. 4to, Francofurti, 1847.

RITUAL—*Ordo administrandi Sacramenta et alia quædam Officia Ecclesiastica rite peragendi in Missione Anglicana ; ex Rituali Romano jussu Pauli V edito extractus, nonnullis adjectis ex Antiquo Rituali Anglicano.* 16mo, Derbiæ, 1856.

Excerpta ex Rituali Romano, pro Administratione Sacramentorum ad commodiorem Usum Missionariorum in Septentrionalis Americæ Fœderatæ Provinciis. 32mo, Baltimori, 1860. Vid. n. 297.

Epitome Ritualis Romani ad commodiorem Usum Clericorum

Missionis Scotiæ.   32mo, Glasgow, 1859.

ROMALE.   *Praxis Celebrandi Missam*, etc. Edit. J. H. HAZÉ. 3 vols. 8vo, Mechlinæ 1854.

SANCTI THOMÆ AQUINATIS, *Summa Theologica*. Edit. Migne, 4 vols. imp. 8vo, Parisiis, 1861.

SCAVINI.   *Theologia Moralis Universa*. 3 vols. 8vo, Bruxellis, 1847.

SUAREZ.   *Opera Omnia*.   26 vols. imp. 8vo, Parisiis, 1856–61.

SYLVESTER.   *Compendium Theologiæ Classicum*. Petropoli, 1799.

TOURNELY.   *De Baptismo* edit.

in *Theologiæ Cursu Completæ*. Vol. XXImo, Parisiis, 1840.

VAVASSEUR.   *Cérémonial selon le Rite Romain*.   3me édition, 2 vols. 12mo, Paris, 1865.

WATERWORTH.   *Canons and Decrees of the Council of Trent, translated*. 1 vol. 8vo, London, 1848.

WHEATLY.   *A Rational Illustration of the Book of Common Prayer*.   1 vol. 8vo, London, 1842.

WILKINS.   *Concilia Magna Britanniæ et Hiberniæ*.   4 vols. folio, Londini, 1737.

ZACCARIA.   *Bibliotheca Ritualis*.   2 vols. 4to, Romæ, 1776.

GENERAL INDEX.

SUPPLEMENT

TO THE

NOTES ON THE RUBRICS.

—◦◦◦—

PENANCE AND MATRIMONY.

SUPPLEMENT.

---◆◇◆---

Cum igitur pœnitentem absolvere voluerit, injuncta ei prius, et ab eo accepta salutari pœnitentia, primo dicit: Misereatur tui omnipotens Deus, et dimissis peccatis tuis, perducat te ad vitam æternam. Amen.

981. The rubric prescribes that the confessor impose the sacramental penance before he gives absolution. It can rarely happen, unless the penitent be "in articulo mortis," that there is sufficient reason for acting otherwise. Theologians, however, commonly teach that the penance may be imposed after absolution. (Vid. Lig., lib. vi, nn. 514–8 in parenth.) There is no doubt that it will have the same sacramental effect whether it is imposed before or after absolution; and, therefore, the confessor, if he forgets to impose it before absolving, should take care to impose it immediately after. (Gury, vol. ii, n. 523.) It is in accordance with the judicial order, which should here be followed, that the penance be imposed and accepted before the penitent is absolved; and as the rubric prescribes this order, it cannot, we think, be looked on as merely directive. The confessor is clearly bound to follow it, unless there be some reasonable cause for acting otherwise. He may be easily excused, however, by inadvertence, especially when, after hearing the confession, he spends some time in giving advice and direction.

It is certain that the mere inversion of the order is not in any case a grievous sin; and some even hold that the confessor may, without any fault, defer the imposition of the penance until after the absolution, when he fairly presumes that the penitent is willing to accept it. (Gury, n. 523.)

982. "Misereatur tui," etc. This prayer is to be said always in the singular.

Deinde dextera versus pœnitentem elevata, dicit : Indulgentiam, absolutionem, et remissionem peccatorum tuorum tribuat tibi omnipotens et misericors Dominus. Amen.

Dominus noster Jesus Christus te absolvat ; et ego auctoritate ipsius te absolvo ab omni vinculo excommunicationis, suspensionis, et interdicti, in quantum possum, et tu indiges.

The priest is directed to raise his right hand towards the penitent while pronouncing the words, *Indulgentiam*, etc. It was the practice in many places to raise the hand over, and even to place it on, the head of the penitent. This was in fact the usage of the Church for many ages (De Herdt, 204—Catal.), and it is permitted by the ritual of Mechlin, where the confession is heard " extra sedem confessionalem." (De Herdt.)

Considerable latitude is admitted in interpreting the expression, even when the ceremony which it implies is necessary to the validity of a sacrament. Still greater latitude may easily be admitted when, as in the present case, the ceremony does not in any way affect the validity of the sacrament. It is not improbable, therefore, that the " im-" positio" prescribed by the ancient rituals was often little in practice more than the raising of the hand, as prescribed by the present rubric.

983. But in the confessional as now constructed, the priest can do no more than raise his hand towards the penitent. It is recommended, however, that the priest do so, by directing the palm rather than the little finger towards the penitent, so that the ceremony may approximate more to the literal "impositio manus" which was formerly in use. (De Herdt, *ibid.*) He keeps the hand in this position until he has pronounced the words, *Ego te absolvo a peccatis tuis.* He then makes the sign of the cross, as if blessing the penitent, while he says, " In nomine Patris et Filii," etc. ; and for this purpose he turns his hand so as to direct the little finger towards the penitent.

984. It is the common opinion of theologians that the essential form of the sacrament is found in the words, " absolvo " te." (St. Lig., 430, Dub. 1.) This may be inferred from the Council of Trent (Sess. 14, cap. 3), and from the Catechism of the Council (p. ii, n. 14 : Est autem forma, *Ego te absolvo*). Some, however, maintain that the words, " a peccatis tuis," are also essential, while all are agreed that it would be a mortal sin to omit them.

985. The forms given by the most ancient rituals are in-variably found to contain the foregoing words, although not always in juxtaposition as we have them here.

The words, "In nomine Patris," etc., are certainly no essential, but it is commonly held that the omission of them would be a venial sin. (St. Lig., l. c., Dub. 3.)

We find them sometimes mixed up with the words of a long prayer, in which several words intervened between " a "peccatis tuis" and "in nomine Patris," etc. (Catal., page 229.)

Deinde, Ego te absolvo a peccatis tuis, in nomine Patris, ✠ *et Filii, et Spiritus Sancti. Amen.*

986. The word *deinde* is, in some editions of the Ritual, printed in rubric type, and in others in the same type as the words immediately before and after it. A question, there-fore, has been raised whether the priest should regard it as part of the text, and say . . . "et tu indiges. Deinde ego te," etc., or look on it simply as a rubric, and say . . . "et tu indiges. "Ego te," etc. The question was proposed by the Bishop of Verona to the Congregation of Rites in the following form: "Utrum in forma absolutionis verbum *Deinde*, in nonnullis "editionibus rubro charactere impressum, omittendum sit?" and the Sacred Congregation answered simply, "Nihil in-"novandum." (Veronen., 11 Martii, 1837.) The same answer was sent some years afterwards to a priest of Vigevano, who proposed the same question. (Vigevanen., 27 Febr., 1847.) The meaning of this answer, however, is not very clear, for it may still be doubted which *is* the innovation—the use or the omission of the word. The vote of the consultor might clear up the point; but, this not being published, the ques-tion to a great extent resolves itself into one of accuracy and authority as between different editions of the Ritual.

987. There is no doubt that recent editions of the Ritual printed in Rome have the word in rubric type. The latest Propaganda edition has it so printed. Now, there is a strong presumption that in this edition the word is correctly printed, not only on account of the careful supervision to which books —especially liturgical books—printed at the Propaganda are subjected, but also because particular attention would most probably be directed to the printing of this very word on account of the controversy raised about it. Hence, we find that those who touched on the question within the past few

years, as Ballerini (Annot. ad Gury *De Pœnitentia,* n. 426),
and Vavasseur (Du Sacrement de Penitence, n. 101, note),
are inclined to regard the word as a rubric. Baruffaldi is
often cited, amongst others, by Vavasseur (loc. cit.), as holding this view, but he seems to us to hold the opposite. He
says, indeed, that "deinde" does not belong to the substance
of the form in such a way that without it the absolution
would be null; but he is far from saying or implying that it
is not to be pronounced by the priest, since he concludes by
recommending in practice the opinion of Nicole: "Æquum
"esse pronunciari tale verbum." "Quærunt nonnulli," he
says, "inter quos Nicolius, Flosc., (Verb. *Absolutio*), et Sar-
"nell (*Epist., Eccl.* tom. 4, ep. 42), an adverbium illud *deinde*
"sit necessario pronunciandum in forma absolutionis adeo
"ut, eo verbo prætermisso, absolutio sit invalida. Nicolius
"respondet æquum esse pronunciari tale verbum; Sarnellus,
"vero, posse stare absolutionem licite et valide opinatur abs-
"que tali verbo. In tali dubio quid resolvendum ? Quicquid
"sibi libuerit aget confessarius, adverbium enim illud nòn est
"de substantia formæ absolutionis: tutiorem opinionem
"crederem illam Nicolii."

988. Catalani expressly rejects the opinion that the word
belongs to the rubric, and insists . . . "adverbium illud
"*deinde,* quod eodem charactere exaratum absolutioni pecca-
"torum inmediate præmittitur, ut in nostro § II videre est,
"recitandum esse cum ipsa absolutione velut ejusdem con-
"textum." The edition of the Ritual which Catalani had
before him, and to which he here appeals, was that published
by order of Benedict XIV, as appears from what he states
in the dedication of his work to that Pontiff. He cites
also, in favor of the same view, the "Instructiones" of St.
Charles (Act. p. iv, De Sacramento Pœnitentiæ, p. 434), which
are very minute both as to the ceremonies to be observed and
the words to be used by the priest in giving absolution ; and
in them "deinde" is printed in type indicating that it is
to be pronounced by the confessor. Now, there is reason to
believe that the Roman Ritual was compiled in great part
from these "Instructiones." In fact its rubrics are taken from
them verbatim. It is not unreasonable, then, to conclude
that, when two editions of the Ritual differ as to a word, the
more exact is that which agrees with the text of the "In-
"structiones," and that the innovation, if any, should be put
down to that which differs from it.

989. Fornici, who was a consultor of the Sacred Congregation of Indulgences and professor of Sacred Liturgy in the Roman Seminary, adopts the view, and almost the very words, of Catalani. As a reason why the priest should use the word, he says: " Præmittitur illud (deinde) peccatorum ab- " solutioni, quia primo confitens absolvendus est a censuris; " deinde a peccatis. Et cum absolutio a peccatis sequatur illam " a censuris, sacerdos qui utramque impertitur, in formulâ " absolutionis recitare debet etiam adverbium conjunctivum, " ut evidenter dignoscatur diversas esse absolutiones, quæ in " uno actu jurisdictionali conjunguntur."

990. De Herdt makes no reference to the controversy, nor does he even give the words of the Ritual. Falise simply gives the formula of the Ritual with " deinde " as part of the text. (Du Sacrement de Penitence, § II, n. 7.) Bauldry understands the Sacred Congregation, in the answer above cited, to condemn the omission of the word as an innovation. (Expositio Rubricarum, pars iv, De Sacramento Pœnitentiæ.) Schneider states the doubt almost in the words of Baruffaldi above cited, and resolves it by saying: " Vocabulum ' deinde,' licet " in nonnullis editionibus Ritualis Romani rubro sit charactere " impressum, ad formam tamen integram spectat." (Manuale Sacerdotum, etc.; De Sacramento Pœnitentiæ, § Forma Absolutionis, in nota. Editio sexta, Coloniæ, 1871.) As he refers, in support of this opinion, to the answer of the Sacred Congregation, he evidently understands it in the sense in which it is understood by Bauldry. And in fact this interpretation derives some probability from the form in which the question is put. For it is simply asked whether the word should be omitted, because in some editions it is printed in red type. Now, this seems to imply that, up to the date of the question, 1, the word was in most editions printed as part of the text, and, 2, that usage was against the omission. The Sacred Congregation therefore, by answering, " Nihil innovandum," may be, not unreasonably, understood as deciding that the word should not be omitted.

991. The editions of the Ritual hitherto in common use in Ireland, England, and America, have " deinde " printed as part of the text, and confessors in these countries have universally pronounced it as such. The same, we believe, holds also for France, Belgium, and Germany. Some very recent editions, as, e. g., that of Mechlin, 1869, have the word in red, as it is in the Propaganda edition; but that this has not

affected the practice of the clergy, may be inferred from the note of Father Schneider above cited.

992. In the present state of the controversy, and until the Sacred Congregation gives a clear decision on the point, we think the confessor is free to follow in practice whatever opinion he pleases; for it is hardly necessary to observe that the use or the omission of the word does not in any way affect the validity of the sacramental form. We rather incline, however, to the use of the word, for, without doubt, in most countries, the use was, so to speak, in possession, when the answer of the Sacred Congregation was given; and, therefore, to continue that use cannot well be regarded as the innovation forbidden by the answer.

ON THE SACRAMENT OF MATRIMONY: "DE SACRAMENTO MATRIMONII."

993. Matrimony is so called, according to the common opinion, because the female who contracts it undertakes the office and duty of a mother—the words, "Matris munia," from which it is derived, signifying *the duties of a mother*.

994. This sacred contract was instituted by God himself in the terrestrial paradise, and was elevated by Christ to the dignity of a sacrament of the New Law. For a statement of the Catholic doctrine on this subject, and its vindication against the heretics, see Bellarmine, de Sacramento Matrimonii, tom. iii, p. 725. (Edit. Prag. 1721.)

I.

Parochus admonitus de aliquo matrimonio in sua parochia contrahendo, primum cognoscat ex his ad quos spectat, qui et quales sint, qui matrimonium contrahere volunt: An inter eos sit aliquod canonicum impedimentum: Utrum sponte, libere, et secundum honestatem sacramenti velint contrahere: Utrum sint in aetate legitima, ut vir saltem quatuordecim, mulier vero duodecim annos expleverit: et uterque sciat rudimenta fidei, cum ea deinde filios suos docere debeant.

995. When the parish priest gets notice that a marriage is about to be contracted in his parish, he is directed by this rubric to ascertain, in the first place, whether the parties concerned are in a condition to contract validly and licitly; whether there is between them any canonical impediment, and especially whether they are acting freely; whether they have attained the proper age, which is fourteen years com-

plete for males, and twelve for females; and whether they
know the Christian doctrine, which it will be their duty
afterwards to teach to their children.   The inquiries regarding
the liberty of the parties and their ages are particularly
necessary in the case of young persons whose marriage is
arranged by their parents.   Great prudence and caution are
necessary where there is question of a marriage without the
knowledge or consent of parents.   Pastors are directed, in
the Catechism of the Council of Trent, to instruct children
in their duties towards parents and guardians on this head,
and to exhort them not to contract marriage without their
knowledge or against their wishes.   (P. ii, cap. 8, No. 32.)
As a general rule, such marriages are not contracted without
sin.   It is the common opinion of theologians that children
are bound to consult their parents and follow their advice on
this matter, at least so far as not to contract a marriage
against their just and reasonable wishes.   (Lig., 6, 849.)
On the other hand, it is certain, from the declaration of the
Council of Trent (Sess. 24, cap. i, de Reform. Mat.), that the
consent of parents is not necessary for the validity of marriage;
and theologians teach that their objections may be in some
cases so very unreasonable, that the children are not bound
to attend to them.   (Lig., *ibid.*, *conveniunt autem.*)   The
priest, therefore, when asked to assist at such a marriage,
must carefully weigh all the circumstances, and, if possible,
arrange matters so that the parents may be induced to consent, or at least may have no reason to complain of him for
assisting at the marriage.

996. A sufficient knowledge of the rudiments of faith or of
the Christian doctrine is a necessary disposition for worthily
entering into the married state.   The Ritual directs the
pastor's attention to this, and assigns one very urgent reason
why this knowledge should be required : that parents are
bound to teach their children the rudiments of faith.   The
Synod of Thurles, adopting the words of the Ritual, directs
special attention to the same point.   Benedict XIV expressly
teaches that the pastor should refuse to marry those who are
ignorant of the Christian doctrine, because they are bound
sub gravi to acquire a knowledge of it; and if they fail to do
so when, as is supposed, they have the opportunity, they are
in a state of mortal sin, and, consequently, would be guilty
of sacrilege by receiving the sacrament in this state.   Now,
though the priest be not the minister of the sacrament, his

obligations in regard to it are in many respects the same as if he were Nor is it lawful for him to sanction, by his presence and authority, a contract which, in the circumstances, would be an act of sacrilege. (De Syn. Dioec., lib. viii, cap. xiv, nn. 4 and 5.) Should the priest, then, find, on interrogating the parties, that they have not this necessary knowledge, he should admonish them of their obligation of acquiring it before the celebration of the marriage, which he is not to permit until he is satisfied that they have acquired it. He must bear in mind, however, what the same great authority observes (ibid., n. 6), that a person may know and believe the principal mysteries of faith, and may have a sufficient knowledge, in his own rude way, of whatever else he is required to know, *necessitate præcepti*, and yet be so stupid and so deficient in memory as to be unable, even after diligent application, to remember and repeat them. Such persons are not to be refused marriage, but the pastor must take care that what they have learned be frequently repeated to them, so that they may not completely forget it. (*Ibid.*)

II.

Noverit ex probatis auctoribus quæ sint canonica impedimenta matrimonii contrahendi, et quæ contractum dirimant ; et qui sint gradus consanguinitatis et affinitatis, et item cognationis spiritualis ex Baptismi vel Confirmationis sacramento contractæ.

997. The pastor must know, out of approved authors, what are the impediments of matrimony—those which render the contract illicit, as well as those which would render it null. We need not here enumerate the several impediments, as it would be beyond our scope to treat of them. Our object is simply to explain the rubrics of the Ritual, and develop the instructions which they contain ; and we touch on theological questions only so far as we deem it necessary for this object. Beyond some hints here and there, we cannot often allude even to many controverted points. Amongst those who have written on the impediments of marriage, there is, perhaps, no author that may be consulted with greater advantage than Carriere. We do not mean to recommend all his opinions and decisions, for he is generally inclined to the side of rigor, and his opinion on the power of the state to institute impediments is quite untenable; but, for lucid arrangement of the matter, and for clearness and

precision in the discussion of each question, we do not know any writer on the subject that can be compared with him. Moreover, when theologians are divided on any point, he is careful to state the several opinions, with accurate references to the places in which they are given by the authors; so that the student who desires fuller information on any point, is put in the way of finding it at once.

998. The rubric mentions those impediments that are of most frequent occurrence, and directs the special attention of the pastor to them. He must know how to reckon the degrees of consanguinity and affinity, and when a spiritual relationship is contracted by baptism or confirmation. In tracing degrees of kindred, it is recommended to form a kind of genealogical tree by writing down the name of the common ancestor, and under it the names of his descendants; those of each succeeding generation being placed under those of the preceding, until you reach the names of the parties of whom there is question. Otherwise, by writing down the names of the parties, and over them the names of the parents through whom they are likely to be related, until you reach the common ancestor.

III.

Habeat in primis ipse bene cognita præcepta illa omnia, quæ in matrimoniis rite conficiendis servare oportere, sacri Canones, et præcipue sancta Synodus Tridentina jussit: dabitque operam ut illa in parochia sua accurate exacteque serventur.

999. It is the manifest duty of the pastor to make himself acquainted with the laws of the Church, and especially those of the Council of Trent, relating to the celebration of marriage, and to endeavor, as far as he can, to have them fully observed in his parish. This duty is strongly inculcated in the decrees of the Provincial Councils that have been lately held in almost every country. The Synod of Thurles admonishes parish priests to observe accurately whatever is prescribed by the Roman Ritual with regard to the celebration of marriage. (De Mat., n. 51.)

IV.

Præsertim vero meminerit matrimonia inter raptorem et raptam, dum ipsa in raptoris potestate manserit, inita, nec non clandestina. et quælibet matrimonia, quæ aliter quam præsente Parocho, vel alio Sacerdote de ipsius Parochi vel Ordinarii licentia, et duobus vel tribus testibus contrahuntur, ex ipsius Concilii decretis irrita omnino ac nulla esse.

1000. The forcible abduction of a female, with intent to marry her, constitutes the impediment of "raptus." (Lig., 1107.) It is certain that a marriage between the raptor and his victim, while she remains in his power, would be null. This is expressed by the Ritual in the words used by the Council of Trent: "Dum ipsa in potestate raptoris "manserit." For a full discussion of this impediment, and the cases in which it arises, see Carriere (905 et seq.).

1001. The word "clandestine" was formerly applied to marriages celebrated without a previous proclamation of the banns, or certain other prescribed solemnities, as well as to those celebrated without the presence of the parish priest and witnesses. It may be used, and is still sometimes used, in this wide sense; but, since the Council of Trent, it is commonly applied only to those marriages that are celebrated "without the presence of the parish priest, or some "other priest with permission from him or the ordinary, and "two or three witnesses." Understood in this restricted sense, a clandestine marriage is null and void, according to the decree of Trent. The Council, however, requires that the decree be published in every parish, and it is not binding until after thirty days from its first promulgation. (Sess. 24, De Rit. Mat., cap. 1.) If it be observed in any place, for a considerable time, as a decree of the Council, it is held to be sufficiently promulgated in that place. (Car., 1181.) The decree is at present in force everywhere in Ireland, but is not yet published in England and Scotland.

1002. Many questions of great practical importance regarding the interpretation of this decree are discussed by theologians and canonists; and some of them have been decided by the Sacred Congregation of the Council, and even in Papal Constitutions.

1003. 1°. If the parties belong to a place where the decree is received, and there contract, the marriage must, of course, be celebrated in the form prescribed; otherwise it is null.

1004. 2°. If they go to a place where the decree is not received, and there contract a clandestine marriage, without having previously acquired a domicile or quasi-domicile in the place, the marriage is invalid. (Car., 1187 ; Lig., 1080, *Si quis vero*.) This is quite certain for the case in which they go for the purpose of evading the law, or, as is said, "in fraudem legis," as is clear from the responses of the Sacred Congregation, approved by a decree of Urban VIII, and republished and confirmed by Benedict XIV, in the constitution, "Paucis abhinc hebdomadis," of which we have much to say a little further on. But is the decision to be restricted to this case? Carriere maintains (loc. cit.) that no such restriction is to be admitted, and contends (1188) that the decisions are to be understood, and were understood by Benedict XIV, as against the validity of the marriage, even though the parties had no intention of evading the law, unless they had previously acquired a sufficient domicile. Many eminent authorities, however, maintain that the restriction is to be admitted, and that the marriage would be valid unless the parties acted " in frandem legis." (Schmalzgrueber lib. iv, tit. iii, 110) De Lugo holds the same opinion. (Resp. Mor. Dub. xxxvi, n. 5.) St. Liguori does not mention the restriction, but simply states that the marriage would be null (l. c.).

1005. Up to the time of Urban VIII it was the more common opinion of theologians that parties going from a place where the decree of the Council of Trent concerning clandestine marriages was in force, to a place where it was not, for the very purpose of evading the decree, could contract a clandestine marriage validly in the latter, even though they neither abandoned their domicile, nor acquired a domicile or quasi-domicile in the place where the marriage took place. Since the publication of the Responses confirmed by Urban VIII, this opinion is no longer tenable; but before the publication of the Responses, the validity of such marriage was maintained by the most celebrated writers on matrimony. Amongst these, Sanchez, who indisputably holds the first place, maintains this opinion. (De Matrimonio, lib. iii, disp. 17, n. 29.) It is also supported by Basil Pontius (lib. v, De Mat., c. 9, n. 4), although this author is ever on the watch to controvert the opinions of Sanchez. Many other celebrated authors who maintained the same opinion are cited by Benedict XIV, in the constitution referred to. They relied on the axiom that *locus regit contractum*, which is especially true as to the *forms* to be observed in entering into a contract. To the objection that the parties who leave their own parish for the purpose of contracting clandestinely, go there "in fraudem legis," they answer that the parties only use their lawful right by passing from one place to another, where they contract according to the forms prescribed by the Church for that place; or that, if there be fraud, it is one which only renders the marriage illicit, but not invalid. Hence some theologians and canonists of great authority regard the Responses confirmed by Urban VIII and Benedict XIV, not as a mere interpretation of the law of the Council of Trent, but as a new enactment established by the Supreme Pontiffs for the purpose of preventing the law of Trent from being evaded. But, however this may be, it is certain that parties, retaining a domicile in a place where the decree of Trent is in force, and proceeding to a place where it is not in force, for the purpose of contracting marriage there clandestinely, cannot intermarry validly until they have acquired a domicile or quasi-domicile in the latter place.

1006. But can they contract marriage validly before the parish priest of the place to which they have betaken themselves and two witnesses? Certainly not; because, as they have neither a domicile nor a quasi-domicile there, he is not their *proprius parochus*, whose presence is required by the Council of Trent. How, then, can they contract a valid marriage in the place where they now are? Their parish priest, or bishop, or the vicar-general of the diocese, provided he has jurisdiction over the parish where their domicile is situated, can either personally assist at the marriage, as far as the validity is concerned, or delegate any other priest to do so. But if the parties named, on being applied to, refuse to do either one or other of the things mentioned, they must either wait until they shall have acquired a domicile or quasi-domicile in the place to which they have gone, and then they can marry validly, but illicitly, without the presence of any priest; or they must return to their place of residence, where they can contract immediately before their own parish priest or his deputy.

1007. The Responses confirmed by Urban VIII and Benedict XIV are of so much importance that we transcribe them from the constitution, *Paucis abhinc Hebdomadis*. (Vol. ii, Bull. Bened. XIV, pp. 390, 391. Ed. Mechlin., 1827.)

Quæritur humiliter a Sacra Congregatione: An incolæ tam masculi quam fœminæ, loci in quo Concilium Tridentinum in puncto matrimonii est promulgatum et acceptatum, transeuntes per locum in quo dictum Concilium non est promulgatum, retinentes idem domicilium, valide possint in isto loco matrimonium sine Parocho et testibus contrahere?

Secundo. Quid, si eo prædicti incolæ tam masculi quam fœminæ, solo animo sine Parocho et testibus contrahendi, se transferant, habitationem non mutantes?

Tertio. Quid, si iidem incolæ tam masculi quam fœminæ, eo transferant habitationem illo solo animo, ut absque Parocho et testibus contrahant?

Die 5 Septembris: Sacra Congregatio Cardinalium Concilii Tridentini Interpretum, ad primum et secundum respondit. non esse legitimum matrimonium inter sic se transferentes cum fraude.

Ad tertium respondit, nisi domicilium vere transferatur, matrimonium non esse validum.

Urban VIII, in 1627, issued a brief confirming these Responses.

1008. It is quite certain, therefore, that, if the parties go from a place in which the decree is in force, to a place in which it is not, *for the purpose of evading the law*, and there contract clandestinely, the marriage is invalid. But is the decision to be restricted to this case? We have seen that Carriere (n. 1188) maintains that it is not, and that the decisions are to be understood, and were understood by Benedict XIV, as against the validity of the marriage, even though the parties had *no intention of evading the law*, unless they had previously acquired a domicile or quasi-domicile.

And this would certainly appear to be implied by the response to the first and second questions proposed by the Archbishop of Cologne; which were answered by the Sacred Congregation, and confirmed, as already stated, by Urban VIII. The sole difference between the first and second questions is, that in the first there is no mention of the parties having gone to the place where the decree against clandestine marriages was not in force, *for the purpose of* contracting there; and in the second it is supposed that they have gone *with such intention.* The same answer is given to both interrogatories: "Non esse legitimum matrimonium inter sic se "transferentes cum fraude." The only reason for doubting that the marriage would be invalid, whether the parties went to the place for the purpose of contracting marriage there, or for some other purpose, must be derived from the words *cum fraude*. But to this it may be replied that, for instance, if two Catholics, having their domicile in Ireland, should go for a few days to England for recreation or on business, and contract marriage there, either privately or in presence of a priest and witnesses, without obtaining the authority of their own parish priest, they would act " in fraudem legis." It certainly appears to us that such a marriage would be regarded as invalid. No doubt some eminent authorities, as Schmalzgrueber (lib. iv, tit. iii, n. 110), hold the contrary. But this great author treats the question very briefly, and Lugo (Resp. Moral., lib. 1, Dub. 36, n. 5), though often quoted for the same opinion, does not maintain that the marriage would be valid, even if the parties did not go to the place for the purpose of contracting a clandestine marriage, nor does he rely much on the words *cum fraude*. As he is often said to have *shown that the decisions can be understood only* of the case in which the parties act " in fraudem," it may be well to quote his words : " In quo cardinalium responso illos doctrinam " restrinxisse ad eos qui ex industria per breve tempus trans- " ibant ad locum alium, ut sine parocho et testibus contraherent, " et ideo addiderunt *fortasse* in responso verba illa, *cum fraude*, " quæ in interrogatione non fuerunt *formaliter expressa :* quo " casu negari non potest, communem doctorum sententiam " negare matrimonium illud posse valide fieri, *quidquid sit,* " *un in aliis casibus valeat, quando ad negotia, vel mercimonia,* " *aut ob alios eventus ibi contrahentes inveniuntur, de quibus* " *cardinales nihil voluerunt definire.*" But we have already shown that the question as to the intention was formally put in the second question, and therefore designedly left out of the first ; and we therefore think that the marriage would be invalid, even if the parties had not gone to the place without the intention of contracting clandestinely in it.

1009. Moreover, Benedict XIV proves that the Sacred Congregation *always* adhered to the response given to the interrogatories of the Archbishop of Cologne, by citing a decision given by it on the 16th of December, 1640, which was as follows : " Sacra Congregatio censuit non valere matri- " monium contractum coram parocho loci, ubi contrahentes " reperiuntur non animo ibi domicilium contrahendi." Now, this decree, as well as all those which declare to be void all marriages contracted " coram parocho rurali," whether the parties have gone there to get married, or for recreation, or on business, clearly shows that all marriages contracted by parties in a place where they happen to be at the time, without the intention of acquiring a domicile or quasi-domicile in said place, are invalid.

1010. We have said above that the marriage would be invalid, *unless the parties have previously acquired a domicile or quasi-domicile in the place;* for, if they have, the clandestine marriage would be valid, according to all, because they would then be in the same condition as the inhabitants of the place, enjoying its privileges, as well as subject to its laws. And this holds, even though they may have left their former residence for the very purpose of evading the decree of Trent. This is clear from the answer to the third of the queries contained in the constitution, *Paucis abhinc,* already quoted. (See also Car., 1194; Lig., loc. cit.) But if they have not acquired at least a quasi-domicile in the place, it is necessary, for the validity of the marriage—or, at least, to remove all doubt about its validity—that it be celebrated according to the form prescribed by the decree; and, consequently, the parish priest of one of the parties must be present to assist at it, or some other priest with his permission. Hence, for instance, if two persons from Dublin go to London, and wish to get married there, before either of them *has* acquired a quasi-domicile, the marriage must be celebrated before the parish priest of either (who might happen to be in London at the time), or before another priest, with his permission or the permission of the Ordinary of Dublin.

1011. 3°. If the parties belong to a place where the decree is not received, but contract marriage in a place where it is received, the marriage would be invalid, unless celebrated according to the form prescribed. This is the common opinion according to Carriere, 1187, and St. Liguori, 1080, who quote several authors, Sanchez, Pontius, etc. Carriere, while admitting it to be the opinion of most theologians, thinks the opposite opinion more probable (1194). Gury, however, gives it as certain (p. 640), and in practice we must regard it as such.

1012. But who is the parish priest in this case? Is it the parish priest of one of the parties, or of the place in which the marriage is celebrated?

1013. On the one hand, it might be maintained that since,

if the marriage took place in their own country, the presence of the parish priest of one of the parties would not be required for its validity, it is hard to suppose that it would become necessary, when they, in some manner, withdraw from his jurisdiction by going to a place where the decree of Trent is received. It might be said, moreover, with Carriere (1190), that, since the decree is not published in his parish, he is not that authorized witness deputed by the Church to assist at the marriage, however his presence might be desirable in other respects; and if this be true, when the marriage is celebrated in his parish, it ought to hold *a fortiori* when it is celebrated elsewhere. Again, it is a general principle in the law of contracts, that the forms or the formalities to be observed in making them are those that are required in the place where they are entered into, according to the axiom, "locus regit actum :" and it is on this very principle that theologians and canonists maintain the necessity of complying with the decree of Trent in the case now under consideration; but this principle founds a kind of presumption in favor of the parish priest of the place, unless when it is clearly shown that not he, but some other, is authorized to assist.

1614. On the other hand, it is certain, as we shall see, that the parish priest whose presence is required by the Council is the parish priest of one of the parties, and not the parish priest of the place *as such ;* and therefore, since it is supposed they have a parish priest, and are not "vagi," whose case is exceptional, it would seem that his presence is required; and, in fact, Lacroix (lib. vi, pars 3, n. 713) infers that, because, according to the common and true opinion, the marriage, even if contracted before the parish priest of a parish in which the parties now are, but where neither of them has a domicile or quasi-domicile, would be invalid, therefore their own parish priest, in whose parish the decree of Trent is not in force, or his deputy, should assist at the marriage to render it valid. Lacroix does not give the authority of a single theologian or canonist for this opinion; and he quite overlooks the hypothesis, that neither the parish priest of the place where the parties have neither a domicile nor quasi-domicile, nor the parish priest of the place where they have a domicile, but in whose parish the decree of Trent has not been published, can assist validly at the marriage when contracted where the decree binds; and that such parties cannot contract a valid marriage except by acquiring a domicile or quasi-domicile in the place where they now are, or by returning to their own country, where, as far as the validity is concerned, the presence of a priest is not required. We do not say that this case has been settled, as we have not seen an express decision on the point; but we consider it so probable, that, until a decision shall have been given by the Holy See, no priest could act on the contrary opinion without grievous sin. Then, if two Catholics come from England or Scotland to Ireland, in order to marry validly, they must acquire a domicile or quasi-domicile in the latter country, or return to the former.

1015. It follows from what we have stated, that, if a Catholic domiciled in Ireland agrees to marry a Catholic domiciled in England, the marriage, if contracted in Ireland, will be invalid unless solemnized before the parish priest and witnesses; but, if contracted in England or Scotland without the presence of the parish priest or witnesses, it will be valid, but illicit. The decision in both cases rests on the principle, that *locus regit contractum.* This case had been decided by the Sacred Congregation. (Lacroix, loc. cit., n. 714.)

1016. It may be observed that a clandestine marriage is always valid when one of the parties is exempt from the law of Trent, even though the other may be subject to it. (Car., 1227.) Hence, e.g., a person from Ireland who contracts a clandestine marriage in Scotland with a native of the place, or one having a sufficient domicile there, is married validly.

1017. Another priest, with the permission of the parish priest or of the ordinary, can validly assist at the marriage, according to the words of the decree, which are here given in the Ritual. The permission must be clear and express. It is not sufficient that it be presumed, or that it certainly would be given, if asked for. (Car., 1330 et seq.) It must be a permission that actually has been given, and in virtue of which he assists. It is sometimes a question whether it be included in a general permission or appointment to administer sacraments in a parish. Whether it be or not, evidently depends on the intention of the bishop or parish priest; and this may often be determined by the circumstances, or by the recognized custom in the place.

1018. If the curate has this permission, without any expressed or implied limitation, it is certain, 1°, that he can himself assist at the marriage of any parishioner when the marriage is celebrated in the parish (Car., 1344); and 2°, that he can assist, just as we shall see the parish priest can, at the marriage of his parishioner, even in another parish, unless his delegated powers be specially restricted.

1019. The presence of the priest must be such that he can, morally speaking, be a witness of the marriage ; and, therefore, he must have some notice of the intention of the parties to contract before him. (Car., 1263, 1264.)   The same may be said of the witnesses. (*Ibid.*, 1265.)

1020. At least two witnesses must be present with the parish priest.   It is the common opinion of theologians that any persons having sufficient intelligence to testify to the marriage may be admitted as witnesses. (Car., 1350.)   Both must be present at the same time with the priest, and must be present also in such a way that they could afterwards bear testimony to the marriage, if called on. (*Ibid.*, 1351.)

V.

Est autem proprius Parochus, qui adesse debet, is, in cujus parochia matrimonium celebratur, sive viri, sive mulieris.

1021. The "parochus" whose presence is required, is here stated to be the parish priest in whose parish the marriage is celebrated, whether he be the parish priest of the man or of the woman.   When the parties are from different parishes, it would seem from the rubric that the parish where the ceremony is performed should determine the parish priest whose presence is required; but the matter having been referred to the Sacred Congregation, it was decided that the presence of the parish priest of either is sufficient, no matter in which of the parishes the marriage is celebrated (Car., 1275); no matter, indeed, where, in what parish or what diocese it may be celebrated (Car., 1266, Lig., 1081).   In Ireland, however, as in most other countries, the ceremony usually takes place in the parish of the bride, and is performed by her parish priest, or at least with his permission ; and it is but right and proper in all cases to have the consent of the parish priest of the parish where the marriage takes place (Car., l. c.) : and it would certainly be a grievous sin to give the solemn nuptial benediction without it (Lig., 1087).

1022. The chief point to be here determined is, the residence necessary in any place in order that a person may be able validly to contract marriage before the parish priest of that place.

1023. 1°. It is certain that the fact of being born in any

parish is not enough, if the person has ceased to reside there. (Bened. XIV, Inst. xxxiii, n. 6.)

1024. 2°. It is certain also that it is sufficient to have a fixed residence or domicile in a parish. (Car., 1273.) A person is said to have a "domicile" in a place when he resides in it, and intends to reside in it permanently. He can acquire it at once on coming to a place, if his intention of residing permanently be sufficiently manifested, as it often is by the circumstances (*ibid.*), as, *e g.*, if he has transferred his movable property to a house which he has purchased and fitted up as a residence, etc.

1025. 3°. If a person has two domiciles in two different parishes, which he may have, if he resides in them alternately, and for about an equal length of time in each, he is free to marry before the parish priest of either. (Car., 1274.)

1026. 4°. If a person, having a domicile in one parish, goes to another with the intention of residing there for a considerable time ("per tempus notabile"), and sufficiently manifests this intention, he acquires a "quasi-domicile" in that place. This is not unfrequently the case with students, lawyers, and other professional men, persons holding situations in certain public offices, etc.   Theologians seem to be agreed that a person acquires a quasi-domicile at once if he sufficiently manifests his intention of residing in a place for a tempus notabile, and really has such intention: but the question is, whether such a quasi-domicile would suffice for marriage without the previous residence. Carriere is of opinion that it does suffice (1277). Bouvier is inclined to the same opinion (De Mat., Art. v, § i).   We consider this opinion to be true, from the number and authority of theologians and canonists who hold it, some of whom we shall quote further on.   In the meantime we consider it practically certain: 1°, because Benedict XIV (Inst. xxxiii, n. 11, in fine) cites a decision of the Sacred Congregation to the following effect: "An valeat matri-"monium contractum coram parocho illius loci, ubi contra-"hentes reperiuntur, *non animo ibi domicilium contrahendi*, sed "recreationis causa? Et quid, si contrahens *ibi moretur tan-*"quam* prætor, judex, seu medicus temporalis." The Sacred Congregation answered that, in the first case, the marriage was invalid, in the second, valid. Secondly, because this opinion, as we have said, has been maintained by the greatest writers on matrimony. It will be sufficient to quote here Sanchez (De Mat., lib. iii, disp. xxiii, n. 14), who says: "Hinc

" infertur 1°, non opus esse expectare ut majori anni parte hi
" in parochia aut diœcesi habitarint, *sed statim ac animum*
" habitandi majori anni parte habentes, incipiunt habitare, effici
" parochianos, et posse omnia dicta" (amongst which. assisting
at their marriage is included) " erga illos exerceri. Sicut enim
" ad domicilium nullius temporis habitatio requiritur, sed statim
" ac quis incipit habitare; cum animo perpetuo habitandi, illud
" acquirit. . . sic statim ac quis incipit habitare animum habens
" habitandi toto tempore requisito, efficitur parochianus." The
same doctrine is held by the Canonists. (Cf. Barbosa De
Officio Parochi, Part II, c. xxi, n. 36, and many more, a few
of whom we shall quote further on.)

1027. It is, therefore, commonly admitted by theologians
and canonists that two things are necessary and sufficient to
constitute a quasi-domicile: 1°. That the person shall have
the intention of dwelling in a place for a notable time; and
2°, that he shall have actually commenced to dwell in such
place, and that he shall have sufficiently manifested his intention of dwelling there for a *notable* time. When these two
things concur, the quasi-domicile is acquired at once. The
animus, being essentially an act of the mind, can only be known
by external acts, such as taking a house, or apartments, or a
shop in which a person is to dwell, for a " tempus notabile."
The decision of the Sacred Congregation, quoted by Benedict
XIV, in the constitution, " Paucis abhinc," which we shall
presently transcribe, proves at least this much—that the
actual dwelling of a person in a place for a month, in the
absence of any sufficient indication that he is going to leave
it soon afterwards, may generally be regarded as a sufficient
external manifestation of his *intention* to remain there for a
notable time. But supposing that the intention must in this
case extend beyond a month, the marriage would be invalid
unless such intention actually existed; for the mere external
indication would not supply the intention, any more than the
former indications. such as taking a house for six months,
would, supposing the person only intended to remain in the
place until he should succeed in getting married.

1028. We say an intention of remaining for six months
would certainly suffice, but we do not say that it should
necessarily extend to so long a period. Schmalzgrueber,
with many other canonists of great authority, thinks that a
few (*aliquot*) months may be considered a *tempus notabile
anni*, and that therefore the intention of remaining for this

period will suffice. " Conformius autem juri sentire videntur " qui dicunt, sufficere propositum habitandi per aliquot menses, " præcipue si domus, conclave, taberna, etc., fuerunt conducta." (Schmalzgrueber, lib. ii, tit. ii, n. 19.) Who adds: " *Nullum* " vero dubium, conditionibus hisce verificatis *statim post* " *habitationem acceptam quasi domicilium acquiri.*" The opinion that the quasi domicile, the requisite conditions being observed, is acquired at once, is taught by Barbosa de Parocho (p. 2, c. xxi. n. 35), by Giraldi, Sanchez, et aliis passim ; so that, as already stated, we regard it as practically certain that a person actually dwelling in a place with the intention of continuing to dwell there for six months, who has sufficiently manifested that intention, may be married before the parish priest of that place, immediately after he has commenced to dwell in it.

1029. Nor is this opinion opposed to the teaching of Benedict XIV, in the constitution, " Paucis abhinc," in which he says : " Post hæc necessarium fore censemus nonnihil " adjungere, ut in propatulo sit quidnam requiratur ad quasi " domicilium adipiscendum.   Verum hac in re non alio " pacto responderi potest, nisi quod antequam matrimonium " contrahatur, *spatio saltem unius mensis ille*, qui contrahit, " habitaverit in loco ubi matrimonium celebratur."   Because, the Pontiff adds : " Definitiones Cong. Conc. hac de re ob- " servari poterunt apud Fagnanum *in cap. Significavit de* " *Parochis*, ubi eorundem contextu perpenso, hæc habet *sub.* " *num.* 39. Vir et mulier Trajectenses timentes impedimentum " a parentibus, cum ad vicinam urbem Aquisgranum se " contulissent, et ibi aliquamdiu morati matrimonium con- " traxissent, Sacra Congregatio, consulta super validitate, " censuit, exprimendum tempus quo contrahentes Aquisgranæ " manserunt ; quod si fuerit saltem unius mensis, dandam esse " decisionem pro validitate ; *alias de novo referendum in* " *congregatione.*"   From these last words, which, though given by Fagnan, from whom Benedict XIV has taken the decision, are strangely omitted by the Pontiff, it is clear that the Sacred Congregation did not regard the previous residence of a month as absolutely necessary, provided it should be proved from other circumstances that the parties had manifested h r intention of residing *per tempus notabile* in the place where the marriage took place.

1030. It is clear also from what the Pontiff adds, immedi- ately after quoting the decision of the Sacred Congregation,

that he did not regard a month's previous residence as absolutely necessary to constitute a quasi-domicile *in ordine ad
mat. contrahendum:* "Natalis Alexander," says the Pontiff
(in Theol. Dog et Moral., lib. ii, De Sac. Mat., c. ii, a. ii, Regul.
6), " animadvertit, ad acquirendum quasi domicilium, oportere
" ut contrahentes, antequam matrimonium celebrent, *tanto tem-
"pore* eo in loco ubi copulantur, fuerint commorati, *ut ibidem
" cogniti jam sint, atque perspecti.*" In this passage there is no
mention of a month's previous residence being necessary, but
only that the parties should have resided in the place where
the marriage is to be contracted for a period long enough to
make them well known in it. It is clear that a previous
residence regarded in this light concerns the lawfulness rather
than the validity of the marriage; for it is equally applicable
to all strangers, whether they come to a strange place to
reside permanently or only temporarily in it. And, in fact,
although Natalis Alexander, in the Rule quoted ·by the
Pontiff, treats the question of quasi-domicile, yet, iu the little
paragraph which he adds at the end, to which the Pontiff
alludes, he clearly includes the domicile as well as quasi-
domicile. His words are: " Observari tamen oportent *statuta
" moresque Diœcesium* quoad tempus constituendo domicilio,
" seu domicilii juri acquirendo, ad effectum matrimonium con-
" trahendi præfixum. Eo certe tempore contrahentes in
" Parochia mansisse necesse est, quod sufficiat ut ibi noti sint."
These words certainly apply to all strangers, whether they
acquire a domicile or a quasi-domicile, and regard the licitness
rather than the validity of their marriages.

1031. The next question is, whether a month's residence
in a place is sufficient to render valid all marriages contracted
after the lapse of this period, although the parties intend to
return to their former domicile immediately afterwards. Carriere (n. 1285), and the author of the *Prælectiones Juris
Canonici habitæ in Seminario S. Sulpitii* (pars i, a. 3, n. 244),
Gury (n. 846, who, however, excludes the case of parties who
reside in the country for the purpose of recreation, or *ad negotia
ruralia agenda*), hold that the residence of a month in any
place is sufficient *per se* to render valid a marriage contracted
after the lapse of this period. But all these rely on the
authority of Benedict XIV, in the constitution, "Paucis ab-
" hinc," and on another decision confirmed by Gregory XVI,
which is as follows:—

" Joannes et Maria, Mechliniæ domicilia habentes, Lon-

" dinum veniunt, et sine anctoritate vel licentia suoru n paro-
" chorum, uno solummodo mense elapso. Londini matrimonium
" contrahunt. Quæritnr utrum hoc matrimonium invalidum sit
" propter decretum Conc. Trid. (Seas. 24, cap. i. de ref. Mat.)
" necne.

" Feria 4ª die 6ª Decembris, 1842, Sanctissimns D. N. Div.
" Provid. Gregorius Papa XVI, in solita audientia R. P. D.
" Assessori S. Officii impertita, audita relatione suprascriptæ
" epistolæ una cum EE. et RR. DD. Cardinalium Gen. Inq.
" suffragiis dixit: Stet Epistola Bened. XIV ad Archiep.
" Goanum." (*Mélanges Théologiques*, vol. ii, p. 451.)

1032. As far, therefore, as this last decision concerns the
matter of which we are speaking, it is clear that it adds
nothing to the decision of Benedict XIV, which we have
already considered, concerning the necessity of an actual previous residence of a month being necessary in order to
acquire a quasi-domicile. Now, in reference to this whole
matter, it is clear that Benedict XIV does not make any new
law, but merely undertakes to exemplify the law of clandes-
tinity, from the decree of Urban VIII, and the decision of
the Sacred Congregation in the Utrecht case; because he
expressly avoids entering into the question of the quasi-domicile, and refers the reader to the decisions contained in Fagnan,
and especially to the Utrecht case. Then, in the end of the
paragraph, he adds: " Dubitari autem posset, num ad quasi
" domicilium acquirendum matrimonii causa, uti diximns, non
" solum requiratur præcedens habitatio, verum etiam subsequens
" ad aliquod temporis spatium: verum cum observaverimus,
" subsequentem habitationem ab iis auctoribus, qui hanc
" tractarunt materiam, tanquam magni momenti *adminiculum*
" reputari, ut *novum domicilium quæsitum dicatur*, nihil vero de
" illa præscriptum fuisse a Conc. Congreg. in adducta paulo
" ante definitione penes Fagnanum, *nolumus de hac re quid-*
" *quam novi decernere.*"

1033. Let us, therefore, consider what has been decided in
the Utrecht case. This being a particular case, we cannot
arrive at a certain conclusion without knowing all the circumstances. Now, in order that this case should prove that a
month's residence in a place is sufficient to constitute a quasi-
domicile, in which marriage may be validly contracted, we
should know, 1st, that the parties had not abandoned their
former domicile; and 2dly, that they intended to return to
their former domicile immediately after the lapse of a month.

Because, if they did not intend to return to their former
domicile at all, or intended spending a considerable time at
Aix-la-Chapelle, where the marriage was contracted, which is
extremely probable, from the circumstance that they had fled
from their parental abode to avoid the opposition of their
parents to the marriage, the fact of the marriage contracted
a' Aix-la-Chapelle, after a month's residence in that place,
having been pronounced valid, would prove nothing as to a
month's residence being *per se* sufficient to constitute a quasi-
domicile, or habitation in *ordine ad matrimonium*. It is also
remarkable that Benedict XIV (Inst. xxxiii, n. 9), referring
to this very case and some others, makes the following comment: "Advertendum tamen est matrimonium hoc pacto
"ineuntes, antequam rem perficerent, domicilium in eo loco vel
'quasi domicilium assecutos fuisse. Nam diu morati ibidem
'ante matrimonium fuerunt, neque inde postea decesserunt, *ut*
"*primam sedem, ac domicilium repeterent*, quemadmodum Cle-
"ricatus recte perpendit."

1034. Secondly, Fagnan, on whose authority the authenticity of this decision rests, does not himself draw the conclusion from it that a month's residence is sufficient to
constitute a quasi-domicile. The question he discusses is
this: A woman was banished by order of a secular prince
from the city in which her domicile was, on account of her
scandalous life, and she was commanded to reside in another
place during the prince's pleasure. After four months'
residence in her new abode (which she was clearly resolved
to leave and return to her former domicile, whenever the
prince should permit her to do so), she contracted marriage
before the parish priest of her present residence with a man
who had his domicile in the city from which she had been
banished. The question was, had this marriage been contracted so as to fulfil the forms prescribed by the Council of
Trent in the decree already cited? (Fagnan, loc. cit., n. 29.)
Then, having adduced many opinions regarding the things
required to render a stranger a *parishioner*, so that the parish
priest of the place where he actually dwells can administer to
him the sacraments and assist at his marriage, he approves of
the opinion which holds that, when a person goes to a parish,
not merely for recreation or some other temporary cause, but
to reside there, he becomes immediately a parishioner of that
parish. This, he says, is not only the more common and
true opinion, but also the most equitable in the case of the

woman who was forced to live in a city at a distance from that in which she had her domicile (nn. 31, 32.)

1035. " Non obstat," ait, " quod hæc mulier non habuerit " animum in dicto oppido perpetuo morandi. Quoniam satis " est ut habuerit animum morandi quamdiu necessitas et jussus " principis durarent: nam et hi qui pestis aut belli causa alio " divertunt, non habent animum illic manendi, nisi quoad " duraverit necessitas. . . . Ad hoc enim ut dictum est, jura " non considerant domicilium, sed *simplicem habitationem*, et " satis est, ut causa submovendi scandalum, ob quam princeps " jussit mulierem alio transferri, non fuerit talis, *ut potuerit* "*probabiliter* incontinenter cessare. . . . Secus si per transi- "tum alicujus exercitus transeuntis hostiliter per comitatum " quis contulisset se ad civitatem. . . . Nam primo casu venit " animo commorandi; secundo non" (n. 34). He then cites various decisions of the S. C. The first case concerned the marriage of a noble youth who resided at Sienna. He wished to marry a harlot, who also resided at Sienna; but fearing that, if he attempted to marry her at Sienna accord- ing to the form prescribed by the Council of Trent, his friends would interpose, he went to Rome, where, having remained for some time (aliquantisper), he contracted mar- riage with the harlot before the parish priest of St. Anastasia, in which parish they resided at the time; and this marriage was declared to be valid by the S. C., " because he is the "*proprius parochus* in whose parish the contracting parties " dwelt at the time when the marriage took place." And the Congregation, being consulted generally: " An proprius " parochus quis dicatur, in cujus parochia contrahentes habi- " tant tempore quo matrimonium contrahitur. Respondit ita " dici" (n. 36).

1036. Afterwards, *following the example*, he continues, of the decision given in the Sienna case, the S. C. declared to be valid the marriage of a student, who, fearing opposition from his parents, remained five or six months in the city where his university was situated, and there contracted mar- riage with a girl of inferior condition before the parish priest of the parish in which he resided. The next case was that of two persons, who, fearing opposition from their parents, came to England, and contracted there before the parish priest of the parish in which they resided for some time (aliquantisper). Finally, Fagnan adduces the Utrecht case, and from all these concludes as follows: " Ex quibus non

" videtur dubitandnm quominus validum sit præsens matri-
" monium contractum coram parocho *habitationis* post
" quartum habitationis mensem.   Et in hanc sententiam S. O.
" respondit."

1037. Now, it will be observed, 1°, that the word quasi-domicile, with which we are now so familiar, does not occur either in the decisions of the S. C., or in the comments of Fagnan.   According to these decisions, a person could become a parishioner, *in ordine ad matrimonium*, not only by acquiring a domicile, but by a *residence* in the parish for some time, even though he has the intention of returning afterwards to his former domicile.

1038. 2°. That in all these cases the parties either left their domicile, or did not return to it until they contracted marriage, because they feared that *their parents would oppose their marriage.*

1039. 3°. That it is never stated in any of the decisions that a residence of a month is *per se* sufficient, for this period is only mentioned in one decision, whilst in two others a period of four, of five, or six months is mentioned; and in two others a residence for some time, no definite period being mentioned, is declared to have been sufficient.

1040. 4°. That in the decisions of Urban VIII, and in many decisions of the S. C., the word domicile comprises not only a permanent residence, but also such temporary residence in a place as will enable parties to contract marriage validly before the parish priest of the parish in which they reside. We have already quoted the decisions of Urban VIII, and a decree of the S. C., which is given by Benedict XIV, in the constitution, " Paucis abhinc hebdomadis," in which both the Pope and the Congregation declare null a marriage contracted " coram parocho loci, ubi contrahentes reperiuntur non animo " ibi *domicilium* contrahendi."   In the decisions cited by Fagnan, what we call quasi-domicile is called a *habitation.*

1041. 5°. That Benedict XIV, and the other theologians who distinguish between a domicile and a quasi-domicile, never add any third mode by which a person may become a parishioner *in ordine ad matrimonium contrahendum.*   On the contrary, Benedict XIV distinctly calls the month's residence mentioned in the Utrecht case a quasi-domicile: " Post hæc," ait, " necessarium fore censemus nonnihil adjungere, ut in " propatulo sit quidnam requiratur ad *quasi domicilium* adipis-" cendum.   Verum in hac re non alio pacto responderi potest,

" nisi quod antequam matrimonium contrahatur, spatio saltem
" unius mensis ille, qui contrahit." etc. He then quotes the
Utrecht case, and adds: " Dubitari antem potest, num ad
" *quasi domicilium* acquirendum matrimonii causa, uti diximus,
" non solum requiratur præcedens habitatio," etc.

1042. 6°. Consequently that Carriere, and those who follow
him, in making a simple habitation distinct from a quasi-
domicile, are totally deceived, because, as far as the validity
of marriage is concerned, they mean one and the same thing.
For the same reasons it also follows that nothing can be
deduced in favor of a month's residence previous to the
celebration of marriage in any place being *per se* sufficient to
render the subsequent marriage valid. Because Carriere, and
those who agree with him, rely entirely on the Utrecht case,
and the constitution, "Paucis." Now, we have already shown
that they are entirely wrong in distinguishing a simple
residence *in ordine ad matrimonium* from a quasi-domicile.
Nor does Benedict XIV ever affirm that a month's residence is
per se sufficient to constitute a residence or quasi-domicile for
marriage. On the contrary, the Pontiff expressly declares
that, as the authors who have written on the subject lay great
stress on the *subsequent residence* as *magni momenti adminiculum*, he will make no new decree on this head. Nor does
the decree of the S. C. settle anything on the question that a
month's residence is *per se* sufficient to render a marriage
subsequently contracted valid, but simply that in the Utrecht
case this was sufficient. It only follows:—

1043. 7°. That a month's habitation is sufficient to render
the subseqnent marriage valid *positis ponendis*, that is, when it
is such as to constitute a quasi-domicile; and, consequently,
as the words, *quasi-domicile*, and *habitation*, and *simple
habitation*, are used by canonists and theologians to express
the same thing, the Holy See was perfectly justified in leaving
the words, quasi-domicile and simple habitation, sufficient to
constitute a quasi-domicile *in ordine ad matrimonium*, as it
has done, in the Acts of two French Provincial Synods;
because, as we have shown, where there is question of a
residence sufficient to make a person a parishioner, " in ordine
" ad matrimonium contrahendum," these words mean exactly
the same thing, and it is perfectly true that either a quasi-
domicile or a *simplex habitatio, positis ponendis*, is sufficient
to enable a person to marry in presence of the parish priest of
the place.

1044. 8°. That, to acquire a quasi-domicile or habitation *in ordine ad matrimonium*, both the *intention* and the *fact*, or *actual* residence, are necessary. It is not enough that a person intends to reside for a "tempus notabile" in a place, or that he has taken a house for six months or a year, and furnished it. He must have actually commenced to *reside* there as in his dwelling-place; and he must also have the intention of making it his *dwelling-place* for a notable period. Hence it has frequently been decided that a person who goes to the country for recreation, or to transact business, or for any other temporary cause, or for the purpose of *contracting marriage*, and not of acquiring a domicile or quasi-domicile, cannot marry validly there. Hence, if Bertha, even though she be already engaged to be married to Caius, goes on a visit to a friend to a lodging in the country to recruit her health, or takes apartments in a neighboring town by the week or fortnight, in order to prepare dresses, etc., but without the intention of acquiring a residence in these places, although her stay may be unexpectedly protracted from time to time until a period of one, two, three, or even six months has elapsed, she cannot contract marriage in the place where she is staying, because she never intended to acquire a habitation (quasi-domicile) in that place.

1045. 9°. But the question is, if she takes a house or lodgings in town or country, still retaining her proper domicile, how long must she intend to dwell in the place in order to acquire a residence sufficient for marriage? 1°. Is a month's residence previous to the marriage necessary? 2°. Is it sufficient, if she intends to marry at the expiration of the month, and leave the place immediately afterwards? To the first question we answer: that, if she has taken a house or lodgings for five or six months, and bound herself to pay rent for that time, she can be married in that place at once, if she took the house or lodgings before she was engaged to be married; because she acquired a quasi-domicile the moment she commenced to reside in that parish, for her intention of remaining there for a *tempus notabile* was sufficiently manifested by the circumstances we have mentioned. And in this case the marriage would be both licit and valid, even though she changed her mind before the marriage took place, and intended after her marriage to reside in a different parish with her husband; because, when a domicile or quasi-domicile is once validly acquired, it is only lost by the *intention* and the *fact.* Neither the fact of a *brief* absence, whilst the *intention* of returning to the place *tanquam in locum domicilii aut quasi domicilii* remains, nor the *intention* of leaving the place, so long as the person continues to *actually* reside in it, deprives him of either.

1046. 10°. But if she were engaged to be married before she took the house or lodgings for five or six months other circumstances should be taken into consideration. If she took the place as a residence both for herself and her husband, or if the marriage were not to take place for five or six months, we think her intention of residing in the place for a " tempus " notabile" would be sufficiently manifested; and therefore that, not only in the first, but even in the second case, she could contract validly *coram parocho loci*, if for some unforeseen cause it should be considered expedient to solemnize the marriage at an earlier period. For instance, if, on account of urgent business, the *sponsus* should be unexpectedly obliged to go to America or Australia, we think the marriage could be validly contracted at once before the parish priest of the place where the girl resided, whether she intended to remain on in it or to accompany her husband, because, having already acquired a sufficient residence, she would not lose it until she actually ceased to dwell in it.

1047. 11°. But if she only took the lodgings by the week, with accommodation for both herself and her intended husband, even though she declared that she would reside there for six months, after which she would leave it, we think the intention of remaining there for a " tempus notabile" would not be in many cases sufficiently manifested, at all events until she should have dwelt for some time in the place. It is supposed that she retains her former domicile, and that her intended husband does not reside in the parish where she lodges, but in some other parish: for, in either of these cases, the marriage would be valid for other reasons. But, we say, supposing the validity to depend on the sufficiency of her own residence, the intention of remaining for a " tempus notabile" would not generally be sufficiently manifested from the beginning. But after the lapse of a fortnight or a month this might be clear: as, if she had made permanent improvements at her own expense, had got paper put on the walls, got the doors and windows painted, purchased furniture specially suited to the place, or furnished it in a manner suitable to carry on her own trade or calling. All this might be made manifest in a fortnight or in a month, or it might require the lapse of two or three months to make it so.

1048. 12°. The same is to be said of servants, clerks, and others, who are engaged by the week, month, or quarter; for, if they are engaged by the half-year or year, they can be married as soon as they commence to reside in the place where they are employed. If the engagement be in the former case for a period of a week, month, or quarter, at the expiration of which they are definitely *to leave the place*, they cannot (supposing the month's residence to be insufficient) contract marriage in that place at all during the periods mentioned. But if the engagement, although entered into by the week, month, or quarter, is not understood to terminate definitely after the lapse of the above periods, but only that the servant may leave if he does not like the place, or that the master may dismiss him, we think that if the servant shall continue to reside in the place without interruption, then, as soon as circumstances render it morally certain that he will continue to reside for a *tempus notabile*, he will have contracted a quasi-domicile *in ordine ad matrimonium*. Thus, if after the lapse of a month or two the master appoints a servant engaged by the quarter to a permanent office, which he accepts, with the intention of remaining for an indefinitely long period, or even for a second quarter, we think he has a quasi-domicile. The same we hold to be true, if at the expiration of the quarter the engagement be renewed without the servant having given up his residence, because he never intended to leave at the end of the quarter, and the continuance of the engagement comprises a *tempus notabile*, and, consequently, immediately after the new engagement, he acquires a quasi-domicile. So, also, when the servant who has been engaged by the month continues in the service for two or three months, and all the circumstances indicate that he will remain in the place for a considerable time, as soon as this becomes morally certain, he acquires a quasi-domicile. The same is to be said of the servant engaged by the week. In all these cases a certain period must elapse before the person acquires a quasi-domicile; not because this is necessary *per se* for this purpose, but because in the circumstances the intention of remaining in the place for a *tempus notabile* is not at once manifest. But if the engagement, either by the provisions of the law, or by express contract, be entered into for half a year, or for any longer period, the person acquires a quasi-domicile from the moment he comménces to dwell in the place.

1049. 13°. Now, from these observations we think we can explain the decisions of the S. C. In all those cases cited by Fagnan, in which the persons left their home, or stayed away from it, to avoid the opposition which they knew or feared their parents would make to their marriage, for the purpose of getting married in a different place, and of returning afterwards to their native parish,—no doubt these persons asserted that they intended to reside in the place in which they wished to get married, for a "tempus notabile," because in the Utrecht case the parties did actually reside a considerable time in Aix-la-Chapelle after their marriage. which, with the month they had lived there before it, showed their intention of remaining there for a tempus notabile, and because, as Benedict XIV says, the authors who had written on the matter of quasi-domicile considered a subsequent residence a great *adminiculum* in favor of its validity. Now, this adminiculum could not directly affect the marriage, which, if it were invalid at the time it was contracted, would not be made valid by a subsequent residence. It was, therefore, a great *adminiculum* in support of the assertion of the parties that they came there, not for the mere purpose of getting married, but to acquire a quasi-domicile by residing in it for a notable time.

1050. 14°. But it may be said truly that the S. C. did not inquire in the Utrecht case as to the subsequent residence of the parties in Aix-la-Chapelle. We therefore infer that the S. C. must have known this circumstance, otherwise the answer should have been (in the opinion of those very theologians who maintain the sufficiency of the month's residence, and who hold the marriage had been declared valid on this ground) that, if the parties had resided at Aix-la-Chapelle for an entire month before the marriage, it was invalid, for no one ever held that an actual residence for a shorter period, without the intention of remaining longer, would be sufficient. But the S. C. does not answer in this way, but that, in case the parties had not resided in Aix-la-Chapelle for a month previous to the marriage, "*the case should be referred to it* "*again*." The month's previous residence, therefore, did not *directly* affect the validity or invalidity of the marriage, but the sufficiency of the manifestation of the intention of the parties to remain for a tempus notabile. The S. C.

considered a month's previous residence sufficient for this purpose; but in case they had not resided at Aix-la-Chapelle for a month previous to the marriage, it desired the case to be referred to it again, because the sufficiency of the intention might be inferred from other circumstances, if this one were wanting.

1051. 15°. And certainly, in all cases where the parties left home to avoid the opposition of their parents, a grave suspicion would exist that they merely came to another place in order to get married there, and not to acquire a quasi-domicile. Hence we see that the S. C. laid great stress on the parties having resided some time in the place previous to the marriage; but no fixed period was necessary, not only because in some of the cases no fixed time is mentioned, as we have shown from the words, *aliquantisper morati*, but also because, from the answer in the Utrecht case, it is clear that no fixed period was required.

1052. 16°. As to the cases concerning persons who go into the country for recreation, or on business, or for some other temporary cause, the authors who hold the sufficiency of the month's residence are greatly puzzled. Some of them are driven to the necessity of saying that persons who go to the country for recreation, commonly remain only for a few days. (See *Prælectiones Juris Canonici in Sem. S. Sulpitii*, vol. i, n. 244.) But we respectfully submit that this is not the fact, and that a great many families go to the country in summer time for one, two, or three months.

1053. 17°. If the S. C. acknowledged the validity of a marriage contracted anywhere after a month's residence, it certainly could not have made these general assertions concerning the *parochus ruralis*, for a great many persons go to the country for one, two, or three months, taking their whole family with them; and, consequently, they have both the intention and fact of residing there during this period. The true solution is this: that to acquire a quasi-domicile or habitation *in ordine ad matrimonium*, it is necessary that the parties should intend to reside in the place "per tempus nota-"bile anni." An intention of residing for about six months is certainly sufficient. But we think about five months constitute a *tempus notabile anni*, and it is very probable that four are sufficient. "Conformius autem juri videntur sentire, qui dicunt, *sufficere propositum* habitandi per *aliquot* menses, præcipue si domus, conclave, taberna, etc., fuerint conducta."

(Schmalz., lib. ii, tit. ii, n. 19.) He adduces in this place Suarez, Laymann, and others, in support of this opinion. On this account we think an intention of dwelling in a place for four months successively sufficient to constitute a quasi-domicile. Schmalzgrueber adds (loc. cit.), there is no doubt when a person takes up his residence in a place where he intends to remain *per tempus notabile anni*, that he at once (*statim*) acquires a quasi-domicile there. So also Barbosa de Parocho (p. ii, c. xxi, n. 35), Giraldi, Sanchez, etc., cum communi. We repeat these passages, as we consider them most important.

1054. 18°. From what we have said in discussing the necessity of a previous residence, as far as the validity of marriage is concerned, we have been led to express our opinion that a month's residence *per se* is never sufficient to constitute a habitation in which a person can validly contract marriage, provided·he retains a domicile of his own, or a paternal, fraternal, or other real domicile elsewhere, if he intended from the first to leave the place immediately after the expiration of the month. We have shown that there is no decision in which it is stated that a month's residence is *per se* sufficient. In addition to this, we may mention that the Bishop of·Southwark begged that his Holiness, Pius IX, would declare that the mere fact of residing in a place for the space of thirty days would suffice to prove and constitute a sufficient domicile *ad effectum contrahendi matrimonium*, without the animus, either before, or at the beginning of, or during, the thirty days, *contrahendi domicilium vel quasi domicilium*. This proposition having been submitted to the Holy Office, their Eminences, after having carefully examined it, replied, *Non expedire*. (See Synods of the Diocese of Southwark, p. 51.) This decision, however, only refuses to make a new law by which the mere fact of *staying in a place for a month*, without even the *intention of residing for the whole or for any portion of that time*, would constitute a quasi-domicile *in ordine ad matrimonium*.

1055. 19°. What, then, is to be said of the parochus ruralis? Simply that, *as such*, he can never validly assist at the marriage of strangers unless, they acquire a domicile or quasi-domicile in his parish, supposing them to have a domicile elsewhere. But if they come into his parish with the intention of residing in it "per tempus notabile," or make up their minds to do so whilst sojourning there, and make this intention sufficiently plain, he can assist at their marriage, because he ceases to be the "merus parochus ruralis," and becomes the "parochus quasi-domicilii."

1056. 20°. There were some other arrangements made by Benedict XIV, when Cardinal Archbishop of Bologna, respecting the marriage of servants and others, who, besides a quasi-domicile in the place where they actually reside, have a paternal, fraternal, or other domicile in a different parish. When the domicile and quasi-domicile are in the same city, he orders the marriage to be contracted coram parocho domicilii; but if the domicile be at a considerable distance, then the marriage is to be contracted coram parocho quasi-domicilii. But as the mere distance of the places from each other cannot change the nature of the residence, it is quite clear that the marriage could be validly contracted before either of the parish priests. In this country, when a person, such as a servant, has a domicile in one parish and a quasi-domicile in another, the parish priest before whom the marriage shall be contracted should be selected according to the custom of the diocese.

1057. 21°. Although we consider it extremely probable that any period exceeding four months may be considered a *tempus notabile anni*, for the reasons already given and for others which we shall now add, yet we think it would be sinful for any priest to act on this opinion, and therefore that he should practically require, before assisting at the marriage of parties who have a domicile in a different parish, that one of them should have sufficiently manifested his intention of residing in the parish where the marriage is sought to be contracted, for six months. But we think the opinion which holds that the intention of residing in a place for a period of four or five months is sufficient, is strongly confirmed by all the recent decisions, in not one of which is the inquiry made as to whether the parties had the intention of remaining for the greater part of the year,—a question which would undoubtedly have been put if the intention of residing for this period at least were necessary. It is useless to quote on this head Sanchez and the older theologians, who had not seen these decisions. We are quite aware that a Belgian canonist has asserted that he learned, whilst attending the Vatican Council, from an authentic document, that the *mens* of the Holy See is that the intention of dwelling for the greater part of the year is necessary. We confess we should like to see the document, in which, after all, it may be only laid down that this is the ordinary way of acquiring a quasi-domicile. We are strongly of opinion that *tempus notabile* being a thing to be determined *ex communi æstimatione*, is not a precisely determined period. Certainly the woman whose case Fagnan treats at such length, and whose marriage, contracted after a lapse of four months, was declared by the S. C. to be valid, had no intention of dwelling in the place for a greater part of a year. She simply intended to dwell there as long as the prince obliged her to do so, and this intention at the time of the marriage had comprised four months. She would have left the next day had she obtained leave, and still the marriage would have been valid. We cannot see how she had manifested her intention of remaining for at least six months.

1058. 22°. The same remarks apply to the cases already noticed, in which the marriages were declared valid, which took place where the parties had resided *for some time* previously in the place, nor was it even asked whether they had intended to reside there for the greater part of a year. Nor can it be objected that no inquiry was made as to their intention of residing *per tempus notabile*, because the necessity of such residence was sufficiently declared by the decisions in which it was laid down, that persons could not contract in a place where they only tarried for recreation or *ad negotia ruralia agenda.* Nor does Benedict XIV, who certainly knew the *mens Sanctæ Sedis* as well as any theologian, indicate, in any of his many writings on this subject, that the intention of residing *per tempus notabile* in any place must extend to the greater part of a year. We therefore think that the precise period necessary to constitute a *tempus notabile* is not defined, but that the various decisions show it must extend over several months.

1059. But as we do not lay down this opinion as certain, and admit that practically the intention should embrace a period of six months, it may be asked what use there is in discussing it. We answer, that it is of very great practical use, because we know that cases have actually occurred, in which persons intended to reside in the place where they contracted marriage, from the first, a little longer in some cases than four, and in others than five months, and then to return to their proper domicile. Now, we consider the opinion we have been advocating so probable, that such persons should not be disturbed as to the validity of their marriage, so long as the Holy See shall not have definitively decided the question, because, especially when there is question of the validity of matrimony: *In dubio standum est pro validitate actus, seu contractus.*

1060. With respect to prisoners, they are distinguished into two classes. Some are imprisoned for life, or a fixed term of punishment; others are merely kept in custody awaiting their trial. It is decided that the former have a sufficient domicile in the parish where the prison is situated; but that the latter have not, and must therefore have recourse to the parish priest of the domicile which they may have elsewhere. (Inst. xxxiii, n. 12.) The reason of the difference is, that persons detained in custody until their trial shall take place have no intention of acquiring a domicile in the prison, and are generally not detained for a *tempus notabile;* whilst those who have been sentenced to imprisonment for a considerable period, must make the prison their dwelling for that time.

1061. With regard to foundlings brought up or placed in public institutions for the purpose, their parish priest is that of the parish where the institutions are. (*Ibid.,* n. 14.)

1062. Many of the difficulties that may arise regarding the residence necessary for contracting marriage are best solved in practice by a reference to the parish priest, whose presence or permission would *certainly* be sufficient. Thus, for instance, if it be doubted whether a person has a sufficient quasi-domicile in any place, all difficulty about the marriage would be removed if the parish priest of his domicile were referred to and gave his consent.

1063. It may be observed, 1°, that, though a person may contract marriage before the parish priest of his quasi-domicile, he is still free to contract it before the parish priest of his domicile. (Car., 1284; Bouvier, De Mat., art. v, § 1.)

1064. 2°. That the presence of the ordinary (and by the ordinary is meant the bishop or his vicar-general), or of a priest authorized by him, is sufficient for the marriage of any one who is a subject of the diocese. (Car., 1346.)

1065. We need hardly observe that most of what we have said in this rubric regards merely the validity of the marriage; because, for its licitness, the ceremony should be performed as is prescribed in the Ritual.

VI.

Caveat præterea Parochus, ne facile ad contrahendum matrimonium admittat vagos ac peregrinos, et qui incertas habent sedes; neque item eos, qui antea conjugati fuerunt, ut sunt uxores militum, vel captivorum, vel aliorum qui peregrinantur; nisi diligenter de iis omnibus facta inquisitione, et re ad Ordinarium delata, ab eoque habita de ejusmodi matrimonii celebrandi licentia, quæ gratis concedatur.

1066. Those who have no domicile or fixed residence are called "vagi." Even those who have but recently left their domicile, and are on their journey to another place where they intend to fix their residence, are, for the time being, "vagi." A person absent from his domicile, but intending to return to it, is a "peregrinus." Such is the distinction made by Benedict XIV. (Inst. xxxiii, 10.) It is evident that great caution is necessary when there is question of the marriage of these, as well as of the others mentioned in the present rubric; and nothing can dispense the pastor from the obligation of making diligent inquiry regarding them, as is here prescribed.

1067. Much of what we have said on the subject of residence under the preceding rubric applies to those who are "peregrini."

1068. A "vagus" must be married by the parish priest of the place where he is for the time being, who is to be regarded as the "proprius parochus." (Bened. XIV, l. c.)

A priest should not assist at the marriage of any "vagus" until he has not only made diligent inquiry regarding him, but has referred the matter to the ordinary, and obtained permission from him. This is expressly prescribed by the Council of Trent; and the Synod of Thurles ordains that it be strictly observed. (De Mat., 55.) According to the common opinion of theologians, the priest is bound to this sub gravi (Car., 1303; Lig., 1089), though it is not required for the validity of the marriage. (Car., 1304; Lig., l. c.)

1069. The same thing is here prescribed in the case of those who were married before, and whose husbands or wives are alleged to have died abroad. The most careful inquiry must be made; and, at least if any doubt remains, the priest should not proceed without referring the matter to the bishop. (Car., 807.)

VII.

Antequam matrimonium contrahatur, ter a proprio contrahentium Parocho continuis diebus festis in Ecclesia intra Missarum solemnia, ad ipsius Concilii præscriptum, publice denuntietur inter quos matrimonium sit contrahendum.

1070. The publication of the banns, or the announcement of a marriage about to take place between such and such parties, is here prescribed by the Ritual, in accordance with the decree of Trent. This was in use in some form from the earliest times, but was not made a penal law of the Church until the fourth Council of Lateran, held in 1215. (Car., 377, Catalani in locum.) Having fallen into disuse in some countries, it was renewed in its present form by the Council of Trent. (Catal., l. c)

1071. The principal object of the law is to discover any impediment which might prevent a marriage between the parties; and there can be no doubt that a parish priest who fails to comply with it, unless he has obtained a dispensation, is guilty of grievous sin (Car., 379; Lig., 990), though the omission does not invalidate the marriage. (Car., 380.)

1072. According to the words of the decree which are here given in the Ritual, the proclamation must be made three times, on three continuous festival days. By these days are understood days on which there is an obligation of hearing Mass, at least in the place where the proclamation is made. (Car., 383.)

1073. By *continuous* is meant, not that they should immediately succeed each other, as was formerly the case, on Sunday, Monday, and Tuesday in Easter or Pentecost week, but that no great interval should intervene between them, as would ordinarily be the case if a Sunday or festival were allowed to pass between any two. (Car., 384.)

1074. The publication must take place in the church and at the parochial Mass, which is to be understood by "Missarum solemnia." (Car., 385, 386.) It would not suffice if it took place elsewhere, or at a private Mass at which only a few were present. Where there are several Masses that may be called parochial, the banns may be published at each; but we think it would suffice to publish them at any one, at all events at what is regarded as the principal one. In like manner, where there are several churches or chapels in a parish, they may be published in each; but we think it would suffice to publish them either in the principal one or

in that one which the person concerned usually attends. (Car.,
l. c., and Bouvier, cap. 4, art. 2.)

1075. Some maintain that the banns may be published on
any day or in any place where there is a sufficient concourse
of people, for the end of the law is thus sufficiently attained.
St. Liguori thinks this might be done without grievous sin
(991, 992); but the words of the decree should be strictly
adhered to, unless in case of necessity.

1076. The publication should be made by the parish priest,
or with his consent. It may be made at the time when he
usually gives an instruction—after the Gospel, or after the
Communion, or any other convenient time before the people
disperse.

VIII.

Si vero vir et mulier Parochiæ sint diversæ, in utraque Parochia
fiant denuntiationes : quibus denuntiationibus factis, si nullum legitimum
opponatur impedimentum, ad celebrationem matrimonii procedatur.
Sed si quid obstat, ultra Parochus non procedat.

1077. If the parties be from different parishes, the banns
are here directed to be published in each ; and many theologians require the same, if either has two domiciles in two
different parishes, in the manner mentioned before. (Sect. v.)
In the case of "vagi," they commonly require the publication, not only in the parish where they now are, but in their
native parish, or in that in which they have spent longest
time.   Also, in the case of servants, soldiers, minors, etc.,
they require a publication in the previous domicile, or the
parish of the parents, etc., according to circumstances. (Car.,
389 et seq.; Bouv., l. c.)   Such was the custom in many
places, founded on the motive of the law.   Most of the
difficulties, however, in such cases are removed by obtaining
a dispensation; but, of course, the priest is bound to make
careful inquiry.   After the publication of the banns, if there
be no canonical impediment or other obstacle, the marriage
may be proceeded with; but not, according to many theologians, till after the lapse of at least one day from the last
publication.   (Car., 384; Baruff., 123.)   This is very reasonable, considering the motive of the law, and is expressly
prescribed in many dioceses ; but the rubric does not seem to
require any delay, and hence some maintain that the marriage
may take place on the very day of the last publication.
(Busemb. ap. St. Lig., 993.)

1078. If the priest comes to know, or has good reason to suspect, that an impediment exists, he should proceed no farther till the matter is cleared up; and if, after careful inquiry, a doubt still remains, he should refer the matter to the bishop. (Baruff., 125, 126; Car., 421.) According to the common opinion, a single witness to the existence of an impediment is enough to prevent the priest from assisting at the marriage (Lig., 996; Car., 422); but whenever an impediment is revealed to him, he should be careful to require a statement of it in writing, such as would justify himself, should his conduct or his motives be afterwards impugned.

IX.

Quod si aliquando probabilis fuerit suspicio, vel alia rationabilis causa subsit, arbitrio Episcopi, matrimonium malitiose impediri posse, si tot præcesserint denuntiationes, tunc de licentia Ordinarii. vel una tantum fiat denuntiatio, vel saltem Parocho et duobus vel tribus testibus præsentibus, Matrimonium celebretur. Deinde ante illius consummationem, denuntiationes in Ecclesia fiant, ut si aliqua subsunt impedimenta, facilius detegantur, nisi aliter Ordinarius ipse expedire judicaverit.

1079. The Council of Trent leaves to the judgment and discretion of the bishop to dispense, in whole or in part, from the publication of the banns. The words of the rubric are taken almost verbatim from the decree of the Council (Sess. 24, cap. 1), and they seem to convey that a dispensation should be given only when there is reason to apprehend that the marriage might be maliciously prevented, if delayed till after the third publication; and even then they seem to require that there be one publication, or at least that, after the marriage has been solemnized in the usual form, the publication shall take place before it is consummated. There are other causes, however, which are commonly admitted as sufficient. 1°. If there be an apprehension of infamy or scandal, as when the parties are commonly supposed to be already married. 2°. When there is such an enormous disparity between them, in respect of age or condition, as would expose them to ridicule. 3°. When the marriage is to put an end to concubinage, which might be continued during the delay. 4°. When a person "in extremis" is about to marry one with whom he has been living in sin. 5°. When there is danger in delay—e. g., of change of mind of one of the parties to the great injury of the other, or of serious dissension amongst their relatives, etc. (Car., 437; Lig., 1005–6.) It may be maintained, also, that a dispensation can be lawfully granted in consideration of a sum of money given for charitable purposes. (Car., 436, 3°, 1112.)

1080. When the banns are omitted by dispensation previous to the marriage, they are seldom published after it, as there are generally good grounds for believing that this would not be expedient.

1081. By the ordinarius in the decree, we are to understand, not only the bishop, but his vicar-general, and also the vicar-capitular, when the see is vacant. (Car., 430; Lig., 1007.) When the parties are from different dioceses, some are of opinion that the dispensation of one ordinary is enough (Sanchez. Kugler, ap. Car., 432); but it is more commonly maintained that a dispensation should be obtained from each. (Car., l. c.; Gury, ii, 555.)

X.

Has autem denuntiationes Parochus facere non aggrediatur, nisi prius de utriusque contrahentis libero consensu sibi bene constet.

1082. The priest should make himself certain that the marriage has been agreed on with the full consent of the parties, before he publishes the banns. This is a precaution which ordinary prudence would naturally suggest. St. Charles Borromeo required the priest to ascertain from the parties themselves whether they are willing to have the banns published. (Ap. Catal. in locum.)

XI.

Si vero intra duos menses post factas denuntiationes matrimonium non contrahatur, denuntiationes repetantur, nisi aliter Episcopo videatur.

1083. If the marriage does not take place within two months after the publication of the banns, they must be again published, unless the bishop grants a dispensation. This rubric is sufficiently explained by the motive of the law. The previous publication might be forgotten; and, besides, a new impediment might have arisen. Hence there is good reason for what is here prescribed.

XII.

Denuntiationes autem fiant hoc modo: inter Missarum solemnia Parochus populum admoneat in hanc sententiam vulgari sermone:

*Notum sit omnibus hic præsentibus, quod N. vir et N. mulier, ex tali
vel tali familia et Parochia, Deo adjuvante, intendunt inter se contrahere
matrimonium. Proinde admonemus omnes et singulos, ut si quis noverit aliquod consanguinitatis, vel affinitatis, aut cognationis spiritualis, vel
quodvis aliud impedimentum inter eos esse, quod matrimonium contrahendum invicem impediat, illud quamprimum nobis denuntiare debeat; et hoc
admonemus primo si fuerit prima; vel secundo, si fuerit secunda; vel
tertio, si fuerit tertia denuntiatio.*

1084. The banns are directed to be published, for obvious
reasons, in the vulgar tongue.   It does not appear necessary
to adhere strictly to the form here given; but it would be
difficult, perhaps, to find another better or more convenient
for the purpose.   It may be translated thus: " Be it known
" to all here present that N. (*of such a family and place, giving
" the name and place of residence*) and N. (*of such a family, etc.,
" giving the name and residence*) intend, with God's blessing, to
" be united in the holy state of matrimony.   Wherefore, if any of
" you know that there is between them an impediment of con-
" sanguinity, affinity, or spiritual relationship, or any other to
" prevent their marriage, we hereby admonish each and all of
" you that you are bound to make it known to us as soon as
" possible.   This is the first (*second* or *third*) publication."   It
is usual to give not only the Christian and surnames of the
parties, but also the names of their parents, and, in case of a
widow, the name of her deceased husband; but the priest
must carefully avoid the mention of any name or circumstance
that would be a reproach to the person—as, *e. g.*, if he were
illegitimate.   It is enough in such a case to give the name by
which the person is commonly known. (Car., 398–9.)

1085. The publication is to be made, of course, in a clear,
distinct voice, that it may be heard by the congregation; and
if there be a dispensation from one or two publications,
this should be distinctly notified, so that those who know of
any impediment may understand their obligation of declaring
it without delay. (Car., 400–1; Baruff., 152–3.)

1086. Whoever knows of an impediment is bound, according to the common opinion (Lig., 994, Car., 403), under pain
of mortal sin, to declare it, except in a few cases.   If the
knowledge has been acquired under the seal of confession,
there is no conceivable case in which it can be used; but of
course the confessor will instruct the penitent who reveals it

in what he is bound to do. (Car., 408.)   A person is also, according to the common opinion, exempt from the obligation
of revealing, when he knows it only as one of those professional secrets which the public good requires to be kept inviolate (*ibid.*, 409 ; Gury, 557) ; or when he cannot reveal it
without serious injury to himself in character or otherwise.
(*Ibid.*, 411 et seq.)

1087. Charity may sometimes require that a person knowing of the impediment should first admonish the parties to
desist from the marriage or seek a dispensation, and, if they
do so, he is not bound to go farther. (Car., 415.)

XIII.

Moneat Parochus conjuges, ut ante benedictionem sacerdotalem in
templo suscipiendam, in eadem domo non cohabitent, neque matrimonium consumment, nec etiam simul maneant, nisi aliquibus propin-
quis vel aliis præsentibus; quæ benedictio a nullo alio, quam ab ipso
Parocho, seu ab alio Sacerdote de ipsius Parochi vel Ordinarii licentia,
fieri debet.

1088. The solemn nuptial benediction which is given in
the church at Mass must be carefully distinguished from the
marriage ceremony, properly so called.   It usually follows it
immediately, but not always, as we shall see ; and when it is
deferred, the newly married couple are exhorted by the Council of Trent (Sess. 24, c. 11), and are here admonished, not to
live together until they have received it.   If they do so, some
maintain that they are guilty of sin ; but it is much more
probable that they are not, for the words only convey a
counsel and not a precept. (Lig., 984, Dub., 2, Bened., Inst.
xxx, n. 17.)   This benediction can be given only by the
parish priest, or a priest authorized by him or the ordinary.
Any other priest, by giving it, would incur suspension *ipse
facto*. (Con. Trid, Sess. 24, cap. 1.)

XIV.

Caveat etiam Parochus, ne, quando conjuges in primis nuptiis benedictionem acceperint, eos in secundis benedicat, sive mulier, sive etiam
vir ad secundas nuptias transeat.   Sed ubi ea viget consuetudo, ut si
mulier nemini unquam nupserit, etiamsi vir aliam uxorem habuerit,
nuptiæ benedicantur, ea servanda est.   Sed viduæ nuptias non benedicat,
etiamsi ejus vir nunquam uxorem duxerit.

1089. The nuptial benediction is not to be given when
either of the parties received it in a previous marriage ; but

where it is usual to give it in all cases in which the female
was not previously married, the custom, according to the
rubric, may still be retained.   The benediction, from its form,
seems directed chiefly to the female, and hence, probably, the
custom, as well as the sanction given to it.   In Ireland, until
recently, marriages were usually celebrated in private houses,
and the parties were seldom, if ever, required to receive the
solemn benediction in the church.   With us, therefore, custom
can decide nothing regarding it, and we should adhere to what
is prescribed in the Ritual.

1090. It is to be observed that the benediction is not to be
withheld at the second marriage, unless it was given at the
first; and, therefore, may be given even to a widow who did
not receive it at her first marriage, whatever may have been
the cause of the omission. (Caval., De Benedict. Nupt., Dec.
1, n. iii.)

XV.

Matrimonium in Ecclesia maxime celebrari decet : sed si domi cele-
bratum fuerit præsente Parocho et testibus, sponsi veniant ad Ecclesiam
benedictionem accepturi, et tunc caveat Sacerdos, ne iterum a contrahen-
tibus consensum exigat, sed tantum benedictionem illis conferat, celebrata
Missa, ut infra dicetur.

1091. The Synod of Thurles has ordered that all marriages
in Ireland be celebrated in the church, unless in case of
necessity, or for some grave reason to be determined by the
bishop. (De Mat., 57.)   When the marriage takes place in the
church, the solemn nuptial benediction should never be
omitted, unless in the cases excepted by the rubric itself.
When it is celebrated elsewhere, it is here prescribed that the
newly married pair should come to the church to receive the
benediction, which is to be given at Mass in the manner
hereafter described; but the priest must take care not to ask
a renewal of the consent, or repeat any part of the marriage
ceremony which has been already performed.

1092. The nuptial benediction can be given only in the
church, according to a decree of the Sac. Cong. (17 Ap., 1649,
ap. Caval., De Bened. Nupt., Decr. iv); but this is because,
according to another decree (13 Jul., 1630, ibid., Dec. v), it
can be given only at Mass.   Such, at least, is the opinion of
Cavalieri, who further maintains that, if there be an oratory
annexel to the house where the marriage takes place, the
nuptial benediction may be given at Mass celebrated there.

(Sup. Decr. iv., n. ii.) Suppose, then, that a marriage is, for some sufficient reason, celebrated in a private house, and that there is at the same time permission to say Mass there, it would appear to us that the nuptial benediction may and should be given.

1093. According to the decree already cited, the benediction can be given only at Mass; but Cavalieri (l. c.) is of opinion that by the dispensation of the bishop it may be given, with the usual prayers of the Missal, without Mass, and, when necessary, even "*extra ecclesiam*"—and in some countries a custom prevails of giving it in this manner; and the Sac. Cong., being consulted on the subject as regards Bavaria, replied that this might be done. (1 Sept., 1838.) The same is done also in England. The edition of the Roman Ritual recently published for the use of the English Mission, gives the prayers of the benediction taken from the Missal, and directs that these be not omitted when, as is often the case, Mass cannot be celebrated.

1094. We think Ireland is circumstanced, in this respect, very much as England is: hence it might, perhaps, be desirable to adopt the same practice when Mass for the nuptial benediction cannot conveniently be said. But this is a point for the determination of the bishops of this country; for we do not think a priest would be justified in adopting it of his own authority. (See Rev. Theol., vol. iv, p. 191; Dec. Authent., p. 37.)

XVI.

Admoneantur præterea conjuges ut, antequam contrahant, sua peccata diligenter confiteantur, et ad SS. Eucharistiam, atque ad Matrimonii Sacramentum suscipiendum pie accedant, et quomodo in eo recte christiane conversari debeant, diligenter instruantur ex divina Scriptura, exemplo Tobiæ et Saræ, verbisque Angeli Raphaelis eos edocentis, quam sancte conjuges debeant convivere.

1095. Marriage, being one of the "sacramenta vivorum," must be received in the state of grace. A person conscious of mortal sin must, therefore, according to all, either go to confession, or make an act of perfect contrition before he receives it. Some theologians maintain the necessity, in this case, of previous confession; but, according to the more probable opinion, it is sufficient to have contrition, since there is no precept requiring confession before any of the "sacra- " menta vivorum " except the Blessed Eucharist. (Lig., lib. 6,

n. 86.) The Council of Trent, indeed, exhorts (Sess. 24 c.
1), and the Ritual, in nearly the same words, here admonishes, those who are about to get married to go to confession
and communion before the marriage is contracted, or. at
least, as the Council adds (l. c.), three days before it is consummated; but this is not regarded as imposing a strict
obligation. (Baruff., 181; Car., 63, 2°.) Although confession is not strictly required, it is, nevertheless, to be most
earnestly recommended by the pastor, not only as the most
secure means of recovering the state of grace for those who
may be conscious of mortal sin, but as a most useful preparation for all, and a means in some cases morally necessary in
order to detect certain occult impediments, which would
otherwise be unknown, and might afterwards come to light
with most disastrous consequences. Hence, in some places
confession is strictly required by a special law, or custom
having the force of law, and the parish priest should not
assist at the marriage until he is satisfied that the parties have
confessed. This is the case in France. (Car., 62, 3° ; Bouv.,
c. i, art. 2, § ii, Quær. 1°.) We believe the same is the case
in Ireland, but there may be circumstances in which it would
not be expedient to insist on it; and in these the bishop should
be consulted.   (Car., 63 ; Bouv., l. c.; Gury, ii, 585.) It is
very important that the confession be not delayed till all
things are prepared for the marriage, for it may happen, as
we have said, that an impediment would then become known,
so that it would be necessary to break off the marriage, or
obtain a dispensation; and it is easy to see the embarrassment
that would be caused if the confession, in such a case, were
deferred till the very day of the marriage.   For the duty of
the confessor in this most perplexing case, see St. Liguori
(lib. 6, De Pœnit., n. 613).

1096. The communion here recommended is admitted by
all to be only of counsel, and is nowhere strictly required.

It is manifestly of great importance that those who are
about to enter the marriage state should be well instructed
in its duties.   The Ritual here recommends the pastor to
place before them the example of Tobias and Sara. who
were taught by the Angel Raphael the holiness in which
they should live together.   Other passages of the Sacred
Scripture also, especially from the Epistles of St. Paul (1
Cor. vii; 1 Thess. iv; Ephes. v, 22), are very appropriate.
In an instruction on this subject, the priest must be very

careful in the selection of his language, so as to avoid as far as possible any expression that might offend against modesty, or convey a knowledge of sins which might be to some an occasion of committing them. Many Rituals contain a carefully written instruction to be addressed to the contracting parties immediately before marriage, and another to be addressed to them after the nuptial benediction at the time prescribed in the rubric; but the pastor should take occasion, in some of his instructions to the faithful generally, to explain to them the holiness of the married state, and the dispositions required in those who enter it. Such an explanation would save himself a great deal of trouble, and probably also prevent many unhappy marriages.

XVII

Postremo meminerint Parochi, a Dominica I Adventus, usque ad diem Epiphaniæ, et a Feria IV Cinerum, usque ad Octavam Paschæ inclusive, solemnitates nuptiarum prohibitas esse, ut nuptias benedicere, sponsam traducere, nuptialia celebrare convivia, matrimonium autem omni tempore contrahi potest. Nuptiæ vero qua decet modestia et honestate fiant: sancta enim res est matrimonium, sancteque tractandum

1097. It was forbidden from the very earliest times, as is shown by Catal., to solemnize marriage during Lent or Advent. In some churches it was forbidden at other times also, which were set apart for penance. The Council of Trent renewed these ancient prohibitions, and ordered them to be everywhere observed during the times here specified in the rubric; *i. e.*, from the first Sunday of Advent till the Epiphany, and from Ash-Wednesday till the Sunday after Easter, or Low Sunday, the days mentioned being included.

1098. Some theologians maintain that the prohibition extends not only to the solemnities of marriages, but to the contract itself, or at least to its consummation: and there can be no doubt that the intention of the Church was to withdraw the people at those times from sensual pleasures, that they might more fully devote themselves to exercises of piety. (Catal. in locum, S. Thom., St. Anton. ap. St. Lig., 984.) It is evident, however, from the present rubric that by the common law the mere contract is not prohibited—neither is its consummation, as is also quite certain (Bened. XIV, Inst lxxx, 14, 17; St. Lig., l. c.), but all nuptial *solemnities* are prohibited; and by these we are to understand, as the rubric itself here explains, the giving of the solemn nuptial benediction—not the benediction, "Ego vos conjungo," etc.; the solemn escort of the bride to the house of the husband—not the bringing her home privately and without pomp; and nuptial banqueting and festivities—not a moderate entertainment. (St. Lig., l. c.)

10:9. But it may happen that in certain countries, by a particular law or interpretation of the decree having by custom the force of law, marriage itself is prohibited during these times, so that it cannot be celebrated even without pomp or solemnity, unless by dispensation from the bishop. (Bened. XIV, l. c., n. 14; Car., 921.) This is the case in France and several parts of Germany (Car., l. c.), and we believe the same is the case in every part of Ireland. It is to be observed that when in these countries a dispensation is granted for the celebration of marriage, it is not supposed to include a permission to give the solemn nuptial benediction. (Bened. XIV, l. c., n. 12.) This benediction, and the Mass "pro sponso et sponsa," or even a commemoration of it, are prohibited altogether during Lent and Advent, as has been declared by the Sac. Con. (Aug. 31, 1839); and it is doubtful whether a bishop is competent to dispense in this prohibition. (Bened. XIV, l. c., n. 15.)

1100 When the parties are from different dioceses it is enough in this case, according to Cærem. (l. c.), to have a dispensation from the ordinary of the diocese in which the marriage takes place.

XVIII.

Quæ omnia fere ex sacri Concilii Tridentini decretis desumpta, et item alia, quæ ibi de matrimonio rite contrahendo præcipiuntur sunt diligenter servanda.

1101. It has been already observed that some of the preceding rubrics are taken verbatim from the decrees of the Council of Trent; others are taken from them in substance, but are more precise and enter into details. This is here stated in general terms by the Ritual itself, which orders that not only the preceding rubrics, but whatever else has been prescribed by the Council concerning marriage, be carefully observed.

CHAPTER II.

RITE OF CELEBRATING THE SACRAMENT OF MATRIMONY: "RITUS CELEBRANDI MATRIMONII SACRAMENTUM."

1102. Before treating of the ceremonies to be observed in the celebration of marriage, it is necessary to premise that the Council of Trent expresses an earnest desire (*vehementer optat*) that, in addition to what it has itself prescribed in this matter, the laudable rites and customs of particular countries or provinces shall be also retained. (Sess. 24, cap. i, De Ref. Mat.) The Roman Ritual also mentions this, as we shall see. In the present chapter, therefore, we cannot confine ourselves to the rubrics of the Roman Ritual, but must also dwell on the ceremonies usually observed at marriages in these countries.

I.

Parochus igitur matrimonium celebraturus, publicationibus factis tribus diebus Festis, ut dictum est, si nullum obstet legitimum impedimentum, in Ecclesia Superpelliceo et alba Stola indutus, adhibito uno saltem Clerico Superpelliceo pariter induto, qui Librum et vas Aquæ Benedictæ cum aspersorio deferat, coram tribus aut duobus testibus, virum et mulierem, quos parentum vel propinquorum suorum præsentia cohonestari decet, de consensu in matrimonium interroget utrumque singillatim in hunc modum, vulgari sermone:

N., *vis accipere* N. *hic præsentem, in tuam legitimam uxorem, juxta ritum Sanctæ Matris Ecclesiæ?*

Respondeat Sponsus: *Volo.*

Mox Sacerdos Sponsam interroget: N., *vis accipere* N. *hic præsentem, in tuum legitimum maritum, juxta ritum Sanctæ Matris Ecclesiæ?*

Respondeat: *Volo.*

1103. All that has been prescribed in the preceding rubrics regarding the publication of the banns, etc., etc., having been duly complied with, the parties present themselves in the church on the day fixed for the marriage. They should be accompanied by their parents or relatives: at least this is very becoming, and should be required, if circumstances do not render it impossible.

1104. An altar should be prepared for the celebration of Mass, at which the nuptial benediction, unless prohibited by the rubric, is to be given; and two seats or prædieus should be prepared for the bride and bridegroom, or at least convenient places assigned them, near to and in front of the altar, but not within the sanctuary. According to many ancient Rituals, they should present themselves before the priest at the door of the church, where the mutual consent was expressed, and the ceremony, as far as the nuptial Mass, was performed. They were then introduced into the church, where they assisted at Mass, and received the solemn nuptial benediction. (Mart., lib. 1, cap. ix, art. iii, nn. vi, viii.)

1105. The priest should vest in surplice and white stole, according to the rubric; but, if he is to celebrate Mass, the Rituals of many dioceses permit him to vest in amice, alb, cincture, and stole (De H., p. 6, n. 38, iv); the chasuble and maniple being in this case placed on the Gospel side of the altar. He issues from the sacristy, preceded by two clerks, or at least one, vested in surplice, and carrying the vase of holy water, with the aspersory and the Ritual. Arrived at the foot of the altar, he kneels and says a short prayer, having given his cap to the clerk on his right, who holds the Ritual, or, if there be only one clerk, having himself put it aside on the altar step. He then rises up, and having made the due reverence at the foot of the altar, advances, accompanied by the clerks, to where the bride and bridegroom are standing, the former being on the left. The priest then interrogates them in the vulgar tongue, in presence of the witnesses, who should be looking on and listening. He puts the question as it is given in the ritual : *N. Wilt thou take,* etc., first to the bridegroom and then to the bride.

1106. It is usual to mention not only the Christian name, but the surname of each, though the words, " *hic præsentem,*"— " here present," leave no doubt about the person. Any words, or even any sign, which clearly expresses the consent of the parties, would be sufficient; and hence, if one or both of them be mute, any sign or writing expressive of consent may be admitted; but it is right, except in such cases of necessity, to insist on an adherence to the form given in the Ritual. The consent of the parties may be expressed even by proxy, as is here stated in the rubric; but marriages by proxy, unless in the case of princes, are very rare, and should not be permitted by a priest of his own authority. (Catal., n. x; Car., 139.) For the validity of a marriage by proxy, it is necessary, 1 , that the procurator be specially commissioned for the purpose; 2°, that he do not depart from the terms of his commission; 3°, that the person for whom he acts shall not have revoked his consent before the celebration of the marriage. These conditions are expressly required by the canon law. (Car., 141 et seq.) In expressing the consent, the procurator should use words which clearly convey that he is speaking and acting in the name and on behalf of another.

1107. In the Ritual, which has been from time immemorial used in Ireland and England, immediately after the interrogations, when the bride has expressed her consent, saying, " I " will," we have the following rubric : " *Deinde detur fœmina a* " *patre suo vel ab amicis suis ; quæ si puella sit, discoopertam* " *habeat manum, si vidua, tectam ; et vir eam recipiat in Dei* " *fide et sua servandam et teneat eam per manum dexteram in* " *manu suâ dexterâ ; et ad hunc modum, docente Sacerdote, det* " *ei fidem per verbum de præsenti dicens :*

" I, N., take thee, N., to my wedded wife, to have and to " hold from this day forward, for better, for worse, for richer. for " poorer, in sickness and in health, till death do us part, if holy " Church will it permit; and thereto I plight thee my troth.

" *Mox manum retrahendo, iterumque jungendo, dicat mulier,* " *docente Sacerdote :*

" I, N., take thee, N., to my wedded husband, to have and " to hold from this day forward, for better, for worse, for richer, " for poorer, in sickness and in health, till death do us part, if " holy Church will it permit; and thereto I plight thee my " troth."

As soon then as the bride has said, " I will," she should, according to this rubric, be " given away," as it is called, by her father or some of her friends. This may be done by taking her right hand and placing it in that of the bridegroom, as Raguel gave his daughter in marriage to Tobias. (Tob. vii.) If a widow, she should have on a glove; if not, her hand should be uncovered.

1108. This distinction between the first and second marriages, of presenting the hand naked in the former and covered in the latter, is mentioned in many very ancient Rituals. Catalani cites one about six hundred years old, in which it is ordered to be observed. (De Mat., tit. vii, cap. ii, § 2. n 2.) Baruff., however, says: " Decet manus esse nudas et " ab-que chirothecis," without making any distinction. (In loc., n. 37.)

1109. The bridegroom, having thus taken her right hand, repeats after the priest the words given above, " I, N., take "thee," etc. Both then withdraw their hands for an instant, and she takes his right hand in the same manner, and says, "I. N., take," etc.

1110. We have then the following rubric: "*Data sic* "*utrimque fides junctisque dexteris dicat sacerdos :* Ego con-"*jungo vos in matrimonium,* in nomine Patris ✠ et Filii et "Spiritus Sancti. Amen. *Et mox aspergat eos aquá benedictá.*"

1111. The Ritual does not state at what time the parties should kneel, or even that they should kneel at all, nor is the question decided by any uniform practice; it is usual, how-ever, to require them to kneel before the priest pronounces the words, "Ego conjungo vos," etc. We think they may be conveniently required to kneel after the bride has been "given away" and the bridegroom has taken her by the right hand, so as to say, on their knees, "I, N., take thee," etc. At all events, it is right that they should be on their knees when the priest pronounces the words, "Ego conjungo "vos," etc., and sprinkles them with holy water; and there is no reason why they should not remain in this posture, as they commonly do, until the end of the ceremony. The priest, saying the words, "*in nomine Patris,*" etc., makes the sign of the cross over their hands (Baruff., l. c. 39); then, taking the aspersory, which is presented to him by the clerk, he sprinkles them with holy water.

II.

Mutuo igitur contrahentium consensu intellecto, Sacerdos jubeat eos invicem jungere dexteras, dicens: *Ego conjungo vos in matrimonium, in nomine Patris* ✠ *et Filii et Spiritus Sancti. Amen.*

1112. All that is prescribed in this rubric is carried out in the ceremony above described. We may observe that there is a great variety in the ceremonies prescribed in different places for the joining of right hands, etc. In Belgium the priest envelops their hands with the extremities of his stole. (De Herdt, pt. 6, No. 38, vii.) In the Ritual of Rheims and in that of Milan, he is directed to place the extremities of his stole over their hands in the form of a cross. (Catal., l. c. ii.)

1113. Instead of the words, "Ego conjungo," etc., the priest is permitted by the present rubric to use any other words sanctioned by the received Ritual of the province. This latitude is expressly permitted by the Council of Trent, and in the very words here given by the rubric. It is certain that in many ancient Rituals the form, "Ego vos conjungo," etc., is not mentioned. Catalani cites one of the church of Rouen, in which it is given, but not earlier than the thirteenth century. Martene says it was quite unknown in the early Church. (De Ant. Eccl. Rit., lib. 1, cap. ix, art. 3, n. vi.; From this it is inferred, with great probability, that these words do not constitute the form of the sacrament. (Car., 79 et 110.) At all events it is now almost universally admitted that the priest is not the minister of the sacrament, the contract itself between Christians being, by the institution of Christ, a true sacrament. This seems to have been at all times the common opinion of theologians, except at most in France and Germany (Bellarmin, De Mat., cap. 7; St. Lig., 897); and it appears to us that at present it can hardly be doubted, since it is clearly conveyed in the Brief of the present Pope, Pius IX, to the King of Sardinia, which sets forth as the doctrine of the Catholic Church : "Sacramentum " de ipsa Matrimonii essentia esse, ita ut unio conjugalis inter " Christianos non sit legitima, nisi in Matrimonii Sacramento, " extra quod *merus concubinatus tantum invenitur*."

1114. Since the words, "Ego vos conjungo," etc., are used in these countries and given in all our Rituals, the priest is not at liberty to omit them, or to substitute others for them.

Lightning Source UK Ltd.
Milton Keynes UK
UKHW02n1342050718
325281UK00003B/137/P